Globalization, Uncertainty and Women's
Careers

Globalization, Uncertainty and Women's Careers

An International Comparison

Edited by

Hans-Peter Blossfeld

Bamberg University, Germany

Heather Hofmeister

RWTH Aachen University, Germany

Edward Elgar

Cheltenham, UK • Northampton, MA, USA

Published by
Edward Elgar Publishing Limited
Glensanda House
Montpellier Parade
Cheltenham
Glos GL50 1UA
UK

Edward Elgar Publishing, Inc.
William Pratt House
9 Dewey Court
Northampton
Massachusetts 01060
USA

Reprinted 2008
Paperback edition 2008

A catalogue record for this book
is available from the British Library

Library of Congress Control Number: 2005055933

ISBN 978 1 84542 664 4 (cased)
ISBN 978 1 84720 625 1 (paperback)

Printed by Biddles Ltd, King's Lynn, Norfolk

Contents

List of contributors   *viii*
Preface   *xiv*
Foreword   *xvi*

PART I   INTRODUCTION

1. Globalization, uncertainty and women's mid-career life courses:
    a theoretical framework   3
    Heather Hofmeister, Hans-Peter Blossfeld and Melinda Mills
2. Women's employment in times of globalization: a comparative
    overview   32
    Dirk Hofäcker

PART II   COUNTRY-SPECIFIC CONTRIBUTIONS ON
CONSERVATIVE WELFARE REGIMES

3. Women's employment in West Germany   61
    Sandra Buchholz and Daniela Grunow
4. Changes in women's employment and occupational mobility in
    the Netherlands: 1955 to 2000   84
    Matthijs Kalmijn and Ruud Luijkx

PART III   COUNTRY-SPECIFIC CONTRIBUTIONS ON
SOCIAL-DEMOCRATIC WELFARE REGIMES

5. Globalization, deindustrialization and the labor market experiences
    of Swedish women, 1950 to 2000   115
    Tomas Korpi and Charlotta Stern
6. Danish women's unemployment, job mobility and non-employment,
    1980s and 1990s: marked by globalization?   142
    Daniela Grunow and Søren Leth-Sørensen

PART IV   COUNTRY-SPECIFIC CONTRIBUTIONS ON POST-SOCIALIST WELFARE REGIMES

7. Women's career mobility in Hungary   171
   Erzsébet Bukodi and Péter Róbert
8. Women's employment in Estonia   199
   Jelena Helemäe and Ellu Saar
9. Women and the labor market in the Czech Republic: transition
   from a socialist to a social-democratic regime?   224
   Dana Hamplová
10. Women and the labor market in Poland: from socialism to
    capitalism   247
    Ania Plomien

PART V   COUNTRY-SPECIFIC CONTRIBUTIONS ON LIBERAL WELFARE REGIMES

11. Women's employment in Britain   275
    Katrin Golsch
12. Women's employment transitions and mobility in
    the United States: 1968 to 1991   302
    Heather Hofmeister

PART VI   COUNTRY-SPECIFIC CONTRIBUTIONS ON FAMILY-ORIENTED WELFARE REGIMES

13. Labor force dynamics and occupational attainment across
    three cohorts of women in urban Mexico   329
    Emilio A. Parrado
14. Mid-career women in contemporary Italy: economic and
    institutional changes   352
    Maurizio Pisati and Antonio Schizzerotto
15. Hard choices: can Spanish women reconcile job and family?   376
    Carles Simó Noguera

PART VII   CONCLUSIONS

16. The impact of gender role attitudes on women's life courses   405
    Detlev Lück
17. Women's careers in an era of uncertainty: conclusions from a
    13-country international comparison   433
    Heather Hofmeister and Hans-Peter Blossfeld

Index   *451*

Contributors

Hans-Peter Blossfeld is a Professor of Sociology at the Department of Social and Economic Sciences, Bamberg University, Germany. He was a Professor of Sociology at the European University in Florence and the universities in Bremen and Bielefeld. He is editor of the *European Sociological Review*. He was the Director of the GLOBALIFE project and is the Director of the 'Staatsinstitut für Familienforschung an der Universität Bamberg (ifb)' (State Institute for Family Research at Bamberg University). His research interests include social inequality, youth, family and educational sociology, labor market research, demography, social stratification and mobility, cross-national comparative research, modern methods of quantitative social research and statistical methods for longitudinal data analysis. He has 16 books and over 100 articles to his name. Address: Lehrstuhl für Soziologie I, Otto-Friedrich-Universität Bamberg, Postfach 1549, 96045 Bamberg, Germany. [e-mail: hans-peter.blossfeld@sowi.uni-bamberg.de]

Sandra Buchholz works as an Assistant Professor at Bamberg University, Germany. Previously she served as a Research Scientist in the GLOBALIFE project at Bamberg University and in the DFG-project 'Flexibility forms at labor market entry and in the early career – a cross-national comparison of the development of social inequality' at the State Institute for Family Research at Bamberg University. Her research addresses the influence of increasing labor market flexibility on employment patterns in different career stages. In her dissertation she focuses on labor market entry and exit in East and West Germany. Address: Lehrstuhl für Soziologie I, Otto-Friedrich-Universität Bamberg, Postfach 1549, 96045 Bamberg, Germany. [e-mail: sandra.buchholz@sowi.uni-bamberg.de]

Erzsébet Bukodi is currently a Research Officer at the Center for Longitudinal Studies at the University of London. From 2005-2006 she worked as a senior researcher at the Department of Sociology I at Bamberg University, Germany. Previously she was the Head of the Section of Social Stratification within the Department of Social Statistics of the Hungarian Central Statistical Office, Budapest, Hungary. Her research interests involve educational inequalities and different aspects of life-course analysis. Her PhD dissertation studies marriage timing and educational homogamy of couples. Further publications examine career differences of married couples and the main features of regional and social stratification based on the Hungarian Census data. Address: Centre for Longitudinal Studies, Institute of Education, University of London, 20 Bedford Way, London WC1H 0AL UK. [e-mail: e.bukodi@ioe.ac.uk]

Katrin Golsch is currently an Assistant Professor at the Faculty of Economics, Business Administration and Social Sciences, University of Cologne, Germany. Prior to this she was a researcher in the GLOBALIFE project and a lecturer in the Department of Sociology, Bielefeld University, Germany. She received her doctorate in sociology in 2004 about labor market insecurity and its impact on the work and family life of men and women in Germany, Great Britain and Spain. Her core interests include statistical methods for the analysis of survey data and longitudinal data analysis in particular, life-course analysis, social structure, labor market research and comparative sociological research. Address: The Faculty of Economics, Business Administration and Social Sciences, Universität Köln, Herbert-Lewin-Str. 2, 50931 Cologne, Germany. [e-mail: golsch@wiso.uni-koeln.de]

Daniela Grunow served as a Research Scientist in the GLOBALIFE project at Bielefeld University and at Bamberg University and in the DFG-project 'The household division of domestic labor as a process' at the State Institute for Family Research at Bamberg University, Germany. She took a postdoctoral appointment from 2006 to 2008 at the Center for Research on Inequalities and the Life Course at Yale University. Her research addresses the interaction of market work, domestic work and gender relations in divergent welfare regimes from a life-course perspective, applying qualitative as well as quantitative methods. Her dissertation, 'Convergence, Persistence and Diversity', tackles these themes for male and female employment careers over time in international perspective. Address: Staatsinstitut für Familien-forschung an der Universität Bamberg (ifb), Heinrichsdamm 4, 96047 Bamberg, Germany. [e-mail: daniela.grunow@yale.edu]

Dana Hamplová works as a Senior Researcher at the Institute of Sociology, Academy of Sciences of the Czech Republic and finished her PhD in Sociology at the Charles University, Prague, Czech Republic. From 2002 to 2004 she worked as a research associate within the GLOBALIFE project at Bamberg University, Germany. In 2006 she accepted a postdoctoral position at McGill University, Montreal, Canada. Her main research interests focus on family and labor market dynamics. Address: Institute of Sociology, Jilska 1, 110 00 Prague 1, Czech Republic. [e-mail: dana.hamplova@soc.cas.cz]

Jelena Helemäe is Senior Research Fellow at the Department of Social Stratification, Institute of International and Social Studies at Tallinn

University, Estonia. Her research fields include social mobility and ascriptive stratification. She has published on occupational mobility and job values, age and ethnic inequalities. Her current research project is re-stratification processes in the post-Soviet Estonian society. Address: Institute for International and Social Studies at Tallinn University, Uus-Sadama 5, Tallinn 10120, Estonia. [e-mail: helemae@iiss.ee]

Dirk Hofäcker works as a Research Scientist at the State Institute for Family Research at Bamberg University, Germany and is the coordinator of the ESF TransEurope Research Network. He was a researcher in the GLOBALIFE project from 2002 to 2005. His main research interests lie in the field of international comparisons, attitude research as well as in quantitative social science data analysis. His work has concentrated on cross-national comparisons of female employment patterns and its institutional backgrounds, and the comparative analyses of retirement processes. Address: Staatsinstitut für Familien-forschung an der Universität Bamberg (ifb), Heinrichsdamm 4, 96047 Bamberg, Germany. [e-mail: dirk.hofaecker@sowi. uni-bamberg.de]

Heather Hofmeister is a Professor of Sociology at RWTH Aachen University in Aachen, Germany. From 2002 to 2007 she was an Assistant Professor at Bamberg University, Germany and served as the Deputy Director and a Senior Research Scientist in the GLOBALIFE project at the universities of Bielefeld and Bamberg. She earned her PhD at Cornell University where she was a predoctoral fellow at the Cornell Careers Institute. Her award-winning research focuses on families, couples and gendered occupational and geographical career path-ways in international comparison and under forces of social change. Address: RWTH Aachen University, Institut für Soziologie, Kármán Forum, Eilfschornsteinstr. 7, 52062 Aachen, Germany. [e-mail: heather.hofmeister@rwth-aachen.de]

Matthijs Kalmijn is a Professor in the Department of Social and Cultural Sciences, Tilburg University, Netherlands. His research focuses on the sociology of marriage, family and the life course. Important current research projects are on divorce and separation in the Netherlands and on kinship solidarity in the Netherlands. He is also a member of Netspar, the Network for Studies on Pensions, Aging and Retirement, which was initiated and is coordinated by Lans Bovenberg, Arie Kapteyn and Theo Nijman. Within this institute, he focuses on the sociological aspects of the later stages in the life course. He has a PhD from the University of California, Los Angeles, USA. Address: Department of Social and Cultural Sciences, Tilburg University, P.O. Box 90153, 5000 LE Tilburg, The Netherlands. [e-mail: M.Kalmijn@ uvt.nl]

Tomas Korpi is Associate Professor at the Swedish Institute for Social Research, Stockholm University, Sweden and researcher at the Swedish Research Council. His research broadly focuses on inequality, stratification, mobility and life-course analysis. More specifically it deals with labor market research, including both education and (un)employment, and the relationship between the labor market and public policy. Address: Swedish Institute for Social Research, Stockholm University, S-106 91 Stockholm, Sweden. [e-mail: tomas.korpi@sofi.su.se]

Søren Leth-Sørensen is a sociologist employed as Senior Adviser in a Research Service Unit at Statistics Denmark. Currently, his office is at the University of Aarhus. His responsibilities include managing projects for outside researchers using data from Statistics Denmark. His main research interests focus on labor market and family changes in Denmark. He has taken part in establishing the so-called IDA database. This is a longitudinal database for persons, jobs and firms in Denmark starting in 1980. Address: Forskningsservice, Danmarks Statistik, Forskerfilialen, Århus Universitet Bygning 447, Tåsingegade 1, 8000 Århus C, Denmark. [e-mail: sls@dst.dk]

Detlev Lück works as a senior researcher on the project 'Job Mobility and Family Lives in Europe', funded by the EU and located at the University of Mainz. His dissertation analyzes change of gender roles and of gender-related attitudes and his research interests are value change, social inequality, gender and international comparison. From 2002–05 he served as a research scientist in the GLOBALIFE Project at Bamberg University, and from 2005–06 he was an Assistant Professor at the University of Hohenheim, Germany. Address: University of Mainz, FB 02, Institut für Soziologie, Colonel-Kleinmann-Weg 2, D-55099 Mainz, Germany. [e-mail: lueckd@uni-mainz.de]

Ruud Luijkx is a Lecturer of Sociology at the Department of Social Cultural Sciences, Tilburg University, Netherlands. He contributed to international benchmark studies on social mobility and published further in the field of (educational) heterogamy, social inequality, career mobility, labor market transitions and loglinear and latent class analysis. Recently his focus shifted partly towards research on values, norms, beliefs and voluntary associations and at this moment he is chief of data processing for the European Values Study and responsible for the integration and harmonization of the European and World Values Surveys. Address: Department of Social Cultural Sciences, Tilburg University, P.O. Box 90153, 5000 LE Tilburg, the Netherlands. [e-mail: R.Luijkx@uvt.nl]

Melinda Mills is a Rosalind Franklin Fellow and Assistant Professor at the Department of Sociology, University of Groningen, the Netherlands. She is currently Editor of the journal *International Sociology.* She was previously a member of the GLOBALIFE project at Bielefeld University, Germany. Her research interests include cross-national comparative research, demography, family sociology, inequality, and time and causality. Recent publications examine globalization, partnership histories, labor market flexibility, time, and interdependent processes using event history models. Address: Department of Sociology, University of Groningen, Grote Rozenstraat 31, Groningen, 9712 TG the Netherlands. [email: m.c.mills@ rug.nl]

Emilio A. Parrado is an Assistant Professor at Duke University, USA. His main research interests include migration, family and fertility behavior, educational inequality and Latin America. Publications include articles in *American Sociological Review, Comparative Education Review, Demography, International Migration Review, Journal of Marriage and the Family, Perspectives on Sexual and Reproductive Health, Population and Development Review, Social Forces, Social Problems, Sociological Methods and Research, Social Science Quarterly,* and *World Development.* Address: Department of Sociology, 277B Soc/Psych Bldg, Box 90088, Duke University, Durham, NC, USA. [e-mail: eparrado@soc.duke.edu]

Maurizio Pisati is an Associate Professor of Sociology at the University of Milano Bicocca, Italy. His main research interests are in the fields of social mobility, inequality of educational opportunities, religious behavior, residential segregation and quantitative data analysis techniques. Address: Department of Sociology, Milano-Bicocca University, Via Bicocca degli Arcimboldi, 8, Edificio U7, 20126 Milano, Italy. [e-mail: maurizio.pisati@ galactica.it]

Ania Plomien is a Research Assistant and Tutorial Fellow at the London School of Economics and Political Science. She earned her doctorate at the University of Bremen, Germany in the Graduate School of Social Sciences. Her work concentrates on the position of women within the labor market in Poland, and more specifically on the influence of the European Employment Strategy on the domestic labor market policy-making of a new member state. Her research interests include: welfare state, work, labour, labour market policy, transition societies, social movements, gender, European Employment Strategy, Open Method of Coordination. Address: London School of Economics, Houghton Street, London WC2A 2AE, UK. [e-mail: a.plomien@lse.ac.uk]

Péter Róbert is an Associate Professor at the Department of Sociology, Faculty of Social Sciences, ELTE University, Budapest, Hungary. He is also a Senior Researcher at the TÁRKI Social Research Center. His research interests include social stratification and mobility with special focus on educational inequalities and life-course analysis. He also does research on lifestyle differentiation and on attitudes toward social inequalities. Recent publications examine career differences of married couples, educational transition from secondary to tertiary school, comparison of students' performance in state-owned and church-run schools. Address: Faculty of Social Sciences, ELTE University, Pázmány Péter sétány 1/A, 1112. Budapest, Hungary. [e-mail: robert@tarki.hu]

Ellu Saar is a Senior Researcher at the Institute for International and Social Studies, Tallinn University, Estonia. Her research areas are social stratification, educational inequalities, life-course analysis. She is a coordinator of the Sixth Framework Project 'Towards a lifelong learning society in Europe: the contribution of the education system.' Address: Institute for International and Social Studies at Tallinn University, Uus-Sadama 5, Tallinn 10120, Estonia. [e-mail: saar@iiss.ee]

Antonio Schizzerotto is a Professor of Sociology at the Milano-Bicocca University, Italy, and the scientific director of the Italian Household Longitudinal Survey (ILFI). His main interests include research on social mobility, social change and the life cycles, comparative analysis of the transition from school to work as well as research on unemployment and inequalities by gender and generation. Address: Department of Sociology, Milano-Bicocca University, Via Bicocca degli Arcimboldi, 8, Edificio U7, 20126 Milano, Italy. [e-mail: antonio.schizzerotto@unimib.it]

Carles Simó Noguera is a researcher at the Department of Sociology and Social Anthropology, Universitat de València Estudi General, Spain. His research interests include aging, divorce, fertility, early labor market careers, adulthood transitions and job mobility. Recent publications examine the transition to parenthood and adulthood in the era of globalization and immigrant care of the elderly in Spain. Address: Departament de Sociologia i Antropologia Social, Universitat de València Estudi General, Edifici Departamental Oriental, Campus dels tarongers. Av. dels Tarongers s/n, 46022 València, Spain. [e-mail: carles.simo@uv.es]

Charlotta Stern is a researcher at the Swedish Institute for Social Research, Stockholm University. She is currently doing research in labor market sociology, but her research has also involved analyzing effects of social networks on outcomes such as health, participation in collective action, diffusion of and competition between social movements. Address: Swedish Institute for Social Research, Stockholm University, S-106 91 Stockholm, Sweden. [e-mail: lotta.stern@sofi.su.se]

Preface

This volume is one of four books of research from the international and multidisciplinary research program 'GLOBALIFE – Life Courses in the Globalization Process,' funded by the Volkswagen Foundation (Hanover, Germany) and established and directed by Hans-Peter Blossfeld. The project was a 2006 finalist for the EU Descartes Prize for Collaborative Research. Beginning in 1999 at the University of Bielefeld, Germany, it moved to Bamberg University from 2002 to 2005. The project employed 23 scientists and had an additional 44 external collaborators from 17 different countries. It produced 80 working papers and many other publications in addition to these edited volumes. Our thanks go to the Volkswagen Foundation in Hanover for their financial support that made this ambitious project possible.

GLOBALIFE studied the implications of the globalization process for the life courses of individuals in various OECD-type societies. The project examined how globalization impacts four aspects of the life course: (1) the transition to adulthood, (2) men's mid-career mobility, (3) women's mid-career employment transitions; and (4) late careers and retirement. This volume represents the work generated in the third phase of this project.

We examine how women in 13 industrialized societies navigate work and family careers in an era of globalization and rising economic uncertainty. Globalization has powerfully shaped both national economies and individual life courses during the last decades. The emergence of a single worldwide market has therefore enhanced the number of competitors and increased the demand for flexible labor forces. Mid-career women may be affected by globalized working environments due to their outsider position in many labor markets and the various competing demands for their time across paid employment and unpaid caregiving.

There are many people to thank in a project of this magnitude. During the preparation of this volume, the project consisted of core project members located at Bamberg University, including: Sandra Buchholz, Daniela Grunow, Dana Hamplová, Steffen Hillmert, Dirk Hofäcker, Karin Kurz, Detlev Lück, Štěpanká Pollnerová and Kadri Täht. We thank all for their counsel and support. We especially recognize project members on site who contributed chapters to this volume, including Sandra Buchholz, Daniela Grunow, Dana Hamplová, Dirk Hofäcker and Detlev Lück. Our gratitude goes to Melinda Mills for advice and support throughout the research and manuscript preparation, and to Fabrizio Bernardi for valuable editorial advice. We also thank Karin Kurz who trained the student assistants and gave us helpful advice for preparing the typescript in addition to substantive research support. We also thank Ingeborg McIntyre, Petra Ries and Kathrina Schafhauser for competent administrative support.

Many student assistants were involved in the research phase whom we would like to thank, including Wiebke Paulus, Simone Bloem, Katrin Busch, Cathrin Conradi, Fabian Czerwinski, Melanie Flügel, Lena Gehringer, Eva-Maria Goertz, Daniel Halbritter, Karin Handke, Evelyn Hock, Stefan Kirsch, Juliana Körnert, Jens Kratzmann, Kerstin Künsebeck, Jochen Landes, Alexander Lenz, Nicole Maul, Sonja Meixner, Corinna Mergner, Jan Mewes, Monika Schmich, Anna-Maria Thomas, Joanna Urban, Pia Wagner, Ulrike Wolf, Dagmar Zanker and Markus Zielonka.

Christian Haag, Wolfgang Kraus, Susanne Lindner, Ilona Relikowski and Susanne Stedtfeld showed exceptional dedication and assistance in the preparation and deserve special thanks for assisting with the typescript in addition to their research support. Extraordinary thanks go to John Bendix who came in at the right moment to improve the consistency, accuracy and readability of the chapters in our book, well beyond our expectations.

An important goal of the GLOBALIFE project was to create and utilize an international research network that would collectively pursue specific substantive and methodological issues in the analysis of life courses in the globalization process. This volume would not be possible without the external contributors to this volume, experts in their respective countries, who devoted time and energy to the project by traveling for workshops, corresponding regularly over the course of several years, and above all producing top-quality research to illuminate the life courses of mid-career women. Our gratitude goes to Matthijs Kalmijn, Ruud Luijkx, Thomas Korpi, Charlotta Stern, Søren Leth-Sørensen, Erzsébet Bukodi, Péter Róbert, Jelena Helemäe, Ellu Saar, Ania Plomien, Katrin Golsch, Emilio A. Parrado, Maurizio Pisati, Antonio Schizzerotto and Carles Simó Noguera for their enthusiastic, professional, and cooperative teamwork throughout.

Our appreciation goes to David Vince, Jo Betteridge, Catherine Elgar and Felicity Plester at Edward Elgar Publishing for their kind and helpful support through the process of publication. We would also like to thank Phyllis Moen, Karl Ulrich Meyer, and the many individuals who responded to our work when it was presented at various conferences and who helped improve the final outcome. Finally, we are in debt to the hundreds of thousands of women who gave their time and information to surveys over the course of decades that enable this work to be possible.

Hans-Peter Blossfeld
Bamberg University, Germany
Heather Hofmeister
RWTH Aachen University, Germany

Foreword

Phyllis Moen

Across the European and American labor markets, the 'story' of the latter half of the twentieth century consists of trends in women entering, remaining in, or reentering employment at different ages and life-course stages. Hans-Peter Blossfeld and Heather Hofmeister make a convincing case that the 'story' in the first decade of the twenty-first century will be globalization and its varied impacts, especially as they intersect with women's lives in different policy contexts.

Globalization, Uncertainty and Women's Careers: An International Comparison is the third in a quite remarkable series of edited volumes chronicling an impressive array of comparative, cross-national longitudinal research findings from the GLOBALIFE project. Most extant studies of globalization focus largely on the developing world. By contrast, this series charts the ecology of globalization in economically developed regions: North America and Europe, including countries in Eastern Europe. Taken together, these researches examine micro-level, life-course impacts of globalization processes, within as well as across nations, within as well as across age and gender divides.

In this edited volume, Blossfeld, Hofmeister and colleagues demonstrate the ways that the globalization of markets together with existing institutional disadvantages exacerbate women's position as outsiders. But this outcome is nuanced, in that women's increasing vulnerability is contingent on both their prior biographies and the policy regimes under which they live.

Mayer (1986, p. 167) describes institutional careers as the orderly flow of persons through segmented institutions. A number of life-course scholars (for example, Blossfeld and Drobnič 2001; Blossfeld, Drobnič and Rohwer 1995; Kohli 1986; Mayer 1986; Moen 2003, Riley and Riley 1989; 1994) have pointed to the development of occupational careers as providing the organizational blueprint for the life course, beginning with a period of education, followed by years of continuous, full-time productive work, and then retirement. By the middle of the twentieth century across the West, this became a *career mystique* institutionalizing a 'primary' labor market, with continuous (throughout adulthood) full-time employment the expected and rewarded norm (Moen and Roehling 2005). The career mystique promised success and fulfillment in return for a lifetime of hard work and commitment.

Indeed, in the United States uninterrupted full-time (or more) employment in the primary labor market became the *only* path to security, status, and success, including the provision of health care insurance, pensions, and even paid (typically two-week) vacations. Those outside this primary labor market were, literally, outsiders.

The career mystique belief, and the social organization of paid work it fostered, was predicated on the *feminine mystique* (Friedan 1963), the myth that women could (and should) find fulfillment as homemakers, supporting their husbands who, in turn, were freed to devote their time, effort, and commitment to their paid jobs. Thus the career mystique of the good worker was conveniently isomorphic with men's roles as family breadwinners. With the identification of the feminine mystique as a false myth in the 1960s, the re-energized women's movement in Europe and America argued for equality in access to educational and occupational opportunities, as well as in pay. Feminists in the 1960s and 1970s saw paid work as the path to gender equality, and this meant replacing one false myth (the feminine mystique) with another (the career mystique), using men's employment experiences as the yardstick for equality.

In the 1970s and 1980s, women in Europe and North America pushed for equality at school and at work, moving into universities and employment in unprecedented numbers. But they did so while still encumbered with a second shift (Hochschild 1989) of housework, family care and the details of daily living. Most employed women in most developed countries were part of the secondary labor market. This meant working part-time, temporarily, or in low-level jobs that came without the career mystique expectation of continuous, total commitment but also without the internal mobility ladders, skill development, security or rewards associated with it (Blossfeld and Hakim 1997). This two-tier arrangement offered a bifurcation of opportunities. 'Good jobs' in the primary labor market were disproportionately occupied by middle-class men, along with men in unionized blue-collar occupations. Women, immigrants, minorities, and the poorly educated, by contrast, worked in the secondary labor market with few job protections or possibilities. The lack of job protections or possibilities have been especially but not exclusively the case in the United States, where health insurance, pensions, unemployment insurance, disability insurance, and Social Security all rest on the edifice of the lock-step career mystique. Whether or not employees may have actually believed in the career mystique script, it nevertheless became the yardstick against which job success and status are gauged and resources are allocated.

Feminists in the 1980s turned to the concept of comparative worth. If women and men were not to occupy the 'same' jobs, at least those doing comparable jobs (in terms of educational and skill requirements) should earn comparable pay (Reskin 1998). The next phase of feminism in the 1990s addressed the second shift of unpaid care work, presuming that women's double day accounted for the enduring disparities in men's and women's occupations, status, mobility and pay. The call was for men to accept their fair share of domestic work. But men's 'good jobs' remain 'greedy' (Coser 1984) and men remain the principal breadwinners in most households. Even dual-earner couples prioritize husbands' jobs (Pixley and Moen 2003) and follow a neotraditional division of paid work and domestic work (Moen and Sweet 2003).

While women are now doing less housework and men are doing somewhat more of the unpaid family care work in some modern societies, this has not appreciably lessened women's work–family conflicts and strains. And even though opinion surveys show that women (and men) give primacy to family and personal life over paid work in their hierarchy of commitments, their actual adaptive strategies suggest otherwise (Moen and Orrange 2002; Orrange 2003). Across Europe and North America, the evidence is that women are seeking to lessen the family demand side of the work–family equation: having no or fewer children, bearing them later in life, marrying later or not at all, or not remaining married.

Feminist scholars in the United States are beginning to frame gender disparities as originating in and sustained by the social organization of paid work (Bailyn 1993; Moen 2003; Moen and Roehling 2005). Many Americans are calling for more flexibilities in the clockworks of paid work – the social arrangement of workdays, workweeks, work years, career and retirement paths. But, as Blossfeld and Hofmeister show, this call for greater temporal flexibility at work (especially in the United States) comes at a time when global forces are creating a different kind of flexibility, in the form of job uncertainties and insecurities. *Globalization, Uncertainty and Women's Careers* shows that continuities and changes in women's roles and adaptations are occurring side by side with dramatic shifts in technologies and in labor markets that are rewriting seniority and security conventions. The traditional contract between employers and employees is dissolving in many countries, and even workers with established seniority and skills find they are disposable in times of mergers, bankruptcies, and restructuring. Risk and uncertainty may be blurring age-graded rules and scripts based on the career mystique, but women are still especially vulnerable to the forces of global change.

Blossfeld and Hofmeister, along with their other chapter authors, use women's life courses as a *strategic research site* (Merton 1968) to empirically investigate the micro (changing biographical) consequences of these macro forces of globalization. In doing so they are reframing the work–gender–life course discourse, chronicling what I call *converging divergences* (Moen and Spencer 2005) in life paths and life chances. Global forces are dismantling the lock-step life course, producing *divergences* in biographical paths. These divergences are occurring across social locations, meaning that the experiences of subgroups are *converging* in the range of their variation. Combining both concepts captures the growing heterogeneity by age and by gender in the strategic selections and opportunity structures of men and women. Thus within-gender distinctions may be as diverse and as consequential as across-gender (or age or cohort) differences.

This edited volume charts the converging divergences in women's lives brought about by globalization in distinctive national contexts. It encompasses a complex but rich theoretical and research agenda: locating gendered life courses within global forces of change, even as these forces are themselves embedded within the very national borders globalization is seeking to blur. Each country chapter models how national constellations of roles, risks and relationships serve to moderate (or exacerbate) the impacts of the forces of globalization on women's life chances and life quality.

Globalization, Uncertainty, and Women's Careers shows how women's position as outsiders in the labor force in many countries is being exacerbated by the globalizing of markets, including the labor market. Equally important, the unique contribution of this edited volume is that it captures the dynamics and cross-national contextual distinctions in women's relative vulnerability, given the culture and structure of women's 'expected life course' embedded in within-nation (as well as within welfare regime) institutions and ways of thinking.

This book, and especially as part of the set of four books on life courses under globalization, highlights the often outdated shared understandings and taken-for-granted rules, roles and risks within and across policy regimes in the face of the uncertainties and ambiguities of twenty-first century life on a global playing field. This volume highlights different *within gender* differences, depending on the institutional ecologies of women's lives. The books taken together show that the social organization of the life course remains *gender graded*, typically producing diverging paths for men and women even though they may begin life with similar backgrounds and abilities. By viewing macro-level forces of global change from the micro-level of women's lives, this edited volume offers a unique angle on globalization. Pathbreaking too is its contextual, comparative and dynamic framing of gendered policy regimes, careers and life courses. Women's lives are being reconfigured in light of dramatic shifts in the larger social fabric of society, but in different ways in different settings.

BIBLIOGRAPHY

Bailyn, L. (1993) *Breaking the mold: women, men, and time in the new corporate world*, New York: Free Press.

Blossfeld, H.-P. and Drobnič, S. (2001) *Careers of couples in contemporary societies: from male breadwinner to dual earner families*, Oxford: Oxford University Press.

Blossfeld, H.-P. and Hakim, C. (1997) *Between equalization and marginalization: women working part-time in Europe and the United States of America*, Oxford: Oxford University Press.

Blossfeld, H.-P., Drobnič, S. and Rohwer, G. (1995) 'Employment patterns: a crossroad between class and gender', *Sfb-Arbeitspapier*, no. 33, Bremen.

Coser, L.A. (ed.) (1984) *Greedy institutions: patterns of undivided commitment*, New York: Free Press.

Friedan, B. (1963) *The feminine mystique*, New York: Bantam Doubleday Dell.

Hochschild, A. (1989) *The second shift*, New York: Avon Books.

Kohli, M. (1986) 'The world we forget: a historical review of the life course', in V. W. Marshall (ed.), *Later life: the social psychology of aging*, Beverly Hills, CA: Sage, pp. 271-303.

Mayer, K.U. (1986) 'Structural constraints on the life course', *Human Development*, 29: 163-70.

Merton, R.K. (1968) *Social theory and social structure*, New York: Free Press.

Moen, P. (ed.) (2003) *It's about time: couples and careers*, Ithaca, NY: Cornell University Press.

Moen, P. and Orrange, R. (2002) 'Careers and lives: socialization, structural lag, and gendered ambivalence', in R. Settersten and T. Owens (eds) *Advances in life course research: New frontiers in socialization*, London, UK: Elsevier Science, pp. 231-60.

Moen, P. and Roehling, P. (2005) *The career mystique: cracks in the American dream*, Boulder, CO: Rowman & Littlefield.

Moen, P. and Sweet, S. (2003) 'Time clocks: couples' work hour strategies', in P. Moen (ed.) *It's about time: Couples and careers*, Ithaca, NY: Cornell University Press, pp. 17-34.

Moen, P. and Spencer, D. (2005) 'Converging divergences in age, gender, health, and well-being: strategic selection in the third age', in R. Binstock and L. George (eds) *Handbook of aging and the social sciences* (6th edition) San Diego, CA: Academic Press.

Orrange, R. (2003) 'The emerging mutable self: gender dynamics and creative adaptations in defining work, family, and the future', *Social Forces*, 82(1): 1–34.

Pixley, J.E. and Moen, P. (2003) 'Prioritizing careers', in P. Moen (ed.) *It's about time: couples and careers*, Ithaca, NY: Cornell University Press, pp. 183-200.

Reskin, B.F. (1998) *The realities of affirmative action*, Washington, D.C.: American Sociological Association.

Riley, M.W. and Riley, J.W. (1989) 'The lives of older people and changing social roles', *Annals of the American Academy of Political and Social Science*, 503: 14–28.

Riley, M.W. and Riley, J.W. (1994) 'Structural lag: past and future', in M.W. Riley, R.L. Kahn and A. Foner (eds), *Age and structural lag: society's failure to provide meaningful opportunities in work, family and leisure*, New York: Wiley, pp. 15–36.

PART I

Introduction

1. Globalization, uncertainty and women's mid-career life courses: a theoretical framework

Heather Hofmeister, Hans-Peter Blossfeld and Melinda Mills[1]

INTRODUCTION

Since the early 1960s, rates of mid-life women's paid work have been steadily increasing in all modern societies. In most of the countries in the Organisation for Economic Co-operation and Development (OECD), this integration has been coupled with a rise in more flexible types of non-standard employment (Blossfeld and Hakim 1997; Daly 2000) or an expansion of the informal sector, most notably in Southern Europe (Gonzalez, Jurado and Naldini 2000). Since the late 1980s these phenomena seem to be enhanced by the process of globalization, which has dramatically accelerated the demand for a more disposable labor force with lower fixed costs and thereby accelerated the 'feminization of the labor market' (Standing 1989). The dominant (male) Fordist standard full-time and lifelong employment relationship that ties the worker to one occupation or firm over the life course has been gradually eroding in many countries (Fromm 2004; Mayer 2001; Myles 1990). Women's rising labor force participation has been associated with this process.

Globalization therefore appears to have ambivalent implications for women's employment, largely depending on the welfare state and the country-specific employment regime. In some countries, it may foster women's employment by allowing more women to (re-)enter the labor market than in the past, because more flexible jobs may bring a large group of mid-life women into the labor market that previously had no or only a marginal attachment or difficulties reconciling paid work with unpaid care duties. Yet, in other countries that already have achieved higher levels of women's full-time secure employment, the employment restructuring fueled by globalization has the potential to jeopardize that security. Based on the increasing global flexibilization of work, more and more of these women might find themselves in flexible and more insecure jobs than in the past. The goal of this book is to examine both the labor market attachment of mid-life women over time and the quality of that attachment. We ask whether globalization has the potential to enhance gender equality by integrating more women into the labor market or reverse trends toward equality by weakening the position of women in the labor market via a reduction in the quality of their employment, and to examine how this varies across 13 different countries.

Four mutually reinforcing processes, often referred to as globalization, contribute to radical changes in labor relations and women's employment in modern OECD-type countries (Mills and Blossfeld 2005). First, we have witnessed the declining importance of national borders for all kinds of economic transactions, coupled with increased competition in terms of capital, labor and goods, particularly from low-income countries where labor costs and labor rights are less developed and from countries where foreign direct investments produce higher profits. Second, the rising worldwide interconnectedness through the information and communication technology (ICT) revolution has given rise to more options of flexible work re-organization and the creation of virtually instantaneous and real-time international competition. A third change is the tougher tax competition between welfare states, which is accompanied by the deregulation, privatization, and liberalization of domestic industries and markets. This in turn results in a notable rise in part-time jobs, work designed into reduced hours or marginal work that sometimes replaces full-time jobs and is connected with an explicit erosion of employment conditions. Finally, the rising importance of, and firms' exposure to, a world market that has increasingly unpredictable disruptions puts firms under mounting pressure to adapt faster and more flexibly to the changes in their environment. In other words, globalization produces increasing uncertainty on the side of employers who have to compete within an increasingly worldwide market by reducing costs through a decrease in wages and commitments to workers: in short, through creating more flexible employment (Kalleberg 2000).

In general, employment flexibility can be introduced to the labor market through several major types: functional, numerical, wage, temporal and outsourcing (Atkinson 1984). The meaning of 'flexibility' varies by national labor market context and industry, and can be as simple as a change in the number and scheduling of working hours in the day or workweek or as pro-found as the ease of labor market exit and re-entry, reduced job security, more short-term contracts and fewer long-term ones, lower pay and fewer protections (for example, benefits, coverage by unions or collective agree-ments). Of central importance in this volume is the extent of functional and numerical flexibility, which leads to a division of labor market insiders and outsiders. Functional flexibility strategies mean that existing job positions are becoming more flexible (in other words, the traditional standard employment contract weakens, mainly affecting internal labor markets or the 'organizational insiders'). Numerical flexibility strategies create new kinds of jobs that are designed with flexible conditions (mainly non-standard work arrangements or 'organizational outsiders') (Kalleberg 2003). It seems that rising flexibility does not signal a break from the preponderance of internal labor markets in shaping available employment careers of mid-career men, but rather enhances the scope and relevance of a second tier of employment lying outside its protections and promotions (Blossfeld, Mills and Bernardi 2006).

As globalization encourages and enhances processes of labor market flexibility, mid-life women in OECD countries stand uniquely poised, by choice or by default, to move into such positions because of their structural location between competing demands (Mills 2004a). On the one hand, mid-life women still hold primary responsibility for the household, a role that has remained relatively stable over time and across national contexts (Blossfeld and Drobnič 2001; Chapter 16, this volume). This heavy responsibility and the likelihood of women interrupting work careers for caregiving responsibilities at various points along the life course make it difficult for mid-life women to compete with unencumbered workers (men) in internal labor markets and for full-time secure positions. For men, there is no irreconcilability between the traditional definitions of a good family man and a good worker (Brines 1994). A man can satisfy the conditions of both spheres by being a good provider, and in fact, this is important gender work for recodifying a male identity (West and Fenstermaker 1993; 1995).

By contrast for women, the roles in each sphere still lie at odds, with tremendous tension between fulfilling the roles of an ideal worker and an available caregiver (Williams 2000). The result is an asymmetry within the household and within the labor market (Blossfeld and Drobnič 2001). Strong segregation exists between men and women's positions at home (Blossfeld and Drobnič 2001; Gerson 1985; Moen 1992) and in the workplace (Charles and Grusky 2004; Williams 2000), and structural constraints exist to varying degrees that limit the options available to women to balance their competing demands. Women's heavy responsibility for family also often culturally legitimizes their structural allocation to the secondary labor market and segregation into 'feminized' occupations, often characterized by higher turnover and a lower human capital requirement, as well as lower earnings and less authority, autonomy, power or opportunity for career advancement (Aschaffenburg 1995; Bielby and Baron 1986; Rosenfeld 1990).

But on the other hand, women are increasingly involved in paid employment. Since women are more educated across progressive cohorts in all advanced societies, they also can obtain better jobs and access to careers (Blossfeld 1987) as well as higher real wages in comparison to their predecessors (Hannan, Schömann and Blossfeld 1990). Thus, persistent gender segregation of jobs does not necessarily mean that women's career opportunities would not improve relative to where they had been (Blossfeld

1987). Rather, with the tertiarization of the occupational structure and the trend towards a knowledge society, accelerated by globalization forces, we expect that there is also a shift across cohorts from relatively unskilled production and service jobs to more skilled service jobs, for which women are increasingly well qualified. It is, however, still an open empirical question as to which extent the integration of qualified women into skilled jobs goes together with more flexible and precarious employment forms for women in the various countries under study.

To explore the seemingly ambivalent implications of globalization on women's careers, we address four main research questions. Our first question asks: does globalization foster a rise in women's mid-life employment? Here we explore whether the flexible jobs that globalization generates pull more mid-career women into the labor market, perhaps by satisfying the tensions inherent between work and family roles.

Second, what are the consequences of globalization for the *quality* of women's employment? Here we specifically examine whether increased employment flexibilization hinders the further integration of women into the skilled, secure and mostly full-time positions of the internal labor market, or whether skilled women are particularly integrated through the knowledge-intensive economy. We also study whether the escalating restructuring of employment conditions affects the movement of mid-life women into un-skilled jobs (downward mobility), skilled jobs (upward mobility), unemployment and unpaid caregiving. We view globalization therefore as reinforcing existing trends in women's labor market participation by speeding up the process by which mid-life women are re-entering the labor market and participating in skilled as well as unskilled paid work.

Third, are there certain groups of women who are more likely to be in lower-quality jobs? Of course, not all women are in the same structural position. Individual characteristics, family structure and the particular arrangements between spouses also determine women's positions in the labor market. National contexts and sets of regulations and alternative structures may likewise enhance or alleviate women's responsibilities in either the work or family sphere.

A final question therefore asks: how do national contexts and welfare regimes influence the availability of the compromises between work and family demands for mid-career women, the quality of women's employment and inequality among women? More specifically, how do the diverse domestic institutions across the different nations filter the transformations brought about by the globalization process and create incentives or disincentives for certain life-course options at the individual level? Countries differ significantly with respect to the configuration of employment relationships among employers, workers, families and the state (Esping-Andersen 1999; Orloff 2002). There are distinct variations among modern countries in terms of the importance of not only labor market agreements but also the availability of state-sponsored family supports or market-driven alternatives to women's unpaid caregiving. How do these impact on the mid-life options and pathways of women in a globalizing world? In particular, how do these affect mid-life women's upward and downward job moves as well as their transitions into unemployment and from unemployment to employment?

This volume examines the relationship between globalization and the changes in women's mid-life courses in and out of paid work and its alternatives in 13 OECD countries. The countries are divided into five different welfare regimes: the conservative (the Netherlands and Germany), social-democratic (Sweden and Denmark), post-socialistic (Estonia, Czech Republic, Hungary and Poland), liberal (Great Britain and the United States) and family-oriented regimes (Mexico, Italy and Spain). We do not intend to address all questions that are implied in the relationship between globalization and women's household and economic activity. Rather, we will focus on the more specific task of describing the changes in women's mid-life work entries, exits and re-entries to paid work and family caregiving and their job mobility within paid work over the last few decades. The inclusion of countries that are structurally different will allow us to gain an empirically grounded theoretical understanding of how globalization, and the apparent uncertainty that it generates at the employment level, has impacted on women's mid-career life courses across a variety of contexts.

For our purposes, we have defined women's mid-life course trajectories by a series of transitions. Each nation-specific chapter within this book examines the impact of globalization on the life courses of women via three transition types: (1) upward, lateral and downward job mobility; (2) transitions from paid employment into unemployment, unpaid caregiving, paid caregiving or out-of-labor-force status; and (3) re-entry into paid employment from unemployment, unpaid caregiving, paid caregiving or out-of-labor-force status.

It is valuable to focus on women's mid-career intragenerational mobility as a topic in its own right. The majority of previous research on social mobility has primarily examined the *inter*generational mobility of *men*, meaning that comparative research on *intra*generational mobility, particularly of women, is rare. That which does exist demonstrates that the mobility experiences of women differ significantly from those of men (Aschaffenburg 1995; Rosenfeld 1990; 1992). For example, men are generally protected insiders to the labor market, less impacted on by flexibilization, and seldom leave the labor market for family-related interruptions. Women's careers have undergone more extensive change in recent decades, and women are increasingly developing their own individual social identity via the workplace. Despite this development, a woman's social position within classical stratification research is attributed to her husband or father rather than her own achievements (for example, Giddens 1973; Parsons 1953). To do justice to the topic of women's mid-career mobility, in this volume we focus exclusively on the experiences of women and address the consequences of globalization on men's mid-career life courses in an accompanying book (Blossfeld, Mills and Bernardi 2006). However, both books work with the same longitudinal approach and generally examine the same transitions so that many of the results for men and women are easily comparable.

This chapter reviews the core concepts and theories applied to the 13 case studies in this volume. We first clarify the four central dimensions of our definition of globalization and outline how they are affecting women's work. We then explain the role played by national institutions in 'filtering' these universal forces of globalization, with a focus on welfare regimes, educational systems, employment systems and family and cultural systems. The discussion then turns to the importance of individual resources and family strategies, followed by a specification of the main pathways in women's mid-life employment careers. The data and methods used in this volume are summarized, and the chapter concludes with a description of the structure of this book.

GLOBALIZATION AND MID-LIFE WOMEN

As described in the introduction, we define globalization by four interrelated structural shifts: (1) the internationalization of markets in terms of labor, capital and goods and decline of national borders; (2) intensified competition through deregulation, privatization and liberalization; (3) accelerated spread of networks and knowledge via new communication and information technologies; and (4) the rising importance of world markets and their increasing dependence on random shocks (see Figure 1.1). We share the perspective of Mayer (2001) that these globalization forces create a set of similar pressures and challenges that interact with existing institutions and cultural differences within nation-states, which together impact on the life courses of mid-life women. The following description of globalization is informed by the work of Mills and Blossfeld and adds a focus on how globalization affects women's employment (Mills and Blossfeld 2005; Mills, Blossfeld and Bernardi 2006).

These four universal structural shifts together generate rising uncertainty broadly but influence the level of uncertainty felt by employers and experienced by mid-life women themselves based on the degree of intervention from country-specific institutions including employment relations, educational systems, welfare regimes and family systems. Women in some countries may be either more protected or more exposed to uncertainty based on the type of family organization, labor market and the level of risk-protection afforded by the welfare state in various nations.

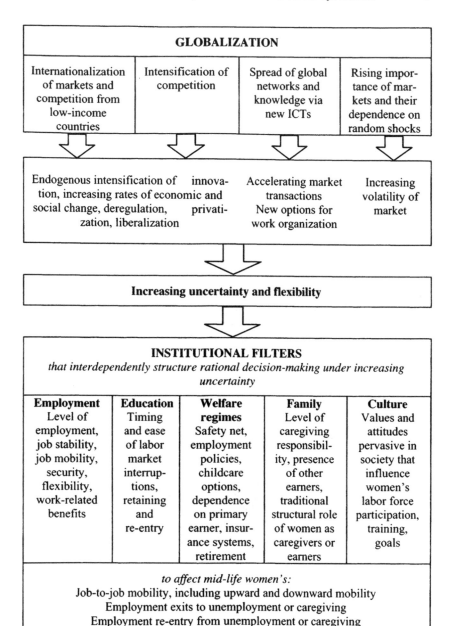

GLOBALIZATION			
Internationalization of markets and competition from low-income countries	Intensification of competition	Spread of global networks and knowledge via new ICTs	Rising importance of markets and their dependence on random shocks

Endogenous intensification of innovation, increasing rates of economic and social change, deregulation, privatization, liberalization   Accelerating market transactions New options for work organization   Increasing volatility of market

Increasing uncertainty and flexibility

INSTITUTIONAL FILTERS
that interdependently structure rational decision-making under increasing uncertainty

Employment	**Education**	**Welfare regimes**	**Family**	**Culture**
Level of employment, job stability, job mobility, security, flexibility, work-related benefits	Timing and ease of labor market interruptions, retaining and re-entry	Safety net, employment policies, childcare options, dependence on primary earner, insurance systems, retirement	Level of caregiving responsibility, presence of other earners, traditional structural role of women as caregivers or earners	Values and attitudes pervasive in society that influence women's labor force participation, training, goals

to affect mid-life women's:
Job-to-job mobility, including upward and downward mobility
Employment exits to unemployment or caregiving
Employment re-entry from unemployment or caregiving

Source: Modified from Mills and Blossfeld (2005)

Figure 1.1   Model of globalization and increasing uncertainty in women's employment

Internationalization of markets and decline of national borders

The internationalization of markets and decline of national borders is the first driving engine of globalization we discuss. Internationalization is caused by changes in laws, institutions and practices. In the era of globalization, these changes are often designed to make transactions easier and less expensive across borders. For instance, we are now experiencing the integration of previously isolated nations into the world economy that were closed to global forces for reasons such as a dictatorship (Spain) or communism (Estonia, Hungary, Czech Republic, Poland). For these countries, the integration into the world economy has resulted in rapid technological catch-up processes and periods of painful social and economic adjustments. For the rest of the highly industrialized countries in the world market, in particular for the countries in Western Europe, the integration of former socialist countries means increasing international competition from countries where labor costs and labor rights are less developed and less expensive (Standing 1989). The ease of transactions across national borders also results in an intensification of innovation and an increased rate of economic and social change in all societies.

We anticipate that the internationalization of markets will have several impacts on women's mobility patterns. First, changes in the labor market increase demand for flexibility and new skills. The consequence is that women with the right educational qualifications may be adaptable to shifting job circumstances, requirements and conditions. In national contexts with increased opportunities for re-training, we hypothesize that women's absences from the labor market should be less penalizing for later job entry or re-entry across cohorts.

The internationalization of markets also intensifies competition among firms, who compete for cheap labor and expanding markets. The most successful firms in such a climate create a workforce that can expand and contract as the market requires. This competition affects women at several levels. They may be more likely to find employment in cases where their labor is valued at lower rates than the labor of women in a neighboring country; for example, in Mexico the northern border is dotted with industries employing women at much lower wages than in the United States. In general, demand for workers with flexibility and new (service and information-based) skills should rise, with the consequence that in times of globalization, women with the appropriate educational qualifications will be recruited by firms for their ability to adapt to shifting job circumstances, requirements and conditions. Workers in some regions are finding their industries are leaving and their training is obsolete, while workers in other regions are realizing new employment opportunities. This means that some regions are experiencing surges in employment opportunities in traditionaly feminized industries and occupations while other regions experience losses of jobs. We expect that increased competition will urge firms to compete by lowering labor costs, which they will partly achieve by reducing benefits for more marginal workers such as those in part-time positions, starting a 'race to the bottom' (Mills 2004a). Benefits taken disproportionately by women for caregiving responsibilities (paid time off for parental leave, job security after parental leave, flexible or reduced hours) may decrease, reducing the quality of jobs available for women, especially regarding job security and earnings.

Competition: deregulation, privatization, liberalization

A second central feature of globalization is the intensification of competition and the need for nations to heighten their competitiveness via deregulation (relaxing government regulation of economic activities), privatization (transferring to private ownership previously public or state-owned enterprises) and liberalization (relying on price mechanisms to coordinate economic activities). With the awareness that capital and labor are increasingly mobile and in a move to improve the functioning of their domestic markets, many nations have modified their tax structures. There are several consequences for women's labor market experiences. First, in order to add a competitive advantage and improve the functioning of their domestic markets, many countries have deregulated Employment Protection Legislation (EPL). Previous research has shown that when there is less EPL, such as in liberal regimes like the United States and the United Kingdom, companies have fewer constraints for downsizing, lay-offs and the introduction of further labor market flexibility measures (Auer and Cazes 2000).

Second, the shift to privatization should expose more women to employment uncertainties. Employment in the public sector is farther removed from the impetus of productivity and profitability of global competition compared to the private sector (Esping-Andersen 1993). We expect, therefore, that the sector of employment should be a key factor in determining how women are sheltered from risk, with those employed in the public sector more protected than their counterparts in the private sector. But as the public sector shrinks during privatization, fewer women may benefit from this protection and more may be exposed to uncertainty.

Information and communication technology revolution

The spread of information and communication technologies speeds up interactions and dissolves many information barriers; it allows processing of information to happen anywhere at any time and reduces the transaction time and costs of information movement. We anticipate several consequences for women's employment experiences. First, we assume that the spread of these technologies will have country-specific effects on the flexibility and availability of paid work, with rising employment opportunities in the technology-service sector in lower-cost, lower-welfare-benefit countries, but less employment in countries with higher levels of welfare benefits and firm costs because of competition from abroad. Second, the integration of new technologies in the workplace means that workers with more skills, and the 'right' skills, will fare better in the new 'knowledge-based economy' (Gera and Massé 1996). Third, and conversely, new technologies not only create positions for new knowledge workers, but can also be used to increase efficiency through the mechanization of low-skilled positions and thus create redundancy for workers from unskilled manual classes (Beck 2000). In some economies, this means that there is less work for unskilled labor. Returning to employment may be difficult and require retraining for jobs that require more technological skill, which may be time and cost intensive. Fourth, the growth in ICT affects individuals' access to information about the labor market itself. Finally, new technologies may provide more flexible working conditions such as telecommuting and flexible work hours, which can facilitate (high-capital-holding) women's dual roles as caregivers and workers (Mills 2004a; Mills and Blossfeld 2005; Moen and Roehling 2005).

Rise in the importance of markets

Finally, globalization is inherently related to the rise in the importance of markets. Not only do we experience the intensification or speeding up of processes, but globalized markets also increasingly take the lead and set the standards to which individuals, firms and nations then try to comply. The escalating dynamics and volatility of outcomes of globalizing markets makes it more difficult for individuals, firms and governments to predict the future and to make choices between different alternatives and strategies. This increasing uncertainty results in the need for firms and governments to leave their options 'open' and thus promotes labor market flexibility and the shifting of risk to the individual. Firms react by implementing various measures of labor market flexibility (described previously), which vary depending on the institutional context. The increasing volatility of the market results in the shifting of risk from the firm and the government to the individual, especially the most vulnerable, including youth (Mills, Blossfeld and Klijzing 2005) and women who attempt to re-enter paid employment after periods of extended caregiving. The consequence for women is a heightened and repeated unemployment risk or downward mobility after labor market re-entry.

INSTITUTIONAL STRUCTURES: NATION-SPECIFIC REACTIONS TO GLOBALIZATION

As Figure 1.1 illustrates, institutions are central to our understanding of how individuals' options and decisions are shaped by universal globalization forces (Esping-Andersen 1999; Mayer 2004a; Mayer 2004b). Institutions initiate very different responses to similar pressures by affecting the costs of having and raising children, the economic value of family responsibilities and the choices available between family activities and paid employment. Relevant institutions that shape women's labor market responses to globalization include the welfare regime with its particular labor market and family policies, education systems that regulate re-entry chances in the workplace, employment relation systems and family and cultural systems.

Welfare regimes

Welfare regimes are a crucial organizing characteristic of women's life courses owing to the ways the regimes value women's unpaid work and/or share it (Lewis 1992). Institutional supports available in some countries and their absence in others influence the ways that women and their partners make decisions about the timing, spacing and number of births (Blossfeld 1995a; Blossfeld 1995b), the ability to return to paid work after giving birth and the level of trust women and men can put in institutions (if any exist) that care for their children while they are at work. Institutions that define welfare regimes also reflect and create cultures that may encourage, tolerate or discourage births or women's paid employment after childbirth. In addition, welfare regimes configure the processes of globalization, the ways in which the uncertainties are shifted to specific groups while protecting others, and the degree to which types of flexible employment, and flexible life courses, are tolerated, welcomed or avoided (Mayer 2001). We categorize welfare regimes according to a modified Esping-Andersen typology (Mills and Blossfeld 2005) of conservative, social-democratic, post-socialist, liberal and family-oriented. Owing to these configurations of institutions, mentioned above, women's labor force participation and part-time employment levels vary by welfare regime (Blossfeld and Hakim 1997; Chapter 2, this volume).

Obstacles to women's secure employment may be many, as the nation-specific chapters of this volume describe in detail. Some welfare regimes discourage female employment through taxes, labor laws, training regulations and lack of alternative institutional supports (such as childcare). Discriminatory hiring and payment practices may discourage women from working for pay or bar them access to the kinds of jobs they want or need. Maternity leave policies discourage employers from investing in a female labor force because the costs of hiring women who interrupt their jobs for caregiving are higher than the costs of hiring workers who do not interrupt. The more generous the leave policies, the more 'expensive' women are to hire. Even women who do not plan to interrupt their employment can be suspected of having a higher likelihood to interrupt and are either not hired, passed over for promotions or relegated to lower-paid, lower-status work. Furthermore, the lack of affordable and available childcare or active work/family policies may further inhibit women's ability to participate actively in the labor market.

The log-logistic S-curve in Figure 1.2 conceptualizes the relative labor market involvement of mid-life women by welfare regime and the expected direction in which globalization produces shifts in women's labor market involvement over time. These shifts likely reach a threshold, perhaps one that the post-socialist and social-democratic welfare regimes have already reached for reasons that will be described below. At these high levels of women's labor market participation, women's continuous attachment to the labor market is likely made more difficult through globalization forces and the concomitant introduction of uncertainty, flexibility, unemployment and a rise in the chance of downward mobility. By contrast, rates of women's labor market participation in family-oriented and conservative welfare regimes may increase with the expansion of flexible job types. This increase may be welcomed by mid-life women who otherwise would have been excludedd from paid work opportunities (and thus benefit from globalization forces) because more opportunities for flexibly timed employment may help these women to accommodate alternative responsibilities or to achieve an easier re-entry after work interruptions. We therefore hypothesize that, for mid-life women in conservative and family-oriented welfare regimes with low levels of overall female employment, the globalization process increases women's attachment to the labor market; while for social-democratic, post-socialist and to a lesser extent for liberal welfare regimes the higher level of more secure full-time employment should be likely to decrease, or at least be replaced by more flexible employment arrangements.

Conservative
In conservative welfare regimes (the Netherlands and Germany), the male breadwinner model is the primary family form. National policies in these regimes assume and encourage families to conform to a single (male) bread-winner template. Policies include long maternity leaves and, in the case of Germany, tax structures that reward single-earner families, and part-time over full-time second earners, by heavily taxing a second income into a household (Blossfeld and Drobnič 2001; Blossfeld and Hakim 1997). But these countries are shifting slowly toward alternatives with more than one earner. For example, the Netherlands has strongly adapted what is termed a 'one-and-a-half' breadwinner model for couples with children, with the man's full-time paycheck supplemented by the woman's part-time income (Schippers and Plantenga 2001). Therefore, women in conservative countries like (West) Germany and the Netherlands may be more accommodating to the kinds of jobs generated by globalization because the potential female workforce can more easily tolerate flexible part-time contingent employment based on their structural position as secondary earners in a system that supports the employment and high pay of the primary earner.

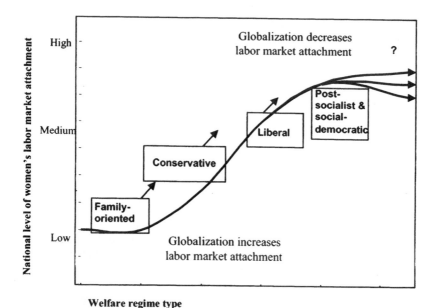

Figure 1.2 shows a plot with vertical axis "National level of women's labor market attachment" (Low, Medium, High) and horizontal axis "Welfare regime type".

Text within figure:
- Globalization decreases labor market attachment   ?
- Post-socialist & social-democratic
- Liberal
- Conservative
- Family-oriented
- Globalization increases labor market attachment

Key:
⟶ = Conceptual direction globalization forces push women's employment
Family-oriented = Italy, Spain, Mexico
Conservative = Germany, the Netherlands
Liberal = Great Britain, United States
Post-socialist = Czech Republic, Estonia, Hungary, Poland
Social-democratic = Sweden, Denmark

Figure 1.2   Conceptual model of macro-level changes in women's labor market attachment over time under processes of globalization

More flexible work for women fits well with the logic of the male breadwinner model. We expect, therefore, that mid-life women in conservative regimes will experience a continuation of the changes already under way, especially via increases in marginal part-time work over time, which will allow further integration of women into the labor market and the continued growth of the 'one-and-a-half' earner model. This hypothesis is supported by empirical evidence of the first GLOBALIFE book where young women have been more likely than men to be in fixed-term contract, part-time and other more precarious jobs (see Mills, Blossfeld and Klijzing 2005). Considering the cultural propensity for mothers to work part-time and the institutional difficulties they face with full-time paid work (for example, lack of childcare, school system where children are free many afternoons), we do not anticipate a substantial move to the dual-earner model that would permit or encourage mothers to work full-time.

Social-democratic

Social-democratic welfare regimes (Sweden and Denmark) are characterized by a strong welfare state, a high proportion of women in public sector and abundant reduced-full-time work. These regimes individualize and decommodify men and women, making them more equal in the eyes of the state and legal system. Men and women in these regimes theoretically should be exposed equally to globalization, but in reality, these regimes have exceptionally high gender segregation, with men and women employed in different industries. One reason for this high level of gender segregation is that many mothers of young children who remain in the labor force are on parental leave, while, still, only few men take up these leaves. Another reason is that even when caregiving work is paid, it still tends to be 'women's work' (Orloff 2002). Women often also work in service industries that are the growth industries for globalization, which means that they may also experience an expansion of 'flexible' employment opportunities.

In social-democratic regimes, it is easier to move in and out of employment owing to an active labor force policy that includes mandatory additional training and re-skilling for the unemployed. Citizens enjoy high labor market flexibility because of a state-cushioned flexible labor market (a model often called flexicurity). Flexibility is thus supported by the state via the way the state supports the individual. Globalization may, however, put pressure on the welfare state to reduce costs in a competitive environment, ultimately giving citizens less security, particularly if the state chooses to cut back in family policy areas. One piece of early evidence of globalization's effects on workers in social-democratic countries is that cutbacks in the public sector jeopardize firm tenure. But the biggest risk population is male workers with blue-collar vocational training, who are the most likely to be unemployed (Blossfeld, Mills and Bernardi 2006).

Within social-democratic regimes, we anticipate few additional fluctuations in job mobility and labor market attachment changes across cohorts. These countries already experience high levels of mobility and attachment to the labor market, so are already at the virtual 'ceiling.' However, it is not unlikely that globalization pushes mid-career women to take up more flexible forms of employment such as part-time work (as opposed to reduced full-time, which is virtually equivalent to full-time), more precarious jobs in the growing service sector or reduced employment in the public sector (attributed to potential welfare state retrenchment).

Post-socialist

Post-socialist countries (Estonia, Czech Republic, Hungary and Poland) have a twentieth-century legacy of encouraging dual-earner families. Full-time employment for women has been the norm for the past 40 years owing to the socialist practice of setting salaries at levels that required two salaries for each family and enacting legislation that required men and women to be in the labor market. Wage policies encouraged women into some occupations that are, in other countries, male-dominated, such as medicine.

After the fall of the Iron Curtain, however, full employment was no longer guaranteed by the state. More insecure employment has replaced lifelong jobs in these transition economies, and unemployment is a growing trend. However, some strict employment protections remain, making these countries less liberalized than Western Europe, although more liberalized than they used to be. The service sector has grown in the process of modernization that followed the collapse of communism. In addition, social and economic inequalities have expanded.

Now that women are not required by law to be employed, some might leave the labor force because they have the option. We therefore expect that women in some of the post-socialist countries with a strong (Catholic) conservative tradition (such as Poland) prefer part-time work. Because there are not many part-time jobs to be found in these former socialist countries (Blossfeld and Hakim 1997), women are forced to choose between working full-time or withdrawing from the labor force. Two explanations exist for the lack of part-time jobs; both are to be discussed in more detail in the respective nation-specific chapters in this book. In brief, the public sector, which is a large employment sector, has no policy of providing part-time employment to women. The private sector, as in other countries, avoids creating part-time jobs because employers perceive these jobs as expensive to firms, owing to the equivalent levels of benefits for workers who invest less time.

Because of economic upheaval and the transition to a market economy in these welfare regimes, being out of the labor force is a situation many women cannot afford, increasing the probability that women will work full-time. Post-socialist welfare regimes do provide long maternity leaves (three years in some countries) and well-protected jobs in some sectors, but the sectors operate quite differently. Public service sectors are secure but low paid. Among families with stable breadwinners, such employment may be a desirable option for women. Some state-owned factories remain but tend to be low paid and insecure. The private sector operates using short-term contracts, but it also pays more (see Chapters 7, 8, 9 and 10, this volume). We can also envision a scenario where the rapid changes and deregulation of emerging Eastern European economies creates turmoil for both men's and women's careers, causing a crisis for both breadwinners in the household.

Public childcare services, especially public nurseries for very young children, have diminished sharply since the early 1990s in varying degrees in post-socialist countries, with some public childcare remaining. This lack of public childcare creates clear difficulties for women who combine work and family responsibilities when private options have not filled the demand.

Liberal

Liberal welfare regimes (Great Britain and the United States) have a market-based approach to their policies. By creating favorable business climates, these regimes are designed to provide employment for their citizens mainly through the private sector. Compared with other welfare regimes, they have small public sectors and low levels of job security. High levels of employment flexibility and fewer regulations from unions and government give firms the opportunity to hire and fire workers as their demands require. Therefore, women in liberal welfare regimes find a variety of employment forms, from full-time to marginal. The drawback is that employment benefits are weak, especially in part-time and marginal work, and there is comparatively little job security.

For women working in liberal welfare regimes, barriers to employment include a lack of public childcare and expensive private childcare. There is also a tradition, particularly in the United States, of linking benefits like health insurance, paid time off and pension contributions to full-time jobs only (Kalleberg, Reskin and Hudson 2000). Part-time employees are also often exempt from the restrictive employment regulations in the primary labor market, and are subjected to less stringent firing policies. Many occupations in female-dominated industries are only available in part-time work, and/or they have low pay, less employment protection and/or a combination of these. This means that single mothers who are employed in these kinds of work arrangements, and women with unemployed or low-income partners, are especially financially vulnerable. If the welfare state or kinship ties do not step in, women must find secure jobs to protect the well-being of the family (Oppenheimer 1988). Many cannot, resulting in financial hardship especially for single mothers. Men and women are treated equally by law in a way that seeks not to privilege women with exceptions like maternity leave but rather attempts to regard all workers in the same job status as equal, with equal responsibilities and benefits, regardless of need. We therefore expect that the impact of globalization on these welfare regimes will further intensify the move towards contingent, part-time and insecure jobs for women, particularly those in the lower occupational classes. The minimal welfare safety net and 'business-friendly' state policies pass uncertainty and flexibility more directly to the workers.

Family-oriented

Centralized, Catholic, 'family-oriented' welfare regimes (Mexico, Italy, Spain) have tended to rely on families and kinship networks instead of the state to take care of the sorts of supports offered by more generous welfare regimes (Bernardi 2001; Gonzalez, Jurado and Naldini 2000; Saraceno 1994). In particular, this type of welfare regime offers less public childcare and fewer services for dependent elderly than other regime types (Bernardi 2001). Alternatively, they have among the longest paid maternity leave, which has the opposite effect of what would be expected: instead of acting to reserve a woman's job for her after the birth, an extremely long maternity leave sends the message to mothers that they belong at home to care for children rather than in the labor force. The consequences for women's labor force participation are apparent. For one, women face few options for combining paid work and motherhood (Bernardi 1999; 2005). Childcare is difficult to find, part-time work is unavailable, and social policies discourage mothers' employment. Many young women are choosing to postpone or forgo having children: Italy and Spain's birth rates, for example, are the lowest in the world.

We expect that women in family-oriented welfare regimes may be affected by globalization in several ways: globalization may face an alteration of regimes' childcare policies as countries try to keep up with international competition to reduce labor market costs (and related expenses). Or, under economic duress, the welfare regime may limit or shorten unemployment benefits, forcing women back into employment more quickly over time and thus also likely increasing the probability of downward job mobility. Finally, we expect that there will be an increase in more flexible employment arrangements, giving family-oriented women in Italy and Spain a better opportunity to combine family and paid work. A problem arises that the family-oriented welfare states in Spain and Italy do not have a history of (female) part-time work, as conservative welfare states do (Blossfeld and Hakim 1997). Thus, in the course of globalization, flexible employment forms have to be created from scratch and might therefore take a long time to become established.

Education systems

Educational systems have an influence on women's labor force participation by either tracking women into certain occupational training paths early in their careers (Blossfeld and Huinink 1991) that reduce their overall earnings potential (Hannan, Schömann and Blossfeld 1990) or providing encourage-ment and opportunity to attain high-earnings and high-prestige occupations. Women's mid-life labor market participation and success is partly dependent on whether educational systems allow women to get additional training and skill-updating after family responsibilities have lessened, which would allow them to compete in the labor force on equal footing with those who have had continuous careers. As the chapters in this volume will elaborate, some educational systems have excellent 'off-time' training programs, whereas other systems make little or no allowance for adult education.

Employment systems shift to a post-Fordist model

There are also country-specific variations in employment relations and systems that emerge in relation to aspects such as the types of work councils, collective bargaining systems, strength of unions and labor legislation. These differences produce distinct variations in occupational structures and industries, labor conditions and the degree, level and type of labor market flexibility that is allowed within each country. The differences between these systems are often characterized by the degree of 'open' or 'closed' employment relations (Sørensen 1983) or as 'individualist' or 'collective' regimes (DiPrete et al. 1997). The type of employment relation regime in turn impacts on how the 'outsiders' of the labor market, who are often women, experience globalization. We argue that the relationship of women to employment systems must be examined in a unique way, particularly in relation to how this relationship has drastically shifted in conjunction with the evolution from a Fordist to a post-Fordist model of life-course organization.

A central factor in understanding variation in employment systems is the level of job security, which is often linked to the strength of unions and employer associations. We anticipate that women who live under more open or deregulated employment regimes that are dominated by the market mechanisms of globalization will have a higher risk of unemployment, being in more precarious or lower-quality jobs, lower levels of compensation and less protection or recourse than those in more regulated regimes.

We likewise expect recent shifts towards globalization to be experienced more directly by the outsiders of the labor market (Mills, Blossfeld and Klijzing 2005), particularly those in the more open or individualistic employment regimes. Unpaid labor in the home and paid labor in secondary labor markets or informal 'black' markets are outside of traditional employment protections. Thus women, especially mothers, are often outsiders in most labor markets, even as their unpaid labor at home has made possible men's insider labor market status and uninterrupted employment. Outsiders in a paid labor market tend to experience less security, lower wages and fewer benefits. As women in some countries are increasingly likely to be the sole breadwinners for their families, this outsider status has profound repercussions for the lives and health of children and women, as well as for the relationships between women and men. Few secure jobs that pay a living wage with benefits that also allow for entry and exit for childbearing are available to women, but this varies by country.

In a historical sense, the relationship of women to the paid, formal labor market and employment systems in general, can be thought of in terms of the evolution from Fordist to post-Fordist models of life-course organization (Mayer 2001; Myles 1990). The 'pre-contemporary-globalization' reference point is a Fordist model of life-course organization that had, as one of its hallmarks, an extremely strong differentiation of men's and women's roles in the household and in the labor market.

The Fordist model is based on mass-production technology, with products having a relatively long life cycle. Correspondingly, worker skills, once acquired, are useful throughout a career and the productivity level of workers is relatively static throughout their working lives. The auto industry is a good example of the leading sectors in the Fordist type of industrial economy. Under such a model, firms could offer a 'family wage' organized around a single, stable breadwinner, typically a man, whose secure income was enough to provide for an entire family. Correspondingly, women's lives became closely linked to men's lives and decisions owing to women's financial dependency on the male wage (Moen 1992; 2001; Moen and Roehling 2005). As we elaborate in the next section, structural and cultural assumptions emerged to further support this dependency by emphasizing that women's central organizing life-course priority should be family care, justified through biological differences.

Economic rationality arguments have also been applied to justify the division of labor between husbands and wives based on a Fordist model of household and labor market organization. According to Becker (1981), there is an economic rationality that drives the division of household labor: the worker who is earning the most should be 'specializing' in the work domain, with the other worker specializing in the home domain. In this model, gender differences in human capital investments and acquisition and in the levels of responsibility for household tasks and childcare are all linked to husbands and wives' roles (Blossfeld and Drobnič 2001). Often wives' work is secondary in the household because of the earnings differences between men and women.

In contrast, a post-Fordist economy is more oriented to the application of information technology and the production of information and services with a relatively short life cycle, requiring continuous innovation. Computer software and telecommunications industries represent the leading sectors of this type of economy. Worker skills must be constantly upgraded, and workers must repeatedly be trained and seek multiple careers in their lifetimes. The transition from the Fordist to a post-Fordist life-course model has been accelerated by globalization forces and leads to the heterogeneous life-course patterns that characterize mid-life women in contemporary societies.

Family and cultural systems

As described above, the explanation for women's relegation to this secondary or outsider flexible labor market position likely lies in the cultural and structural requirement for women to be the family members responsible for caregiving. On the one hand, some kinds of labor market flexibility answer the needs of women who try to combine paid work with the full responsibility for family care. On the other hand, this very need for job flexibility stems from institutional constraints such as lack of childcare or adequate parental or sickness leave to care for children or other family members. Therefore women may favor labor market flexibility in some countries out of a desire to minimize their labor market involvement, but in other cases because these are the only positions women can obtain within the structural constraints of their situation (Mills 2004a).

Despite the rapid changes in the economy and in the skills required to compete in the labor market, change of attitudes does not shift from a Fordist model so quickly. Cultural norms toward male breadwinning and female homemaking (or the appearance of it) persist (Bielby and Bielby 1992; Lück, Chapter 16, this volume). For example, the probability of quitting a job increases for women (but decreases for men) with more traditional family styles (Camstra 1996). Men perceive themselves as having something to lose by taking on additional housework, especially if their masculinity, as defined through a secure Fordist-type career, is in jeopardy from the potential weakening of that security (Brines 1994). Couples 'do gender' through the ways in which they choose to divide work, avoid work and create work from among their available options (Bellah et al. 1985; Brines 1994; Hochschild 1989; West and Fenstermaker 1993; 1995). As women change faster than men in their expectations and roles at home and work (Blossfeld and Drobnič 2001), the distribution of home labor in couples becomes lopsided, with women often working a 'second shift' of home-care work in addition to a full-time job (Hochschild 1989). These additional felt responsibilities further hamper women's ability to compete effectively in the labor market against those who do not assume such responsibilities (Moen and Roehling 2005).

When the overwhelming cultural messages are against women's paid employment, employed women are likely to experience a lack of institutional and community support. As globalization forces alter institutions, we must ask: will dominant cultural norms shift toward women's labor market participation and generate attitudinal and institutional support growing within the other relevant institutions, or will culture bifurcate into extremes that reflect the access of different groups to power and privilege? The conclusion section of this volume (Lück, Hofmeister and Blossfeld) will address these issues.

INDIVIDUAL RESOURCES AND FAMILY STRATEGIES

Up to this point, we have portrayed how macro-level institutional effects enable or constrain the employment careers of women. However, our theoretical model also acknowledges the importance of individual competencies and resources (Elder 1999) and the interdependency between agency and structure (Giddens 1984; Mills 2004b). Individual human capital plays a central role in determining the success of the adaptations of women and families to the labor market. Human capital consists of individual characteristics such as educational attainment, skills, labor market experience and age. We anticipate that women with lower levels of human capital – such as those with lower levels of education, skills, experience and are younger – may experience the impact of globalization in more direct ways. Particularly considering the growth of the knowledge economy and ICTs, we expect that there will be rising employment opportunities for women in the technology-service sector in lower-cost, lower-welfare-benefit countries, but less employment for women in countries with higher levels of welfare benefits and firm costs.

However, it is not only nation-specific institutions or individual-level characteristics that define women's employment careers. A particularly important aspect to consider when examining women's labor market behavior is the fact that their employment decisions are often strategized within a broader context: the family. Families can be seen as adaptive units (Moen and Wethington 1992) who seek to maximize benefit to the household. Some women try to stagger their work and family commitments as a strategy, and so they invest first in one sphere (whether it be family or employment) and then later switch. Evidence indicates that women who prioritize family responsibilities by exiting paid employment in their early career-building years never reach the level of pay they would have obtained if they had not left the labor force (Jacobsen and Levin 1995). Women with early investments in careers are likely to see higher and higher dividends over the life course. Women are thus not only likely to retain their priority in their careers, but also to make decisions that continually reinforce that priority, including forgoing or postponing family formation. For other women, globalization may create opportunities that were not available at earlier stages of their life courses, opportunities that facilitate movement between employment and non-employment over time. In short, the globalized economy leaves many life-course chances to individuals' own agency, but path dependencies within women's life courses (the accumulation of advantage in the labor market or disadvantage out of the labor market) is likely to modify the effects of globalization on an individual woman's occupational trajectory.

PATHWAYS IN WOMEN'S MID-LIFE

The theoretical framework up to this point has described how globalization generates increasing uncertainty in paid work, meaning that employees in general and mid-life women in particular are likely to experience rising levels of insecurity owing to rapid shifts in employment conditions and the restructuring of the workplace. This uncertainty is subsequently 'filtered' by nation-specific institutions and impacted by individual-level resources and family strategies, which in turn generate distinct strategies or pathways that women develop to cope with uncertainty. Insofar as individual actors have agency, we can expect that when faced with a loss of one kind of security, they will seek security through other means. In doing so, individuals create new life-course pathways and trajectories. At the aggregate level, these new trajectories should form discernable patterns as the most successful new pathways under globalization diffuse. Even if globalization creates only the perception that previously reliable sources of security are becoming less secure, individuals are likely to create alternative pathways in an attempt to secure themselves and their families against vulnerability.

Figure 1.3 illustrates these potential pathways for mid-career women. We start with the assumption that there are three main sources of economic security, which vary in availability depending on several national, regional and personal contexts: (a) state support, (b) own employment and (c) partnership with an earner (see pathways in Figure 1.3). Globalization introduces uncertainty through (a_1) weakening welfare state support, (b_1) weakening women's labor market position through underemployment, below-subsistence wages or unemployment, (c_1) the weaker labor market performance of the partner/earner on whom mid-life women rely or (c_2) relationship dissolution, meaning the loss of earners on whose incomes women depend.[2]

In this volume, we evaluate many of these pathways and the routes out of these pathways available to women in the wake of such rising uncertainty. The country studies will examine several questions. Do we find a weakening of state support in each country and, if so, what action do women take against it: do they move to their own employment (a_{1a}) or increase their partnering to male breadwinners (a_{1b})? Do mid-life women experience underemployment or unemployment at higher rates than in the past? If so, do we find evidence that they solve this uncertainty through (b_{1a}) depending on state support, (b_{1b}) trying to get back into better employment or (b_{1c}) increasing their partnership dependence? Or, does the employment uncertainty affect women via their attachment to earners who are becoming more vulnerable on the labor market? If so, do they use state support (c_{1a}) or their own employment (c_{1b}) as a way out?

Not in the scope of this volume, but nonetheless relevant to the total picture and called for in future research, is the question of how women resolve

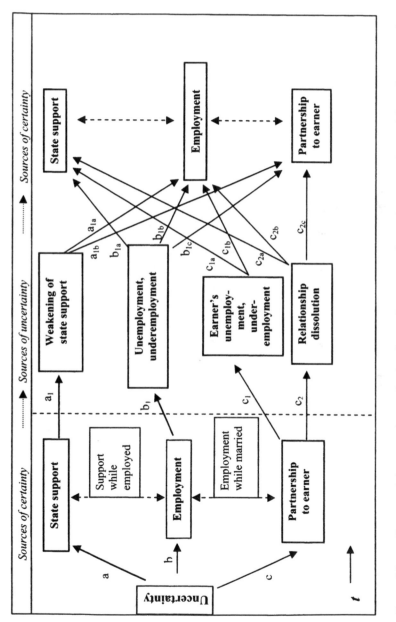

Figure 1.3   Conceptual diagram of micro-level pathways from an initial state (uncertainty) to and through sources of certainty and uncertainty over time (t)

uncertainty following relationship dissolution: are there differences over time in the dependence of women on support from (c_{2a}) the welfare state, (c_{2b}) employment or (c_{2c}) remarriage? We anticipate that these pathways' ease of movement varies based on institutional filters and country contexts as described above.

DATA AND METHODS

The empirical techniques used in the chapters to follow draw upon individual-based event history data and undertake longitudinal analytical methods and techniques (Blossfeld and Rohwer 2001). The majority of data used in this study come from retrospective or longitudinal panel surveys collected in the 1990s. These include the German Life History Study (birth cohorts 1939–41; 1954–56; 1964) for Germany and data pooled from three surveys of the Netherlands Family Survey, the Survey of Households in the Netherlands and the Family Surveys of the Dutch Population (data for years 1955–2000) for the Netherlands. The Swedish analysis draws on the Level of Living Survey and Labor Force Surveys (data for years 1950–2001) with Denmark using the Integrated Database for Labor Market Research (data for years 1980–99). The Hungarian Household Panel Survey (1991–97) is used in Hungary, the Estonian Labor Force Survey (data for years 1991–97) in Estonia and the Stratification Survey (data for years 1989–99) in the Czech Republic. The Polish chapter relies on secondary analyses from Labor Force Surveys, 1990–2001. The British Household Panel Survey (data for years 1970–90) is used for the United Kingdom, and the United States chapter draws upon the National Longitudinal Survey of Young Women (birth cohorts 1942–1953). The analysis of Italy draws upon the Italian Household Longitudinal Survey (data for years 1920s–97), Spain uses the 1995 Fertility and Family Survey and Spanish Labor Force Survey (data for years 1955–94) and Mexico uses the National Retrospective Demographic Survey (birth cohorts 1936–68).

For our purposes, event history methods are ideal as they allow for 'causal-type' analysis of events that represent changes from one discrete life-course state to another. Since we also want to examine empirical consequences at the individual level, this general approach is the most desirable.

As stated earlier in this introduction, each nation-specific chapter within this book examines the impact of globalization on the life courses of women via three transition types: (1) upward, lateral and downward job mobility; (2) transitions from paid employment into unemployment, unpaid caregiving, paid caregiving or out-of-labor-force status and (3) re-entry into paid employment from unemployment, unpaid caregiving, paid caregiving or out-of-labor-force status. Statistical applications included piecewise exponential, piecewise constant exponential, logistic and Cox semi-parametric proportional hazard models. Technical and mathematical aspects of the models and methods have been specified elsewhere (Blossfeld and Rohwer 2001). We therefore focus on substantive results instead of explanations of the methods. As with any secondary data analysis, comparability of analyses is dependent on the various available data sets. All authors explored the transitions in a way befitting their country-specific context. The analyses for each country sometimes differ slightly also owing to data availability.

STRUCTURE OF THE BOOK

The next chapter provides an overview detailing changes in women's employment trajectories in direct comparison from a variety of perspectives, testing the globalization hypotheses using macro-level data. The overview is followed by two country studies on conservative welfare regime countries, Germany and the Netherlands, which are nation-states that tend toward protectionism, particularly of male breadwinners, resulting in strong insider-outsider labor markets. But the Netherlands is changing over time toward a more social-democratic welfare regime, and this comparison can easily be seen by its position next to the chapters on Sweden and Denmark that follow. The role of women in labor markets that expect and welcome women workers, while segregating them into specific industries and sectors, is demonstrated in these chapters as well as in the unique pressures and advantages that social-democratic countries face competing in a global economy.

The following section covers the post-socialist countries: Hungary, Estonia, the Czech Republic and Poland. Here the consequences of the economic and political transformations of the 1990s are presented. The struggles of women to find, maintain or voluntarily reduce labor market attachment in these transitioning countries gives important information about the true costs and benefits of the economic transformation. Chapters on Hungary, Estonia and the Czech Republic use micro-level longitudinal data on women. The chapter on Poland provides an overview of the experiences of Polish women in relation to women in other post-socialist countries, using macro data, and takes a careful look at the unique and competing influences of the legacy of communism and the strength of the Catholic Church in this Central European country.

We then move to the liberal welfare regimes: Great Britain and the United States. Women in these countries have a history of integration in the labor market, and we ask how this has been influenced by globalization forces. Finally, the countries with the strongest female-homemaker tradition are the family-oriented/Catholic conservative countries of Mexico, Italy and Spain. Despite their strong legacies of the male provider and female caregiving, these nations have experienced financial struggles that have shaken the roots of the family system, requiring the employment of women at levels that have not been seen in recent history. The ways in which these women are reconciling their financial provider and caregiving demands completes the 13 country studies that demonstrate the wide range of women's involvement in paid and unpaid labor.

Our final part presents two chapters, one taking up the question of women's attitudes toward employment and family care, comparing the attitudes of women from diverse countries and cohorts over time. In the final chapter, we conclude with a summary of the main findings of the volume and their policy implications.

NOTES

1   The authors would like to thank members of the GLOBALIFE project and especially John Bendix, Daniela Grunow and Fabrizio Bernardi for detailed comments on a previous version of this chapter and Ilona Relikowski for extensive editing support.

2   The presence of relationship dissolution as a source of uncertainty is not directly related to globalization but might be a consequence of the influences of other sources of certainty or uncertainty (such as adequate state support for divorced women, employment possibilities for divorced women or declines in earnings capacities of former breadwinners that decrease the utility of the marriage).

BIBLIOGRAPHY

Aschaffenburg, K.E. (1995) 'Rethinking images of the mobility regime: making a case for women's mobility', *Research in Social Stratification and Mobility*, 14: 201–35.

Atkinson, J. (1984) 'Manpower strategies for flexible organizations', *Personnel Management*, 16: 28–31.

Auer, P. and Cazes, S. (2000) 'The resilience of the long-term employment relationship: evidence from the industrialized countries', *International Labour Review*, 139(4): 379–408.

Beck, U. (2000) 'What is globalization?', in D. Held and A. McGrew (eds) *The global trans-formations reader: an introduction to the globalization debate*, Cambridge: Polity Press.

Becker, G.S. (1981) *A treatise on the family*, Cambridge, MA: Harvard University Press.

Bellah, R.N., Madsen, R., Sullivan, W.M., Swidler, A. and Tipton, S.M. (1985) *Habits of the heart: individualism and commitment in American life*, Berkeley, CA: University of California Press.

Bernardi, F. (1999) 'Does the husband matter? Married women and employment in Italy', *European Sociological Review*, 3: 285–300.

Bernardi, F. (2001) 'The employment behaviour of married women in Italy', in H.-P. Blossfeld and S. Drobnič (eds) *Careers of couples in contemporary societies: from male breadwinner to dual earner families*, Oxford: Oxford University Press.

Bernardi, F. (2005) 'Public policies and low fertility: rationales for public intervention and a diagnosis for the Spanish case', *Journal of European Social Policy*, 2: 27–42.

Bielby, W.T. and Baron, J.N. (1986) 'Men and women at work: sex segregation and statistical discrimination', *American Journal of Sociology*, 91: 759–99.

Bielby, W.T. and Bielby, D.D. (1992) 'I will follow him: family ties, gender role beliefs, and reluctance to relocate for a better job', *American Journal of Sociology*, 97(5): 1241–67.

Blossfeld, H.-P. (1987) 'Labor market entry and the sexual segregation of careers in the Federal Republic of Germany', *American Journal of Sociology*, 93: 89–118.

Blossfeld, H.-P. (1995a) 'Changes in the process of family formation and women's growing economic independence: a comparison of nine countries', in H.-P. Blossfeld (ed.) *The new role of women*, Boulder, CO: Westview Press.

Blossfeld, H.-P. (1995b) *The new role of women: family formation in modern societies*, Boulder, CO: Westview Press.

Blossfeld, H.-P. and Drobnič, S. (2001) *Careers of couples in contemporary societies: from male breadwinner to dual earner families*, Oxford: Oxford University Press.

Blossfeld, H.-P. and Hakim, C. (1997) *Between equalization and marginalization*, Oxford: Oxford University Press.

Blossfeld, H.P. and Huinink, J. (1991) 'Human-capital investments or norms of role transition? How women's schooling and career affect the process of family formation', *American Journal of Sociology*, 97(1): 143–68.

Blossfeld, H.-P. and Rohwer, G. (2001) *Techniques of event history modeling: new approaches to causal analysis*, Hillsdale: Lawrence Erlbaum.

Blossfeld, H.-P., Klijzing, E., Mills, M. and Kurz, K. (2005) *Globalization, uncertainty, and youth in society*, Routledge: London.

Blossfeld, H.-P., Mills, M. and Bernardi, F. (2006) *Globalization, uncertainty and men's careers: an international comparison*, Cheltenham, UK and Northampton, MA, USA: Edward Elgar.

Brines, J. (1994) 'Economic dependency, gender, and the division of labor at home', *American Journal of Sociology*, 100(3): 652–88.

Camstra, R. (1996) 'Commuting and gender in a lifestyle perspective', *Urban Studies*, 33(2): 283–300.

Charles, M. and Grusky, D.B. (2004) *Occupational ghettos: the worldwide segregation of women and men*, Stanford, CA: Stanford University Press.

Daly, M. (2000) 'A fine balance: women's labor market participation in international comparison', in F. Scharpf and V. Schmidt (eds) *Welfare and work in the open economy: diverse responses to common challenges*, New York: Oxford University Press.

DiPrete, T.A., deGraaf, P.M., Luijkx, R., Tahlin, M. and Blossfeld, H.P. (1997) 'Collectivist versus individualist mobility regimes? Structural change and job mobility in four countries', *American Journal of Sociology*, 103(2): 318–58.

Elder, G.H. Jr. (1999) *Children of the great depression: social change in life experience* (25th Anniversary Edition), Boulder, CO: Westview Press.

Esping-Andersen, G. (1993) 'Post-industrial class structures: an analytical framework', in G. Esping-Andersen (ed.) *Changing classes*, London: Sage.

Esping-Andersen, G. (1999) *Social foundations of postindustrial economies*, Oxford: Oxford University Press.

Fromm, S. (2004) *Formierung und Fluktuation: Die Transformation der kapitalistischen Verwertungslogik in Fordismus und Postfordismus*, Berlin: Wissenschaftlicher Verlag Berlin.

Gera, S. and Massé, P. (1996) 'Employment performance in the knowledge-based economy', Industry Canada Working Paper, Ottawa, Canada.

Gerson, K. (1985) *Hard choices: how women decide about work, career, and motherhood*, Berkeley, CA: University of California Press.

Giddens, A. (1973) *The class structure of advanced societies*, New York: Harper Torchbooks.

Giddens, A. (1984) *The constitution of society: outline of the theory of structuration*, Cambridge: Polity Press.

Gonzalez, M.J., Jurado, T. and Naldini, M. (2000) *Gender inequalities in southern Europe: women, work and welfare in the 1990s*, London: Frank Cass.

Hannan, M.T., Schömann, K. and Blossfeld, H.-P. (1990) 'Sex and sector differences in the dynamics of wage growth in the FRG', *American Sociological Review*, 55: 694–713.

Hochschild, A. (1989) *The second shift*, New York: Avon.

Jacobsen, J.P. and Levin, L.M. (1995) 'Effects of intermittent labor force attachment on women's earnings', *Monthly Labor Review*, 118(9): 14–19.

Kalleberg, A.L. (2000) 'Nonstandard employment relations: part-time, temporary and contract work', *Annual Review of Sociology*, 26: 341–65.

Kalleberg, A.L. (2003) 'Flexible firms and labor market segmentation: effects of workplace restructuring on jobs and workers', *Work and Occupations*, 30: 154–75.

Kalleberg, A.L., Reskin, B.F. and Hudson, K. (2000) 'Bad jobs in America: standard and nonstandard employment relations and job quality in the United States', *American Sociological Review*, 65(2): 256–78.

Lewis, J. (1992) 'Gender and the development of welfare regimes', *Journal of European Social Policy*, 2(3): 159–73.

Mayer, K.U. (2001) 'The paradox of global social change and national path dependencies: life course patterns in advanced societies', in A. Woodward and M. Kohli (eds) *Inclusions and exclusions in European societies*, New York: Routledge.

Mayer, K.U. (2004a) 'Life courses and life chances in a comparative perspective', Mannheimer Vorträge no. 26, Mannheimer Zentrum für Europäische Sozialforschung.

Mayer, K.U. (2004b) 'Whose lives? How history, societies, and institutions define and shape life courses', *Research in Human Development*, 1(3): 161–87.

Mills, M. (2004a) 'Demand for flexibility or generation of insecurity? The individualization of risk, irregular work shifts and Canadian youth', *Journal of Youth Studies*, 7: 1.

Mills, M. (2004b) 'Stability and change: the structuration of partnership histories in Canada, the Netherlands and the Russian Federation', *European Journal of Population*, 20: 141–75.

Mills, M. and Blossfeld, H.-P. (2005) 'Globalization, uncertainty and the early life course: a theoretical framework', in H.-P. Blossfeld, E. Klijzing, M. Mills and K. Kurz (eds) *Globalization, uncertainty, and youth in society*, London: Routledge.

Mills, M., Blossfeld, H.-P. and Bernardi, F. (2006) 'Globalization, uncertainty and men's employment careers: a theoretical framework', in H.-P. Blossfeld, M. Mills and F. Bernardi (eds) *Globalization, uncertainty and men's careers in international comparison*, Cheltenham, UK and Northampton, MA, USA: Edward Elgar.

Mills, M., Blossfeld, H.-P. and Klijzing, E. (2005) 'Becoming an adult in uncertain times: a 14-country comparison of the losers of globalization', in H.-P. Blossfeld, M. Mills, E. Klijzing and K. Kurz (eds) *Globalization, uncertainty, and youth in society*, London: Routledge.

Moen, P. (1992) *Women's two roles*, New York: Auburn House.

Moen, P. (2001) *The career quandary*, Washington, DC: Population Reference Bureau.

Moen, P. and Roehling, P. (2005) *The career mystique*, Lanham, MD: Rowman & Littlefield.

Moen, P. and Wethington, E. (1992) 'The concept of family adaptive strategies', *Annual Review of Sociology*, 18: 233–51.

Myles, J. (1990) 'States, labor markets, and the life cycles', in R. Frieland and A.F. Robertson (eds) *In beyond the marketplace: rethinking economy and society*, New York: Aldine de Gruyter.

Oppenheimer, V.K. (1988) 'A theory of marriage timing', *American Journal of Sociology*, 94(3): 563–91.

Orloff, A.S. (2002) 'Gender equality, women's employment: cross-national patterns of policy and politics', in *Welfare, work and family: Southern Europe in comparative perspective*, Florence: EU Institute.

Parsons, T. (1953) 'A revised analytical approach to the theory of social stratification', *Essays in Sociological Theory*, Glencoe, IL: Free Press.

Rosenfeld, R.A. (1990) 'Race and sex differences in career dynamics', *American Sociological Review*, 45: 583–609.

Rosenfeld, R.A. (1992) 'Job mobility and career processes', *Annual Review of Sociology*, 18: 39–61.

Saraceno, C. (1994) 'The ambivalent familism of the Italian welfare state', *Social Politics*, Spring: 60–82.

Schippers, J. and Plantenga, J. (2001) 'Het combinatiescenario en de noodzakelijke veranderingen in het emancipatiebeleid', in N. van der Heuvel, F. Holderbeke and R. Wielers (eds) *De Transitionele Arbeidsmarkt*, Den Haag: Elsevier.

Sørensen, A.B. (1983) 'Processes of allocation to open and closed positions in social structure', *Zeitschrift für Soziologie*, 12(3): 203–24.

Standing, G. (1989) 'Global feminization through flexible labor', *World Development*, 17(7): 1077–95.

West, C. and Fenstermaker, S. (1993) 'Power, inequality, and the accomplishment of gender: an ethnomethodological view', in P. England (ed.) *Theory on gender/feminism on theory*, New York: Aldine de Gruyter.

West, C. and Fenstermaker, S. (1995), 'Doing difference', *Gender & Society*, 9(1): 8–37.

Williams, J. (2000) *Unbending gender: why family and work conflict and what to do about it*, New York: Oxford University Press.

2. Women's employment in times of globalization: a comparative overview

Dirk Hofäcker

INTRODUCTION

This chapter provides an internationally comparative overview of key features of female labor market participation and links their development patterns to key aspects of globalization processes. In doing so, this overview intends to serve as contextual background for the subsequent country studies in this volume.

At the outset of the twentieth century, paid employment was a strongly male activity, and a clear division of labor existed in most middle-class families between a male breadwinner and a female homemaker. However, recent social processes have challenged this division of labor. Women's increasing integration into the labor market has even led in some countries to a partial replacement of the traditional division by new patterns that are given labels such as 'adult worker' or 'dual earner' (Korpi 2000; Lewis 2004). Where they occur, these developments are often interpreted as significant advances towards dismantling gender differences.

However, feminist theorists have criticized this positive view for several reasons (Daly 2000; Fagan and Rubery 1999; Hakim 1997; Sainsbury 1999). First, despite changes in female labor market participation, the division of housework has only marginally changed. Second, empirical studies have shown that the use of crude labor force participation rates may well obscure important differences in the *extent* and *quality* of women's integration in the labor market (Hakim 1993; Jonung and Persson 1993). The emergence of 'atypical' forms of work (such as part-time work or flexible work arrangements), heralded as creating opportunities for women to find new places in the labor market, was seen by feminists as a reflection or continuation of enduring gender-based labor market inequalities. Thus despite rising levels of women's employment, women's careers are often not as secure, prestigious or high-earning as men's and do not imply the same level of economic security for women or their families as the traditional male career does. Third, cross-national statistical comparisons suggested that political regimes, welfare arrangements and especially family policies supported women's labor participation to varying degrees, with consequent marked international differences in the actual labor market integration of women (Lewis 1993; Sainsbury 1999).

I ask, how has the integration of women in the labor market occurred in various country contexts during an era of globalization? Does globalization point to systematic developments across all or most western industrialized countries, or do nation-specific institutions filter the development of women's labor market attachment in a specific way (Mills and Blossfeld 2005; Hofmeister, Blossfeld and Mills, this volume)?

I first develop hypotheses about globalization and its expected effects on the female life course. I then test these hypotheses using the most recent empirical figures available and describe the quantitative and qualitative position of women in the labor market in different national contexts. The particular focus is on women's overall integration into employment and their most common work patterns. In this respect, I pay special attention to cross-national differences and review selected institutional characteristics of the countries before summarizing the results and pointing toward the next step – the country studies.

GLOBALIZATION AND FEMALE EMPLOYMENT

The GLOBALIFE research project uses three theoretical levels when describing and explaining life-course patterns under the influence of globalization (see Blossfeld 1999; 2000).

On a macro-theoretical level, it assumes globalization has effects that can be observed in most modern societies, including the growing importance of knowledge work, rapid shifts from industrial to service-based economic structures and an increasing global competition between welfare states that leads to a stagnation and reduction in welfare state measures (Mills and Blossfeld 2005; Hofmeister, Blossfeld and Mills, this volume).

These macro processes however lead to very different results nationally. The reason lies at the institutional level: country-specific institutional 'packages' (such as welfare, education, employment or family systems) filter the influences of the globalization process. Such institutions show considerable developmental inertia and therefore have a 'tendency to persist in the process of globalization' (Blossfeld 2000, p. 2).

Filtering processes at the institutional level can lead to differing results at the individual level. In some countries, the globalization process can be expected to lead to profound changes in individual life courses, while other countries may show much lesser effects at the individual level.

General hypotheses

With this theoretical framework in mind, I develop general hypotheses about women's labor force participation in the globalization process.

On the labor supply side, educational expansion has led to increasing participation in higher education, hence to women's greater chances to be employed even in highly qualified jobs. The increasing inability for one earner to support a family has also fostered female labor market participation. Finally, the increasing instability of marriage has generally supported a more individual design of female life courses rather than an orientation towards sole reliance on a male breadwinner.

On the labor demand side, the rise in the service sector has created new working opportunities for women. The erosion of the employment contract and its gradual replacement by 'atypical' forms may also have favored female employment, as women could be expected to be more inclined to take up reduced, restricted or flexible work owing to their frequently interrupted career paths or competing family commitments.

One can thus posit a 'Globalization Hypothesis I': *female employment should have clearly increased during the last decades*, for these supply-side and demand-side reasons, many of which are triggered by globalization. It is unlikely that this integration takes place uniformly across work sectors and work forms. Certain sectors are expanding under globalization, for example the service sector, and many firms are designing their work in ways that push risk to the individual, such as offering only part-time work and temporary contracts instead of secure full-time jobs. Outsiders in the labor market, such as women, are more likely to gain access through these new, less protected routes. I therefore posit a 'Globalization Hypothesis II': *the impact of globalization should be evident in the concentration of female employment in specific economic sectors (specifically the private and public service sectors) as well as in flexible working arrangements* (part-time work, temporary contracts, self-employment).

However, there will be country-specific differences in the patterns of female employment owing to the institutional filters noted above, including varying national labor markets, welfare states and value systems. My 'Institutional Hypothesis' is thus that *internationally different outcomes can be attributed to institutional filtering processes*. This hypothesis is complementary to the globalization hypothesis, which describes an overall process within which national variations may occur, in turn explained by the institutional approach.

GLOBALIZATION AND FEMALE EMPLOYMENT: TRENDS

The following evaluates recent data on women's labor market participation and asks:

1   To what extent are women integrated into the labor market?
2   If women participate in employment, what is their labor force status and in which sectors of the economy are they typically found?
3   What are the typical job characteristics of women in terms of working hours and types of contracts?

Where available, data for all countries represented in this volume are examined, ordered according to the welfare state/labor market typology used in this book: conservative (Germany and the Netherlands, with France as a comparison case in this chapter), social-democratic (Sweden and Denmark), post-socialist (Hungary, Estonia, Czech Republic and Poland), liberal (Great Britain and the United States, with Canada included for comparison) and family-oriented (Mexico, Italy and Spain) (Blossfeld et al. 2005; Blossfeld, Mills and Bernardi 2006; Esping-Andersen 1990; Ferrera 1996). For achieving a maximum of cross-national comparability, trends are analyzed using data from large-scale international data sources such as the *Key Indicators of the Labor Market* (KILM) of the International Labour Organization (ILO) or the *Historical Statistics* of the OECD. Depending on data availability, the longitudinal range is from the 1970s or 1980s until 2000.

WOMEN'S OVERALL LABOR FORCE PARTICIPATION

Figures 2.1a and 2.1b provide an overview of women's labor force participation by country and as a percentage of the female working age population, defined here as women aged 15 to 64 in some representative sample countries.[1] Overall, there has been a notable increase in female participation ratios during the last three decades, with signs of stabilization during the 1990s.

Despite this overall trend, one can observe clear differences between the countries. High and rising participation rates can be seen in two sets of countries with an increase of about 20 points: in the social-democratic countries (represented by Sweden, with Denmark [not shown] within three percentage points), where female labor force participation has a longer history, and in liberal countries (represented by the United States, with Canada and the United Kingdom being within five percentage points), where current levels are a result of substantive increases in the last decades. The liberal countries began at a lower level in 1970 and converged towards the

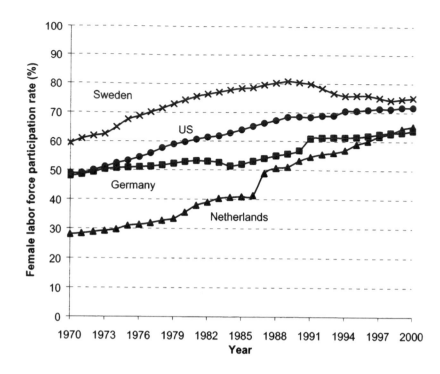

Source: OECD (2002)

Figure 2.1a   *The rise in female labor force participation as percentage of all*
                 working age women (15–64 years) in representative social-
                 democratic, liberal and conservative countries, 1970–2000

social-democratic levels in the 1990s. The conservative countries (Germany
and the Netherlands) also show signs of increasing female labor force
participation, though at a lower level than the liberal cluster. The Netherlands
constitute an exceptional case because female labor force participation
doubled in only 20 years (near 30 percent in 1974 to near 60 percent by
1994). The lowest level of female labor force participation is found in the
family-oriented countries (Italy, Spain, Mexico) where women's labor force
participation has, despite increases, remained below 50 percent until very
recently.

Post-communist countries are a special case with female labor force
participation varying between a minimum of 50 percent (Hungary in the mid-
1990s) and around 80 percent (Estonia in the early 1990s). Initially high
participation rates are probably due to a socialist ideology which strongly
supported female labor force participation. However, in the course of the

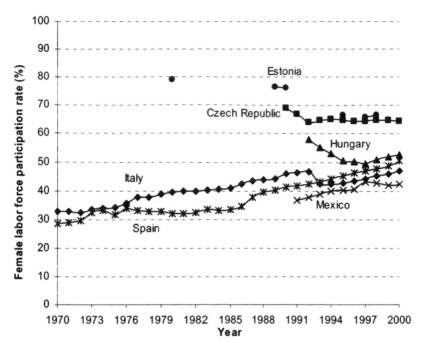

Source: OECD (2002)

Figure 2.1b *The rise in female labor force participation as percentage of all working age women (15–64 years) in family-oriented and post-socialist countries, 1970–2000*

economic 'transition shock' (Lück and Hofäcker 2003), the changes in the labor market had gender consequences: women were mostly employed in the public services and light industries that declined, while the heavy industries that were protected – at least initially – mostly employed men. At the same time, women were less likely to take up new jobs in the private market sector, partly due to employer discrimination. Furthermore, early retirement schemes as well as parental leave schemes fostered a withdrawal of women from the workforce (Blossfeld, Buchholz and Hofäcker 2006; Ruminska-Zimny 2002; Sasser 2001; UNICEF 1999).

The aggregated nature of labor force participation ratios obscure variation within female employment, for example across the life course. While rates of women's labor force participation within each age group in mid-life have risen drastically from the 1970s to the 1990s (Hofäcker 2004), there still remain institutionally distinctive patterns of female employment among welfare regimes.

Figure 2.2 depicts the structure of age-specific labor force participation rates for women by country in an example year, 1990. In liberal welfare regimes (represented in Figure 2.2 by the United States, with similar rates in Canada and the United Kingdom), women participate in the labor force already at early ages, reaching the highest levels of aggregate participation when in their 30s and subsequently remaining in at stable rates until close to retirement age. Over time, women's labor force participation has increased in the age groups from 30 to 50 (Hofäcker 2004). In all three liberal countries, this upward shift has reduced or even eliminated the decline of participation rates around the mean age of first childbirth in their mid-20s (the 'baby effect'). An even more continuous and high labor force integration of women until their mid-60s prevails in social-democratic countries (represented by Sweden). Only around the official retirement age do female participation rates decline sharply, and again no 'baby effect' is visible.

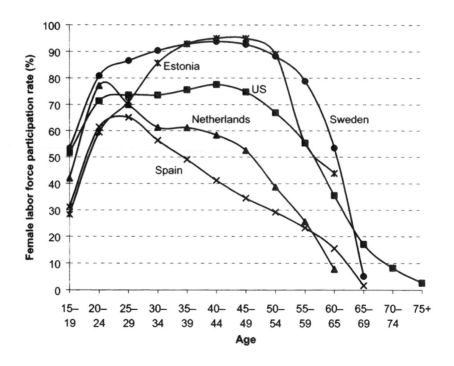

Source: OECD (2003)

Figure 2.2   The distribution of women's employment across
*   age groups in representative countries from each*
*   welfare regime type, 1990*

Conservative countries (represented here by the Netherlands) show a different pattern with a high for women in their early 20s, and a drop around the ages when women enter motherhood. In the consecutive age groups, female labor force participation then remains moderately stable until reaching (early) retirement age. Though declines in Figure 2.2 may partly be due to cohort differences, there is visible evidence of a 'baby effect' in family-oriented countries (represented by Spain). Women in these countries show a delayed labor market entry, lower rates of labor force participation at all ages and steep declines with parenthood. Post-socialist countries (represented by Estonia) again reveal a very distinct pattern. Low female participation rates in early adulthood that might indicate significant barriers to female employment in younger age groups or high rates of education are followed by a sharp increase to nearly 100 percent in mid-life. Until the mid-50s, labor force participation remains stable, but visibly declines after this age, possibly an indication of the usage of early retirement policies to battle the adverse effects of the economic shock in transition countries (Blossfeld, Buchholz and Hofäcker 2006; Lodahl and Schrooten 1998). The 'Institutional Hypothesis' is therefore supported by the observation that in some countries women drop their involvement in paid labor during mid-life while in other countries women in the same life stages remain in the labor market at high rates.

WOMEN'S FAMILY WORK AND SELF-EMPLOYMENT

National-level data that distinguishes between women classified as salaried workers, self-employed or as family workers[2] indicates that close to 90 percent of women participating in the labor market are found in dependent work, with the exception of Spain (83 percent), Italy (78 percent) and Mexico (64 percent). In these family-oriented countries, 20 to 30 percent of women's economic activity is in self-employment and family work, largely attributable to the important role agricultural employment played in these countries (agricultural employment is often connected with working in family-based businesses). But family work has declined significantly in these countries in the years 1985 to 2000, more evidence of the ways in which globalization forces are impacting on the lives and livelihoods of women in unique ways based on differences among countries.

Women's self-employment hangs at around 10 percent in all countries except Sweden, where it is around 5 percent, and the family-oriented countries and, to a lesser extent, Canada, where it is closer to 15 percent or more. Nonetheless, it deserves special attention in a study on globalization. To explain the role of self-employment in women's lives, one needs to recognize that self-employment is not a homogeneous category (Bögenhold and Staber 1991; 1993) but, as extreme cases, includes both the successful management of one's own company as well as a 'contract worker arrangement,' dependent upon the receipt of work contracts from a firm. The ILO KILM database splits self-employment into self-employment as 'employers' and as 'own account workers,' the former referring to individuals who work on their own account and engage one or more persons to work for them, while the latter denotes those self-employed who engage no employees on a permanent basis (ILO KILM 2001 Manual, Indicator 3). It is among the latter group that one can expect to disproportionately find precarious work forms: at-home work, telecommuting, subcontracting or the like. The ILO data suggest that, at least in the family-oriented countries, self-employment can largely be attributed to high values of own-account workers and may therefore be regarded as a new form of marginal employment for women in these countries.[3]

FEMALE PARTICIPATION IN DEPENDENT EMPLOYMENT: WORK CHARACTERISTICS

The 'Globalization Hypothesis II' suggests women will cluster in flexible employment forms such as part-time and/or fixed-term employment. To test this assumption, one can examine these two work forms more closely for the countries featured in this volume.

Part-time work

In all countries studied, part-time employment, where it exists, has clearly been a female phenomenon with women making up around two-thirds of all part-timers (ILO 2001). Figures 2.3a and 2.3b indicate the relative rates of part-time employment within female employment as a whole for selected countries over time.[4] Liberal countries of the United States, Canada and the United Kingdom are omitted from this figure because their rates of part-time work among all employed women have remained extremely stable from 1980 to 2000. Female part-time employment is of clearly higher importance in the United Kingdom (at 40.8 percent) than in Canada (27.8 percent) or the United States (20.8 percent), possibly indicating differences between the liberal countries in terms of 'work cultures' (Walsh and Wigley 2001) and regulatory frameworks for working time (Rubery, Smith and Fagan 1998).

Some national differences exist in the development of part-time rates over time. In the social-democratic countries, part-time work had accounted for about a third of women's jobs in the 1980s, but is now losing its share of female employment. Clear differences emerge between conservative countries: while part-time employment is of rather moderate importance in both France and Germany, it has become the dominant form of employment for women in the Netherlands (Figure 2.3a).[5] Lowest part-time shares are

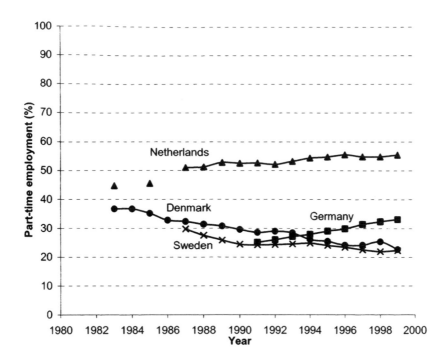

Source: ILO (2001)

Figure 2.3a   *Part-time employment as percentage of overall female employment in social-democratic and conservative countries, 1980–2000*

found in post-socialist and family-oriented countries where reduced working hours have largely been unavailable for both men and women (Figure 2.3b). Part-time work is a minority phenomenon in Southern Europe (but is around 30 percent in Mexico), and virtually unheard of for working women in Hungary and the Czech Republic. Despite occasional changes in some countries, the overall importance of women's part-time employment has remained largely stable in most countries. However, recent research has pointed to the limited comparability of harmonized part-time employment rates between countries (Van Bastelaer, Lemaître and Marianna 1997). Using a standard demarcation line – as with the OECD 30-hour limit used by the ILO indicator – obscures important differences in terms of actual working hours. For example, when one compares the United Kingdom with the United States, one finds only about 20 percent of the US women working less than 30 hours per week, while the comparable United Kingdom figure is closer to 40 percent. A similar comparison can be drawn in the conservative countries: about 30 percent of the Dutch women work less than 20 hours a week, but the same is true of only about 10 to 15 percent of German women. In social-democratic countries, very short working hours only play a marginal role. 'Part-time employment' in these countries usually means working only slightly less than full-time.

To what extent increases in women's part-time work should be judged as reflecting the 'precariousness' of female employment is open to question, as part-time employment can provide a supplementary 'half income' for married couples to help reconcile family and working life (Blossfeld and Hakim 1997; ILO 2001; Klijzing 2005), while for women (and men) who seek and need full-time work, part-time work is wholly inadequate.

Furthermore, the actual precariousness of part-time work strongly depends on how welfare state institutions address it. In the Netherlands, for example, part-time employment is favorably treated as part of a strategy to establish it as the standard work form, as a 'combination scenario,' for both men and women (Knijn 2002).

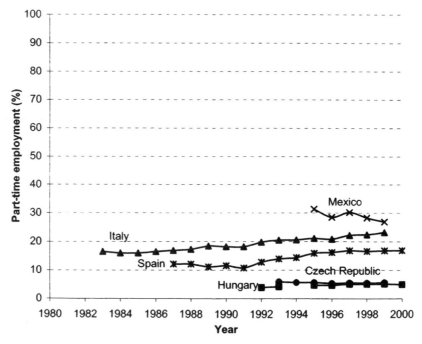

Source: ILO (2001)

Figure 2.3b   *Part-time employment as percentage of overall female employment in family-oriented and post-socialist countries, 1980–2000*

Fixed-term employment

Can one find similar results for fixed-term employment? Of all fixed-term work, men and women equally share about half, varying slightly by countries (except for the post-socialist regimes) with women taking from 42 percent of all fixed-term work in Spain to 55 percent in the Netherlands in 2000 (European Industrial Relations Observatory 2001). But as a share of women workers, fixed-term employment plays a visible but clearly less important role than part-time work, hovering consistently around 10 percent of women workers over time. The exceptions are found among the post-socialist states where the percentages are even lower, reinforcing the observation that the overwhelming norm in these countries is for working women to work full-time, and Spain, where 35 percent of Spanish women in the labor market are in fixed-term employment, an outcome of the increasing importance of fixed-term employment for both sexes in this country (see Klijzing 2005).

INTERIM SUMMARY

The evidence thus supports 'Globalization Hypothesis I' across welfare regimes: female labor force participation rates have increased during the last decades (see Figure 2.1). 'Globalization Hypothesis II,' however, that female employment will be concentrated and rising in flexible working forms as a result of globalization, can only be partly confirmed. That is, the data on part-time employment indicates that though it is an important category of female employment, in many of the countries surveyed here the proportion of women in this category has changed little in the last two decades of the twentieth century. Where it is changing, the change moves in opposite directions (Figure 2.3). Similarly, fixed-term employment, though a smaller category of female employment, has also remained relatively unchanged over time. Notably, in some of the countries where flexibility in terms of working time and contract type in dependent employment forms has been restricted, self-employment plays a considerable role as a relevant alternative work form for women.

More relevant are variations in the degree to which women are integrated in the labor force across their life courses (Figure 2.2) and the extent to which their work is full time. Differences here fit well along the lines of the extended Esping-Andersen regime typology:

1   Social-democratic countries are characterized by a high and stable labor market integration of women over the life course. Most women are engaged in near to full-time jobs with only slightly reduced working hours, with atypical work forms (fixed-term contracts, self-employment) playing only a marginal role. This pattern has remained very stable over

the observed time period, pointing to a longer history of gender equality measures and active labor market integration policies in these countries (DiPrete et al. 1997).

2   Liberal countries also show a high integration of women into the labor force, though with an earlier onset of exit from employment, as well as lower maximum levels, than in the social-democratic countries. Part-time work is of considerably greater importance in the United Kingdom than in the United States or Canada, though there is little difference from other nations either in fixed-term contracts or self-employment (with the partial exception of Canada, whose high self-employment figures resemble those of Spain).

3   Family-oriented countries show the opposite pattern. Here women are far less integrated into the labor force as salaried workers and at far lower levels by age group (see Figure 2.2), yet when they work, then it is much more likely to be in full-time or near full-time jobs. Simultaneously, we can observe the high standardization of work (little flexibility in terms of working hours) as well as the simultaneous existence of precarious work forms (Spain has a comparatively high percentage of fixed-term contracts) or self-employment.

4   Conservative regimes take a middle position. Female labor force integration is on the rise but is still lower than in liberal and social-democratic countries. While female employment was still characterized by a temporary exit from employment during the 1970s, now these countries seem to be gradually moving toward a pattern of a more stable participation over the life course. However, while the Netherlands largely accomplishes integration through part-time jobs, in Germany longer working hours tend to prevail instead. Other atypical work forms have yet to establish themselves as significant components of female workforce participation.

5   Finally, post-socialist countries still seem characterized by the inertia of past employment standardization. Despite recent declines, female employment in the Czech Republic and Estonia remains comparatively high and full-time, with atypical employment forms playing only a marginal role. The steep accelerations of women out of paid employment across the life course points to policies promoting age-related movement.

WOMEN AND THE LABOR MARKET: INSTITUTIONAL PATTERNS

The 'Institutional Hypothesis' that regime- or country-specific institutions filter globalization influences in different ways does appear to be confirmed, and the following examines some of the institutional backgrounds responsible for the differing outcomes that are observed.

One can assume that two kinds of factors influence female labor force participation. One is that there need to be available job positions for women, or in other words that labor force demand must be present. The other is that women need to reconcile workforce participation with family responsibilities, making their participation dependent on the institutional support that is available, or in other words, on the factors influencing labor force supply.

One can also assume both demand and supply can be provided either by the state or the market (see Figure 2.4). A welfare state can create demand for female labor mainly through providing an adequate number of jobs in public services, but it can also foster women's labor force supply by public 'reconciliation policies,' such as organized childcare or family-friendly social policies (Sainsbury 1999). By comparison, the market can stimulate female labor force demand through an adequately sized service sector, or encourage women's labor supply through private 'reconciliation support measures,' such as employer-provided childcare or flexible work arrangements. If neither the state nor the market stimulates female labor force demand or supply, welfare responsibility will need to be transferred to other institutions, particularly the family. A conceptual typology of how this process is at play can be summarized as follows (see Figure 2.4): the state and the market both provide various sources of demand and supply for women's employment. The state creates demand for women's employment through the public sector, and the market creates demand via the service sector. Supply of women for employment is aided by reconciliation between dual roles (caregivers and employees). The state aids in the supply of women workers by offering public childcare, and the market aids in the supply of women by offering employer-provided childcare.

	STATE	MARKET
DEMAND	Public sector employment	Service sector employment
SUPPLY (reconciliation support)	Public childcare	Employer-provided childcare

Figure 2.4   Typologies of sources of supply and demand for women's labor market participation

Female labor force participation will strongly depend as well on the characteristics and regulations of national labor markets, and women's chances to enter and move within the labor market will vary with the degree of openness of the economy. Labor markets with a low level of regulation and low barriers to (re-)employment will therefore be able easily to integrate women into the labor force (liberal countries), as will countries with a high degree of employment promotion programs (social-democratic countries).

Female labor demand: public and service sector employment

If we then seek empirical confirmation for such considerations, we can plot female labor demand through the state and the market (see Figures 2.5 and 2.6).

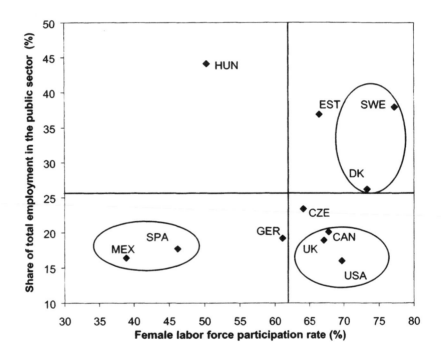

Source: OECD (2002; 2003); Hammouya (1999)

Figure 2.5   *Women's labor force participation rate and overall employment
                  share of the public sector, 1995–1997*

Looking at overall labor force demand induced by the state via the public sector (Figure 2.5), social-democratic countries, especially Sweden, show a high share of public sector employment paralleled by a high integration of women into employment. By contrast, the liberal countries show a very low public sector employment despite high female labor force participation rates, and instead have high service sector employment levels (see Figure 2.6) much like social democratic nations.[6] The difference between social-democratic and liberal countries, one can summarize, lies in the role of the state (Sainsbury 1999). Germany as a conservative country lies near but below the mean on both public sector employment and labor force participation (see Figure 2.5). Service sector employment is diverse in the conservative countries: the Netherlands has a service sector share considerably above that of Germany (Figure 2.6).

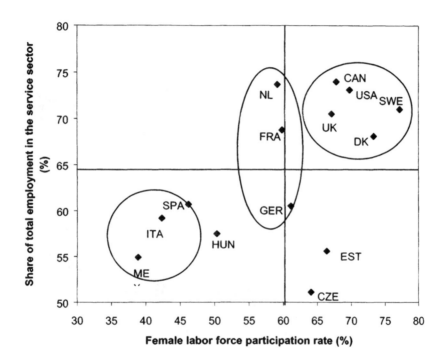

Source: OECD (2002; 2003); Hammouya (1999)

Figure 2.6   *Women's labor force participation rate and overall employment share of the service sector, 1995–97*

Family-oriented countries are well below the mean in public and service sector employment and in labor force participation rates, reflecting the role that both industrial and agricultural employment still play in these nations.

The above discussion indicates that examining the state or market in isolation does not explain female employment patterns. Countries with similar state or market involvement may have very different employment profiles. However, the simultaneous examination of both market and state influences enables one to achieve a more comprehensive approximation of institutional background patterns for female employment.

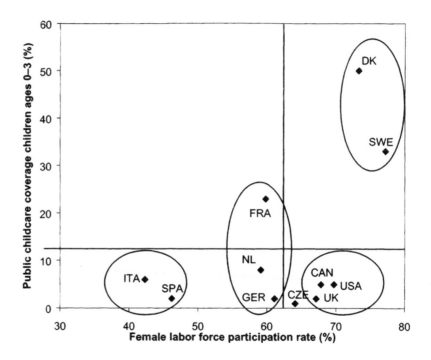

Source: Hofäcker (2002); Meyers and Gornick (2000); OECD (2001; 2003)

Figure 2.7   *Women's labor force participation rate and support for female labor force participation in terms of publicly provided care for children 0–3 years*

Social-democratic countries create demand for female employment mainly through a large public sector, which in turn also accounts for a high number of service jobs. In comparison, while public sector employment is comparatively low in the liberal countries, this lack of state-induced demand for women's labor is partly compensated through market demand in the form of a well-developed service sector. Family-oriented countries show below-average demand on both the state and market side, which may provide one explanation for their comparatively low levels of female employment.

Female labor supply: public and private childcare services

If we then turn to 'reconciliation support' (for example, of family with work life), one can examine the provision of public vs. private childcare services as indicators.[7] Figure 2.7 shows the coverage rates for public childcare facilities (children aged 0-3)[8] while Figure 2.8 shows the number of women reporting employer-provided childcare.

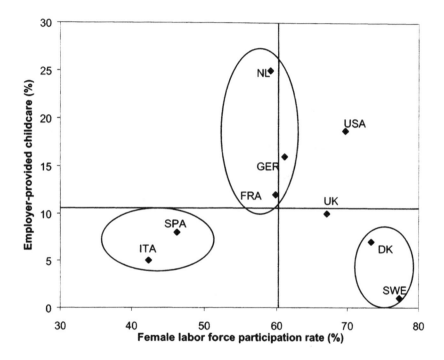

Source: OECD (2001; 2003)

Figure 2.8   Women's labor force participation rate and support for female labor force participation in terms of employer-provided childcare reported

If one looks at childcare provided by the state, the distinct position of social-democratic countries is notable. These countries combine high female labor force participation rates, a high level of public sector involvement and the highest levels of public childcare. While France also displays moderately high values of childcare coverage, all other countries in this volume for which data were available have only rudimentary early childcare facilities. The private provision of childcare facilities reverses the picture to some extent, with social-democratic countries having low levels of market-based childcare but clearly higher levels in liberal countries, especially the United States. The conservative countries diverge, with the Netherlands clearly exceeding the average. Family-oriented countries score low on both public and private dimensions (Figure 2.7 and 2.8).

The interplay of state and market is similar to what was noted above for employment: while social-democratic countries stimulate female labor force participation through generous state involvement in childcare, liberal countries partly compensate for the lack of public institutions through greater involvement by employers in 'reconciliation support.' Family-oriented countries again score low on both dimensions, while conservative countries reveal considerable heterogeneity.

Little comparable data is available for the post-socialist countries, but recent reports for Central and Eastern Europe suggest that the presence of childcare institutions for very young children (0-3 years) had been moderate but sufficient to enable women to be employed (Kamerman 2003). However, as a consequence of welfare retrenchment in the course of the transition process, such institutions have clearly declined (Schnepf 2001), thereby lowering public support for female labor force supply. Private replacements have not yet developed to replace the public childcare institutions.

Labor market characteristics

To round out this discussion of institutional filters at a country level, one can include measures of labor market rigidity and employment protection. The expectation is that little labor market rigidity as well as low entry restrictions would provide the most favorable conditions for female employment participation.

Figure 2.9, showing the duration of female short-term unemployment in different countries, is a proxy for rigidity, as indicated by the percentage of unemployment lasting less than three months as a proportion of overall female unemployment. High levels of short-term unemployment can be seen as an indicator of high labor market flexibility. As could be expected, we find comparatively high shares of short-term unemployment in the liberal welfare regimes, though with clear differences between the United States and Canada (very high) and the United Kingdom (average). Labor market flexibility is also high in Mexico, indicating the impact of recent political and economic changes. In all other countries for which data were available, short-term unemployment is a less typical form of unemployment (Denmark is the exception; its level, however, is comparable to the United Kingdom, hence average). This diagnosis is especially true for the family-oriented countries, where it accounts for less than 20 percent of overall unemployment.

Figure 2.10 complements the above discussion by adding two OECD Employment Protection Indices. These are measures of how difficult dismissal is and how many procedures are required to dismiss workers

(OECD 1999). These two dimensions can be read as rough proxy variables for labor market regulation by the state. The patterns tend to confirm what has already been observed. Liberal countries, where labor market flexibility is high, constantly show very low levels of state regulation. This pattern also holds true for Denmark and therefore distinguishes it within the social-democratic cluster from Sweden in labor market terms. One possible conclusion is that though highly flexible labor markets make it easy for women to enter employment, a simultaneous absence of stronger public employment protection in such countries suggests a correspondingly higher volatility in women's employment.

Both conservative and family-oriented countries combine a moderate to low labor market flexibility with rather high state regulations, although larger cross-country differences can be observed. Regulatory differences between the Czech Republic (high) and Hungary (weak) again point to a not-yet-determined institutional pattern in post-socialist countries.

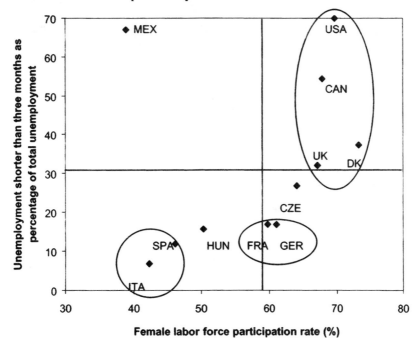

Source: OECD (1999; 2003)

Figure 2.9   *Women's labor force participation rate and female short-term*
unemployment (that is, less than three months) as percentage of
female unemployment as a whole

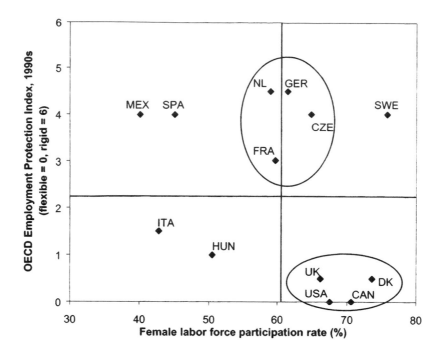

Source: OECD (1999; 2003)

Figure 2.10   *Women's labor force participation rate and combined OECD*
Employment Protection Legislation Index

SUMMARY

A summarizing overview of the results from the institutional comparisons
shows that the systematic regime-specific structure of patterns in female
employment could partly be supplemented by a systematic structure of
institutional design features:

1   Social-democratic countries have a high, continuous and nearly full-time
     integration of women into the labor force. This pattern is mainly
     achieved through a central role of the state in accounting for both the
     demand and the supply of female labor. The generous provision of public
     childcare in particular fosters female employment through the facilitation
     of reconciling competing demands of family and working life even when
     children are still infants.

2   Liberal countries are similar in terms of women's *quantitative* labor force integration, though it is achieved by a completely different institutional design. While public involvement in stimulating female labor force demand and supply is low, there is a comparatively high share of service sector employment and fairly generous market-based childcare provisions, both of which foster female employment. Furthermore, labor markets in these countries are highly flexible, allowing for an easier, but at the same time also more vulnerable, integration of women into the workforce. In liberal countries, flexible labor markets as well as market-based demand and supply measures therefore constitute a functional equivalent to the strong Scandinavian welfare state in terms of enabling high female employment participation. However, these similar results are achieved via different routes: on the one hand, the 'individualization' of the work-family reconciliation conflict in liberal countries and on the other hand, strong state protection of women in the labor market in the countries representing the social-democratic regime type.

3   Family-oriented countries show a weak performance in both the public and private dimensions of female labor force demand and supply. Furthermore, labor markets in these regimes are highly rigid and mostly organized around a standard employment contract. It is this combination of institutional patterns, as well as the central role of the family in these regime types, that can be held responsible for a relatively low and problematic integration of women into the labor force. It is therefore not surprising that women in family-oriented countries in need of a second income may move into marginal employment forms such as fixed-term employment and self-employment (as in Spain).

4   Conservative countries have been observed to take a 'middle position' in the realization of female employment. Similar results were also found for the institutional support patterns with varying but mostly moderate values of state- and market-provided promotion of female labor supply and demand. Clear differences between the conservative states, for example the exceptional position of France in terms of childcare or the high importance of the service sector in the Netherlands, point to important institutional mechanisms at the country level, which will be examined in more detail in the following country chapters.

5   Finally, for post-socialist countries, only a limited number of observations could be made owing to the lack of data. However, the results suggest that a unique pattern of institutional design has not yet developed in these countries. Again, these differences may point to country-level variation, which will be examined further in the following country studies. Future research will have to deal more explicitly with the interaction of processes of globalization, on the one hand, and the transformation from a planned to a market economy, on the other. It is

this superimposition of processes and their associated possibilities and constraints that one will have to bear in mind when analyzing institutional responses of transition countries to globalization forces. This qualification by no means challenges the general applicability of the globalization argument to post-socialist countries. It is rather the high dynamic of current social processes and the accompanying youthfulness of institutional responses that can be held responsible for the observed variations in results.

CONCLUSION

In conclusion, the results have shown that there is an increased involvement and a certain sector-specific concentration of women in the labor force, consistent with the 'Globalization Hypotheses.' I have also found clear cross-country differences in terms of women's labor force integration. These differences could generally be brought in line with institutional background features of welfare states and labor markets consistent with the 'Institutional Hypothesis,' that international variation can systematically be attributed to institutional filters. These macro-level results can serve as a general guideline for the following country analyses at the micro-level. But the country-specific chapters that follow are not bound by the same limitations as this comparative overview and so should serve to give a more precise window into the exact and country-specific mechanisms altering women's life courses in an era of globalization.

First, following my aim to describe major longitudinal developments and characteristics of female labor force participation in different country contexts, and the data availability shortages associated with this ambitious goal, this chapter had to concentrate on a limited number of female employment characteristics. This picture could be extended by a more detailed analysis of women's occupational positions in employment or of the gender-specific wage gap women experience compared with men. Furthermore, while this chapter is restricted to an illustrative overview of stylized facts, the following chapters describe concrete institutional backgrounds influencing female employment patterns including factors such as the demographic background of the countries and detailed analyses of family policy or labor market institutions.

Finally, this comparative overview is restricted to highly standardized cross-sectional data in order to meet preconditions for possibly broad international comparability. This standardization may, on the one hand, require appropriate methodology carefulness in the comparison of statistical indicators across countries (see, for example, the discussion of part-time work). On the other hand, the concentration on cross-sectional data meant that I had to neglect movements between different labor market states, mobility patterns and the development of individual life-course histories. These topics will, however, be considered in generous detail in the following country studies.

NOTES

1 For a more detailed consideration of other countries featured in this volume see Hofäcker (2004).
2 Employees are 'those workers who hold the type of job defined as paid employment, jobs based on explicit or implicit employment contracts which provide for a basic remuneration not directly dependent upon the revenue of the unit for which they work'. The self-employed are those working in a job 'where the remuneration is directly dependent upon the profits derived from the goods and services produced', while family workers are 'those workers who hold a "self-employment job" in a market-oriented establishment operated by a related person in the same household'.
3 It needs to be noted that, even in countries where self-employment is high, it is not a purely female phenomenon, as male values everywhere exceed female values (ILO KILM 2001). Nonetheless, due to its occasionally remarkable quantitative extent, its importance for female labor force participation remains and calls for a more explicit consideration of this aspect in future studies.
4 In keeping with the standard OECD definition, part-time employment was defined as employment for less than 30 hours per week (ILO KILM 2001 Manual, Indicator 5).
5 In fact, recent research argues part-time employment was responsible for the strong increase in Dutch overall female employment rates in the 1970s (Daly 2000).
6 The surprisingly high score of social-democratic countries on the service dimension is probably due to the fact that a large number of public sector employment is actually in jobs classifiable as 'personal services'.
7 Childcare is, of course, not the only means of reconciling family and working life; paid leave schemes or specific tax advantages serve the same purpose (Sainsbury 1999). However, childcare clearly favors female employment and it easily allows for direct stylized comparison of welfare state and labor market measures.
8 Childcare facilities have a special importance for this age group, since they allow women an early re-entry into the labor market soon after the childbirth.

BIBLIOGRAPHY

Blossfeld, H.-P. (1999) 'Bildung, Arbeit und soziale Ungleichheit im Globalisierungs-prozeß. Einige theoretische Überlegungen zu offenen Forschungsfragen', GLOBALIFE Working Paper No. 1, University of Bielefeld.
Blossfeld, H.-P. (2000) 'Globalization, social inequality and the role of country-specific institutions', GLOBALIFE Working Paper No. 11, University of Bielefeld.

56 *Introduction*

Blossfeld, H.-P. and Hakim, C. (1997) *Between equalization and marginalization: women working part-time in Europe and the United States of America*, Oxford: Oxford University Press.

Blossfeld, H.-P., Klijzing, E., Mills, M. and Kurz, K. (2005) *Globalization, uncertainty and youth in society*, London: Routledge.

Blossfeld, H.-P., Buchholz, S. and Hofäcker, D. (2006) *Globalization, uncertainty and late careers in society*, London: Routledge.

Blossfeld, H.-P., Mills, M. and Bernardi, F. (2006) *Globalization, uncertainty and men's careers: an international comparison*, Cheltenham, UK and Northampton, MA, USA: Edward Elgar.

Bögenhold, D. and Staber, U. (1991) 'The decline and rise of self-employment', *Work, Employment and Society*, 5(2): 223–39.

Bögenhold, D. and Staber, U. (1993) 'Self-employment dynamics: a reply to Meager', *Work, Employment and Society*, 7(3): 465–72.

Daly, M. (2000) 'A fine balance. Women's labor market participation in international comparison', in F.W. Scharpf and V.A. Schmidt (eds) *Welfare and work in the open economy, Volume II: Diverse responses to common challenges*, Oxford: Oxford University Press, pp. 467–510.

DiPrete, T.A., de Graad, P.M., Luijks, R., Tåhlin, M. and Blossfeld, H.-P. (1997) 'Collectivist versus individual mobility regimes? Structural change and job mobility in four countries', *American Journal of Sociology*, 103: 318–58.

Esping-Andersen, G. (1990) *The three worlds of welfare capitalism*, Cambridge: Polity Press.

European Industrial Relations Observatory (2001) Gender Perspectives: Annual Update 2000, www.eiro.eurofound.ie/2001/03/update/tn0103201u.html, October 2003.

Fagan, C. and Rubery, J. (1999) 'Gender and labour markets in the EU', paper presented at the COST workshop 'Gender, labor markets and citizenship', 19–20 March 1999, Vienna, Austria.

Ferrera, M. (1996) 'The "southern model" of welfare in social Europe', *Journal of European Social Policy* 6(1): 17–37.

Hakim, C. (1993) 'The myth of rising female employment', *Work, Employment & Society*, 7(1): 97–120.

Hakim, C. (1997) 'A sociological perspective on part-time work', in H.-P. Blossfeld and C. Hakim *Between equalization and marginalization: women working part-time in Europe and the United States of America*, Oxford: Oxford University Press, pp. 22–70.

Hammouya, M. (1999) 'Statistics on public sector employment: methodology, structures and trends', ILO Working Paper, Geneva: ILO.

Hofäcker, D. (2002) *Typen europäischer Familienpolitik: Konvergenz oder Divergenz*, unpublished diploma thesis, University of Bielefeld.

Hofäcker, D. (2004) 'Differing welfare regimes: decomposing patterns of female employment in international comparison', GLOBALIFE Working Paper No. 66, University of Bamberg.

International Labour Organization (2001) *Key indicators of the labour market*, CD-ROM, Geneva: ILO.

Jonung, C. and Persson, I. (1993) 'Women and market work: the misleading tale of participation rates in international comparisons', *Work, Employment & Society*, 7(2): 259–74.

Kamerman, S. (2003) 'Welfare states; family policies and early childhood education, care and family support: options for the Central and Eastern European (CEE) and Commonwealth of Independent States (CIS) countries', paper prepared for the consultation meeting on family support policy in Central and Eastern Europe, Council of Europe/UNESCO, 3–5 September, Budapest, Hungary, www.childpolicyintl.org, May 2004.

Klijzing, E. (2005) 'Globalization and the early life course: a description of selected economic and demographic trends', in H.-P. Blossfeld, E. Klijzing, M. Mills and K. Kurz, *Globalization, uncertainty and youth in society*, London: Routledge.

Knijn, T. (2002) 'Was kommt als Nächstes? Dilemmas in einer Zeit nach dem Familienernähermodell', *WSI-Mitteilungen*, 55(3): 184–9.

Korpi, W. (2000) 'Faces of inequality: gender, class, and patterns of inequalities in different types of welfare states', *Social Politics*, 7(2): 127–91.

Lewis, J. (1993) *Women and social policies in Europe. Work, family and the state*, Aldershot, UK and Brookfield, US: Edward Elgar.

Lewis, J. (2004) 'Auf dem Weg zur "Zwei-Erwerbstätigen-Familie"', in S. Leitner, I. Ostner and M. Schratzenstaller (eds) *Wohlfahrtsstaat und Geschlechterverhältnis im Umbruch. Was kommt nach dem Ernährermodell?*, Opladen: Verlag für Sozialwissenschaften, pp. 62–84.

Lodahl, M. and Schrooten, M. (1998) 'Probleme der Rentenversicherung in Osteuropa. Zur Lage in Polen, Tschechien und der Slowakei', *Soziale Sicherheit*, 47(3): 104–10.

Lück, D. and Hofäcker, D. (2003) 'Rejection and acceptance of the male breadwinner model: which preferences do women have under which circumstances?', GLOBALIFE Working Paper No. 60, University of Bamberg.

Meyers, M.K. and Gornick, J.C. (2000) 'Early childhood education and care (ECEC): cross-national variation in service organization and financing', paper prepared for the consultative meeting on international developments in early childhood education and care, Columbia Institute for Child and Family Policy, 11-12 May, New York.

Mills, M. and Blossfeld, H.-P. (2005) 'Globalization, uncertainty and the early life course: a theoretical framework', in H.-P. Blossfeld, E. Klijzing, M. Mills and K. Kurz, *Globalization, uncertainty, and youth in Society*, London: Routledge.

Organisation for Economic Co-operation and Development (OECD) (1999) 'Employment protection and labour market performance', *OECD employment outlook*, June 1999, 49–132.

Organisation for Economic Co-operation and Development (OECD) (2001): 'Balancing work and family life: helping parents into paid employment', *OECD employment outlook*, June 2001, 129–66.

Organisation for Economic Co-operation and Development (OECD) (2002) *Historical statistics 1970–2000*, CD-ROM, Paris: OECD.

Organisation for Economic Co-operation and Development (OECD) (2003) *Statistical compendium, online version*, http://195.243.213.172/scripts/LogIn.dll/login?lg=d, March 2003.

Rubery, J., Smith, M. and Fagan, C. (1998) 'National working-time regimes and equal opportunities', *Feminist Economics*, 4(1): 71–102.

Ruminska-Zimny, E. (2002) 'Gender aspects of changes in the labour markets in transition economies', UN Economic Commission for Europe Issue Paper, Geneva: United Nations.

Sainsbury, D. (1999) *Gender and welfare state regimes*, Oxford: Oxford University Press.

Sasser, B. (2001) 'Gender and labor markets in transition countries', Workshop Report, Warszaw, 15–17 January 2001, www.worldbank.org, October 2003.

Schnepf, S.V. (2001) 'Transformations of gender relations in Central and Eastern Europe', Working Paper, Bremen: Virtual Women's University, www.vifu.de/new/students/, October 2003.

United Nations Children's Fund (UNICEF) (1999) 'Women in transition: a summary, the MONEE Project regional monitory report summary no. 6 – 1999', Florence: UNICEF International Child Development Centre.

Van Bastelaer, A., Lemaître, G. and Marianna, P. (1997) 'The definition of part-time work for the purpose of international comparisons', OECD Labour Market and Social Policy Occasional Papers No. 22/97, Paris: OECD.

Walsh, M. and Wigley, C. (2001) 'Womanpower: the transformation of the labour force in the UK and the USA since 1945', *ReFRESH – Recent Findings of Research in Economic and Social History*, 30: 1–4.

PART II

Country-specific contributions on
conservative welfare regimes

3. Women's employment in West Germany

Sandra Buchholz and Daniela Grunow[1]

INTRODUCTION

Modern societies are profoundly affected by processes of economic and technological change, here referred to as globalization forces. The process of globalization is marked by the internationalization, privatization, deregulation, liberalization and rising importance of markets, as well as the rapid transfer of information and the movement to a knowledge-based economy (Mills and Blossfeld 2005). We are especially interested in the ways these transitions have affected the employment careers of women, who traditionally form a marginal group in the labor market, inasmuch as they are less protected by unions, and typically have less seniority in the job market. We compare the involvement of women in the labor market of West Germany over the past four decades, and pay special attention to the institutional and family contexts that influence women's labor force participation as well as employment chances. We assume globalization likely affects women's labor force participation in two ways: through increasing labor market attachment and/or through rising employment insecurity.

The first set of arguments about the effects of globalization on women's attachment to the labor force says that globalization will strengthen women's labor market ties due to several converging phenomena. For one, the expansion of women's educational opportunities means that women have become more attractive in the labor market, and that they also stand to gain from investments in paid work. For another, globalization is increasing the uncertainty in men's careers in particular industries and sectors. So as the formerly secure employees in households experience greater uncertainty, it has become more rational for women to keep their own ties to the labor market to compensate for the loss of household income security. This will cause women (and men) to postpone family decisions, to invest in careers, and thus to attach themselves more firmly to the market in order to increase their personal sense of security (Mills and Blossfeld 2005). Finally, uncertain times and unstable male careers (especially among younger men) are associated with higher divorce risks. When women fear divorce, they invest more heavily in careers as a form of security against future financial losses and vulnerability.

The second set of arguments maintains that women's careers under processes of globalization may become even more insecure. Castells (2000a) assumes that globalization leads to increasing international competition, which urges firms to react faster and more flexibly to market changes. According to this argument, firms try to pass the insecurities they face on to their employees in order to gain more flexibility in their fiscal and personnel policies (Kurz, Hillmert and Grunow 2002). Outsourcing strategies lead to a reduction in firm sizes, which may result, together with the increasing use of fixed-term contracts, in a shrinking amount of employment security for employees. The most vulnerable, unprotected individuals – labor market outsiders, newcomers and, thus, often, women – are the most affected by these increased insecurities. If so, we should observe a rising risk of unemployment across cohorts and worsening re-entry chances for women who have interrupted their careers. In order to falsify both the 'labor market attachment' argument and the 'employment insecurity' argument, we test for evidence of (1) changing employment relations, (2) changes in the labor market value of female workforce and (3) the erosion of the male-breadwinner model of family organization.

Historically, labor market insecurity has been distributed unevenly to women based on institutional structures that support and protect men, and we can expect that under globalization this pattern is not likely to change. For women in West Germany, frequent job interruptions for caregiving responsibilities, fixed-term contracts and part-time employment increase insecurity. Possible outcomes from the rise in labor market insecurity include increasing unemployment risk, a rising risk of downward mobility and more difficulty re-entering the labor market after an employment interruption or a spell of unemployment.

The aim of this chapter is to examine whether and how globalization might affect women's life courses. Therefore, we study employment careers of three female birth cohorts in West Germany (birth cohorts 1939–41, 1954–56 and 1964) using life history data. The structure of our chapter is as follows: we begin by discussing recent developments in the labor market and other West German institutions, linking them first to the timing and experiences of the West German cohorts before turning to our hypotheses. We then introduce our data and methods and present our empirical results before concluding with a summary and discussion of our findings.

MARKET TRENDS AND INSTITUTIONAL FILTERS

We start from the assumption that the core mechanism through which globalization forces are channeled to individuals at the micro-level is via institutions (Mills and Blossfeld 2005). Therefore we first provide an overview of the relevant developments in those institutional systems that have a major impact on employment structure and career patterns: the educational system, the economic system and the welfare state. We then describe our cohorts' relationships to these institutions during the second half of the twentieth century.

Education

The German educational system has been typified as highly standardized and stratified, when compared with those of other countries (Allmendinger 1989). Although the authority over education is in the hands of individual federal states (*Bundesländer*), a national standardization of school-leaving certificates is still ensured.

Stratification in West Germany starts after the first four years of primary school (around age ten). Pupils are selected into three different tracks of the lower secondary school (*Hauptschule*), middle school (*Realschule*) and the upper secondary school (*Gymnasium* or *Fachoberschule*), the latter leading to the university entrance qualification (*Abitur*). Transitions between the different school types are possible but quite rare.

After general schooling, a period of vocational training or attendance at a technical college or university usually follows. Most young people (about 60 percent) enter a vocational training in the dual system for about three years where general education is combined with occupational training in a firm. Successful participants receive a standardized certificate, which allows employees to move between firms. But as the certificate is highly occupation-specific, it is at the same time difficult to move between occupations.

As in many other OECD countries, educational reforms during the 1960s and 1970s led to considerable expansion in both secondary and tertiary education. While the aims included increasing both access to higher education and the total number of universities, one of the specific targets were women, who on average at that time had a much lower educational level than men. In general schooling, girls began to catch up to boys, and the opportunities for women in higher education have expanded rapidly. At the beginning of the reforms in the mid-1960s, only 25 percent of all students were women, but only ten years later, this had grown to 36 percent. While there was some stagnation during the 1980s, the share of female students today stands at about half of all university graduates (45 percent) (BMBF 2001; Geißler 1996). However, differences are still marked in the choice of university subject or vocational training that female students make (Geißler

1996). These 'female types' of education lead to jobs that are typically connected with lower income, less security and worse career chances compared with men (Beck-Gernsheim 1984; Geißler 1996; Osterloh and Oberholzer 1994).

Employment

As in most developed countries, West Germany has experienced severe changes in employment share by major sectors: (1) a sharp decline in the agricultural sector, (2) cyclical fluctuation and reduction in the manufacturing sector since the end of the 'golden age' in the early 1970s, (3) the expansion of the public sector until the mid-1980s and (4) a rising labor demand in personal and business services (Carlin 1996; Schmid 1998). The share of the manufacturing sector has remained comparatively high in Germany (Castells 2000b; Kaelble 1997), while the growth of the tertiary sector has been moderate due to the high costs of personal services (Schmid 1998). Still, it is the service sector where women's employment is concentrated in Germany.

Women have also been affected by the changes in the manufacturing industries, where fast technical improvements have led to rapidly growing productivity rates over the last decades. At the same time, firms have made intensive use of rationalization, decentralization, downsizing and outsourcing strategies. This has led to a reduction in firm size and, moreover, to a decrease in the demand for labor, with unskilled positions in the industrial sector being especially affected (Kurz, Hillmert and Grunow 2002).

How might these developments impact on women's careers? The international globalization discourse (Beck 1986; 1997; Castells 2000b) as well as the German discussion on the future of paid work (Giarini and Liedke 1998; Senghaas-Knobloch 1999) suggest that employment instabilities and increasing unemployment have been on the rise, a process that is supposed to have started with the oil price shock in the 1970s. In Germany, this discussion mainly focuses on the erosion of the standard employment relationship (continuous full-time employment, highly standardized in terms of working hours, determined by negotiation), which is a key feature of the German welfare state arrangement, but the dominant type of employment for men, not women (Kohli 2000).

Female careers, by contrast, have in the past decades already been comparatively flexible and discontinuous, with employment spells frequently interrupted by phases of unpaid caregiving. Moreover, women are often found in so called 'atypical' forms of employment: part-time work, fixed-term contracts or other forms of marginal employment. They often work in lower hierarchical positions and in secondary labor market segments, and they typically have lower income, less upward and more downward mobility than men (Geißler 2002; Hall 2001; Maier 1993). Still, from an internationally comparative point of view, in West Germany, where major institutional features help to strengthen a work environment of long-term cooperative exchange and trust, the majority of female workers have enjoyed a certain amount of security.

During the last decades, the preconditions and opportunities for West German women's paid employment have changed noticeably, leading to an overall growth in their labor market participation across cohorts, though it is mostly part-time employment.[2] West German women in general experience a greater disparity between their employment chances and earnings than do men, and suffer a greater depression of earnings upon having children (DiPrete and McManus 2000).

Given the rising pressures on the German labor market due to forces of globalization, women's disadvantaged position within this labor market might have worsened for recent cohorts. That is, considering the historical trend in unemployment rates as well as women's relatively weak position in the labor market, a higher individual risk of becoming unemployed and worsened re-entry chances should be observed for women in the younger cohorts.

Welfare state, employment relations and gender

Following Esping-Andersen's typology (1990), Germany belongs to the 'conservative' welfare cluster, with welfare policies traditionally including only very limited attempts to free women from tasks such as childcare and housework (Esping-Andersen 1990; 1999; Orloff 1993). The assumption that women will take up these tasks has always made it difficult for women with children to stay continuously employed full-time. At the same time, the German system to ensure social security, as through pension and unemployment benefits, has been predicated upon the standard employment relationship (*Normalarbeitsverhältnis*), namely continuously, lifelong full-time employment, the dominant employment pattern for men, not women. This implicit social contract is directly connected to a traditional conception of gender roles in which the female partner does the unpaid reproductive and caregiving work at home (Holst and Maier 1998). This implies that while men's integration into and contribution to the German welfare state arrangement came *directly* via paid work, a woman's social status and social security was supposed to derive *indirectly* from the employment status of the head of her household, whether her father or husband.

Until 1977, married women were by law explicitly expected to focus on unpaid caregiving and housework, subordinating their work careers and even needing their husbands' permission to enter into paid employment (Buchholz 2002). No other area mirrors West Germany's social transformation and value change as clearly as the legal reforms to family policy during the 1970s do. One major goal was to bring about sexual equality, explicitly already asserted in the German constitution as of 1949, in the private sphere as well by returning decisions about the household division of labor back to the married couples (Borowsky 1998). In combination with educational expansion and the rising demand for female labor by employers at that time, these changes in legislation pushed the door towards women's paid employment a great deal further open.

Divorce legislation was also changed at the time, making it possible to divorce not only in cases of one partner's 'guilt' concerning the failure of the partnership, but also in cases of disruption, after a separation period. Perhaps the most important aspect of the legislation change, in the present context, was to obligate the economically stronger partner (usually the man) to financially maintain the other partner, and to split property claims such as pension benefits based on the duration of the marriage. Such changes enhanced women's capacity to form and maintain economically independent households.

Attitudes and options for women's paid employment have changed noticeably since that time. Still, the German welfare state keeps supporting the traditional household division of labor (a) *directly*, through legal regulations as well as (b) *indirectly* through a disinclination to provide care services (Esping-Andersen 1999). A key prescription in this respect is the parental leave legislation, which allows for an interruption of employment for up to three years for either father or mother and forces job protection during the leave. In West Germany, though, it is still predominantly women who claim this leave. Thus parental leave legislation supports the discontinuous employment of women rather than that of men (Brumlop 1994; Jungwirth 1999; Landenberger 1990). Joint taxation for married couples gives strong incentives for the spouse with lower earnings, usually the woman, to reduce working hours or to quit employment (Dingeldey 2001; Esping-Andersen 1999; Kurz 1998). At the same time, public childcare is very limited, especially in the daily hours covered, and market solutions to the childcare problem are rather expensive and therefore not widely used.

This policy framework makes discontinuous careers, part-time work, flexible work arrangements and less secure employment relationships attractive, or at least tolerable, to women who have a family (Kurz, Hillmert and Grunow 2002). Employers interested in a flexible workforce could therefore hire women for the less secure positions and keep secure, full-time employment for men. This would be in line with the interests of men, too: given the institutional and cultural support for the male-breadwinner model, they have strong motivations for working in secure, well-paid full-time positions (Kurz, Hillmert and Grunow 2002).

In sum, a trade-off between work and family is characteristic for female labor market participation in Germany (Buchholz 2002). As a result, women's mid-career phase cannot be defined as clearly as it can be for men. Instead, women's careers are marked by substantial periods of interrupted employment (Lauterbach 1994; Mayer 1991). This implies that while men usually step into the labor market as outsiders once – namely, at the beginning of their careers – and then establish themselves in the labor market, the majority of women experience this outsider status and endure establishment phases several times, often in combination with their caregiving duties.

Changing macro conditions for the cohorts under study

We compare women of three different birth cohorts (1939–41, 1954–56 and 1964), who entered the labor market and developed their work and family careers under very different conditions. Three major trends affected women's (and men's) labor market participation: the educational expansion and shift in the occupational structure, increasing female labor force participation and demographic fluctuations (Corsten and Hillmert 2001). As empirical studies have shown, the shift in the occupational structure from rather unskilled production and service jobs to skilled service and administrative occupations has been more pronounced, across cohorts, for women than for men (Blossfeld 1989; Blossfeld and Drobnič 2001).

Women born around 1940 entered the labor market during the 'economic miracle' phase, when labor market conditions were excellent and unemployment practically non-existent. At the same time, however, women usually worked until they married or expected their first child, and then left the labor market. Women of the 1940 cohort belong to the 'baby-boom' generation, where women married and had their first child at younger ages than the generations on either side. Re-entering the labor force after a phase of unpaid caregiving usually meant re-entering on a part-time basis. From 1950 to 1975, the share of part-time working women rose from 6 to 29 percent, a development connected to the expansion in the public sector in West Germany (Blossfeld and Rohwer 1997).

Women born around 1955 entered the labor market around 1975 when the macroeconomic conditions were deteriorating, but with unemployment rates still comparatively low. This phase was marked by slow growth in overall female labor market participation rates. Women of this birth cohort had already taken part in the educational expansion; that is, they had spent a longer time in the educational system and were as a group more highly educated than earlier cohorts.

The 1964 birth cohort was the largest cohort ever born in West Germany. Moreover, it is this cohort that was most confronted with the rising uncertainties attributed to globalization at the beginning of their careers. Women born in 1964 clearly faced the worst labor market conditions, compared with the two older cohorts. Unemployment started to rise in the early 1980s, and firms increasingly faced international competition in the globalizing markets. Moreover, the 1980s were marked by several structural crises in the automobile and steel sectors, key industries in Europe (Springer

1996; Zink 1995). As a reaction to the rising pressure on the German economy to be more flexible, the use of fixed-term contracts grew and other deregulation measures were introduced in the following years, with young people being especially affected (Kurz, Steinhage and Golsch 2001). On the other hand, women of the youngest cohort grew up in a period influenced by the legacy of the feminist movement. Women of this youngest cohort have, at least in some areas, even overtaken their male cohort members with regard to educational performance and ultimate educational level. In sum, members of the 1964 cohort should be the *best prepared for* and at the same time the *most concerned by* rising labor market insecurity and job competition, as compared with the two older cohorts.

HYPOTHESES REGARDING THE EFFECTS OF GLOBALIZATION ON WOMEN IN WEST GERMANY

We focus on three primary hypotheses. First, that changing employment relations are under way; second, that the role of education in women's labor market involvement is becoming more important; and third, that the male-breadwinner model of family support is in decline.

Changing employment relations – increasing employment instability for women in younger cohorts?

If increasing international competition urges firms to react faster and more flexibly to market changes, and firms try to pass the insecurities to their employees, then we should see employment instabilities increasing for the younger cohorts. We expect, then, rising unemployment risk across birth cohorts. Considering the historical trend in unemployment rates as well as women's relatively weak position in the labor market, a higher individual risk of becoming unemployed and worsening re-entry chances after unemployment should be observed, especially for women of the younger cohorts. As indicated by the term 'changing employment relations,' this might imply a loosening of ties between employers and employees.

In their investigation of men's employment careers in West Germany, Kurz, Hillmert and Grunow (2002) find that, contrary to what could be expected based in the globalization discourse, employment instability has not generally increased for German men, apart from the higher unemployment risk faced by the two younger birth cohorts under study. These scholars suggest that the relatively high stability in men's careers might be coming at the expense of women's career stability ('buffering effect'). They argue that within the framework of institutional support for the male-breadwinner model, the interests of married women, married men and employers work in the direction of reserving secure positions for men and leaving less secure positions to women (Kurz, Hillmert and Grunow 2002). If this argument proves to be true, women of the younger cohorts should face less employment stability than women in older cohorts.

Female workforce: do women benefit from educational upgrading and growing needs for a flexible workforce in the labor markets?

Qualification as such has become an increasingly important resource in the German labor market. As Schmid (2000) points out, most of the newly emerging jobs require specific skills as well as high educational attainment. Rudolph and Grüning (1993) conclude that the changes in economic conditions owing to rising international competition have led to a partial convergence of interests between well-educated women on the one hand and innovative firms on the other. They argue that organizations increasingly need 'soft skills,' teamwork and flat hierarchies, which in return require flexible workers with social competences, abilities that have long been attributed to women. Hence, skilled women have become a 'talent reserve' that is more and more desirable to employers (Riegraf 1996). If this view is not too optimistic, it is reasonable to expect that higher education improves women's career prospects in the younger cohorts.

Gender relations: does globalization lead to an erosion of the male-breadwinner model?

As men's risk of becoming unemployed rises, women should, in general, increasingly feel forced to stay in employment while married or having children in order to protect themselves and their families. Another argument for women's growing labor market attachment is the increasing instability of partnerships and marriages. As is indicated by the rising divorce rates, marriage increasingly does not guarantee secure payoffs for women's family investment. Owing to longer education phases, young women also tend to postpone marriage and children. This implies that they – at least for a certain period of time – do not invest mainly in family formation but rather in their own education and careers, which leads to higher opportunity costs for leaving the labor market. Taken together, it is reasonable to expect that the impact of *marriage* on the likelihood of leaving a job for family reasons should decrease over cohorts.

However, staying continuously employed when having children could still be difficult for West German women of the younger cohorts, as German welfare policies have included only very limited attempts to provide alternatives to maternal childcare. That is, state-provided daycare for children under age three is very limited, and market solutions to the childcare problem play only a minor role (Kurz, Hillmert and Grunow 2002). So the impact of *having children* on the transition from job to family work should still be strong for women of the younger cohorts.

DATA AND METHODS

We use data from three surveys of the West German Life History Study (GLHS). The GLHS provides a rich set of detailed retrospective information on educational and employment histories as well as on household- and family-related issues on a monthly basis. It covers a comparatively long time frame and consists of a set of singular retrospective interviews with persons belonging to specific birth cohorts (Brückner and Mayer 1995; Corsten and Hillmert 2001; Mayer and Brückner 1989).

We selected data for the cohorts born between 1939 and 1941 ('cohort 1940'), between 1954 and 1956 ('cohort 1955') and those born in 1964.[3] The cohorts were interviewed between 1981 and 1983 (cohort 1940), in 1989 (cohort 1955) and between 1998 and 1999 (cohort 1964). This means our respondents were between 34 and 44 years old when reporting their life histories. Our sample includes women of German nationality only, followed up to age 40 (at maximum).

In the analyses we control for characteristics of career development and current job, qualification and family-related variables. The effects are calculated using piecewise-constant exponential transition rate models and exponential transition rate models (Blossfeld and Rohwer 2002). We used the latter in order to include period-specific information on job duration and on the duration of employment interruptions.

According to our hypotheses and research interest we focused on the following transitions:

1   To study *employment instability*, we look at transitions from employment to *unemployment* and *out of unemployment*. The underlying time axis for transitions to unemployment is 'job duration.' For transitions out of unemployment the underlying time axis is 'duration of the unemployment spell.' In both cases we distinguish between time periods up to 12, from 12 to 24, from 24 to 36 and more than 36 months. Because of the low case numbers for the two older cohorts for unemployment, we excluded cohort 1940 from this analysis and extended our sub-sample for the transition out of unemployment to the unemployment spells of women born between 1959 and 1961 ('cohort 1960'), added to the cases of cohort 1955.

2   We regard direct and indirect *career mobility* up and down the Treiman prestige scale (Treiman 1977). To distinguish between direct and indirect job mobility, we use period-specific information on the duration of the job and on the duration of employment interruption. An upward move is

defined as entering a new job that has at least a 10 percent higher value in the Treiman prestige rankings than the position before. Transitions to a job at least 10 percent lower in prestige than the position before are regarded as downward moves. Any other job shifts are defined as lateral moves. In exponential transition rate models, we distinguish job durations up to 12, from 12 to 24, from 24 to 36 and more than 36 months as well as the duration of employment interruptions up to six, from six to 12 and more than 12 months.

3   For the analyses on women's transitions *to unpaid caregiving* and *back to employment* after such an interruption, we study the duration of each employment and unpaid caregiving spell observed in a person's career. We distinguish between time periods up to 12, from 12 to 24, from 24 to 36 and more than 36 months.

RESULTS

Rising employment instabilities in younger cohorts?

Women of younger cohorts are more affected by *unemployment* than women of cohort 1940 – although the younger cohorts are much better qualified (table not shown, see Buchholz and Grunow 2003). The effect seems to become even stronger across cohorts (1.54 v. 1.78). Further analyses have shown that the difference between the two younger cohorts is nearly significant (with a significance of 0.9485): women of cohort 1964 seem to have an even higher unemployment risk than women of birth cohort 1955.

The assumption that women of the youngest cohort in general face worse employment chances is also supported by our findings on *women's re-entering into the labor market after unemployment* (table not shown, see Buchholz and Grunow 2003). Women of birth cohort 1964 have more problems re-entering employment after unemployment than women born around 1955 and 1960.

As further analyses on exiting unemployment have shown, having children particularly hinders women from getting re-employed, perhaps because women with children are less mobile or flexible competitors for new jobs. Moreover, the number of potential jobs that suit women with childcare obligations is limited. The effect of 'having a child' seems to be much stronger for women born around 1964 compared with women of the older cohorts. Apparently the stigma 'being a mother' increases its negative power on the chances of leaving unemployment. This finding suggests that alternative-role motivated discrimination is more severe in difficult economic times: in times of increasing labor market competition, employers can afford to be more selective about whom they hire.

Unemployment-to-job transitions are becoming more difficult for women of the youngest cohort.

Benefiting from a rising need for a female workforce?

For testing the hypothesis that women of younger cohorts have benefited from educational upgrading and the need for a flexible workforce, we made a cohort comparison for women's *upward, lateral and downward career mobility*. The results are shown in Table 3.1.

Table 3.1   West German women's upward, lateral and downward career mobility[a]

	Upward mobility	Lateral mobility	Downward mobility
Constant	−6.14**	−5.25**	−6.75**
Period specific information, including job duration and job interruption duration Job duration up to 12 months (ref.)			
Job duration			
12 to 24 months	−0.20	−0.22**	−0.14
24 to 36 months	−0.18	−0.21**	−0.35
36 months and more	−0.55**	−0.62**	−0.60**
Employment interruption duration			
Up to six months	0.87**	0.98**	1.24**
Six to 12 months	0.09	0.43**	0.65**
12 months and more	−0.25**	−0.41**	0.07
Birth cohort			
1939–41 (ref.)			
1954–56	0.20	0.62**	0.34**
1964	0.29**	0.48**	0.56**
Events	568	1 734	437
Total episodes	28 205	28 503	28 473
Censored episodes	27 637	26 769	28 036
−2*diff (logL)	84.41	485.02	132.76

Notes:
[a]   Exponential models including period-specific covariates for job duration and duration of employment interruption phases
**   Significant at $\alpha \leq 0.05$

Source: German Life History Study (GLHS)

Interestingly, though women of younger cohorts are in general more (career) mobile than women born around 1940, women of these younger cohorts experience more downward mobility. This is noteworthy because they are much higher qualified than earlier cohorts and have, to speak in labor market terms, more human capital. Although the effect seems to be even stronger for women of birth cohort 1964, they do not significantly differ from women born around 1955.

At the same time, women of the youngest cohort are also more likely to take a step up the career ladder compared with women of the 1940 birth cohort. Further analyses show this cannot exclusively be attributed to the higher average qualification level in younger cohorts, but is also connected to labor force experience. The greater likelihood of upward moves in the youngest cohort apparently can be attributed to the fact that these more highly qualified women show greater labor market attachment.

So far our results do not support the thesis of a 'march through' of female workforce: on the one hand, women of later cohorts improved their career chances compared with women born around 1940, and on the other hand, we find that women of younger cohorts face higher status insecurity. They are more likely to make a downward move or to become unemployed.

Further investigation on German women's *upward and downward career mobility* (Tables 3.2 and 3.3) support our assumption that women did not really benefit from educational upgrading and the growing need for flexibility in the labor market. Instead, a high level of education even loses its formerly strong protective power against downward mobility. This means that the value of high qualifications in protecting women's careers has diminished over time.

The labor market situation for women of younger cohorts has also worsened, as can be seen from the fact that employment interruptions have become more costly across cohorts: for women born around 1955 and in 1964, an interruption leads to a higher risk of downward mobility. In contrast, for the 1940 cohort, long interruptions (more than 12 months) used to have the opposite effect: women who interrupted their employment for more than 12 months even experienced less downward mobility than employed women. Maybe these long interrupting women had no financial pressure to re-enter the labor market as quickly as possible and could therefore wait for an attractive offer. Moreover we find a gap emerging between public and private sector for women of younger cohorts, indicating that economic turbulence mostly affects the private sector while the traditionally secure public sector jobs are still sheltered.

Erosion of the male-breadwinner model?

Based on our arguments concerning the erosion of the male-breadwinner model, one might expect women of younger cohorts to experience fewer

Table 3.2   West German women's upward mobility[a]

	Birth cohort 1939–41	Birth cohort 1954–56	Birth cohort 1964
Constant	−2.63**	−2.84**	−3.59**
Period-specific information, including job duration and job interruption duration			
Job duration up to 12 months (ref.)			
Job duration			
12 to 24 months	0.03	−0.41	−0.08
24 to 36 months	0.21	−0.47	−0.10
36 months and more	−0.47	−0.52**	−0.36
Employment interruption duration			
Up to six months	0.53	0.73**	0.97**
Six to 12 months	0.18	−0.14	0.02
12 months and more	−0.91**	−0.12	−0.04
Characteristics of career development and current job			
Treiman prestige	−0.11**	−0.09**	−0.08**
Labor force experience	−0.13**	−0.07	−0.05
Number of previous jobs	0.25**	−0.04	0.08
Qualification			
Lower secondary degree without occupational qualification	−0.12	−0.20	−0.51
Lower secondary degree with occupational qualification (ref.)			
Upper secondary degree without occupational qualification	0.94**	1.13**	1.14**
Upper secondary degree with occupational qualification	0.20	0.74**	0.75**
College or university degree	1.47	1.01**	1.01**
Sector			
Private sector (ref.)			
Public sector	0.06	0.10	−0.34
Events	166	173	229
Total episodes	8162	8801	11 242
Censored episodes	7996	8628	11 013
−2* diff (logL)	170.23	170.67	163.75

Notes:
[a]   Exponential model including period-specific covariates for job duration and duration of employment interruption phases
**   Significant at $\alpha \leq 0.05$

Source: German Life History Study (GLHS)

Table 3.3   *West German women's downward mobility*[a]

	Birth cohort 1939–41	Birth cohort 1954–56	Birth cohort 1964
Constant	−8.65**	−8.94**	−8.42**
Period specific information, including job duration and job interruption duration			
Job duration up to 12 months (ref.)			
Job duration			
12 to 24 months	0.02	−0.38	−0.17
24 to 36 months	−0.36	−0.22	−0.47
36 months and more	−0.79**	−0.33	−0.72**
Employment interruption duration			
Up to six months	1.03**	1.30**	1.37**
Six to 12 months	−0.66	0.92**	0.95**
12 months and more	−0.76**	0.69**	0.29
Characteristics of career development and current job			
Treiman prestige	0.06**	0.06**	0.06**
Labor force experience	−0.08**	−0.08**	−0.08**
Number of previous jobs	0.14	0.18**	0.14**
Qualification			
Lower secondary degree without occupational qualification	0.83**	0.36	0.31
Lower secondary degree with occupational qualification (ref.)			
Upper secondary degree without occupational qualification	−0.12	−0.25	0.19
Upper secondary degree with occupational qualification	−0.42	−0.13	−0.22
College or university degree	−2.51**	−1.46**	−0.31
Sector			
Private sector (ref.)			
Public sector	−0.13	−0.91**	−0.62**
Events	112	128	197
Total episodes	8231	8839	11 403
Censored episodes	8119	8711	11 206
−2* diff (logL)	71.46	79.89	141.22

Notes:
[a]   Exponential model including period-specific covariates for job duration and duration of employment interruption phases
**   Significant at $\alpha \leq 0.05$

Source: German Life History Study (GLHS)

transitions to unpaid caregiving than women of the oldest cohort. The opposite is the case: women of younger cohorts are even more likely to drop *out of employment* for caregiving reasons compared with the 1940 cohort (table not shown, see Buchholz and Grunow 2003). We put this result down to the fact that women of younger cohorts have a higher labor force participation rate and labor market attachment than women of cohort 1940 and therefore have a higher general probability of interrupting their careers. While women of older cohorts left the labor market permanently in mid-life, women of younger cohorts try to have periods of employment in mid-life. This is connected with more interruptions (that is, employment exits *and* re-entries). Other findings for West Germany support this argument: studies show German women of successive cohorts differ in their interruption and re-entry behavior – the interruption phases become shorter and the proportion of women re-entering employment increases across cohorts (Lauterbach 1994). What can be concluded is that women's employment careers are still perturbed by the institutional framework provided by the German conservative welfare state, which continues to favor the male-breadwinner model: although the younger female cohorts are better qualified and have more human capital than the oldest cohort members, they still cannot avoid dropping out of the labor market for caregiving reasons.

We examined this finding more closely in Table 3.4. We expected to find a declining impact of *marriage* on women leaving the labor force. At the same time we assumed that due to the lack of childcare option (for example, for structural reasons), *becoming a mother* should still be an important reason for women to leave the labor market.

Both hypotheses are supported by the data. The impact of marriage on women's employment interruption decreases systematically across cohorts: for women born around 1940, marriage was the strongest dropout reason (2.50), but sharply declined by the 1955 cohort (0.84) and the 1964 cohort (0.51). Yet at the same time, the effect of giving birth is statistically significant across cohorts and becomes much stronger (1940: 2.02; 1955: 3.88; 1964: 6.54). For the youngest cohort, having children of any age is the most important reason for leaving employment and becoming a homemaker.

We also find that women of younger cohorts are more likely to *re-enter employment after unpaid caregiving* compared with women born around 1940 and therefore show a higher labor market attachment than women of earlier cohorts (table not shown, see Buchholz and Grunow 2003). Even when controlling for education this difference remains significant.

Higher education seems to increase women's labor market attachment. Further analyses on *women's re-entry to employment after unpaid caregiving* show that educational level positively affects West German women's transitions from unpaid caregiving to employment in all birth cohorts[4] (Table 3.5). Education serves, then, as a magnet to the labor market. On the other hand, having a child of a care-intensive age, not surprisingly, hinders women

Table 3.4   *West German women's transition to unpaid caregiving*[a]

	Birth cohort 1939–41	Birth cohort 1954–56	Birth cohort 1964
Job duration			
One to 12 months	−7.33**	−7.47**	−9.84**
12 to 24 months	−6.80**	−7.28**	−9.60**
24 to 36 months	−6.54**	−7.21**	−9.93**
36 months and more	−6.86**	−7.21**	−9.49**
Labor force experience	−0.13**	−0.04	0.04**
Qualification			
Lower secondary degree without occupational qualification	−0.05	0.15	0.20
Lower secondary degree with occupational qualification (ref.)			
Upper secondary degree without occupational qualification	−0.33	−0.25	−0.09
Upper secondary degree with occupational qualification	−0.39	−0.06	0.29**
College or university degree	−1.28**	−0.49	0.16
Marital status			
Unmarried (ref.)			
Married	2.50**	0.84**	0.51**
Divorced/widowed	−7.48	−0.11	−7.93
Children in the household			
No child (ref.)			
Pregnancy/birth	2.02**	3.88**	6.54**
Preschool child	−0.40	1.45**	1.86**
School child	−1.88**	−0.01	1.96**
Number of children	−0.06	−0.10	−0.15**
Events	233	280	376
Total episodes	2481	3109	3766
Censored episodes	2248	2829	3390
−2* diff (logL)	659.04	830.69	1851.03

Notes:
[a]   Piecewise constant exponential models
**   Significant at $\alpha \leq 0.05$

Source: German Life History Study (GLHS)

from going back into employment. Nevertheless, we find differences across cohorts. The members of the youngest female birth cohort stay at home only

Table 3.5   West German women's re-entry to employment after unpaid caregiving[a]

	Birth cohort 1939–41	Birth cohort 1954–56	Birth cohort 1964
Duration in caregiving			
One to 12 months	−4.36**	−3.56**	−4.44**
12 to 24 months	−4.91**	−4.39**	−3.73**
24 to 36 months	−4.55**	−4.17**	−3.99**
36 months and more	−5.62**	−4.62**	−4.72**
Qualification			
Lower secondary degree without occupational qualification	0.12	−0.04	−0.34
Lower secondary degree with occupational qualification (ref.)			
Upper secondary degree without occupational qualification	0.39	0.59**	0.53
Upper secondary degree with occupational qualification	−0.14	0.40**	0.29**
College or university degree	1.38**	0.08	−0.08
Marital status[b]			
Married (ref.)			
Unmarried	0.54	−1.36	0.84**
Divorced/widowed	2.64**	1.11**	0.97**
Children in the household			
No child (ref.)			
Pregnancy/birth	−2.00**	−0.79**	−1.13**
Preschool child	−0.74**	−0.88**	−0.29
School child	−0.35	−0.39	0.05
Number of children	0.10	0.17	0.10
Events	170	183	290
Total episodes	2695	1637	2879
Censored episodes	2525	1454	2589
−2*diff (logL)	114.46	60.26	108.36

Notes:
[a] Piecewise constant exponential models
[b] In our analysis on re-entering employment after unpaid caregiving we introduced marital status as a controlling variable and did not interpret the results for this variable. In Germany women doing unpaid caregiving are usually married (in our analysis between 307 and 506 cases), and we have too few cases of 'unmarried' (between 18 and 29 cases) and 'divorced/widowed' (between 11 and 23 cases) to provide interpretations for this transition. The effect of 'divorced/widowed' is highly significant and positive in all cohorts; however, widowhood or divorce may require women to exit unpaid caregiving to earn an income.
** Significant at $\alpha \leq 0.05$

Source: German Life History Study (GLHS)

as long as their youngest child is a toddler and then re-enter employment. For women born around 1940 and 1955 we find significant effects also for having a preschool child. German women of later cohorts apparently keep the time of depending on a sole male breadwinner to a minimum.

The empirical findings support the argument that a male-breadwinner-model-oriented gender contract in Germany is eroding. Moreover this erosion could not simply be attributed to the fact that women of younger cohorts have higher overall qualifications and therefore show more interest in their careers. Even when controlling for qualification we find robust evidence for our thesis. Yet avoiding employment interruptions is still difficult for women, especially when they have children. Women of younger cohorts apparently feel forced to stay in employment to economically (and, through the attendant benefits, socially) protect themselves and their families in times of rising economic insecurity. On the other hand, young mothers are unable to stay continuously employed because of the restrictive German welfare state, and therefore try to reduce their 'unavoidable' time of unpaid caregiving to a minimum.

DISCUSSION AND CONCLUSIONS

The aim of this chapter was to examine whether and how globalization might affect women's life courses via paid employment. We presented evidence for globalization leaving its mark on women's employment careers in West Germany in two directions. As hypothesized, we found women's increasing labor market attachment on the one hand and rising employment insecurity on the other.

The first aspect is mirrored in our findings for transitions in and out of unpaid caregiving. German women show an increasing labor market attachment across cohorts, thereby becoming less dependent on male-breadwinner support. Women of later cohorts:

1   have a higher re-entry rate after unpaid caregiving;
2   try to reduce their time out of the labor market because of family reasons to a minimum; and
3   the normative character of the male-breadwinner model seems to have lost power for women of younger generations, since marriage is no longer the main reason for leaving the labor market.

Still, women's employment in Germany is strongly affected by the lack of institutionalized childcare structures.

In line with our second argument, we find that women's careers have become more insecure under the processes of globalization. Women of later cohorts have a higher risk of becoming unemployed and of being downwardly mobile. Moreover, the chances of finding a job have become worse for unemployed women across cohorts.

In contrast to the thesis of Rudolf and Grüning (1993), we could not find evidence for an improvement of female careers across cohorts. Instead we find:

1   a rising overall unemployment risk and worsening exiting chances from unemployment across female birth cohorts;
2   more downward mobility across cohorts (although women of younger cohorts invested much more in their education);
3   a strengthening of the outsider position of women in Germany (re-entering after unpaid caregiving is connected to a higher risk of downward mobility for women of younger cohorts); and
4   a weakening or fading effect of high qualifications on career security.

The increasing labor market attachment of women in Germany is closely related to the rising employment insecurity these women face. Furthermore, our findings indicate that Germany is still far from achieving full labor market integration of women: structural obstacles of the conservative welfare regime still mark women's employment careers. Moreover, German women could not improve their employment chances – though they invested much more in their education and are higher qualified than women of earlier cohorts.

In line with the assumption of Kurz, Hillmert and Grunow (2002), our findings support the thesis that in Germany economic insecurity due to globalization is systematically channeled to women. In times of increasing labor market insecurity and competition, German women experience a strengthening of their outsider status and do not manage to turn their investment in higher qualifications into secure positions in the labor market.

NOTES

1   The authors are listed in alphabetical order. We would like to thank Karin Kurz for helpful comments and support.
2   Unfortunately, the German Life History Study did not collect the information on working hours very precisely for the earlier birth cohorts. The persons questioned do not report if they work in a job with part-time contract or marginal working hours, but they report how many hours they work per week (includes overtime hours). Furthermore, there is a large amount of missing working hours information. Because of this restricted data situation we have not included working hour effects in our models. However, other exploratory models (not reported here) have shown that the inclusion of working hours neither has an effect on its own nor does it change other effects.

3   Analyses for the youngest cohort are based upon an 85 percent sample (checked and edited data) of the overall sample.
4   The finding of no significant effect for college and university degree for the two younger cohorts reflects data limitation problems: women of the 1955 and 1964 cohorts were only followed up to age 35. These women were too young to finish university, enter the labor market, drop out of the labor market for family reasons and then re-enter into employment again by age 35.

BIBLIOGRAPHY

Allmendinger, J. (1989) 'Educational system and labour market outcomes', *European Sociological Review*, 3: 231–50.

Beck, U. (1986) *Risikogesellschaft: Auf dem Weg in eine andere Moderne*, Frankfurt am Main: Suhrkamp.

Beck, U. (1997) *Was ist Globalisierung?*, Frankfurt am Main: Suhrkamp.

Beck-Gernsheim, E. (1984) 'Frauen zurück in die Familie', *WSI-Mitteilungen*, 37: 23–32.

Blossfeld, H.-P. (1989) *Kohortendifferenzierung und Karriereprozeß: Eine Längsschnittstudie über die Veränderung der Bildungs- und Berufschancen im Lebenslauf*, Frankfurt and New York: Campus.

Blossfeld, H.-P. and Drobnič, S. (2001) *Careers of couples in contemporary societies: from male breadwinner to dual earner families*, Oxford: Oxford University Press.

Blossfeld, H.-P. and Rohwer, G. (1997) 'Part-time work in West Germany', in H.-P. Blossfeld and C. Hakim (eds) *Between equalization and marginalization. Women working part-time in Europe and the United States of America*, Oxford: Oxford University Press.

Blossfeld, H.-P. and Rohwer, G. (2002) *Techniques of event history modeling. New approaches to causal analysis*, Mahwah, NJ: Lawrence Erlbaum Associates.

BMBF (2001) *Die wirtschaftliche und soziale Lage der Studierenden in der Bundesrepublik Deutschland 2000*, Berlin: BMBF.

Borowsky, P. (1998) 'Sozialliberale Koalition und innere Reform', *Informationen zur Politischen Bildung*, 258 (Family Policy, Ehe- und Familienpolitik).

Brückner, H. and Mayer, K.U. (1995) *Lebensverläufe und gesellschaftlicher Wandel: Konzeption, Design und Methodik der Erhebung von Lebensverläufen der Geburtsjahrgänge 1954–1956 und 1959–1961*, Berlin: Max-Planck-Institut für Bildungsforschung.

Brumlop, E. (1994) 'Betriebliche Frauenförderung. Bisherige Konzepte, Umsetzungs-erfahrungen, notwendige Neuorientierungen', *Gewerkschaftliche Monatshefte*, 7 (94): 458–68.

Buchholz, S. (2002) *Berufliche Mobilität in Westdeutschland. Eine vergleichende Betrachtung für die Geburtskohorten 1939 bis 1941 und 1954 bis 1956*, Bielefeld: University of Bielefeld, Faculty of Sociology.

Buchholz, S. and Grunow, D. (2003) 'Globalization and women's employment in West Germany', GLOBALIFE Working Paper No. 47, Chair of Sociology I, University of Bamberg.

Carlin, W. (1996) 'West German growth and institutions', in N. Crafts and G. Toniolo
(eds) *Economic growth in Europe since 1945*, Cambridge: Cambridge University
Press.

Castells, M. (2000a) 'The global transformations reader', in D. Held and A. McGrew
(eds) *An introduction to the globalization debate*, Cambridge: Polity Press.

Castells, M. (2000b) *The rise of the network society*, Oxford and Malden, MO:
Blackwell Publishers.

Corsten, M. and Hillmert, S. (2001) 'Qualifikation, Berufseinstieg und Arbeitsmarkt-
verhalten unter Bedingungen erhöhter Konkurrenz: Was prägt Bildungs- und
Erwerbsverläufe in den 80er und 90er Jahren?', Ausbildungs- und Berufsverläufe
der Geburtskohorten 1964 und 1971 in Westdeutschland Arbeitspapier No. 1, Max-
Planck-Institut für Bildungsforschung, Berlin.

Dingeldey, I. (2001) 'European tax systems and their impact on family employment
patterns', *Journal of Social Policy*, 30: 654–72.

DiPrete, T.A. and McManus, P.A. (2000) 'Family chance, employment transitions,
and the welfare state: household income dynamics in the United States and
Germany', *American Sociological Review*, 65(3): 343–70.

Esping-Andersen, G. (1990) *The three worlds of welfare capitalism*, Princeton, NJ:
Princeton University Press.

Esping-Andersen, G. (1999) *Social foundations of postindustrial economies*, Oxford:
Oxford University Press.

Geißler, R. (1996) *Die Sozialstruktur Deutschlands: Zur gesellschaftlichen
Entwicklung mit einer Zwischenbilanz zur Vereinigung*, Opladen: Westdeutscher
Verlag.

Geißler, R. (2002) *Die Sozialstruktur Deutschlands: Zur gesellschaftlichen
Entwicklung vor und nach der Vereinigung*, Wiesbaden: Westdeutscher Verlag.

Giarini, O. and Liedke, P. (1998) *Wie wir arbeiten werden: der neue Bericht an den
Club of Rome*, Hamburg: Hoffmann und Campe.

Hall, A. (2001) 'Berufliche Karrieremobilität in Deutschland und Großbritannien:
Gibt es Differenzen zwischen Frauen und Männern?', in P.A. Berger and D.
Koniezk (eds) *Die Erwerbsgesellschaft: Neue Ungleichheiten und Unsicherheiten*,
Opladen: Leske + Budrich.

Holst, E. and Maier, F. (1998) 'Normalarbeitsverhältnis und Geschlechterordnung',
Mitteilungen aus der Arbeitsmarkt- und Berufsforschung, 31: 506–18.

Jungwirth, C. (1999) 'Soll der Erziehungsurlaub verkürzt werden?', *Zeitschrift für
Personalforschung*, 2(99): 188–200.

Kaelble, H. (1997) 'Der Wandel der Erwerbsstruktur in Europa im 19. und 20.
Jahrhundert', *Historical Social Research*, 22(2): 5–28.

Kohli, M. (2000) 'Arbeit im Lebenslauf: Alte und neue Paradoxien', *Geschichte und
Zukunft der Arbeit*, Sonderdruck.

Kurz, K. (1998) *Das Erwerbsverhalten von Frauen in der intensiven Familienphase.
Ein Vergleich zwischen Müttern in der Bundesrepublik Deutschland und in den
USA*, Opladen: Leske + Budrich.

Kurz, K., Hillmert, S. and Grunow, D. (2002) 'Increasing instability in employment
careers? Men's job mobility and unemployment in West Germany. Birth cohorts
1940, 1955, 1964', GLOBALIFE Working Paper No. 34, Faculty of Sociology,
University of Bielefeld.

Kurz, K., Steinhage, N. and Golsch, Katrin (2001) 'Case study Germany: global competition, uncertainty and the transition to adulthood', GLOBALIFE Working Paper No. 16, Faculty of Sociology, University of Bielefeld.

Landenberger, M. (1990) *Wirkungen des Erziehungsurlaubs auf Arbeitsmarktchancen und soziale Sicherung von Frauen*, Berlin: Wissenschaftszentrum.

Lauterbach, W. (1994) *Berufsverläufe von Frauen. Erwerbstätigkeit, Unterbrechung und Wiedereintritt*, Frankfurt and New York: Campus.

Maier, F. (1993) 'Zwischen Arbeitsmarkt und Familie: Frauenarbeit in den alten Bundesländern', in G. Helwig and H.M. Nickel (eds) *Frauen in Deutschland: 1945–1992*, Berlin: Akademie Verlag.

Mayer, K.U. (1991) 'Berufliche Mobilität von Frauen in der Bundesrepublik Deutschland', in K.U. Mayer, J. Allmendinger and J. Huinink (eds) *Vom Regen in die Traufe: Frauen zwischen Beruf und Familie*, Frankfurt and New York: Campus Verlag.

Mayer, K.U. and Brückner, E. (1989) 'Lebensverläufe und Wohlfahrtsentwicklung: Konzeption, Design und Methodik der Erhebung von Lebensverläufen der Geburtsjahrgänge 1929–31, 1939–41, 1949–51, Teile I, II, III', *Materialien aus der Bildungsforschung*, 35, Berlin: Max-Planck-Institut für Bildungsforschung.

Mills, M. and Blossfeld, H.-P. (2005) 'Globalization, uncertainty and the early life course: a theoretical framework', in H.-P. Blossfeld, E. Klijzing, M. Mills and K. Kurz (eds) *Globalization, uncertainty, and youth in society,* London: Routledge.

Orloff, A.S. (1993) 'Gender and the social rights of citizenship – the comparative analysis of gender relations and welfare states', *American Sociological Review*, 58(3): 303–28.

Osterloh, M. and Oberholzer, K. (1994) 'Der geschlechtsspezifische Arbeitsmarkt: Ökonomische und soziologische Erklärungsansätze', *Aus Politik und Zeitgeschichte*, 6.

Riegraf, B. (1996) *Geschlecht und Mikropolitik*, Opladen: Leske + Budrich.

Rudolph, H. and Grüning, M. (1993) 'Neue Jobs für neue Frauen? Frauenförderung und die Dynamik gespaltener Arbeitsmärkte', in B. Strümpel and M. Dierkes (eds) *Innovation und Beharrung in der Arbeitsmarktpolitik*, Stuttgart: Schäffer-Poeschel Verlag für Wirtschaft, Steuern, Recht.

Schmid, G. (1998) 'Arbeitsmarkt und Beschäftigung', in B. Schäfers and W. Zapf (eds) *Handwörterbuch zur Gesellschaft Deutschlands*, Opladen: Leske + Budrich.

Schmid, G. (2000) 'Arbeitsplätze der Zukunft: Von standardisierten zu variablen Arbeitsverhältnissen', in J. Kocka and C. Offe (eds) *Geschichte und Zukunft der Arbeit*, Frankfurt and New York: Campus.

Senghaas-Knobloch, E. (1999) 'Von der Arbeits- zur Tätigkeitsgesellschaft? Zu einer aktuellen Debatte', *Arbeit. Zeitschrift für Arbeitsgestaltung und Arbeitspolitik*, 2.

Springer, R. (1996) 'Effektivität von unterschiedlichen Formen der Gruppenarbeit in der Automobilindustrie', in C. Antoni, E. Eyer and J. Kutscher (eds) *Das flexible Unternehmen: Arbeitszeit, Gruppenarbeit, Entgeltsysteme*, Wiesbaden: Gabler.

Treiman, D.J. (1977) *Occupational prestige in comparative perspective*, New York: Academic Press.

Zink, K.J. (1995) *TQM als integratives Managementkonzept – Das europäische Qualitätsmodell und seine Umsetzung*, München, Wien: Carl Hanser.

4. Changes in women's employment and occupational mobility in the Netherlands: 1955 to 2000

Matthijs Kalmijn and Ruud Luijkx[1]

INTRODUCTION

In the process of modernization, women's employment patterns have changed dramatically. In virtually all western countries, an increasing number of married women remain in the labor force, even when they have children. In addition, the motivation to work for pay has shifted, with fewer women working as a secondary breadwinner in the home, and more women working to have an independent and attractive occupational career (Blossfeld and Hakim 1997; Van der Lippe and Van Dijk 2001). These changes entail that women's employment patterns have become more stable and more continuous. In essence, their careers have come to look more like the careers of men. Underlying causes for this convergence in employment patterns lie in the fundamental elements of the modernization process: an increasing demand for service sector workers, the expansion of higher education and the erosion of traditional norms and values about gender and family roles (Davis 1984).

In the last two decades of the twentieth century, societies faced new structural changes. Although these changes were probably a logical consequence of the modernization process, they were so different in nature that they are believed to add up to a new transformation (Alderson 1999; Blossfeld et al. 2005). Central elements of this transformation are the internationalization of markets and the rise of new information and communication technologies. These alterations have led to a process of globalization in which economic, social and cultural relations between individuals and between countries have changed. One of the more important consequences of globalization, so it is believed, lies in the labor market. An influential hypothesis is that globalization has led to heightened competition among firms and to an increase in the power of markets. On the individual level, these changes result in increasing uncertainty on the labor market and an increasing need to be flexible in one's employment behavior. In practical terms, globalization is believed to mean more temporary work, fewer fixed-term contracts, more part-time work, more job changes and higher risks of short-term unemployment.

The globalization hypothesis about employment patterns is particularly interesting when applied to the position of women in the labor market. In the modernization process, women's careers became more standardized, more continuous and more secure. Although important differences between men and women remain, modernization has led to a convergence to the male pattern. In the globalization process, careers are believed to become less standardized, less continuous and less secure. Essentially, this would mean that women's careers are changing back to the traditional female pattern. The reasons for a feminization of careers have of course changed: in the past, discontinuity was primarily related to supply-side factors (women's own life-course transitions), now discontinuity is more strongly related to demand-side factors (the changing circumstances of employers). Because it is also believed that men's careers will have been affected by globalization (Blossfeld, Mills and Bernardi 2006), globalization may also mean that a new type of convergence has occurred, a convergence to the female pattern.

Although men and women will both face the consequences of the globalization process, it is an important question whether they will be affected to the same extent. Several authors suggest the hypothesis that the change will be more pronounced for women. Two different reasons for this expectation are given (see Hofmeister, Blossfeld and Mills, this volume). One reason is that women are relative outsiders in the labor market and hence are less well protected from uncertainty. In this scenario, the forces of globalization are negative for outsiders in the labor market, such as youth, ethnic minorities and women. Another reason is that the flexibility that is increased by globalization coincides with what many women want. In this interpretation, the consequences of globalization are not per se negative and can even be positive. In the new flexible context, women can make transitions in their demographic career if they face temporary problems in the labor market and women who interrupt their work for family reasons may not be penalized later on in their career (again, see Hofmeister, Blossfeld and Mills). However we are to evaluate the two interpretations, they both imply an important break with the past. Whereas modernization meant that women increasingly opted for an uninterrupted and continuous occupational career, globalization may mean that women again have more precarious and discontinuous careers.

In this chapter, we examine these hypotheses for women's employment and occupational careers in the Netherlands. Using four retrospective life-history surveys, we examine movements in and out of the labor force as well as different types of job mobility. To examine the implications of globalization, we focus on a comparison of career transitions in different periods.

The Netherlands provides a particularly interesting testing ground for the thesis of globalization. The smaller a country, the more sensitive it is to the forces of globalization, and the Netherlands is no exception to this rule. When looking at indicators concerning international trade, communication technology, foreign investments and international tourism, the Netherlands is definitely a forerunner in the globalization process (Liefbroer 2005). High scores on globalization indicators in the Netherlands are coupled with a strong international orientation of the population. At the same time, however, the Netherlands is not a special case when looking at employment patterns. Dutch employment relationships have been characterized as relatively closed. There are many rules and regulations about employment and the labor unions play an important role in determining wages and secondary labor conditions. It is generally difficult to lay off employees in the Netherlands and there are limitations in hiring temporary workers. Comparative studies show that the Netherlands is more or less similar to the European Union as a whole when looking at the relative share of temporary workers, the share of fixed-term contracts and the number of people with a secondary job (De Grip, Hoevenberg and Willems 1997; Smulders and Klein Hesselink 1997). In other words, flexible work is not especially common in the Netherlands.

What is special in the Netherlands is the high degree of part-time work. The Netherlands has been called 'the only part-time economy of the world.' Almost 70 percent of the women who work for pay work part-time and this is high compared with the European Union as a whole, where only a third of working women work part-time (Blossfeld and Hakim 1997). Part-time work is also relatively high among Dutch men: between 10 to 20 percent of men work part-time, depending on the data source. Although part-time work is part of the trend toward flexibilization, part-time work is not flexible in all respects. In fact, most part-time jobs are tenured in the Netherlands so that part-time work is only flexible in the sense that it allows employers to organize the workforce in a more flexible manner.

The high level of part-time work has contributed to low levels of unemployment in the Netherlands. Part-time work in combination with wage restraints have often been considered the main ingredients of the so-called Dutch 'polder model' (Visser and Hemerijck 1997). The Dutch economy is regulated by a corporatist structure in which the government, employer organizations and labor unions jointly come to agreements about a whole range of work aspects, ranging from wages to childcare facilities. Even though by themselves such organizational structures do not foster economic growth, the particular way in which they have operated in the Netherlands has been successful. In the last two decades, the three institutional actors have jointly placed emphasis on wage restraints on the one hand, and on the redistribution of labor on the other hand. This not only led to a reduction in the standard workweek for many sectors of the labor market, but it also contributed to the rapid rise of part-time jobs. This change reflected a desire on the part of employers to be more flexible in the way they organize their firms, which in turn was a response to the forces of globalization. The desires of employees coincided with the desires of many women to work part-time. Part-time work is now a legally defined right in all collective labor agreements.

It is important to emphasize that changes in working hours have been made in the context of strong regulations about hiring and firing. To characterize employment relations in the Netherlands, we can borrow Atkinson's distinction between internal and external flexibility (Atkinson 1984). Internal flexibility pertains to the degree to which firms are able to change the allocation of their existing workforce, whereas external flexibility pertains to the degree to which firms can change the workforce itself by hiring and firing employees. The Netherlands is high in terms of internal flexibility but it is about average or even below average in terms of external flexibility.

CHANGING GENDER DIFFERENCES IN THE NETHERLANDS

Before discussing the possible consequences of globalization for women's employment patterns, it is important to review what has happened to women's employment in the preceding era of modernization. Women's employment in the Netherlands has been characterized by radical and rapid change over the past decades. Between 1970 and 2000, the percentage of women participating in the labor market has risen from 29 to 54 percent (Keuzenkamp and Oudhof 2000). Among married women, the change has been even more pronounced (De Graaf and Vermeulen 1997; Van der Lippe and Van Doorne-Huiskes 1995). Although all western countries have witnessed an increase in women's labor supply, the change in the Netherlands has been so rapid that its position in the list of western countries has shifted from being among the most traditional countries to being a little above average in the European Union.

Important gender differences remain when looking at indicators of flexible or insecure work. First, as discussed above, the share of part-time workers is higher among women than among men, and this difference is particularly striking in the Netherlands. A second and less well-known fact is that the share of workers who have a flexible contract is higher among women than it is among men. About 12 percent of women have a temporary contract (for less than a year) or have an uncertain number of weekly hours. For men, this figure is much smaller, 6 percent (Keuzenkamp and Oudhof 2000). The greater prevalence of flexible workers among women is not entirely due to part-time work because many part-time jobs in the Netherlands work on fixed contracts. Third, as in many other countries, unemployment is higher among women than among men, but unemployment itself is low, as discussed above.

Gender convergence in employment has also resulted in declining gender differences in the type of work men and women do. In general, it appears that there has been an increase in the level of occupation that women occupy, while there are persisting differences in the detailed occupations of men and women (Van der Lippe and Van Doorne-Huiskes 1995). It is not fully clear whether women are more or less likely to work in sectors that have been most strongly affected by globalization. On the one hand, women are overrepresented in government jobs and these jobs have probably been less strongly affected by the forces of globalization. On the other hand, women are well represented in other globalized labor market sectors, such as finance and trade. In one of the most globalized sectors of the labor market – information and communication technology – women are underrepresented.

Changing employment in the Netherlands is associated with four other important changes: increasing demand for service jobs, educational change, changes in family structure and changing gender roles.

In virtually all western countries, educational expansion has coincided with a decline of gender inequality in schooling. In the Netherlands, differences between men and women in terms of education were originally rather small, although certainly not absent. In younger generations, educational differences between men and women at the higher levels have disappeared. The percentage of recent generations receiving university training or higher vocational training is about 30 percent for both men and women (about 10 percent received university training) (Keuzenkamp and Oudhof 2000). The rise in women's level of schooling is an important cause of the rise in married women's employment, although it is not a sufficient cause. Increases in married women's employment have occurred within educational categories as well, particularly among better educated women, suggesting that other causes are important as well (SCP 1998).

Changes in family structure are connected in complex ways with changes in women's employment patterns. The Netherlands has experienced the 'second demographic transition' quite rapidly. The total fertility rate has declined from 3.1 in 1960 to well below replacement level (1.7) in 2000 and the age at the birth of the first child (for women) is now 29 years, which is the highest in the European Union (Garssen et al. 1999). Marriage rates have declined as well since the 1970s, a decline that in the Netherlands is primarily due to the rise of unmarried cohabitation. The divorce rate (per 1000 married women) has increased from 2.1 in 1960 to 9.2 in 2000 and the number of marriages expected to end in divorce is about one in three, which is about average for Western European countries. Declining fertility is both cause and consequence of the rise of women's employment.

The rise of women's work is also affected by changing attitudes about the appropriate roles of men and women in society. Empirical indicators show that in virtually all western societies there is decreasing support for a rigid division of labor between husbands and wives, that acceptance of married women's work has increased rapidly, and that men are expected to become more involved in traditional female activities like child rearing. In the Netherlands, these changes have been particularly rapid: in 1970, 68 percent of Dutch men and women found it unacceptable for a mother of young children to work for pay if that meant that the children would go to daycare. In the late 1990s, this percentage declined to 34 percent (SCP 1998). Although gender values have changed rapidly in the Netherlands, cross-country studies suggest that the share of women who work lags behind the high degree of egalitarian gender attitudes. In terms of gender values, the Netherlands belongs to the most liberal countries, but in terms of women's work, the Netherlands is about average or even below average when we look at full-time working women (Kalmijn 2003). A possible explanation of this discrepancy is that even though the tolerance of married women's work is high in the Netherlands – people think everyone should be free in how to organize his or her own life course – the preference to work among women is not so high. Many women consider paid work as an option they can choose, and not as the 'default' in the way it is for men.

HYPOTHESES REGARDING GLOBALIZATION'S EFFECTS ON WOMEN IN THE NETHERLANDS

In this contribution, we examine the consequences of globalization for the employment and occupational careers of women. The consequences of globalization for employees are believed to be largely indirect. Globalization results – through heightened competition in international markets – in an increased need for firms to engage in flexible labor relations and an increased degree of uncertainty for both employers and employees. To test this hypothesis, we consider several labor market outcomes. We distinguish between the following career transitions:

1   transition to non-employment (exit);
2   transition to employment (re-entry);
3   change to an occupation with a lower status;
4   change to an occupation with a similar status;
5   change to an occupation with a higher status.

Transitions to non-employment can be made for family reasons or for other reasons but we make this distinction indirectly, by looking at the effects of having children and by looking at effects during episodes without children. Because we are focusing on mid-career women (that is, ages 25–55), it is also important to look at re-entry transitions.
    To test the globalization hypothesis, several strategies can be followed. One strategy is to compare the career transitions of women in countries that

differ in the degree to which these countries are affected by globalization. Another strategy is to focus on differences within countries and to compare women's careers in labor market sectors that have been heavily involved in the globalization process (for example, information and communication technology) to women's careers in sectors that are less involved (for example, education). A third strategy, which is used here, is to rely on a comparison over time within a country. Because globalization is a process, this seems a logical approach.

An important question that needs to be answered in this approach concerns the timing of the globalization process. When did globalization occur? It is usually believed that globalization began in the mid- or late 1980s and developed further into the twenty-first century. We will therefore compare careers in four decades: the 1960s (roughly), the 1970s, the 1980s and the 1990s. From the 1960s to the 1980s we should see the usual signs of modernizing gender roles, but from the 1980s to the 1990s we should also see signs of globalization (see Hofmeister, Blossfeld and Mills, this volume). Note that we apply a period rather than a cohort perspective. Even though cohort comparisons are usually more easy to interpret (especially when the focus is on the link between demographic transitions and labor market outcomes), globalization is a period phenomenon that will probably affect all birth cohorts. There may be cohort differences that are related to differences in experience, but we take experience into account.

There are two ways in which time can play a role. First, the general chances of experiencing certain transitions may have changed. The chances of making any type of moves during the career will have increased, the chances of experiencing a labor market exit will have increased, and the chances of moving back into the labor market will have increased as well. Our first hypothesis is that women's labor market careers have become more transitional. A second way in which time plays a role is that the effects of other variables may have changed over time. Interaction hypotheses can be formulated for a number of characteristics. Before we do this we need to specify hypotheses about the main effects of these characteristics. We consider three types of characteristics that have often been considered in individual studies of women's labor force participation: job characteristics, women's career investments and women's life-course transitions (Alon, Donahoe and Tienda 2001; De Graaf and Vermeulen 1997; Dekker, Muffels and Stancanelli 2000; Desai and Waite 1991; Lehrer 1999; Moen 1991; Van der Lippe 2001).

Our first individual hypothesis is that certain types of jobs are better protected than other jobs and that women in such jobs will be less likely to experience a departure from the labor market. We consider a range of occupational characteristics. We expect that higher status occupations, occupations in the government sector, full-time jobs and occupations with a higher percentage of male employees are better protected in the labor market.

In some cases, we also expect positive effects of these job characteristics on upward and downward mobility. More specifically, we generally expect that better protected jobs also imply better chances of upward and lower chances of downward mobility. An exception is occupational status. Occupational status will have a different effect on upward and downward mobility owing to ceiling and bottom effects. The higher the status, the more difficult it is to move up and the lower the status, the more difficult it is to move down.

Will the effect of job characteristics change over time? In the globalization period, we may expect an increase in the effects of certain job characteristics. Government jobs have probably been shielded from the forces of globalization and we therefore expect that differences in mobility and exit rates between government and other types of jobs will have increased. Similarly, we expect that other well-protected jobs, such as male jobs and full-time jobs, will be more strongly protected from increasing uncertainty than other jobs. Formulated differently, we not only expect changes in the labor market as a whole, but we also expect the effects of job characteristics to increase over time.

Our second individual hypothesis is that the more women have invested in the labor market, the less likely they will experience a departure from the labor market, the more likely they will experience re-entry, and the more likely they will experience favorable patterns of mobility. This notion parallels the well-known insider–outsider distinction. By investing in paid work, women can strengthen their tie to the labor market, and this gives them an insider position, which is generally a better protected position. We look at several aspects of career investments: educational attainment, labor market experience, the length of job tenure and the number of times a woman has switched jobs. We expect job changes to be positive investments, on top of tenure and experience effects. Positive career investments are believed to decrease employment exit chances, increase favorable job mobility and increase re-entry chances.

Are there reasons to believe that the role of career investments has changed? It is generally argued that in open employment systems, where employees are not protected by rules, regulations and labor unions, the role of personal qualities becomes essential. Because globalization implies a move toward a more open system, we believe that investment effects on careers will have become stronger as well. This suggests that globalization intensifies inequality. This effect is believed to be indirect in the sense that insiders on the labor market will be less likely to experience the negative consequences of globalization than outsiders. This argument can also be associated with the finding that youth are more strongly affected by globalization whereas middle-aged men are less strongly affected. The more women have invested in their career, the more they have become insiders, and the more they will be able to avoid the job insecurity that globalization entails. This is our third hypothesis.

Our fourth hypothesis concerns the well-known role of life-course transitions. Marriage and children will increase exit chances, reduce job mobility and reduce entry chances. We expect that these life-course effects will increase over time. Initially, women's careers were heavily dependent on their marriage and family life. During the modernization period, this linkage will have become weaker: marriage is no longer a reason to leave the labor market and the effects of motherhood on employment exits will have declined as well. During the more recent globalization period, this process may have been reversed. In the present era, employer needs of flexible labor may coincide with women's desire to have a career that is flexible and this may have resulted in a return to strong life-course effects on careers. More specifically, we expect the connection between employment exits and fertility to become stronger in the more recent period. Women can more easily withdraw from the labor market when they have children, and women may decide to have children in anticipation of an involuntary employment exit, thereby strengthening the connection between non-employment and fertility.

DATA

To test our hypotheses, we analyze four retrospective life history surveys based on (stratified) random samples of the Dutch population:

1   the Netherlands Family Survey 1992–1993 – FNB1992 (Ultee and Ganzeboom 1993);
2   the Survey Households in the Netherlands 1995 – HIN1995 (Weesie and Kalmijn 1995);
3   the Family Survey Dutch Population 1998 – FNB1998 (De Graaf et al. 1998);
4   the Family Survey Dutch Population 2000 – FNB2000 (De Graaf et al. 2000).

All four surveys used face-to-face interviews with respondents at home. For married and cohabiting couples, the partners also were interviewed, using more or less similar questionnaires. Because the surveys were couple-oriented, they had an undersample of single persons. The number of women interviewed in the four surveys is: 898 (FNB1992), 1655 (HIN1995), 1029 (FNB1998) and 782 (FNB2000), yielding a total sample of 4364 women. As we focus on women between 25 and 55 years of age, we selected all women 25 and over at the time of the interview. After also deleting records for women who never worked and for women with missing values on central variables, our effective sample size was 3614 women (739, 1430, 845 and 600 respectively for the four surveys). Of all women over 25, 3.7 percent never worked for pay.

The surveys gathered retrospective information on work histories. For all the jobs that the respondent held in his or her life, respondents reported beginning and ending dates, as well as additional information on the content of the job. In the FNB1992 interviews, the work history was organized by jobs, while in the other three surveys, the career history was organized by employer. Within employer spells, additional data were gathered on the jobs held. For the HIN1995 data this was limited to the first and last occupation with an employer. All information was based on monthly data.

METHODS

For each person, we consider multiple job spells that can end with a change in jobs or with an exit from employment. We also have multiple spells without work and these can end in the re-entry into employment. The first job entry is ignored in our models since the focus is on mid-career women. We estimate three separate models:

1 Model A: the chance of leaving employment, given that a woman is employed;
2 Model B: the chance of re-entering employment, given that a woman is not employed and was employed before;
3 Model C: the chance of a job change given that a woman is employed, separated into downward, lateral (not shown) and upward moves.

Upward and downward moves are defined in absolute terms: these are any moves on the International Socio-economic Index (ISEI) scale. Lateral moves are moves to a job with the same ISEI, which most often will be a move to the same occupation in a different job. We estimated two versions of Model C. The first version includes only employed women, the second version also includes women who re-enter. In this model, we compare the new job with the job women had before they left.

Note that job changes are treated as censored spells in Model A, whereas employment exits are treated as censored spells in Model C. Three-month periods of not-working are not considered as nonemployment. The data contain a sufficient number of events for each model: 1757 employment exits, 1445 re-entries (497 downward, 572 lateral and 376 upward re-entries) and 2019 job changes (430 downward, 1071 lateral moves and 518 upward moves).

To analyze the data, we apply discrete-time event history models (Yamaguchi 1991). The data were re-organized into a person-month file, which contained time-constant and time-varying variables for each respondent in each month. The person-month file is analyzed by (multinomial) logistic regression models in which the occurrence of an event rather than experiencing no event is the dependent variable.

All models are also estimated for each historical period separately. The coefficients for the four periods are presented in the same table that contains the pooled result. We tested whether the differences in the coefficients are significant using interaction effects. Testing was done in a parsimonious fashion by including only the interaction of period and the independent variable of interest. We tested no linear trends since the hypotheses suggest different changes in the modernization period and the globalization period.

MEASURES

Job characteristics

Occupational status: the current (or most recent) occupational status of the job a woman held, coded to ISEI-scores (Ganzeboom, De Graaf and Treiman 1992). The mean was 46 in our sample.

Full-time work: three categories for the number of hours a woman works for pay: a small part-time job (less than 20 hours, 23 percent of the jobs), a large part-time job (20–31 hours, 28 percent of jobs) and a full-time job (32 hours or more, 46 percent of jobs).

Government job: whether the job is in the government sector (34 percent of jobs).

Proportion of women in an occupation: obtained from external survey sources and matched to the two-digit occupational codes of the current or most recent occupation. In an average job held by a woman in our sample, 64 percent of the workers in that occupation are female.

Career investments

Educational attainment: highest completed level of schooling, coded to the approximate number of years needed to complete the level (mean 10.4 years).

Job tenure and non-employment duration: the number of months in the current job or in a non-employment spell, expressed in months and separated into four categories: 12 or fewer months; 13–24 months; 25–48 months; and more than 48 months. Note that the first month of a job spell is excluded from all models since no event can logically occur in the first month. For job tenure and non-employment, more than half the spells are longer than 48 months.

Paid work experience: the number of months of experience in all jobs except the current job, expressed in months (a logged transformation was used to take into account diminishing marginal returns to experience; a quadratic specification did not turn out to be significant).

Number of job changes: the number of jobs a woman held in her career (lagged one month). Since this measure is time-varying – summarizing a woman's career 'so far' – it is highly correlated with age. We standardized this measure for age, which was done by calculating the degree to which a woman's number of jobs or unemployment spells deviates from the average in her five-year age group.

Life course

We distinguished the combination of marital and child status in five mutually exclusive groups and coded these with cumulative contrasts:

1 single (that is, living alone, unmarried or divorced; seven percent of spells);
2 married without children (that is, married, remarried or cohabiting; 18 percent);
3 young children (that is, married, remarried or cohabiting, with any child under age six; 36 percent);
4 old children (that is, married, remarried or cohabiting, with all children over age six and at least one child under age 18; 29 percent);
5 empty nest (that is, married, remarried or cohabiting, with children, all children over age 18; 10 percent).

Single mothers are treated as if they were married when they had their first child (N = 67). After divorce, women are treated as single again.

Control variables

Age and age squared: age is included because employment behavior also depends on age, given a certain amount of experience. Age and experience can simultaneously be included because for women, the correlation is not so strong (r = 0.33). The average age is 35.7 with a standard deviation of 7.8 years (women are 25 to 55 based on our selection of the data).

Father's occupational status: included because upward and downward moves may depend on ascriptive factors.

Survey: dummy-variables indicating from which survey the data come; reference is 1992.

Period: broken down in four categories: 1955-69, 1970-79, 1980-89 and 1990-2000. Note that periods before 1955 were not considered in the analyses. The number of women observed in each of the four periods is sufficient: 700 in the 1960s, 1506 in the 1970s, 2703 in the 1980s and 3419 in the 1990s. Note that we do not include cohort or year of birth since this is highly correlated with period (r = 0.69). We also estimated cohort instead of period effects and concluded that the main effects do not tell a different story.

Conservative welfare regimes

Therefore, we ignore in this chapter the important question of whether trends in female careers are a cohort or a period phenomenon.

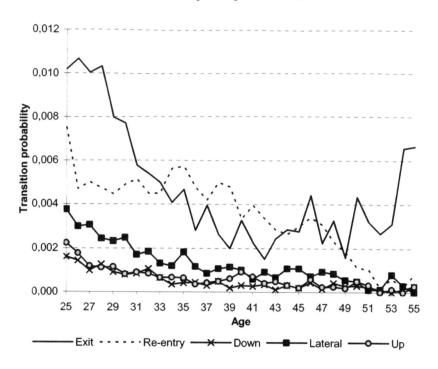

Sources: Netherlands and Dutch Family Surveys 1992–93, 1998, 2000; Survey Households in the Netherlands 1995

Figure 4.1   Transition probabilities by age for women in the Netherlands

RESULTS

We begin with a descriptive analysis in which we look at the various transition chances in detail in a bivariate fashion. Figure 4.1 depicts the chances of employment exits, employment re-entries and job mobility by age. The figure shows that employment exit chances follow a U-shaped pattern, they are highest at the lowest ages, decline rapidly during the twenties and thirties, and then increase again, although not to levels as high as in the beginning. Re-entry chances follow a more continuous pattern and decline with age. A similar pattern is observed for job moves. Women change jobs most frequently when they are young. Lateral moves are not uncommon, even though they are defined as a change to jobs with exactly the same ISEI score (mostly moves to the same occupation in a different job). Upward and downward transition chances are about equal when women are young, but when women are older, upward chances are greater than downward chances, which is consistent with an upward career pattern.

Figure 4.2 depicts employment levels by stage in the life course separately for the different periods. The figure shows that in all periods, most single women were employed (80 percent). Note that women who never worked for pay (3.7 percent) are not included in this figure.

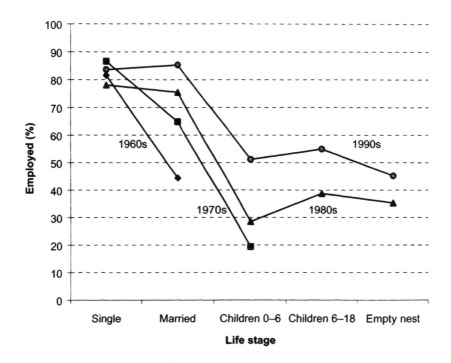

Sources: Netherlands and Dutch Family Surveys 1992–93, 1998, 2000; Survey
           Households in the Netherlands 1995

*Figure 4.2   Percentage employed in different periods by life stage of women in the
           Netherlands*

When women marry or start living with a partner, the proportions of women who are employed decline sharply. This effect declines continuously from the 1960s to the 1990s and in the 1990s, employment levels are the same for women before and after marriage (or cohabitation). When married or cohabiting women have their first child, employment levels decline again, as is well known from other research in the Netherlands (Dekker, Muffels and

Stancanelli 2000). A new finding is that this decline is not so much reduced across the different periods. In each period, there is a sharp reduction in employment levels after the birth of a first child. What has changed is that in the early periods, both marriage and fertility led to a decline in employment, whereas in the more recent period, it is only fertility that has an effect. The declining effect of marriage is also the main reason why the level of employment of mothers is higher in the 1990s than in the 1970s. Another interesting pattern is that employment levels increase again when all the children have passed the age of six, although not to levels preceding the birth of the first child. There is no clear trend in this increase. We have to keep in mind that the levels of employment depicted in Figure 4.2 are the result of many underlying exit and (re-)entry chances. It is to these transition chances we now turn.

Period effects

We begin with the effects representing changes in the nature of women's careers. The exit model in Table 4.1 (first column) shows that the chances to leave employment have decreased continuously since the 1960s. There does not appear to be a slowdown or reversal of the trend when moving from the 1980s to the 1990s. In other words, the trend fits in with the modernization process and there are no signs supporting the globalization thesis. Women's hold on the labor market has continuously become stronger.

When looking at the re-entry model in Table 4.2 (first column), we see evidence for the reverse change: the chances of non-employed women to re-enter the labor market have increased across successive periods. Although the changes are not of similar magnitude in all successive decades, we do not see a clear acceleration in the 1990s, as suggested by the globalization thesis.

The models for job changes in Tables 4.3 and 4.4 provide partial confirmation for the globalization thesis. For downward and upward moves (and also lateral moves, see Kalmijn and Luijkx 2003), we observe an increase across periods. In other words, the chances to change jobs have increased over time. Because this increase started in the 1960s, it is unclear whether modernization or globalization is at work here. The finding of increased job mobility is nevertheless important.

Job characteristics

We now turn to our other hypotheses. First, we see that being in a government job leads to a lower chance of leaving employment, in line with our expectation (see Table 4.1).

Table 4.1   Exits from employment for women in the Netherlands

	All periods	1960s	1970s	1980s	1990s
Survey					
1992 (ref)					
1995	0.01	−0.08	0.28*	−0.13	−0.17
1998	−0.07	0.37+	0.11	−0.18	−0.39*
2000	−0.24**	−0.30	−0.10	−0.29*	−0.51**
Period					
1970s	−0.34***				
1980s	−0.60***				
1990s	−0.86***				
Age	−0.37***	−0.04	−0.23+	−0.46***	−0.32***
Age/10 squared	0.45***	−0.06	0.22	0.57***	0.38***
ISEI/10	−0.02	−0.02	−0.04	−0.02	−0.04
Work hours per week					
32+ hours (ref)					
20–31 hours	−0.32***	−0.67**	−0.14	−0.41***	−0.36*
1–19 hours	−0.52***	−0.70+	−0.49**	−0.66***	−0.65***
Missing hours	−0.80***	−0.56	−0.49	−0.81**	−1.35**
Government job	−0.13*	−0.08	0.21+	−0.17+	−0.37***
Women in occup. /10	0.04***	0.05	0.03	0.05**	0.04*
Years of education	−0.03*	−0.07*	0.01	−0.04*	−0.03
Job tenure					
< 13 months (ref)					
13–24 months	0.10	0.20	0.48*	0.07	−0.04
25–48 months	0.02	0.10	0.50**	0.14	−0.32*
> 48 months	−0.22**	0.31	0.34+	−0.17	−0.76***
Experience paid work (ln)	−0.08+	−0.29*	−0.13	−0.21**	−0.01
Number of jobs	0.03	0.11	0.08+	0.08*	−0.02
Life course					
Single (ref)					
Cohabiting/married no children	0.81***	1.79***	1.21***	0.67***	0.26
Youngest child 0–6	0.54***	−1.19***	0.27*	1.07***	0.93***
Youngest child 6–18	−0.66***		−0.73***	−0.88***	−0.68***
Empty nest	0.32*			−0.12	0.40+
Father's occupation	0.03*	−0.01	0.02	0.05+	0.02
Constant	2.31***	−2.55	−1.34	3.39**	1.48
Number of events	1 757	202	364	606	585
N	299 772	16 039	42 821	105 448	135 464
Chi-squared	892.5	170.1	203.5	333.6	260.7
Df	25	20	21	22	22

Notes: *** p < 0.001, ** p < 0.01, * p < 0.05, + p < 0.10. Logistic regression coefficients

Sources: Netherlands and Dutch Family Surveys 1992–93, 1998, 2000; Survey Households in the Netherlands 1995

Being in a government job does not increase the chances to re-enter the labor market later on, as Table 4.2 shows. In Tables 4.3 and 4.4, we observe that women who work in government jobs have a lower chance of experiencing downward and upward mobility (and the effect of a government job on lateral mobility is not significant). Together, these findings suggest that women in government have flatter and more stable careers.

Have the effects of government jobs changed over time? In other words, have the differences between the government sector and other sectors increased, as we expected? Table 4.1 suggests that the effect of government jobs on employment exits becomes (more) negative over time. In other words, there has been a general decline in women's chances of leaving employment, but this decline is weaker outside the government sector. Another way of evaluating this is to estimate the period effects in Table 4.1 only for women who are not in government jobs. When we do this, we see that the decline in the chances of leaving the labor market is weaker for women outside the government sector. In other words, the profit sector has become less secure in a relative way.

A second important job characteristic is the proportion of women in the occupational group (two-digit level). In line with expectations, we see that women in male jobs are less likely to move out of the labor force. Apparently, male jobs protect women from employment exits. Male jobs do not lead to higher re-entry chances, however, as Table 4.2 shows. Moreover, women in male jobs are more likely to experience downward mobility and less likely to experience lateral mobility. These latter findings suggest that women fare less well in male jobs than in female jobs. No clear trends can be seen in the effects of male and female jobs.

Table 4.1 further shows that occupational status has no effect on employment exits. We do see a positive effect on re-entry, showing that women in higher status positions are more likely to return to the labor market. This is in line with what we would expect. Even stronger effects exist for occupational status on job mobility (Tables 4.3 and 4.4). We observe both bottom and ceiling effects: the higher the status, the lower the chances of upward mobility and the higher the chances of downward mobility. More interesting is that occupational status also has a positive effect on lateral mobility, which is defined as a movement to another job with the same status. In other words, high-status careers are more versatile in terms of job and employer changes than low-status jobs (Kalmijn and Luijkx 2003).

Have the effects of occupational status changed over time? We see one important trend, which is a decline in the effect of occupational status on re-entry chances. In the past, returning to the labor market was more common among women in higher status occupations, whereas in recent times there is no difference between high- and low-status women. Another way of saying this is that the period- increase in re-entry chances has occurred more strongly among women in low-status occupations.

Table 4.2 Re-entry to employment for women in the Netherlands, logistic regression coefficients

	All periods	1960s	1970s	1980s	1990s
Survey					
1992 (ref)					
1995	−0.06	0.39	−0.44**	0.07	−0.01
1998	−0.22**	0.55	−0.19	−0.24+	−0.32*
2000	−0.09	0.76+	−0.32	−0.15	−0.06
Period					
1970s	0.67***				
1980s	0.88***				
1990s	1.46***				
Age	0.11*	0.08	0.00	0.04	0.26***
Age/10 squared	−0.27***	−0.12	−0.11	−0.19+	−0.44***
ISEI/10	0.07**	0.41**	0.12*	0.07+	0.02
Government job	0.06	−0.14	0.08	−0.02	0.10
Women in occupation/10	0.00	0.04	0.00	0.03	−0.03
Years of education	0.09***	0.05	0.10***	0.07***	0.10***
Duration of non-employment					
< 13 months (ref)					
13–24 months	−0.55***	−0.82+	−0.33	−0.70***	−0.48**
25–48 months	−0.39***	−0.40	−0.41+	−0.33*	−0.39**
> 48 months	0.23**	−0.42	0.46*	0.16	0.33*
Experience paid work (ln)	0.00	−0.04	−0.07	0.20*	−0.21*
Number of jobs	0.21***	−0.05	0.22***	0.16***	0.27***
Life course					
Single (ref)					
Cohabiting/married, no children	−0.55***	−1.27**	−1.26***	−0.62**	−0.15
Youngest child 0–6	−0.82***	−1.09**	−0.57**	−0.85***	−0.86***
Youngest child 6–18	0.80***		0.70***	0.96***	0.69***
Empty nest	−0.11			0.00	−0.16
Father's occupation	0.01	0.05	0.03	0.04	−0.05+
Constant	−7.17***	−8.37	−4.35*	−5.14***	−8.11***
Number of events	1445	70	285	518	572
N	340 763	38 961	86 003	128 074	87 725
Chi-squared	1161.0	82.3	182.8	335.9	465.6
Df	22	17	18	19	19

Notes: *** $p < 0.001$, ** $p < 0.01$, * $p < 0.05$, + $p < 0.10$

Sources: Netherlands and Dutch Family Surveys 1992–93, 1998, 2000; Survey Households in the Netherlands 1995

The effects of full-time work (32 or more hours a week) are puzzling at first observation. We expected that full-time jobs would be in an advantageous position in the labor market. In contrast to this expectation, we see that the exit chances are higher in full-time jobs than in part-time jobs (Table 4.1).

In addition, an exit from a large part-time job (20 to 32 hours a week) is more likely than an exit from a small part-time job (under 20 hours a week). There appears to be a continuous decline in exit chances with a decline in hours. These results first suggest that the notion that full-time jobs are better protected is not valid for the Netherlands. Why full-time jobs have a higher exit chance is more difficult to explain. Perhaps it is more difficult for women in full-time jobs to reduce their hours. If a woman wants to work less, she will then be compelled to look for another job, which may also imply a temporary withdrawal from the labor market. The models for job changes support this interpretation (Tables 4.3 and 4.4). Full-time working women are more likely to change jobs than part-time working women. That this applies especially to upward mobility seems consistent with our original expectation (Tables 4.3 and 4.4).

Career investments

We now turn to the effects of career investments. We start with investments that are made before the career begins: educational attainment. We see that better educated women are less likely to move out of the labor force (Table 4.1), more likely to return (Table 4.2), less likely to experience downward mobility and more likely to experience upward (and lateral) mobility (Tables 4.3 and 4.4). These results are fully in line with previous research and with theoretical predictions on the role of human capital. We also expected to see an increase in the role of education for women's labor market careers over time, but this does not turn out to be the case. The effects of education across all transitions fluctuate somewhat from period to period, but differences are small and no clear trend is visible.

In line with expectations, we observe important experience effects. When women have been in a job for more than four years, they are less likely to leave the labor market. In addition, the more experience women have in previous jobs, the less likely it is that they will leave the labor market. Prior investments in a career strengthen the tie to the labor market. Does experience also affect job mobility? In Tables 4.3 and 4.4, we generally see negative tenure effects. The longer women have been in the labor market, the less likely it is that they change jobs laterally, and the longer women have been in a job, the less likely it is that they change jobs in any direction. This suggests that women are especially mobile at the beginning of their career, which seems plausible. We further expected that the effects of experience and tenure would increase over time, but the tables do not suggest any systematic change. Just like education, experience remains an important factor in the labor market, but it has not become *more* important.

We also consider a more specific aspect of prior career investments: the number of job spells. The evidence is not fully consistent with what the more standard measures of career investments reveal. Women who held more jobs in the past are more rather than less likely to move out of the labor force. Apparently, job changes in the past are more an indicator of flexibility or instability than of investments. For re-entry, we see a positive effect as well.

Women who held more jobs in the past are more likely to return to the labor market. This is consistent with an investment idea, but it is also consistent with an interpretation in terms of instability. The job change models reveal exactly the same pattern: the more jobs a woman has had in her career, the more likely it is that she will change jobs in the future. Clear trends in these effects cannot be found, although the effect of job changes on re-entry is stronger in the more recent period.

The final investment factor we look at is the effect of employment on job mobility. More specifically, we can look at the chances of being upwardly or downwardly mobile for women who are working and for women who are returning to the labor force. This model is similar to the initial model and adds a dummy-variable for whether a woman is employed. In this model, we see a strong negative effect of employment on downward mobility presented in Table 4.4 ($b = -0.88$, $p < 0.01$), a smaller negative effect on upward mobility in Table 4.4 ($b = -0.32$, $p < 0.01$) and a positive effect on lateral mobility ($b = 0.14$, $p < 0.05$; model not shown). These figures show that mobility from within the labor market is somewhat more favorable than mobility from the outside. If non-employed women return, they are more likely to end up in a lower-status job than employed women. They are also more likely to end up in a higher-status job, but this effect is weaker.

Note that the duration variable in this model pertains to job tenure for women who are employed, while it pertains to the non-employment period for women who are not employed. These duration effects may be different, but a model that includes interaction effects of employment and duration shows that at most durations, the employment effects are similar (results available in Kalmijn and Luijkx 2003).

Has the insider effect on mobility of being employed changed over time? The comparisons show that the negative effect of employment on downward mobility has increased (become more negative). In other words, the disadvantage of being outside the labor market has increased over time. This is consistent with the globalization hypothesis.

Life-course effects

Life-course effects on employment exits, as presented in Table 4.1, are in line with what is already known about women's employment patterns from

Table 4.3 Direct downward and upward job-to-job mobility for women in the Netherlands, logistic regression coefficients (lateral not shown)

	Downward mobility					Upward mobility				
	All periods	1960s	1970s	1980s	1990s	All periods	1960s	1970s	1980s	1990s
Survey										
1992 (ref)										
1995	-0.29+	-0.22	-0.52	-0.06	-0.13	-0.69***	-0.48	-0.71+	-0.65**	-0.71**
1998	0.02	0.20	-0.24	0.11	0.31	-0.07	0.43	0.20	-0.29	-0.03
2000	0.34*	0.58	-0.09	0.14	0.68*	0.08	0.50	0.25	-0.34	0.15
Period										
1970s	0.34					0.24				
1980s	0.47+					0.24				
1990s	0.72**					0.60*				
Age	-0.15+	0.40	-0.01	-0.06	-0.22+	-0.04	2.88	-0.33	0.03	-0.05
Age/10 squared	0.11	-0.79	-0.10	0.01	0.20	-0.03	-5.14	0.44	-0.15	-0.01
ISEI/10	0.37***	0.06	0.19	0.38***	0.43***	-0.44***	-0.77**	-0.47***	-0.48***	-0.42***
Working hours										
32+ hours (ref)										
20-31 hours	-0.19	-1.06	-0.28	-0.43+	0.00	-0.37**	-0.50	-0.10	-0.43+	-0.35*
1-19 hours	-0.41*		-0.81	-0.54+	-0.18	-0.62***		-0.64	-0.02	-0.86***
Missing hours	-0.43	-0.89	-0.91	-0.00	-0.82	-0.81*	-1.69	-1.16	-0.34	-0.94
Government job	-0.38**	-0.48	-0.42	-0.53**	-0.26+	-0.49***	0.09	-0.84**	-0.60***	-0.38**
Women in occ/10	-0.09***	-0.07	-0.14*	0.10*	-0.07*	0.03	-0.12	0.10+	0.08*	0.00
Years of education	-0.06**	0.01	-0.09	-0.05	-0.07*	0.17***	0.10	0.14**	0.18***	0.19***
Job tenure										
<13 months (ref)										
13-24 months	-0.20	-0.28	0.44	0.00	-0.42*	-0.12	0.07	0.29	0.06	-0.29
25-48 months	-0.11	-0.87	0.05	0.51+	-0.36+	-0.17	-0.08	-0.28	0.20	-0.28+
>48 months	-0.56***	-0.74	-0.27	-0.09	-0.81***	-0.46***	-0.12	-0.22	0.24	-0.82***

104

Table 4.3   Continued

	Downward mobility					Upward mobility				
	All periods	1960s	1970s	1980s	1990s	All periods	1960s	1970s	1980s	1990s
Experience paid work (ln)	0.08	−0.06	0.17	−0.12	0.17	0.08	0.37	−0.42+	0.23	0.03
Number of jobs	0.09*	0.02	0.21+	0.23***	0.01	0.08*	−0.28	0.27*	0.14*	0.04
Life course										
Single (ref)										
Cohabiting/married no children	−0.22+	−0.20	−0.59+	−0.21	−0.04	−0.16	0.75	−0.02	−0.64**	−0.01
Youngest child 0–6	−0.43**	−0.95	−0.75	−0.46	−0.33	−0.50***	−1.51*	−0.86*	−0.78*	−0.25
Youngest child 6–18	0.27		0.88+	0.07	0.24	0.64***		0.58	0.67*	0.68**
Empty nest	−0.40			−0.18	−0.42	0.11			0.65	−0.10
Father's occupation	0.01	−0.15	−0.05	0.05	0.03	0.12***	0.24	0.07	0.15**	0.11*
Constant	−3.64*	−9.81	−3.78	−5.25*	−2.26	−4.86***	−45.11	0.22	−6.25*	−4.10*
Number of events	430	20	57	133	220	518	21	63	151	283
N[a]	300 034	15 937	42 719	105 469	135 909					
Chi-squared[a]	1 463.2	91.6	210.0	514.7	866.0					
Df[a]	75	57	63	66	66					

Notes: [a] Information for downward, lateral, and upward mobility together (lateral mobility not shown)

*** $p < 0.001$, ** $p < 0.01$, * $p < 0.05$, + $p < 0.10$

Sources: Netherlands and Dutch Family Surveys 1992–93, 1998, 2000; Survey Households in the Netherlands 1995

Table 4.4 Downward and upward job mobility including re-entries for Netherlands women, logistic regression coefficients (lateral not shown)

	Downward mobility					Upward mobility				
	All periods	1960s	1970s	1980s	1990s	All periods	1960s	1970s	1980s	1990s
Survey										
1992 (ref)										
1995	-0.21*	-0.01	-0.51*	-0.12	0.07	-0.40***	-0.13	-0.31	-0.35*	-0.41*
1998	-0.18+	0.08	-0.39+	-0.19	0.17	-0.11	0.46	-0.19	-0.22	0.00
2000	0.08	0.27	-0.44+	-0.13	0.57**	0.06	1.14*	-0.15	-0.18	0.21
Period										
1970s	0.46**					0.81***				
1980s	0.75***					0.83***				
1990s	1.19***					1.23***				
Age	-0.01	-0.37	0.05	-0.05	0.02	0.06	-0.06	-0.18	0.11	0.06
Age/10 squared	-0.09	0.50	-0.19	-0.04	-0.14	-0.19*	-0.02	0.15	-0.27+	-0.19
ISEI/10	0.38***	0.40**	0.24**	0.43***	0.40***	-0.42***	-0.68***	-0.47***	-0.43***	-0.38***
Government job	-0.27***	-0.57	-0.09	-0.31*	-0.28*	-0.34***	-0.02	-0.48*	-0.41**	-0.24*
Women in occ/10	-0.06***	-0.02	-0.11**	-0.07*	-0.05*	0.00	-0.05	0.04	0.06*	-0.03
Years of education	-0.04*	-0.03	-0.04	-0.06*	-0.02	0.19***	0.16+	0.23***	0.17***	0.19***
Job tenure										
<13 months (ref)										
13–24 months	-0.36**	-0.77	0.33	-0.38	-0.53**	-0.22+	0.07	0.23	-0.37	-0.24
25–48 months	-0.10	-0.51	-0.03	0.20	-0.24	-0.22*	-0.02	0.06	-0.06	-0.32*
>48 months	0.13	-0.59	0.54+	0.40*	-0.09	-0.06	0.44	0.66*	0.18	-0.39**
Experience paid work (ln)	0.08	0.00	0.00	0.04	0.11	0.13*	0.61+	0.16	0.13	0.07
Number of jobs	0.14***	0.01	0.28***	0.18***	0.11***	0.14***	-0.11	0.22**	0.18***	0.12***

Table 4.4 Continued

	Downward mobility					Upward mobility				
	All periods	1960s	1970s	1980s	1990s	All periods	1960s	1970s	1980s	1990s
Life course										
Single (ref)										
Cohabiting/married no children	-0.47***	-0.86+	-0.72*	-0.45*	-0.22	-0.32**	0.40	-0.45	-0.63***	-0.05
Youngest child 0–6	-0.66***	-0.80+	-0.78***	-0.65***	-0.59***	-0.94***	-1.58**	-0.77**	-1.07***	-0.84***
Youngest child 6–18	0.67***		0.89***	0.68***	0.55**	0.96***		0.91***	1.09***	0.94***
Empty nest	-0.41+			-0.83+	-0.22	0.08			0.54	-0.25
Father's occupation	0.00	-0.03	-0.05	0.05	-0.01	0.13***	0.36**	0.11+	0.15***	0.10**
Employed	-0.88***	-0.61	-0.69**	-0.87***	-1.05***	-0.32***	1.39**	-0.15	-0.39**	-0.47***
Constant	-5.82***	-0.11	-4.94+	-4.67**	-5.82***	-7.24***	-7.53	-3.26	-6.97***	-5.88***
Number of events	927	48	149	313	417	894	30	141	286	437
N^a	640 801	54 898	128 722	233 545	223 636					
Chi-squared^a	2 733.0	210.8	445.7	930.3	1 179.9					
Df^a	69	54	57	60	60					

Notes: [a] Information for downward, lateral, and upward mobility together (lateral mobility not shown)

*** p < 0.001, ** p < 0.01, * p < 0.05, + p < 0.10

Sources: Netherlands and Dutch Family Surveys 1992–93, 1998, 2000; Survey Households in the Netherlands 1995

cross-sectional work in the Netherlands (Van der Lippe 2001) and from an earlier retrospective study based on a much smaller data set (De Graaf and Vermeulen 1997). Marriage and children have strong positive effects on employment exits, with the stronger effect coming from marriage (Table 4.1). Note that marriage and cohabitation are combined here. Given that women remain employed, however, we see negative effects of older children (as compared with younger children) on the chances of leaving employment. This is probably due to the fact that women who remain employed while having children are a more selective group. The transition to the empty nest stage has no significant effect on employment exit.

The re-entry model in Table 4.2 also provides interesting results. We find that when women marry and have children, they have a lower chance of re-entering the labor market. Both effects exist so that they are cumulative, but the stronger effect comes from children. In addition, we see that there is a positive effect of older children, which shows that when the children become older, women are more likely again to re-enter the labor market. In other words, women return once their children are older. Moving into the empty nest stage has no further effect.

We also see effects on job mobility. The pattern of effects generally suggests that transitions to marriage and motherhood reduce mobility, in line with expectations. We should note that these effects apply to women who experience family transitions while staying employed. For these women, we see that the entry into the stage of motherhood makes them less likely to move up or down the ladder (Table 4.3). Lateral mobility, however, is not reduced by marriage and motherhood. We expected that children would primarily hamper women's chances of being upwardly mobile. Although the data do show this effect, they also show that downward moves become less likely once women have children. We think that the latter finding calls for a different interpretation, however. When women are at risk of being downwardly mobile after they have children, they may instead choose to leave the labor market. The negative effect on downward mobility may therefore be different in nature than the negative effect on upward mobility.

We now come to the question of how life-course effects have changed over time. In the early period, the marriage transition had a very strong effect on women's departure from the labor market and this effect has continuously decreased over time. The effect of children on employment exit has changed as well. In comparison to the married stage, the effect of becoming a mother on employment exits has changed from negative to positive. We should note at the outset that the sample included in this model pertains to married women who remained employed after their wedding (or who became employed during marriage). Married women who remained at work in the past were probably a more select group, which may explain why the transition to becoming a mother did not lead to increased exit chances.

For re-entry chances, we see that the marriage transition has become less influential (Table 4.2). Women who marry initially experienced a decline in the chances of returning to the labor market, but this effect has disappeared at the end of the period we consider. The additional negative effect on re-entry from becoming a mother has also declined, but this decline is much weaker. Children thus remain an important hindrance for returning to the labor market. The aging of the children increases the chances to return to the labor market, but this is true to the same degree in all periods.

The effects of the life course on women's career mobility did not change in a systematic fashion.

DISCUSSION AND CONCLUSIONS

We have analyzed retrospective life-history data from the Netherlands in order to describe the occupational and employment careers of women in the period 1955–2000. In line with cross-sectional studies, our results show that the chances of leaving the labor market have continuously declined while the chances of re-entering the labor market have continuously increased. In addition, we see that job mobility has increased over time. In other words, the careers of women have become more stable in the sense that attachments to the labor market have become stronger. But the careers have also become more versatile in the sense that women more often change jobs when they are in the labor market.

We find no evidence for a reversal of the trend that was set in motion by modernization. The globalization thesis suggests that labor markets have become more uncertain in recent decades, but we do not observe such a trend. We also expected to find increases in the effects of job characteristics and career investments on careers. Contrary to these expectations, we find stability in most of the individual effects we look at. One exception is the role of government jobs. The protective effect of being in a government job has become stronger in recent decades. Put differently, jobs in the profit sector have become more insecure in a relative sense, but we should note that even in the profit sector, exit chances have declined continuously.

While this chapter has not found a reversal of trends, it did provide new longitudinal analyses of the individual determinants of women's careers in the Netherlands over a broad span of years. We distinguished between three sets of individual determinants of women's careers.

The first set of determinants we refer to as career investments. We generally find support for the notion that investments in the labor market have a positive influence on the career. Education, tenure, experience and the number of jobs held, all tend to reduce the chances of employment exits and they increase the chances of returning to the labor market. We also find that education leads to upward mobility while reducing the chances of being downwardly mobile. The number of jobs held seems to promote further job mobility in all directions, rather than simply promoting upward mobility. A final interesting finding is that women who are non-employed more often move back to a lower job when we compare them with women who are experiencing job mobility while being employed. In other words, being out of the labor market is a disadvantage, even after controlling for experience and the number of prior jobs.

There are also important differences depending on the type of job, our second set of individual characteristics. Women in government jobs are less likely to move out of the labor market and less likely to be upwardly or downwardly mobile. In other words, the government provides a stable and flat career. Mixed evidence is obtained for the difference between male and female types of jobs. One would expect that male (or rather, less female) jobs are better protected than female jobs and that they can provide a more attractive career. We find that women in male jobs are indeed less likely to exit employment, in line with expectations, but women in male jobs are also more likely to be downwardly mobile, which is not what we would expect. In addition, we find that women in high-status jobs are more likely to return to the labor market. An unexpected finding is that women in full-time jobs are more likely to leave the labor market. It may be more difficult to reduce the number of hours in such jobs, which can create an incentive to leave the job and look for another one. Women in full-time jobs also seem to be more mobile in terms of job changes.

Our third factor is the life-course stage. Our analyses show that life-course stages have become less influential over time, with a particularly strong shift from the role of marriage to the role of children. While marriage no longer leads to employment exits, children remain a hindrance. We also find important effects on job mobility: the transitions to marriage and motherhood generally reduce mobility. Interestingly this not only applies to upward mobility – which is often suggested in the literature on gender inequality (Budig and England 2001) – but also to downward mobility. We believe that women who have children may prefer to leave the labor market if they run the risk of being downwardly mobile.

The globalization thesis suggests that life-course factors would have become more influential again because increased uncertainty and flexibility on the side of the employer is combined with women's own desires to combine work and family demands. We see no evidence for such a trend. As Figure 4.2 clearly shows, changes away from the traditional life-course employment pattern are continuing into the 1990s.

NOTES

1   We want to thank the Department of Sociology, Radboud University, Nijmegen for making available the Family Surveys Dutch Population 1998 and 2000.

BIBLIOGRAPHY

Alderson, A.S. (1999) 'Explaining deindustrialization: globalization, failure, or success?', *American Sociological Review*, 64: 701–21.
Alon, S., Donahoe, D. and Tienda, M. (2001) 'The effects of early work experience on young women's labor force attachment', *Social Forces*, 79: 1005–34.
Atkinson, J. (1984) 'Manpower strategies for flexible organizations', *Personnel Management*, 16: 28–31.
Blossfeld, H.-P. and Hakim, C. (1997) 'A comparative perspective on part-time work', in C. Hakim (ed.) *Between equalization and marginalization. Women working part-time in Europe and the United States of America*, Oxford: Oxford University Press.
Blossfeld, H.-P., Klijzing, E., Mills, M. and Kurz, K. (2005) *Globalization, uncertainty, and youth in society*, London: Routledge.
Blossfeld, H.-P., Mills, M. and Bernardi, F. (2006) *Globalization, uncertainty, and men's careers: an international comparison*, Cheltenham, UK and Northampton, MA, USA: Edward Elgar.
Budig, M.J. and England, P. (2001) 'The wage penalty for motherhood', *American Sociological Review*, 66: 204–25.
Davis, K. (1984) 'Wives and work: consequences of the sex role revolution', *Population and Development Review*, 10: 397–417.
De Graaf, P.M. and Vermeulen, H. (1997) 'Female labour-market participation in the Netherlands: developments in the relationship between family cycle and employment', in C. Hakim (ed.) *Between equalization and marginalization: women working part-time in Europe and the United States of America*, Oxford: Oxford University Press.
De Graaf, N.D., De Graaf, P.M., Kraaykamp, G. and Ultee, W.C. (1998) *Family survey Dutch population 1998* (machine-readable data file), Nijmegen: Department of Sociology, Nijmegen University (producer), Amsterdam: Netherlands Institute for Scientific Information Services (NIWI) – P1583 (distributor).
De Graaf, N.D., De Graaf, P.M., Kraaykamp, G. and Ultee, W.C. (2000) *Family survey Dutch population 2000* (machine-readable data file), Nijmegen: Department of Sociology, Nijmegen University (producer), Amsterdam: Netherlands Institute for Scientific Information Services (NIWI) – P1609 (distributor).
De Grip, A., Hoevenberg, J. and Willems, E. (1997) 'Atypical employment in the European Union', *International Labour Review*, 136: 49–71.
Dekker, R., Muffels, R. and Stancanelli, E. (2000) 'A longitudinal analysis of part-time work by women and men in the Netherlands', in D.E. Meulders (ed.) *Gender and the labor market: econometric evidence of obstacles to achieving gender equality*, New York: St. Martin's Press.
Desai, S. and Waite, L.J. (1991) 'Women's employment during pregnancy and after

the first birth: occupational characteristics and work commitment', *American Sociological Review*, 56: 551–66.

Ganzeboom, H.B.G., De Graaf, P.M. and Treiman, D.J. (1992) 'A standard international socio-economic index of occupational status', *Social Science Research*, 21: 1–56.

Garssen, J., de Beer, J., Hoeksma, L., Prins, K. and Verhoef, R. (1999) *Vital events: past, present, and future of the Dutch population*, Voorburg/Heerlen: Statistics Netherlands.

Kalmijn, M. (2003) 'Country differences in sex-role attitudes: cultural and economic explanations', in W. Arts, J. Hagenaars and L. Halman (eds) *The cultural diversity of European unity: findings, explanations and reflections from the European values study*, Leiden: Brill.

Kalmijn, M. and Luijkx, R. (2003) 'Changes in women's employment and occupational mobility in the Netherlands between 1955 and 2000', GLOBALIFE Working Paper No. 50, Chair of Sociology I, University of Bamberg.

Keuzenkamp, S. and Oudhof, K. (2000) *Emancipatiemonitor 2000*, Den Haag: Sociaal en Cultureel Planbureau/Centraal Bureau voor de Statistiek.

Lehrer, E. (1999) 'Married women's labor supply behavior in the 1990s: differences by life-cycle stage', *Social Science Quarterly*, 80: 574–90.

Liefbroer, A.C. (2005) 'Transition from youth to adulthood in the Netherlands', in H.-P. Blossfeld, E. Klijzing, M. Mills and K. Kurz (eds) *Globalization, uncertainty, and youth in society*, London: Routledge.

Moen, P. (1991) 'Transitions in mid-life: women's work and family roles in the 1970s', *Journal of Marriage and the Family*, 53: 135–50.

Smulders, P. and Klein Hesselink, J. (1997) 'Nederland lang geen koploper flexibilisering', *Economisch Statistische Berichten*, 82: 888–90.

Social and Cultural Planning Office (SCP) (1998) *Sociaal en cultureel rapport 1998: 25 jaar sociale verandering*, Den Haag: Staatsuitgeverij.

Social and Cultural Planning Office (SCP) (2000) *Sociaal en cultureel rapport 2000: Nederland in Europa*, Den Haag: Staatsuitgeverij.

Ultee, W.C. and Ganzeboom, H.B.G. (1993) *Netherlands family survey 1992–1993* (machine-readable data file), Nijmegen: Department of Sociology, Nijmegen University (producer), Amsterdam: Netherlands Institute for Scientific Information Services (NIWI) – P1245 (distributor).

Van der Lippe, T. (2001) 'The effect of individual and institutional constraints on hours of paid work of women; an international comparison', in L. Van Dijk (ed.) *Women's employment in a comparative perspective*, New York: Aldine de Gruyter.

Van der Lippe, T. and Van Dijk, L. (2001) *Women's employment in a comparative perspective*, New York: Aldine de Gruyter.

Van der Lippe, T. and Van Doorne-Huiskes, A. (1995) 'Veranderingen in stratificatie tussen mannen en vrouwen', in J. Dronkers and W.C. Ultee (eds) *Verschuivende ongelijkheid in Nederland: Sociale gelaagdheid en mobiliteit*, Assen: Van Gorcum.

Visser, J. and Hemerijck, A. (1997) *A Dutch miracle: job growth, welfare reform and corporatism in the Netherlands*, Amsterdam: Amsterdam University Press.

Weesie, J. and Kalmijn, M. (1995) *Households in the Netherlands 1995* (machine-readable data file), Utrecht: ICS/ISCORE, Utrecht University (producer), Amsterdam: Netherlands Institute for Scientific Information Services (NIWI) – P1458 (distributor).

Yamaguchi, K. (1991) *Event history analysis*, Newbury Park, CA: Sage Publications.

PART III

Country-specific contributions on
social-democratic welfare regimes

5. Globalization, deindustrialization and the labor market experiences of Swedish women, 1950 to 2000

Tomas Korpi and Charlotta Stern[1]

INTRODUCTION

Globalization is a word with cultural, social and economic connotations. The economic meaning of the word is perhaps the most unequivocal, namely as an increase in international trade and the internationalization of financial markets. In recent decades, the industrialized world has seen an increase in both areas, and the consequence of these developments at the individual level is an area of intense public and academic debate. Heated disputes around the ratification of various multilateral agreements (North American Free Trade Agreement – NAFTA, General Agreement on Tariffs and Trade – GATT, European Union – EU) are mirrored by a wealth of research on the development of wages and employment. Of particular concern has here been the situation of less educated/unskilled workers. Increasing wage inequality and/or unemployment has thus been linked to international trade, skill-biased technical change and investment patterns.

For a thorough investigation of the consequences of globalization on Swedish women's labor market involvement, we would need a counterfactual, that is, a case describing what would have taken place on the Swedish labor market if globalization had never occurred. Empirical research normally tries to construct relevant comparisons of this kind either through an experimental design or through multivariate analysis. A comparative approach such as the one used in this project may be seen as an alternative in which other countries act as control groups.

A study based on a single country may nonetheless be informative in itself, and the analyses in this chapter are based on two observations. Almost by definition, the links that have been posited between globalization and national labor markets are most likely to affect the sector directly exposed to international competition, that is manufacturing. Although not immune to international developments, private services and the public sector are much more indirectly affected. Consequently, globalization would appear to have less import if changes in labor market mobility in the manufacturing sector are matched by similar developments in other sectors. Likewise, many of the links between globalization and domestic labor markets identify the less educated as the most exposed group. However, if one found changes in mobility among the less educated that were matched by similar changes among the more educated, these would also seem to be driven by other factors.

In this analysis of the impact of globalization on employment and labor market mobility among Swedish women, we therefore focus on differences in the evolution of employment stability, unemployment risk and job mobility between sectors and educational categories. Our results show that during the period analyzed here, the labor market position of Swedish women has been strengthened and the relative position of women in different sectors and with different levels of education has remained stable. These results are thus at odds with the thesis that globalization has had a dramatic impact on all domestic labor markets.

TRADE, CAPITAL MOBILITY AND DOMESTIC LABOR MARKETS

Analyses of the patterns of international trade and of their impact on a country's use of productive resources have a long tradition. In the eighteenth century, Adam Smith examined absolute costs, stating that goods would be produced where the costs were the lowest. Ricardo, writing in the nineteenth century, instead focused on relative costs. He hypothesized that a country that could produce two goods at a lower cost than another country would benefit from specializing in the good in which its advantage was greatest. This is the concept of comparative advantage or, more precisely, comparative advantage in production costs. Later in the twentieth century, Heckscher and Ohlin focused on comparative advantage in productive resources, arguing a country would prosper by specializing in goods requiring resources in which it had a relative advantage.

The Heckscher-Ohlin model is still the standard tool in analyses of international trade (see Wood 1994; 1995). In its original formulation, the productive resources were land, labor and capital. A country's relative endowment of the production factors was thus believed to influence what was produced and what was traded. A country with a relatively abundant supply of labor would, for instance, specialize in the production of labor-intensive goods, whereas a country with an extensive supply of capital would concentrate on goods requiring large amounts of capital.

In more recent years, these ideas have been further elaborated with respect to the assumptions of homogeneous labor and capital (see OECD 1994 for a review). A distinction has been introduced between infrastructure capital and other forms of capital on the one hand, and between skilled and unskilled labor on the other. The basic ideas have remained, however, so that a country with a wealth of skilled labor will focus on production requiring skilled workers, leaving the production of other goods to other countries.

The ideas inherent in the two forms of comparative advantage have in turn been applied to trade between industrialized and developing countries. The basic prediction of Ricardian trade theory is straightforward: the difference in costs (for example, wages) would generate a shift in production from the industrialized to the developing countries. Likewise, the Heckscher-Ohlin model suggests that the production of low-skilled, labor-intensive goods is likely to shift to developing countries, with high-skilled (and capital-intensive) production remaining in industrialized nations. The industrialized countries will, in other words, see a shift in the demand for different types of labor, as well as in the types of goods produced.

International trade may thus affect the long-term aggregate level of labor demand through its effect on growth and Gross Domestic Product (GDP). It may also have an impact on domestic labor demand, with respect to industry and skill requirements. In industries/skill groups experiencing increasing imports, there will be a decrease in demand, and vice versa in industries/skill groups experiencing increasing exports. Adjustment to such changes may come in the form either of wage and/or employment changes, with the latter in turn potentially taking the form of job mobility, unemployment or exits from the labor force. Which of these various adjustment routes will be followed will depend on both economic and institutional factors. Job mobility may, for instance, be the outcome if demand reductions in some parts of the labor market are offset by demand increases elsewhere. If this is not the case, relative wage changes, unemployment and/or labor force exits may occur. The path (or paths) chosen will also depend on the institutional setting in which adjustment takes place.

The predictions based on comparative advantage have been used to explain inter-sectoral employment shifts, in particular the continuing decline of the manufacturing sector in industrialized nations. A comparative advantage in low-skilled labor-intensive manufacturing production in developing countries has affected the demand for these products from industrialized countries, and also reduced demand in the manufacturing sector relative to other sectors.

In addition to long-term aggregate and sectoral/group effects, international trade may also change the volatility (that is, the short-term variation) in demand (Garrett 2001; Rodrik 1997). Specialization will increase vulnerability to variations in external demand, thereby increasing labor demand volatility, yet increasing openness also means greater access to world trade and less reliance on domestic markets. Since a drop in demand among consumers in one country may be compensated by increases among other consumers, increased international trade may also reduce demand volatility.

Such developments need not come about through trade between companies in different countries; multinational corporations may instead be 'trading' with themselves. This brings in the other major factor in the globalization debate: international capital mobility and foreign direct investment (FDI). The process here is basically one of relative production costs, and therefore closely related to that described above under the heading 'Ricardian trade theory.' However, rather than being the outcome of international 'competitive' trade, this now takes place within firms. In addition to this direct effect of FDI on domestic employment, a potentially negative impact on manufacturing employment of changes in domestic investment decisions and long-term consequences of investments abroad have also been discussed (see Alderson 1999 for a review).[2]

It should be noted that the central tenets of economic globalization would seem to apply most directly to manufacturing, and it is therefore necessary to examine the development of the manufacturing sector more closely. This, however, immediately leads in to another major debate, that on deindustrialization and the service society.

The demise of manufacturing (or industrial production more generally) was proclaimed long before globalization became a household word. Clark thus predicted 'the movement of working population from agriculture to manufacture, and from manufacture to commerce and services' (1951, p. 395). His conclusion was primarily based on the differences in the income elasticity of demand for various goods postulated by Engel's Law. With increasing wealth, spending would first shift from agricultural products to manufactured goods and then in a subsequent stage to service consumption (see also Bell 1973).

Fuchs (1968) focused on a second strand of Clark's work, namely the productivity differences between sectors and their changes. Greater productivity increases in the manufacturing sector would slowly lead to an increase in the proportion employed in the service sectors. As Rowthorn and Ramaswamy (1999) emphasized, differences in productivity and relative prices between the manufacturing and service sectors may lead to shifts in their relative importance, though what shifts to expect remain uncertain. Productivity growth will allow more production per unit of labor, thereby reducing demand, but faster productivity growth will also reduce the relative price of manufactured products, thereby raising product demand. The overall employment prediction is thus ambiguous.

To conclude, increasing globalization may affect domestic labor markets in a number of potentially conflicting ways, and these different aspects of globalization should be seen as potential forces. The extent to which these apply to a specific country may, of course, vary, and depend on the industrial structure of the country as well as on national policies and institutions. Furthermore, in all theoretical accounts manufacturing and unskilled labor play a prominent role. This indicates that any evidence of globalization 'effects' is most likely to be found in the manufacturing sector and/or in the position of low-skilled labor.

THE SWEDISH LABOR MARKET IN INTERNATIONAL CONTEXT

Sweden is a small economy whose GDP in 2001 was approximately 2 percent of that of the US, and 43 percent of the EU average. This means that it was roughly on a par with Belgium and Switzerland. As with most small economies, Sweden has a history of open trade, but international capital mobility is of a more recent vintage.

International trade and investment

A country's trading patterns can be examined along a number of different dimensions: openness, geographic structure and inter-industrial as well as intra-industrial structure. A primary source of information is provided by the OECD Jobs Study (OECD 1994), which offered a comprehensive overview of employment-related developments up until the early 1990s.

This study provided several interesting pieces of the globalization puzzle. Openness (defined as international trade in relation to GDP), for example, tended to increase over time, and this held for trade between industrialized OECD countries, as well as between OECD and developing non-OECD nation-states. Even though the latter increased, there was much less trade between OECD and non-OECD states than between OECD nations. Looking specifically at manufacturing, the OECD's trade surplus vis-à-vis the non-OECD area declined after the early 1980s, though it remained positive. This was particularly the case in textiles, clothing and footwear, while machinery, transport equipment, chemicals and plastics showed little change or even an increase in the surplus. Services (specifically non-factor services) are more difficult to examine, since they are less well recorded, but it was believed that the OECD ran a modest surplus.

Apart from a temporary decrease in the early 1990s, Swedish evidence for the period 1950 to 2000 also shows a steady increase in international trade (Heston, Summers and Aten 2002). During the period 1975 to 1993 this primarily stemmed from an increase in trade with other OECD countries. Trade with Central and Eastern European countries, as well as trade with other less developed countries, in contrast, remained stable and accounted for a very small part of Sweden's trade (Edin, Fredriksson and Lundborg 2004).

The Jobs Study also reviewed the evolution of FDI, which can be examined according to both level and structure. Most FDI by OECD countries took place in other OECD nations. Yet there were sizable transfers from OECD to non-OECD countries, as well as between non-OECD nations. Two-way FDI investment flows were also common within the OECD. As for

OECD investments in the non-OECD area, they increased during the 1980s. This surge was mainly directed at newly industrialized countries (NICs) in Asia; investments in the rest of the non-OECD area were small and mainly in the petroleum industry. Relative to total investment in these countries, the inflow from the OECD was rather small. This also held for manufacturing, and it was noticeable that OECD investment in the NICs mainly originated in Japan. After the increase in the 1980s, OECD investment activities in non-OECD countries dropped off markedly in the early 1990s.

With regard to Sweden, evidence for the period 1965/1970 to 1992 shows an increase in both inward and outward FDI (Andersson 1994; OECD 1994). Outflows exceeded inflows, a difference that increased dramatically in the late 1980s. Employment in Swedish multinational companies (MNCs) abroad rose. However, most of the increase in outward investment involved investment in the European Community (EC) countries (Andersson 1994). Indeed, during the period from 1978 to 1990, employment in Swedish multinationals in less developed countries dropped (Andersson and Hellström 1994), and the recession in the early 1990s practically stopped investment activities. Nonetheless, in the latter half of the decade, MNC employment in non-OECD countries increased markedly due to an expansion in the former Central and Eastern European countries (Hansson 2005).

This review in many ways suggests that the impact of international trade and investment on the labor markets of the industrialized world probably is more limited than commonly assumed. As is the case for most industrialized nations, Swedish trade and investment almost exclusively involves other industrialized countries, and this engagement has undoubtedly increased. The Swedish presence in less developed countries appears rather small. While it is unclear how the steady increase in Sweden's international engagement will affect Swedish employees in the long run, it seems unlikely that it thus far will have produced landslide changes. That Swedish companies interact with less developed countries only to a limited extent may also suggest that any labor market effects are more evenly distributed across educational/skill groups rather than disproportionately to lower skill groups as is generally argued by the globalization hypothesis.

Deindustrialization and the rise of the service sector

Before reviewing the evidence on industrial development, two things are worth noting. First, services are difficult to pin down, both as a sector and as an activity. In sectoral terms, it thus tends to be defined as a residual category or as what is left after accounting for agriculture and manufacturing. One consequence is that outsourcing of services that were formerly performed within the boundaries of a manufacturing firm will lead to a change in the balance between manufacturing and services without there being a real change in activities. Another is that only activities carried out within a workplace are normally taken into account, leaving out activities within the household. Problems such as these also lead to different definitions of sectors that in turn lead to very diverse estimates regarding sector size. Second, the deindustrialization thesis may take different forms, as there may be a relative reduction in employment or a relative reduction in production. Although the former seems to be more frequent, these alternatives add to the confusion caused by the definitional vagueness of services.

Putting definitional difficulties aside, the overall trend is that manufacturing has receded and been replaced by services both in Sweden and elsewhere. Focusing on Sweden, agriculture's share of employment declined from approximately 70 percent in the late nineteenth century to around 5 percent of total employment today (Schön 2000). Manufacturing (and construction) started out with around 20 percent, peaked at 45 percent in 1960 and in the early 1990s accounted for around 30 percent of total employment. Services, not including those provided within the household, increased at the same pace as manufacturing, and became the largest sector in the first half of the 1960s. Today, almost 70 percent of all employment is in services. This increase in service sector employment during the post-war period took different forms at different times. Up until 1985, there was a steady increase in public sector employment, particularly dramatic during the 1970s, but it then stagnated, and growth instead shifted over to private services.[3]

Evidence on the causes of structural change

Globalization could thus have an impact on domestic labor markets in three ways: through long-term aggregate effects, sectoral/group effects and volatility effects. At the same time, deindustrialization effects on employment could occur through productivity and price changes, as well as changes in domestic demand.[4] The empirical evidence on these issues comes in various guises. Comparative studies of employment development and the factors driving it exist, as do studies based only on Swedish data.

Rowthorn and Ramaswamy (1999) examined manufacturing employment in 18 industrialized countries between 1963 and 1994, trying to trace the relative importance of different explanations for the successive decline of industry. They concluded that the major impetus for deindustrialization stems from factors internal to industrialized countries: productivity growth and changes in relative prices and domestic demand. North–South trade accounts for less than one-fifth of the change in industrial employment. On a similar note, Alderson (1999), analyzing an almost identical sample of 18 OECD nations from 1968 to 1992, concluded that 'deindustrialization would have been considerable even if the performance of manufacturing had been stronger or the upswings in direct investment and southern imports had not occurred' (p. 718).

Another strand of research examines trade openness and business cycle volatility. Here, results are rather mixed. Rodrik (1997; 1998) found that openness to trade significantly increases variation in economic growth for a wide range of countries, whereas Garrett (2001) and Iversen (2001) arrived at the opposite conclusion.[5]

As could be expected, the impact of changes in international trade on Swedish employment appears to be roughly analogous to variations in domestic demand, such that increased exports within an industry reduce exits from it and increased imports stimulate exits (Edin, Fredriksson and Lundborg 2000). There is also evidence indicating that trade with non-OECD countries in the period from 1970 to 1993 decreased the demand for less-skilled workers, primarily until 1985 (Hansson 2000). The effect of non-OECD trade was judged to be small relative to the demand shift induced by technological change, and was basically confined to developments in the textile industry.

There have also been some Swedish analyses of the domestic employment consequences of FDI. There is thus some evidence indicating that during the period from 1970 to 1994, the foreign investments of Swedish MNCs were associated with increased employment in Sweden (Blomström, Fors and Lipsey 1997). This positive employment effect decreased over the period, driven by a decline in the effect of investment in less developed countries. With the exception of the recession in the early 1990s, the positive employment impact of investment in developed countries remained stable throughout the period.[6] This may have changed during the 1990s, as the expansion of FDI in the former Central and Eastern European countries during the latter half of the decade coincided with employment reductions in Sweden and other OECD countries (Hansson 2005). This development seemed to affect the position of less-skilled workers in the Swedish MNC parents adversely, for though employment among high-skilled workers remained constant, the number of less-skilled workers dropped.

While overlapping predictions and measurement problems makes definite conclusions premature, one preliminary conclusion may be that labor market developments in industrialized countries are driven primarily by internal factors that come in the form of technological change and/or changes in consumption patterns. Although it clearly is of importance, and is probably of greater importance than originally believed, globalization still plays a secondary role. Trade and investments have had positive as well as negative effects on Swedish employment, with the involvement in less developed countries seeming to have affected the less educated negatively, particularly during the 1970s and the late 1990s.

Institutions that matter

To understand changes in women's employment patterns, country-specific institutional structures and their internal changes are crucial, as institutional structures may encourage or discourage labor force participation and specific patterns of employment. In the following, we focus on institutions that are important for Swedish women's labor market participation: parental leave, (public) daycare, part-time work and taxation.

Maternity leave was introduced in 1937, entitling almost all women to six months of paid leave following childbirth. In 1974, this was transformed into parental leave when Sweden became the first country to implement a system where both parents had the right to paid parental leave. The duration of parental leave has been extended, and Swedish parents currently share 12 months of paid parental leave for each child (one month is here earmarked for each parent, the so-called 'father-month'). Even so, Swedish women still take the lion's share of the time available to the family; in 2000, it amounted to almost 88 percent.

Yet the generous parental leave system gives prospective parents incentives to work: to have access to the system requires employment during the 34 weeks preceding the birth of the child. Swedish parents can also remain employed while on parental leave. At the same time, the generous system gives employers plenty of reasons to practice statistical discrimination towards women. The current Swedish policy discussion therefore focuses on increasing the earmarked period for each parent, in practice forcing men to claim parental leave or forfeit their right to the benefit.

Public daycare centers were introduced in the early 1960s, although mainly as a metropolitan phenomenon. Public childcare has expanded significantly since then, and in 2002, 81 percent of all children between ages one and five attended some form of public or private childcare (Swedish National Agency for Education 2004). This expansion was partly due to threats of a new era of labor shortages, as subsidized childcare such as daycare centers increases female labor force participation (Gustafsson and Stafford 1992).

Part-time work increased in the 1960s and 1970s, accounting for a substantial proportion of the rise in women's labor market participation (Sundström 1987). It peaked in the early 1980s at 47 percent of women's overall employment (Båvner 2001, p. 18). Most social benefits, such as sickness insurance and pension rights, do not depend on work time. In Sweden, part-time work has been 'supply driven,' and a majority of the women working part-time do so because it suits them best (Båvner 2001; Sundström 1983, pp. 73–80). There is substantial mobility out of part-time and into full-time jobs over the life course (Sundström 1999). Empirically, there is no evidence suggesting clear-cut positive or negative effects of part-time work (Båvner 2001; Sundström 1983).

Separate taxation was introduced in 1971 (Gonäs and Spånt 1997, p. 1). However, to avoid adverse effects on single-earner households, an earlier 'housewife tax deduction' was maintained (Gustafsson 1992), a deduction that to some extent may be said to neutralize separate taxation. Nonetheless, the deduction was kept at the same nominal value until its elimination in the 1980s, leading to the gradual establishment of separate taxation. As was the case with subsidized childcare, separate taxation had a positive impact on married women's employment in manufacturing (Gustafsson 1992).

In sum, the Swedish welfare state provides Swedish parents with an institutional structure aimed at simplifying the combination of parenting and labor market participation. It is clearly an institutional structure that stimulates women to partake in the labor force, and to a lesser extent it has also stimulated men to partake in parenting. The high degree of part-time work Swedish women engage in, together with their larger share of parental leave than men, indicate that Swedish families maintain a rather traditional division of household labor after becoming parents. However, studies also suggest that Swedish women, at least since the 1980s, base their labor market decisions on their own opportunity costs (their labor market wage) rather than on the income of their husbands (Gustafsson and Stafford 1992; Henz and Sundström 2001). In any case, these reforms have affected Swedish women's labor force participation in a way that has to be taken into account in a discussion of the impact of globalization.

SWEDISH WOMEN ON THE LABOR MARKET 1950–2000

The working hypotheses in the subsequent analyses are based on the suggestion that any effects of globalization are most likely to be visible in the exposed manufacturing sector and in the relative position of the less skilled. Conversely, changes within manufacturing and among the less skilled that are matched by similar developments in other sectors and among other groups are less likely to be related to globalization.

With these conjectures as our guide, we examine various aspects of labor market mobility in Sweden and how these have evolved over half a century. We pursue the following questions: what characterizes female employment in Sweden? In particular, has general employment stability declined? How has the risk of unemployment changed? How have different kinds of job mobility evolved? More specifically, have upward, downward, firm internal moves and shifts between employers changed? These analyses allow a direct comparison with the results for Swedish men (Korpi and Tåhlin 2006), but extend the analyses through the addition of information pertaining to the 1990s.

Data and methods

We have used a number of data sets and methods. In the description of employment patterns, as well as in the analyses of general employment stability, we have used the Level of Living Surveys (*Levnads-nivåundersökningarna*) from 1968, 1974, 1981, 1991 and 2000 (Jonsson and Mills 2001). These surveys were carried out as face-to-face interviews with national probability samples of individuals aged 18 to 75 (15 to 75 through 1981). The number of respondents was between 5000 and 6000 at each occasion. For the analysis of employment stability, we have carried out cross-sectional and pooled cross-sectional ordinary lease squares (OLS) regressions.

For the unemployment analyses, we have used the Labor Force Surveys (*Arbetskraftsundersökningarna*, AKU) covering the period 1963–2001. The surveys are conducted monthly by Statistics Sweden as telephone interviews with national probability samples of individuals aged 16 to 64 (16 to 74 through 1985). Sample sizes have varied over time, from 6500 in 1963 to 24 000 in 1977 and to 17 000 in 2001 (Statistics Sweden 1996; 2002). In these analyses, we have examined changes in the distribution of unemployment across sectors and educational categories.

In the analyses of job mobility, we have used the work–life biographies collected for the respondents in the 1991 and 2000 Level of Living Surveys. The retrospective biography encompassed information on monthly labor force status, commencing at the time of labor force entry (defined as the first job of at least six months' duration). Around 3800 respondents aged 25 to 65 provided complete information on their work–life careers. The information provided by the work histories has been examined using duration analysis, or more precisely, using Cox proportional hazard models.

As far as possible, given the focus of the present volume, we have restricted the empirical analyses to women aged 20 to 50. However, the available Labor Force Surveys do not always permit breakdowns by age and sex. With regard to the retrospective biography data, the survey design implies that the full age range from 20 to 50 is not reached until 1975, and only lasts until 1995. We have dealt with this problem by including age as a time-varying covariate in all models based on the retrospective data (in addition to employment experience measured at the start of each job spell).

Employment patterns 1968–2000

Changes in Swedish women's labor force participation since the late 1960s are shown in Table 5.1. As can be seen in Panel A, the female participation rate increased steadily until 1991. There is a drop between 1991 and 2000, probably partly due to an increase in young women's likelihood of attending tertiary education as well as an increase in the probability of being unemployed. Part-time employment (less than 35 hours per week) also grew initially, but started to decrease in the 1980s, and is now lower than in the 1960s.

The impact of young children on Swedish women's labor force participation is examined in Panel B, and it is noticeable that the employment rates found in Panel B have converged with that in Panel A. The difference in labor market participation between women with or without young children has, in other words, disappeared over time. In the year 2000, women with small children are even slightly more likely to be employed, but also more likely to work part-time (< 35 hours/week). The high participation rates are almost identical to those of Swedish men, but the high degree of part-time work suggests that the uneven distribution of parental responsibilities prevails. Nonetheless, the proportion of women who are full-time home-makers has declined over time. Overall, these data suggest that Swedish women have steadily strengthened their position on the labor market.

Table 5.1   Employment status as percentage of Swedish women aged 20 to 50, 1968 to 2000

	1968	1974	1981	1991	2000
Panel A: All women					
Homemakers[a]	36.7	26.0	11.3	5.0	5.8
Employed	55.6	67.2	80.1	81.3	75.2
of whom part-time[b]	39.7	43.7	47.4	37.6	32.0
Panel B: Women with small children[c]					
Homemakers[a]	62.4	45.5	20.0	10.2	8.9
Employed	34.7	53.3	74.9	80.5	75.8
of whom part-time[b]	60.9	58.5	66.1	55.9	40.5
N	1603	1556	1591	1512	1509

Notes: [a] A woman is considered a homemaker when she is not a student, unemployed or retired. These three categories are excluded from the table
[b] Part-time employment is defined as working less than 35 hours per week
[c] Defined as under age seven from 1968 to 1981, and under age nine in 1991 and 2000

Source: Sweden Level of Living Survey

Table 5.2 provides further information on employment among Swedish women and how this has progressed over time. The increasingly secure labor market position of Swedish women is also reflected in the average tenure with the current employer. As shown in Panel A, this increased throughout most of the period. In the private service and in the manufacturing sector, average tenure increased until 1991, but decreased in the year 2000. One possible explanation is that demand for labor was high(er) in the private sector after the recession in the 1990s, increasing entry and causing a decline in average tenure. An alternate, or complementary, explanation is that the reduction in tenure is a result of an increased use of short-term contracts. By contrast, average seniority in the public sector increased over the period examined.

Table 5.2   Employment among Swedish women aged 20 to 50, 1968 to 2000

	1968	1974	1981	1991	2000
Panel A: Average tenure with current employer (in years)					
All employed	5.0	5.5	6.5	8.1	7.4
Public service	5.4	6.0	6.5	8.8	8.9
Private service	4.1	4.6	6.2	6.5	4.8
Manufacturing	6.0	5.6	7.2	8.2	6.8
Panel B: Sector of employment (%)					
Public service	42.6	51.4	61.6	59.2	56.4
Private service	33.4	29.8	21.4	25.8	30.0
Manufacturing	20.0	16.5	14.3	12.8	11.8
Panel C: Women with compulsory schooling (% within sector)					
All women	48.3	35.8	27.7	15.0	7.0
Public service	37.9	26.8	20.1	11.6	5.6
Private service	52.7	42.1	37.0	18.1	7.0
Manufacturing	64.1	56.4	42.7	27.8	10.0
Homemakers	62.8	53.4	49.7	36.1	17.3

Source: Sweden Level of Living Survey

As seen in Panel B, employment in manufacturing has decreased steadily throughout the period, from 20 to below 12 percent. Employment in public services peaked at approximately 62 percent in 1981. It has since declined, but still accounts for around 56 percent of total employment. Private services show the reverse trend, bottoming at less than 22 percent in 1981 and subsequently increasing to 30 percent.

The number of women with compulsory schooling has declined continuously from 48 percent in 1968 to only 7 percent by 2000 (see Panel C). This development is reflected in all sectors of the economy. In 1968, female employees with compulsory education were approximately twice as common in manufacturing as in the public services. This proportion has remained roughly constant throughout, with the private services constantly falling in between. The reduction in the proportion of homemakers with compulsory education has been somewhat less dramatic.

The evolution of job stability is examined more closely in Table 5.3. Stability is measured through job tenure, that is, the number of years that respondents have been with their employer at the time of interview. The continuous trend toward *more* employment stability between 1974 and 1991 is broken in 2000. The reference female worker in the estimated models (one holding a medium-skilled job in manufacturing and having an average amount of experience, namely, 13 years) had stayed 6.4 years with her current employer in 1974 and 9.2 years in 1991 (as revealed by the constant terms in the equations). The corresponding figure for 2000 is 7.2 years. Given changes over time in average experience and in the distribution of skill categories and industries, the differences among the years are significant.

Table 5.3   Job tenure among female employees aged 20 to 50 in Sweden, 1974 to 2000, OLS regression, unstandardized coefficients

	All years	1974	1981	1991	2000
Constant	8.50	6.39	8.07	9.21	7.15
1974	−0.99***				
1981	−0.65***				
2000	−0.98***				
Experience (yrs.)	0.50***	0.42***	0.48***	0.52***	0.56**
Low-skill job	−1.21***	−0.90**	−1.50***	−1.26***	−1.10*
High-skill job	0.18	−0.15	0.26	−0.18	0.84*
Private service	−1.45***	−1.18**	−1.19**	−1.46**	−1.71**
Public service	0.08	0.33	−0.60	−0.12	0.95
R^2	0.37	0.35	0.39	0.34	0.37
N	4117	919	1126	1141	928

Notes:
Tenure is the number of years spent with current (at the time of interview) employer. Reference categories are 1991, Mid-skill job, and Manufacturing, respectively. Coefficients for other industries are omitted in the table. Experience is measured as deviation from sample mean
Significance levels:
*** p <= 0.01
** p <= 0.05
* p <= 0.10

Source: Sweden Level of Living Survey

As for the various worker categories, women in low-skill jobs have less stable employment than others do, yet there is no obvious trend in the evolution of this difference over time. On the contrary: the variation in job stability between employees with low- and medium-skilled jobs began to diminish during the 1980s and then fell significantly in the 1990s. Likewise, the difference between those with high- and medium-skilled positions stayed roughly constant from 1974 to 1991. Nonetheless, it is notable that tenure among those in high-skilled jobs rose dramatically in relation to that of the two other groups during the 1990s.

Job–worker matches in manufacturing and in public services have been significantly more stable than in private services. Over time, the relatively short job durations in private services compared with manufacturing have become steadily more rather than less marked. In all, this pattern of job duration among Swedish women corresponds well to earlier reported patterns of duration among Swedish men (cf. Korpi and Tåhlin 2006). Thus, it is not possible to detect any significant gender differences in job duration in Sweden. It is also worth noting that an inclusion of part-time work and having young children did not change the overall results (analyses not presented).

To summarize, the impact of small children on female labor force participation has diminished over time, and employment and (to a lesser extent) working hours among women with and without children have also become more similar. Women's labor force participation has also become more stable over time, which means labor market mobility has decreased. Taking the period as a whole, these trends towards increasing stability apply to women in all educational categories. They also apply equally to women in manufacturing and in public services, while the reduced employment stability in the private services probably is owing in part to the strong employment growth of this sector. Such patterns appear to violate the predictions of the globalization thesis.

Unemployment 1963–2001

By international standards, the Swedish unemployment rate remained very low until the cataclysmic slump of the early 1990s. This change from full employment to mass unemployment may conflate different trends. Still, a marked increase in unemployment among manufacturing workers (and workers with relatively little education) relative to developments among workers in other industries and educational categories could be an indication of a globalization effect on unemployment risks. We can therefore contrast the evolution of unemployment among workers in manufacturing with that among workers in non-manufacturing industries and among workers with different amounts of schooling. Due to data limitations (the labor force survey does not allow breakdowns of unemployment by sector and sex) the former contrast is between men and women in different sectors of the economy.

The evolution of unemployment from 1963 to 2001 for workers in manufacturing and other workers show that relative to other workers, the unemployment risk among manufacturing workers has been a little lower throughout most of the period. Unemployment among manufacturing workers even passed the rates among other workers in the early 1990s, yet also declined more rapidly. The dominant impression is a clear correspondence in unemployment risks across both manufacturing and non-manufacturing sectors, both in levels and trend (a graph of the sector differences in unemployment is presented in Korpi and Tåhlin 2006).

The unemployment rate can be disaggregated into inflow rate and duration. Behind the tendency toward rising unemployment from the early 1960s to the 1990s lies an increase in average unemployment duration and not a growing inflow (not shown). Until the late 1980s, transition rates from employment to unemployment actually decreased somewhat, and during the economic recovery in the late 1990s inflow also diminished faster than duration. Both inflows and duration have tended to differ more between sectors than the compound unemployment rate. Inflow rates into unemployment among manufacturing workers have generally been lower than among other workers (other than in the recession of the early 1990s), but the average duration of unemployment spells has been longer.

Turning then to unemployment risk by educational level (see Figure 5.1), one can note that unemployment is consistently lowest for those with tertiary education. The difference between those with compulsory and secondary education is less clear. Relative differences between the educational levels seem to have remained roughly constant over time. A plot of the development of these differentials (not shown) reveals that this is true for the gap between those with compulsory and with secondary education. The differential between university educated and the other two groups did however decrease up until 1985 and increase thereafter, leaving the relative risks largely unchanged.

The evolution of Swedish unemployment does not provide much evidence in line with the globalization thesis. The difference in unemployment between manufacturing and other sectors has remained unchanged over a 30-year period. This also holds for the relative unemployment rates of the different educational categories. The support for the globalization thesis is, in other words, rather limited in the Swedish case.

Job mobility 1940–2000

In the analyses of job mobility, we have used the questions on monthly labor force status in the retrospective work–life biographies in the Level of Living Surveys of 1991 and 2000. A job change is defined as a move from one job to the next, irrespective of whether this subsequent job follows immediately upon the first. Periods of non-employment, or self-employment falling in

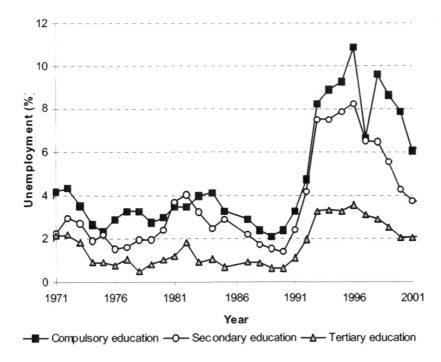

Year

—■— Compulsory education —○— Secondary education —△— Tertiary education

Source: Labor force surveys (AKU), Statistics Sweden

Figure 5.1 Swedish women's unemployment rates (%) by education 1971–2001, ages 16–64 (1971 through 1985 ages 16–74)

between two jobs, have in other words been included in the time at risk (modeled with the help of a time-varying dummy variable). These job changes are, in turn, divided into internal and external job mobility according to whether the second job was with the same employer as the previous one. We have also distinguished between upward, downward and lateral moves. This categorization is based on Treiman's (1977) prestige scale. An upward move was defined as a job shift involving an increase on the prestige scale of at least 10 percent, and a downward move as a job shift with an identical loss in prestige. All other job changes have been treated as lateral moves. Internal and external mobility as well as vertical moves have been modeled as competing risks, with right censoring occurring only at the time of interview (in 2000).

For each type of mobility, we have estimated Cox proportional hazard models, where individuals have been considered to become at risk of making a transition at the time of each job entry. We have followed workers over

their entire career until the time of interview, and corrected for the resulting
non-independence of observations (job spells) by estimating robust standard
errors.

Our interest has centered on the variables period, industrial sector and
education. We have therefore distinguished between the 1940s and 1950s, the
1960s, the 1970s, the 1980s and the 1990s; between manufacturing, private
services, public services and other industries; and between a low
(compulsory), middle (upper secondary) and high (tertiary) level of
education. Education has been modeled as a time-varying covariate,
indicating the highest educational level attained. All models have also
contained a set of control variables: employment experience (including a
square term), number of previous jobs and workplace size have been
measured at the start of each job, while age and periods of non-employment
or self-employment included in time at risk have been time-varying
covariates. In the analyses of vertical mobility, we have also included the
prestige of the present job among the control variables.

Table 5.4 provides an overview of job mobility differentials among
Swedish women, over time, between educational groups and between sectors.
With regard to development over time, most analyses show fairly constant
mobility up until the 1960s. Mobility then increases before leveling off in the
1990s. Internal mobility is an exception here, with mobility actually falling in
the last decade. Increasing education is generally associated with increasing
mobility, the only exception being downward mobility, which is less
common among the more educated. The private service sector displays less
downward and internal mobility than the manufacturing sector, but otherwise
there are hardly any mobility differences. The public service sector evinces
less vertical mobility, which given similar job-to-job rates, implies
substantial lateral mobility. Not surprisingly, there is also more internal and
less external mobility in the public sector.

Of greater interest for the globalization thesis is, however, the development
of these inter-educational and inter-sectoral differences over time. Tables 5.5
and 5.6 present evidence on the evolution of mobility within the educational
categories and the industrial sectors, respectively. These analyses have been
carried out by including a period-education (alternatively a period-sector)
interaction term in the regression models of Table 5.4. In order to simplify
the interpretation of results, we have calculated the total (main plus
interaction) effect for each sub-category based on the estimated coefficients.
The effects presented thus show the mobility difference between each sub-
category and the reference category (low education and manufacturing,
respectively, in the 1990s).

We are primarily interested in differences in mobility among educational
categories or employment sectors. While we also mention changes in the
estimated rates of mobility over time for the various categories, we do not
present significance tests of these within group developments. Nonetheless,

Table 5.4   Labor market mobility among Swedish women aged 20 to 50, Cox models, standard errors in parentheses

	Job-to-job	Upward	Downward	Internal	External
Period					
1940s and 1950s	−0.61***	−0.78***	−0.97***	−0.91***	−0.53***
	(0.09)	(0.17)	(0.19)	(0.18)	(0.09)
1960s	−0.62***	−0.70***	−1.02***	−0.66***	−0.60***
	(0.05)	(0.11)	(0.13)	(0.11)	(0.06)
1970s	−0.36***	−0.48***	−0.42***	−0.10	−0.50***
	(0.04)	(0.09)	(0.10)	(0.08)	(0.05)
1980s	−0.00	0.00	−0.03	0.27***	−0.16***
	(0.03)	(0.08)	(0.09)	(0.07)	(0.05)
Education					
Compulsory (ref.)					
Secondary	0.12***	0.44***	−0.33***	0.20***	0.09**
	(0.03)	(0.07)	(0.08)	(0.07)	(0.04)
Tertiary	0.22***	0.87***	−1.28***	0.42***	0.10*
	(0.03)	(0.11)	(0.12)	(0.07)	(0.05)
Sector					
Private service	−0.01	0.02	−0.41***	−0.23**	0.02
	(0.05)	(0.10)	(0.09)	(0.11)	(0.05)
Public service	−0.01	−0.28***	−0.76***	0.47***	−0.29***
	(0.04)	(0.09)	(0.09)	(0.09)	(0.05)
N	1 709	1 709	1 709	1 709	1 709
Number of job spells	6 373	6 373	6 373	6 373	6 373
N non-events (failures)	5 278	1 191	890	1 833	3 444
Log L	−40 649.8	−8 888.6	−6 714.0	−13 520.4	−27 764.7

Notes:
In addition to the variables shown, the models have also included the variables experience and experience squared, previous number of job changes, workplace size, and two time-varying covariates, indicating age and periods of self-employment, farming, and non-employment included in time at risk. The models of upward and downward mobility have furthermore included prestige of current job
Significance levels:
*** $p <= 0.01$
** $p <= 0.05$
* $p <= 0.10$

Source: Sweden Level of Living Survey

the trends have been tested for significance and the changes described have all been found significant. Instead, we concentrate on relative rates of mobility and changes therein, and we present two different tests. First, we examine within period differences in mobility among the categories, and significance is here indicated by the presence or absence of asterisks in the table. As an example, in Table 5.5, we see that total job-to-job mobility among the less educated in the 1990s (the reference category in the table with an implicit point estimate of 0.00) differs from mobility among those with a middle level of education (point estimate 0.22), as well as those with a high level of education (point estimate 0.20). Second, we test for changes in these relative mobility differentials over the period 1960 to 2000, and here, significance is reported in the two bottom rows of the table. Again, taking total job-to-job mobility as an example, we see that the hypothesis of unchanged relative mobility rates cannot be refuted in the case of the low and middle educated. In the case of the less and highly educated, the alternative hypothesis of changes in the relative rates is significant at the 6 percent level.

The employment prospects of the less educated/less skilled are a central component in much of the globalization literature. As is evident in Table 5.5, the development of job mobility among the less educated basically corresponds to the general pattern found in Table 5.4. Stable mobility rates up until the 1960s are followed by increases before leveling off in the 1980s. Also evident from the table is that the evolution of job mobility among those with a medium and high level of education is largely similar. There is, of course, 'cross-sectional' variation during a particular decade, as evinced by the significant period-specific differences (the asterisks). Nonetheless, as is shown by the p-values at the bottom of the table, the cross-sectional differences between those with low, and those with a medium level of education remain fairly stable. The sole exception refers to downward mobility. However, inspection of the differences in the point estimates show that, rather than increasing, the gap between the two groups has narrowed.

This also holds for the two cases where the mobility differential between the low and the highly educated has changed, that is, job-to-job and internal mobility. Instead of increasing diversity, the analysis shows increasing similarity. While the employment prospects of the less educated are an important issue in the discussions around increasing economic integration, there is no indication of a marked worsening of their situation in these data. This conclusion is bolstered by the fact that it holds for both women and men (cf. Korpi and Tåhlin 2006).

Any globalization effect on the Swedish labor market ought to be apparent in inter-sectoral differences in mobility. These are examined in Table 5.6, and the sector-specific changes in mobility follow the by now well-demonstrated pattern of early stability followed by an increase and subsequent stability. More interesting, however, is that there are almost no indications of any changes in these differentials over time. Furthermore, the two instances where a changing differential is documented do not comply with the globalization thesis. In the case of downward mobility, the disparity between manufacturing and the private service sector decreased during the 1970s and

Table 5.5 *Education-specific period effects: labor market mobility among Swedish women aged 20 to 50, Cox models*

	Job-to-job	Upward	Downward	Internal	External
Low education					
1940s & 50s	−0.62	−0.75	N.e.	−1.18	−0.49
1960s	−0.62	−0.67	−0.64	−0.92	−0.52
1970s	−0.32	−0.42	−0.16	−0.20	−0.38
1980s	0.04	0.10	0.21	0.16	−0.02
1990s (ref.)					
Mid education					
1940s & 50s	−0.53	−0.14*	N.e.	−1.26	−0.32
1960s	−0.55	−0.07***	−1.21***	−0.69	−0.48
1970s	−0.25	0.03***	−0.55***	−0.08	−0.33
1980s	0.16**	0.47***	−0.23***	0.45***	0.01
1990s	0.22***	0.46***	0.09	0.16	0.23**
High education					
1940s & 50s	−0.00***	−0.31	N.e.	0.24***	−0.14
1960s	−0.13***	−0.11	−3.14***	0.03***	−0.24*
1970s	−0.09***	0.38***	−1.58***	0.29***	−0.36
1980s	0.19***	0.88***	−0.97***	0.53***	−0.03
1990s	0.20***	1.08***	−1.05***	0.16	0.23**
Log L	−40 640.2	−8886.0	−6706.0	−13 505.7	−26 759.8
$P(\text{Low}_{60} - \text{Mid}_{60} = \text{Low}_{70} - \text{Mid}_{70} = \text{Low}_{80} - \text{Mid}_{80} = \text{Low}_{90} - \text{Mid}_{90})$	0.49	0.78	0.02	0.70	0.39
$P(\text{Low}_{60} - \text{Hi}_{60} = \text{Low}_{70} - \text{Hi}_{70} = \text{Low}_{80} - \text{Hi}_{80} = \text{Low}_{90} - \text{Hi}_{90})$	0.06	0.43	0.51	0.03	0.15

Notes:
Point estimates calculated from models with period, education, and period*education variables. Variables sector, experience and experience squared, previous number of job changes, workplace size are included, and two time-varying covariates, indicating age and periods of self-employment, farming, and non-employment are included in time at risk. The models of upward and downward mobility have furthermore included prestige of current job. Asterisks indicate periodwise tests of equal education effects relative to low education, with ***, ** and * indicating significant at the 1, 5 and 10 percent levels. $P(\text{Low}_{60} - \text{Mid}_{60} = \text{Low}_{70} - \text{Mid}_{70} = \text{Low}_{80} - \text{Mid}_{80} = \text{Low}_{90} - \text{Mid}_{90})$ shows significance levels for tests of equal period differences between low and middle educated, and $P(\text{Low}_{60} - \text{Hi}_{60} = \text{Low}_{70} - \text{Hi}_{70} = \text{Low}_{80} - \text{Hi}_{80} = \text{Low}_{90} - \text{Hi}_{90})$ for low v. high educated. N.e. (not estimated) indicates that the two time periods 1940s/50s and 1960s have been combined into one due to a lack of observations. The period difference tests for downward mobility have here been adapted and span the period 1970s to 1990s

Source: Sweden Level of Living Survey

Table 5.6   Sector-specific period effects: labor market mobility among Swedish women aged 20 to 50, Cox models

	Job-to-job	Upward	Downward	Internal	External
Manufacturing					
1940s & 50s	−0.92	−1.30	−1.23	−1.73	−0.69
1960s	−0.81	−0.79	−1.00	−1.38	−0.59
1970s	−0.59	−0.61	−0.74	−0.83	−0.49
1980s	−0.13	−0.17	−0.36	−0.13	−0.14
1990s (ref.)					
Private services					
1940s & 50s	−0.75	−0.80	−1.67	−1.87	−0.52
1960s	−0.83	−0.79	−1.90***	−1.62	−0.62
1970s	−0.49	−0.53	−0.92	−0.94	−0.38
1980s	−0.12	−0.06	−0.60	−0.35	−0.07
1990s	−0.20**	−0.28	−0.74***	−0.54***	−0.11
Public services					
1940s & 50s	−0.72	−1.21	−1.82	−0.74*	−0.74
1960s	−0.72	−1.18	−1.86***	−0.54***	−0.84*
1970s	−0.52	−0.97**	−1.47***	−0.04***	−0.89***
1980s	−0.18	−0.44*	−1.00***	0.24***	−0.50***
1990s	−0.15*	−0.28	−0.94***	−0.14	−0.17
Log L	−40 645.2	−8883.9	−6708.9	−13 505.6	−26 752.8
$P(Man_{60} - PrS_{60} =$ $Man_{70} - PrS_{70} =$ $Man_{80} - PrS_{80} =$ $Man_{90} - PuS_{90})$	0.15	0.36	0.04	0.42	0.53
$P(Man_{60} - PuS_{60} =$ $Man_{70} - PuS_{70} =$ $Man_{80} - PuS_{80} =$ $Man_{90} - PuS_{90})$	0.25	0.97	0.68	0.00	0.45

Notes:
Point estimates calculated from models with period, sector, and period*sector variables. The variables education, experience and experience squared, previous no. job changes, workplace size, and two time-varying covariates indicating age are included, and periods of self-employment, farming, and non-employment are included in time at risk. The models of upward and downward mobility also include prestige of current job. Asterisks indicate periodwise tests of equal sector effects relative to manufacturing, with ***, ** and * indicating significant at the 1, 5 and 10 percent levels. $P(Man_{60} - PrS_{60} = Man_{70} - PrS_{70} = Man_{80} - PrS_{80} = Man_{90} - PrS_{90})$ shows significance levels for tests of equal period differences between manufacturing and private services, and $P(Man_{60} - PuS_{60} = Man_{70} - PuS_{70} = Man_{80} - PuS_{80} = Man_{90} - PuS_{90})$ for manufacturing v. public services

Source: Sweden Level of Living Survey

1980s before increasing somewhat in the 1990s. In the case of internal mobility, the gap between the public sector and manufacturing was markedly greater during the period of public sector expansion in the 1960s and 1970s, and has since narrowed. The changes that have taken place in the most global sector are thus largely matched by similar developments in the other two sectors, a pattern indicating a rather limited impact of globalization. As with the other analyses presented here, this reiterates the result obtained in the analyses for men (Korpi and Tåhlin 2006).

CONCLUSION

Taking globalization as shorthand for increasing economic integration, we have pursued two different hypotheses. The literature suggests that if globalization has had an impact on the labor market experience of Swedish women, such an impact is most likely to be visible in the relative position of the manufacturing sector and/or in the relative position of the less educated. Examining the developments in the different sectors of the economy and among different educational groups for the whole post-war period, we find no clear-cut evidence indicating relative changes of the hypothesized kind.

Swedish women have acquired increasingly secure positions on the labor market: employment rates, working hours and job stability have all increased. These trends also seem to apply more or less equally to women in all sectors of the economy and with different levels of education. While there has been a gradual growth in the risk of unemployment, topped off with mass unemployment in the 1990s, there are no signs that this increase involves manufacturing more than the other sectors or that the unemployment risks have evolved differently among the various educational groups. Likewise, the changes in job mobility that have been documented were either temporary and related to the expansion of the public sector or indicated increasing similarity in the mobility of the different educational groups. The dramatic changes in the working life of adult Swedish women thus seem largely unrelated to changes in economic integration, a conclusion echoing the result from the analysis of the labor market experiences of Swedish men (Korpi and Tåhlin 2006).

This might be taken to suggest that the Swedish labor market has been left unaffected by the force of economic integration. In our view, such a conclusion is premature. First, changes may have occurred in other areas than those examined here. Particularly relevant here would seem to be changes in relative wage rates, inter-sectoral labor mobility and exits from the labor force. Second, while Sweden has seen an increase in trade, this is an increase at a relatively high level of economic integration. As is true of most small industrialized economies, Sweden's exposure to international competition has long been greater than the exposure of other (larger) countries, and the changes may therefore have been less than elsewhere.

The primary forces driving the changes on the Swedish female labor market examined here appear to have been domestic rather than international. The expansions of the public sector and reforms in regulations regarding parental leave, daycare, part-time work and taxation have drastically transformed the conditions for female employment. This would seem to indicate that there is substantial leeway for domestic policy even in the face of extensive international economic integration.

NOTES

1   We would like to thank seminar participants at the Swedish Institute for Social Research, in particular Marianne Sundström, for helpful comments on an earlier version of this chapter.

2   High rates of return on foreign investments may raise the required rate of return on domestic investments in manufacturing. The consequence could be shifts from real to financial investments and from investments in manufacturing to investments in services, both to the detriment of employment in manufacturing. The other effect is with regard to the long-term consequences of investments abroad. To the extent that these investments are successful and generate a profit that is transferred 'back home,' they could induce an increase in imports, a rise in exchange rates and a further worsening of the employment situation in the tradable sector.

3   This development in sector-specific employment may be contrasted with the evolution of sector-specific production. Examining service sector production as a proportion of GDP and excluding unpaid work within the household, Schön (2000, p. 456) finds that this is basically stable over the period 1800 to 2000. When household services are included; there is a steady reduction of the service sector during the same 200 years. Also, there are breaks in the trends. The first (excluding household services) drops until 1870 and increases thereafter, the second increases after 1970.

4   Globalization and deindustrialization are not the only development pressures acting on the labor markets of industrialized nations. There are also close parallels between the literatures on trade, on deindustrialization and on skill-biased technical change (see Feenstra and Hanson 2003).

5   The link between trade and domestic labor markets has also been examined in analyses of the rise in inequality (and unemployment) in many industrialized nations. This could be explained by a drop in demand for unskilled workers owing to either an increase in trade or to technological change. Since trade between high- and low-income nations is still small and has grown relatively little, and since relative prices have not moved in the expected direction, many saw technology as the main causal factor (see Krugman 1995). However, this conclusion was largely based on trade in finished consumer products, and it has been argued that trade in intermediate goods as well as trade and FDI between developed countries also must be considered. Skill upgrading within firms and

industries (rather than across) may therefore be the outcome of international trade and capital mobility, as well as of technological change (see in particular Feenstra and Hanson 2003; Wood 1994). Trade may thus be more important than previously believed, although it is still uncertain exactly how important. The discussion of relative importance is also complicated by trade and technology to some extent being interdependent.

6   There were also indications that the positive impact of investment in less developed countries was roughly similar on white- and blue-collar employment, and that investments in developed countries were associated with a smaller increase in blue-collar employment and reduced or unchanged white-collar employment.

BIBLIOGRAPHY

Alderson, A.S. (1999) 'Explaining deindustrialization: globalization, failure, or success?', *American Sociological Review*, 64: 701–21.

Andersson, T. (1994) 'Foreign direct investment and employment in Sweden'. Working Paper No. 418, Industrial Institute for Economic and Social Research, Stockholm.

Andersson, T. and Hellström, H. (1994) 'Swedish direct investment in low-cost countries', Working Paper No. 420, Industrial Institute for Economic and Social Research, Stockholm.

Båvner, P. (2001) *Half-full or half empty? Part-time work and well-being among Swedish women*, Stockholm: Swedish Institute for Social Research.

Bell, D. (1973) *The coming of post-industrial society*, New York: Basic Books.

Blomström, M., Fors, G. and Lipsey, R.E. (1997) 'Foreign direct investment and employment: home country experiences in the United States and Sweden', *Economic Journal*, 107: 1787–97.

Clark, C. (1951) *The conditions of economic progress*, London: Macmillan.

Edin, P.-A., Fredriksson, P. and Lundborg, P. (2004) 'The effect of trade on earnings—evidence from Swedish micro data', *Oxford Economic Papers*, 56: 231–241.

Feenstra, R.C. and Hanson G.H. (2003) 'Global production sharing and rising inequality: a survey of trade and wages', in K. Choi and J. Harrigan (eds) *Handbook of international trade*, Oxford: Blackwell.

Fuchs, V.R. (1968) *The service economy*, New York: NBER and Columbia University Press.

Garrett, G. (2001) 'The distributive consequences of globalization', Leitner Working Paper 2001-02, Yale University.

Gonäs, L. and Anna Spånt (1997) 'Trends and prospects for women's employment in the 1990s', *Arbete och Hälsa* 1997: 4, National Institute for Working Life, Stockholm.

Gustafsson, S. (1992) 'Separate taxation and married women's labor supply. A comparison of West Germany and Sweden', *Journal of Population Economics*, 5: 61–85.

Gustafsson, S. and Jacobsson, R. (1985) 'Trends in female labor force participation in Sweden', *Journal of Labor Economics*, 3: 256–74.

140   Social-democratic welfare regimes

Gustafsson, S. and Stafford, F. (1992) 'Child care subsidies and labor supply in Sweden', *Journal of Human Resources*, 27: 204–30.

Hansson, P. (2000) 'Relative demand for skills in Swedish manufacturing: technology or trade?', *Review of International Economics*, 8: 533–55.

Hansson, P. (2005) 'Skill upgrading and production transfer within Swedish multinationals', *Scandinavian Journal of Economics*, 107: 673–692.

Henz, U. and Sundström, M. (2001) 'Partner choice and women's paid work in Sweden. The role of earnings', *European Sociological Review*, 17: 295–316.

Heston, A., Summers, R. and Aten, B. (2002) 'Penn world table version 6.1', Center for International Comparisons at the University of Pennsylvania (CICUP), www.pwt.econ.upenn.edu, October 2002.

Iversen, T. (2001) 'The dynamics of welfare state expansion: trade openness, de-industrialization, and partisan politics', in P. Pierson (ed.) *The new politics of the welfare state*, Oxford: Oxford University Press.

Jonsson, J.O. and Mills, C. (2001) *Cradle to grave. Life-course changes in modern Sweden*, Durham: Sociologypress.

Korpi, T. and Tåhlin, M. (2006) 'The impact of globalization on men's labor market mobility in Sweden', in H.-P. Blossfeld, M. Mills and F. Bernardi (eds) *Globalization, uncertainty, and men's careers: an international comparison*, Cheltenham, UK and Northampton, MA, USA: Edward Elgar.

Krugman, P. (1995) 'Growing world trade: causes and consequences', *Brookings Papers on Economic Activity*, 1: 327–77.

Organisation for Economic Co-operation and Development (OECD) (1994) *The OECD jobs study. Part I: Labour market trends and underlying forces of change*, Paris: OECD.

Rodrik, D. (1997) *Has globalization gone too far?*, Washington, DC: Institute for International Economics.

Rodrik, D. (1998) 'Why do more open economies have larger governments?', *Journal of Political Economy*, 106: 997–1032.

Rowthorn, R. and Ramaswamy, R. (1999) 'Growth, trade, and deindustrialization', IMF staff papers, 46: 18–41.

Schön, L. (2000) *En modern svensk ekonomisk historia. Tillväxt och omvandling under två sekel*, Stockholm: SNS Förlag.

Statistics Sweden (1996) *De svenska arbetskraftsundersökningarna (AKU)* (The Swedish labor force surveys), Bakgrundsfakta till arbetsmarknads- och utbildningsstatistiken 1996: 2, Statistics Sweden, Stockholm.

Statistics Sweden (2002) *Arbetskraftsundersökningarna 2001* (The labor force surveys 2001), Statistiska meddelanden, AM 12 SM 0201, Statistics Sweden, Stockholm.

Sundström, M. (1983) 'Kvinnor och deltidsarbete', in M. Lundahl and I. Persson-Tanimura (eds) *Kvinnan i ekonomin*, Malmö: Liber Förlag.

Sundström, M. (1987) *A study in the growth of part-time work in Sweden*, Stockholm: Arbetslivscentrum.

Sundström, M. (1999) 'Part-time work in Sweden – an institutionalist perspective', Stockholm Research Reports in Demography No. 138, Stockholm University.

Swedish National Agency for Education (2004) 'Descriptive data about childcare, school, and adult education 2003', Swedish National Agency for Education Report No. 236, Swedish National Agency for Education, Stockholm.

Treiman, D. (1977) *Occupational prestige in comparative perspective*, New York: Academic Press.

Wood, A. (1994) *North–south trade, employment, and inequality: changing fortunes in a skill-driven world*, Oxford: Clarendon Press.

Wood, A. (1995) 'How trade hurts unskilled workers', *Journal of Economic Perspectives*, 9: 57–80.

6. Danish women's unemployment, job mobility and non-employment, 1980s and 1990s: marked by globalization?

Daniela Grunow and Søren Leth-Sørensen

INTRODUCTION

The Danish variant of the 'Scandinavian welfare-state model' was based on a strong ideology of equality and state-facilitated female labor market participation; it also actively promoted market flexibility largely through the absence of employment protection measures. Yet it was established at a time when labor market conditions became more favorable and unemployment was lower, so how have Danish women's careers fared in the late twentieth century under globalization pressures? This chapter addresses this question with respect to job mobility, unemployment risk, labor market exits and women's subsequent chances of re-employment. Globalization theorists have argued that women, and especially mothers, face severe disadvantages in the labor market during times of increasing flexibilization and large-scale unemployment (Beck 1986).

Using linked register data from the IDA database (Integrated Database for Labor Market Research, for which see Leth-Sørensen 1997), mid-career employment transitions of two female birth cohorts are studied longitudinally for the period between 1980 and 1999. The analyses focus not only on the effects of macro-economic and legislative changes 'in times of globalization,' but also take women's human capital and career investments as well as changes in women's family situation into account.

As previous research has shown, Denmark is a special case because of its long tradition of combining a high level of labor market flexibility (hire and fire labor market) and trade openness with high levels of social security (Braun 2003; Grunow and Leth-Sørensen 2006; Madsen 1999; 2002). Another peculiarity is that about half the female workforce is employed in the public sector. High job stability for women, as well as a favorable balance between work and family, have been ascribed to the sheer size of this sector (Esping-Andersen, Rohwer and Leth-Sørensen 1994), but that has come at the expense of lower earnings and worse career chances for women relative to men (Pedersen and Deding 2000). In addition, it was largely the public sector during the 1990s that provided jobs for the unemployed within the new framework of activation and re-employment measures. These programs belong to a broader set of employment activation and flexibilization concepts that have been introduced since 1992, in response to persistent unemployment. Since 1994, however, private sector employment has benefited from an economic upswing, and unemployment has dropped considerably. Despite the ups and downs on the Danish market throughout the 1980s and 1990s, male careers have not, in general, been marked by increased employment instability, which is one hypothesized consequence of globalization. Rather, specific groups with specific qualifications have been exposed to unemployment risk and to flexibility demands, even while overall employment opportunities for men improved (Grunow and Leth-Sørensen 2006).

Given Danish gender equality precepts on the one hand, and the relatively high level of sex-specific labor market segregation on the other, has this been the case for women as well? Do we find different mobility and employment patterns for specific female groups, depending on their level of education, their employment sector or their family status? Do labor force exits and job interruptions increasingly become an option for individual women as labor market competition rises? Or has the norm of continuous female employment proven persistent, even for those who became mothers or those with high-earning spouses?

We assume that women's careers are affected largely by changes in the institutional and legislative framework, by economic – and therefore, labor market – trends and by individual factors, which in their interplay shape individual women's options and restrictions on the job market. We start with an overview of female employment since the 1960s. Then we describe some of the central features of the Danish welfare state, shifts in women's enrolment in family providership, and changes in labor market and family policies. This provides the framework within which the female cohorts under study pursued their employment and family careers throughout the 1980s and 1990s. Special attention is paid to the extensive labor market and family policy reforms of the mid-1990s. The Danish case is then summarized with respect to the discourse on globalization, allowing us to derive hypotheses of women's labor market performance 'in times of globalization.' Data and methods are discussed in the subsequent section, and we conclude with a discussion of results and key findings.

SHIFTS IN WOMEN'S EMPLOYMENT

Global processes of economic and technological change, concomitant with the internationalization, privatization, deregulation and liberalization of markets, are supposed to have an impact on the life course of individuals, especially through their participation in paid employment (Mills, Blossfeld and Klijzing 2005). Evidence for this is seen in the massive increase in female employment, as well as the high levels of educational attainment that have characterized the second half of the twentieth century; employment and education have resulted in shifts in household structures and family formation. Such changes are heralded as the 'beginning of a new epoch' in the transformation of modern societies (for example, Beck 1986; Castells 2000).

Women's work and family lives in Denmark have been affected by two key developments in recent Danish history: the so-called 'second industrial revolution' of the 1960s, the basis for Denmark's present material wealth, and the concomitant expansion of the 'welfare society' during the 1960s and 1970s, which included extensive public assistance and tax-based income redistribution. During the economic boom there was a rising demand for unskilled labor as well as an increase in white-collar, public sector jobs, and both developments worked to the benefit of women from groups that had not previously participated in paid work. Women's participation in higher education increased strongly, and by the mid-1980s female employment had shifted toward white-collar work – particularly in education, social-care and healthcare and administration – in the public sector where 45 percent were employed (StatBank Denmark 2004).

THE INSTITUTIONAL FRAMEWORK AND WOMEN'S RESPONSES IN THEIR WORK AND FAMILY ARRANGEMENTS

Educational upgrading and increase in female employment were embedded in national education, family and labor market policies that for decades had fostered women's labor force participation. These policies were implemented through tax legislation but had also been inspired by a sense of public sector responsibility. We assume that changes in these regulations go hand in hand with prevailing normative assumptions about the work and family roles of women and men (Grunow, Hofmeister and Buchholz 2006).

Education

Education influences not only employment opportunities and career choices for women but is also an important factor in choices women make about balancing family and paid work (Gustafsson, Kenjoh and Wetzels 2002; Oppenheimer, Blossfeld and Wackerow 1995; Pylkkänen and Smith 2003).

The Danish educational system is governed at the national level. Access to higher education depends on school grades, and like Germany, Denmark also has a system of apprenticeship that combines schooling with on-the-job training. Educational degrees are standardized, and especially for those who have completed an apprenticeship the kind of training attained is, as in Germany, closely linked with later occupational career tracks. With the expansion of women's educational participation, beginning in the 1960s, women became more valuable to the labor market and their gains from investment in paid work increased. Adult education also has increased in importance, in conjunction with the activation policies introduced in the mid-1990s (Munk 2001).

The public sector

The Danish welfare model as it exists today would hardly be imaginable without the large growth in the public sector over the last several decades. This has been financed mainly by tax revenues (including value-added tax – VAT), and the egalitarian or solidaristic ideological orientation that has justified such growth has meant steeply progressive taxation levels in the interest of redistribution or fairness. Spouses are taxed separately on their individual incomes, a system considered both 'neutral' and 'encouraging' with respect to the incentives of both partners to work (Pylkkänen and Smith 2003).

The most important component for women is doubtless the extensive provision of care-related services provided by the state, as they lead to making work and family responsibilities far more compatible, and are abetted by accommodating institutional arrangements. The public sector not only takes responsibility for kindergartens and schools, but also provides care services for the elderly. Though women are still considered the primary caregivers at home, female homemaking has become an exception. Daycare rates for infants and toddlers are extraordinarily high, considerably higher even than in Sweden (Danmarks Statistik 2001; Pylkkänen and Smith 2003).

That the public sector provides such extensive services also means it accounts for nearly 30 percent of total employment, and half of the female workforce is employed in this sector (Danmarks Statistik 2001).

The shift towards a dual-earner family model

As in the other Scandinavian countries, Danish families have become naturally dependent on two incomes and both men and women usually work long hours (Leth-Sørensen and Rohwer 1997). Between 1974 and 1991 the labor market participation rate for women with small children rose from 48 percent to 90 percent (Christoffersen 1993). In the same period the share of women with small children who said that they were 'housewives' dropped from 43 percent to 3 percent (Christoffersen 1993). Overall female activity rates increased steadily until 1980, and since that date the level has remained constant at about ten percentage points lower than for males. Nowadays activity rates for both males (~ 80 percent) and females (~ 71 percent) are among the highest in Europe, though men continue to predominate in the higher-level jobs, even in the public sector (Datta Gupta, Oaxaca and Smith 1998; Danmarks Statistik 2001; Naur and Smith 1996).

Family policies

An important means for enhancing women's labor market attachment is through parental leave measures (Pylkkänen and Smith 2003), though it has been argued that such arrangements are also associated with a reduction in relative female wages and can imply negative effects on further career development. Others have argued the opposite, that maternity leave schemes have a positive effect on women's careers and, in particular, on women's wages, since they shield mothers from losing tenure and tenure-related promotion in the firm (Waldfogel 1998). Having children does not have a negative effect on women's wages in Denmark, holding labor force experience constant (Datta Gupta and Smith 2002), though because such experience decreases when taking leave, there is a de facto wage penalty upon re-entry into work.

Maternity leave and parental leave mandates

Though the regulations changed in 2002, maternity leave during the period under study here (1980s and 1990s) was from one to two months before birth and three months after birth, depending on employment sector; this placed Denmark in an 'intermediate' position among comparable developed countries (Alewell and Pull 2001). As of 1985, benefits were available to mothers who had worked at least 120 continuous hours in the 13 weeks before birth (the level of wage compensation depended upon the sector the woman worked in), fathers could take a two-week leave in connection with childbirth (this was superseded by the 2002 regulations) and an additional ten weeks of parental leave could be taken by either mother or father. Danish employers faced no direct financial costs related to maternity leave, although as in Germany, they have had a job guarantee obligation, that is, women who take maternity leave have a legal claim to return the same (or similar) job during the leave (cf. Alewell and Pull 2001; Human Rights and Equal Opportunity Commission 2002; Pylkkänen and Smith 2003).

Taking advantage of all available maternity and parental leaves could thus result in paid leave for seven or eight months, the time frame planned by most Danish mothers (Pylkkänen and Smith 2003, p. 21). About half the mothers (and considerably fewer of the fathers) were entitled to full wage compensation during their leaves, male partners usually had higher earnings and so the leave schemes invited a fairly unilateral care accountability. So while parental leave could be taken by either father or mother, both direct economic and indirect social incentives resulted in having vastly more mothers taking leaves than fathers. It is worth parenthetically noting that the 2002 reforms have resulted in a still *more* generous policy: 32 weeks of parental leave, offering additional ring-fenced leave for fathers and entitlement to full compensation for the parent on leave.

Childcare

A second precondition of women's high employment rates and career continuity has been the availability of subsidized, high-quality, public childcare facilities. Parents cover only one-third of the operating costs of childcare institutions, on average, and means-tested support programs for low-income families also exist (European Commission 2002; Pylkkänen and Smith 2003).

Childcare rates are very high in Denmark, in international comparative perspective, and the standards of the facilities are also judged to be good (Pylkkänen and Smith 2003; Rostgaard and Friedberg 1998). Fifty-six percent of the infants (to age two) are in subsidized nursery or daycare in private homes in 2000 (Pylkkänen and Smith 2003). In 2000, 92 percent of the three- to five-year-olds were in daycare, and many schoolchildren participate in preschool and after-school programs (Danmarks Statistik 2002), all of which is to the advantage of working women with young children. However, many families have experienced temporary problems in finding a care place for their child, since the demand for childcare has often been higher than the supply.

Labor market policies and the 'Employment Miracle' of the 1990s

Danish labor market policies have been estimated as being very successful, as they have been able to combine little employment protection (hire and fire labor market, consequently a high degree of labor market flexibility) with high standards of social security (Albæk, Van Audenrode and Browning 1999; Döhrn, Heilemann and Schäfer 1998; Emmerich and Werner 1998; Werner 1998).

As employment protection measures are largely absent, employers can easily adjust the number of employees according to their current needs, reinforcing high individual job mobility and a large number of transitions in and out of unemployment (Emmerich, Hoffman and Walwei 2000; Grunow and Leth-Sørensen 2006). At the same time, the unemployment benefit system is generous and the legal period for entitlement to unemployment benefits used to be very long (until 1994) compared with other industrial countries, if not practically unlimited (Albæk, Van Audenrode and Browning 1999). In other words, there has been a strong tradition of compensating for the labor market risks Danish citizens face by providing state support through fiscal transfers.

Until 1994, the Danish labor market policy had been to buffer individuals from the material component of unemployment. However, that involved a relatively passive employment strategy, which was abandoned in reforms introduced in 1994 (Westergaard-Nielsen 2001). The main components of the new employment policies include early 'activation' of the unemployed, increasing the quality of such 'activation' measures and tightening the conditions for obtaining unemployment benefits (Grunow and Leth-Sørensen 2006; Westergaard-Nielsen 2001).

Prior to this, a set of paid leave arrangements (PLAs), financially supported by the state, had been enacted starting with a pilot scheme in 1992, permitting a leave period of up to one year, and including a job guarantee for employed leave-takers. The PLAs gave employees the option to go on an education leave, a sabbatical leave or, for parents, an additional childcare leave (Madsen 1999). The intention was to enable more flexible transitions between work, education, family care and leisure time for both the employed and the unemployed. In this sense, PLAs increase work-time flexibility over the individual life cycle (Madsen 1999). As extended leave possibilities create temporary vacancies on the job market, these positions can be taken up by unemployed persons for a time, and they might thereby have better chances of finding a permanent job afterwards (Madsen 1999).

Although PLAs were open to both men and women, the share of women taking these leaves has been disproportionately high (Figure 6.1), an unintended effect (Madsen 1999). However, as Danish family norms still regard women as the primary caregivers (and therefore as the secondary breadwinners), and as men's jobs on average command higher pay, and because men have better career prospects than women, the gender difference in PLA participation is less startling.

Thus it is unsurprising that gender differences were exceptionally large (90 percent women) with regard to taking additional childcare leave. For various reasons, including lack of childcare options and an expansion in coverage and compensation for such leaves, the number of women going on leave rose dramatically after 1994, even resulting in employment bottlenecks in some female-dominated jobs (Pylkkänen and Smith 2003). Subsequent reforms reduced these numbers again, and in 2002 the additional childcare leave was finally abolished (Pylkkänen and Smith 2003).

The 'Danish employment miracle' after 1994 attracted international attention, since the pattern of high unemployment that had held since the mid-1970s was broken, with unemployment dropping relatively quickly from

12 percent (1993) to 5.5 percent (1999) (Westergaard-Nielsen 2001). It was not just state policies such as the 1994 labor force 'activation' or changes in leave policies that occurred in this period, but also expanded production in the private sector as well as increased private consumption that resulted in the recovery of the Danish economy, reflected in the yearly 2 to 3 percent increase in GDP after 1994 (Danmarks Statistik 2001). Because political and market changes occurred in the same period, however, it is hard to disentangle the policy effects on reduced unemployment from the effects of the economic upswing. The role of women, as they took an increased number of childcare leaves after 1994, is particularly unclear.

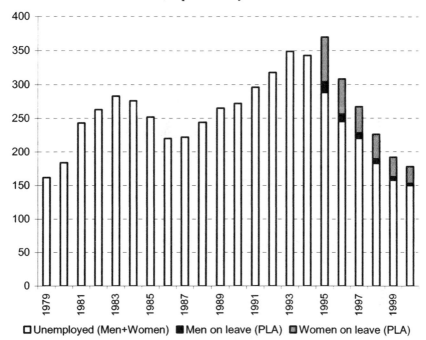

□ Unemployed (Men+Women)   ■ Men on leave (PLA)   ▨ Women on leave (PLA)

Note: No information on participation in paid leave arrangements is available prior to 1995

Source: StatBank Denmark (2004)

Figure 6.1   *Development in Danish women's and men's unemployment and participation in paid leave arrangements across the 1980s and 1990s (in thousands)*

HYPOTHESES

Institutional and economic changes

Increasing career interruptions for women in the 1990s?
Given the Danish framework of (a) strong normative support and actual demand for female employment, (b) living costs assuming two breadwinners and separate spousal taxation, (c) a combination of intermediate-term maternity and parental leave mandates with good (yet not sufficient) availability of childcare and (d) a high proportion of women working in a sector that offered particularly favorable conditions for combining wage work and family work, women and mothers had strong incentives for being continuously employed, even during the care-intensive family phase. However, in the early 1990s, a series of measures were introduced that made it suddenly attractive to leave the job temporarily, at least in a physical sense. Therefore, we assume an increase in women's temporary career interruptions (labor market exits) in the 1990s relative to the early 1980s, when the option to take care leave was not as generous or institutionally supported. The likelihood of exit should be higher particularly from 1994 to 1996, when legal incentives to take childcare leave were especially strong.

A weakened labor market position for women, despite the economic upswing?
Globalization theorists have argued that it is especially women and mothers who face severe disadvantages in the labor market in times of rising flexibilization pressures and threat of unemployment (cf. Beck 1986, pp. 129, 145ff). In fact, the rising trend in female employment came to an end by the early 1990s, at a time of high unemployment, a relative shortage in public childcare places and the invention of PLAs. Madsen (1999, pp. 61ff) believes the introduction of PLAs might have weakened women's position on the labor market, given both the critical attitude of employers toward PLAs and the high proportion of women who took advantage of this new opportunity. However, negative effects may have been negated by the economic upswing after 1994, inasmuch as the overall labor market conditions improved.

Against this background, it is hard to predict the labor market outcomes in terms of job mobility, unemployment risk and re-employment chances for women in the 1990s. The empirical question is whether the career dynamics of mid-career women in the 1990s are indeed different than in the 1980s, and if they are, do the observed differences indicate a weakening of women's labor market position?

The impact of individual characteristics on women's careers
While political and economic changes might be important in externally framing women's career chances and choices, individual factors such as

qualifications, family situation and current position in the labor market play a crucial role as well, and might account for considerable variation among the cohorts being studied.

Does family context matter, and does it matter more in the 1990s?
Women's work-life balance decisions are particularly tied to the life courses of their partners and children (Blossfeld and Drobnič 2001; Moen 2003). However, labor force exits in favor of 'full-time' childcare used to be the exception among Danish mothers in the 1980s. Given the availability of additional phases of paid leave, exiting might have become more likely during the 1990s, particularly among those women whose income is not essential for supporting the family, that is, for women with a breadwinning partner or spouse. Still, with the new possibility of temporary career interruptions in the framework of the 1990s PLAs, taking additional leaves might have become a feasible (and affordable) option for most women owing to financial compensation. Against this background, we control for family context variables in an effort to determine whether the relevance of family context for women's labor market attachment changed in the 1990s as compared with the 1980s.

Does educational attainment alter women's career choices and employment chances, despite family events, policy changes and economic cycle?
Education is known to be a strong predictor for women's labor market chances. It is reasonable to assume that high levels of education increase the opportunity costs of labor force exits, owing to either temporary earnings losses during the time spent out of the labor force or because of uncertain career prospects after returning to the labor market. Highly educated women thus should be less likely to interrupt employment, as compared with less well educated women. Such differences in women's labor market attachment should be especially evident in the 1990s, when the enactment of PLAs provided Danish employees with new – however temporary – alternate roles outside of paid employment.

Human capital theory argues that individual skills determine the productivity of a person and thus their market chances. Moreover, it has been argued that globalization leads to a skill-biased demand for labor (Castells 2000), with skilled employees becoming more desirable on the job market as knowledge intensity and the task complexity of jobs increase. Highly educated employees, with greater skills, should thus face a lower unemployment risk and better career chances (upward moves) than those with lower skill levels.

At the same time, it is reasonable to assume that unskilled women should be especially concerned by the ups and downs of the Danish labor market and economy during the 1980s and 1990s, as labor market turbulence can imply higher job-to-job mobility, income loss due to downward job mobility and unemployment risk (Grunow and Leth-Sørensen 2006). Unskilled workers can more easily be hired and fired because their jobs usually require little knowledge and training of a specific person. Employers in the Danish setting might also see layoffs as an easy and inexpensive way of adjusting to market changes (numerical flexibility). However, aside from moving into un-employment, unskilled women have the alternative of (temporarily) leaving the labor force, even more so since 1992. It is an empirical question whether and how unskilled women's patterns of career interruptions have changed during the 1990s.

DATA AND METHODS

The hypotheses presented above are tested using a sub-sample of Danish women from the IDA database (Integrated Database for Labor Market Research, for which see Leth-Sørensen 1997). This register-based data set allows one to follow persons as well as workplaces over time. The information is collected each November on a yearly basis, beginning in 1980.[1]

The women selected for this analysis were divided into two large birth cohorts, in order to be compared across time, the 1980s against the 1990s. Both decades were marked by a phase of economic upswing, and by a phase of recession. However, the 'Danish employment miracle' occurred during the 1990s, and it was also a phase when the continuity of women's employment careers, long taken for granted in Denmark, was put into question through the introduction of PLAs.

For those women born between 1949 and 1958 (the earlier cohort), the observation window opens in 1980 and closes in 1989, while the later cohort contains women born between 1959 and 1968, with the observation window from 1990 to 1999. Both cohorts have the same age ranges (22 to 31 at the beginning, 32 to 41 at the end) for the respective decade under observation, and were selected because it is in this mid-career phase that most women have already entered the labor market. These are also the ages in which career chances interact with family formation, making women more susceptible to labor market and family policy changes.

Owing to data limitation, jobs, unemployment spells or phases out of the labor force that started before 1981 (for the earlier cohort) or 1991 (for the later cohort) were excluded from the analyses. We therefore accept a selection bias: by excluding spells in progress at the starting of the observation windows, we exclude the most stable persons who do not move to another firm, exit the labor force or become unemployed at all.

We investigate how women in both cohorts might be affected by transitions out of the labor force (this transition as defined here includes all moves into PLAs), upward and downward mobility (significant gains and losses in salary in connection with a change of employer), entry into unemployment, chances of exiting unemployment and the likelihood of re-entering a job after a phase spent out of the labor force or in paid leave.

All effects are calculated using discrete time logistic regression models (Allison 1982), and we focus only on dependent workers. For the first four transitions noted, the underlying time axis is 'time spent within the same establishment or firm,' for the chance of exiting unemployment, it is 'time spent in registered unemployment,' while for the last transition it is 'time spent neither in a job, nor in registered unemployment,' including phases of paid leave from employment in the 1990s (PLAs). [2]

We study upward and downward mobility in terms of increase or decrease in deflated wages (measured by approximate gross wages, and based on the taxes paid). An upward move is defined as having achieved a new job that brings about a 10 percent increase in pay, compared with the position held before. Downward mobility is associated with a new position that entails a 5 percent decrease in wages. [3]

In each of the two observation windows we control for personal characteristics including the highest level of education (time-varying), labor force experience in years, squared labor force experience, number of previous unemployment spells, unemployment status in the previous year, number of previous jobs and firm tenure (time-varying). We also control for women's family characteristics, the number of children (time-varying), age of youngest child (time-varying) and the partner's characteristics (time-varying, with dummy variables for partners with high earnings – highest wage quartile for male full-time employees, partners with medium or low earnings – lower three wage quartiles for male full-time employees, and no partner). Job characteristics, such as wage level (high/medium/low), full-time v. part-time employment (job with greater or equal/less than 30 hours/week), industrial sector (public v. private sector) and establishment size (dummies for one to ten, 11 to 50, 51 to 500 and >500 employees) are also included.

To capture changes in the economic and labor market situation, we include time-trend dummies, when we expect a non-monotonic effect of time. Thus, the time dummies for the earlier cohort distinguish between 1980 to 1983, 1984 to 1986 (the end of the first economic upswing, when the overall employment situation was good and unemployment started to decline) and 1987 to 1989 (when GDP dropped from 4 to 0 percent, where it remained until 1993). For the later cohort, the 1990 to 1993 dummy captures the second half of this low GDP economic phase. The second and third time-trend dummies cover 1994 to 1996 (the second economic upswing and the beginning of decreasing unemployment, as well as the introduction of the new employment policy measures) and 1997 to 1999. For the transition out of unemployment we use a metric variable for the time trend and include an extra dummy to flag the time period prior to the 1994 changes in legislation and economic upswing.

RESULTS

In this section we present the results of our logistic regression model estimations. Our description first compares cohorts of mid-career women in the 1980s (cohort 1949 to 1958) and 1990s (cohort 1959 to 1968) with respect to labor force exits, transitions to unemployment and job mobility (Table 6.1). In line with our hypotheses, special attention is paid to the impact on these transitions of having children, as well as the impact of women's educational levels. The other independent variables work as controls. Subsequent to the direct cohort comparison, we report the results of selected cohort-specific models on women's transitions from employment to out of labor force status, and from job to unemployment; these indicate changes in the impact of explanatory variables across cohorts (Table 6.2). Findings on cohort differences for women's re-entry into employment from non-labor market participation and from unemployment are presented in Table 6.3.

Labor force exits and transitions to unemployment across cohorts

The first column in Table 6.1 addresses the question of women's response to the 1990s policy changes. As hypothesized, members of the later cohort have a much higher likelihood of exiting the labor force (b = 1.09**) than to members of the earlier cohort. Further analyses (not reported here) have confirmed that the finding is robust for various model specifications. Strong cohort discrepancy – with a reverse sign – can also be observed with regard to the transition to unemployment (column 2). Here our findings indicate that the later cohort is less likely (b = −0.50**) to become unemployed than the earlier cohort.

Both transitions, labor force exits and entries into unemployment, are most likely to occur for women with small children below age three, and for the lowest educational group of women with lower secondary education without vocational training. High educational qualifications, namely a college or university degree or long vocational education, is by contrast the most powerful predictor, aside from firm tenure, for staying in a job. An increasing number of children in the household has a negative impact on women's labor force exits and transition to unemployment. However, for labor force exits the effect is not statistically significant. Career characteristics are used as controls and operate in expected directions.

It is interesting how similarly very high and very low educational skills as well as the presence of small children affect both transitions out of employment for Danish women. The finding that having small children increases the likelihood to become unemployed is especially startling since parental leave mandates include a job guarantee, and childcare facilities for

Table 6.1 Cohort comparison of Danish women's transitions from employment to out of labor force and to unemployment and upward and downward mobility chances in the 1980s (birth cohorts 1949–58) and 1990s (birth cohorts 1959–68), common models for both cohorts

	Job to out of labor force	Job to un-employment	Upward mobility	Downward mobility
Constant	−2.36**	−1.47**	−1.33**	−2.67**
Birth cohort				
1949–58 (ref.)				
1959–68	1.09**	−0.50**	−0.06	−0.20**
Family characteristics				
Number of children	−0.02	−0.10**	−0.04	−0.01
No child (ref.)				
Youngest child 0–2	0.45**	0.49**	−0.18**	0.03
Youngest child 3–6	0.11	0.08	−0.12	−0.09
Youngest child 7–17	−0.14	−0.05	−0.13*	−0.19**
Job/employment history				
LF experience	−0.21**	−0.10**	−0.01	−0.08**
LF experience squared	0.00**	−0.00**	−0.00*	−0.00
No. of previous jobs	0.03	−0.07**	0.18**	0.09**
No. of prev. unempl. episodes	0.15**	0.42**	0.00	0.06*
Firm tenure two years or more	−1.11**	−1.90**	−1.66**	−1.70**
Education				
Lower secondary education without occ. training	0.21**	0.41**	−0.07	0.03
Upper secondary education without occ. training	0.12	−0.35**	0.38**	−0.03
Lower secondary education with short occ. training (ref.)				
Lower secondary education with middle occ. training	−0.34**	−0.84**	0.20**	−0.14**
College/university degree/ long voc. training	−0.99**	−1.15**	0.89**	−0.73**
Wage (deflated)				
Low wage (ref.)				
Medium wage	−0.45**	0.28**	−1.35**	0.94**
High wage	−0.40**	0.12	−2.07**	1.86**
No. of person year observations	67 204	67 204	67 204	67 204
No. of events	2 987	4 182	4 979	4 769
−2*diff (logL)	3 989.36	7 994.03	6 999.11	5 482.48

Note: Discrete-time logistic regression models. Statistical significance: * $\alpha \leq 0.05$, ** $\alpha \leq 0.01$

Source: Calculations based on female random sample of IDA database 1980–99

the very young are widespread and widely used in Denmark. We guess that shortage of childcare facilities and associated queue-lists for childcare places are part of the explanation, insofar as entering into unemployment enables a mother to take care of her child herself while receiving financial transfers (unemployment benefits). Another interesting finding is that women with low earnings more often experience labor force exits, while women with medium wages instead enter into unemployment. Given the generous Danish social security system and the high replacement rates for those who become unemployed, unemployment might not necessarily be perceived as a blow by every woman, and perhaps be even less so by those who are the primary caregivers for small children.

Upward and downward mobility across cohorts

In Table 6.1 columns 3 and 4, we find the later cohort is as upwardly mobile as, but less downwardly mobile than, the earlier cohort. Job moves that entail substantial gains or losses in earnings have not become more frequent for mid-career women in the 1990s than they were for comparable women in the 1980s. All kinds of mobility, including lateral moves, have not become more likely for the later cohort, additional analyses show, or put differently, the later cohort does not seem to enjoy a lower job stability than does the earlier cohort.

Hence, we find no support for Madsen's (1999) conjecture of a weakening of women's labor market position, either for women's job mobility or when considering women's unemployment risk. Even granting that the high proportion of women claiming paid leave in the 1990s entailed negative labor market consequences for the younger cohort in general, these were obviously cancelled out by the positive labor market effects associated with the economic upswing after 1994.

We now turn to the issue of family cycle impacts on women's upward career chances and downward mobility. Mothers have a lower likelihood of being upwardly mobile than women without childcare responsibilities. Not surprisingly, upward career chances are considerably lower when having a baby or toddler at home. Mothers of schoolchildren are both, less upwardly and less downwardly mobile, indicating a higher job stability and firm attachment for this group.

High educational level is a powerful predictor for both types of directional mobility and, in line with the expectations raised by human capital theory, upward career chances are highest for women with college or university degrees and for those with long vocational education (b = 0.89**). This group of highly educated women is at the same time sheltered best from downward mobility, compared with all other educational groups.

Mid-career women's labor force exits and moves into unemployment during the 1980s and 1990s

We analyzed job exits for the two cohorts separately (Table 6.2). The findings for the earlier cohort reflect 1980s career patterns, at a time when women's labor force participation rates were already high, labor force exits were rare and there was little institutional support for them. Job exit findings for the later cohort result from 1990s transitions, when labor market conditions changed considerably, and when temporary job interruptions were institutionally favored through the PLAs.

From Table 6.1 we know that the later cohort of women have a significantly higher likelihood of exiting the labor force, as defined here, than does the earlier cohort, lending support to our argument of women's strong response to the 1990s policy changes and introduction of the PLAs. Table 6.2 provides additional information in line with our hypothesis that women's job interruptions were especially pronounced from 1994 to 1996, when the childcare leave policy was especially generous.

Family context impacted differently on women's careers in the 1980s and 1990s: in contrast to the earlier cohort, where the presence of children seems to have no effect, mothers with preschool children in the younger cohort have a significantly higher likelihood to exit their job. We included information on women's partners to establish whether women's leaves are associated with having a male breadwinner at home capable of supporting the household on his earnings alone. Our findings indicate that the presence of a partner has a negative influence on women's labor force exits in the earlier cohort, regardless of his absolute contribution to the household income. There is no such effect for the later cohort. However, analyses that exclusively focus on women's transition from job to paid leave in the 1990s show that the presence of a partner has a significant positive effect on women's paid leave participation, regardless of his earnings (Grunow 2006).

Education, in contrast, has remained an important factor influencing women's labor market attachment. The findings indicate that labor force exits in both cohorts are highly stratified according to women's educational attainments and vocational qualifications. As hypothesized, labor force attachment is considerably higher among the highly educated, while the less highly educated groups are more likely to exit the labor force. However, in the earlier cohort labor force exits are especially pronounced for women who have completed high school but lack further occupational qualifications (b = 0.55**), while in the later cohort, we find no significant differences among women with medium and low educational resources.

Table 6.2   *Danish women's transitions from employment to out of labor force and to unemployment in the 1980s (birth cohort 1949–58) and 1990s (birth cohort 1959–68)*

	Job to out of labor force		Job to unemployment	
	Birth cohort 1949–58	Birth cohort 1959–68	Birth cohort 1949–58	Birth cohort 1959–68
Constant	−2.55**	−2.08**	−1.15**	−0.41**
Time trend (for each cohort resp.)				
1980–83 (ref.) 1990–93 (ref.)				
1984–86 1994–96	0.06	0.13*	−0.35**	−0.53**
1987–89 1997–99	0.01	−0.45**	−0.45**	−1.25**
Family characteristics				
Number of children	−0.07	−0.01	−0.03	−0.04
No child (ref.)				
Youngest child 0–2	0.20	0.62**	0.48**	0.39**
Youngest child 3–6	−0.06	0.25**	0.00	0.13
Youngest child 7–17	−0.08	−0.13	−0.09	0.02
No partner in household (ref.)				
Partner with med./low earnings	−0.58**	−0.02		
Partner with high earnings	−0.37**	−0.03		
Job/employment history				
LF experience	−0.19**	−0.15**	−0.11**	−0.26**
LF experience squared	0.00	0.00	−0.00	0.00**
No. of previous jobs	0.07	0.02	0.06*	−0.07*
No. of prev. unempl. episodes	0.46**	0.18**	0.74**	0.37**
Unemployed in the prev. year	0.30	0.16	0.82**	0.44**
Firm tenure two years or more	−1.51**	−0.95**	−1.76**	−1.49**
Education				
Lower secondary education without occ. training	0.47**	0.10	0.48**	0.24**
Upper secondary education without occ. training	0.55**	−0.08	−0.24*	−0.35**
Lower secondary education with short occ. training (ref.)				
Lower secondary education with middle occ. training	−0.37*	−0.35**	−0.79**	−0.97**
College/university degree/long voc. training	−0.61*	−0.96**	−1.56**	−1.05**
Wage (deflated)				
Low wage (ref.)				
Medium wage			0.20**	0.19**
High wage			−0.01	0.11

Table 6.2 continued

Establishment size				
1–10 (ref.)				
11–50	−0.01	−0.06	−0.18*	−0.13
51–500	0.06	−0.06	−0.22**	−0.19*
500+	0.04	−0.06	−0.39**	−0.44**
Sector of employment				
Private sector (ref.)				
Public sector	−0.06	0.32**	0.14**	−0.34**
Hours worked				
Full-time (ref.)				
Part-time	0.77**	0.67**	−0.77**	−0.71**
Birth cohort increments (resp.)				
Born 1949–53 (ref.) 1959–63 (ref.)				
Born 1954–58 1964–68	−0.05	−0.07	−0.25**	−0.31**
No. of person year observations	32 645	34 559	32 645	34 559
No. of events	843	2 144	2 453	1 729
−2*diff (logL)	1 602.68	2 259.97	4 709.04	4 103.51

Notes: Discrete-time logistic regression models
　　　　Statistical significance: * $\alpha \leq 0.05$, ** $\alpha \leq 0.01$

Source: Calculations based on female random sample of IDA database 1980–99

Furthermore, the decision to exit the labor force seems to depend on the hours worked. Interestingly, the likelihood of exit is higher among those women who work on a part-time basis. Either these women are less interested in (and/or less dependent on) working for pay, or they still face severe problems in managing to balance work with family care, since part-time jobs may be as long as 29 hours per week. Analyses that exclusively focus on transitions to paid leave in the 1990s, however, indicate that part-time employed women are less likely to interupt (Grunow 2006).

We control for establishment size and employment sector, assuming that the organizational requirements for organizing and enabling temporary job exits, anticipated by the introduction of PLAs, might be more easily (and willingly) fulfilled by larger firms with larger internal labor markets as well as by public sector institutions, with their longer traditions of providing conditions permitting a balance between work and life that favors their employees. Establishment size turns out to be irrelevant, but working in the public sector mattered in the 1990s: among the members of the later cohort, public sector employees had a significantly higher likelihood of exiting the labor force (b = 0.32**) than did private sector employees.

As with the transition out of the labor force, the results of cohort-specific models for the transition to unemployment largely confirm robustness of the findings from Table 6.1. Unemployment risk has significantly decreased across cohorts, and the time-trend dummies in the Table 6.2 models show that for each individual cohort, unemployment has been decreasing over time.

For both cohorts transitions to unemployment are more likely when small children are present.

As hypothesized, educational differences influence women's unemployment risk in both cohorts. Establishment size has a negative effect on the transition to unemployment, indicating that women's individual unemployment risk is considerably higher in smaller firms. Unlike the transition out of the labor force, being part-time employed *de*creases women's likelihood of becoming unemployed in both cohorts.

The most interesting finding in Table 6.2 is the switch in sign for public sector employment. During the 1980s, female public sector employees were significantly more likely to enter unemployment, as compared with private sector employees (b = 0.14**), and this finding is robust, although startling. For the 1990s, the situation is reversed, with public sector employees significantly *less* likely to enter unemployment (b = −0.34**), despite the general improvement and increase in private sector employment during this decade. It is interesting to note that the decrease in women's unemployment risk in the public sector is paralleled by a significant increase in female public sector employee transition out of the labor force and into unpaid caregiving in the 1990s.

Women's re-employment chances

Table 6.3 presents the findings for re-entry into paid employment from being out of the labor force (or in paid leave) and from unemployment.

Not surprisingly, re-entry into a job, either from being out of the labor force or from unemployment is most likely to occur within one year of observed non-employment. For women on paid leave, the time spent out of the labor force is legally defined (with a maximum leave period of one year) and normally ends by re-entering the job held before the woman went on leave (PLA). Re-entries from unemployment are concentrated in the first year of observed unemployment, probably because the Danish labor market is open and highly flexible. In addition, longer phases of non-employment are often associated with loss of human capital, so potential employers usually prefer not to hire the long-term unemployed.

Cohort differences are pronounced for both dependent processes. However, we do not interpret this coefficient for the transition from being out of the labor force, owing to the – institutionally fostered – heterogeneity between

Table 6.3 Danish women's transitions from out of labor force and from unemployment back to paid employment in the 1980s (birth cohort 1949–58) and 1990s (birth cohort 1959–68)

	Out of labor force to job[a]	Unemployment to job[a]	Unemployment to job[a]
	Both birth cohorts	Both birth cohorts	Birth cohort 1959–68
Constant	−0.68**	−0.18**	2.70**
Time trend			
General time trend			−0.18**
Previous to 1994			−0.69**
Duration			
< 1 year (ref.)			
≥ 1 year, < 2 years	−1.46**	−0.71**	−0.85**
≥ 2 years, < 3 years	−2.12**	−1.55**	−1.38**
≥ 3 years	−3.17**	−2.16**	−1.84**
Birth cohort			
1949–58 (ref.)			
1959–68	0.18**	−0.33**	
Family characteristics			
Number of children	−0.08**	0.01	0.02
No child (ref.)			
Youngest child 0–2	0.21*	−0.15*	−0.17*
Youngest child 3–6	0.30**	−0.15*	−0.16
Youngest child 7–17	0.19*	−0.11	−0.03
No partner in houshold (ref.)			
Partn.with med./low earnings	0.34**	0.18**	0.18**
Partn. with high earnings	0.40**	0.27**	0.29**
Education			
Lower secondary education without occ. training	−0.42**	−0.28**	−0.41**
Upper secondary education without occ. training	0.10	−0.13	−0.04
Lower secondary education with short occ. training (ref.)			
Lower secondary education with middle occ. training	0.35**	0.25**	0.24*
College/university degree/ long voc. training	0.17	0.42**	0.41**
No. of person year observations	11 118	10 839	5 422
No. of events	3 657	4 530	2 045
−2*diff (logL)	4 536.14	1 925.06	795.98

Notes: Discrete-time logistic regression models. * $\alpha \leq 0.05$, ** $\alpha \leq 0.01$
[a] Columns 1 and 2 are common models for both cohorts; column 3 models re-entry into paid employment from unemployment separately for birth cohort 1959–68

Source: Calculations based on female random sample of IDA database 1980–99

the two female cohorts at risk of making this transition. Interestingly, for the transition from unemployment, we find the later cohort is significantly less likely to re-enter than is the earlier cohort. Members of the later cohort were observed during a period initially marked by high unemployment rates, and later by a strong decline in unemployment, but that decline is not reflected in the cohort comparative model. Thus, the earlier cohort of 1980s mid-career women was in general more likely to re-enter. The finding probably reflects unobserved heterogeneity among our 'at risk' samples in the 1980s and 1990s. It could be speculated that a similar group of women who opted for paid leave in the 1990s might have entered into temporary unemployment in the 1980s, owing to lack of alternatives.

We ran a separate unemployment exit model for the later cohort, to examine the relative changes for the period of economic upswing and enactment of activation measures. The findings shown in column 3 indicate that women's chances to exit unemployment have changed from 1994 onwards. However, as further analyses have shown, the coefficient is only significant in a model that controls simultaneously for the general time trend throughout the 1990s.

Educational characteristics influence both processes, with low-skilled women being least likely to move back into paid employment, and more highly educated women more likely to do so. However, while the re-entry chances from unemployment are highest for women with college or university degrees, or with long vocational education, transitions from being out of the labor force and into employment are more pronounced for the second-highest group in our sample, that is, women with lower secondary education and middle occupational training. Given that women with college or university degrees or with long vocational education are least likely to exit employment altogether, the highly educated women at risk of re-entering employment after a phase out of labor force are a selective group.

Having (small) children has a positive effect on women re-entering paid employment after a phase spent out of the labor force, probably because many of the re-entries are from child-minding leave and follow the PLA regulations, independent of other factors, but leaving unemployment seems to be less likely when preschool children are at home. Having a partner has a positive effect on women's re-entry into a job, regardless of that partner's income or ability to support the family on his earnings alone. Having a partner means sharing work and family responsibilities (to varying degrees), so cohabiting and married women might be more flexible in balancing the responsibilities, and are therefore more competitive on the labor market, as compared with women without a partner to support them at home.

DISCUSSION AND CONCLUSIONS

The aim of this chapter was to study patterns of Danish mid-career women's labor market transitions in the late twentieth century, the time period that is often associated with accelerating labor market pressures, flexibilization demands and individualization of market risks in a 'globalizing' economy (for example Beck 1986; Beck and Beck-Gernsheim 1994; Castells 2000).

We have argued, and our analyses have confirmed, that applying these hypotheses to the Danish case is made problematic by the fact that labor market flexibility and trade openness have always been high in this country. The current economic developments point to an improvement in the overall employment conditions for Danish women and, most notably, to a declining unemployment risk. We find that female mid-career employees in the 1990s are less likely to become unemployed or to move to another firm, compared with mid-career women in the 1980s. In other words, our findings indicate that women's employment careers have not become more unstable in the 1990s, nor do they have a higher risk of being downwardly mobile.

However, prior to the economic upswing of the mid-1990s, labor market conditions had been tightening, with a doggedly persistent, relatively high level of unemployment. Our study of Danish women's changing career patterns over the past two decades makes a strong case for the argument that mid-career women were indeed facing changing employment conditions. Yet this was not so much a result of globalization pressures that were increasing labor market insecurity and the threat of unemployment (Beck 1986, pp. 129, 145ff) but, rather, through institutional changes domestically that suddenly opened new options and incentives for temporary job interruptions in the 1990s.

Women clearly responded to these policy changes. We find a significant increase in mid-career women's likelihood of career interruptions in the 1990s, and especially high exit rates for the short period when paid parental leave options were especially generous. Prior to the invention of such paid leave arrangements, women's non-labor force participation had been an exception, even during the care-intensive family phase, and the institutional framework had widely promoted and encouraged women's continuous employment.

Whether to interpret the option of extended leave phases as a new and desirable level of employment flexibility in women's life courses, or as a backlash or threat to women's labor market success, depends on one's viewpoint. At least in terms of Madsen's argument that women's labor market position might have weakened, our evidence is mixed. On the one hand, our findings indicate that women's jobs have not become more unstable, but rather more secure in the 1990s than in the 1980s. On the other hand, women's likelihood of exiting unemployment has decreased for the 1990s cohort.

It is also important to note that women's education and motherhood strongly affect their employment transitions, and in the expected ways. Highly educated women, especially those with college or university degrees, as well as those with long vocational training, have a stronger job and labor market attachment, better upward career chances and a lower downward mobility risk, than do those in the medium and lower educational groups. Unskilled women face the worst career chances with regard to these transitions, and their likelihood of becoming unemployed or of exiting the labor force is highest relative to all other skill groups. Having to care for small children also significantly increases women's unemployment risk (despite legal job protection measures for the early phases of motherhood!), and it seems that the likelihood of exiting a job for childcare reasons has become stronger in the 1990s as compared with the 1980s.

NOTES

1   We have no information on women's job histories before November 1980, except for an approximate measure of the cumulated labor force experience (EXPATP), which was constructed by Niels Westergaard-Nielsen and the Center for Corporate Performance (CCP) at the Aarhus School of Business. The authors would like to thank Niels Westergaard-Nielsen and the CCP for making this information available.

2   Employees on paid leave actually do not 'exit' their job in a legal sense. This includes that leave-takers do not lose their firm tenure and that they return to their old job, for example. However, interrupting a job for paid leave means being absent from the workplace for a considerable time span. Therefore phases of paid leave work like labor force exits in the sense that they entail stagnation or decline in firm-specific human capital accumulation. Second, apart from maternity leave and the option to go on paid leave in the 1990s, Danish employees who intend to become a homemaker carry no financial or legal status for unpaid caregiving. They either become unemployed or exit the labor force. For this reason we technically define the 1990s entries into paid leave as (temporary) labor force exits, our indicator of unpaid caregiving, therefore accepting somewhat blurred findings. Notable differences from respective results for entry into and exits from paid leave are reported but not shown in the tables. Empirical findings for women's transition to paid leave are presented in Grunow (2006).

3   Our definitions of upward and downward mobility are arbitrary. However, further tests have shown that the effects for the independent variables remain stable even when using modified definitions of upward and downward mobility.

BIBLIOGRAPHY

Albæk, K., Van Audenrode, M. and Browning, M. (1999) *Employment protection and the consequences for displaced workers: a comparison of Belgium and Denmark*, University of Copenhagen: Institute of Economics.

Alewell, D. and Pull, K. (2001) 'An international comparison and assessment of maternity leave regulation', *Comparative Labor Law & Policy Journal*, 22(2/3): 297–326.

Allison, P.D. (1982) 'Discrete-time methods for the analysis of event histories', in S. Leinhardt (ed.) *Sociological methodology*, San Francisco, CA: Jossey-Bass.

Beck, U. (1986) *Risikogesellschaft: Auf dem Weg in eine andere Moderne*, Frankfurt/Main: Suhrkamp.

Beck, U. and Beck-Gernsheim, E. (1994) *Riskante Freiheiten: Individualisierung in modernen Gesellschaften*, Frankfurt/Main: Suhrkamp.

Blossfeld, H.-P. and Drobnič, S. (2001) *Careers of couples in contemporary societies: from male breadwinner to dual earner families*, Oxford: Oxford University Press.

Braun, T. (2003) 'Ein neues Modell für Flexicurity – der dänische Arbeitsmarkt', *WSI Mitteilungen*, 2(2003): 92–9.

Castells, M. (2000) *The rise of the network society*, Oxford and Malden, MO: Blackwell Publishers.

Christoffersen, N.M. (1993) *Familiens ændring – en statistisk belysning af familieforholdene*, Copenhagen: Danish National Institute of Social Research.

Danmarks Statistik (2001) *50-års oversigten*, Copenhagen: Statistics Denmark.

Danmarks Statistik (2002) *Nyt fra Danmarks Statistik*, no. 433, Copenhagen: Statistics Denmark.

Datta Gupta, N. and Smith, N. (2002) 'Children and career interuptions: the family gap in Denmark', *Economica*, 69: 609–629.

Datta Gupta, N., Oaxaca, R.L. and Smith, N. (1998) *Wage dispersion, public sector wages and the stagnating Danish gender wage gap*, Aarhus: Centre for Labour Market and Social Research.

Döhrn, R., Heilemann, U. and Schäfer, G. (1998) 'Ein dänisches "Beschäftigungs-wunder"?', *Mitteilungen aus der Arbeitsmarkt- und Berufsforschung*, 2/1998: 312–23.

Emmerich, K. and Werner, H. (1998) 'Dänemark: Erstaunlicher Umschwung am Arbeitsmarkt: Erfolge durch angebots- und nachfrageorientierte Strategien', *IAB Kurzbericht*, 13: 3–8.

Emmerich, K., Hoffman, E. and Walwei, U. (2000) 'Beschäftigung von Gering-qualifizierten in Dänemark', *IAB-Werkstattbericht*, 3: 1–17.

Esping-Andersen, G., Rohwer, G. and Leth-Sørensen, S. (1994) 'Institutions and occupational class mobility: scaling the skill barrier in the Danish labour market', *European Sociological Review*, 10/1998, 119–34.

European Commission (2002) 'Annex V – country studies: Denmark', in *The role of women in the fisheries sector. Study carried out on behalf of the European Commission*, Bruxelles: European Commission.

Grunow, D. (2006) *Convergence, persistence and diversity in male and female careers: does context matter in an era of globalization? A comparison of gendered employment mobility patterns in West Germany and Denmark*, Bamberg: Faculty of Social and Economic Sciences, Otto-Friedrich University.

Grunow, D. and Leth-Sørensen, S. (2006) 'Mobility of men in the Danish labor market', in H.-P. Blossfeld, M. Mills and F. Bernardi (eds) *Globalization, uncertainty, and men's careers: An international comparison*, Cheltenham, UK and Northampton, MA, USA: Edward Elgar.

Grunow, D., Hofmeister, H. and Buchholz, S. (2006) 'Late 20th century persistence and decline of the female homemaker in Germany and the United States', *International Sociology*, 21(1): 101–132.

Gustafsson, S., Kenjoh, E. and Wetzels, C. (2002) 'The role of education on postponement of maternity in Britain, Germany, the Netherlands and Sweden', in E. Ruspini and A. Dale (eds) *The gender dimension of social change: the contribution of dynamic research to the study of women's life courses*, Bristol: Policy Press.

Human Rights and Equal Opportunity Commission (2002) 'Valuing parenthood: options for paid maternity leave', Interim Report 2002, Sex Discrimination Unit, Sydney.

Leth-Sørensen, S. (1997) 'The IDA database: a longitudinal database of establishments and their employees', Danmarks Statistik: IDA Project.

Leth-Sørensen, S. and Rohwer, G. (1997) 'Women's employment and part-time work in Denmark', in H.-P. Blossfeld and C. Hakim, (eds), *Between equalization and marginalization: women working part-time in Europe and the United States of America*, Oxford: Oxford University Press.

Madsen, P.K. (1999) 'Denmark: flexibility, security and labour market success', paper for European Foundation for the Improvement of Living and Working Conditions, University of Copenhagen.

Madsen, P.K. (2002) 'The Danish model of "Flexicurity" – a paradise with some snakes', Paper presented at the *European Foundation for the Improvement of Living and Working Conditions* meeting on 'Interactions between Labour Market and Social Protection', Brussels, 16 May 2002.

Mills, M., Blossfeld, H.-P. and Klijzing, E. (2005) 'Becoming an adult in uncertain times: a 14-country comparison of the losers of globalization', in H.-P. Blossfeld, E. Klijzing, M. Mills and K. Kurz (eds) *Globalization, uncertainty and youth in society*, London: Routledge.

Moen, P. (2003) 'Linked lives: dual careers, gender, and the contingent life course', in V.W. Marshall (ed.) *Social dynamics of the life course: transitions, institutions, and interrelations*, New York: Aldine de Gruyter.

Munk, M.D. (2001) 'The same old story? Reconversions of educational capital in the welfare state', in A. Bolder, W.R. Heinz and G. Kutscha (eds), *Deregulierung der Arbeit – Pluralisierung der Bildung? Jahrbuch Bildung und Arbeit 1999/2000*, Opladen: Leske + Budrich.

Naur, M. and Smith, N. (1996) *Cohort effects on the gender wage gap in Denmark*, Aarhus: Centre for Labour Market and Social Research.

Oppenheimer, V.K., Blossfeld, H.-P. and Wackerow, J. (1995) 'United States of America: new developments in family formation and women's improvement in educational attainment', in H.-P. Blossfeld (ed.) *The new role of women: family formation in modern societies*, Boulder, CO: Westview Press.

Pedersen, L. and Deding, M. (2000) *Lønforskelle mellem kvinder og mænd i Danmark*, Copenhagen: National Institute of Social Research.

Pylkkänen, E. and Smith, N. (2003) 'Career interruptions due to parental leave: a comparative study of Denmark and Sweden', OECD Social, Employment and Migration Working Papers, Paris.

Rostgaard, T. and Friedberg, T. (1998) *Caring for children and older people: a comparison of European policies and practices*, Copenhagen: Danish National Institute of Social Research.

StatBank Denmark (2004) www.statistikbanken.dk.

Waldfogel, J. (1998) 'The family gap for young women in the United States and Britain: can maternity leave make a difference?', *Journal of Labor Economics*, 16: 505–45.

Werner, H. (1998) 'Beschäftigungspolitisch erfolgreiche Länder: Was steckt dahinter?', *Mitteilungen aus der Arbeitsmarkt- und Berufsforschung*, 31(2): 324–33.

Westergaard-Nielsen, N. (2001) *Danish labour market policy: is it worth it?*, Aarhus: Aarhus School of Business, Centre for Labour Market and Social Research.

PART IV

Country-specific contributions on
post-socialist welfare regimes

7. Women's career mobility in Hungary

Erzsébet Bukodi and Péter Róbert

INTRODUCTION

Hungary is one of the countries that experienced transformation away from a socialist regime type in the 1990s. Individuals were hit by the transition away from socialism at different points of their employment careers, but the overall effect on mobility in Hungarian society was a strengthened relationship between social origins and occupational class position in the last decade of the twentieth century (Róbert and Bukodi 2004). The aim of this chapter is to investigate changes in women's employment opportunities caused by economic and social transformation as well as by worldwide globalization, and our questions include identifying the major factors that influence female career mobility and asking what the role of human capital investments or prior employment insecurities might be. We focus on the 1990s and employ the Household Panel Survey (1992 to 1997) conducted by the Tárki Social Research Center. We investigate upward and downward career mobility, measured by changes in job status, and the transition between labor market and other positions (unemployment, paid and unpaid caring activities).

There is a large body of literature (Beck 1992; Giddens 1999) that argues that globalization is the driving force behind increased risk and insecurity in the life course of individuals. However, other scholars emphasize the national path-dependence of this process (Blossfeld 2001). In this latter view, nation-specific institutional arrangements such as the educational system, the deregulation of the labor market or changing welfare state provisions may structure the impact globalization has on individual life chances. For Hungary, the recent transition may need to stand as a proxy for globalization effects (Róbert and Bukodi 2005). What is known about Hungarian career mobility, outside of its globalization context, is as follows.

A recent study investigated the occupational careers of Hungarian couples in the communist period, and its finding, that educational attainment was one of the strongest predictors of occupational success, provided strong support for human capital theory (Róbert and Bukodi 2002). In addition, life cycle and household characteristics influenced women's occupational careers more than men's, indicating that family attributes are key in analyzing Hungarian women's employment chances. Additional evidence points to the positive effect of a partner's assets on an individual's occupational success and failure. This suggests that the relatively traditional gender role attitudes coexist with the advantage during the socialist era to increase the pooled income potential of the family (Róbert and Bukodi 2002).

The study of couples, however, predates the collapse of socialism in Hungary. The following study of male employment mobility during the 1990s (Bukodi and Róbert 2006) confirmed the general view of Hungarians that more status loss than status gain occurred after the collapse of socialism. Some men faced increasing career insecurities, in particular the long-term unemployed who were unable to re-enter the labor market owing to a lack of appropriate educational resources, and those for whom recurrent unemployment became a frequent experience and who existed at the periphery of the labor market.

This chapter examines mobility under transformation for women. We first outline the possible driving forces influencing women's career mobility in Hungary, and we show the most influential economic and institutional factors that shape their employment over the life course. Then we predict the impact of these factors on women's career movements and we describe the measures and methods used in the analysis and then turn to a general description of career events in the 1990s. Estimates from event history analysis that predict the chance of different types of employment shifts are then presented, and the chapter ends with a discussion of the results.

DRIVING FORCES AND INSTITUTIONAL CONTEXT OF WOMEN'S EMPLOYMENT CAREERS

Investments in human capital

Changes in the nature of paid work and technological developments have a self-evident impact on employment structures and the type of labor required. To compete internationally, and to attain a high level of productivity, firms require highly skilled employees, and an increase in the demand for such highly skilled labor can be investigated from various perspectives.

One effect is that unemployment rates are higher, and have increased at a faster pace, for individuals with low-level education. Those without any qualifications are forced to face the negative consequences of structural changes in the labor market: the number of jobs for them has decreased, and the likelihood of becoming unemployed or inactive has increased (OECD 2000a). However, the relative labor market (dis)advantages connected to various qualification levels show significant differences between countries. A review of 14 countries conducted by the OECD's Education Committee in 1996 indicated that Hungary was one of four OECD countries where the gap between the highly educated and the poorly qualified was the greatest in terms of labor market outcomes (OECD 2000b, p. 34).

When we examine the specific educational context in Hungary, it is noteworthy that two basic features seem to have survived the transformation from the socialist system. The Hungarian system follows a German model, which means that education is still characterized by tracking (both a general and a vocational path) at both secondary and tertiary levels. Vocational training continues to play a dominating role and combines abstract knowledge with job-related skills and practical work experience, though there has been an increase in the proportion of individuals enrolling in general education.

In both principle and practice, this system provided a relatively smooth transition from school to paid work under the planned socialist economy. The highly standardized acquisition of qualification through recognized certificates served as a good indicator of skills and knowledge to employers about potential employees. Yet this advantage may turn out to be more of a disadvantage in the market system, as the close relationship between vocational certificate and occupational opportunity may result in a high degree of rigidity in labor market entry and may block other career opportunities.

Educational opportunity also expanded at secondary (particularly vocational) and tertiary (particularly college) levels in Hungary during the last decades of the twentieth century. This particularly benefited women, who have increasingly been acquiring higher skill levels, and it can be seen by the fact that the relative proportion of women without any qualification has been declining over time. At the same time, the proportion of graduates from lower secondary school with vocational training has also been rising. For women aged 25 to 64, the share of vocational secondary school graduates has increased from 5 percent in 1973 to 21 percent in 2000, and the proportion of women with a university or college degree has increased at a comparable rate, from 3 percent to 16 percent in the same time period. According to the 2001 census, the share of the employed with a tertiary school diploma was higher for women than men (20 v. 17 percent); women were also much more likely than men to be graduates of secondary schools (40 v. 27 percent).

In other words, in the last decades, and particularly during the 1990s, the pace of educational upgrading was higher for women than for men in Hungary. To some extent, this contradicts the predictions of family human capital theory, according to which women show different resource-investment behavior than men (Polachek 1981). Women, this argument posits, who are expecting marriage and childbearing, invest less in their education and skills, whereas men, whose 'task' is to maintain their (future) family, try to attain a higher level of education to be more successful in the labor market.

174   *Post-socialist welfare regimes*

Another aspect of human capital investment is in lifelong learning, namely, by participating in different forms of training after completing initial education. When compared with Western European countries, a much smaller share of Hungarians obtain some kind of skill outside of their initial education (OECD 1999). In part, this is a consequence of the nature of the Hungarian educational system that embeds vocational training in the curriculum. But a lack of further investment in training and knowledge may lead to higher unemployment risk and to a lower chance of getting a high-paying job.

According to time-use data, there was a slight increase in the last decade of the twentieth century in the proportion of individuals (aged 25 to 64) spending time studying, which indicates the growing importance of human capital investment in people's everyday lives. However, significant differences exist by employment status and initial educational attainment. In 2000, 3.3 percent of working people spent any time on studying on an average day, and those not employed are even less likely to invest in their training (only 1.2 percent) on an average day. Among women, and irrespective of their employment status, the incidence of studying is somewhat higher. Those with less initial education appear to lack incentives or opportunities to acquire more education in later life, which may increase their risk of labor market exclusion, and this problem is particularly relevant if they have only primary and basic vocational education: the proportion who spent any time on studying on an average day decreased between 1986 and 2000 for both sexes.

Previous research showed that educational attainment had a significant impact on individuals' employment careers in the socialist era, with women's educational levels significantly influencing the odds of choosing maternity leave or becoming housewives. A wife's human capital investment decreased the chance of exit from the labor force, and women with higher education levels were more likely to re-enter into employment – irrespective of the form of employment interruption (Róbert, Bukodi and Luijkx 2001). Qualification exerted a substantial effect on the odds of career improvement as well: well-educated couples had the best chances to climb up the occupational ladder and the lowest risk of losing their privileged positions (Róbert and Bukodi 2002).

In light of prior research, the role of human capital investments seemed to have become even more important after the end of socialist rule. For the non-employed in the 1990s, the chance of re-employment was much higher for the well-educated than for the poorly educated. The positive effects of qualifications on the likelihood of re-entry into the labor market appeared to be stronger for women than men. This is supported by the fact that in the last decade, women without any training had lower odds of finding a job after employment interruption than men (Köllő 2001).

Educational attainment proved salient for male occupational opportunities in the 1990s, especially when moves with status change were predicted (Bukodi and Róbert 2006). The chance of upward mobility and the risk of downward mobility are clearly influenced by different qualification levels. Those holding a university diploma have the highest chance of status gain and the lowest risk of status loss, while men with only compulsory schooling face the highest risk of downward mobility.

The amount of human capital influences the financial position of households or individuals through the employment opportunities it makes available, with education appearing to exert a large impact on the distribution of and the changes in income inequalities in Hungary. In 1987, according to a recent study, only 8 percent of total household income inequalities were explained by educational attainment of the head of the household; by 2001, this figure had risen to 27 percent (Tóth 2003). The biggest 'losers' of the last decade's transition were households headed by the poorly educated: their relative income position has declined the most. The 'winners' were young people with tertiary educations, whose relative income position improved substantially during the 1990s (Kertesi and Köllő 2002).

EMPLOYMENT PATTERNS

Employment, unemployment

The economically active population declined from 60 percent in 1992 to 52 percent in 1996, but it has increased slightly since. No gender difference was evident in this time period, though the share of the employed was always much lower among women than among men. The activity rate is lower for younger people, and their pace of temporal decrease was the largest, owing to both educational expansion and the growing difficulties concerning career entry (Róbert and Bukodi 2005).

Immediately after the system changed, the unemployment rate climbed to 12 percent, but it has been decreasing since 1993 and stood at 5.7 percent in 2001. In the early 1990s, the share of those unemployed for more than a year rapidly increased, but that came to a halt by 1996. However, the share of individuals excluded from the labor market was about 5 percent in the 15- to 74-year-old population, even in 2001 – among both women and men. In contrast to many developed countries, male unemployment in Hungary was always somewhat higher than female unemployment.

We also assume that many people leave unemployment only for short-term, insecure jobs, and then return to the unemployment rolls. Unemployment experience does influence the risk of labor market mobility, as it exerts a positive impact on downward moves along the occupational hierarchy (Bukodi and Róbert 2006). It implies that certain groups live on the periphery of the workforce who, after initial unemployment, can only find jobs at lower status than before upon re-entering the labor market. On the basis of this research, we argue that there is a certain proportion of the Hungarian population whose labor market position is particularly insecure: it comprises the long-term unemployed who are unable to re-enter the labor market owing to a lack of appropriate human resources and those who move between unemployment and low-status jobs.

Occupational structure, earnings differences

In the past, women were found in a narrow range of occupations, especially in routine clerical, unskilled and agricultural jobs. However, there has been a shift by women away from such jobs and into service or administrative jobs that require higher levels of qualification. Comparison of data from 1973 and 2000 shows a 22 percent increase in the proportion of women in professional and managerial occupations (EGP I-II), and a decrease from 55 to 30 percent in the proportion of women in unskilled jobs (EGP VII) during this same period. The proportion working in industrial jobs has also decreased.

In 2001, almost 75 percent of employed women worked in the service sector, especially governmental services (33 percent) and distributive services (sales, transport: 25 percent). Older women are overrepresented in semi-skilled or unskilled service occupations: among those aged 50 to 74 who are employed, 16 percent work in these kinds of jobs as compared with less than 5 percent in all younger age cohorts.

Taking a job reduces the likelihood of living in poverty. Though in the EU, one earner in the household is sufficient to reduce the poverty risk to below average; this is not the case in post-socialist countries. In transitional Central European societies, in households where the head is in paid employment, the risk of poverty is almost 80 percent of the average – compared with 69 percent in the EU (Klugman, Micklewright and Redmond 2002). This means that in transitional countries, employment does not help as much to pull people out of poverty, either because work is poorly paid, or there are not enough members of the household in paid employment, or both. Thus, the majority of women are forced to take a job (if they can), as the man's income alone is not enough to support a family. In addition, in the last decade there was a sharp increase in earning differences among those who have paid employment in transition countries. Changes in the Gini-coefficients for earnings are larger than for household income, even in countries where overall income inequalities have risen modestly (UNICEF 2001).

In the first years, differences between male and female earnings declined significantly, with the earning gap halving between 1989 and 1992. There were no substantial changes after that, and the gap has stabilized since at around 20 percent (Köllő 2002). However, there are important differences in the gender pay gap by sub-group (Kertesi and Köllő 1996). An initial drop in the gender wage gap occurred in the traditionally low-paid sectors (farming, food processing, construction, healthcare) and among middle-aged employees. The gender pay gap for occupations requiring higher education increased. Owing to declining wages in regions of high unemployment, which hit women harder than men, earning differences increased in the first few years of transformation in these regions.

The pay gap for unqualified women continued to decline after 1995. Following 1992, earnings for moderately educated women grew more slowly than for women with only a primary education. In this category, however, male wages grew even more slowly, and the result was a nearly 10 percent drop in the earnings gap. As for tertiary school graduates, the gap increased somewhat in the first half of the 1990s before becoming significantly wider in 1995–98 (Köllő, 2002).

Job flexibility, job insecurity

European labor market patterns show an increasing share of flexible employment that deviates from a pattern of secure, lifelong careers, with the OECD reporting an increase in the number of individuals experiencing employment insecurity or flexibility between the 1980s and 1990s (OECD 1997). A definition of employment flexibility emphasizes its diverse character: 'Flexibility policies trigger the emergence or reappearance of various forms of atypical jobs characterized by factors as diverse as working hours, the duration and type of contracts, schedules, workplace and forms of remuneration' (Maruani 1998, p. 6).

Working schedules may influence women's opportunities to combine paid employment with family life, though the relationship between work time and family life may be complex. Some forms of irregular work schedules (part-time work, irregular and evening shifts) are more widespread in the youngest and in the oldest cohorts, indicating that those in the weakest positions in the labor market are more likely to have temporally flexible jobs.

At first sight, working evenings, nights or weekends could be considered disruptive to family life, as it may result in difficulties in coordinating daily schedules, raising children or managing the household. On the other hand, such schedules may offer employment opportunities for some mothers with young children at the times when other family members or childcare services are available to take care of the children.

For balancing employment and family responsibilities, one of the most obvious solutions is to take a part-time job, which, for some people, means an advantageous work schedule that provides opportunities to supplement family income and/or helps to maintain ties to the labor market. But for others, particularly those unable to get full-time work, it is a 'forced' employment status. According to a recent study (Sik and Nagy 2002), there are sharp differences between men and women in their work time flexibility.

While part-time work is more frequent among women (almost 9 percent of employed women worked in part-time jobs in 2001, but only 2.8 percent of employed men, according to the 2001 Census), all other types of temporal flexibility are overrepresented among men. Part-time work is overrepresented among women in professional and in unskilled jobs, in other words at the extremes of the occupational hierarchy.

The incidence of part-time work in Hungary is very low compared with EU countries. In 1999, the EU average for part-time employment was 16.4 percent, but according to a 1997 survey conducted by the Labor Research Institute, the proportion of employees working shorter hours in Hungary was around 2.1 percent (of whom 1.8 percent were part-time workers; by 2000, these figures had increased to 2.8 and 2.0 percent, respectively; see Laky 2001). There may be several reasons for the low prevalence, including that the public sector has no priority on part-time employment and the private sector avoids creating part-time jobs, because it increases their transaction costs and is perceived to be too expensive: part-time jobs have the same degree of security as full-time jobs, even though part-time employees invest less time (Laky 2000). Plus owing to the relatively low wage levels, two 'full-time' earnings are needed for most families to make ends meet.

According to Sik and Nagy (2002), about one-third of workers have a 'flexible' job contract in Hungary, meaning those who work without a written contract (11 percent), those who are self-employed (9 percent) and individuals with a fixed-term contract (7 percent). The remainder is a mixture of various flexible contracts, such as temporary or casual jobs. But are 'flexible' positions stepping-stones to secure employment or a path to unemployment and worsened socio-economic status? There is no clear answer to this question, because it depends upon the context. Most 'flexible' jobs are filled by younger and less educated employees, and are more poorly paid than permanent jobs, and sometimes give less access to sick leave, paid time off, and so on (OECD 2002).

Family matters

As was shown in a recent study on entry into adulthood (Róbert and Bukodi 2005), marriage behavior has undergone a radical change in the last decade. The proportion of people married by age 25 is much lower for those born after 1970 than for those cohorts born before: younger generations tend to postpone marriage. However, the lower incidence of marriage is compensated by a higher incidence of cohabitation. The non-marital relationship is the most widespread among poorly educated individuals with limited career prospects. For getting married it appears to be very important to maximize certainties around labor market entry. First parenthood has also been delayed in recent cohorts.

Marital instability increased substantially after 1992. Divorce risk is higher when the wife has greater labor force involvement, but lower when the husband has stronger labor force involvement (Bukodi and Róbert 2003a). Career mobility has a positive impact on the likelihood of divorce, indicating that any deviation from the status relations between spouses at the time of marriage makes the partnership more vulnerable.

Women's career chances have been influenced substantially by their husbands' employment status and by the number of children. In terms of women's career mobility until the early 1990s, childless women tended to move up the occupational ladder more often at early stages of their careers, while women with children were 'obliged to postpone' their career advancement until after the childbearing period (Bukodi 1998). Also, many of the downward occupational transitions occurred over the first childbirth break. Thus one can outline a consistent picture of the effect of children on women's careers: a small proportion of upward mobility and a larger proportion of downward moves occurred over childbirth phases.

For women, upward transition was the largest in the last decades, when their occupational status was lower than that of their husbands (Bukodi 1998; Róbert and Bukodi 2002). At the same time, if a woman's status was better than that of her husband, the odds of her moving downward was much higher than in other cases. Consequently, spousal occupational position meant some kind of barrier for female mobility or job opportunity. The husband acted in the economic interest of the family as long as his wife's position did not exceed his own occupational standing (he 'enabled' his partner to move up). But if his wife's status improved so it was above her husband's position, he probably 'pulled' his partner down.

The role of the welfare state

Welfare coverage in Hungary is extensive. Benefits are paid for pregnancy, birth, childcare, family and schooling, as well as for child protection and child sickness. The family allowance and child protection benefits are considered the income of the children, but the rest are considered the income of the parents caring full-time for their children.

The childcare fee (GYED) is an insurance-based benefit, available for the first two years of a child's life to those parents who have paid social security contributions for at least 180 days in the two years prior to the birth. The benefit is equal to 70 percent of the parents' previous wages (but can be no more than twice the minimum wage) and is paid to either parent who takes care of the child full-time. Childcare aid (GYES) is a universal insurance-related benefit, first introduced in 1967, and is available to those parents who do not qualify for GYED (for example, less than two years of insurance payments) for the first three years of a child's life: it is equivalent to the minimum old-age pension. During the entitlement period, the parent may not be employed until the child is 18 months old. After that time, the recipient may work for pay part-time, or even full-time if he or she works for pay at home. Child-raising support (GYET), starting in 1993, was designed to serve the interests of families with three or more children (in their own households) as long as the youngest child is aged three to eight. The monthly benefit, irrespective of the number of children, is equal to the minimum pension. Parents receiving GYET can work for pay part-time, but full-time employment is allowed only if the parent works for pay at home.

Despite the declining birthrate, the number of women receiving childcare benefits of any kind has continued to rise every year. In 1999, 27 percent of the inactive female population of working age received benefits, most of them GYED or GYES.

The family allowance is currently a universal benefit paid for children until the age of six, and it has accounted for the largest share of family and child benefits. After age six, it is replaced by the schooling allowance, also universal, paid until age 16 (20 for those studying full-time), which is supplemented by the child protection benefit in the case of low-income families.

Family benefits have significantly reduced child poverty in Hungary, but the pace of this reduction decreased between the first and the second half of the 1990s (Förster and Tóth 2001) and the amount of benefit per child relative to average earnings and the share of family allowance in total household income have also declined, a trend accompanied by increasing attempts to exclude higher income households from the benefit system.

Occupational welfare was a key source of entitlement under state socialism. Paid work was not only a moral obligation for women but an essential welfare passport. Social security was managed by trade unions; healthcare as well as childcare was available at work. Firm-provided welfare institutions still exist, but they have declined and coverage has become more uneven. The capacity of employers to provide care has become more unequal, and differences in provisions between employees in firms are growing (Pascall and Manning 2000).

Municipal kindergarten enrollment has slightly increased to 92 percent by the end of the 1990s. This can make it easier for women to take a job after maternity leave, but it is an open question whether this is 'enough help' for women aiming to return to paid employment after childbirth.

HYPOTHESES

The role of education

Our first hypothesis is that the impact of educational attainment on employment and career has increased or held stable in the 1990s. Well-educated women have advantages in the labor market compared with their poorly educated counterparts; they have had minimal risk of becoming unemployed or experiencing status loss, and if they exit paid employment, the odds of their quickly returning to it had been very high. The counter-hypothesis is that the role of high education levels in securing good employment opportunities has decreased. The labor market has not properly adjusted to the rapid expansion of educational opportunity inasmuch as it has not kept pace in creating jobs that require qualified personnel, with the result that the value of higher education has been declining. More and more well educated (young) people are forced to choose lower-status and less well paid positions. Some researchers consider this a temporary phenomenon in an individual's life course, confined to the early career stages that can be 'corrected' later during the employment career (Aberg 2003). Others argue that over-education may persist over the whole occupational life course, indicating a structural character of the future labor market (Brynin 2002).

Both hypotheses emphasize the worsening position of low-educated women in paid employment. They have moderate chances to get a regular job or to work as 'core' employees in the globalizing labor market. On the one hand, they will be pushed out of those positions that are – in theory – matched to their (lack of) human capital, as these jobs will be filled by better educated workers, at least temporarily. On the other hand, they are less inclined to participate in adult education after completing their initial schooling, which may lead to their labor market exclusion.

The role of occupational status and branch of industry

We believe that the industrial restructuring process has created career turbulence. While restructuring may partly increase upward career opportunities especially in service fields, including both distributive and producer services, we expect it to lead to downward moves in agriculture or traditional heavy industry. For women, government service occupations may play a unique role, for while this sector does not provide good career opportunities for men, it may 'protect' women from becoming unemployed or from losing status thanks to its secure employment conditions. Our predictions are straightforward with respect to occupational position: employees working in higher status jobs are less likely to move up the occupational ladder (ceiling effect) while those working near the bottom of the occupational status hierarchy are less likely to experience further downward mobility (bottoming effect).

The role of family

Previous research showed that family attributes influenced women's career chances in the socialist era, and we expect they have exerted an even larger impact on women's employment opportunities in the 1990s.

According to our hypothesis, for a married woman whose spouse does not work for pay, the likelihood of becoming unemployed and experiencing status loss is larger than for a female whose partner has paid employment. There are three reasons behind this prediction. First, there has been a substantial increase in educational status homogamy in Hungary, especially at the two extremes, namely, for highly and poorly educated people (Bukodi 2004; Bukodi and Róbert 2003b). Since there is a strong relationship between education and employment chances, the number of 'work-poor' couples with no employed member at all may be increasing. Second, there are striking regional differences in Hungary in the incidence of unemployment and in the employment structure, and so 'work-poor' families may be concentrated in certain regions. Third, a spouse's education and occupational status can be interpreted as 'informational' capital (Róbert and Bukodi 2002). A partner's non-employment results in losing this additional capital, which leads to a higher risk of becoming unemployed and a lower chance of career improvement.

In addition to the partner's resources, we expect that the effect of children on women's employment opportunities remained substantial in the 1990s. Though various welfare measures have been carried over from socialist times, women with small children, particularly after maternity leaves, have higher risks of becoming occupationally inactive, or if they managed to keep their jobs, the probability of (temporal) status loss is quite high. Private firms may reduce their demand for the labor of mothers of small children.

Official statistics show that women experienced lower risks of unemployment in the 1990s than did men. However, their overall labor force involvement is also lower due to their higher incidence of other types of out-of-employment experiences. Women are thus more readily pushed out of the labor force during unfavorable labor market conditions and more frequently interrupt their employment trajectories. As it is well known from the human capital literature that frequent career interruptions result in a substantial devaluation of career resources, this may lead to a vicious cycle of employment failures. So women – in spite of their lower unemployment ratio – may be the 'losers' of the transitions in the last decade of the twentieth century. Still, some claim that women are not necessarily the victims of economic and social transformations or of globalization (Fodor 1997). Women have become as well educated as men (in some fields, even better educated); more generations of women have accumulated employment experiences, and women are concentrated in sectors (such as in services rather than in heavy industry) affected less by economic recessions.

CONCEPTUALIZATION, DATA AND METHODS

In this chapter, five types of employment moves are taken into account: the risk of becoming unemployed; the chance of finding a job; the mobility between unpaid caregiving activity and the labor market; exit to as well as entry from maternity leave; and upward and downward occupational status mobility. Upward mobility and (re-)entry into the labor market are considered employment success, while downward moves, the transition into unemployment and the entry into unpaid caregiving status are the alternatives. These types of career moves are defined as follows:

1   Transition into unemployment from the labor market: all unemployment episodes, whether registered or unregistered, are considered if the individual worked for pay before. Those individuals who have not yet entered the labor force were omitted.
2   Transition into the labor market from unemployment: all women are taken into account if they were unemployed at the beginning of the observation window or at any time during the investigated period. Only the fact of re-employment is studied; the type of new job is not considered.
3   Entry into unpaid caregiving activity: similar to the transition into unemployment, all episodes in unpaid caregiving status (homemaker, taking care of elderly persons, and so on) are included in the analysis if the woman worked for pay before.
4   Exit from unpaid caregiving status into the labor market: all individuals are considered if they were in an unpaid caregiving status at the start of the observation window or at any point of the period under study.
5   Moving into maternity leave: again, all episodes in caregiving status are incorporated into the analysis if the woman held employment before.
6   Moving from maternity leave into the labor market: those women are involved who were in maternity leave at the beginning of the observation window or at any point of the investigated time span.
7   Upward/downward status mobility: these moves are sub-groups in the category of job-to-job mobility, where moves are accompanied by (a) changes in occupational standing defined by the ISEI scores and/or (b) alteration in supervisory status. Upward (downward) mobility is defined as a status gain (loss) of 10 percent on the ISEI occupational status scale. In the case of self-employment, the definition of status mobility is based on changes in the ISEI score or in the number of employees.

When individuals were not in the labor force, the variables on status mobility have no values, and these records are omitted from the analysis because, in these periods, individuals were not at risk of making any occupational moves. This rule also applied in cases when the score of the job was at the top or at the bottom of the occupational hierarchy; individuals here are unable to move further up (or down) the occupational ladder.

The analyses use the longitudinal data of the Hungarian Household Panel Survey (HPS) conducted by the Tárki Social Research Center. The first wave of this survey in 1992 was based on a random sample of households in which all members aged 15 years and older were interviewed. All those surveyed were re-interviewed in March for the next five years, which allows us to reconstruct their employment histories from April 1991 to March 1997, because a retrospective question was always included in the panel survey to record employment moves in the previous 12 months. Information on partnership and fertility history can be linked to employment changes, which makes it possible to investigate the impact of marital status and partner's employment as well as the effect of the number of children of different ages on career moves. Only those respondents are included whose labor market career can be followed for the entire period from 1991 to 1997 (N = 1202 women).

The discrete-time method of event-history analysis has been used to investigate employment transition rates because events of interest are tied: several individuals experience the events investigated at the same time (in fact, in the same month). The at-risk period of having a transition for each respondent begins in April of 1991 and continues up to the year in which she exits from the labor market or until the last interview in March of 1997. If a respondent leaves the labor market somewhere between these two points (because of study, retirement, early retirement), she is treated as a right-censored case. The dependent variable is the occurrence of a given mobility event (coded as 1 for occurrence and 0 for non-occurrence).

Several time-varying covariates have been included. One is age, as it is well known that employment mobility decreases with age, irrespective of structural changes. For Hungary, age plays a unique role because age at the time of the collapse of socialism determines the time available for any labor market moves in the new era. In addition to age, we include indicators for career insecurity after system transition (the incidence of employment interruptions and unemployment experience); measures of career resources (an individual's education, occupational status, branch of industry); marital status and the spouse's employment position; and the family life cycle (number and age of children). Variables are detailed in the tables.

FINDINGS

An overview on women's employment mobility in the 1990s

Almost half (49 percent) of women aged 15 to 74 reported at least one career transition (either different forms of non-employment or occupational status mobility) between 1991 and 1997. Ten percent experienced only employment moves (entry into paid/unpaid caregiving or unemployment), 23 percent reported only status mobility (at least a 10 percent change) and 15 percent experienced paid caregiving, unemployment and status loss or status gain. This indicates a large mobility 'boom' for Hungarian women in the 1990s. But the summary of career movements does not control for individual characteristics, nor does it take the heterogeneity of the observation period into account.

Figure 7.1 displays the rates of upward and downward mobility between 1991 and 1997.[1]

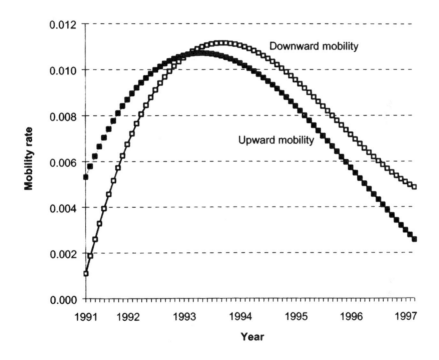

Source: Hungarian Household Panel Survey

Figure 7.1 *Smoothed monthly rates for Hungarian women's upward and downward career mobility between 1991 and 1997 showing large career mobility in the first half of the 1990s*

These rates are calculated by taking the number of events of a given mobility type – an upward or downward move by at least 10 percent – in a certain month and dividing it by the number of individuals at risk of experiencing status change. The curves indicate that the period after system transformation can be divided into two parts. The first period shows more turbulence in the labor market than the second one. In the early 1990s, both types of mobility increased, reaching a peak at the end of 1993, while the rate of status moves decreased thereafter. The restructuring process thus led to considerable career mobility in the early 1990s.

WHO ARE THE 'WINNERS' AND 'LOSERS' OF THE LAST DECADE'S ECONOMIC AND SOCIAL CHANGES?

Different forms of employment interruption and the chance of re-employment

Table 7.1 displays the causal factors on the risk of moving between the labor market and different kinds of non-employment for the period from 1991 to 1997.

From employment to unemployment

The probability of losing a job appeared to be unaffected by age – controlling for individual and household factors. Two indicators on career insecurities were included in the analysis. The first is the amount of employment experience in relation to the time elapsed between March 1991 and the transition or end of 1997. Women with less involvement in paid employment have a higher risk of becoming unemployed compared with those who remained attached to the labor market during the 1990s. The second is related to previous unemployment spells, as those who have experienced unemployment were at significantly more risk to be pushed out of the labor force again than women without it. These results call attention to an important feature of the recent Hungarian labor market: many women (and men) were forced to move between employment and different kinds of non-employment episodes, thereby being drawn into a vicious cycle as it became more and more difficult for them to re-enter the labor market.

The link between qualification and the odds of becoming unemployed seems quasi-linear: women with only primary education have the highest risk of losing their jobs, and women with tertiary diplomas have the lowest. These findings confirm our hypothesis that educational qualifications serve as an 'effective buffer' from labor market insecurities.

Women in high-status jobs have a significantly lower risk of becoming unemployed than women in low-status jobs. However, the relationship between occupational position and the likelihood of becoming unemployed is not linear. The odds of becoming unemployed do not substantially differ between those working at unskilled (bottom quarter on ISEI occupation

Table 7.1 Beta values indicating the effects of different characteristics on the hazard of Hungarian women's moves out of employment, 1991–97

	From employment to unemployment	From employment to unpaid caregiving	From employment to paid caregiving
Age			
15–29	0.21	0.47	4.05***
30–39	0.27	−0.02	2.97*
40–49	0.10	0.07	−0.47
50–x (reference)			
Career insecurity			
Employment experience, months	−0.02***	−0.02***	0.00
Unemployment experience, dummy	0.24*	0.39	−0.46
Education			
No training	0.42*	0.13	0.97***
Vocational training	0.02	−0.39	0.50*
Secondary school (reference)			
Lower tertiary	−1.19*	−0.47	−0.36
Higher tertiary	−2.31*	−0.63	−0.14
Occupational status			
Very low [unskilled]	0.29	−0.46	−0.17
Low [semi-skilled] (reference)			
High [skilled and supervisory]	−0.46*	−0.55	0.39
Very high [controllers]	−0.32*	−0.65*	0.06
Branch			
Industry (reference)			
Agriculture	0.48*	0.58*	0.42
Distributive service	0.23	−0.78*	0.16
Producer service	0.12	−0.80*	0.65
Social service	−0.68**	−0.74*	−0.09
Personal service	−1.58*	1.07**	−0.44
Marital status/spouse's employment			
Single (reference)			
Married, husband working	0.26	−0.91*	1.25***
Married, others	0.63*	0.17	1.44***
Divorced/widowed	0.51	−0.69	0.86
Family life cycle			
Number of children aged 0–2	−0.93	−0.57	3.27***
Number of children aged 3–6	−0.04	0.42*	−0.23
Number of children aged 7–14	−0.02	0.42**	−0.15
Number of children aged 15–18	−0.37	−0.03	−0.64*
Constant	−4.17***	−5.01***	−10.66***
Chi-square	194.53	106.25	546.14
Degrees of freedom	24	24	24
-2 log-likelihood	2 683.20	1 142.88	1 631.46
Number of events	226	85	162
Number of person months	49 056	48 915	48 992

Note: Significance: *** p<0.001; ** p<0.01; * p<0.05

Source: Hungarian Household Panel Survey (HPS)

ranking) and at semi-skilled (second-quarter) jobs. As was true for men, the effect of education for women became statistically significant only after incorporating occupational status in the equation (stepwise models not shown) (Bukodi and Róbert 2006). For two women in the same occupational position, the likelihood of entering unemployment is lower for the educated one. With regard to type, employment in social and personal services provides the greatest protection from unemployment, while women working in agriculture had the highest risk of becoming unemployed.

Finally, the model includes two linked family factors: marital status combined with information on the partner's labor market attachment. The likelihood of becoming unemployed is the highest for married women with a non-employed partner, confirming our hypothesis of 'coupled unemployment.' In other words, the spouse's labor market involvement decreases the risk of job loss. The presence of children did not influence the odds of becoming unemployed after controlling for the above-mentioned explanatory variables.

From employment to paid and unpaid caregiving

With regard to age effects, there is an important difference between the chance of entering into unpaid and into paid caregiving (maternity leave). The probability of entering unpaid caregiving is unaffected by the age of the woman whereas moves into paid caregiving are more frequent among younger women with small children. Cumulative work experience has a negative impact on the odds of entry into unpaid caregiving, and higher career investments decrease the likelihood of leaving employment.

Educational attainment only significantly influences the transition between employment and paid caregiving. Unskilled women, and their counterparts with vocational training, have higher odds of entry into paid caregiving than women with secondary school diplomas. However, prior job status exerts a significant effect only on the likelihood of leaving the labor market for unpaid caregiving. Women in high positions are less likely to choose unpaid caregiving than those in semi-skilled occupations.

The effect of the sector in which women were employed differs markedly for the two types of exits. For unpaid caregiving it is a significant predictor, whereas in the case of maternity leave, there is no effect. As in the case of unemployment, working in agriculture increases the chance of existing the labor market, while service employment (other than personal services) 'protects' women from the transition between employment and homemaker status.

Whether the spouse has paid employment or not, rather than marital status alone, influences the odds of leaving the labor market to become a homemaker. Women with a working partner have significantly lower risks of becoming unpaid caregivers than their single counterparts – after controlling for the different individual characteristics and the number of children. This finding is in line with our hypotheses on the effects of spousal attributes on employment mobility.

From unemployment to employment

According to the estimates in Table 7.2, both young and elderly women are less likely to re-enter employment than their middle-aged counterparts. We had an opportunity to examine the impact of the duration of unemployment on the likelihood of finding a job, specifying it with both a linear and a quadratic term. The effects are significant, implying that the odds of employment re-entry initially increase, and then begin to decline as the time spent unemployed increases. In other words, if a woman could not find paid employment within several months, it then became progressively more difficult to do so.

Educational level has an impact on the likelihood of finding a job. Estimates suggest that women without qualifications have the greatest difficulty in returning to the labor market; women with tertiary education have a considerable advantage over secondary school graduates, and women with vocational training have lower chances of re-entering paid employment than their counterparts with secondary school diplomas.

The linked 'marital status/spouse's employment' measure exerts a significant effect on re-entry into the labor market, as the likelihood of job-finding is lower for married women than for their single or divorced/ widowed counterparts. A woman whose spouse is not employed appears to have the greatest disadvantage in returning to paid employment. This can be interpreted in light of the lack of accumulation of informational, human or social capital in the family. In jobless households, it is particularly difficult to obtain the appropriate information about the labor market, and individuals in these families are subjected more to the negative effects of skill inflation.

From paid and unpaid caregiving to employment

Unlike the odds of entry into unpaid caregiving, the chance of returning to paid employment is affected by age: the younger the woman, the higher the probability of finding a new job (Table 7.2). There is no difference between paid and unpaid caregiving with respect to its effects on career insecurity, but the impact of time spent in non-employment on the chances for re-employment does depend on the type of caregiving.

For paid caregiving, the pattern is similar to that of unemployment. The chance of re-entry into the labor force initially increases before it begins declining (the underlying reason for it is an institutional one: women are entitled to maternity leave for at most three years). In the case of unpaid family care, only the linear term of duration is significant: the more

Table 7.2   Beta values indicating the effects of different characteristics on the hazard of Hungarian women's re-employment moves, 1991–97

	From unemployment to employment	From unpaid caregiving to employment	From paid caregiving to employment
Age			
15–29	1.00	1.99***	−0.10
30–39	1.69**	1.96***	0.13
40–49	0.68	1.48**	0.37
50–x (reference)			
Career insecurity			
Employment experience, months	0.00	0.01***	0.01*
Months out of employment	0.11***	−0.03*	0.03***
Months out of employment, squared	−0.00*	0.00	−0.00***
Education			
No training	−0.43*	−0.90**	−0.26
Vocational training	−0.42*	−0.63*	−0.42
Secondary school (reference)			
Lower tertiary	1.31**	−0.76	0.33
Higher tertiary		−0.70	0.34*
Personal service			
Marital status/spouse's employment			
Single (reference)			
Married, husband working	−0.90**	−0.58	0.74
Married, others	−1.13***	−0.86*	0.78
Divorced/widowed	−0.71	−0.50	1.11
Family life cycle			
Number of children aged 0–2			−1.59***
Number of children aged 3–6	−0.25	0.16	0.53***
Number of children aged 7–14	0.04	0.00	−0.45***
Number of children aged 15–18	−0.20	−0.26	−0.40
Constant	−4.01***	−4.03***	−4.62***
Chi-square	89.46	175.88	196.12
Degrees of freedom	17	17	17
−2 log-likelihood	1 467.41	989.89	1 700.97
Number of events	192	113	191
Number of person months	4 200	7 405	10 091

Note: Significance: *** p<0.001; ** p<0.01; * p<0.05

Source: Hungarian Household Panel Survey (HPS)

time spent in this status, the lower the likelihood of re-employment, owing to the devaluation of human capital or losing the proper networks.

Educational effects are strong here, as unpaid caregivers without qualifications have a very small chance of returning to the labor market, taking other factors into account. However, women with university degrees on paid caregiving leave re-enter employment much faster than their more poorly educated counterparts.

Women with non-working spouses have the smallest chance of re-integration into the labor market, another sign of the polarization between 'work-poor' and 'work-rich' couples. However, the likelihood of returning to paid employment from paid caregiving is affected neither by marital status nor by the spouse's employment position. Not surprisingly, the number of children and having young children substantially impact on the odds of re-entry into the labor market after maternity leaves, and women with children under age two have the lowest probability of taking a job. The chance of returning into employment is the highest for women with preschool children (after exhausting maternity benefits). But having a school-aged child decreases the odds of transition between maternity leave and the labor market.

The risk of downward mobility, and the chance of upward shifts

Recall that Figure 7.1 shows that Hungarian women experienced greater career mobility in the early 1990s, peaking in around 1994. The majority of moves before the middle of 1993 were upward moves; since then, the majority are downward moves.

The coefficients shown in Table 7.3 indicate slightly different underlying processes taking place for upward and downward status mobility. Middle-aged women have significantly higher chances of making an upward occupational shift than their younger or older counterparts, but downward mobility appears to be unrelated to age.

Greater involvement in paid employment increases the odds of upward moves on the career ladder, while previous unemployment experience increases the risk of downward mobility. It implies that an unsecured employment career makes it more difficult to be successful in the labor market in the future.

Experiencing an upward occupational shift decreases the likelihood of further status gain and increases the odds of downward status move. Conversely, previous status loss has a positive impact on the likelihood of

Table 7.3 Beta values indicating the effects of different characteristics on the hazard of Hungarian women's occupational status mobility, 1991–97

	Upward, 10%	Downward, 10%
Age		
15–29	−0.05	0.07
30–39	0.28*	0.20
40–49	−0.14	0.15
50–x (reference)		
Employment experience, months	0.01*	0.00
Unemployment experience, months	0.23	0.48**
Career instability		
Upward move, dummy	−0.38***	0.48**
Downward move, dummy	0.69***	−0.41***
Education		
No training	−1.15***	0.62***
Vocational training	−1.01***	0.27*
Secondary school (reference)		
Lower tertiary	0.32*	−0.43**
Higher tertiary	0.90***	−0.48*
Occupational status		
Very low [unskilled]	0.10	−0.66***
Low [semi-skilled] (reference)		
High [skilled and supervisory]	−0.89***	−0.02
Very high [controllers]	−1.78***	0.91***
Branch		
Industry (reference)		
Agriculture	0.24	−0.32
Distributive service	0.19*	−0.23*
Producer service	0.04	−0.01
Social service	−0.33**	−0.36**
Personal service	−0.48*	0.09
Marital status/spouse employment		
Single (reference)		
Married – husband working	0.24*	−0.17*
Married – others	0.17	−0.01
Divorced/widowed	−0.15	−0.05
Family life cycle		
Number of children aged 0–2	−0.36	0.77**
Number of children aged 3–6	−0.23*	0.33**
Number of children aged 7–14	0.04	−0.01
Number of children aged 15–18	−0.05	0.00
Constant	−3.83***	−5.03***
Chi-square	432.22	275.10
Degrees of freedom	26	26
-2 log-likelihood	6 568.90	6 503.53
Number of events	667	644
Number of person months	47 113	46 088

Note: Significance: *** p<0.001; ** p<0.01; * p<0.05

Source: Hungarian Household Panel Survey (HPS)

making an upward transition later in the career, while also decreasing the chance of experiencing a further downward move. These results indicate that some of the status mobility during the 1990s may have been owing to the turbulence in the labor market immediately after the end of socialist rule. Upward mobility might be status reconstruction once the initial, transitional phase has passed, while downward mobility may be interpreted as a return to the 'original' occupational status.

The risk of downward mobility is clearly determined by differences in educational qualification. Women with university diplomas had the lowest probability of status loss, while women without educational qualifications have the highest. The coefficients underline a clear trend in upward mobility, as women with university diplomas had the highest chance of making an upward shift and their non-educated counterparts had the lowest.

Our prediction was that socio-economic status would significantly influence career movement, such that the higher the occupational status, the fewer upward and more downward moves would be expected (ceiling effect) and, the lower the status, the more upward and fewer downward moves would be expected (bottoming effect). Generally, the results are in line with these expectations, though women in unskilled occupations have no more chance of experiencing status gain than women in semi-skilled positions. It implies that women with few qualifications are pushed into 'dead-end' jobs without career improvement possibilities.

Working in distributive services (trade, transport, and so on) increases the likelihood of upward shifts and decreases the odds of downward moves. This result suggests expanding sectors such as distributive services have opened opportunities for women to improve their careers. At the same time, social services (education, health, and so on) appear to protect women from any status mobility.

The linked marital status/partner's employment variable appears relevant to upward and downward career mobility as well. Married (or cohabiting) women with employed partners have the highest chance of improving their occupational career and the lowest risk of status loss.

The presence of an infant and a preschool child substantially influences downward movement. The positive sign indicates that the more small children women have, the greater the chance of moving down the occupational ladder. For upward mobility, only having a preschool child appears significant, implying that the presence of a child aged three to six has a postponing effect on women's upward mobility. Hungarian women have three years of paid maternity leave, but after this employment interruption it is quite difficult to re-enter the labor market. To preserve their prior employment status is even more difficult, as our figures show.

DISCUSSION

Women's career mobility decreased between the early and the late 1990s, and the prevailing tendency was for transitions between different employment statuses as well as for shifting between various occupational positions. In this respect, the last decade can be divided into two parts. In the first years after the collapse of communism, there was a sharp increase in female career movements, but since then, employment mobility has been declining and appears to be stabilizing. However, women experienced fewer career transitions in the 1990s than do men.

The risk of becoming unemployed seems to be attached to occupational – in most cases downward – career mobility. On the other hand, a high proportion of women experienced status loss as well as status gain in a relatively short period, namely, in the first half of the decade. The nature of this movement was different from the life-course mobility pattern of the socialist era, probably owing to the rapid economic and social changes as well as to globalization processes. There also seems to be a new phenomenon in the Hungarian labor market as some employees found it more and more difficult to preserve their former employment status. Forced to leave the labor market, they were unable to re-enter paid employment, which pushed them into different types of non-employment statuses. The majority of these women chose unpaid caregiving as an escape from long-term unemployment.

Our previous study on male employment careers showed that macro-economic changes had large impacts on career movements irrespective of age (Bukodi and Róbert 2006). For women, the probability of career shifts appears highest from age 30 to 39, particularly for upward occupational mobility and the chance of re-entry into the labor market after unemployment. This may be because of women's employment profile, as women with children tend to postpone their career after their childbearing period. In other words, the career-investment profile of married women is not monotonic (Mincer and Ofek 1982). Non-participation in paid employment during the childbearing period may cause a deterioration in acquired skills, leading to a lower chance of upward occupational mobility.

This explanation is supported by our findings of the effect of children on women's career chances and risks. One of the most important factors in shaping women's employment opportunities is childbearing. Women with preschool children face the largest difficulties when they want to re-enter paid employment. A substantial proportion of such women are forced to enter another inactive status and become unpaid caregivers. Those able to re-enter paid employment may experience a substantial status loss.

The labor market position of the spouse significantly influences women's employment profile. For women with non-employed partners the probability of becoming unemployed (or a homemaker) or experiencing downward occupational moves is higher than for their counterparts with an employed husband. In other words, unemployment (or non-employment) comes in couples in Hungary, similar to other European countries. These results support our hypotheses on the polarization of households. Owing to high-status homogamy and regional differences in employment opportunities, an increasing proportion of households has become 'work-poor' and without any member in paid employment, while other households have become 'work-rich' and all adult members have secure jobs.

One of our most important findings is that employment career insecurity has an impact on women's further occupational opportunities: unemployment 'attracts' unemployment. For women who experienced unemployment earlier, the odds of recurrent unemployment, as well as the probability of status loss, is much higher than for those who had no previous experience of unemployment. Similarly, career 'raggedness,' or the lack of the proper amount or kind of employment experiences increases the hazard of exit from the labor market or the odds of downward occupational shifts.

According to general human capital theory, higher education leads to gains in status. The higher the level of education, the greater the chance one has to be successful in the labor force. However, this approach holds that the labor market is imperfect, with some employees under-rewarded while others are over-rewarded. That means resources (qualifications) do not match employment position. Under these circumstances, it is predicted that status gain, and the chance of re-entry the labor market after non-employment, is more likely for employees who are under-rewarded, and the likelihood of being under-rewarded increases with educational attainment. For downward mobility, or for the risk of becoming unemployed, the prediction is reversed: these transitions are less likely for over-rewarded employees, and the likelihood of being over-rewarded decreases with educational level.

Findings are in line with these predictions. Education, in general, has not lost its significance for protecting from the risk of becoming unemployed or inactive and from the odds of downward mobility in the 1990s. Women without any qualifications, by contrast, have fewer and fewer chances in the job market and are forced to leave the labor market (to become unemployed or not employed), and they experience status loss to a greater extent than their educated counterparts. This indicates that uncertainties generated by the system transformation and globalization processes are passed to the most marginal groups of the labor force who have no, or only moderate, educational credentials.

According to our hypothesis, the role of career mobility generated by the mismatch between education and (prior) job status will increase in the future because of educational expansion, the pace of which is outstripping the demand for graduates in the labor market. In this situation, an increasing proportion of young graduates are forced to enter the labor market in under-rewarded jobs, though most of them correct the mismatch between their qualifications and their occupational status mid-career.

Our analysis also revealed that working in social services protects women from career failures, as the risk of becoming unemployed or the odds of status loss is lower for those employed in this sector, though women working in distributive services have the best chances to improve their careers.

The transitional processes and globalization waves have affected various groups of women differently. Those who lacked the appropriate resources were the losers, and their labor market position has become particularly insecure. Pushed out of paid employment, their odds of re-entering the labor force appeared very low, forcing them to 'choose' paid or unpaid caregiving as an 'escape' from this situation – and the more time they spent in non-employment, the more difficult it became to re-integrate into the labor market. Women with only a moderate amount of human capital, and who have experienced an unsecured employment career, are more exposed to the risk of downward occupational mobility and they tend to move between non-employment and low-status jobs.

However, there is another group of women who are 'rich' in career resources and are employed in protected sectors that are less exposed to economic recessions. They have managed to preserve their relatively good position in the labor market. So, in line with the emerging knowledge-based society, our findings indicate that human capital (or career) investments have become more and more relevant for success in the labor market, and without an appropriate amount of these kinds of capital, it is becoming more difficult to become integrated into the labor market.

NOTES

1   For calculating the mobility rates, we applied the method of moving averages. We found that the distribution of mobility shows relatively more transitions from March to April each year. This may be a consequence of the retrospective calendar method used in collecting data. As respondents were asked to report about the previous year (from April to the following March), this meant that the job in March in a given year was always a 'present' job, though the job in April in the same year comes from the calendar information collected the next year. This artificial break in reporting data could result in an overrepresentation in observed status mobility.

BIBLIOGRAPHY

Aberg, R. (2003) 'Unemployment persistency, overeducation and the employment chances of the less educated', *European Sociological Review*, 19: 199–216.
Beck, U. (1992) *Risk Society. Towards a new modernity*, London: Sage.
Blossfeld, H.-P. (2001) 'Globalization, social inequality and the role of country-specific institutions. Open research questions in a learning society', in P.

Conceicao, M.V. Heitor and B.-A. Lundvall (eds) *Towards a learning society: innovation and competence building with social cohesion for Europe*, Oxford: Oxford University Press.

Brynin, M. (2002) 'Overqualification in employment', *Work, Employment and Society*, 16: 637–54.

Bukodi, E. (1998) 'Women's occupational career mobility and family formation: the case of Hungary', Joint ECE/INSTRAW/UNSD Work Session on Gender Statistics, Working Paper No. 25.

Bukodi, E. (2004) *Ki, kivel (nem) házasodik? Párválasztás Magyarországon, (Who marries whom? Partner selection in Hungary)* Budapest: Századvég.

Bukodi, E. and Róbert, P. (2003a) 'Union disruption in Hungary', *International Journal of Sociology*, 32: 64–94.

Bukodi, E. and Róbert, P. (2003b) 'Who marries whom? Life-course and historical variations in educational homogamy in Hungary', in H.-P. Blossfeld and A. Timm (eds) *Who marries whom? Educational systems as marriage markets in modern societies*, European Studies of Population Series, Dordrecht, Boston and London: Kluwer.

Bukodi, E. and Róbert, P. (2006) 'Men's career mobility in Hungary during the 1990s', in H.-P. Blossfeld, M. Mills, and F. Bernardi (eds) *Globalization, uncertainty and men's careers: an international comparison*, Cheltenham, UK and Northampton, MA, USA: Edward Elgar.

Fodor, É. (1997) 'Gender in transition: unemployment in Hungary, Poland and Slovakia', *East European Politics and Societies*, 11: 470–500.

Förster, M.F. and Tóth, I.G. (2001) 'Child poverty and family transfers in the Czech Republic, Hungary and Poland', *Journal of European Social Policy*, 11: 324–41.

Giddens, A. (1999) *Runaway world: how globalisation is reshaping our lives*, London: Profile Books.

Kertesi, G. and Köllő, J. (1996) 'A bér alakulását meghatározó tényezők' ('Factors determining wage trends'), in L. Halpern (eds) *Bérköltség és versenyképesség, (Wage costs and competitiveness)*, Budapest: MTA Közgazdaságtudományi Intézet.

Kertesi, G. and Köllő J. (2002) 'Economic transformation and the revaluation of human capital – Hungary, 1986–1999', in A. De Grip, J. van Loo and K. Mayhew (eds) 'The economics of skills obsolescence: theoretical innovations and empirical application', *Research in Labour Economics*, 21: 235–73.

Klugman, J., Micklewright, J. and Redmond, G. (2002) 'Poverty in the transition: social expenditures and the working-age poor', Innocenti Working Papers No. 91, Florence, United Nations Children's Fund, Innocenti Research Centre.

Köllő, J. (2001) 'The patterns of non-employment in Hungary's least developed regions', Budapest Working Papers on Labour Market, 1, Labour Research Department, Institute of Economics, Hungarian Academy of Sciences.

Köllő, J. (2002) 'Gender earnings differences', in K. Fazekas and J. Koltay (eds) *The Hungarian labour market. Review and analysis*, Institute of Economics, Budapest: HAS Hungarian Employment Foundation.

Laky, T (2000) 'Labour Market in Hungary – 1999', in K. Fazekas (ed.) *Munkaerőpiaci Tükör (Labour Force Mirror)*, Budapest: MTA KTK.

Laky, T. (2001) *Az atipikus foglalkozások (Atypical jobs)*, Budapest: Struktúra Munkaügyi Kiadó.

Maruani, M. (1998) *Flexibility and the challenge of equality employment flexibility and gender equality*, Paris: OECD.

Mincer, J. and Ofek, H. (1982) 'Interrupted work careers: depreciation and restoration of human capital', *Journal of Human Resources*, 17: 1–23.

Organisation for Economic Co-operation and Development (OECD) (1997) 'Is job insecurity on the increase in OECD countries?', in *Employment outlook 1997*, Paris: OECD.

Organisation for Economic Co-operation and Development (OECD) (1999) 'Training of adult workers in OECD countries: measurement and analysis', in *Employment outlook 1999*, Paris: OECD.

Organisation for Economic Co-operation and Development (OECD) (2000a) *Literacy in the information age. Final report of the international adult literacy survey*, Paris: OECD, Statistics Canada.

Organisation for Economic Co-operation and Development (OECD) (2000b) *From initial education to working life. Making transitions work*, Paris: OECD.

Organisation for Economic Co-operation and Development (OECD) (2002) 'Taking the measure of temporary employment', in *Employment outlook 2002*. Paris: OECD.

Pascall, P. and Manning, N. (2000) 'Gender and social policy: comparing welfare states in Central and Eastern Europe and the former Soviet Union', *Journal of European Social Policy*, 10: 240–66.

Polachek, S.W. (1981) 'Occupational self-selection: a human capital approach to sex differences in occupational structure', *Review of Economics and Statistics*, 63: 60–69.

Róbert, P. and Bukodi, E. (2002) 'Dual career pathways: the occupational attainment of married couples in Hungary', *European Sociological Review*, 18: 217–32.

Róbert, P. and Bukodi, E. (2004) 'Changes in intergenerational class mobility in Hungary; 1973–2000', in R. Breen (ed.) *Social mobility in Europe*, Oxford: Oxford University Press.

Róbert P. and Bukodi, E. (2005) 'The effects of the globalization process on the transition to adulthood in Hungary', H.-P. Blossfeld, E. Klijzing, M. Mills, and K. Kurz (eds) *Globalization, uncertainty and youth in society*, London: Routledge.

Róbert, P., Bukodi, E. and Luijkx, R. (2001) 'Employment patterns in Hungarian couples', in H.-P. Blossfeld and S. Drobnič (eds) *Careers of couples in contemporary societies*, Oxford: Oxford University Press, pp. 307–31.

Sik, E. and Nagy, I. (2002) 'Households, work and flexibility', Hungarian Research Report for Household, Work and Flexibility Project, www.hwf.at. Accessed 10 October 2003.

Tóth, I.G. (2003) 'Jövedelem-egyenlőtlenségek: tényleg növekszenek vagy csak úgy látjuk?', ('Inequalities of income: are they or do they just seem to be increasing?') *Közgazdasági Szemle* (*Review of Economics*), 50: 209–34.

United Nations Children's Fund (UNICEF) (2001) *A decade of transition*, Florence: Innocenti Research Centre.

8. Women's employment in Estonia

Jelena Helemäe and Ellu Saar

INTRODUCTION

In western developed countries, a combination of economic and technological development, mediated by the sociopolitical environment, creates structural change (DiPrete et al. 1997). In Estonia, the dismantling of state control over the economy led to a rapid rise in structural changes such as private ownership and in the market-based allocation of resources and consumer goods (Gerber 2002). This chapter examines the impact of this rapid structural change on Estonian women's employment by comparing career transitions before, during and after the national transition to a market economy that occurred from 1989 to 1999. We begin with a description of the labor market situation in each of these time periods.

The pre-transformation labor market situation, 1989-91

The main features of the Estonian pre-transition labor market – mostly produced by the rigidities of the Soviet regime and shared by all socialist economies – were job security and hidden unemployment, gender pay equity and high female labor force participation (Haltiwanger and Vodopivec 1999; Riboud, Sánchez-Páramo and Silva-Jáuregui 2002). The Estonian economy in 1989 was part of the economy of the Soviet Union and was closely bound up with its raw material and product markets.

Work structures were heavily dominated by central planning. The supply of jobs and demand for them was subject to direct bureaucratic control by state agencies. Administrative control over job supply and demand was usually envisaged as an ideological project aimed at achieving full employment, which implied not only an absolute guarantee of employment but also strong job security, as dismissals were exceedingly rare (Mach, Mayer and Pohoski 1994). Enterprises were operating under soft budget constraints and were even prepared to employ more workers, contributing to considerable hidden unemployment (overstaffing).

The command system supported lifelong employment with one firm, usually in one profession. Work experience and seniority were the main elements in advancement and remuneration. But, despite the strong support of employment stability, labor turnover was surprisingly high in most transition countries (Cazes and Nesporova 2001).

Full-time employment for women was the norm in the socialist period. While the male labor force participation rate in Estonia was comparable to the rates in most European countries, the female participation rate was much higher than in other countries, partly as the result of official policies aimed at offsetting the growing labor shortage and also reflecting economic pressures: wages were too low to support a family on the income of a single breadwinner. Nonetheless, Soviet norms and institutions rested on the premise that women, but not men, had dual roles; thus legislation favored a traditional division of gender roles; for example, childcare leaves were only available for mothers (Lapidus 1994).

The transformation market situation, 1992-94

The effect of globalization on the labor market of post-socialist countries can be observed from the 1990s onward (Table 8.1). The Estonian reform period during 1992–94 can be interpreted in two contexts: as a transition from state socialism to a market economy and as a movement from an industrial, Fordist economy to a post-industrial, post-Fordist economy (Terk 1999b). One might distinguish two types of structural changes, though they act in parallel and are in fact intertwined: (a) those designed to compensate the inherited misallocation problem, and (b) those created by the functioning of the globalizing market economy. As the main changes occurred over a very brief span, it is difficult to separate the impact of these types of changes: institutional changes 'freed the space' for structural changes, which in turn put more pressure on institutions.

Most Central and East European socialist countries began their transitions in much better shape than Estonia, which had the lowest pre-transition GDP per capita and had a structure of trade relationships only with Eastern bloc countries. The cutoff of subsidized petroleum from Russia at the time of transition forced Estonia to seek new energy sources on the world market. The collapse of the institutional and technological links to the Soviet centrally planned system disrupted the supply of production inputs and the delivery of outputs. The reorientation of industry from eastern markets to western markets was frequently also accompanied by a transition from more complex production to less complicated work, usually subcontracting (Terk 1999b).

In June 1992, Estonia introduced its own currency, a date considered to be the start of serious economic reforms (Arro et al. 2001). In the same year, economic activity collapsed under the combined effects of the breakdown of trade relations with the countries of the former Soviet Union, the collapse of the old central planning system, the extensive price and trade liberalization and the abolition of many subsidies. Real GDP fell by almost 22 percent, and consumer price inflation reached 1069 percent. Estonia had the longest (five years) and deepest (35 percent) recession among all the transition countries (*Transition* 2001).

There was a certain delay before the effects of the transition were felt by employees because enterprises were at first reluctant to dismiss redundant workers. But Estonia took a very liberal approach in embracing a free market-oriented strategy and allowed enterprises to discharge excess labor without imposing undue costs on them (Orazem and Vodopivec 1999). In doing so, Estonia ended the period of near-universal job security and opened up the national economy to world competition (Arro et al. 2001).

Despite the presence of permanent-contract-type jobs, employment security in Estonia was one of the lowest among transitional countries during the most intensive reforms (1992-94) (Cazes and Nesporova 2003). But unemployment only increased gradually, and the fall in GDP did not lead to high unemployment in the first half of the 1990s. Reasons cited for this moderate unemployment growth include: a sharp drop in labor force participation, relatively flexible labor markets, low unemployment benefits and net migration to the former Soviet Union (Eamets 2001). There was no official policy to facilitate early retirement, and owing to the scarce benefits, the unemployed were forced to re-enter the labor market as soon as possible (Noorkõiv et al. 1997), often without any support for finding or getting training for new jobs.

The Estonian employment relation system experienced a rapid shift from a closed to an open one (Mills and Blossfeld 2005). There was a clear need first for intensive numerical flexibility. In Estonia flexibility is achieved through firing and hiring, rather than by using flexible forms of employment. There are thus limited choices of employment forms for women in Estonia, with few forms of flexible employment: short-term contracts, part-time work or self-employment. One indication of these conditions is that even in 2001, 90 percent of employed persons (89 percent of men and 91 percent of women) had permanent job contracts, 92 percent of employed persons (95 percent of men and 89 percent of women) had full-time jobs and 92 percent of employed persons (89 percent of men and 95 percent of women) were employees rather than self-employed (*Labour Force* 2001).

In the pre-reform and reform period, labor market adjustment was partly attained by decreasing supply. Thus, some women turned to unpaid caregiving, while those of pension age were pushed away from the labor market, thereby lowering the inter-age competition among women. But by the end of the twentieth century this form of adjustment was exhausted.

Table 8.1   Developments in Estonia from 1989 to 1999

	1989–91 (Pre-reform)	1992–94 (Reform)	1997–99 (Post-reform)
Internalization of markets	Estonia as one of the USSR republics was an open economy, with Russia as the main trade partner. Estonian's share of foreign trade with OECD countries was negligible	In the second half of 1992 after the introduction of the Estonian national currency, Estonian's share of foreign trade with OECD countries increased to nearly 50 percent of total trade	In 1999 the biggest trade partners were Finland, Sweden, Russia, Latvia, and Germany
Privatization	From Soviet-type co-operatives to small-scale privatization	1992: peak of small-scale privatization; 1993–94: peak of privatization of large enterprises	Most manufacturing firms and banking privatized; privatization of infrastructure continued. Land reform begun
Educational system	Highly centralized and narrowly specialized educational system with high potential to strengthen labor market boundaries. Because of high degree of differentiation, serious difficulties for re-entry into educational system		Introduction and institutionalization of occupational market. Underdevelopment and over-marketization of adult education
Employment system	By early 1990, the government determined only the minimum and maximum wages; after 1991 only the minimum wage	1992: Introduction of Law on Employment Contract; employer right to lay off a worker with a two-month notification; wide use of temporary contracts possible	Poorly developed collective bargaining system; only about 15% of employees are covered by collective agreements, mostly in public sector or privatized enterprises
Employment-sustaining policy	Minimal and passive since the establishment of the National Labor Market Board in 1991		
Welfare-sustaining employment policy	Restrictive since the establishment of the National Labor Market Board; unemployment benefits very low and of short duration; eligibility rules strict; no early exit policy		

Table 8.1   continued

Welfare state	Paid parental leave for mother or father of a child under one; additional six months of unpaid leave	Paid parental leave for mother or father of a child under three. The employment contract is suspended for the period of parental leave. Economic support provided by Estonian state for child under three years is comparable with that in Western Europe, support for older children is one of the more modest in Europe
Family structure		Gradually decelerating trend towards earlier parenthood; since 1993 increase in the mean age of mother at childbirth and the mean age at birth of the first child; continuing juvenescence of first partnership formation; consensual unions as the main route to family building; rising share of children born outside marriage (25% in 1989 to 54% in 1999), most born to cohabiting parents
Culture	Emphasis on traditional gender roles as a rejection of Soviet-style gender equality	Adaptation of 'winner-takes-all' model for gender roles

Sources: Arro et al (2001); Eamets (2001); Hansson (2000); Katus (1998); Narusk (1996); *Statistical Yearbook of Estonia* (2002); Terk (1999a)

Women's labor force participation through the transition

In 1989, the female participation rate in Estonia was 71 percent, similar to Central and East European socialist countries and Scandinavia. This rate began to decline with the onset of the economic transition. Estonian women have become less active in the labor market over the course of the transition, though their rate stayed considerably higher than the EU overall rate; for example, among women aged 25–49 in 1999, the Estonian employment rate is 74 percent, compared with 65 percent in the EU (*Statistical Yearbook of Estonia* 2002).

Women were disproportionately employed in sectors that gained employment share during the transition. The main job losses occurred in heavy industries and in agriculture, where male employment was concentrated. Nevertheless men gained a disproportionate share of the new positions in expanding sectors (Orazem and Vodopivec 1999).

The post-transformation market situation, 1997-99

Estonia has had two recessions, one caused by general transition shock and economic restructuring after the currency reform (1992–94), and the other caused by a domestic crisis in the financial markets that was followed by the external shock of the Russian financial crisis (1998–99). As a result of the first shock, the unemployment rate reached almost 8 percent; as a result of the second, it rose to 15 percent by the beginning of 2000 (Eamets 2001). In 1992–94, the first waves of dismissals affected women more than men (Eamets 2001). But there has been higher unemployment rate among men compared with women in recent years in Estonia, a pattern not typical of other European countries.

In terms of welfare state policies and employment relations, Estonia is similar to an 'individualist mobility regime' (DiPrete et al. 1997). In Estonia, expenditure on labor market policies is the lowest among transition countries and comprises only 0.16 percent of GDP (Eamets 2001). Estonia uses a flat-rate unemployment benefit system with a very low replacement ratio, below 10 percent of the national average wage. Regulations for receiving unemployment benefits are very restrictive, leaving many unemployed persons no possibility of receiving unemployment benefits, and this could be why only half register as unemployed. In relative terms, the active labor policy measures have declined in recent years and only the registered unemployed can obtain access to new job training. The consequence of having weak trade unions – only about 10–13 percent of employees are trade union members (Arro et al. 2001) – is that employers do not always enact regulations and violations are often not investigated. In addition, in a climate of high unemployment, employees do not initiate individual claims against employers for fear of losing their jobs. All this contributes to the lowering of job security: the mean tenure of prime-age women fell during the first half of the 1990s and remained about the same during the second half of 1990s despite the stabilization of the Estonian economy (Helemäe and Saar 2003).

At the same time, the Estonian version of an individualist mobility regime seems to have some distinct features related particularly to entry into the labor market and to the duration of unemployment. While open employment relations and individualist mobility regimes are characterized by relatively easy entry into the labor market and shorter spells of unemployment (Mills and Blossfeld 2005), in Estonia, economically inactive people, especially young people and women, have difficulties entering the labor market (Saar 2005). The share of long-term unemployed (persons unemployed for more than a year) accounted for 46 percent of total unemployment in 1999 (Vöörmann 2001a, p. 56), evidence of two groups of unemployed: those leaving unemployment relatively quickly and those who are unemployed for a very long time (Eamets 2001).

Gender equity and the welfare state

The welfare state regimes in post-socialist countries are moving in quite different directions. Hungary and the Czech Republic, for example, have adopted the social-democratic regime with familistic features (Bukodi and Róbert; Hamplová, both this volume). Estonia has adopted a liberal regime in many ways: few barriers to labor market dislocation or new job creation, meager support for the unemployed, no effective wage floor, low taxation of labor and privatization methods that strengthened corporate governance and thus encouraged labor shedding (Vodopivec 2000). But where liberal welfare states are typically 'defamilistic' (Blossfeld and Drobnič 2001), in the Estonian case, otherwise quite liberal, one finds aspects of familistic regimes, including one of the longest paid maternity leaves. According to Hofmeister, Mills and Blossfeld (this volume) an extremely long maternity leave sends the message to women that after a birth, they belong at home to care for the child – and not in the labor force.

The duration women could spend at home on maternity leave has varied over time. In 1956, the duration of paid maternity leave was set at 16 weeks (eight weeks before and eight weeks after childbirth). This was supplemented by unpaid childcare leave lasting three months, which was extended to a year in 1968. In 1984, the duration of paid leave increased to a year (plus a half year of unpaid childcare leave) and in 1989, to 1.5 years (plus 1.5 years unpaid leave). The available maternity leave doubled in length in 1997, and women with young children were offered up to four years of additional unemployment benefits. At the same time, the existing kindergarten system was intended mainly for three- to six-year-old children. Consequently, as the cost of labor force participation rose for women with young children, the number of women exiting the labor force increased (Orazem and Vodopivec 1999). Based on data from the Estonian Fertility and Family Survey, Figure 8.1 compares work interruptions and returns of different age cohorts, from birth cohorts of 1924 to 1973, grouped in four-year increments (see also Helemäe and Saar 2003). Most work interruptions for women have been connected with childbirth.

The duration of legal maternity leave was very short for earlier birth cohorts (1924–38), so 20 percent or more women returned to the labor market more than a half year later than legal maternity leave granted and few returned before leave was over (see Figure 8.1). The cohorts 1939–53 began to return in higher numbers before the end of leave. Analysis indicates heterogeneity among the later birth cohorts (1954–68). Women with higher education and in professional jobs returned earlier to the labor market than did women with lower levels of education and lower occupational status. It seems that in the 1990s, long work interruptions became risky, especially for women with professional careers.

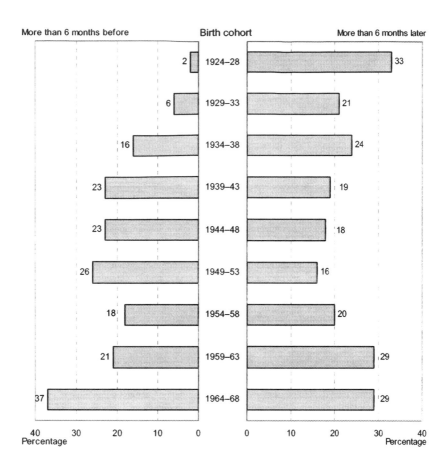

Source: Estonian Family and Fertility Survey data

Figure 8.1   *Percentage of women who return to the labor force after childbirth early or late compared with the legal duration of maternity leave, by birth cohort*

The employment rate among women with preschool children is noticeably lower in Estonia than for example in Scandinavia (Nordic Council of Ministers 1999). But of those who are employed, most have full-time jobs: 84 percent of them work more than 35 hours per week (*Statistical Yearbook of Estonia* 2002). Many young women are choosing to postpone having children because part-time work is unavailable, redistributing working hours is only possible by agreement, and hiring caregivers is not cost-effective because a large percentage of women earn fairly low wages. What differs from a familistic regime is that Estonian women do not rely on support from families, and with the increase in the pension age, grandmothers can also no longer be counted on to serve as babysitters. The divorce rate is also high, so there are many female-headed, single-parent households (Hansson 2000).

In spite of the strong formal protection of the maternity period, there is a risk (especially in small private firms) of informal regulation that penalizes female employees' maternity. When a young woman is hired, she may be obligated to sign a letter promising not to have a child during the time she is employed, or if she does take maternity leave, to accept the punishment of a downgraded job at the time she re-enters employment.

The education system

During the Soviet period, atypical proportions existed in the educational levels of men and women in Estonia. While men with university education outnumbered women in the working-age population until 1959, the 1979 and 1989 Soviet Censuses reported that women's educational level was even higher than men's and had increased more rapidly. Gender-based secondary education explains why there were such large differences in educational levels (Saar 1997). The dual character of secondary education (vocational and academic secondary education) was strongly associated with gender-specific transitions into tertiary education. There was clear gender segregation by fields of study as well, as young men and women were being prepared for different fields considered to be men's or women's work (Helemäe, Saar and Vöörmann 2000). In this sense, human capital obtained under Soviet rule had a clearly gender-specific nature.

A decrease in the proportion of female students at the beginning of the 1990s has been balanced by an increase at the end of the decade, and by 2002, 59 percent of students in the higher schools were female (*Education* 2001/2002). Overall, the education gap between men and women widened in the 1990s: the share of men with higher education decreased while that of females increased, though neither did so dramatically (*Population and Housing Census* 2002).

Yet though women in Estonia, just as women in the USA, attend and complete university at higher rates than men (Grunow, Hofmeister and Buchholz 2003), they have fewer opportunities to enjoy occupational flexibility over the life course. A largely market-oriented system of re-training has also denied them such opportunities. Women are a highly differentiated group in terms of availability of further training and re-training. Those employed in the public sector (primarily teachers but also state employees) have good opportunities and are actively involved in training activities, but those employed in the private sector, and especially those who are unemployed or who are trying to re-enter the labor market after childbearing, are highly dependent on the financial resources of their partners or kin networks because they must pay for training (Helemäe, Saar and Vöörmann 1998).

Family structures

In the 1970s and 1980s, the process of family formation in Estonia differed significantly from the process in Western Europe (Hansson 2000). In most developed western countries, the mean age of marriage continued to rise, but in Estonia, people continued to get married and have their first child at a young age through these decades. One reason was that under Soviet law, many social benefits (such as access to new apartments) were available only to people who were officially married.

The changes in Estonian family patterns and gender roles have been significant in and leading up to the 1990s, inasmuch as more emphasis began to be placed on the idealization of traditional family patterns and gender roles. This kind of ideological pressure can be interpreted as a rejection of Soviet-style gender equality and was consistent with the general political desire to re-establish the pre-war Estonian state (Narusk 1996). This resulted not so much in changes in women's behavior (only a minority of them withdrew from the labor market) as in legitimation of discrimination against women in the job market by both employers and employees as rational behavior (Vöörmann 2001b). The World Values Survey in 1990 found that less than 10 percent of the population disagreed with the opinion that if there was a job shortage, priority should be given to men (Täht and Unt 2002, p. 134).

Thus the 1990s have been marked by sharp reversals in family patterns (Hansson 2000; Katus 1998; Kutsar and Tiit 2002). Marriage and childbirth (especially of the first child) have been postponed, the birthrate has plummeted (in 1998, it was only half of what it had been in 1987), the proportion of registered marriages has dropped while the divorce rate has remained relatively high, and the percentage of children born out of wedlock and the proportion of single-parent households has increased sharply.

HYPOTHESES

This volume focuses on the impact of globalization on women's employment. Because experiences related to globalization are intensified into one decade in Estonia, we compare women's mobility patterns across this decade in three different periods. Two of the periods (1989–91 and 1992–94) were transitional. We call 1989–91 the 'pre-reform' period. This was followed by what we call the 'reform' period from 1992–94 when key market reforms were introduced. By the late 1990s, the major reforms had been enacted and the Estonian economy was considered driven less by transition than by 'real market' logic. We call 1997–99 the post-reform (or globalized market) period.

We expect women's employment mobility patterns to differ by periods owing to structural and institutional changes. Restructuring (deindustrialization and deagriculturalization) combined with the privatization of the economy exerted a dual pressure on women's labor market behavior during the reform period (Rutkowski 2003). But these pressures weakened by the time of the post-reform period, which began in 1997 (Rõõm 2002). The protection that institutions had provided for individuals weakened throughout the examined periods, increasingly displaced in importance by individuals' personal resources and location in the labor market.

We consider three characteristics that might significantly influence the different probabilities of mid-career women's labor market transitions: labor market location, personal resources (education and job tenure) and family-related circumstances.

We expect labor market location to be of greatest importance during the reform years. Certain state-owned enterprises, in particular the large factories, were under severe structural pressure as the economy restructured and privatized, despite the generally high level of employment protection in the state sector. Conversely, and despite the lack of employment protection, workers in newly established small enterprises in some segments of the private sector enjoyed favorable employment conditions. Thus, we suggest that sector and branch of economy together with the size of the firm have influenced the labor market behavior of women. By the post-reform period, we expect to find the usual market economy pattern of greater insecurity in the private sector (whether in moves into unemployment or downward mobility) than in public sector employment.

In individualist mobility regimes, workers gain stability through their own personal characteristics (DiPrete et al. 1997). We hypothesize a growth of educational inequalities in terms of the distribution of labor market risks. We do not expect a significant impact of education on the distribution of labor market risks and opportunities during the pre-reform period, owing to the high level of labor market regulation at the time. During the reform period we expect some kind of interplay between labor market opportunities and education to influence the labor market behavior of women. For women who joined the private economy, as well as for women whose labor market location was most endangered by economic restructuring, education was a very important resource to help avoid risk and to gain a better labor market location. We suggest that the Estonian institutional environment unequally channels uncertainties generated by globalization to the lower-educated groups of women. In the post-reform period, the risk of unemployment or downward mobility would be higher and upward mobility lower for the lower educated than for the higher educated. So we expect education, together with labor market location, to be important determinants in the distribution of labor market risks during the reform years.

Tenure is often seen as a worker's personal resource as well. Owing to the importance of seniority in a command economy (Clarke and Donova 1999), we suggest tenure to be an important predictor of labor market risks during the pre-reform period: the longer the tenure, the lower the risk of unemployment and forced job mobility. During the reform period, we take into account that massive increases in worker flows during the transition were driven by increases in job flows (Haltiwanger and Vodopivec 1999). So short job tenure might be an indication (a) of unfavorable labor market allocation (closed enterprises), (b) of a low level of personal resources (downsized and/or privatized enterprises) or (c) of a high level of labor market resources in the case of women looking for a better job. We expect women with short tenure in the reform period to be both most exposed to labor market risks (moving downward as well as into unemployment) *and* most successful in taking up labor market opportunities (moving upward and directly from job to job). In the post-reform period we expect job tenure to be of great importance as a personal resource, according to individualist mobility regime patterns. Earlier analyses of men's mobility pointed to the division of the Estonian labor market between highly qualified, well-protected, 'core staff' and workers with lower qualifications who failed to integrate into stable jobs (Saar and Helemäe 2002). Men with tenure lasting less than a year were the most vulnerable in terms of the risk of becoming unemployed, and we expect to find the same among women in the post-reform period.

As for the impact of family and children on women's labor market behavior, we suggest an increasing differentiation of women in terms of the opportunity they have to make a choice to work or not to work according to their cultural preferences and not just out of economic necessity, and also to have the job they want. This differentiation is the result of increasing inequalities in both wealth and education, an increasing reliance on market forces in different life domains and a weak welfare system. Under these circumstances, we expect that having a partner is a security resource that enables better (at least short-term) choices, while the existence of a preschool child is an indication of vulnerability.[1] We suggest that women with preschool children are more likely to try to avoid risks and limit voluntary moves than are women with older children or without children. We expect them to change jobs less often as well as experience less upward mobility and more downward mobility. In the reform and post-reform periods, we also expect women (especially those with lower personal resources) to prefer the status of being unemployed to that of being an unpaid caregiver or being employed in a 'bad' job.[2] Thus, we expect mothers of preschool children to have lower chances of transitions from unemployment to employment.

DATA, METHODS AND MEASURES

We combine two different data sets in our analyses: the Fertility and Family Survey (FFS) and the Estonian Labor Force Survey (ELFS). The FFS provides detailed retrospective information on work interruptions among women born from 1924 to 1973, allowing analyses from the 1940s to 1990s for women up to age 45. The target population of the Estonian FFS also included the foreign-origin population (Katus, Puur and Sakkeus 2000), but as more than a third of the foreign born population immigrated to Estonia after 1970 and part of their career had proceeded out of Estonia, we include only the native population in our analysis, bringing our sub-sample to 3307 women.

The ELFS 1995 was the first labor force survey conducted by the Statistical Office of Estonia. We use the data of ELFS 1995 to cover the 1989–94 period and the ELFS 1998, 1999 and 2000 for the period from 1997–99. In 1995, 9608 individuals (aged 15 to 74) were interviewed, but there has been considerable fluctuation in sample size since (1998: 13 090; 1999: 12 073; 2000: 7500). As retrospective data of the different waves of the ELFS cover different periods of time, we use an annual format. We study transitions of women aged 20 to 50: job mobility has been modeled as competing risks with right-censoring at the time of interview:

1   Job transitions: direct job-to-job inter-firm moves (0 = in the same job by the end of the year; 1 = direct move to another firm in that year) and inter-firm upward (0 = in the same job by the end of the year; 1 = move to a higher occupational position) and downward moves (0 = in the same job by the end of the year; 1 = move to lower occupational position). Upward and downward mobility are defined on the basis of occupational position as measured by ISCO-88, which classifies jobs into broad categories: manager, professional, semi-professional, lower non-manual worker, agricultural worker, skilled industrial worker and unskilled worker. Downward (upward) mobility is measured by movement to the next (previous) level except for moves among lower non-manual worker, agricultural worker and skilled industrial worker, which are considered lateral moves.

2   Out-of-employment transitions: moves from job to unemployment (0 = in the same job by the end of the year; 1 = move from job to unemployment in that year) and moves from job to unpaid caregiving (0 = in the same job by the end of the year; 1 = move from job to caregiving in that year). To distinguish moves to caregiving from the other moves into inactivity, we use answers to the question on the reasons for leaving the job.

3   into-employment transitions. moves from unemployment to job (0 –
    remained unemployed by the end of the year; 1 = move from
    unemployment to job in that year).

For job mobility transitions and out-of-employment transitions for every year
between 1989 and 1999, we first specify those who had at least one job spell
in a given year; then all their job spells within a given year were taken into
account. For every period, all job spells of respective years were summarized:
for example, inter-firm mobility in the pre-reform period was studied on the
basis of the sum of job spells for three years (1989, 1990 and 1991); both
right-censored (spells of jobs the respondent did not leave by the end of
respective year) and spells ended by the move to a job were taken into
account. Similarly, for transitions from unemployment into employment, for
every year between 1989 and 1999, the existence of at least one
unemployment spell during a given year was identified. For those who had
such an unemployment spell, all other unemployment spells during the
respective year were taken into account. Data on periods were summarized in
the same way as for job mobility and out-of-employment moves.

   We use logistic regression models both to compare the risk of a respective
event occurring (of job mobility, out-of-employment and into-employment
transitions) by periods, as well as to identify factors of occurrence of these
events.

RESULTS

Transitions among job states vary widely based on the time period studied
(Helemäe and Saar 2003). In the reform period, women's job-to-job moves
became more likely than in the periods before and after reforms. But it
became harder for women to avoid unemployment and to re-enter
employment after unemployment in the post-reform period compared with
the other periods.

Job-to-job moves

For mid-career women, the pre-reform (1989–91) period and the post-reform
(1997–99) period were characterized by lower probabilities of job-to-job
mobility than the reform (1992–94) period (Helemäe and Saar 2003). During
all three examined periods the probability of direct job change was highest
for those with the least job tenure. The probability of job-to-job movement of
any kind (general job churning) was largely dependent on the process of
restructuring the economy and is manifest in differences in women's industry
and education. In the reform period, the chances for mid-career women to
change their jobs diverged depending upon the industrial sector they worked

in: women in social services, the most protected segment of the economy, had the lowest chances of leaving a given job compared with the transformative sector, while those in the agricultural, producer, personal and distributive sectors had higher chances of changing jobs. Compared with higher-educated women, women at all lower levels of education were less likely to change jobs in all three periods, though the statistical significance moves from those with the very lowest education to those with secondary education by the post-reform period. The impact of family factors remained about the same during all three periods examined: marriage reduced job mobility.

Chances of upward mobility, risks of downward mobility

As for women's upward and downward mobility, a kind of crystallization of labor market opportunity structures has occurred: the post-reform period is characterized by lower probabilities of vertical moves both upward and downward when compared with the reform period (Helemäe and Saar 2003).

The predictors of upward and downward mobility changed over the transition period (see Table 8.2). In the reform and the post-reform period, tenure in the current job differentiated the probability of upward moves: those with more job tenure were less likely to rise on the occupation ladder. Long tenure also decreased chances of moving down only in the post-reform years.

We can see that low-qualified women were significantly less likely than those with higher education to have upward job opportunities during the reform period. This effect diminishes significantly by the time of the post-reform period. Education had no impact on the probability of downward mobility during any examined period. As there was no real downward mobility in the pre-reform period, education levels were irrelevant to mobility. The reform and post-reform periods were characterized by gradually shrinking labor market opportunities for everyone, and higher education levels provided little protection.

During the reform period, chances of upward mobility were influenced by the previous job, being lowest for those leaving jobs in social services compared with the transformative industry and relatively high in agriculture, producer services and personal services. In the reform period, women employed in social services and personal and distributive services were protected from downward mobility relative to the transformative sector. Sector has no impact on career mobility.

Family-related characteristics have no effect on women's chances of upward mobility. But, as we expected, women without partners were exposed to greater risks of downward moves when compared with married women.

Table 8.2 Chances of upward and downward mobility for Estonian women by periods: results of logistic regression models

	Pre-reform		Reform		Post-reform	
	Upward	*Downward*	*Upward*	*Downward*	*Upward*	*Downward*
Tenure						
Up to 12 months (ref)						
13–24 months	−0.76	−0.13	−0.49	0.09	−0.32	−0.64
25–60 months	−0.57	0.05	−0.70**	0.10	−0.66*	−0.99**
61+ months	−1.22***	−0.39	−0.89*	0.04	−1.66***	−1.23***
Which job during year	−0.84	−1.18	−2.00***	−1.33**	−0.83*	−1.30*
Education						
Primary and basic	−0.35	−0.77	−1.12**	−0.31	−0.46	0.03
Secondary	−0.53	−0.16	−0.71**	0.15	−0.55*	0.01
Second. specialized	−0.52	−0.16	−0.45	0.32	−0.23	−0.24
Higher (ref)						
Industry						
Transformative (ref)						
Agriculture	−0.07	−0.23	0.72*	−0.11	−0.15	0.21
Producer services	0.14	0.44	0.71*	0.21	0.72	0.82*
Social services	0.11	0.01	−0.69*	−0.78***	0.09	−0.64
Personal and distributive services	0.35	−0.30	0.49*	−0.39*	0.61*	0.21
Sector						
Public (ref)						
Private	−0.22	−0.01	−0.02	−0.19	0.30	−0.51
Age of youngest child						
No child of preschool age (ref)						
Child under six years	0.45	0.32	−0.14	−0.08	0.13	−0.66
Marital status						
Unmarried	0.27	0.58**	0.21	0.38*	0.25	0.23
Married (ref)						
Constant	−2.47***	−2.67**	−0.60	−1.92**	−2.73***	−1.72*
Number of events	86	111	141	188	105	82
Number of episodes	6158	6490	5622	5851	5945	5925
−2 log likelihood	875	1097	1244	1613	993	832

Note: *** $p <= 0.001$, ** $p <= 0.01$, * $p <= 0.05$

Source: Estonian Labor Force Surveys

Transition to unemployment

Our earlier analysis showed that the risks of moves to unemployment in post-reform years were higher than in the pre-reform period and about the same as during the reform period (Helemäe and Saar 2003).

During the pre-reform period, women with job tenure up to one year did not differ from women with job tenure up to five years in terms of exposure to unemployment risks (Table 8.3). From the reform period on, however, women with less than one year in the current job had very special labor market behavior. In the reform years, their mobility had signs of both greater vulnerability (higher risks of unemployment) and attainment (greater chances of upward moves).

Higher education (as well as secondary specialized education) provided women with more security from unemployment than basic education.

Labor market location appears to have had important consequences for unemployment risks first in the reform period. In relative terms, employment in social services provided women with the most security compared with the transformative sector, and employment in agriculture provided the least.[3]

Women employed in the private sector had a lower probability of transition to unemployment compared with women employed in the public sector, certainly a 'transitional' phenomenon related to the first years of privatization, and especially evident due to the annual format of our data.

We can see that the impact of having a preschool child on the job–unemployment transition differed by periods. In pre-reform years, women with children of preschool age were exposed to greater unemployment risks, which may have been a kind of 'hidden' move to caregiving. Under worsening labor market conditions as well as the growing revival of traditional gender role ideology in the reform and post-reform period, women with children aged under three were less likely to move to unemployment. There is a probability that those at risk of losing their jobs chose caregiving instead, thus selecting out of the pool available to become unemployed. During the reform and post-reform periods it might have been preferable and more legitimate to stay at home with a small child as a caregiver than to stay at poorly remunerated workplaces in shrinking enterprises.

During the post-reform period, unmarried women were exposed to a higher risk of unemployment than married women. Taken together with the data on downward mobility, this indicates worsening labor market opportunities for women and the fact that married women who stayed in the market after the reform period are a select group who are less likely to become unemployed or would opt for caregiving if the possibility arose.

Table 8.3   Risks of transition from job to unemployment for Estonian women by periods: results of logistic regression models

	Pre-reform		Reform		Post-reform	
	Beta	*SE*	*Beta*	*SE*	*Beta*	*SE*
Tenure						
Up to 12 months (ref)						
13–24 months	−0.77	(0.49)	−0.83***	(0.19)	−0.87***	(0.16)
25–60 months	−0.32	(0.37)	−0.86***	(0.17)	−1.37***	(0.16)
61+ months	−0.84*	(0.37)	−1.00***	(0.16)	−1.54***	(0.15)
Which job during year	−1.59*	(0.77)	−1.67***	(0.24)	−1.43***	(0.25)
Education						
Primary and basic	1.13*	(0.50)	0.61**	(0.24)	0.95***	(0.21)
Secondary	0.77	(0.42)	0.61***	(0.18)	0.46*	(0.19)
Secondary specialized	0.52	(0.44)	0.36	(0.19)	0.26	(0.20)
Higher (ref)						
Industry						
Transformative (ref)						
Agriculture	0.35	(0.40)	0.57***	(0.18)	0.10	(0.20)
Producer services	0.03	(0.63)	−0.47	(0.30)	0.08	(0.24)
Social services	0.00	(0.36)	−0.89***	(0.18)	−0.51*	(0.24)
Personal and distributive services	0.50	(0.31)	0.10	(0.14)	0.08	(0.13)
Sector						
Public (ref)						
Private	−0.24	(0.31)	−0.36**	(0.13)	0.17	(0.19)
Age of youngest child						
No child of preschool age (ref)						
Child under 6 years	0.70**	(0.26)	−0.12	(0.14)	−0.18	(0.15)
Marital status						
Unmarried	0.28	(0.25)	0.18	(0.12)	0.33**	(0.11)
Married (ref)						
Constant	−3.39***	(1.06)	−0.50	(0.38)	−0.89*	(0.41)
Number of events	75		375		387	
Number of episodes	6893		6529		6868	
−2 log likelihood	796		2721		2748	

Note: *** $p \leq 0.001$, ** $p \leq 0.01$, * $p \leq 0.05$

Source: Estonian Labor Force Surveys

Exit from unemployment

For mid-career women, opportunities to move from unemployment back to a job were lower during the post-reform period than in both pre-reform and reform periods (Helemäe and Saar 2003, pp. 17–18). During the post-reform period, the risks of moves to unemployment were about the same as during the reform period, though for mid-career women the post-reform period brought about a higher risk of experiencing a long unemployment spell than during the reform period (Helemäe and Saar 2003).

For the pre-reform period, women with very short unemployment spells (less than six months) were much more likely than the long-term unemployed (over two years) to become re-employed (Table 8.4). But re-entry chances in the reform and post-reform periods extended to women unemployed up to two years. By the post-reform period, women's duration of unemployment spells, as well as their rate of long-term unemployment, had significantly increased (Venesaar et al. 2004). The change points to worsened conditions for women unemployed longer than 24 months.

During the reform period, women with higher education had significantly better chances of re-employment than women with less education. The pervasiveness of unemployment for all eliminated this advantage by the post-reform period. As we expected, mothers with preschool children had lower chances of transitions from unemployment to employment during the reform and post-reform periods. In the reform and post-reform periods, women had the opportunity to get unemployment benefits until their children went to school. Under unfavorable labor market conditions, to stay unemployed was a quite reasonable solution for women who had restricted opportunities to find good jobs. This is why we suggest that the higher risk for women with young children to stay in the unemployment pool might be not so much a direct consequence of their inability to find a job as a legally legitimate way to avoid 'bad' jobs.

Transition to caregiving

Women were more likely to move to caregiving in the pre-reform period compared with the next two periods (Helemäe and Saar 2003). Women with more job tenure had lower chances of moving to caregiving in the pre-reform period. This effect disappears by the post-reform period (see Table 8.5).[4]

In pre-reform as well as reform years, moves to caregiving were influenced by marital status rather than by having a child under the age of six. By the post-reform period, marital status had no impact on the probability of moving into unpaid caregiving, while having a child of preschool age turned out to be the most important factor. There are several explanations. First, married

Table 8.4   Chances of transition from unemployment to job for Estonian women by periods: results of logistic regression models

	Pre-reform		Reform		Post-reform	
	Beta	SE	Beta	SE	Beta	SE
Duration						
Up to 6 months	1.29*	(0.64)	1.07***	(0.31)	1.48***	(0.19)
7–12 months	−0.30	(0.72)	1.14***	(0.33)	1.22***	(0.21)
13–24 months	−0.23	(0.90)	0.37	(0.34)	0.70**	(0.22)
25+ months (ref)						
Which unemployment spell during year			−1.05*	(0.49)	−1.15**	(0.42)
Education						
Primary and basic	−0.58	(0.80)	−1.08***	(0.31)	−0.34	(0.25)
Secondary	−0.40	(0.70)	−0.56*	(0.24)	−0.11	(0.22)
Secondary specialized	−0.55	(0.75)	−0.66**	(0.25)	−0.17	(0.24)
Higher (ref)						
Age of youngest child						
No child of preschool age (ref)						
Child under 6 years	0.25	(0.38)	−0.47**	(0.16)	−0.37**	(0.14)
Marital status						
Unmarried	0.61	(0.40)	0.15	(0.15)	−0.22	(0.13)
Married (ref)						
Constant	−0.82	(0.86)	0.55	(0.61)	−0.09	(0.49)
Number of events	63		372		418	
Number of episodes	143		881		1175	
−2 log likelihood	175		1146		1440	

Note: *** $p \leq 0.001$, ** $p \leq 0.01$, * $p \leq 0.05$

Source: Estonian Labor Force Surveys

women without small children have changed their behavior: in the post-reform period they moved to caregiving significantly less frequently compared with the pre-reform and reform periods. The second reason relates to job relations during maternity leave: in the pre-reform and reform periods leaves were interpreted (by official rules as well as women themselves) just as temporary leave, not as leaving a job.

Table 8.5 Chances of transition from job to caregiving for Estonian women by periods: results of logistic regression models

	Pre-reform		Reform		Post-reform	
	Beta	SE	Beta	SE	Beta	SE
Tenure						
Up to 12 months (ref)						
13–24 months	−0.32	(0.20)	−0.69**	(0.23)	0.29	(0.25)
25–60 months	−0.62***	(0.19)	−0.46*	(0.20)	0.40	(0.24)
61+ months	−1.46***	(0.19)	−1.45***	(0.23)	−0.03	(0.25)
Which job during year	−1.71***	(0.37)	−1.95***	(0.37)	−0.53	(0.45)
Education						
Primary and basic	−0.72*	(0.31)	0.42	(0.29)	0.66*	(0.33)
Secondary	0.14	(0.17)	0.05	(0.21)	0.35	(0.25)
Secondary specialized	−0.07	(0.18)	0.06	(0.21)	0.48	(0.25)
Higher (ref)						
Industry						
Transformative (ref)						
Agriculture	0.35	(0.21)	0.28	(0.29)	−0.40	(0.36)
Producer services	−0.07	(0.30)	0.55	(0.32)	0.03	(0.38)
Social services	0.09	(0.17)	0.18	(0.23)	0.10	(0.34)
Personal and distributive services	0.27	(0.17)	0.36	(0.21)	0.05	(0.22)
Sector						
Public (ref)						
Private	−0.05	(0.16)	−0.10	(0.18)	0.24	(0.29)
Age of youngest child						
No child of preschool age (ref)						
Child under six years	0.22	(0.13)	−0.05	(0.17)	3.42***	(0.22)
Marital status						
Unmarried	−0.76***	(0.16)	−0.72***	(0.19)	−0.04	(0.19)
Married (ref)						
Constant	−0.50	(0.49)	−0.69*	(0.52)	−5.44***	(0.71)
Number of events	299		200		181	
Number of episodes	7117		6354		6662	
−2 log likelihood	2324		1681		1237	

Note: *** $p \leq 0.001$, ** $p \leq 0.01$, * $p \leq 0.05$

Source: Estonian Labor Force Surveys

DISCUSSION AND CONCLUSION

A comparison of mobility during three periods confirmed the growing uncertainties experienced by mid-career women in Estonia. Deep institutional and structural changes that occurred during a short period of time, a substantial decrease in labor demand, and weak safety nets contributed to growing (both real and perceived) insecurity: at the end of the twentieth century, Estonian women's mobility was predominantly driven by the demand side, and the overall level of mobility depended on the level of involuntary mobility. During the post-reform period, even highly educated women had difficulties with employment security; their chance of re-employment did not differ from that of women with only a basic education. This equality of women with different educational qualification came about not so much because of improved opportunities for the less well educated as due to the shrinking opportunities for the highly educated, as their share of long-term unemployment had increased. In sum, women's chances of longer-term unemployment were growing in the post-reform years. Moreover, the outcomes of direct job-to-job moves were also rather uncertain.

In Estonia women adjust their family behavior to employment opportunities rather than employment adjusting to family. This style began under socialism and has not changed in a globalized economy. Economic necessity was, and is, one important reason, but other reasons are period-specific: under socialism it was ideological pressure, while under post-socialism it is a lack of institutional support to deal with multiple uncertainties.

If, according to DiPrete et al. (1997), *de*commodification does not necessarily contribute to a reduction of job mobility, maybe Estonia is an example of how too rapid *re*commodification does. The strong policies aimed at reducing restrictions on employers' freedom of action were accompanied by weak policies aimed at reducing the impact of forced mobility on individual social welfare.

It would be safe to conclude that the institutional rules worked out during the reform period that were aimed at preventing labor market rigidities have not worked as intended. Further analysis of mobility during more favorable economic circumstances would help to understand whether quick shock-type deregulation, once considered a long-term solution for labor market adjustment, will produce the intended outcomes for women's careers.

NOTES

1   We are aware of limitations of such an approach: under a weak welfare system, an unemployed or inactive partner might indicate vulnerability, and under globalization, women with preschool children might be a pre-selected group with

enough resources to make such a binding decision and thus have better opportunities to make other choices as well. Still, employed prime-age husbands outnumber unemployed and inactive ones, and women have children under many circumstances, not only when economically secure or assured of such security in the future.

2   According to the Law on Social Protection of the unemployed, persons rearing a child under six had the right to state unemployment benefits.

3   While the post-reform period data (Table 8.3) do not reveal significant impacts of labor market industry on probability of transition into unemployment, it could be due to the close connection between industry and sector. Public sector jobs dominate social services, and women are also predominantly located here. Separate analyses showed that public sector jobs and social services jobs both provided women relatively secure employment in the post-reform period.

4   According to our initial analyses (not shown here), age played a crucial role as a factor in the transition to caregiving but had no impact on the probability of other moves.

BIBLIOGRAPHY

Arro, R., Eamets, R., Järve, J., Kallaste, E. and Philips, K. (2001) 'Labour market flexibility and employment security', Employment Paper No. 25, Geneva: International Labour Office.

Blossfeld, H.-P. and Drobnič, S. (2001) 'Theoretical perspectives on couples' careers', in H.-P. Blossfeld and S. Drobnič (eds) *Careers of couples in contemporary societies. From male breadwinner to dual earner families*, Oxford: Oxford University Press, pp. 16–50.

Cazes, S. and Nesporova, A. (2001) 'Towards excessive job insecurity in transition economies?', Employment Paper No. 23, Geneva: International Labour Office.

Cazes, S. and Nesporova, A. (2003) *Labour markets in transition: balancing flexibility and security in Central and Eastern Europe*, Geneva: International Labour Office.

Clarke, S. and Donova, I. (1999) 'Internal mobility and labour market flexibility in Russia', *Europe-Asia Studies*, 51(2): 213–43.

DiPrete, T.A., de Graaf, P.M., Luijkx, R., Tåhlin, M. and Blossfeld, H.-P. (1997) 'Collective versus individualist mobility regimes? Structural change and job mobility in four countries', *American Journal of Sociology*, 103: 318–58.

Eamets, R. (2001) *Reallocation of labour during transition disequilibrium and policy issues the case of Estonia*, Tartu: Tartu University Press.

Education (2001/2002) Tallinn: Statistical Office of Estonia.

Gerber, T.P. (2002) 'Structural change and post-socialist stratification: labor market transitions in contemporary Russia', *American Sociological Review*, 67: 629–59.

Grunow, D., Hofmeister, H. and Buchholz S. (2003) 'Rising uncertainty and the erosion of the male breadwinner family? Comparing the implications of globalization for women's employment in (West) Germany and the U.S.', GLOBALIFE Working Paper No. 43, Chair of Sociology I, University of Bamberg.

Haltiwanger, J.C. and Vodopivec, M. (1999) 'Cross worker and job flows in a transition economy: an analysis of Estonia', Policy Research Working Paper No. 2082, Washington, DC: World Bank.

Hansson, L. (2000) 'The changing family in Estonia and Europe', in R. Vetik (ed.) *Estonian human development report 2000*, Tallinn: UNDP, pp. 42–8.

Helemäe, J. and Saar, E. (2003) 'Women's employment in Estonia', GLOBALIFE Working Paper No. 48, Chair of Sociology I, University of Bamberg.

Helemäe, J., Saar, E. and Vöörmann, R. (1998) 'Adult education and integration', in *Estonian human development report 1998*, Tallinn: UNDP, pp. 24–31.

Helemäe, J., Saar, E. and Vöörmann, R. (2000) *Kas haridusse tasus investeerida?*, Tallinn: Teaduste Akadeemia Kirjastus.

Katus, K. (1998) 'Development of population', in J. Sillaste, S. Laud and U. Kask (eds) *Social trends*, Tallinn: Statistical Office of Estonia.

Katus, K., Puur, A. and Sakkeus, L. (2000) *Fertility and family surveys in countries of ECE region*, Estonia, New York and Geneva: United Nations.

Kutsar, D. and Tiit, E.-M. (2002) 'The individual life course in the context of family development', in D. Kutsar (ed.) *Living conditions in Estonia five years later*, Tartu: Tartu University Press, pp. 7–36.

Labour Force 2001 (2001), Tallinn: Statistical Office of Estonia.

Lapidus, G.W. (1994) 'Gender and restructuring: the impact of Perestroika and its aftermath on Soviet women', in V.M. Moghadam (ed.) *Democratic reform and the position of women in transitional economies*, Oxford: Clarendon Press, pp. 137–61.

Mach, B.W., Mayer, K.U. and Pohoski, M. (1994) 'Job changes in the Federal Republic of Germany and Poland: a longitudinal assessment of the impact of welfare-capitalist and state-socialist labour-market segmentation', *European Sociological Review*, 10: 1–28.

Mills, M. and Blossfeld, H.-P. (2005) 'Globalization, uncertainty and the early life course: a theoretical framework', in H.-P. Blossfeld, E. Klijzing, M. Mills and K. Kurz (eds) *Globalization, uncertainty, and youth in society*, London: Routledge.

Narusk, A. (1996) 'Gender outcomes of the transition in Estonia', *Finnish Review of East European Studies*, 3–4: 22–39.

Noorkõiv, R., Orazem, P.F., Puur, A. and Vodopivec, M. (1997) 'How Estonia's economic transition affected employment and wages (1989–95)', Policy Research Working Paper No. 1837, Washington, DC: World Bank.

Nordic Council of Ministers (1999) 'Women and men in the Nordic countries', Nordic Council of Ministers.

Orazem, P.F. and Vodopivec, M. (1999) 'Male-female differences in labor market outcomes during the early transition to market: the case of Estonia and Slovenia', Policy Research Working Paper No. 2087, Washington, DC: World Bank.

Population and Housing Census 2000 (2002) Tallinn: Statistical Office of Estonia.

Riboud, M., Sánchez-Páramo, D. and Silva-Jáuregui, C. (2002) *Does Eurosclerosis matter? Institutional reform and labour market performance in Central and Eastern European countries in the 1990s*, Washington, DC: World Bank.

Rõõm, M. (2002) 'Unemployment and labour mobility in Estonia: analysis using duration models', Working Papers No. 7, Tallinn: Bank of Estonia.

Rutkowski, J. (2003) 'Rapid labor reallocation with a stagnant unemployment pool: the puzzle of the labor market in Lithuania', Policy Research Working Paper No. 2946, Washington, DC: World Bank.

Saar, E. (1997) 'Transitions to tertiary education in Belarus and the Baltic countries', *European Sociological Review*, 13: 139–58.

Saar, E. (2005) 'New entrants on the Estonian labour market: a comparison with the EU countries', *European Societies*, 7(4):513–46.

Saar, E. and Helemäe, J. (2002) 'Employment careers of men in Estonia', GLOBALIFE Working Paper No. 39, Chair of Sociology I, University of Bamberg.

Statistical Yearbook of Estonia (2002) Tallinn: Statistical Office of Estonia.

Täht, K. and Unt, M. (2002) 'Gender and the Estonian labour market', in E. Saar (ed.) *Up and down – winners and losers in post-socialist Estonia*, Tallinn: Estonian Academy Publishers, pp. 126–44.

Terk, E. (1999a) *Erastamine Eestis: ideoloogia, läbiviimine, tulemused*, Tallinn: Estonian Institute for Future Studies.

Terk, E. (1999b) 'Estonia's economic development: achievements, conflicts, prospects', in R. Vetik (ed.) *Estonian human development report 1999*, Tallinn: UNDP, pp. 60–66.

Transition. The first ten years. Analysis and lessons for Eastern Europe and the former Soviet Union (2001) Washington, DC: World Bank.

Venesaar, U., Hinnosaar, M., Luuk, M. and Marksoo, Ü. (2004) *Pikaajaline töötus*, Tallinn: Tallinn University of Technology.

Vodopivec, M. (2000) 'Worker reallocation during Estonia's transition to market: how efficient and how equitable?', Social Protection Discussion Paper No. 0018, World Bank.

Vöörmann, R. (2001a) *Social trends 2*, Tallinn: Statistical Office of Estonia.

Vöörmann, R. (2001b) 'Sotsiaalsed probleemid Eestis: meeste ja naiste vaatenurk', in E. Heinla (ed.) *Kultuur, Elukvaliteet ja Väärtushinnangud*, Tallinn: Tallinna Pedagoogikaülikool, pp. 50–58.

9. Women and the labor market in the Czech Republic: transition from a socialist to a social-democratic regime?

Dana Hamplová

INTRODUCTION

Former socialist countries attempted to create self-sufficient economic units that stood outside the international marketplace, using central planning and governmental intervention as a substitute for market forces. This was ultimately neither economically nor politically viable. In a sense, such countries engaged in a rather unsuccessful experiment in shutting themselves off from the trends characteristic of globalization. It could therefore be argued that after the collapse of communism, these countries experienced 'globalization shock.' While market economies were able to adapt to globalization trends at a relatively gradual pace, formerly socialist economies faced quite sudden pressures to liberalize their economies. This chapter will address the effects of the transition on women's labor market experiences in the Czech Republic with an eye toward evaluating which welfare regime type is emerging.

Hans-Peter Blossfeld (2000) and others (Layte et al. 2002) have argued that the impact of economic liberalization, free trade and other typical forms of globalization are influenced by country-specific logic, mechanisms and institutions. Though this logic was applied to compare different types of welfare regimes, it is also valid for post-socialist countries. Some socialist countries (such as Hungary or Poland) adopted market-oriented reforms by the late 1970s, while others (such as Czechoslovakia) maintained a rigid, centrally planned economy until the collapse of communism. Country-specific institutional filters and social policies mediated the speed and extent with which these countries undertook the transition to a market economy and were inspired by different types of welfare regimes. For example, while Hungary headed towards a social-democratic regime with familistic features (Róbert and Budoki 2002), Estonia adopted a more liberal market orientation.

Pre-war Czechoslovakia had a social-democratic regime with rather moderate levels of social inequality compared with Northern and Western European countries (Večerník 1996a, p. 3), and it will be argued here that the post-communist Czech Republic is moving back to this pattern. Despite the liberal ideology and rhetoric evident in the first years of transformation, reforms were oriented more towards a social-democratic than a liberal regime (see Hofmeister, Blossfeld and Mills, this volume). That is to say that the country maintains a generous welfare system, and some areas (for example, the housing market) have not been deregulated at all, even 14 years after the end of communist rule. The following sections will elaborate on these events.

This chapter covers the period of economic transition from a centrally planned economy to a market economy, and later to economic stabilization and thus to participation in the globalized world economy. In the first part of the chapter, background is provided on economic reforms. Since women's labor force participation, job mobility and exits from and returns to the labor force are closely connected with their family responsibilities, special attention is also given to childcare and institutional settings related to family caregiving.

I test the globalization hypotheses for the Czech Republic but I argue that Czech women have few choices in whether or not to work full-time. Under socialism, everyone was forced to work for pay (including women) for ideological reasons and because the economy was closed, with wages and prices set centrally. After the fall of the Iron Curtain, rates of full-time employment are still high, but mainly because employers do not offer part-time work or because families need two full-time earners to make ends meet. While the proportion of women in full-time jobs suggests the Czech labor market protects women from job insecurity, the rate of full-time employment stems mainly from the fact that Czech women have few options for part-time work. Despite the fact that one-half of the women with a child of preschool age are working in full-time jobs, only a minority of women do so voluntarily, according to the International Social Survey Program (ISSP) opinion survey from 1994 (see Table 9.1).

In the Czech context, if globalization brings about a higher proportion of part-time jobs and higher flexibility, which women often desire during certain life cycles, women could be 'winners' in the process. However, the development of the Czech labor market does not indicate any such shift. Governmental regulations do not permit the full liberalization of the labor market. Part-time jobs feature the same social benefits and protection as full-time jobs, and this makes them expensive for employers. Though it could be argued that in the future the labor market will have to become more flexible, this kind of development has yet to take place.

Table 9.1   Real and demanded economic activity of Czech mothers (percentage)

	Full-time		Part-time		At home	
	Real	Demanded	Real	Demanded	Real	Demanded
With a child of preschool age	49.9	6.0	19.2	43.4	30.9	50.6
With a child of school age	68.2	20.7	16.8	60.9	15.0	18.4
After children had left home	91.7	85.9	3.1	12.9	5.1	1.2

Source: Čermáková et al. (2000), p. 93; ISSP 1994

ECONOMIC REFORMS AND LABOR MARKETS

In the early 1990s, Czechoslovakia (later the Czech Republic) shifted sharply away from a rigid, centrally planned economy. Domestic prices were liberalized and most foreign trade controls were lifted in January 1991, and the most significant macro-economic reforms, including economic liberalization, macro-economic stabilization and privatization, were introduced by the end of 1993 (Večerník 1996a, p. 1). In response, GDP declined sharply, but by 1993 it started to grow again (see Table 9.2). In 1995, the Czech Republic introduced full current account convertibility, joined the World Trade Organization (WTO) and became a member of the OECD.

Under a command economy, there was a permanent shortage of workers even though the regime pursues a policy of full, compulsory employment (Večerník 1996a, p. 26). Officially, unemployment did not exist, and it was a crime punishable by imprisonment to be outside the labor force. The result was that those who would be most vulnerable in a standard market economy were protected.

The labor market in Czechoslovakia was characterized by high female labor participation in full-time jobs. In the mid-1980s, women constituted 46 percent of the labor force. Household work was not considered 'real work' (Freiová 1998), and both direct and indirect pressure was put on women to enter paid employment. In this respect the policy of income equalization was of particular importance: wages were set at such a level that two incomes were necessary in all social strata; there was no significant difference between education groups or social classes in the need for two incomes.

Economic liberalization in the 1990s meant an initial decline in employment for men and women, and higher-than-before job-to-job mobility. The new labor market conditions required adjustments, and the supply-and-demand side of the labor market had to be redefined.

Table 9.2   Macro-economic development in the Czech Republic, 1991 to 1999

	1991	1992	1993	1994	1995	1996	1997	1998	1999
GDP in constant prices (percentage change)**	−11.5	−3.3	0.6	3.2	6.4	3.9	1.0	−2.7	−0.4*
GDP in capita (US dollars)	2466	2903	3332	3977	5040	5620	5109	5412	5189
Share of trade in GDP (in percentage)	66.9	63.1	82.8	80.9	89.6	85.0	95.2	99.1	104.2
Real exports of goods and services (percentage change)				0.2*	16.7*	8.2*	9.2*	9.1*	6.3*
Real imports of goods and services (percentage change)				7.6*	21.2*	13.4*	8.1*	6.5*	5.4*
Share of private sector in GDP (percentage)	15.0	30.0	45.0	65.0	70.0	75.0	75.0	75.0	80.0

Notes: * Source: OECD (2001)
         ** Constant prices in 1984 up to and including 1993; 1994 prices thereafter

Source: EBDR – Transition Report (2000)

Change in employment in the 1990s

Three factors contributed to the decline in the employment rate of men and women. First, educational opportunities have expanded and a higher proportion of young people stay in school longer. There are no available statistics on age-specific school enrollment, but the number of women studying at university or college at any given time increased by 80 percent between 1993 and 2001 (*Czech Statistical Yearbooks* 1994–2002).

Second, the retirement of employed pensioners and the practice of early retirements were important channels for an outflow from the employment sector. Employed pensioners represented one-tenth of the workforce, and their numbers were nearly halved in the very first year of the economic transformation (Frýdmanová et al. 1999, p. 21). Between 1988 and 1993, the number of retired women of pre-retirement age increased from 10 percent to 16 percent (Matějů 1999, p. 160).

Third, unemployment was a new phenomenon in the labor market after 1991, and decline in employment among middle-aged women is most often attributable to this cause. The start of the economic transformation brought about a temporary spike in unemployment, but at the end of 1991, owing to cuts in the generous long-term unemployment benefits, the level of unemployment dropped. Unemployment has been regionalized, and some

regions (for example, Prague) even experienced an increasing shortage of
workers (Večerník 1996a, p. 30). The trends in unemployment for men and
women are similar, with a slightly higher level for women (see Table 9.3). In
the aggregate, women comprise 45 percent of the labor force by the end of
the 1990s.

Table 9.3   Unemployment rate of Czech men and women, 1990 to 2000

	1990	1991	1992	1993	1994	1995	1996	1997	1998	1999	2000
Men	0.70	3.47	2.15	2.98	2.51	2.32	2.85	3.70	5.10	7.60	7.20
Women	0.76	4.81	3.00	4.10	3.97	3.63	4.29	6.52	8.20	10.70	10.60

Source: Czech Statistical Office

Three main factors contributed to the Czech 'employment miracle': (1) a
reduction in the labor supply, (2) the good initial state of the economy 'in
terms of the industrial structure of employment and skill levels,' and (3)
wage moderation. The last factor is of special importance, as it points to a
governmental policy aimed at offsetting the unregulated development of the
labor market. It was based on a low-wage, low-unemployment trade-off
designed to maintain high employment in the economy. Exchange-rate policy
and wage controls were used to keep Czech wages low in dollar terms, as
well as lower than in other Central European economies, despite the fact that
labor productivity and GDP per capita were higher in terms of purchasing-
power parity than in these other countries.[1] Low wages kept more workers
employed and thus reduced the main initial social and economic costs of
transition – namely, unemployment (Orenstein and Hale 2001, p. 271). In
1995, wage regulations were lifted, and since 1996 unemployment has been
growing and now hovers around 9 percent.

Female unemployment is age-specific: it peaks in the younger age groups
and declines after age 35. It is connected not only with the lack of experience
of new entrants into the labor market, but also with family responsibilities,
employer expectations and especially the shortage of part-time jobs in the
Czech Republic (Čermáková et al. 2000). Women work in full-time jobs
largely owing to the paucity of alternatives: only 5 percent of employment is
part-time, a very low figure in international comparison (OECD 2002). One
can conjecture that the registered unemployment of mothers with small
children is in many cases a sort of 'false unemployment'; it entitles a woman
to collect social benefits and support while allowing full-time childcare.

Job-to-job mobility and sector change

The job market has featured not only a decline in employment but also high job-to-job mobility. More than 70 percent of the labor force experienced at least one job change from 1990 to 1995. This figure does not take into account those just entering or exiting the labor market, privatization or the re-organization of previously existing firms (Večerník 1996a; 1996b), but refers exclusively to job and occupational changes. During the transition period, women experienced a lower level of job-to-job mobility than men, though still higher than pre-transition levels.

Under the socialist system, administrative control led to the suppression of a large range of business services that are normally required to facilitate the operation of markets (accounting, financial services, lawyers, and so on). The liberalization of the economy brought about a rapid increase in the number of people employed in these services. Between 1989 and 1999, the proportion of the labor force in the service sector increased from 41 to 54 percent and the labor force in industrial production declined by 8 percent. This rapid growth in the service sector has also meant more job opportunities for women.

Changes in wage distribution

Even within the Eastern bloc, socialist Czechoslovakia had one of the most equalized levels of income distribution, with wage distribution characterized by three main features: (1) the peak of the age curve was gradually shifting towards older workers (rewards for the 'founding fathers'); (2) redistribution flowed from the service sector into manufacturing and agriculture; and (3) the position of university educated people deteriorated and the differences between various levels of education were diminished (Večerník 1996a). The promotion of the working class (following communist ideology) was thus economically implemented through the manipulation of wages.

Economic liberalization created a different basis for wage differentiation, though until the mid-1990s wages were regulated through taxation. The first year of the transformation saw a short, sharp decline in GDP and in 1991 real wages decreased by 25 percent (Bosworth and Ofer 1995, Večerník 1996a, p. 51), but since 1992 real wages have been rising. The position of the lowest income group seems to have remained unchanged, owing to the introduction of the minimum wage. However, transformation did open up an opportunity for expansion within the highest income groups. Since 1992 the top income has been rising, and in the mid-1990s income inequality reached levels similar to those in Germany (Večerník 1996a, p. 61).

WORK AND THE FAMILY: CHILDCARE AND OTHER SUPPORT INSTITUTIONS

Socialist welfare: maternity leave and public childcare

Despite high rates of female labor participation, women also remain responsible for childcare and the household. This double burden may have contributed to a decline in fertility in the 1950s and 1960s. A set of policies was introduced, in response, to enable women to combine work outside the household with maternity. Paid maternity leave lasting six months was introduced in the later 1960s, and in 1971, this leave was extended to 24 months.

A network of childcare facilities was established in the same era, such that by the late 1980s, nearly 15 percent of infants (up to two years old) attended nurseries, and nearly 90 percent of those aged three to five attended preschools. Despite these high numbers, there was still insufficient capacity and not all applications for preschool were accommodated (Freiová 1998). Therefore grandmothers have played an important role in raising children (Možný 1990; 1991).

High labor force participation led to a particular marriage and fertility pattern common to other Eastern European nations: very high marriage rates (97 percent of women) and early first marriages (for women, at a mean age of 21; mode at 19.7), with the first child born within a few years thereafter. A 'typical' Czech woman had her second (and in most cases last) child by age 26 (Fialová et al. 2000). About half the women had their second child within two years of the first. This allowed these women to combine two maternity leaves, thus to spend four years devoted to childcare while receiving public support. When these women subsequently started their careers, their reproductive phase already lay behind them so no major career-path interruption lay before them.

Social policy in the 1990s

Maternity leave has now been transformed into paid parental leave that now extends to four years. Benefits during the first six months are derived from the level of the woman's prior wages, and a flat rate is applied subsequently. This can be combined with other types of social benefits that are means tested and depend on the income of the household. Parental leave includes social and health insurance until a child turns seven. Employers are obliged to hold a woman's specific position open for six months and to hold a job within the company open for her for three years. Employers may not dismiss a woman during her pregnancy.[2]

There is a widespread belief that public childcare has collapsed in all post-communist countries, but this is not true for all countries nor for all facilities.

On the one hand, public nurseries in the Czech Republic have nearly disappeared, with less than 1 percent of infants cared for by public institutions in 2001; 82 percent of the places available in nurseries are now privately organized.[3] On the other hand, the number of available places in preschools actually exceeds the number of children of preschool age (Czech Statistical Office). Though the number of children in preschool dropped by 23 percent between 1991 and 2001, this reflects a slump in the birth rate rather than in demand.[4] More than 90 percent of three- to five-year-olds attend a preschool, an even higher percentage than in the later 1980s. This explains why, at 2.7 years, the Czech Republic has one of the longest average attendance rates at such facilities (Čermáková et al. 2000). Most preschools offer all-day care and – unlike nurseries – almost none (1.5 percent) are private.

The main explanation for why nurseries and preschools have developed so differently is cultural. Surveys indicate low cultural acceptance of nurseries, and only a minority of women are willing to work for pay before the youngest child turns three (Hamplová 2000). The use of nurseries and public childcare during the communist period was the result of economic pressure rather than deliberate decisions: surveys from the 1960s and the 1970s showed that women would have stayed at home had they had the economic means to do so (Kučera 1994, p. 64).

HYPOTHESES: GLOBALIZATION AND THE FEMALE LABOR MARKET IN THE CZECH REPUBLIC

Cohort differences

No data exist that would allow us to compare job stability under the communist regime with job stability after economic liberalization, nor to compare cohorts. However, we can compare the period before 1995, when reforms were domestically focused, with the more internationally focused era that began in 1995. As noted earlier, the 1991 to 1995 phase was marked by liberalized domestic prices, privatization and economic liberalization and a lifting of foreign trade controls – though wage regulations on firms were maintained. This wage control was lifted in 1995, the same year the Czech National Bank introduced and guaranteed the full convertibility of Czech currency, and in that year the country also joined the WTO and the OECD, which served to increase external or international economic discipline.

Increased internalization of economic activity is sometimes believed to lead to growing labor market flexibility, particularly in terms of marginal work, part-time employment, short-term contracts and flexible working hours (Blossfeld 2000). Reich (1992) predicted more than a decade ago that there would be an end to traditional employment contracts and expected temporary ad hoc teams would be constituted instead to find solutions to specific tasks. The expectation was therefore that younger cohorts and cohorts more exposed to the 'global economy' should experience greater job instability.

However, the job instability hypothesis is not universally supported in the developed countries (Diebold, Neumark and Polsky 1996; 1997; Swinnerton and Wial 1996; Valletta 1999). Moreover, this discussion has pointed out that job instability does not affect both sexes equally. For example, while on average men in the United States have experienced small declines in tenure, women have witnessed increases in average job tenure (Schmidt and Svorny 1998). Booth and Marco (1999) find that men in Great Britain are experiencing higher job instability than are women and have found no cohort trend for females quitting or for layoffs. Farber (1998) has found that the distribution of long-term jobs has shifted against less educated men, and in favor of women in the United States

If there is a 'globalization effect,' then in the Czech case we should expect to find somewhat higher job mobility in the wake of the liberalization and deregulation of the labor market after 1995. There should also be greater job-to-job mobility and a higher risk of unemployment. Conversely, the transition to family caregiving should be lower, since people might wish to avoid long-term, binding commitments (Mills and Blossfeld 2005).

Class differences

Technological innovations and the advance of the 'new economy' require more flexibility on the part of workers. There are two competing theories about the changing distribution of risk in the labor market (Layte et al. 2002). The individualization thesis holds that growing uncertainty means increasing equality of the risk of experiencing atypical work and unemployment. The segmentation argument holds that growing economic risks will be experienced among those on 'labor-type' contracts such as manual workers and especially unskilled manual workers.

I thus assert a number of hypotheses related to occupational class:

1   Occupational class has an influence on job mobility and job security.
2   Manual (qualified and unqualified) workers are usually considered the group whose careers are most at risk and unstable because the increasing importance of new technology and the growing demand for services lead to a shift in the relative labor demand toward higher-skilled and service workers. This tendency is strengthened by the spread of modern transportation technology, which makes it possible to move manufacturing to areas with a cheaper labor force (Reich 1992).

This has implications for the job market in the Czech Republic: manual workers could experience a fate similar to that of their counterparts in more advanced societies, as their jobs could become relatively unstable and they could face a greater risk of unemployment than non-manual workers. On the other hand, as a country with a relatively highly qualified labor force but low labor costs, the Czech Republic remains relatively attractive for outside firms to hire. Therefore, manual workers could occupy a relatively good position in comparison with the workers in more advanced western countries, especially if they work in plants owned by large foreign or multinational companies. In that way, Czech manual workers could be viewed as 'winners' of globalization.

3   The growth of the service sector could have a relatively benign effect on ordinary non-manual workers. I would expect them to have jobs with greater stability. However, the nature of non-manual work does not really require long-term contracts, and employers could be increasingly less willing to offer long-term tenure (Blossfeld 2000). This would especially affect women because they form a higher percentage of the service sector.

4   Information and new technologies are the driving force behind modern societies, and those with high human capital (or those who 'control' such information) are supposed to be the 'winners.' Greater efficiency and productivity and higher returns on human capital should make them less vulnerable to involuntary job changes. On the other hand, the 'new economy' demands more flexible workers, perhaps of the 'symbolic analyst' kind suggested by Reich (1992), who lack stable work contracts.

5   McManus (2000) argues against a recent claim that a new form of low-quality, contingent self-employment is taking hold in advanced societies, and that self-employed jobs are generally of low quality. According to her analyses, self-employment represents the most stable form of job. The Czech Republic experienced a rapid growth in the self-employed sector, and those who are self-employed on average have the highest incomes (Večerník 1996b, p. 33). However, while this 'stability through self-employment' argument appears to hold for Czech men in the 1990s, it may not be true for self-employed women. A lack of part-time jobs may push women who seek part-time work into the kind of self-employment that has the characteristics of a marginal job and lacks the stability of male self-employment.

Family status

While married women's labor force participation has been growing over time, married women remain the main caregivers in the family, with a consequent impact on their labor force participation (Klijzing et al. 1988). Wives typically schedule their paid work and family roles sequentially over the life course, leaving their jobs at the birth of the first child and returning to paid work when the children grow older (Blossfeld and Drobnič 2001).

Women with children tend to work for pay less often than those without children, and family-related job interruptions also reduce the probability of finding suitable jobs later in women's careers (Vlasblom and Schippers 2002). The more children, the bigger the effect on employment should be.

There is a nearly universal model of childcare among Czech women. The majority of women interrupt their jobs for maternity leave and many combine maternity leaves. However, after the period of paid maternity leave ends, nearly all women return to full-time employment and make use of public childcare.

I thus assert a number of hypotheses relating to family caregiving:

1   Once women stay in or re-enter the job market, the number of children should have a relatively low impact on job-to-job or job-to-unemployment mobility. The fact that the woman is back in employment means that the most intensive years of childcare are already over or that she does not have any children.

2   However, the number of children may lead to an increase in downward mobility and hinder upward mobility, since it is likely that the number of children affects a woman's efficiency and availability. Public childcare can only offset some of the demands related to raising children, but not all of them. For example, there is a legally guaranteed parental right to stay on paid sick leave with children, and this provision is mainly used by women. Thus, the hypothesis is that the number of children a woman has may not affect job-to-unemployment mobility, but it will increase the probability of downward mobility.

DATA, VARIABLES AND METHODS

The data in my analysis are drawn from a large stratified survey, *Ten Years of Social Transformation*, that was carried out in the Czech Republic between September and November 1999. The data file contains complete information about respondents' careers after 1989. The target population of the survey was the population of the Czech Republic aged 18–69 in 1999. Respondents were selected on the basis of a stratified multistage sample (the strata consisted of cities, electoral districts, households and individuals), while the selection procedure at each stage was strictly random. A total of 4744 interviews were completed and a response rate of 65 percent was achieved. We have information on 2516 women in total.

The life-history roster of the survey contains complete information on individuals' labor market histories after 1989, including the type of activity, the ending and starting years and, for jobs, a detailed classification of the occupation and ownership sector. The roster begins in 1989, so all jobs that people held in this year are assigned the year 1989 as their start. I expect that the breakdown of the communist regime meant a decisive change in the labor market and we can treat 1989 as the beginning of a new job. No details about the type of contract (fixed term v. permanent, part-time v. full-time) were gathered. Out-of-labor-market statuses were also recorded in the roster.

I analyzed five types of labor-market transitions:

1   job-to-job mobility;
2   job-to-family caregiving;
3   job-to-unemployment;
4   job-to-job mobility, distinguishing between upward, lateral and downward occupational mobility;
5   job-to-job mobility, distinguishing between upward, lateral and downward occupational mobility, including job interruptions related to family caregiving.

Only labor market episodes after the conclusion of an individual's schooling are explored. Other exits from the labor market (retirement, study, and so on) are treated as right-censored. Moreover, we focus only on mid-career occupational mobility; jobs are right-censored when the respondent reaches 50.

The survey records only annual data, and therefore the time at risk is measured in years dating from the beginning of the job. Four levels of education are distinguished: primary, lower secondary, upper secondary and tertiary. Labor force experience is measured at the beginning of each episode. This experience represents the number of years since the conclusion of the respondent's education. Age is measured as a time-constant covariate at the beginning of the episodes. Social class is a nominal variable based on the 'Erikson-Goldthorpe-Portocarero' (EGP) classification of occupations (Erikson and Goldthorpe 1992; Erikson, Goldthorpe and Portocarero 1983; the variable used includes self-employed professionals among the self-employed, unlike in Erikson and Goldthorpe). Five basic classes are distinguished: controllers, routine non-manuals, self-employed, supervisors and skilled workers, and unskilled workers and agricultural laborers. The ownership sector is a nominal variable with three categories: public sector, private sector, other (including cooperative, mixed and all other types of ownership). Two periods are utilized in the analysis: before and after 1995. The number of children is measured as a time-varying covariate. The episodes were split one year before the child was born. The International Socio-Economic Index (ISEI) scale (Ganzeboom, De Graaf and Treiman 1992) is used to model upward, lateral and upward occupational mobility. A shift within 10 percent up or down the scale is treated as lateral mobility. An upward shift of more than 10 percent on the scale is considered as upward mobility, and a downward shift of more than 10 percent is regarded as downward mobility. The jobs at the top and the bottom of the scale are excluded. The first five years in the labor market are controlled by a dummy variable since we are interested primarily in mid-career women.

The event-history method is adopted in the analysis to explore job mobility, and models are estimated by using discrete time logistic models. The models are evaluated with the use of the Bayesian Information Criterion (BIC) (Raftery 1995).

RESULTS

All models include a dummy for the first five years in the labor market and a control for age. The first five-year period in the labor market is characterized by higher job-to-family care mobility and higher job-to-job mobility. The risk of downward mobility is lower during the first five years in the labor market, which may reflect the fact that young people enter first jobs that have a relatively low level of prestige, and chances to move up are high (Table 9.4).

Direct Moves

Class differences
Different social classes face an uneven risk of unemployment and job-to-job mobility. Self-employed women have the lowest job-to-job (and lateral) mobility, but self-employment does not protect women from unemployment or downward mobility and does not increase their chances for upward mobility (see Table 9.5). In their case, lateral mobility means a transition to the same type of job within that employment status. Given the specificity of self-employed jobs, this transition is rather unlikely: stability is more the norm of the self-employed.

The risk of unemployment is comparatively higher only in the case of unskilled manual workers compared with skilled workers. Skilled manual workers do not face a higher risk of unemployment than controllers, non-manual workers or the self-employed. This may reflect two trends. First, the rapid expansion of the service sector has created a high demand for skilled workers. Second, the Czech Republic, as a middle-income country with a highly skilled labor force, offers a benign environment for foreign investors and manufacturing. In this case, the expansion of foreign trade and the possibility of shifting manufacturing to countries with a cheaper labor force establish relatively favorable conditions for skilled manual workers.

There is no significant class difference in the tendency to leave the labor market for family care. This reflects the rather uniform pattern of family formation and the general acceptance of job interruptions pertinent to family care. The data do not confirm that women from higher classes tend to avoid job interruptions.

Education

Education has no impact on the job-to-family care (maternity) and the job-to-unemployment transition when we include social class in the models. Job-to-job transitions are significantly lower only in the case of women with only primary education. They occupy a rather precarious position in the labor market and their chances of changing or finding a new job are relatively small. Women with primary and vocational training also have a lower chance of upward mobility. When social class is excluded from the model, having at least a secondary school education protects women from unemployment, but does not have an impact on job-to-job or job-to-family care transitions.

Number of children

The presence of children proved to be an important labor market factor. Even though the number of children does not affect job-to-unemployment or job-to-job mobility, it does increase the risk of job-to-family care transition. The key difference is between having a child and being childless. There is a general trend among Czech women to leave the labor force when a child is born and to return after maternity leave. The fact that a woman is back in employment means that the most intensive years of childcare are already over, and thus the actual number of children does not have much influence on job-to-job mobility or the risk of unemployment. One hypothesis was that the number of children in the household hinders upward or increases downward mobility. However, the data do not confirm this.

Period effect

It was expected that the period after 1995 would be characterized by higher job-to-job and job-to-unemployment mobility and lower job-to-family care mobility. Only the hypothesis predicting higher job-to-unemployment mobility has been confirmed by the data. Contrary to expectations, lower job-to-job mobility is characteristic of the period after 1995. The high job-to-job mobility that existed in the period between 1989 and 1995 can be explained through the classic job-search theory. A new labor market required new adjustments and a new process of matching jobs and workers. Employers were searching for new workers and people were searching for jobs in which their potential and human capital could be better used. There is no significant period effect on upward mobility, but the 1989–95 period featured higher lateral and downward mobility.

The globalization hypotheses suggest that differences within societies have been growing as markets gain more significance and deregulation takes place. Thus, it could be predicted that class and educational differences and the difference between childless women and women with children would be more profound in the period after 1995. Therefore, a set of models including interactions between class, education, the number of children and the period was also estimated (not reported here). However, the data do not confirm that

Table 9.4   Job-to-job, job-to-family caregiving, job-to-unemployment transitions for Czech women; discrete logistic models, competing risks

	Job-to-family			Job-to-unemployment			Job-to-job		
	Model 1	Model 2	Model 3	Model 1	Model 2	Model 3	Model 1	Model 2	Model 3
Constant	0.77	0.32	−0.34	−4.75**	−4.86**	−4.58**	−5.18**	−5.13**	−5.17**
First five years in labor market	0.95**	1.04**	1.09**	0.42	0.59	0.54	0.89**	0.86**	0.88**
Age at beginning of job	−0.05	−0.05	−0.02	−0.01	−0.01	−0.01	0.16**	0.16**	0.16**
Age square	−0.00	−0.00	−0.00	0.00	0.00	0.00	−0.00**	−0.00**	−0.00**
Education									
Primary	−0.06	0.03		0.35	0.43		−0.64**	−0.66**	
Vocational	−0.27	−0.26		0.29	0.38		−0.04	−0.06	
Secondary	−0.32	−0.32		−0.06	−0.02		−0.05	−0.06	
Tertiary (ref.)									
EGP									
I: Controllers	−0.05	−0.07	−0.02	0.18	0.11	−0.16	−0.28*	−0.27	−0.19
II: Routine, non-manual	0.16	0.14	0.10	0.61	0.55	0.35	−0.23	−0.22	−0.17
III: Self-employed	−1.33	−1.32	−1.37	−0.26	−0.34	−0.52	−0.88**	−0.87**	−0.81**
IV: Skilled, manual (ref.)									
V+VI: Unskilled, agriculture	0.29	0.26	0.29	0.91*	0.88*	0.91*	0.15	0.15	0.07

Table 9.4 continued

	(1)	(2)	(3)	(4)	(5)	(6)	(7)	(8)	(9)
Sector									
Private	-0.41**	-0.45**	-0.45**	0.27	0.06	0.11	-0.28**	-0.24**	-0.24**
Other	-0.24	-0.21	-0.21	0.49	0.55	0.61	0.28*	0.28*	0.28*
Public (ref.)									
Number of children									
None	-2.55**	-2.06**	-2.06**	-0.79	-0.39	-0.40	0.15	0.05	0.06
One	-0.46			-0.36			0.11		
Two	-0.83**			-0.51			0.08		
Three + (ref.)									
Pre-1995 period		-0.14	-0.15		-0.95**	-0.93**		0.16*	0.16**
BIC	-562.82	-591.30							

Notes:
* p < 0.05, ** p < 0.01, *** p < 0.001
Number of events: 1206

Source: Ten Years of Social Tranformation

*Table 9.5   Direct upward and downward mobility for Czech women (lateral mobility not
shown): discrete logistic models*

	Upward		Downward	
	Model 1	Model 2	Model 1	Model 2
Constant	−2.45**	−3.06**	−4.41**	−4.28**
First five years in labor market	−0.13	−0.04	−0.62*	−0.64*
Age at beginning of job	−0.03**	−0.03**	−0.03*	−0.02*
Education				
Primary	−1.14**		0.59	
Vocational	−0.78*		0.20	
Secondary	−0.23		−0.04	
Tertiary (ref.)				
EGP				
I: Controllers	−1.13**	−0.63**	0.84**	0.64*
II: Routine, non-manual	−0.51*	−0.17	0.37	0.21
III: Self-employed	−0.90	−0.60	0.43	0.29
IV: Skilled, manual (ref.)				
V+VI: Unskilled, agriculture	0.80**	0.74**	0.35	0.41
Sector				
Private	−0.15	−0.20	−0.05	0.01
Other	0.51*	0.46*	−0.18	−0.14
Public (ref.)				
Number of children	−0.00	−0.00	−0.16	−0.16
Pre−1995 period	0.15	0.12	1.43**	1.43**
Events	232	232	172	172
BIC	−65.77	−57.05	−59.839	−63.53

Note: *p < 0.05,   ** p < 0.01,   *** p < 0.001

Source: Ten Years of Social Transformation

the importance of class, education or parental status has been systematically
changing over the periods under consideration.

Indirect moves

Two strategies were adopted for analyzing upward, lateral and downward
mobility. In addition to direct job-to-job mobility (Tables 9.4 and 9.5),
indirect mobility was also analyzed (see Table 9.6). In this case, the data set
included women who had been in employment but were out of employment

for family care, and a measurement was made of the change in the ISEI between the pre-interruption and post-interruption jobs. An interruption was indicated by a dummy variable.

Job interruption

The important finding is that job interruptions hinder upward mobility but do not influence lateral or downward mobility for women (see Table 9.6). This means that when a woman returns from maternity leave to the labor market it is unlikely she will directly enter a job with higher prestige. The inclusion of interaction effects (Model 2, Table 9.6) does not indicate that education or social class affects job interruptions, and the effect is rather uniform. The only exceptions are unskilled and agricultural workers, who have higher chances of upward mobility after job interruptions. This may again reflect their low starting position and the possibility that they return only if they have the prospect of a better job.

Class differences

Self-employed women show lower lateral mobility (model not shown) even after interruptions. Women in the higher classes demonstrate a lower tendency towards upward mobility after interruptions, while unskilled workers have, relatively speaking, the highest chances for upward mobility after interruptions. This reflects the fact that women from higher social classes have relatively little space to move up into. The higher chances for upward mobility among unskilled and agriculture workers stem from the fact that there are a relatively small number of such jobs available. Unskilled workers can move up, stay in the job they already have or become unemployed.

Sector

The private sector protects women against the risk of downward mobility and lowers the risk of lateral mobility after interruptions, compared with the public sector. This finding may seem peculiar, but it must be understood in the context of the mass privatization that occurred in the 1990s, which included the inflow of foreign direct investment and the openings made for multinational companies. The private sector has been developing rapidly, and companies with good economic prospects were privatized quickly.

Education

If I control for social class, women with primary education and vocational training have a lower chance of upward mobility after interruptions. However, education does not offer protection against downward mobility. Primary education also lowers the chances of lateral mobility. This again reflects that people with lower education have fewer chances on the job market and low opportunities for changing jobs.

Table 9.6 *Indirect upward and downward mobility for Czech women (lateral mobility not shown): discrete logistic models*

	Upward		Downward	
	Model 1	Model 2	Model 1	Model 2
Constant	−2.65**	−2.63**	−4.52**	−4.53**
First five years in labor market	0.49*	0.50*	0.44	0.43
Age at beginning of job	−0.03**	−0.02**	−0.00	−0.00
Job interruption	−1.40**	−2.11**	−0.43	−0.28
Education				
Primary	−0.19	−0.15	−0.23*	−0.22
Vocational	−0.75*	−0.74**	0.47	0.48
Secondary	−0.15	−0.16	−0.00	−0.00
Tertiary (ref.)				
EGP				
I: Controllers	−1.16**	−1.17**	0.69*	0.70*
II: Routine, non-manual	−0.54*	−0.53*	0.28	0.28
III: Self-employed	−0.87	−0.89	−0.14	−0.12
IV: Skilled, manual (ref.)				
V+VI: Unskilled, agriculture	0.84**	0.75**	0.15	0.28
Sector				
Private	−0.25	−0.25	−0.38*	−0.38*
Other	0.50*	0.51*	−0.10	−0.10
Public (ref.)				
Number of children	0.07	0.06	−0.07	−0.07
Pre−1995 period	0.15	0.15	−0.13	−0.13
Interaction				
EGP V+VI*Interruption		1.37*		−12.01
Events	241	241	184	184
BIC	−109.56	−112.55	10.54	7.76

Note: *p < 0.05, ** p < 0.01, *** p < 0.001

Source: Ten Years of Social Transformation

Period effect

The analyses that included indirect moves did not confirm the possibility that the pre-1995 period featured higher lateral mobility. However, this does not contradict the findings from the analyses of direct mobility, indicating that the new labor market required new adjustments and the occurrence of a new process of matching jobs and workers. In the analyses of indirect transition I worked with a mixed category, comprised of women who were changing jobs and women who were coming back from maternity leave. It is not reasonable to expect that the pattern of returning from maternity leave should change, and thus the inclusion of indirect moves could offset any period effect.

CONCLUSIONS

The analyses do not confirm expectations that job instability is growing, aside from the finding in Table 9.4 that the pre-1995 period had fewer transitions to unemployment than the latter half of the decade. But downward mobility decreased. The data do not confirm either a general growth in job instability, or the growing significance of social class, education or family responsibilities. It could be argued that a ten-year span is too short a period to enable us to detect any significant change.

There has been a long tradition in the Czech Republic of full female full-time employment. The data indicate that this has not changed even after the liberalization and deregulation of the job market. Even though surveys suggest that women's full-time employment is viewed by the women themselves more as an economic necessity than as desirable, work has become a natural part of their standard life course.

Institutional arrangements (long maternity leave and a broad network of childcare services) enable Czech women to combine work and family responsibilities. The number of children or becoming a mother does not increase their risk of becoming unemployed or changing jobs, though it does decrease their chances of upward job mobility relative to women who forgo children. Also, the number of children has no influence on their chances of upward or downward mobility. Generally, most mothers leave the job market for family care and when their maternity leave is over they return to work. If a woman interrupts her job, it is unlikely that she will return directly from maternity leave to a job with higher prestige than the one she had before the job interruption. However, job interruption does not influence her risk of downward mobility.

Unskilled manual workers face a higher risk of unemployment and self-employment is the most stable form of work arrangement. However, skilled manual workers do not appear to be more disadvantaged than non-manual workers or professionals. The results show a mixed picture of class effects on Czech women's careers, indicating a possible benefit, as mentioned, of the low-wage/high-qualified Czech labor pool on the international market.

Generally, the analyses do not reveal any significant period change in women's job market behavior, or in the way they combine their family responsibilities and work. It can be concluded that paid work is an integral part of Czech women's life courses. The number of children and family obligations do not significantly change women's behavior in the labor market.

NOTES

1   Wage control occurred through the punitive taxes put on 'excess' increases in an enterprise's average wage bill beyond the annual percentage limits agreed in the tripartite council.
2   The extension of parental leave should have helped to combat expected unemployment and to reduce the labor force naturally. However, 1990 saw a radical drop in the rates of fertility and marriage and a similar decrease in the number of maternity leaves. The number of children born declined from 130 000 in 1990 to 90 000 in 1996, and has remained stable since that year.
3   Data – see Kučera (2001) on the socialist era, and the Czech Statistical Office for later figures.
4   In 2001 only 2770 cases were registered in which a child could not be accepted due to the low capacity of the pre-school (Czech Statistical Office). By comparison, in 1983 the number of unsuccessful applications reached 69 000 (Freiová 1998). This difference stems in part from the radical change in the fertility rate.

BIBLIOGRAPHY

Blossfeld, H.-P. (2000) 'Globalization, social inequality, and the role of country-specific institutions', GLOBALIFE Working Paper No. 11, Chair of Sociology I, University of Bamberg.
Blossfeld, H.-P. and Drobnič, S. (2001) *Careers of couples in contemporary societies. From male breadwinner to dual earner families*, New York: Oxford University Press.
Booth, A.L. and Marco, F. (1999) 'Job tenure and job mobility in Britain', *Industrial and Labour Relations Review*, 53(1): 43–71.
Bosworth, B. and Ofer, G. (1995) *Reforming planned economies in an integrating world economy*, Washington, DC: Brookings Institution.
Čermáková, M., Hašková, H., Křížková, A., Linková, M., Maříková, H. and Musilová, M. (2000) *Souvislosti a změny genderových diferencí v České společnosti v 90. letech* Praha: SOU AV CR.
Czech Statistical Yearbook (Years 1994–2002) Praha: Scientia.
Diebold F.X., Neumark D. and Polsky, D. (1996) Comment on K.A. Swinnerton and H. Wial: 'Is job stability declining in the U.S. economy?', *Industrial and Labour Relations Review*, 49(2): 348–52.
Diebold F.X., Neumark D. and Polsky, D. (1997) 'Job stability in the U.S.', *Journal of Labour Economics*, 12(4): 554–94.
EBDR Transition Report (2002) London: European Bank for Development and Reconstruction.
Erikson, R. and Goldthorpe, J.H. (1992) *The constant flux. A study of class mobility in industrial societies*, New York: Oxford University Press.
Erikson, R., Goldthorpe, J.H. and Portocarero, L. (1983) 'International class mobility and the convergence thesis: England, France and Sweden', *British Journal of Sociology*, 34: 303–43.

Farber, H.S. (1998) 'Are lifetime jobs disappearing? Job duration in the United States, 1973–1993', in J. Haltiwanger, M. Manser and R. Topel (eds) *Labor statistics measurement issues*, Chicago, IL: University of Chicago Press, pp. 157–203.

Fialová, L., Hamplová, D., Kučera, M. and Vymětalová, S. (2000) *Představy mladých lidí o manželství a rodičovství*, Praha: Slon.

Freiová, M. (1998) *Východiska rodinné politiky*, Praha: Občanský institut.

Frýdmanová, M., Janáček, K., Mareš, P. and Sirovátka, T. (1999) 'Labor market and human resources', in P. Matějů and J. Večerník (eds) *Ten years of rebuilding capitalism, Czech society after 1989*, Praha: Academia.

Ganzeboom, H.B.G., De Graaf, P.M. and Treiman, D.J. (1992) 'A standard international socio-economic index of occupational status', *Social Science Research*, 21: 1–56.

Hamplová, D. (2000) 'Názory na manželství a rodinu mladých svobodných lidí v roce 1997', *Demografie*, 42(2): 92–9.

Klijzing, E., Siegers, J., Keilman, N. and Groot, L. (1988) 'Static versus dynamic analysis of the interaction between female labor-force participation and fertility', *European Journal of Population*, 4: 97–116.

Kučera, M. (1994) *Populace České Republiky 1918–1991*, Praha: Sociologický ústav AV ČR.

Kučera, M. (2001) 'Rodinná politika a její demografické důsledky v socialistickém Československu', in *Česko-francouzský dialog o dějinách evropské rodiny*, Praha: CEFRES, pp. 53–8.

Layte, R., O'Connell, P.J., Fahey, T. and McCoy, S. (2002) 'Ireland and economic globalization: the experience of a small open economy', GLOBALIFE Working Paper No. 21, Chair of Sociology I, University of Bamberg.

Matějů, P. (1999) 'Social mobility and changes in perceived life-chances', in P. Matějů and J. Večerník (eds) *Ten years of rebuilding capitalism. Czech society after 1989*, Praha: Academia.

McManus, P. (2000) 'Market, state, and the quality of new self-employment jobs among men in the U.S. and Western Germany', *Social Forces*, 78(3): 865–905.

Mills, M. and Blossfeld, H.-P. (2005) 'Globalization, uncertainty and the early life course: A theoretical framework', in H.-P. Blossfeld, E. Klijzing, M. Mills and K. Kurz (eds) *Globalization, uncertainty, and youth in society*, London and New York: Routledge.

Možný, I. (1990) *Moderní rodina (Mýty a skutečnost)*, Brno: Blok.

Možný, I. (1991) *Proč tak snadno?*, Praha: SLON.

Orenstein, M.A. and Hale, L.E. (2001) 'Corporatist renaissance in post-communist Central Europe?', in C. Candland and R. Sil (eds) *The politics of labor in a global age. Continuity and change in late-industrializing and post-socialist economies*, New York: Oxford University Press.

Organisation for Economic Co-operation and Development (OECD) (2001) *Employment outlook*, April, Paris: OECD.

Organisation for Economic Co-operation and Development (OECD) (2002) *Employment outlook*, Paris: OECD.

Raftery, A. (1995) 'Bayesian model selection in social research', in P. Marsden (ed.) *Sociological methodology vol. 25*, Oxford: Blackwell Publishers.

Reich, R.B. (1992) *The work of nations: preparing ourselves for 21st century capitalism*, New York: Vintage Books.

Róbert, P. and Bukodi, E. (2002) 'The effects of the globalization process on the transition to adulthood in Hungary', GLOBALIFE Working Paper No. 27, Chair of Sociology I, University of Bamberg.

Schmidt, S.R. and Svorny, S.V. (1998) 'Recent trends in job security and stability', *Journal of Labor Research*, 19(4): 647–68.

Swinnerton, K. and Wial, H. (1996) 'Is job stability declining in the U.S. economy?', *Industrial and Labour Relations Review*, 48(2): 293–304.

Valletta, R.G. (1999) 'Declining job security', *Journal of Labour Economics*, 17(4): 170–97.

Večerník, J. (1996a) *Markets and people. The Czech reform experience in a comparative perspective*, Brookfield: Avebury.

Večerník, J. (1996b) *Změny na trhu práce a v materiálních podmínkách života v České republice v období 1989–1995*, Praha: Národohospodářský ústav Josefa Hlávky.

Vlasblom, J.D. and Schippers J.J. (2002) *The dynamics of employment and motherhood* (draft version), Utrecht: Institute of Economics.

10. Women and the labor market in Poland: from socialism to capitalism

Ania Plomien

INTRODUCTION

Two major external changes affected Central and Eastern European (CEE) countries during the last two decades: the fall of communism (1989) and the protracted membership negotiations that led Poland to accede to the European Union (EU) in 2004. Globalization may not have 'caused' communism to fall or encouraged Poland to join the EU, but the external phenomenon is undoubtedly linked to these internal events. Poland, in addition to implementing deep changes domestically, reoriented its political and economic outlook away from the East and toward the democratic states in the West. Poland's post-transformation role in the international economy, including its closer relationship to competitive international markets, greater vulnerability to market shocks and exposure to technological change, are evidence of the impact of globalization within Polish borders.

This chapter focuses on changing gender relations in Poland and women's position in the labor market, as influenced by these endogenous shifts. From the available literature and an overview of legislative changes, I establish how women (and men) have fared.

Poland poses a particular challenge for the EU, not just because it accounts for over half the working-age population of the new member states. It is also because its employment rate is among the lowest (50.6 percent in 2003) and its unemployment rate the highest (19.3 percent in July, 2004) of the 25 nations that now comprise the EU. Women's access to sustainable employment in Poland, although an acute problem, generally has been a low priority on the agenda of domestic actors, whether governments, trade unions or employers. But the growing importance of an external player – the EU – acts as a stimulus to pay greater attention to women's employment.

My question is whether there has been a change in the Polish gender contract from the socialist to the post-socialist era, and if so, how that contract has evolved and what factors and actors have been relevant to that evolution. The fall of communism appears to have been detrimental to the

~~position of women in Poland, but accession to the EU seems to have been~~
more beneficial. Thus, both internal dynamics (in particular, the Polish
government in power) and external influences (the EU) have shaped
women's labor market position.

The chapter begins by situating the discussion of Poland within the broader
welfare state perspective and points to particular historical contexts
influencing the cultural dimension of gender relations. Next, it traces the
attitudes and actions of the pre- and post-transition governments related to
gendered labor market issues. The following section discusses the realities of
the Polish labor market in its central planning and free market economy
phases. After that, the relative position of men and women is placed in a
broader context. Finally, the changes associated with joining the EU are
discussed.

THE WELFARE STATE DISCUSSION

The importance of the welfare state to labor markets is manifest in the state's
ability to maintain full employment or deal with labor market crises (Bastian
1998). Esping-Andersen (1990) systematized the cross-national differences in
welfare state structures into three ideal-types (liberal, conservative and
social-democratic) based on the two dimensions of decommodification and
social stratification.

The literature on western labor markets also considers the national state as
crucial in shaping the relationship between households and employment, so
welfare regimes are said to contour not only employment systems but also
patterns of gender relations (Rubery 2001). Adding on the issue of unpaid
work (Taylor Gooby 1991) expands the discussion of state–market relations
by stressing the family as the third component in the interaction. Including
family in the analysis is crucial, as western states depend on families
providing welfare (Orloff 1993). Thus, one can view welfare regimes as
gendered, most evident in the gendered division of labor, the family wage
system and in traditional marriages (Orloff 1996).

In the male breadwinner model (Lewis 1992), men are assigned to the paid
economy and women to non-paid domestic and caring duties. Few or only
minimal state provisions are made for maternity leave and pay, for the right
to post-maternity work reinstatement or for childcare. Therefore, women's
labor force participation is predicted to be low, since women privately make
up for the deficiencies in the public provision of social services.
Consequently, women who do not participate in the formal labor market must
depend on their husbands for social security entitlements.

The male breadwinner model can be found in many modern welfare states,
though to different degrees: Britain and Ireland have been characterized as
'strong,' France as 'modified,' and Sweden – with its high female labor force

participation rates, generous childcare provisions and individual taxation policies – is an exemplar of the 'weak' variant (Lewis 1992). Sainsbury (1994) has suggested an alternative to the weak male breadwinner model in which both men and women are wage earners and perform caring duties, where state benefits target individuals, and the bulk of the work of caring is provided or paid for by the state. Still, while the male breadwinner model has eroded since the early 1990s, the shift to the individual model, where both partners are financially independent of each other and in full-time work, has not taken place yet (Lewis 2002).

Can the western mainstream or feminist discussions of the welfare state apply to Poland? The welfare state concept pertains more to contemporary Poland than to the socialist period. The socialist regime and the welfare state seem to be more of a contradiction in terms than compatible concepts owing to the organization of the whole political, economic and social system. While today Poland resembles western democracies based on free market principles, under socialism the reign of the free market was not permitted, and all the parts of the polity, economy and society were centrally regulated. Therefore, the notions of labor decommodification or social solidarities and stratifications do not carry across the two periods equally well. However, the concept is still useful in discussing the impact of the state on the labor market and the overall well-being of citizens. Indeed, governmental policies, whether under command economy or free market conditions, can still be assessed from the perspective of promoting a certain gender contract or regulating the labor market.

THE STATE AND THE GENDER CONTRACT

State policies before 1989

Under socialism, all citizens of Poland were in principle given the same legal rights, all were permitted to participate in political, economic and social domains (although not in a democratic sense), and all were guaranteed employment. The socialist ideology stressed participation in work outside the home as emancipating, and as such supported women as paid employees (Pascall and Manning 2000; Piotrowski 1963). Thus, the official public discourse stressed equality in general but also equality between the sexes (Hauser, Heyns and Mansbridge 1993).

This assertion needs to be qualified. First, the right of all to work did not translate automatically into equalities surrounding work: men were excluded from some of the work benefits related to family care, and women were barred from certain occupational categories. Second, the official stance of the party, government and state-controlled media as to women's desired role fluctuated. It varied from clear efforts to increase active female employment and equalize women's and men's positions in social and professional arenas, through indifference and no active promotion of any roles, to stressing the family role of mother, wife and caregiver and thus slow the professional-ization of women (Piotrowski 1963). In essence, the early socialist state was initially concerned with rebuilding and industrializing post-war Poland and, therefore, promoted an image of woman as employee first. By the mid-1950s, there was a shift to emphasize women as mothers, and by the 1960s, the government supported women's employment if the workplaces were not filled by men (Heinen 2002; Piotrowski 1963).

Women's employment steadily increased from 30.6 percent in 1950 to 46 percent of the labor force in 1990 (Glogosz 2000; *Rocznik Statystyczny Rzeczypospolitej Polskiej* 1998; 2003). Various state and work benefits, although not aimed at eliminating inequalities between men and women, facilitated the reconciliation of women's roles as mothers and workers. Services provided by the state minimized the conflicts between professional and family responsibilities (Lobodzinska 1995). But the gender question remained unresolved and the patriarchal family order unchallenged (Pascall and Manning 2000). At times, however, the socialist government treated the gender question in a more decisive and active way, as when it established the Office of the Government Plenipotentiary for Women's Affairs in 1986 to ensure the equal status of women and men in government, political, economic, social and cultural arenas. Such an institutionalization of women's issues indicates some degree of commitment on the part of the socialist government to the establishment of mechanisms pertaining to and dealing with gender (in)equality.

State policies after 1989

In contrast to the previous era, the state's dedication to equal opportunities (even if mostly superficial) and women's professional activation was not sustained through the transition period. After 1989, the official ideology of defining a suitable or desirable role and place for women changed, together with the change of the politico-economic system. Women were now assigned the position of mother in the private sphere of the home (Fuszara 2000a; Watson 1993). The official stance is evident in the 1991 conversion of the Office for Women's Affairs into the Office of Undersecretary of State for Women and Family with new responsibilities for family, children and youth (Hauser, Heyns and Mansbridge 1993). Moreover, at the beginning of the transformation period, the right-leaning government went as far as advising women to return to their households and take up their motherly and wifely duties in order to make jobs available for men (Sasic Silovic 2000).

The government coalitions between 1993 and 1997 came from the left side of the political spectrum, and were more involved in promoting equal opportunities, especially after the 1995 United Nations (UN) Women's Conference in Beijing. The government developed a National Action Plan for Women, which included plans for fighting women's poverty, ensuring access to education and medical care, addressing violence against women, institutionalizing mechanisms for the advancement of women and facilitating women's involvement in power and decision-making (Martynowicz 2000).

However, the policy of promoting gender equality did not persist for long. The state's course altered yet again with the 1997 elections when a right-wing government with close ties to the Church was formed. This administration was quite clear in its traditional views on the appropriate and desirable roles for women. For example in a UN questionnaire, quoted by Martynowicz (2000, pp. 1, 6), the government expressed its interest in a 'pro-family policy' (including decreasing the number of single mothers through counseling and halting an anti-domestic violence project on the grounds that 'offering help to women and children outside their family home contributes to the break-up of that family') and its belief in the 'role of a woman as mother and family supporter.' While the government did note that there were 'strong egalitarian tendencies in Polish society' that women could take advantage of, this formulation suggests not only a lack of will to do anything about improvement, but also a pledge to weakening women's independence outside of family contexts. This government also questioned the need to introduce an equal status bill, to investigate pay and gender equity in the labor market or to introduce a political quota system.

The change of administration in 2001 (to a left-wing coalition) led the Office of Government Plenipotentiary to alter its tune yet again. Based on an ordinance by the Council of Ministers (2002) it now is responsible for the promotion and realization of the principle of equal treatment of women and men in all areas of social life, and counteracting all expressions of discrimination based on gender (Council of Ministers 2002).

One can thus see that the process of crafting a new gender contract is one characterized by progress and retreat, depending on the political orientation of the administration in power. As it is, the political parties themselves can be divided into three different camps: those that pay no specific attention to the needs of women, those that promise extended maternity leaves and part-time employment for women, and those that address discrimination, reproductive rights, the feminization of poverty, the needs of single mothers and women's unemployment (Fuszara 2000b). Presumably the situation for Polish women will become still more complex with accession to the EU.

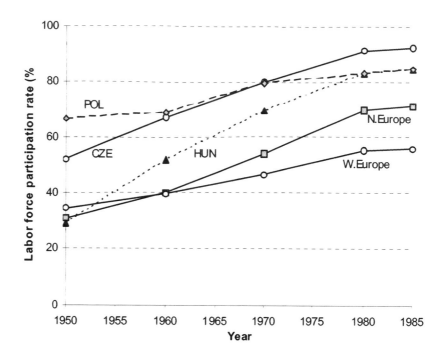

Note: Northern Europe includes Scandinavian countries; Western Europe
                 includes Austria, Belgium, France, FRG, Netherlands, Switzerland,
                 Luxembourg, and UK

Source: Jackman and Rutkowski (1994), based on Kornai (1992)

Figure 10.1   Labor force participation rate of women 40–44 years of age

LABOR MARKET TRANSITION

Labor market participation: employment and unemployment

In the socialist era, women's labor was needed and work was perceived as a
civic duty (LaFont 2001). Work was also a necessity, because one income
was insufficient to support a family (Marody and Giza-Poleszczuk 2000).
Therefore, the state demand was readily met by a supply of women who
combined full-time employment with motherhood. In 1946, the rate of
women working outside of agriculture was nearly 30 percent (Piotrowski
1963). By the end of the 1980s, women comprised about 47 percent of the
entire workforce, a degree of mobilization comparable only with the Nordic
states (Kramer 1995). Among women aged 40 to 44 (Figure 10.1), CEE

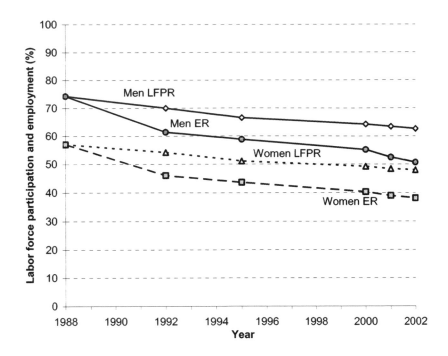

Source: *Rocznik Statystyczny Rzeczypospolitej Polskiej 2003*, as reported in Woycicka et al. (2003)

Figure 10.2   *Labor force participation rates (LFPR) and employment rates (ER) in Poland in the years 1988 – 2002*

countries under command economies achieved higher rates of employment than all other countries in Europe.

Command economies provided numerous work-related benefits: retirement pensions, subsidized canteens, holiday resorts, free transportation to some workplaces and institutionalized childcare. With growing numbers of women in active employment, access to these subsidies was facilitated, though some social services and benefits such as education and healthcare were available free to all citizens.

But the free market system has been detrimental to full employment. Labor force participation as well as the employment rates of men and women declined sharply especially in the initial post-transition years (see Figure 10.2).

The command economy had a low level of, and little growth in, wages and an excess demand for labor; this led to labor shortages and no open unemployment (Brainerd 2000). Once a market economy was adopted,

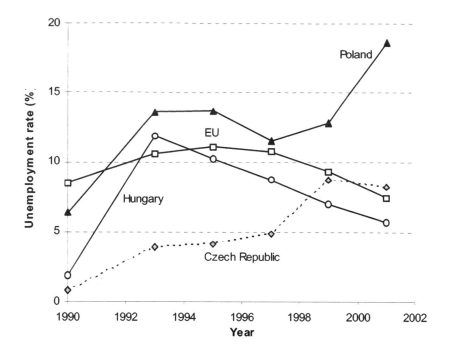

Source: Labour Force Surveys reported in Mickiewicz and Bell (2000); OECD
                Employment outlook 1997, 2002; and as reported in Fultz et al. (2003)

Figure 10.3   *Unemployment rates for selected Central and Eastern European
                countries and European Union countries (EU) in the years 1990–2001*

unemployment jumped for both men and women (see Figure 10.3). After the
initial sharp decline in labor force participation and employment rates the
trend tapers off throughout the 1990s, although the unemployment rate soars
to almost 20 percent. These developments result in a strong increase in non-
employment (Gora 1997) where employment outflows to inactivity surpass
the outflows to unemployment, and outflows from unemployment show the
unemployed leaving the labor force completely instead of moving to new
employment (Mickiewicz and Bell 2000), which is likely due to a
discouraged worker effect, given that some regional unemployment levels
stand at over 40 percent (Churski 2002). Poland is considerably worse off
with respect to its unemployment rate compared with Hungary and the Czech
Republic but also relative to the EU average (see Figure 10.3). Even so,
Poland has lower rates of labor force participation than the Czech Republic or
the EU average (see Figure 10.4).

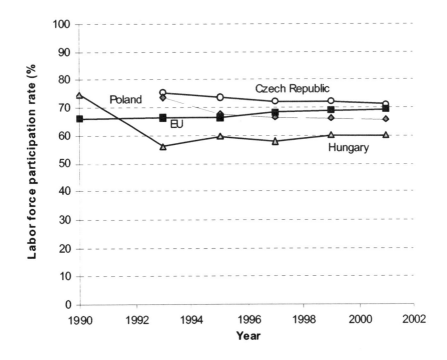

Source: Labour Force Surveys reported in Mickiewicz and Bell (2000); OECD *Employment outlook* 1997, 2002; and as reported in Fultz et al. (2003)

Figure 10.4 *Labor force participation rates for selected Central and Eastern European countries and European Union (EU) in the years 1990–2001*

Unemployed women have also been worse off than unemployed men in the 1992 to 2002 period (see Figure 10.5). Not only do they experience higher unemployment rates, but they also comprise a higher proportion of the long-term unemployed, and their non-employment rate is greater as well (Gora 1997). The demand for female workers appears to be lower than for male workers (Fuszara 2000b) in the now liberalized labor market and, as outsiders, women experience more uncertainty inasmuch as their access to stable jobs with benefits has diminished. The high incidence of long-term unemployment among women is quite serious, as it is strongly associated with poverty.

Source: Badanie Aktywności Ekonomicznej Ludności (BAEL) in GUS
                  www.stat.gov.pl

Figure 10.5   Unemployment rates for Poland in the years 1992–2002 by gender

Wages

The command economy centrally assigned wages based on an occupational
wage scale for specific industries. The wage differential between occupations
was narrow and skewed towards manual workers, especially in heavy
industry and skilled work. As in western economies, women in Poland were
overrepresented in the lower wage sectors, and men dominated the higher
ones (Brainerd 2000), with female wages 20 to 40 percent lower than those of
men even in the same positions (Marody and Giza-Poleszczuk 2000). In fact,
gender was a better predictor of earnings than educational level, occupational
position, age, job experience or membership in the party (Siemienska 1990).

   The demise of the command economy has benefited women, at least to the
extent that it seems to have decreased their relative wage disadvantages.
Mean gender earnings difference changed from 72 percent in 1986 to 81
percent in 1992 (Brainerd 2000). A study by Grajek (2001) confirms that
there was a drop in the gender pay gap in the immediate post-transformation

period, but ascribes this to the fact that most changes occurred in 1989 when the state-owned enterprises were reducing their labor costs. The jobs and wages of men were cut, and that, along with a fraction of well-educated women entering lucrative positions, accounts for the narrowing of the wage differential. After 1992, this narrowing trend ceased (Grajek 2001). Thus, although the relative position of female wages has improved, in real terms women's pay remains well behind men's.

Employment structure

Under the command economy, most employment, whether male or female, was in the public sector, and the much smaller private sector employment was mostly in agriculture or small businesses. With the transition to the market economy via the privatization of state-owned enterprises as well as the establishment of new ventures, the public sector contracted and the private sector expanded. Still, more women than men continue to find employment in the public sector (42.5 percent and 34.2 percent, respectively), and more men than women are attached to the private sector (65.8 and 57.5 percent, respectively) (Kolaczek 2001). Consequently, further privatization or contraction of the public sector would likely be more damaging to the employment of women than to men. In spite of lower wages, public sector employment traditionally provides employment security (Towalski 2003) and is more 'women-friendly' (Balcerzak-Paradowska 2001).

Communism did not eradicate patriarchy or gender inequalities, nor did it enable women to gain positions of power (Graham and Regulska 1997). As a result, men occupied the top professional positions then – and still do so today (LaFont 2001). Throughout the CEE region, horizontal and vertical segregation was the norm, with women found in a narrow range of sectors and occupations such as light manufacturing, caring jobs and services. Professions in medicine, law, education, business and accounting became feminized under socialist auspices, yet this translated into lower status for women working in these areas as well as into lower salaries (Bialecki and Heyns 1993; Towalski 2003). The service sector has been relatively underdeveloped, and women tend to hold low-level jobs in it, except in the financial sector, where female employment is substantial and is attributed to their high qualifications (Pollert 2003).

Part-time employment has not been widespread in Poland, and the number of part-time positions is in short supply (Glogosz 2000). There are calls for the provision of more part-time employment, but such a solution carries both risks and benefits. Given the persistently low income levels, as well as the need for two full-time salaries to ensure basic family needs, part-time employment may actually lower family income to poverty-line levels (Balcerzak-Paradowska 2002). And if part-time work is done in unregulated parts of the labor market, women may be at risk of marginalization in socially unprotected jobs (Sasic Silovic 2000). During the transformation part-time employment has been growing slightly, with women more likely to be employed part-time than men (in 1998, 13.1 percent and 8.1 percent, respectively) (Kolaczek 2001).

Retirement and pensions

Although under socialism the average male pension was higher than the average female pension, there was an element of redistribution from higher to lower benefits. The formula consisted of a constant element as well as a variable component depending on the level of pre-retirement income and work history. Since, on average, women retired at 60 and men at 65, and because women earned less overall, the consequence was to raise women's pensions above 'average' levels, had the strictly actuarial criteria of the duration of time worked and salaries earned been taken into account (Nowakowska and Swedrowska 2000; Woycicka et al. 2003). The different retirement ages of men and women were not as important for pension levels as was the pre-retirement income level (MGiP).

Pension reforms that were introduced when the right-wing government was in power in 1998 increased the gender inequality in pension income, as they retained the different retirement ages, but women who retire earlier than men lose more now than previously. Under the old system, women's average pension was 75 percent of men's average pension, while at equal retirement age it reached 81 percent. On average, the changes will now decrease women's pension to 57 percent of men's pension with different retirement ages and up to 73 percent if the retirement age is equal (Woycicka et al. 2003). Thus, the redistribution of pension income toward low-earning individuals has been restricted and women's relative position has further deteriorated, thus stretching economic uncertainty into old age.

Another change in the calculation of pensions relates to how periods of child-raising leave are treated. The socialist state recognized the value of providing care and such leaves were equal to active employment in calculating pension benefits. Changes introduced in 1991 distinguish between active employment and child-raising, and function to the detriment of care providers by reducing their future pensions (Woycicka et al. 2003). Women's greater responsibilities for and involvement in childcare are thus being penalized, or gender inequality is being reinforced, by extending their effects into post-retirement age.

Under the new rules, pension benefits also depend on the status of unemployment. Those unemployed who receive benefits contribute to their pension fund, and those without benefits do not. Since more women than men are found in the category of unemployed without benefits (their risk of long-term unemployment is greater), their contributions to the pension funds are lower, and as such will translate into lower pensions upon retirement (Woycicka et al. 2003).

The pension reform has, however, some positive aspects. It improves the prospects of persons working part-time (Woycicka et al. 2003), and although part-time work is not prevalent in Poland, more women than men are found in it. Furthermore, a separated or widowed spouse, in case of death or divorce, now also has rights to the pension funds that were accrued by the partner (Woycicka et al. 2003).

Education

Polish women have relatively high educational levels, and their educational achievements surpassed those of men by 1968 (Heinen 2002). Despite their higher human capital, however, they command lower incomes and positions of authority (Hauser, Heyns and Mansbridge 1993), so that educational advantage has not translated into success in the labor market. Greater educational attainment of women is necessary if they want to participate in political or in executive careers at a high level (Fuszara 2000b). Yet education alone is not a sufficient characteristic, as women still have more difficulties than men in attaining higher posts, even when they are better educated. Also, because increased competition in the open economy no longer guarantees secure employment and income, less educated women find themselves in especially vulnerable positions.

Childcare and housework in relation to employment

Under socialism, the state supported the combination of motherhood with employment through generous paid maternity and childcare leave laws and by developing a network of subsidized childcare centers. The particular legislative packages and the coverage of such institutionalized care varied, as did the commitment of various political forces to the idea of women working, but the state did closely coordinate its employment policy with its family policy (Piotrowski 1963). Childcare centers were less numerous in Poland than in neighboring countries, but were nonetheless able to increase the enrollment from nearly 30 percent of the three- to six-year-olds in 1970 to nearly 50 percent by 1980 (Heinen 2002).

Such state support dwindled rapidly during the transition – 40 to 60 percent of nurseries and preschools were closed already by mid-1991 (Titkow 1993) – and many formerly public childcare facilities have been privatized. The decreasing number and high cost of private childcare centers have created a necessity to provide such services at home, a responsibility that more often than not falls to women (Siemienska 2000; Heinen 2002). Poorer families with many young children find private childcare services out of their financial reach.

Mickiewicz and Bell's analysis (2000) indicates that the factor most affecting labor force activity rates among women is the availability of childcare. This single factor is more significant than education level, age, maternity leave provisions, public transportation, the level of urbanization or socio-cultural traits.

Financial support for children, however, has not deteriorated as quickly as institutional childcare coverage. Real values have decreased only slightly, and in 1995 they were still at 97 percent of 1989 values (Pascall and Manning 2000). Maternity leave and benefits, first introduced in Poland in 1924, have been adjusted several times in the post-transition years. In 1989, benefits provided for 16 weeks of leave, at full pay, with the birth of the first child, and during the post-transition period the leave was extended first to 20 weeks, then to 26 weeks. In 2001, part of the leave (two weeks) was also extended to fathers. In 2002, the leave was cut back again to 16 weeks (Woycicka et al. 2003). While the extension of maternity leave to about six months at full salary would seem to ease the tension between motherhood and employment, such an arrangement may also be seen as costly to employers and thus increase discrimination against female workers. In an era in which employment policy is no longer coupled to family policy, generous maternity provisions become associated more with costs than with benefits.

It was only in 1995 and 1996, under a left-wing government, that long extant childcare leave (introduced in 1954) and child-raising leave and benefits (introduced in 1968) were extended to men on an equal basis with women. In principle, both parents have equal rights to 80 percent of the employee's income (Woycicka et al. 2003), and although the extension of this right to fathers is a positive development, there are no incentives for men to opt for such leaves. Introducing legislation consistent with EU standards in this area is insufficient to change the behavior of both parents toward a more egalitarian sharing of childcare duties. Current data show a declining trend among both parents to take child-raising leave; among fathers, it is only 2 percent (Szemplinska 2000). That parents are not exercising their right to time off is ascribed to their fear of losing employment in a precarious labor market, and to the low childcare allowances paid while on leave (Glogosz 2000).

The division of household labor is similarly resistant to change. The official socialist rhetoric of equality found no echo in the home, and the double burden of women during socialism was an acute problem. Time budget studies indicate that the end of socialist rule has meant men on average now do 16 minutes more housework than before and women do 19 minutes less – but that difference hardly matters since women still spend about twice as much time as men on housework – the difference between women's and men's housework diminishes from 2 hours 59 minutes in 1984 to 2 hours 14 minutes in 1996 per day (Woycicka et al. 2003).

Men seem to have a choice whether they will contribute and what form this contribution will take (Fuszara 2000a). The persistent responsibility of women for the household combined with the diminished state support mean that the reconciliation of women's family and professional lives has become more difficult. It remains much harder for women to be available for paid work outside the home, or if they are available, to project the perception of this availability to employers.

A discriminating labor market?

High skill and education levels have become major explanations for higher wages, and are regarded as the best protection for holding on to a job (Rutkowski 1998). However, women's inferior labor market position, both in earning capacity and employment, contradicts their human capital accumulation, as they do, on average, acquire higher qualifications than men. A possible explanation is employers' behavior, as they may view women as mothers and wives first (Balcerzak-Paradowska 2002). As Fuszara (2000a) notes, the regulations intended to uphold equality did not protect women from discrimination in the transformation period. The planned economy was a secure environment in which women's jobs were legally and practically guaranteed even after lengthy parental leaves. The current labor market situation is much more precarious, and women may be discriminated against at the point of entry in order to prevent their potential higher cost to the employer. Men as fathers do not face the same danger, although the legal privilege of caring for children was extended to them as well.

There are numerous examples of women discriminated against in the labor market. Watson (1993) reports that employers have openly indicated a strong preference for male workers: about two-thirds of job vacancies advertised in job agencies preferred men. Other studies (Hebda-Czaplicka and Kolaczek 2001; Kolaczek 2001) found that gender-based discrimination in access to work has increased in Poland during the 1990s. For example, unemployed women seeking jobs were asked far more often (57 percent) than were unemployed men (27 percent) whether they had children (Kolaczek 2001). Furthermore, sometimes employers offered a job to a woman only on condition of her signing a statement that she would not use paid childcare days accorded to her by law while employed. Some young female job candidates were required to provide a doctor's note stating they were not pregnant (Balcerzak-Paradowska 2001). It is thus difficult to disregard the issue of direct gender discrimination in the labor market, though recent modifications to the labor code have clearly banned such discriminatory treatment and penalize violations of the law.

Labor market policy

With unemployment being a new development in post-socialist Poland, the
state laid down legal foundations for labor market policy and to facilitate its
institutionalization. Thus, the first Employment Act, in December 1989,
included a definition of the term 'unemployed person,' introduced
unemployment benefits and made it compulsory for regional employment
offices to take measures to combat unemployment (Churski 2002).

While a gender-based analysis of labor market policy is missing from the
literature on CEE countries, certain policy trends can be detected. Article 33
of the 1997 Constitution, for example, asserts the equal rights of men and
women in family, political, social and economic life, in education, social
security, public office holding, employment and promotion, and stipulates
equal remuneration for equal work (Fuszara 2000a). The Labor Code,
repeatedly revised since 1989, contains regulations that establish an equality
of rights and treatment of men and women, and bans discrimination. Initial
modifications to this code were partial and transitional, according to the
former Economics Minister (Hausner 2002), but more recent changes are in
response to EU regulations and directives from 2000 and 2002. The treatment
of sexual harassment not only replicates EU law but also aligns the Labor
Code with the Polish Constitution and responds to the demands of women's
groups in Poland (European Foundation 2003). The new Labor Code,
effective since January 2004, defines and prohibits all forms of direct and
indirect discrimination, compels employers to counteract discrimination,
defines and prohibits sexual harassment and lifts the upper limits of
compensation to a victim of discrimination. Thus, in terms of equality of
rights and opportunities, progress at the constitutional and administrative
level is evident. The practical impact of these reforms in work relations still
needs to be assessed.

THE POSITION OF WOMEN AND MEN IN A BROADER CONTEXT

Women and political power

Sainsbury (1999, p. 272) argues that women's politics are relevant to policy
outcomes because of 'ideology, power resources, strategies and sites of
influence.' Despite the new Polish Constitution's assertions, equality in
opportunity and equality in outcome leave much to be desired. Although
participation in politics carried a different meaning under socialist rule, the
socialist state did at least put up a façade of women's involvement. Since
then, even the façade is gone, because once the official gender quota was
removed, the proportion of women in positions of power declined (Fuszara
2000b). For example, while women comprised 23 percent of the lower house

representatives (Sejm) in 1980, by 1997 this proportion had fallen to 11 percent. A 1999 proposal to promote equality via quotas, in which the electoral candidate lists would contain at least a third of each sex was not accepted (Fuszara 2000a). The absence of politicized women's issues is also glaring in the trade unions, where women early on were advised not to bring up potentially divisive concerns (Hauser, Heyns and Mansbridge 1993), and which to this day have failed to respond to the new possibilities of achieving greater gender equality (Sasic Saslovic 2000).

A weak representation of women in power may partly explain their relatively poor position in society. A potential new avenue for formulating and articulating issues of specific concern to women could lie in non-governmental organizations (NGOs), but though they are increasing their presence, they are still seen as weak or ineffective (Graham and Regulska 1997) and their cooperation with the government is seen as difficult (Fuszara 2000a). However, their growth may be a real opportunity for women to stretch the boundaries of the public sphere and to engage in politics. This has the potential to engage with the general public in addition to working with national and supranational governing bodies, as it was done after the 1995 Beijing conference by drafting a National Action Plan for Women devised to improve women's situation (Martynowicz 2000).

The role of the EU: membership prospects

The EU included labor market issues early on in its relations with CEE countries. The Europe Agreements provided for cooperation and harmonization of labor law, especially over health and safety, social security and labor market policies (Mickiewicz and Bell 2000). But the politics of equal opportunity is a low priority issue for many CEE governments, especially when compared with what needed to be done to join the EU (Lippert, Umbach and Wessels 2001). The fact that the issue of women in the labor market touches on declining employment and increasing poverty, changing institutions, revamping social policies, as well as evolving gender roles makes it difficult to prioritize policy areas to address (Pollert 2000).

Despite such skepticism, some progress has been made, as Sasic Silovic (2000) observes, CEE countries have passed crucial legislation to prevent gender-based discrimination. In addition, the Polish Constitution permits certain sovereign powers to submit to supra-national regulations, so international law may override domestic legislation and, as such, new opportunities emerge, to alter discriminatory standards (Sasic Silovic 2000). An example comes from retirement regulations, where, as a result of Poland's ambition to join the EU, the principle of equal treatment for men and women now means that an employer cannot fire a woman who has reached the age of 60 if she still wants to work, and must continue to employ her for another five years (Helsinki Foundation Report 2000). Another example is that the

amended 1996 parental leave included fathers without any restrictions
(Heinen 2002).

The positive changes in legislation that have been taking place in recent
years, including changes in the 1997 Constitution and the Labor Code (of
2002 and 2004), are ascribed to the harmonization process and would not
have taken place without the aspiration of joining the EU (Wilkowska 2002).
An EU report on Poland's progress towards accession from 2002 confirms
this in its remarks on gender equality and the Labor Code. But aside from
looking good on paper, the new Labor Code regulations can also serve as a
basis for legal action if the law is not observed (Tokarska-Biernacik 2002).

In the institutional realm, the Office of the Governmental Plenipotentiary
for Equal Opportunities for Women and Men in Poland was established as a
result of the negotiations with the EU (Wilkowska 2002). The Ministry of the
Economy and Labor, together with the European Social Fund, is involved in
the initiative EQUAL, aiming at the study and support of new ways of
fighting all forms of discrimination and inequality in the labor market. In
addition, the government has prepared the *National Strategy for Increasing
Employment and Human Resources Development for 2000–2006* (MPiPS
1999). The document recognizes the inferior position of women in the labor
market and suggests changes, including popularizing the idea of gender
equality through education and media campaigns, and appealing to employers
to provide part-time positions for women with family obligations. While this
document, created during a right-wing administration, does recognize certain
gender inequalities, it still stresses the more traditional role of women as
mothers and attempts to find solutions for their return to work after
childbirth. It does not, however, present women with real choices, nor does it
promote the idea of fathers' role in childcare or part-time employment.
Gender equality, then, is not fully applied nor supported within the document
itself, while the government vows to endorse it within the wider society.

So the prospect of joining the EU does not mean that governments act in a
single direction, or stay the course. A recent example of state action taken
against official EU tendencies and against its earlier proclamations occurred
in the case of abortion law. The Polish left-wing government, facing a
nationwide referendum on joining the EU and under pressure from the
Church, has requested permission from the EU to preserve its existing,
restrictive abortion laws (Penn 2003). That is, the government acting on its
own preferences also responds to pressures from other strong actors,
including the Church and the voters.

In sum, a complete transformation of the Polish system involving all the
political, economic, social and cultural adaptation to the Western European
standard is unlikely. One reason is that a uniform system has not been
established anywhere yet, not even in the longest-standing members of the
EU (Kowalik 1998). Another reason is that applicant or new member states
are active players in the EU integration process and respond not only to the

external structural pressures but also to interests expressed within state borders. A combination of what is demanded as fixed, and what is negotiable causes unique solutions. The resulting outcome for women in Poland and their position within the labor market is, in the end, affected by actions taken by the national governments as well as other sub-national and supra-national actors.

DISCUSSION AND CONCLUSIONS

Although assessing the labor market position of women and men in socialist or post-socialist Poland is a complicated task, it is evident that two recent structural sources of change that reflect globalization, that is, the 1989 collapse of communism and the EU accession process, have resulted in different outcomes for the society. The first external shock worsened the relative position of women in comparison to the socialist period, while the second has brought more beneficial amendments, at least on legislative level.

Throughout the CEE countries, the communist official discourse mostly supported gender equality. The Polish state emphasized women's active participation in employment, so it was relatively high and facilitated by the provision of institutionalized childcare, extensive maternity leave and child benefits, but was also necessary because of low wages. Pension policies partially compensated women for their child-raising leaves. The legal tradition of marriage was based on equality principles and promoted secularization of marriage as well as simplifying divorce procedures (Ferge 1998) and equal property rights in marriage and divorce (Pascall and Manning 2000). Taxes and benefits were tied to individual employment and thus avoided treating women as dependent on their husbands (Pascall and Manning 2000). The liberal abortion laws gave women some control over their reproductive rights. All these characteristics suggest a degree of choice and independence between partners, a pattern of a family approaching a dual/individualized earner model. Still, full equality in socialist Poland was not achieved, and the country had a gendered division of unpaid and paid labor and gender pay differentials as high as in the West.

The collapse of communism changed the official and actual gender relations in Poland. The immediate post-transition government did not engage in women-friendly politics, and women's presence in the labor market became less legitimate than before. The changed overall conditions and economic uncertainty worsened women's relationship to the labor market, where female unemployment levels were rising faster and persisted longer than those of men. The gendered wage gap improved only slightly in the first phase of the transition; the segregation in the labor market did not. The higher human capital of women did not translate into significant improvements in wages or positions of authority, labor market discrimination has increased, and the political power of women has decreased. Household and childcare duties have remained predominantly with women.

Yet, today, the general picture of gender relations and the labor market situation of men and women is mixed, with losers and winners among both groups. Since the guarantees of full employment are unsustainable, the unemployment rates are high. Employment rates are low and women find it more difficult to compete successfully in the labor market. Their labor force participation is lower than before the transformation, but so is that of men. The access to affordable childcare has diminished, but the maternity and child-raising leaves and benefits have been extended to include fathers. Pension reforms became detrimental to persons who take time off to care for children, but benefit part-time workers. In addition, individual wages are generally low and not conducive to the establishment of independent households based on only one income, whether male of female.

The impact of the internationalization of markets, intensified competition, the spread of knowledge and technology, and the rising importance of markets has collided with a set of institutions and a culture that are specific to socialist societies. This collision is still generating the Polish welfare state mix, but in the meantime increased uncertainty is evident (see Table 10.1). The types of labor decommodification and stratification are evolving from more generous and egalitarian to more precarious and stratified. The three pillars of state, market and family have shifted emphasis away from the state toward the market and the family. The patterns of state-promoted gender relations uphold or sometimes intensify the gendered division of labor and traditional marriage, and the change to non-individual taxation hints at a shift to a family wage system (without the family wage). The relatively good maternity leave and post-maternity work reinstatement laws contrast with the diminished state provision of institutionalized childcare. Taken together, it is hard to argue that the employment pattern in Poland has moved from the more individual to the clear male-breadwinner model.

Again, although a more detailed and rigorous analysis is still needed, one can see that structural changes related to globalization pass through the filter of national institutions, interact with agents on various levels and alter the domestic status quo. More specifically, I argue that the commitment to labor market gender equality in a post-socialist state such as Poland depends on the political outlook of the governing administration (with the left more committed to equal opportunities than the right) combined with external and internal actors pressing for such a stance. During the first exogenous shock the domestic environment contained an 'anti-leftist' Solidarity government committed to (male) worker support (decommodification), but grappling with a sudden sharp rise in unemployment, and thus budgetary constraints (a trade-off between unemployment benefits and 'less urgent' services). The increased strength of the Church stressed conservative roles for women, and many unions were in accord with this stance. The weak Women's Movement

Table 10.1   HDI and GDI ranking of select CEE countries, 1990 to 2001

Index/country	1990	1992	1995	1998	1999	2000	2001
HDI[a]							
Czech Republic[b]	27	38	39	34	33	33	32
Hungary	30	50	47	43	36	35	38
Poland	41	51	52	44	38	37	35
GDI[a]							
Czech Republic[b]		15	25	33	32	32	32
Hungary		23	34	38	35	35	36
Poland		22	35	40	36	36	35

Notes: [a]   HDI contains long and healthy life, knowledge, decent standard of living
GDI accounts for differences between men and women. Pollert notes methodological and conceptual modifications in successive UNDP reports, so comparative analysis should be cautious. Still, the ranking position is a valuable indicator of relative changes. The number of countries varies among the surveys, with HDI over 160 and GDI over 140
[b]   For the Czech Republic until 1993, data for Czechoslovakia used

Source: Based on UNDP Human Development Reports from various years[a]

was not in a position to counter the retrenchment in the gender contract. The second external shift met a more fertile ground for supporting gender equality. The power of the right parties committed to the traditional family and the male worker is circumscribed by the leftist groups (no longer viewed as 'old communists') with a more egalitarian outlook and alignment with EU principles, the position of the Church after the initial boost is declining, and issues and non-governmental organizations focusing on commitments to gender equality are maturing and learning to use the EU's commitment to gender equality on the national scene.

BIBLIOGRAPHY

Balcerzak-Paradowska, B. (2001) *Kobiety i mezczyzni na rynku pracy: rzeczywistosc lat 1990–1999*, Warsaw: IPiSS.
Balcerzak-Paradowska, B. (2002) 'Czy uprawnienia pracownicze sprzyjaja zatrudnieniu kobiet?', *Polityka Spoleczna*: 11–12.
Bastian, J. (1998) 'Putting the cart before the horse? Labour market challenges ahead of Monetary Union in Europe', in D. Hine and H. Kassim (eds) *Beyond the market*, London and New York: Routledge.
Bialecki, I. and Heyns, B. (1993) 'Educational attainment, the status of women, and the private school movement in Poland', in V.M. Moghadam (ed.) *Democratic reform and the position of women in transitional economies*, Oxford: Clarendon Press.

Brainerd, E. (2000) 'Women in transition: changes in gender waged differentials in Eastern Europe and the former Soviet Union', *Industrial and Labor Relations Review*, 54(1): 138–62.

Churski, P. (2002) Unemployment and labour-market policy in the new voivodeship system in Poland', *European Planning Studies*, 10(6): 745–63.

Council of Ministers (2002) 'Ordinance of the Council of Ministers on the Government Plenipotentiary for Equal Status of Women and Men of 25 June 2002', Dz. U. z dnia 1 lipca 2002 r.

Esping-Andersen, G. (1990) *The three worlds of welfare capitalism*, Oxford: Polity Press.

European Foundation for the Improvement of Living and Working Conditions (2001–04), *New rules approved on equal treatment and discrimination.* European industrial relations observatory online, www.eiro.eurofound.eu.int. Accessed on 20 December 2003.

Ferge, Z. (1998) 'Women and social transformation in Central-Eastern Europe: the "old left" and the "new right"', *Social Policy Review*, 10: 217–36.

Fultz, E., Ruck, M. and Steinhilber, S. (eds) (2003) *The gender dimensions of social security reform in Central and Eastern Europe: case studies of the Czech Republic, Hungary and Poland*, Budapest: ILO.

Fuszara, M. (2000a) 'The new gender contract in Poland', SOCO Project Paper No. 98, Vienna.

Fuszara, M. (2000b) 'New gender relations in Poland in the 1990s', in S. Gal and G. Kligman (eds) *Reproducing gender. Politics, public and everyday life after socialism*, Princeton, NJ: Princeton University Press.

Glogosz, D. (2000) 'Reconciliation of family and work – situation and trends in Poland – current tendencies and foreseen changes', in M.E. Domsch and D.H. Ladwig (eds) *Reconciliation of family and work in Eastern European countries*, Frankfurt am Main: Peter Lang.

Gora, M. (1997) 'Employment policies and programmes in Poland', in M. Godfrey and P. Richards (eds) *Employment policies and programmes in Central and Eastern Europe*, Geneva: International Labour Office, pp. 115–33.

Graham, A. and Regulska, J. (1997) 'Expanding political space for women in Poland', *Communist and Post-Communist Studies*, 30(1): 65–82.

Grajek, M. (2001) 'Gender pay gap in Poland', Discussion Paper FS IV 01-13, Wissenschaftszentrum Berlin.

Hauser, E., Heyns B. and Mansbridge, J. (1993) 'Feminism in the interstices of politics and culture: Poland in transition', in N. Funk and M. Mueller (eds) *Gender politics and post-communism: reflections from Eastern Europe and the former Soviet Union*, New York and London: Routledge.

Hausner, J. (2002) Interview with Rzeczpospolita journalist Katarzyna Sadlowska. Archives of Rzeczpospolita Online. www.rzeczpospolita.pl. Accessed 17 October 2003.

Hebda-Czaplicka, I. and Kolaczek, B. (2001) 'Przypadki dyskryminacji kobiet i mezczyzn w sferze pracy', in B. Balcerzak Paradowska (ed.) *Kobiety i mezczyzni na rynku pracy: rzeczywistosc lat 1990–1999*, Warsaw: IPiSS.

Heinen, J. (2002) 'Ideology, economics, and the politics of child care in Poland before and after the transition', in S. Michel and R. Mahon (eds) *Childcare policy at the crossroads*, London: Routledge.

Helsinki Foundation Report (2000) 'Poland', pp. 319–44, http//:free.ngo.pl.temida. Accessed 9 September 2003.

Jackman, R. and Rutkowski, M. (1994) 'Labor markets: wages and employment', in N. Barr (ed.) *Labor markets and social policy in Central and Eastern Europe. The transition and beyond*, New York: Oxford University Press.

Kolaczek, B. (2001) 'Zatrudnienie kobiet i mezczyzn w Polsce w latach 1990–1999. Tendencje zmian', in B. Balcerzak Paradowska (ed) *Kobiety i mezczyzni na rynku pracy: rzeczywistosc lat 1990–1999*, Warsaw: IPiSS.

Kornai, J. (1992) *The socialist system: The political economy of communism*. Princeton: Princeton University Press.

Kowalik, T. (1998) 'The systemic conditioning of Polish social policy', *Labour Focus on Eastern Europe*, 59: 53–61.

Kramer, M. (1995) 'Polish workers and the post-communist transition, 1989–1993', *Communist and Post-Communist Studies*, 28(1): 71–114.

LaFont, S. (2001) 'One step forward, two steps back: women in the post-communist states', *Communist and Post-Communist Studies*, 34: 203–20.

Lewis, J. (1992) 'Gender and the development of welfare regimes', *Journal of European Social Policy*, 2(3): 159–73.

Lewis, J. (2002) 'Gender and welfare state change', *European Societies*, 4(4): 331–57.

Lippert, B., Umbach, G. and Wessels, W. (2001) 'Europeanization of CEE executives: EU membership negotiations as a shaping power', *Journal of European Public Policy*, 8(6): 980–1012.

Lobodzinska, B. (1995) *Family, women, and employment in Central-Eastern Europe*, Westport, CT and London: Greenwood Press.

Marody, M. and Giza-Poleszczuk, A. (2000) 'Changing images of identity in Poland: from the self-sacrificing to the self-investment woman', in S. Gal and G. Kligman (eds) *Reproducing gender. Politics, public and everyday life after socialism*, Princeton, NJ: Princeton University Press.

Martynowicz, A. (2000) (on behalf of the Polish Helsinki Committee) 'A perspective on the women's status in Poland', paper presented at the 'Obstacles to the advancement of women's human rights – a regional approach' conference, Sarajevo. 9 September 2003.

Mickiewicz, T. and Bell, J. (2000) *Unemployment in transition: restructuring and labour markets in Central Europe*, Amsterdam: Harwood Academic.

MPiPS (Ministersto Pracy i Polityki Spolecznej – Ministry of Labour and Social Policy) (1999) *Narodowa Strategia Wzrostu Zatrudnienia i Rozwoju Zasobów Ludzkich w latach 2000-2006 – National strategy for increasing employment and human resources development for 2000–2006*. Approved by the Council of Ministers on 4 January 2000. Document accessed from http://www.mgip.gov.pl on 30 October 2003.

Nowakowska, U. and Swedrowska, A. (2000) 'Kobiety na rynku pracy', in B. Gadomska, M. Korzeniewska and U. Nowakowska (eds) *Kobiety w Polsce w latach 90*, Warsaw: Raport Centrum Praw Kobiet.

Organisation for Economic Co-operation and Development (OECD) *Employment outlook*, various years, www.oecd.org. Accessed 29 April 2004.

Orloff, A.S. (1993) 'Gender and the social rights of citizenship: the comparative analysis of gender relations and welfare states', *American Sociological Review*, 58(June): 303–28.

Orioff, A.S. (1996) 'Gender in the welfare state', *Annual Review of Sociology*, 22: 51–78.

Pascall, G. and Manning, N. (2000) 'Gender and social policy: comparing welfare states in Central and Eastern Europe and the former Soviet Union', *Journal of European Social Policy*, 10(3): 240–66.

Penn, S. (2003) 'Poland backs away from liberalizing abortion laws', www. womenenews.org. Accessed 27 October 2003.

Piotrowski, J. (1963) *Praca zawodowa kobiety a rodzina*, Ksiazka i Wiedza.

Pollert, A. (2000) 'Gender relations, equal opportunities and women in transition in Central Eastern Europe', *Labour Focus on Eastern Europe*, 66: 4–49.

Pollert, A. (2003) 'Women, work and equal opportunities in post-communist transition', *Work, Employment and Society*, 17(2): 331–57.

Rocznik Statystyczny Rzeczypospolitej Polskiej 1998 – Statistical Yearbook 1998 (1998) Warszawa: Glowny Urzad Statystyczny (GUS) [Central Statistical Office], www.stat.gov.pl. Accessed 12 December 2003.

Rocznik Statystyczny Rzeczypospolitej Polskiej 2003 – Statistical Yearbook 2003 (2003) Warszawa: Glowny Urzad Statystyczny (GUS) [Central Statistical Office], www.stat.gov.pl. Accessed 12 December 2003.

Rubery, J. (2001) 'Equal opportunities and employment policy', in P. Auer (ed.) *Changing labour markets in Europe: the role of institutions and policies*, Geneva: ILO.

Rutkowski, J. (1998) 'Welfare and the labor market in Poland: social policy during economic transition', World Bank Technical Paper No. 417, Washington, DC.

Sainsbury, D. (1994) 'Women's and men's social rights: gendering dimensions of welfare states', in D. Sainsbury (ed.) *Gendering welfare states*, Thousand Oaks, CA: Sage.

Sainsbury, D. (1999) 'Gender, policy regimes, and politics', in D. Sainsbury (ed.) *Gender and welfare state regimes*, Oxford: Oxford University Press.

Sasic Silovic, D. (2000) 'EU accession – chance for gender equality in CEE countries', *Transfer*, 3: 68–485

Siemieńska, R. (1990) *Płeć, zawód, polityka. Udział kobiet w życiu publicznym w Polsce*, Warszawa: Instytut Socjologii Uniwersytetu Warszawskiego.

Siemienska, R. (2000) 'Factors shaping conceptions of women's and men's roles in Poland', in M.E. Domsch and D.H. Ladwig (eds) *Reconciliation of family and work in Eastern European countries*, Frankfurt am Main: Peter Lang.

Szemplinska, E. (2000) 'Legal possibilities of reconciling family and work in Polish law', in M.E. Domsch and D.H. Ladwig (eds) *Reconcilliation of family and work in Eastern European countries*, Frankfurt am Main: Peter Lang.

Taylor Gooby, P. (1991) 'Welfare state regimes and welfare citizenship', *Journal of European Social Policy*, 1(2): 93–105.

Titkow, A. (1993) 'Political change in Poland: cause, modifier, or barrier to gender equality?', in N. Funk and M. Mueller (eds) *Gender politics and post-communism. Reflections from Eastern Europe and the former Soviet Union*, New York and London: Routledge.

Tokarska-Biernacik, K. (2002) Participant in the seminar 'Kodeks Pracy Szansa dla Kobiet' Secretariat of the Government Plenipotentiary for the Equal Status of Women and Men, Warsaw, 16 April 2002.

Towalski, R. (2003) 'Public sector pay examined', www.eirofound.eu.int. Accessed 20 December 2003.

United Nations, UNDP Human Development Reports from various years, www.undp.org. Accessed 4 December 2003.

Watson, P. (1993) 'Eastern Europe's silent revolution: Gender', *Sociology*, 27(3): 471–87.

Wilkowska, A. (2002) 'Gender equality standards in Poland: the results of the enlargement process', www.ewla.org/wf_dl/Paper_Wilkowska.doc. Accessed 10 October 2003.

Woycicka, I., Balcerzak-Paradowska B., Chlon-Dominczak, A., Kotowska I., Olejniczuk-Merta A. and Topinska, I. (2003) 'The gender dimensions of social security reform in Poland', in E. Fultz, M. Ruck and S. Steinhilber (eds) *The gender dimensions of social security reform in Central and Eastern Europe: case studies of the Czech Republic, Hungary and Poland*, Geneva: ILO.

PART V

Country-specific contributions on
liberal welfare regimes

11. Women's employment in Britain

Katrin Golsch[1]

INTRODUCTION

This chapter examines some implications globalization pressures have for women's work and family life in Britain during the 1990s. Globalization is used here to refer to the complex interactions and growing interdependence between regional and national economies around the world, the intensification of competition, the spread of global networks, the increased volatility of labor, capital and product markets and the pronounced uncertainty in individual, family, social and political life (Mills and Blossfeld 2005).

Prior research indicates that the globalization process may be inherently unstable, segments the occupational structure and hence leads young adults to experience different types of employment insecurity. Aside from its impact on labor market integration, the globalization process and its various types of uncertainty impede the life-course decision-making of men and women (Blossfeld et al. 2005; Mills and Blossfeld 2005). Yet, institutional entrenchment at the aggregate level appears to be a central mechanism through which insecurity is funneled.

Britain provides an interesting case study of transformations in employment relationships, since it has already experienced some effects of the globalization process in increased levels of deregulation and through the liberalization of the labor market (Deakin and Reed 2000). Transitions from school to work appear increasingly complex, and insecure labor market positions hamper partnership and parenthood decisions of young Britons (Francesconi and Golsch 2005). Moreover, there is evidence to suggest that job insecurity has spread to adult men (Golsch 2006). But how do the changes in the degree of social protection under globalization affect adult women's work and family careers? Or more precisely, is there evidence to suggest that globalization leads to more flexible work, flexible families and thus flexible careers? And what are the economic and social consequences for mid-career women?

This chapter takes advantage of the longitudinal data provided in the British Household Panel Survey (BHPS), covering 1991 to 2000, to examine the following events in work and family life: entry into unemployment, exit from unemployment, transitions into and out of unpaid caregiving and downward or upward occupational mobility. It considers the following related research questions. To what extent do women equally face labor market risks, where those risks include unemployment, the probability of re-employment after job loss and occupational downward mobility? In particular, to what extent does inequality arise because of inter-individual differences in educational attainment and occupational status? And what is the role played by women's employment relationship and their lifetime labor market experiences?

In the following sections, I review the most important institutions − degree of social protection, the educational system, and the welfare regime − affecting women's employment decisions in the 1980s and 1990s. I then establish hypotheses and describe the data and methods I use to test these hypotheses. Finally I interpret the results and discuss major findings and their similarities to the case for men in Britain.

THE CHANGES IN THE DEGREE OF SOCIAL PROTECTION IN AN ERA OF GLOBALIZATION

Britain stands out as a country that experienced an increased level of deregulation and flexibility in the labor market during the 1980s compared with previous decades. Owing to employers using flexibility as the guiding principle, firms were able to adjust more swiftly and in less costly ways to competitive demands (Regini 2000). The now prevalent hire-and-fire system imposes almost no restrictions on layoffs or contract lengths, numerical or otherwise, giving employers much flexibility. But this has not led to a tremendous spread of short-term contracts or high unemployment rates as in countries such as Spain (Booth, Francesconi and Frank 2002; Schömann, Rogowski and Kruppe 1998).[2] Rather, the Anglo-Saxon model of strong neoliberalism and free market play has led to substantial job growth. In most other European countries, job growth came to a halt or was even reversed during the 1990s (Mayer 1997; Soskice 1999). Moreover, employers in Britain have used part-time employment to achieve higher levels of labor market flexibility (Dex and McCullogh 1995; Gallie, White and Tomlinson 1998). The collective bargaining system has been intensively decentralized as well, opening the way to introduce wage flexibility in labor relations.

Yet since flexibility is mainly employer–led, workers are relatively exposed to market forces, as welfare state support and third party intervention are lacking compared with many European countries. Conservative governments reformed employment law to restrict the protection against unlawful dismissal; lowered some benefits, tightened eligibility requirements, increased sanction possibilities and work incentives for the unemployed, introduced in-work benefits for low-income households and abrogated wage councils (Deakin and Reed 2000; Dingeldey 1998; Towers 1994). Throughout the 1980s and 1990s, Conservative governments systematically eroded the power of unions through placing restrictions on the right to strike and releasing employers from any obligation to negotiate with unions on wages and working conditions (Heery and Abbott 2000; Ladipo and Wilkinson 2002; Machin 2000). Beyond that, the radical privatization of the public sector led to a decline in firm size and an increasing use of subcontracting and outsourcing strategies. This in turn introduced more insecurity in employment relationships and fostered an increase in own-account workers (Ladipo and Wilkinson 2002; Morgan, Allington and Heery 2000).[3]

Since the change of government in 1997, the so-called Third Way as pursued by the Labour Party determines the British picture (Deacon 2000; Dingeldey 1998). It is mainly characterized by maintaining a high degree of deregulation and flexibility of the labor market. But, at the same time, active labor market policies also aim to increase the rate of movement from welfare benefit receipt to work; at its heart is the need to re-skill the workforce. To combat unemployment, new programs under the rubric of the New Deal were introduced to help the younger and older unemployed, single parents as well as partners of the unemployed back into the labor market. Incentives to work were increased, but national insurance unemployment benefits were cut further and sanctions for not working were sharpened at the same time. To some extent there is also a departure from previous policy, as can be seen in the introduction of a statutory National Minimum Wage in 1999. Owing to changes in fiscal policy (including the Working Families Tax Credit), low-income households are better off. Furthermore, with the implementation of the EU's Part-time Working Directive, benefits to part-time workers have been put on a par with those available to full-time workers. Employment protection and union recognition is also to be strengthened (Deakin and Reed 2000).

In summary, the path Britain has taken during the 1980s and 1990s has led to a highly deregulated labor market with weak social security during times of non-employment. Employment relationships are rather short term and trust relations are of little account (Soskice 1991; Marsden 1995). Labor market deregulation has served to exacerbate insecurity and to increase inequality, leading to a strong polarization between 'work-rich' and 'work-poor' households (Gregg, Hansen and Wadsworth 1999), a phenomenon that describes the difficulty of exiting long-term unemployment as well as the fact that jobs obtained after unemployment spells, though more prevalent than under regulated employment systems, are often lower paid, more likely to be temporary and with limited chances of upward mobility (Arulampalam 2001; Dearden, Machin and Reed 1997; Gregg and Wadsworth 1996). As a result, income inequality has increased (Jenkins 2000; Machin 1999) and poverty rates have gone up (Dickens and Ellwood 2001; Jenkins and Rigg 2001).

THE ROLE OF THE EDUCATIONAL SYSTEM FOR CAREER MOBILITY

The British educational system is coupled to the labor market through informal occupation-specific, on-the-job training rather than through state-mandated certification programs (Allmendinger and Hinz 1997; Blossfeld and Stockmann 1998/99; Heath and Cheung 1998; Kerckhoff 1990; Scherer 2001; Shavit and Müller 1998; Steinmann 1998/99). Occupational qualifications are still undertaken in occupational schools for certain fields but formal apprenticeships, uniform nationwide examination standards and binding curricula are no longer very common. Individuals collect experience rather than specific occupational certificates. This experience is highly valuable to current employers but also to potential future employers, which means that in the deregulated low-trust environment of Britain, employers fear the poaching of their trained workforce (Marsden 1995; Shackleton 1995). At the same time, employees have strong incentives to invest in transferable rather than job-specific business skills because the flexible business climate prevents employers from guaranteeing lifetime or long-term employment (Soskice 1991).

Since the 1980s, the government has attempted to improve both the output and the efficiency of vocational training with programs such as Youth Training, Modern Apprenticeships, National Traineeships and Youth Credits (Steinmann 1998/99). Britain has experienced a tremendous educational expansion over the last three decades of the twentieth century, which should be seen in connection with the increasing need for further education and learning in today's societies (McVicar and Rice 2001). Fluctuations in the labor market, the increasing demand for labor market flexibility, as well as the rise in youth unemployment during the economic recessions in the mid-1980s and early 1990s have also played a part in the demand for education.

Three findings gain importance in the context of this study. First, the practical on-the-job training and the weak connection between educational certificates and entry-level jobs should enhance mobility to find an apt and lasting job match (Blossfeld and Stockmann 1998/99; Steinmann 1998/99). Job mobility in Britain was indeed comparatively high by European standards, especially in the 1990s (Booth and Francesconi 1999). Second, career-entry processes have become less straightforward and might include short-term and part-time employment, job experimentation, periods of non-employment, further education and training or gainful employment while enrolled in educational programs (Gallie, White and Tomlinson 1998; Taylor 2000). One indication of the weakening connection between education and labor market entry can be seen from the fact that between 1989 and 1996, the employment probabilities of school graduates declined by eight percentage points to about 68 percent of new school graduates managing to enter gainful employment within one year of leaving education (OECD 1998). Moreover, there is evidence to suggest that full-time employment as a first labor market destination declined from over 90 percent of men and women in the 1950s and 1960s to one-third in the 1990s (Taylor 2000). Third, employment probabilities and labor market integration seem higher or less difficult for women in Britain than in most European countries. Beyond that, the chances of entering gainful employment seem to have worsened much more for men than women during the 1990s (OECD 1998). Thus, the proportion of men in short-term jobs has increased independently of educational degree. The consequent decline in men's job tenure has been offset by an increase in women's job tenure, particularly among those with dependent children (Gregg and Wadsworth 1999; Gregg, Hansen and Wadsworth 1999). Furthermore, men face substantially higher unemployment risks than women (Booth, Francesconi and Garcia-Serrano 1999) and individual resources play a far more crucial role for men's unemployment risks (Nickell 1999).

THE WELFARE STATE AND THE GENDERED DIVISION OF WORK

Britain, as an example of the liberal welfare state (Esping-Andersen 1999), is characterized by passive labor market policies and only moderate support for those in need. Welfare support for the unemployed and inactive has been cut by British governments over the past decades, and major changes in legal regulations, based on the principles of responsibility and reciprocity, have been made by the Labour Party since its election in 1997 (Deacon 2000). The welfare state is increasingly organized around paid work, so gainful employment is of fundamental importance and marks the doorway back out of neediness. As can be seen in various attempts to make work 'pay' and the New Deal on Welfare to Work, recipients are expected to acquire further qualifications to improve their chances of re-entering the labor market speedily (Deacon 2000). This in turn implies that welfare is understood as a temporary assistance. By and large, a shift from passive to more active labor market policies can be observed in recent years.

The welfare state as well as the labor market structure and employment regulation plays a crucial role in the gendered division of work. State-provided childcare facilities, particularly for preschool children, are rather limited, as are leave entitlements (Burchell, Dale and Joshi 1997; Gornick and Meyers 2003). More particularly, entitlements to reduced working hours, paternity leave (which only came into force in 2003) as well as publicly funded childcare are absent. Hence, childcare provision is mainly market based or through relatives or other informal exchange networks, and this private purchase of daycare affects mothers' work life, particularly mothers in secondary jobs with low remuneration.

In recent years, policy-makers have passed various new laws to make it easier to reconcile parenthood and employment. These have included the Working Families Tax Credit (1999) that includes a Childcare Tax Credit that pays up to 70 percent of childcare costs, an increase in the Child Benefit and Family Credit, the New Deal for Lone Parents that introduces incentives for single parents and those with an unemployed partner to (re-)enter gainful employment and an extension of maternity leave. Despite these changes, policies to help parents balance work and family life remain among the weakest in Europe (Gornick and Meyers 2003; Stier, Lewin-Epstein and Braun 2001). [4]

On the other hand, the female labor force participation rate has remained high and varies between 70 and 75 percent during the 1990s. This has to be seen in connection with a much expanded part-time labor market comprised of a highly heterogeneous set of jobs, which are often work-insecure and mainly taken by women (Burchell, Dale and Joshi 1997; Hakim 1998). [5] Several authors argue that women's increase in long-term employment is connected to the increasing tendency of new mothers only to take maternity leave and return to the labor market rather than to withdraw altogether from labor force participation when children are born as was common in previous decades (Gallie, White and Tomlinson 1998; Desai et al. 1999). For instance, the labor force participation rates of mothers with children under six have increased, and by the late 1990s, around 56 percent of these women perform some paid work (OECD 2001). In summary, a laissez-faire policy, benefit systems that are means tested and work incentives are crucial aspects that imply a high degree of recommodification. At the same time, owing to a lack of affordable childcare facilities and less generous leave entitlements, welfare support for female homemakers is comparatively weak.

HYPOTHESES REGARDING GLOBALIZATION'S EFFECTS ON WOMEN IN BRITAIN

This book argues that globalization is filtered through the country-specific institutions, but also that it can have a direct effect on individual employment security. Britain's liberal welfare regime has accounted for high degrees of flexibility and change in the labor market as measured by the extent to which open employment relationships now exist, the relatively market-driven economy, the weak employment protection available that is related to the decline in trade unions and the dwindling coverage of collective bargaining. In such respects, the workforce is hardly protected against globalization pressures, quite unlike countries with largely closed employment relationships and strong competition for vacancies. Britain is best described as a rather individualistic mobility regime, where employees vie for pay increases and premiums and where differences in wages mirror their marginal productivity (Sørensen and Tuma 1981). Employer-led flexibility, fairly unrestrained competition and a hire-and-fire system result in rather low remuneration and short durations of unemployment but high rates of job mobility and less predictability in occupational moves. By and large, job insecurity is assumed to be more evenly spread among British workers than among workers, say, in the closed labor markets of Germany or Spain.

However, the greater flexibility in the British labor market is expected to have a qualitatively different meaning for men and women, as well as for career maturity, and individual resources should function as significant buffers against labor market pressures. The empirical analysis of this chapter examines current generations of mid-career women and focuses on the following hypotheses.

Hypotheses specific to women

The high degrees of flexibility in the British labor market of the 1990s introduces insecurity in male work careers that in turn may create work incentives for women, as the increased resources of a dual-earner household de-couples the long-term economic prospects of a household from the stability of a male job career. Women's labor force participation may thus be seen as a diversification strategy. However, while the separate taxation system may work as a further inducement for some women to be gainfully employed and to hold a full-time job, the means-tested benefit system might create disincentives that lead to reduced working hours or exiting the labor force for others. Moreover, the weak welfare state renders the gainful employment of mothers with young children difficult and hence fosters their movement between caregiving and employment. In a similar manner, increased labor market flexibility may help some women to reconcile work and family life by creating family-friendly part-time work arrangements. Yet, it is also likely to introduce further instability in their employment careers, particularly as parts of the public sector (in which many women have been employed) become privatized (Bruegel and Perrons 1998). Some women will likely abandon gainful employment in favor of a family if they perceive their job has little protection and low career prospects. Others may not seek a permanent place in the labor market at all, and opt for marriage and motherhood instead (Hakim 2000).

The process of globalization occurs in tandem with educational expansion and growing female labor force participation, with changes in employment and family relations and with changing views on marriage and birth. Women have increasingly extended their educational enrollment, and are more career-oriented than in the past, and, in fact, appear better equipped for job competition than ever before (Blossfeld 1995). But their adaptation strategies dynamically unfold over the life course, and the above considerations suggest that women's employment status as well as the job security of their partners may be very important in the strategies they choose to pursue (Hofmeister, Blossfeld and Mills, this volume; Mills and Blossfeld 2005).

Career maturity hypothesis

This chapter explores the effect of career maturity. In other words, is job insecurity spread over the entire labor market career or confined to early labor market experience? The assumption is that adverse effects of flexibility and deregulation are most pronounced for the young, with little experience in and only weak ties to the labor market. This is because employers make increasing use of flexible work arrangements to screen potential new employees (recruitment strategy), and try to lower labor and non-labor costs in case of mismatches between job and employee, as well as during economic downturns (hire-and-fire strategy). With an advancing career, however, individuals gain work experience and seniority, and this should function as a buffer against new risks in the labor market. Yet owing to the accelerated pace and the flow of work in globalizing labor markets, it is likely more difficult for recent labor market entrants to advance their careers, and insecurity at early stages of the work career may have serious repercussions on the later work life. One can also expect gender-specific effects, as it is substantially more difficult for women with children to accumulate career maturity because of career interruptions and withdrawal as well as to part-time and low-paid employment. At the same time, in a low-trust, hire-and-fire environment, one might expect career maturity not to play a prominent role.

Individual resources hypothesis

One can ask whether recent deregulation and flexible measures are mainly confined to the poorly skilled or those in low occupational classes. Employers are more prone to offer permanent contracts, wage premiums and higher remuneration to highly qualified workers, as they are typically employed in positions carrying greater responsibility. Through this, employers assure continued work commitment, motivation and loyalty. Conversely, manual and poorly qualified non-manual workers are readily recruited and monitored, their duties well defined and constricted (Erikson and Goldthorpe 1992). One can expect that unskilled workers face higher degrees of insecurity than employees belonging to the service class. Moreover, with the shift toward skilled jobs and the growing importance of high educational credentials, insecurity will be particularly channeled toward those who are poorly equipped for job competition, that is, those with no educational qualifications. Differing degrees of insecurity are assumed to be reflected in higher unemployment risks, lower re-entry probabilities for the unemployed and increased downward mobility risk among poorly qualified employees. Previous studies have already examined the role of the individual's resources and established that individual resources are more important determinants of career opportunities in countries with weaker employment protection and weaker labor market boundaries (DiPrete et al. 1997). Hence, in the British low-trust environment, workers should gain stability through their own personal characteristics. From another viewpoint, practical on-the-job training and the flimsy connection between educational certificates and entry-level jobs should enhance mobility to find an appropriate and lasting job match.

DATA, METHODS AND VARIABLES

The data analyzed come from annual panel waves of the British Household Panel Survey (BHPS), 1991 to 2000, using a sample of women born in 1950 and after. The analysis is furthermore restricted to original sample members who are not disabled, provided complete information at each interview date, have entered a first job after full-time education, with at least two years of panel data and an identifiable labor market entry year.[6] These sample selection criteria lead to an unbalanced longitudinal sample of 3169 women with 23 573 person-wave observations. Measures of interest are described in detail in Table 11.1.

The analysis employs discrete-time, competing risks transition models, in which the dependent variable is coded zero for non-occurrence and 1,...j for event occurrence of the j competing mobility events between two panel waves (Allison 1982). The events of interest are risk of entry to and exit from unemployment, transitions to and from unpaid caregiving, and chance of upward mobility and risk of downward mobility.

To investigate to what extent insecurity is owed to lifetime labor market experiences, the chapter starts the analysis at age 16 and runs separate models for two age windows. The first covers the age span from 16 to 29 and hence refers to individuals who are likely to be in their early labor market stages (results not shown because of space limitations, but can be obtained from the author on request). Yet, the focus of the analysis is on mid-career women, defined as between 30 and 49. The subsequent presentation of the results concentrates on the interplay of flexible job positions, individual resources and career maturity.

Table 11.1　Measures used in the analysis of British women's mid-career transitions

Variable	Definitions
Measurement of employment, unemployment and caregiving	
Employed	Having a job and positive working hours
Unemployed	Without work and actively seeking new job within the previous four weeks
Unpaid caregiving	Self-reported activity status (either family care or maternity leave)
Economically inactive	Without work, not actively seeking and not caregiving
Transitions of interest:	
Entry into un-employment and exit from unemployment	Transitions from unemployment to job (economic inactivity = competing risk, results not shown)
	Transitions from employment to unemployment (economic inactivity = competing risk, results not shown)
Transitions of interest:	
Into and out of unpaid caregiving	Transitions from job to unpaid caregiving (unemployment and economic inactivity = competing risks, results not shown)
	Transitions from unpaid caregiving to employment (redundancy and changes into inactivity = competing risks, results not shown)
Transitions of interest:	
Upward and downward mobility	Upward = more than 10 percent increase on the Standard International Socio-economic Index of Occupational Status (ISEI; Ganzeboom and Treimann 2003)
	Downward = more than 10 percent decrease
	Lateral = changes on the ISEI score of less than 10 percent (comparison group; unemployment and economic inactivity = competing risks, results not shown)[a]
Independent predictors	
Type of employment relationship	Seven dummies for: permanent and full-time = reference, fixed-term and full-time, casual and full-time, part-time and permanent, part-time and non-permanent, marginal and permanent, marginal and non-permanent (marginal = 1-14/part-time = 15-29 hours per week)
Career maturity	
Employment experiences and employment experiences squared	Number of years in which individuals are employed
Flexi-worker experiences	Number of years a person has been in a non-permanent employment relationship
Unemployment experiences	Dummy variable that indicates whether respondents have been unemployed at least once in the previous panel waves

Table 11.1   continued

Other individual characteristics

Labor market entry cohort	Four dummies for: before 1970, 1970–79, 1980–90 = reference, 1990 and later
Educational qualification	Five dummies for: higher and first university degree, higher vocational qualification, A level or equivalent, GCSE/O level or equivalent = reference, less than O level and no qualification (see Steinmann 1998/99)
Occupational standing (ISEI)	Four dummy variables for: very low, low = reference, high, and very high ISEI scores; quartiles based on four-digit ISCO codes

Characteristics of the workplace

Industrial sector	Two dummies to separate public from private sector and six dummies to divide within the latter into extractive, transformative, private social (reference), distributive, producer, and personal services. Based on the Browning and Singelman classification (1978) and four-digit SIC codes

Macro-economic conditions and the business cycle

Unemployment rate	Yearly unemployment rate, obtained from www.statistics.gov.uk/ May 2003

Duration effects

Unemployment duration	Dummy variables for: up to one year = reference; one to two years; two years and longer
Caregiving duration	Dummy variables for: up to one year = reference; one to two years; two to three years; three years and longer

Partner characteristics and family cycle

Marital status	Four dummies for: never married, married = reference, cohabiting, separated/divorced/widowed
Number of children by age	Three dummies for: number of children aged 0–4, number of children aged 5–15, no children = reference
Partner's educational qualification	Three dummies for: partner higher qualification, partner lower qualification, equal qualification = reference
Partner's activity status	Three dummies for: unemployed, economically inactive, employed = reference
Partner's employment relationship	Four dummies for: employer, own account worker, flexi-worker, permanent full-time employee = reference
Gender attitude index	Sum of individual item scores for five items: 'A preschool child is likely to suffer if his or her mother works;' 'A family suffers if a woman works full-time;' 'A woman and her family would all be happier if she goes out to work;' 'Both the husband and wife should contribute to the household income;' 'A husband's job is to earn money, a wife's job is to look after the home and family.'

Note: [a] Respondents at extremes are excluded. The analysis uses four-digit ISCO–88 codes and applies the conversion tools provided by Ganzeboom and Treiman (1996).

RESULTS

The analysis in this section is divided into three aspects of women's work life: entry into unemployment and exit from unemployment, the linkage between work and family and, finally, the chances of upward mobility and risks of downward mobility.

Entry into unemployment and exit from unemployment

Table 11.2 documents the estimates from a discrete-time, competing risks transition model for entry into unemployment for women aged 30 to 49 and reflects the risks of employment-to-unemployment transitions by mid-career women who are likely to have already settled in the labor market, have accumulated knowledge and experience, and have developed strong ties.

The estimates document that flexible employment relationships increase unemployment risks net of previous employment experiences, occupational standing and industrial sector. Transition rates into unemployment are higher for women in the categories of fixed-term and full-time, and casual and full-time. Part-time, non-permanent employment and marginal work also increase unemployment risks for women. In contrast, permanent posts seem to protect women from unemployment, even if they are only part-timers.

However, employment experiences and previous spells of flexi-work do not matter for women's unemployment risk: only earlier unemployment spells heighten such risk. Moreover, we do not observe a mediating effect of women's occupational standing. Women in Britain do not only seem less often hit by unemployment than men (Booth, Francesconi and Garcia-Serrano 1999), but instead it is the case that individual resources do not determine women's unemployment risks; rather a cumulation of disadvantage in terms of past unemployment experience and exposure to fixed-term, non-permanent, marginal work makes unemployment more likely. Finally, employees in the public sector and the social services are less likely to become unemployed.

The other specifications of Table 11.2 present the findings for the chances of exiting unemployment. The first specification studies unemployment-to-employment transitions. The second specification separates insiders – women who conclude a permanent contract – from those who enter the labor market as flexi-workers. Employment experiences raise chances of exiting unemployment. Flexi-worker experiences lower women's transition rate into employment and into permanent full-time jobs in particular, though these coefficients do not quite reach the 10 percent level of significance owing to the small number of observations. Finally, higher educational qualification increases the probability of re-entering the labor market speedily. Note, however, that case numbers are small and hence inferences drawn from this analysis should be taken as tentative.

Table 11.2   Risk of entry into and exit from unemployment for British women aged 30 to 49 (multinomial logistic regression)

	Risk of entry to unemployment	Chance of exiting unemployment	
		All	Insiders
Type of employment relationship			
Permanent and full-time (ref.)			
Fixed-term and full-time	0.95*		
Casual and full-time	1.52***		
Part-time and permanent	−0.34		
Part-time and non-permanent	0.75*		
Marginal and permanent	0.28		
Marginal and non-permanent	1.35***		
Employment experience (in years)	−0.12*	0.28**	0.16
Employment experience squared	0.00	−0.02*	−0.01
Flexi-worker experience (in years)	0.12	−0.28	−0.81
Unemployment experience (dummy)	0.78***		
Up to one year (ref.)			
1–2 years		−0.25	−0.34
Two years and longer		−0.42	−0.97*
Labor market entry cohort			
Entered before 1970	−0.26	−0.27	0.39
1970–79	0.08	−0.08	0.03
1980–89 (ref.)			
1990 and later	0.34	0.95	0.63
Educational qualification			
Higher and first degree		1.07*	0.71
Vocational degree		−0.09	−1.32*
A level (or equiv.)		0.51	−0.42
GSCE/O level (or equiv.) (ref.)			
Less than O level		0.18	−0.11
Occupational standing (ISEI score)			
Very low (1st quartile)	−0.07		
Low (2nd quartile) (ref.)			
High (3rd quartile)	−0.28		
Very high (4th quartile)	−0.34		
Unemployment rate	0.18	0.26	0.02
Industrial sector			
Extractive	−1.05		
Transformative (ref.)			
Social services	−1.10**		
Distributive services	−0.52		
Producer services	−0.10		
Personal services	−0.14		
Public	−0.95***		

Table 11.2 continued

	Risk of entry to unemployment	Chance of exiting unemployment	
		All	Insiders
Constant	−4.29***	−1.13	−0.60
Log likelihood	−2121	−375	−496
Number of person wave observations	8087	373	372
Number of events	129	181	33

Notes: Obtained from discrete-time, competing risks transition model. The figures are coefficients from multinomial logistic regressions. Standard errors have been adjusted using the Huber/White/Sandwich estimator of variance. All variables lagged by one period except labor market entry cohort.
*** $p < 0.01$, ** $p < 0.05$, * $p < 0.10$.

Source: British Household Panel Study, 1991–2000, employees only for entry to unemployment risk

In summary, the findings suggest that flexible employment measures matter and that past career experiences affect mid-career women's chances of exiting unemployment. But the latter was not found for women aged 16 to 29 (results not shown). It seems reasonable to link this career instability to women's family commitments, as that may impede the integration of work and family life. Other investigations (not shown) revealed that employment and flexi-worker experience lose their predictive power once the analysis controls for marital status and number of children.

Transitions into and out of unpaid caregiving

The discussion in this section first draws on the results from a discrete-time, competing risks transition model for leaving a job position into unpaid caregiving. The first specification in Table 11.3 takes into account a sub-sample of female employees whereas the second specification examines women in partnerships only. The former provides evidence that women in flexible employment are much more likely to discontinue their employment as compared with their counterparts in permanent full-time positions. As one would expect, increasing work experience makes transitions into unpaid caregiving less probable. However, after an initial decrease in the transition rate, the impact of employment experiences tends to level off. Previous

Table 11.3 Transitions into unpaid caregiving for British women aged 30 to 49
         (multinomial logistic regression)

	All women	Partnered women
Type of employment relationship		
Permanent and full-time (ref.)		
Fixed-term and full-time	0.99*	1.20*
Casual and full-time	0.94**	1.10*
Part-time and permanent	0.64***	0.45*
Part-time and non-permanent	0.95**	0.63
Marginal and permanent	1.17***	1.20***
Marginal and non-permanent	1.64***	1.09**
Employment experience (in years)	−0.27***	−0.24***
Employment experience squared	0.01***	0.01***
Flexi-worker experience (in years)	−0.17	−0.08
Unemployment experience (dummy)	0.01	−0.09
Labor market entry cohort		
Entered before 1970	−0.86***	−0.80**
1970–79	−0.71***	−0.70***
1980–89 (ref.)		
1990 and later	0.15	−0.01
Educational qualification		
Higher and first degree	−0.15	
Vocational degree	−0.15	
A level (or equiv.)	−0.32	
GSCE/O level (or equiv.) (ref.)		
Less than O level	0.42**	
Industrial sector		
Private (ref.)		
Public	−0.59***	−0.46**
Marital status		
Never married	−1.16***	
Married (ref.)		
Cohabiting	−0.08	−0.26
Separated/divorced/widowed	−0.04	
Number of children by age		
No children (ref.)		
Children aged 0–4	0.47***	0.27
Children aged 5–15	−0.06	−0.27**
Gender index	0.12***	0.14***
Educational qualification		
Equal qualification (ref.)		
Partner higher qualification		0.11
Partner lower qualification		−0.60**

Table 11.3 continued

	All women	Partnered women
Partner's activity status		
Employed (ref.)		
Unemployed		0.94**
Economically inactive		1.42***
Partner's employment relationship		
Employer		0.52
Own account worker		0.73***
Permanent full-time employee (ref.)		
Flexi-worker		0.82**
Constant	−3.92***	−4.24***
Log likelihood	−2262	−1184
Number of person wave observations	7356	4380
Number of events	253	166

Note: See Table 11.2. *** $p < 0.01$, ** $p < 0.05$, * $p < 0.10$

Source: British Household Panel Study, 1991–2000, employees only

experience in flexible employment and past unemployment experience does not seem to have repercussions on women's transition rates into unpaid caregiving. This is surprising, since one might expect that career instability discourages women and hence makes them less prone to opt for continuous employment. Several further results are worthy of note. Women with low educational qualification are significantly more likely to interrupt their working career in order to carry the brunt of responsibility for domestic work and child-rearing. Women with preschool children seem more often to suspend their gainful occupation to take care of the household. Finally, women with more traditional work orientations – as captured by the gender index – are significantly more likely to withdraw from paid work.

The estimates also indicate that it is essential to incorporate the partners' characteristics. Keeping constant all other explanatory variables, the partner's educational qualification, activity status and employment relationship turn out to be significant predictors of women's transitions into unpaid caregiving. If the woman is better qualified than her partner, she is less likely to suspend gainful employment in order to do unpaid domestic work, which likely reflects stronger career orientations of women. Yet other results are intriguing, such as the higher transition rates into unpaid caregiving for women whose partner is unemployed or economically inactive, an own-account worker or holds a flexible job. Why is this the case? Before attempting an answer, we can look at a similar analysis of transitions from unpaid caregiving into employment.

Table 11.4 reports the estimates from two different specifications for all women and repeats the analyses with women in partnerships only. As can be seen from the first specification, the more employment experience a woman has, the more likely she is to re-enter the labor market. Interestingly, once I control for the type of entry-level job, this only holds true for exits into permanent employment. Previous career instability – as gauged by flexi-worker experiences and previous unemployment spells – raises the chances of exit from unpaid caregiving. However, women with previous spells of flexible employment or past unemployment experiences seem significantly more likely to accept a temporary rather than a permanent post, and one may assume that these two indicators reflect stronger work orientations. This is particularly clear for previous unemployment spells, operationalized as not working but actively searching for a job. Earlier examinations (not shown here) revealed that estimates for flexi-worker spells and past unemployment experience remain significant even if the analysis controls for gender orientation.[7] The transition rate into employment declines the longer women interrupt their employment career. Finally, women with young infants are significantly less likely to re-enter gainful employment and to find a permanent job position in particular. At the same time, women with schoolchildren are significantly more likely to re-enter the labor market as flexi-workers.

Turning to the results for women in partnerships, I again find that the more employment experience, the higher the chances of exit from unpaid caregiving into permanent employment. By contrast, past spells of flexible work arrangements increase the transition rate into flexi-worker positions. Just as under the specifications for all women, the number of children by age determines women's prospects to find a job and their chances of entering secure employment in particular. But what can one conclude from the estimates for partner's characteristics? If the partner has a higher educational qualification, chances are small that women re-enter the labor market and take up a permanent job. While the partner's employment relationship does not seem to matter, Table 11.4 reveals the intriguing result that women of unemployed or economically inactive men are also significantly less likely to re-enter the labor market.

One would expect that if the husband is unemployed, economically inactive women would be more likely to search for a job to compensate for the loss of income. Likewise, when holding a job, women should be less prone to resigning if the husband is hit by unemployment; and in the literature, this has been called an 'added worker effect.'

Table 11.4 Chances to exit from unpaid caregiving for British women aged 30 to 49 (multinomial logistic regression)

	All women			Partnered women		
	[1]	[2]		[3]	[4]	
	All exits	Permanent position	Flexi-worker	All exits	Permanent position	Flexi-worker
Employment experience (in years)	0.08**	0.10*	0.05	0.08	0.15**	0.03
Employment experience squared	−0.00	−0.01*	0.00	−0.00	−0.01**	0.00
Flexi-worker experience (in years)	0.19**	0.06	0.31***	0.10	−0.22	0.45**
Unemployment experience (dummy)	0.32**	0.18	0.47**	0.37**	0.34*	0.43
Caregiving experience (in years)						
Up to one year (ref.)						
1–2 years	−0.24*	−0.16	−0.95***	−0.29	−0.11	−1.48***
2–3 years	−0.52***	−0.44**	−0.97**	−0.55**	−0.30	−1.20**
Three years and longer	−0.82***	−1.01***	−0.50**	−0.77***	−0.95***	−0.43
Labor market entry cohort						
Entered before 1970	−0.73***	−1.04***	0.07	−0.73***	−1.00***	−0.02
1970–79	−0.03	−0.17	0.14	−0.14	−0.14	−0.29
1980–89 (ref.)						
1990 and later	0.16	0.10	0.50*	0.03	0.06	0.23
Educational qualification						
Higher and first degree	−0.02	−0.49	0.52			
Vocational degree	0.03	−0.04	0.08			
A level (or equiv.)	0.33*	0.06	0.54*			
GSCE/O level (or equiv.) (ref.)						
Less than O level	0.04	0.03	−0.17			
Marital status						
Never married	−0.37*	−0.37	−0.20			
Married (ref.)						
Cohabiting	−0.13	−0.15	−0.05	−0.16	−0.21	0.05
Separated/divorced/ widowed	−0.19	−0.18	−0.06			

Table 11.4   continued

	All women			Partnered women		
	[1]	[2]		[3]	[4]	
	All exits	Permanent position	Flexi-worker	All exits	Permanent position	Flexi-worker
Number of children by age						
No children (ref.)						
Children aged 0–4	−0.28***	−0.32***	−0.15	−0.18*	−0.23*	0.01
Children aged 5–15	0.04	−0.00	0.19*	0.15*	0.10	0.37***
Educational qualification						
Equal qualification (ref.)						
Partner higher qualification				−0.93***	−1.36***	−0.37
Partner lower qualification				0.04	0.07	0.05
Partner's activity status						
Employed (ref.)						
Unemployed				−0.70***	−0.47*	−2.03***
Economically inactive				−0.76***	−0.99***	−0.63
Partner's employment relationship						
Employer				0.09	0.14	−0.56
Own account worker				−0.16	−0.23	−0.60
Permanent full-time employee (ref.)						
Flexi-worker				−0.17	0.17	−1.53*
Constant	−0.88***	−1.02***	−2.91***	−0.73***	−1.05***	−2.57***
Log likelihood	−2368	−2587		−1410	−1572	
Number of person wave observations	2847	2847		1830	1830	
Number of events	511	330	115	332	216	78

Note: See Table 11.2. *** $p < 0.01$, ** $p < 0.05$, * $p < 0.10$

Source: British Household Panel Study, 1991–2000

The analysis here provides considerable contrary evidence. Prior research indicates that in Britain the labor force participation rate of the wives of jobless men is markedly lower than that of wives of working men. In fact, McGinnity (2002) suggests that wives of unemployed men are significantly less likely to make inactivity-to-employment transitions, though they do not have a higher propensity to exit gainful employment. She links these results to a potential disincentive effect of the means-tested benefit system, flat-rate entitlements, and low earnings in Britain. As most of the unemployed receive means-tested benefits, these results cast some important light on the documented rise in workless households (Gregg, Hansen and Wadsworth 1999).

Occupational mobility

Table 11.5 analyzes the risk of downward and the chance of upward mobility. The proxy variables for flexible employment clearly determine women's occupational mobility: holding a fixed-term or casual full-time job significantly increases the risks of downward mobility. By contrast, those in permanent job positions with reduced working hours seem less likely to be upwardly mobile. At the same time, non-permanent part-time posts and marginal work generally make downward moves more probable. From this it can be concluded that flexible work arrangements carry a considerable degree of career instability, not only in terms of unemployment risk, but also with respect to downward mobility. Furthermore, the estimates for employment experience show that the risk of downward mobility is higher during the first years of employment: the more experience women have accumulated, the lower the probability that they will move downward. The significant quadratic term of employment experience indicates that after an initial decrease in the transition rate, this impact levels off. Also, previous mobility experiences (whether upward or downward) make future career moves more likely. Overall, the longer a woman has been in insecure, flexible employment relationships, the less likely it is there will be an upward movement in occupation. Yet, previous unemployment spells do not play a role in occupational mobility.

Moreover, the International Socio-Economic Index (ISEI) score of the first job after completing full-time education determines the chances of subsequent upward mobility, as well as the risk of experiencing any movement downward. Taken together, this lends further support to the hypothesis that increased insecurity during the early labor market career is linked to increased instability during the subsequent career. Previous socioeconomic status and educational qualification also have a clear effect: the better the previous occupation, the lower the chances of upward and the higher the risks of downward mobility.

Table 11.5   Chances of occupational upward, risks of occupational downward mobility
for British women ages 30 to 49 (multinomial logistic regression)

	Upward	Downward
Type of employment relationship		
Permanent and full-time (ref.)		
Fixed-term and full-time	0.18	1.01***
Casual and full-time	0.24	0.74**
Part-time and permanent	−0.50***	−0.09
Part-time and non-permanent	0.09	0.62**
Marginal and permanent	−0.52***	0.36**
Marginal and non-permanent	0.05	0.53*
Employment experience (in years)	−0.05	−0.11***
Employment experience squared	0.00	0.00***
Mobility experience (dummy)	1.22***	1.20***
Flexi-worker experience (in years)	−0.12**	−0.02
Unemployment experience (dummy)	0.19	0.14
Labor market entry cohort		
< 1970	0.02	−0.09
1970–79	−0.16	0.01
1980–89 (ref.)		
1990 and later	0.10	0.17
Educational qualification		
Higher and first degree	0.38**	−0.76***
Vocational degree	−0.29***	−0.34***
A level (or equiv.)	−0.09	−0.38**
GSCE/O level (or equiv.) (ref.)		
Less than O level	−0.41***	0.35***
Previous occupation (ISEI score)		
Very low (1st quartile)	0.14	−0.74***
Low (2nd quartile)(ref.)		
High (3rd quartile)	−0.91***	0.85***
Very high (4th quartile)	−2.11***	1.48***
ISEI score 1st job	0.02***	−0.01***
Unemployment rate	0.02	0.01
Industrial sector		
Extractive	0.24	−0.55
Transformative (ref.)		
Social services	−0.15	−0.11
Distributive services	0.05	0.15
Producer services	0.32**	−0.26*
Personal services	0.03	0.19
Public	−0.25**	−0.20
Constant	−1.81***	−1.73***
Log likelihood	−6385	
Number of person wave observations	7576	
Number of events	989	963

Note: See Table 11.2. *** p < 0.01, ** p < 0.05, * p < 0.10
Source: British Household Panel Study, 1991–2000, employees only

Furthermore, the higher the educational qualification, the lower the downward risk, and as one might expect, the highly skilled seem to have better, the poorly skilled significantly lower, chances to experience any occupational upward move.

In sum, I find that, first, insecurity adheres to flexible employment relationships. Second, individual resources not only protect against downward mobility but foster women's upward mobility. Third, the repercussions of flexible employment seem higher for mid-career women: upward career paths are blocked and the chance of loss in socioeconomic status high. Moreover, the longer adult women hold flexible jobs, the less likely upward career moves become. Such women are largely switching between flexible work and caregiving, so one may conjecture that flexibility has a different meaning for women than for men, inasmuch as it facilitates combining work and family life. However, this comes at the cost of a highly unstable work career.

DISCUSSION AND CONCLUSIONS

This chapter has examined increased labor market flexibility and its consequences for the work and family life of women in Britain in the 1990s. Other research has argued that young adults (and mid-career men in the British case) have been the losers in highly flexible labor markets (Blossfeld et al. 2005; Blossfeld, Mills and Bernardi 2006). Flexible jobs seem to offer British women lower advancement possibilities and higher unemployment risks but are also used interspersed with caregiving exits.

The analysis presented here, seen in conjunction with a parallel analysis of men in Britain (Golsch 2006), suggests that there are important differences by gender. At first view it is intriguing that men seem to bear much greater costs of flexibility than women. But the difference may lie in the gender-specific role of flexible work, career maturity and individual resources in the British mobility system. Not only do flexible work arrangements influence men's and women's careers differently, but career maturity and individual resources have differing implications for men and women.

A central finding was that flexible employment introduces a high degree of insecurity into work careers of men and women. No matter what their employment experience and age, flexi-workers are more likely to be hit by unemployment and confront higher risks of downward mobility. Given the low-trust, hire-and-fire environment of Britain, this result is not surprising. On the other hand, employment experience is a vital source of security, whereas previous spells of flexible work or unemployment destabilize the future labor market career irrespective of a person's current employment relationship. To summarize, the less employment experience and the more experience of insecurity a person has, the more likely he or she will enter a 'low pay – no pay cycle.'

However, there is an important gender difference here. For men, the results indicate that insecurity at labor market entry entraps men in a 'flexible employment – unemployment – flexible employment cycle' and may thus be seen as the onset of an unstable job career.

For women, flexibility has a different meaning, inasmuch as career maturity does not determine women's employment-to-unemployment transitions but appears instead to be a predictor of re-entry into the labor market by unemployed mid-career women. Career maturity is likely to be a crude approximation of women's work orientation, which is substantiated by the finding that it is an important parameter for exits into unpaid caregiving (along with rehiring after periods of unpaid caregiving). Moreover, mid-career women with flexi-worker experiences face few career opportunities. A further striking finding is that men's career instability shapes women's employment decisions, making them less prone to be gainfully employed – perhaps due to the disincentives to work built into the means-tested benefit system. By the same token, flexible work arrangements may well fit with women's work orientations and their family life, thereby increasing their labor market attachment and job tenure. In these terms, flexible work may introduce more stability in women's careers, even though it often means being employed in the lower segments of the labor market. For mid-career women, one can suggest they thus switch between 'flexible employment - caregiving - flexible employments' and thus follow a pattern that is structurally similar pattern to that found among young men.

Gender differences exist in individual resources as well, though the expectation was that they functioned as important buffers against labor market insecurity. While such resources indeed determined men's and women's work careers, it was in different veins. In terms of the risk of job loss, re-employment after job loss and career mobility, educational attainment and high occupational standing loomed large for men, particularly for young job holders. For mid-career women, however, individual resources do not make any difference with respect to unemployment risks and seem of little account for the chances of re-entering into a job. Instead, individual resources merely matter for women's career mobility.

NOTES

1   The data used in this chapter were made available through the ESRC Data Archive and were originally collected by the ESRC Research Centre on Micro-social Change (now incorporated within the Institute for Social and Economic Research) at the University of Essex. Neither the original collectors of the data nor the Archive bear any responsibility for the analyses or interpretations presented here.

2   Not least due to the hire-and-fire system, unemployment rates are comparatively
     low (ILO 2001–02). Also, when studying fixed-term employment as a percentage
     of total dependent employment in European countries in 2000, the UK ranks
     fairly low at about 7 percent.
3   Between 1983 and 1997, the shares of own-account workers increased markedly
     from around 62 to 74 percent (OECD 2000).
4   More information can be obtained at: www.soci.ucalgary.ca/fypp/family_policy_
     databases.htm and http://www.childpolicyintl.org/ [19 May 2004].
5   Between 1983 and 1999, the percentage of women working part time remained
     high and fairly stable (ILO 2001–02). In 2000, 23 percent of total employment is
     part-time employment and women's share in part-time employment equals 80
     percent (OECD 2001). The marginal part-time labor market is highly gender-
     segregated with women more than twice as often in a marginal, part-time post
     (ILO 2001–02).
6   For details on the BHPS questionnaire and survey methods, see Taylor et al.
     2005.
7   More traditional orientations measured on the gender index seem to lower the
     transition rate into employment, but the estimates were insignificant under all
     specifications. Since the items measuring gender roles have only been part of the
     survey biannually, the study would be based on considerably less person wave
     observations; thus, the specifications of Table 11.4 do not include the gender
     index.

BIBLIOGRAPHY

Allison, P. (1982) 'Discrete-time methods for the analysis of event histories', in S.
     Leinhard (ed.) *Sociological methodology*, San Francisco, CA: Jossey–Bass.
Allmendinger, J. and Hinz, T. (1997) 'Mobilität und Lebensverlauf: Deutschland,
     Großbritannien und Schweden im Vergleich', in S. Hradil and S. Immerfall (eds)
     Die Westeuropäischen Gesellschaften im Vergleich, Opladen: Leske und Budrich.
Arulampalam, W. (2001) 'Is unemployment really scarring? Effects of unemployment
     experiences on wages', *Economic Journal,* 111(475): 585–606.
Blossfeld, H.-P. (ed.) (1995) *The new role of women. Family formation in modern
     societies*, Boulder, CO: Westview Press.
Blossfeld, H.-P. and Stockmann, R. (1998/99) 'The German dual system in
     comparative perspective', *International Journal of Sociology*, 28(4): 3–28.
Blossfeld, H.-P., Klijzing, E., Mills, M. and Kurz, K. (2005) *Globalization,
     uncertainty, and youth in society*, London: Routledge.
Blossfeld, H.-P., Mills, M. and Bernardi, F. (eds) (2006) *Globalization, uncertainty,
     and men's careers: an international comparison,* Cheltenham, UK and
     Northampton, MA, USA: Edward Elgar.
Booth, A. and Francesconi, M. (1999) 'Job mobility in 1990s Britain: does gender
     matter?', Paper 1999-26, Institute for Social and Economic Research, University of
     Essex.
Booth, A., Francesconi, M. and Frank, J. (2002) 'Temporary jobs: stepping stones or
     dead ends?', *Economic Journal*, 112(480): 585–606.

Booth, A., Francesconi, M. and Garcia-Serrano, C. (1999) 'Job tenure and job mobility in Britain', *Industrial and Labor Relations Review*, 53(1): 43–70.

Bruegel, I. and Perrons, D. (1998) 'Deregulation and women's employment: the diverse experiences of women in Britain', *Feminist Economics*, 4(1): 103–25.

Burchell, B., Dale, A. and Joshi, H. (1997) 'Part-time work among British women', in H.-P. Blossfeld and C. Hakim (eds) *Between equalization and marginalization*, Oxford: Oxford University Press.

Deacon, A. (2000) 'Learning from the US? The influence of American ideas upon "new labour" thinking on welfare reform', *Policy & Politics*, 28(1): 5–18.

Deakin, S. and Reed, H. (2000) 'River crossing or cold bath? Deregulation and employment in Britain in the 1980s and 1990s', in G. Esping-Anderson (ed.) *Why deregulate labour markets?*, Oxford: Oxford University Press.

Dearden, L., Machin, S. and Reed, H. (1997) 'Intergenerational mobility in Britain', *Economic Journal*, 107: 47–64.

Desai, T., Gregg, P., Steer, J. and Wadsworth, J. (1999) 'Gender and the labour market', in P. Gregg and J. Wadsworth (eds) *The state of working Britain*, Manchester: Manchester University Press.

Dex, S. and McCullogh, A. (1995) 'Flexible employment in Britain: a statistical analysis', Research Discussion Series No. 15, Equal Opportunity Commission (UK).

Dickens, R. and Ellwood, D. (2001) 'Whither poverty in Great Britain and the United States? The determinants of changing poverty and whether work will work', Working Paper No. 8253 (April), National Bureau of Economic Research (USA).

Dingeldey, I. (1998) 'Arbeitsmarktpolitische Reformen unter New Labour', *Aus Politik und Zeitgeschichte*, 11: 32–8.

DiPrete, T., de Graaf, P., Luijkx, R., Tahlin, M. and Blossfeld, H.-P. (1997) 'Collectivist versus individualsit mobility regimes? Structural change and job mobility in four countries', *American Journal of Sociology*, 103(2): 318–58.

Erikson, R. and Goldthorpe, J. (1992) *The constant flux. A study of class mobility in industrial societies*, Oxford: Clarendon Press.

Esping-Andersen, G. (1999) *Social foundations of post-industrial economics*. Oxford: Oxford University Press.

Francesconi, M. and Golsch, K. (2005) 'The process of globalization and transitions to adulthood in Britain', in H.-P. Blossfeld, E. Klijzing, M. Mills and K. Kurz (eds) *Globalization, uncertainty, and youth in society*, London: Routledge.

Gallie, D., White, Y. and Tomlinson, M. (1998) *Restructuring the employment relationship*, Oxford: Clarendon Press.

Ganzeboom, H.B.G. and Treiman, D.J. (1996) 'International stratification and mobility', File: Conversion Tools. Utrecht: Department of Sociology, www.fss.uu.nl/soc/hg/ismf/index.htm. Summer 1996, Accessed May 2003.

Ganzeboom, H. and Treiman, D. (2003) 'Three internationally standardised measures for comparative research on occupational status', in J. Hoffmeyer-Zhlotnik and C. Wolf (eds) *Advances in cross-national comparison. A European working book for demographic and socio-economic variables*, New York: Kluwer Academic/Plenum Publishers.

Golsch, K. (2006) 'Globalization, labor market flexibility and job insecurity. Men's labor market mobility in Britain', in H.-P. Blossfeld, M. Mills and F. Bernardi (eds)

Globalization, uncertainty, and men's careers: an international comparison, Cheltenham, UK and Northampton, MA, USA: Edward Elgar.

Gornick, J. and Meyers, M. (2003) *Families that work. Policies for reconciling parenthood and employment,* New York: Russell Sage Foundation.

Gregg, P. and Wadsworth, J. (1996) 'More work in fewer households?', in J. Hills (ed.) *Income and wealth: new inequalities,* Cambridge: Cambridge University Press.

Gregg, P. and Wadsworth, J. (1999) 'Job Tenure, 1975–98', in P. Gregg and J. Wadsworth (eds) *The state of working Britain,* Manchester: Manchester University Press.

Gregg, P., Hansen, K. and Wadsworth, J. (1999) 'The rise of the workless household', in P. Gregg and J. Wadsworth (eds) *The state of working Britain,* Manchester: Manchester University Press.

Hakim, C. (1998) *Social change and innovation in the labour market,* Oxford: Oxford University Press.

Hakim, C. (2000) *Work-lifestyle choices in the 21st century. Preference theory,* Oxford: Oxford University Press.

Heath, A. and Cheung, S.Y. (1998) 'Education and occupation in Britain', in Y. Shavit and W. Müller (eds) *From school to work: a comparative study of educational qualifications and occupational destinations,* Oxford: Clarendon Press.

Heery, E. and Abbott, B. (2000) 'Trade unions and the insecure workforce', in E. Heery and J. Salmon (eds) *The insecure workforce,* London: Routledge.

International Labour Organization (ILO) (2001–02) *Key indicators of the labour market,* International Labour Organization, Geneva.

Jenkins, S. (2000) 'Trends in the UK income distribution', in R. Hauser and I. Becker (eds) *The personal distribution of income in an international perspective,* Berlin: Springer Verlag.

Jenkins, S. and Rigg, J. (2001) 'The dynamics of poverty in Britain: Routes in and out of poverty', unpublished paper, University of Essex.

Kerckhoff, A. (1990) *Getting started. Transition to adulthood in Great Britain,* Boulder, CO: Westview Press.

Ladipo, D. and Wilkinson, F. (2002) 'More pressure, less protection', in B. Burchell, D. Ladipo and F. Wilkinson (eds) *Job insecurity and work intensification,* London: Routledge.

Machin, S. (1999) 'Wage inequality in the 1970s, 1980s and 1990s', in P. Gregg and J. Wadsworth (eds) *The state of working Britain,* Manchester: Manchester University Press.

Machin, S. (2000) 'Union decline in Britain', *British Journal of Industrial Relations,* 38(4): 631–45.

Marsden, D. (1995) 'Deregulation or cooperation? The future of Europe's labour markets', *Labour* (IIRA): 67–91.

Mayer, K.-U. (1997) 'Notes on the comparative political economy of life courses', *Comparative Social Research,* 16: 203–26.

McGinnity, F. (2002) 'The labour-force participation of the wives of unemployed men. Comparing Britain and West Germany using longitudinal data', *European Sociological Review,* 18(4): 473–88.

McVicar, D. and Rice, P. (2001) 'Participation in further education in England and Wales: an analysis of post-war trends', *Oxford Economic Papers,* 53(1): 67–93.

Mills, M. and Blossfeld, H.-P. (2005) 'Globalization, uncertainty and the early life course: a theoretical framework', in H.-P. Blossfeld, E. Klijzing, M. Mills and K. Kurz (eds) *Globalization, uncertainty, and youth in society,* London: Routledge.

Morgan, P., Allington, N. and Heery, E. (2000) 'Employment insecurity in the public services', in E. Heery and J. Salmon (eds) *The insecure workforce,* London: Routledge.

Nickell, S. (1999) 'Unemployment in Britain', in P. Gregg and J. Wadsworth (eds) *The State of Working Britain,* Manchester: Manchester University Press.

Organisation for Economic Co-operation and Development (OECD) (1998) *Employment outlook,* Paris: OECD.

Organisation for Economic Co-operation and Development (OECD) (2000) *Employment outlook,* Paris: OECD.

Organisation for Economic Co-operation and Development (OECD) (2001) *Employment outlook,* Paris: OECD.

Regini, M. (2000) 'Between deregulation and social pacts: the responses of European economies to globalization', *Politics and Society,* 28(1): 5–33.

Scherer, S. (2001) 'Early career patterns: a comparison of Great Britain and West Germany', *European Sociological Review,* 17(2): 119–44.

Schömann, K., Rogowski, R. and Kruppe, T. (1998) *Labour market efficiency in the European Union. Employment protection and fixed-term contracts,* London: Routledge.

Shackleton, J.R. (1995) *Training for employment in Western Europe and the United States,* Aldershot, UK and Brookfield, US: Edward Elgar.

Shavit, Y. and Müller, W. (eds) (1998) *From school to work. A comparative study of educational qualifications and occupational destinations,* Oxford: Clarendon Press.

Sørensen, A. and Tuma, N. (1981) 'Labor market structures and job mobility', *Research in social stratification and mobility,* 1: 67–94.

Soskice, D. (1991) 'The institutional infrastructure for international competitiveness: a comparative analysis of the UK and Germany', in A.B. Atkinson and R. Brunetta (eds) *The economics of the New Europe,* London: Macmillan.

Soskice, D. (1999) 'Divergent production regimes: coordinated and uncoordinated market economies in the 1980s and 1990s', in H. Kitschelt, P. Lange, G. Marks, and J. Stephens (eds) *Continuity and change in contemporary capitalism,* Cambridge: Cambridge University Press.

Steinmann, S. (1998/99) 'The vocational education and training system in England and Wales', *International Journal of Sociology,* 28(4): 29–56.

Stier, H., Lewin-Epstein, N. and Braun, M. (2001) 'Welfare regimes, family-supportive policies, and women's employment along the life-course', *American Journal of Sociology,* 106(6): 1731–60.

Taylor, M. (2000) 'Work, non-work, jobs and job mobility', in R. Berthoud and J. Gershuny (eds) *Seven years in the lives of British families. Evidence on the dynamics of social change from the British household panel survey,* Bristol: Policy Press.

Taylor, M., Brice, J., Buck, N. and Prentice-Lane, E. (2005) *British household panel survey user manual volume A: introduction, technical report and appendices,* Colchester: University of Essex.

Towers, B. (1994) 'Unemployment and labour market policies and programmes in Britain: experience and evaluation', *Journal of Industrial Relations,* 36(3): 370–93.

12. Women's employment transitions and mobility in the United States: 1968 to 1991

Heather Hofmeister[1]

INTRODUCTION

This chapter will assess the indicators of globalization forces in terms of rising uncertainty on the careers of women born in the United States between 1942 and 1953 based on their exits, re-entrances and job mobility in the 1970s and 1980s, comparing the earliest born with the latest born.

The United States is the most populous country described in this volume, with 141 million women representing an enormous scope and complexity of women's experiences. With its individualist-orientation and labor market/family policies that vary in each of the 50 states, the pathways women take to and through employment over the life course can bear many variations but, despite this diversity, some patterns are found throughout the country. Labor market pathways in the United States are uncertain in comparison with many other countries in this volume, where labor protections are stronger and seniority, state intervention and large public sectors protect many jobs. But women tend to experience more uncertainty than men, even within a particular country, and the United States is no exception. American women, like women in other countries, are concentrated in radically unequal fields of study and institutions (Charles and Bradley 2002) and they still average less pay and security than men in the labor market even for the same jobs.

Much evidence shows that American women began a rapid rise in employment in the twentieth century due to a variety of factors, including delayed age at marriage, rising levels of education, postponement of first births, declining birth rates and rising divorce rates, as well as the decline in the earnings of male breadwinners (Fuchs 1988). The idea that a macro process – globalization – could be operating on women's labor market attachment will be assessed here (Blossfeld et al. 2005). If it is, we should see more women employed across cohorts, and staying in employment longer, regardless of personal characteristics or structural locations, including marriage and motherhood. If globalization is a force that unseats women

302

from their relatively secure employment, we should see more downward mobility for the youngest cohort, particularly for the highly qualified. Globalization forces are filtered through institutions, so it is possible that more uncertainty is felt by women in some structural locations (such as those with low education status) than in others. Whether uncertainty is rising across cohorts in the case of the United States will be indicated through rising levels of downward mobility, more specific allocation of upward mobility only to those women with higher educational qualifications, reduced exits from employment due to family formation and earlier re-entries to employment after children have grown.

I compare three cohorts of women in the United States, one born between 1942 and 1945, one between 1946 and 1949 and the last born between 1950 and 1953 to examine changes in their respective levels of labor market mobility and work careers during a time of rising uncertainty. I assume that women's career mobility and the likelihood of unemployment are filtered through institutions, including the labor market, education system and the family. I link recent developments in the labor market and other institutions in the United States to the timing and experiences of my specific American cohorts.

I find that four contexts hinder women's career mobility: long job interruptions, low-level education, young children and being African-American. Helping women's careers are higher education, which is increasingly important across cohorts, and living in the South for the earlier cohort. Movement along the mobility ladder, up or down, is reduced by long job tenure, full-time work and marriage. Across cohorts, part-time work and dual jobs contribute to more turmoil (increasing risks of upward and downward movement), and a greater number of past jobs create a higher risk over time away from upward mobility and toward downward mobility.

GLOBALIZATION IN THE UNITED STATES

Globalization is defined in this volume as the interaction of economic, technological, cultural and political changes, fueled by technological change, the dependence on worldwide market events and the internationalization of markets and global competition (see Hofmeister, Blossfeld and Mills, this volume). For American women's careers, some of these aspects apply more directly than others. American women are overrepresented in service-sector and knowledge-based jobs, which are strongly affected by the diffusion of knowledge and the spread of networks due to information and communication technologies. Telecommuting, boundary-less contract work and information-based jobs have expanded the range of employment opportunities available and made the workplace and the workday more flexible, which contributes to a rise in United States women's employment as women who would otherwise not enter the labor market choose to participate in one of these new, technology-based ways (Marler, Tolbert and Milkovich 2003; Moen and Roehling 2005). Technological advances also encourage educational expansion by requiring more and different, often computer-related, skills (Erikson and Goldthorpe 1993). In the American context, continuing education programs, especially those that teach computer skills, are widely available and draw many women who have raised families and are interested in returning to the labor market.

Women's returns to the labor market are of crucial importance for many American families in particular for several reasons. The rising importance of markets and their susceptibility to random shocks happening throughout the world means that men's careers are less secure in recent decades than they were at the middle of the twentieth century (Mills, Blossfeld and Bernardi 2006). This has consequences for the affordability of 'housewifery' in American households based on the threat of the cessation of cash flow (unemployment benefits last only six months in the United States, and not all jobs qualify), but the risks of an unstable breadwinner are even deeper. In the United States, health insurance and retirement pensions are primarily dependent on the employer or the fact of being employed. Health insurance is a benefit offered by employers or can be purchased if the potential insured are healthy enough, but at high prices. Private or company-provided pension savings form the bulk of old-age financial security because federal retirement payments (which in turn are based on lifetime earnings) are designed only as a supplement to private savings (Warner and Hofmeister 2006). These private retirement savings are either aided by matching funds from the employer or merely administrated by the employer through pre-tax retirement accounts. If there is only one earner in a household and he or she either loses his or her job or his or her employer does not offer health insurance or retirement security, the entire household suffers. Many American families reduce the uncertainties of health care and retirement security, as well as immediate living expenses, by having two employed adults. This means women are entering and staying in the labor market at high rates relative to other countries, in large part based on the financial uncertainties of the United States system (see also Blossfeld, Buchholz and Hofäcker 2006; Warner and Hofmeister 2006).

The other chapters in this volume point to the intensification of competition owing to deregulation and privatization forces as sources of women's employment changes over the last half of the twentieth century. The story is different for American women than for women in Europe because of the longer history of deregulation and privatization in the United States market and the emphasis on individualism and free-market forces that have long governed the economy (Lipset 1995). Nonetheless, late twentieth-century firm-level efforts to improve 'market share' and competitiveness, including lowering starting salaries, sending jobs offshore and opening the labor market via free trade agreements such as the North American Free Trade Agreement (NAFTA), likely also affected the employment of women, particularly in some industries.

The United States has an employment climate where frequent job changes are not uncommon, and even lower-earning workers move to find new jobs. Unemployment benefits are minimal compared with West European welfare states. Thus, willingness to move – often far from kinship networks – for work-related reasons is a characteristic of some parts of the American labor market. Divorce rates are also high in the United States and have remained so since the 1970s (Cherlin 1989). Thus, many American women face the multiple insecurities of higher divorce probabilities, more job insecurities for male breadwinners, the possibility of living far from kin and lower job security for themselves than women in other country contexts. These multiple insecurities mean that it is relatively more difficult for individuals to make assumptions about the future in the United States, as benefits, investments, jobs, created kin networks and geographic locations shift over time. Some (market-based) institutions may help alleviate the job-related insecurities, for example, market-based childcare, a relatively open labor market and chances for re-training and re-entry into employment at all stages of the life course. They are discussed in more detail below.

Employment

The United States is categorized as a liberal welfare regime (Esping-Andersen 1999) and has what is known as an 'open economy,' which means high levels of employment and job turnover, short-term contract labor, inequalities in wages and intense competition for jobs. Such economies also tend to have low levels of unemployment, low minimum wages and an abundance of low-wage, low-skill jobs. Labor market insecurity is relatively high owing to lower levels of government and union job protection.

Women are still more likely than men to leave the labor market when children are born and raised. In the more open labor market of the United States with high turnover, the boundary between labor market insiders and outsiders is less distinct than in other systems, and therefore re-entry can be easier by comparison (Grunow, Hofmeister and Buchholz 2006). It is, nonetheless, not easy even in the United States for women to return to jobs at the level they left, and the 'mommy penalty' in wages and retirement savings for leaving the labor market is high (Avellar and Smock 2003).

The open economy also creates many part-time jobs, which some workers piece together to create a full-time work schedule. The problem with part-time work, particularly when full-time work is needed, is not only that the pay is lower, but also that those crucial employer-provided benefits are not usually available for part-time jobs. The open economy also provides for re-skilling throughout the life course, a point I take up in the next section.

The consequences for women of working in an open economy are several. While high turnover in the labor market may open opportunities for women to re-enter after child-rearing on the one hand, it can disadvantage all women because the risk of being forced out due to downsizing is higher and the threat of being replaced by outsourcing is ever-present. Work interruptions still have high economic costs for women (Stier and Lewin-Epstein 2001). However, one difference from many European countries is that infant and childcare is available on the market, enabling employed mothers with financial means to compete with non-caregiving men more easily than elsewhere (Grunow, Hofmeister and Buchholz 2006; Stier and Lewin-Epstein 2001). Poorer mothers have few options than to rely on informal arrangements of kin and neighborhood networks or to take work shifts opposite their husbands. High levels of short-term contract labor give women the flexibility some prefer in order to combine employment and caregiving. On the other hand, such contracts are not in the best interests of women who prefer or need long-term contracts and job security (Marler and Moen 2002). Low wages mean long hours, multiple jobs or multiple – perhaps intergenerational – earners for women who must support families (Ehrenreich 2001).

Education

The United States' education system expanded drastically in the twentieth century. By 2000, 88 percent of women aged 18 to 24 had completed high school (against 85 percent of men) (US Department of Commerce 2000). The secondary education system is flexible and deregulated, with content and quality varying widely by state, within states, by district, as well as by individual school, and typically does not train workers directly for jobs, so American workers are highly flexible for the type of job they can take. The post-secondary education system is large, with 63 percent of high school completers enrolling in 2000 (US Department of Labor 2002) and over 14 million people enrolled in colleges and universities in the year 2000 (US Department of Education 2001). It is also growing, with total enrollments rising nearly 14 percent between 1987 and 1992; among non-traditional aged students (aged 25 and older), the growth rate was 41 percent (Dortch 1997). And since 1979, women have surpassed men in American college enrollments and graduation rates (1997). The colleges and universities compete with each other for students and therefore strive to offer relevant and flexible courses: new degree programs and fields of specialization are founded regularly. Non-traditional students make up a growing proportion of college enrollments: 43 percent in 1992 to 1993, up to 46 percent in 1999 to 2000 (US Department of Education 2000). Twenty-two percent of undergraduates in the United States in 1992 to 1993 had non-spouse dependents (usually children), and that figure rose to 27 percent by the 1999 to 2000 school year (US Department of Education 2000). Not all adult education is taking place in 'traditional' colleges and universities, though. In 1991, 58 million adult Americans enrolled in adult education programs, a figure that rose to 90 million, with 23 percent of these participants taking work-related courses, not including post-secondary enrollment (Kim and Creighton 1999). This evidence suggests that the United States is a nation where training, and re-training, are available – and used – throughout the life course, not just fitting into a narrow life stage window before employment. Education often takes place concurrently with paid work; nearly 40 percent of undergraduates in the 1999 to 2000 school year also worked full-time, and an additional 48 percent work part-time (US Department of Education 2000). The ties between education and labor market have never been stronger for women (Blossfeld and Huinink 1991; Cohen and Bianchi 1999; Herring and Wilsonsadberry 1993; Jacobsen and Levin 1995; Leibowitz and Klerman 1995; Yoon and Waite 1994).

Welfare state

The United States orients protection against social risks via the market, through both the availability of risk protection purchased privately (various kinds of insurance) and 'job benefits' offered as partial compensation for certain kinds of full-time employment in larger firms (health insurance, retirement savings). These programs were started in the 1950s, increased through the 1970s via federal tax incentives encouraging firms to provide such protection, and have declined considerably since then. At a time when most women did not have full-time work through large firms, these protections were available to women and families typically only through the breadwinner's career. These protections are dwindling and were never mandated for part-time work or employment in small firms.

In the 1970s and 1980s, women's careers were influenced by the 1963 Equal Pay Act, which reduced but did not eliminate pay differentials between men and women doing the same jobs. And in 1987, the first family leave legislation was passed in four states, paving the way for the first federal protection against job loss for caregiving, enacted in the 1993 Family and Medical Leave Act (though protected leave is unpaid and limited to 12 weeks per 12 months). In 1988, in an effort to assist low-income single mothers, the Family Support Act provided federally funded job training and job-finding assistance, coupled with childcare, transportation and healthcare benefits. The minimum wage was finally increased in 1990 from $3.35 to $3.80 per hour as well (US Department of Labor 2004). In the 1980s and 1990s under Republican and Democratic administrations, the federal programs designed to protect women and children from extreme poverty, which originated in the 1930s welfare programs and the 1960s 'Great Society' programs, were cut back in favor of programs to encourage full employment and individual self-sufficiency. The welfare programs that do exist are organized within guidelines set by the federal government but are administered by states. Thus it is difficult to make national generalizations about use, qualifying criteria, durations of poverty program use, and levels of poverty, to say nothing of the difficulty of comparing the United States welfare state to those of other countries in this volume.

In sum, throughout the 1980s and 1990s, the United States government has introduced a number of policy reforms that foster the trend towards increasing the labor market participation of mothers by institutionalizing the idea of an 'adult worker model,' therefore penalizing those who have difficulties combining paid work and carework, such as single parents (Guthrie and Roth 1999; Woods 2004).

Family structure

As in other countries, families in the United States have also undergone transformation since the early 1970s, with high divorce rates (Coontz 1992; Stacey 1991). In the face of limited or non-existent welfare benefits for single mothers in the United States, many American women can expect to be the sole income provider for themselves and their children for at least some of their adult lives, a life stage not associated with affluence (Hirschl, Altobelli and Rank 2003). And, unlike in some European contexts where the birthrate has plummeted in recent decades to rates well below replacement levels (under 2.1 children per woman), women in the United States on average have not significantly reduced their rate of childbirth.

HYPOTHESES

We argue in this volume and series that globalization is felt by individuals through the rise in insecurity and uncertainty in their specific circumstances. So I expect that women will experience such rising insecurity directly through their labor market participation and indirectly through their connection to would-be male breadwinners. I therefore have three sets of hypotheses:

Increasing uncertainty in employment

Increasing uncertainty in employment is defined as more downward job moves, more exits and longer durations before re-entering the market. But as men, especially in some industries, are experiencing more turbulent careers, women may be hired to replace them, at lower wages and with better chances for promotion, given their overrepresentation at the bottom rungs of the occupational hierarchy.

Differential distribution of uncertainty

As uncertainty rises, the insecurities in the labor market will be differentially distributed between labor market insiders (those who have more experience, full-time work and longer job tenure) and outsiders (newcomers to the labor market, part-time workers, those with long gaps between jobs), thus expanding inequalities. Women who exit may have a harder time re-entering over time. I expect more upward mobility for women who remain in employment and with an employer longer. Downward mobility should be greater for women if they have shorter tenure in their jobs, more and longer job interruptions, lower job prestige, lower levels of education, have a higher number of previous jobs[2] and fewer work hours.

Women with lower levels of education and skill will be more vulnerable to shifts and fluctuations in employment rates and wages. These women are likely to have less security from the incomes of their partners due to marital homogamy and less of their own job security or job availability than highly educated women.

Family circumstances

I expect that across cohorts, married women will have fewer moves out of the labor market and faster returns to employment than earlier cohorts; essentially, marriage will make less difference to women's employment exits as most men's real incomes are declining. This pattern should go against a within-cohort pattern for the earliest-born cohort that married women are more likely to exit the labor market and less likely to re-enter given the presence of another earner because they can be more selective about employment opportunities. The effect will be most acute for women with lower levels of education, who, owing to marital homogamy, are likely to be married to a man also with lower levels of education, the group most affected by declining wages and job opportunities.

Within cohorts, women with more children should have more moves out of the labor market, presumably for caregiving responsibilities, especially for younger children. But under conditions of rising uncertainty, I expect that *across* cohorts, owing to the rising insecurity of the male breadwinner, women with more children will become less likely to exit employment over time, because of financial necessity. Living in the southern United States and racial background are likely to be important moderators of these relationships. The southern United States had an economic boom in the 1970s while the North experienced oil price shocks. African-American women have a longer history of labor market involvement than other women, but with many more labor market disadvantages compared with caucasian American women. The complexities of how race is lived in America go beyond the scope of this chapter in its context in this comparative volume (Lelyveld

2001), so its use here is limited to a control indicator. Proper investigation of career transitions of black versus caucasian and Hispanic women in the United States would require more elaborate analyses.

DATA AND METHODS

I use a panel study called the National Longitudinal Survey (NLS) of Young Women,[3] a nationally representative, semi-annual panel study of the civilian, non-institutionalized female population of women aged 14 to 22 living in the United States in 1968. There have been 19 annual and biennial interviews between 1968 and 1999, and the young women born 1942 to 1953 (for example, containing the three cohorts of interest here) were surveyed nationwide. The entire sample size in 1968 was 5159, and by 1999, 2900 respondents remained for a retention rate of 56 percent. This study oversampled black women (at a rate twice their representation in the population) and includes extensive questions about education, labor force participation, fertility and household composition.[4] I right-censor the study in 1991 to keep the sample in the age range that is firmly in mid-life and is comparable with other cohorts in this volume.

I divide the sample into three birth cohorts (1942 to 1945, 1946 to 1949 and 1950 to 1953) who entered the labor market and developed their work and family careers under different conditions. Models of the center cohort are in the tables but will not be highlighted in the text in order to better contrast. the two cohorts with more diverse experiences.[5]

Women in the earliest birth cohort, born 1942 to 1945, were born during World War II and thus precede the United States baby boom that began in 1946. For these women, the recent feminist revolution was only beginning in the early and mid-1960s as they were entering their twenties and probably did not affect their early career choices to nearly the same extent that later cohorts were affected. This cohort turned 30 by the early 1970s, in time for the oil price shocks and higher unemployment rates. If they entered employment after child-rearing, it would likely have been in the 1980s when the economy started to rebound.

The latest birth cohort, born 1950 to 1953, was born toward the peak years of the baby boom. These women participated in the women's movement of the late 1960s and early 1970s as teenagers, likely affecting their career options and outlook towards paid work. Their career-building and child-rearing years occurred during the energy crisis, the same era when popular discourse centered on the idea of the 'Supermom' who could both have a successful full-time career and be equally successful in traditional roles ascribed to women.

The context of American women's employment is different from that of European countries, especially with regard to the meaning of unemployment and unpaid caregiving. To determine the difference between whether a woman is unemployed (seeking work but unable to find it) or out of the labor force (for any reason, including caregiving), one must ask the woman herself whether she considers herself to be looking for work. If she is, then the question is when she last looked for work.

Unemployment status is quite fluid in the United States, since a woman with alternative financial support (such as an employed husband) might become officially unemployed but then could abandon the job search to focus on unpaid caregiving instead. Conversely, a woman might begin a spell out of paid employment owing to providing unpaid caregiving, and then begin to look for work months or years later. The demarcation points between these shifts are difficult if not impossible to pinpoint in retrospectively reported life history panel data, as the precise questions about when a woman ceased to look or began looking for work are often not asked. The definitions of unemployment or unpaid caregiving are more subjective categories for American women than for women in countries where specific government benefits are assigned based on status. Furthermore, unemployment benefits in the United States are limited (26 weeks) and contingent (on previous full-time employment, ongoing job search and other restrictions) compared with European countries. Therefore, some women's 'unemployment' looks and acts exactly like other women's experience out of the labor force (OLF).

In light of these difficulties, I use two kinds of labor force possibilities, or technically 'state spaces,' among which women may move during their employment career: employed and not employed. The possibility of not being employed includes women who are unemployed, out of the labor force or 'not working (status not determined).'

Women could therefore have the following types of labor force transitions in these analyses:

1   Movement into paid employment from a time of non-employment lasting at least one month. I use the portion of the sample not in a job who are therefore 'at risk' of entry, or able to enter, which excludes women who are employed continuously throughout the observation window and includes women (N = 571) who never report paid employment during this time (total N = 4352).

2   Movement out of paid employment for one month or longer. I use the portion of the sample who are in employment at any point in time. I omit those 571 women who never reported a job and including women who never had an interruption (but who are always 'at risk'). Employed women work for pay either full-time – 35 or more hours per week total in all jobs (69 percent of job spells) – or part-time, defined as working one to 34 hours in one or more jobs or in their main job (25 percent of job spells). I also include a category to identify the 6 percent of job spells for which weekly work hours are not available (total N = 4413).

3   Movement from one job to another, with or without a job interruption,
     measured in terms of upward, downward or lateral job mobility. I use the
     same sample of employed women as in transition type 2. Job changes are
     determined by a change in the occupational code or an interruption of
     longer than one month between jobs. Upward mobility is identified when
     the new job's occupational prestige measure (on a 100-point scale) is at
     least 10 percent higher than the job that was left. Downward mobility is
     indicated when the new job's occupational prestige measure is at least 10
     percent less than the previous job (Ganzeboom and Treiman 1996).
     Lateral mobility means movement to a job whose prestige is within the
     10 percent range. For example, a woman working in a job with an ISEI
     prestige value of 60 would have an *upwardly* mobile transition if her
     next job had a prestige value at or above 66; a *downward* move would be
     at or below a prestige score of 54. A *lateral* move would be a move to a
     job whose prestige code is between 55 and 65.

Explanatory variables

My only time-constant covariate is race, defined as 'African-American' or
'all others' owing to constraints given by the racial categories available in the
1968 data (28 percent of the sample is African-American). Each job episode,
I categorize job characteristics such as hours worked, the job prestige score
and whether the woman also had a second job. My time-varying covariates
include education, marital status, region and number of children in the
household (see Table 12.1).

During the data collection process, several pieces of time-varying
information, such as the births or adoptions of children, the completion of
education or the fact of having moved into or out of the southern United
States, were collected only at the interview following the event. Dates of the
event were not collected (limited information exists for births that occurred in
the mid-1970s). To approximate the dates at which these events took place
and to standardize the errors, I made several assumptions. I adjust education
to change at the most typical graduation month in the United States, May,
from the year before the survey (surveys were given yearly during the most
intensive education-building years for the women in the survey). I change the
region of the country and the number of children in the household at the point
halfway between the two interviews that report a change. This means a six- to
12-month window within which the birth or move took place, with a normal
error – approximately half the reports are assumed to be too early and half are
assumed to be too late. These adjustments are not ideal, but without actual
dates of moves and births it is the best possible way to vary these events over
time. All children's ages were calculated yearly, and at the point that the
youngest child in the household changed category, this calculation was also
made halfway between interviews.

Table 12.1   *Explanatory variables and operationalizations used. Variables are from the 'National Longitudinal Survey of Young Women' in the United States, panel surveys from 1968 to 1991*

Variable	Operationalization	Update point
Employment interruption (time-dependent)	Duration of employment interruption between two jobs	Monthly
Prestige (time-dependent)	ISEI score for current job, converted from 1960 and 1980 Census occupational codes[a]	Monthly
Labor force experience (time-dependent)	In months; cumulated along the life course, measured at the beginning of the episode	Monthly
Number of jobs (time-dependent)	Measured at the beginning of the previous job episode	Monthly
Work hours (time-dependent)	Full time, 35 or more hours per week (reference) Part-time, 1–34 hours per week	Monthly
Holding a second job (time-dependent)	Respondent reported additional job spells	Monthly
Educational qualification (time-dependent)	Less than high school High school degree (reference) Some college College degree or more	The month of May before each survey
Marital status (time-dependent)	Married Not married (reference)	Monthly
Age of youngest child (time-dependent)	Preschool (0–5) School age (6–13) Teenager (14–17)	Halfway between interviews
Number of children (time-dependent)	Number of children (including step-children) in the household (across all spells: Range 0–11, Mode 2)	Halfway between interviews
Region (time-dependent)	South Non-South (reference)	Halfway between interviews
Race (time-constant)	African-American All others (reference)	At 1968 interview

Note: [a] Ganzeboom and Treiman (1996)

Analyses

Mobility transitions are modeled with continuous time event history analysis, with time measured in months since the beginning of each episode – for job episodes, this means time since the start of the current job, measured whether the woman is in the current job for 12 or fewer months, 13 to 24 months, 25 to 36 months or 37 or more months (true for 66 percent of the job episodes). When the current job is separated from the next job by an interruption in employment, as was the case in 67 percent of the job episodes, the time is also measured in increments of zero to six months, seven to 12 months and 13 or more months (55 percent of interruptions). I treat non-interviews (due to attrition) and observations after the age of 41 as right-censored (beyond the window of analysis) so that my cohorts reach approximately the same ages during the analyses, from 22 to a maximum of 41.

RESULTS

I begin by describing entries into and exits from paid employment, followed by a discussion of findings for upward and downward movement within the job career.

Transitions from nonemployment to employment

In terms of movement from non-employment into the labor market, cohort 1942 to 1945 is significantly different from both of the other cohorts (see Table 12.2).

For all cohorts, longer duration out of employment means a lower chance of returning. This makes sense from several perspectives. The women who are out of employment may lack skills for employment or have strong religious or cultural values against women's employment. From the perspective of employers, a job candidate who has had a long duration out of the market is assumed to have rusty skills or a lack of drive.

Education's effect on job entry is changing across cohorts. Women who lack even a high school degree are less likely to return to the market across all cohorts, but college-educated women experience a decline in the value of their degrees for gaining re-entry for the later-born cohort. This might represent the effect of educational expansion, where a college degree ceases to be a signal of exceptionally educated women. The college degree might make a difference for the kind of job one qualifies for (as we will see in Table 12.4), but the effect on the chance of employment is not significantly different for women with a college degree compared to women with a high

Table 12.2   Non-employment-to-job transitions for women in the United States[a]

Variable	Cohort 1942–45		Cohort 1946–49		Cohort 1950–53	
	Coeff	*Sig.*	*Coeff*	*Sig.*	*Coeff*	*Sig.*
Period-specific information						
Months in interruption < 6	−2.82***		−2.33***		−2.63***	
Months in interruption 7–12	−1.82***		−1.79***		−1.83***	
Months in interruption 13–24	−1.98***		−1.91***		−1.91***	
Months in interruption 25–36	−2.12***		−2.28***		−2.12***	
Months in interruption ≥ 37	−2.77***		−2.73***		−2.59***	
Highest education obtained						
Less than HS degree	−0.10***		−0.16***		−0.15***	
HS degree (ref)						
Some college	0.06*		0.05**		0.11***	
College degree	0.25***		0.12***		−0.02	
Family measures						
Married	−0.00		0.02		0.14***	
No children under 18 (ref)						
Youngest child is 0–5	0.20***		0.10***		0.08***	
Youngest child is 6–13	0.05		−0.02		−0.03	
Youngest child is 14–17	0.12*		−0.02		−0.21**	
Number of children	0.05***		0.08***		−0.01	
Contextual measures						
Reside in South	0.03		0.02		0.07***	
African-American	−0.08***		−0.14***		−0.14***	
Episodes	14 870		20 612		19 897	
Total episodes	24 421		34 122		31 535	
Censored episodes	9 551		13 510		11 638	
−2*diff log likelihood	2 865		3 442		2 671	
Log likelihood (starting values)	−48 536		−67 816		−65 116	
Log likelihood (final estimates)	−47 104		−67 816		−63 780	

Notes:
[a] Transition rate models; cohort differences are significant between earliest cohort and each of the other cohorts
* $p < 0.05$, ** $p < 0.01$, *** $p < 0.001$

Source: National Longitudinal Survey of Young Women, N = 4352

school degree. This could reflect an effect of globalization, where even a college degree does not protect women or aid them in the labor market, as we see in the German case study (Buchholz and Grunow, this volume).

Family factors have a powerful effect on women's entry to jobs. At this point in the analysis we see the confounding of effects that are likely related to moves out of unemployment versus moves out of unpaid caregiving (which are not modeled distinctly in these analyses). The effect of marriage on women's chances of entering jobs changes across cohorts, from having no effect to having a strong positive effect: married women are more likely to enter/re-enter than non-married women. The selection effect of 'who is out of the market to be able to re-enter' is probably a strong component here; many of the women at risk of entry are married to another earner because non-married women are likely employed and not at risk of re-entry. But the fact that this effect manifests itself only in the latest cohort implies a globalization effect as well. Where once married women had the choice whether or not to be employed in the United States, because the financial support of the family came from a breadwinner husband, the later cohort experiences more financial and security pressure for all able-bodied adults in the household to earn a living.

The effect of parenthood on women's returns to jobs follows another path. Mothers of all small children in each cohort are more likely than women without children under age 18 to return to the labor market. This seems at first counterintuitive, but the United States, as a liberal welfare regime, lacks financial supports and legal requirements for mothers of young children to stay out of the labor market. Thus women do interrupt, contributing to the representation of mothers at risk of re-entry, but many return within the first year, definitely the first five years, of their youngest child's life. School-aged children have no effect on their mother's employment because, by and large, the mothers who will re-enter already have by the time their youngest is at least six. The other counterintuitive result, that teenagers decrease the probability of re-entry for the latest cohort, is easily explained by the demographics of the later cohort: those women who have teenagers before the time window of this study closes gave birth to those teenagers when they, themselves, were teenagers. The last year of data for this study is 1991, and this cohort was born from 1950 to 1953, therefore for a woman's youngest child to be 17 already in 1991 means that child was born in 1974 to a woman who was in her late teens or very early 20s. Such young mothers are either more likely to be in a traditionally-oriented household where female employment is discouraged, or they have already returned to the labor market when their child was younger.

The demographic controls special to the United States bear discussion. Women residing in the South in the latest cohort were experiencing the boom in the economy in the 1980s, and this could explain the significant result of southern residence on job entry. African-American women, on the other hand, experience consistently reduced chances to enter the labor market.

Transition from employment to non-employment

Cohort differences are significant only between the 1946–49 cohort and the 1950–53 cohort. Therefore the 1942–45 cohort is not discussed in the analyses of employment to non-employment but can be viewed as an indicator of trends across cohorts (see Table 12.3).

Who moves out of jobs? Findings here confound unemployment and unpaid-caregiving exits, but the results nonetheless give indicators about under which circumstances women exit paid employment. Tenure and prestige keep women in the labor market: duration in the current job decreases the odds of exit across cohorts, as do the total months spent in the labor force to date and a higher level of job prestige. For the later cohort, part-time work compared with full-time work acts as a 'stepping stone' from employment.

Educational qualifications' effects on labor market exits appear to be changing across cohorts. College degrees reduce women's chances of exiting in the later cohort. Married women with college degrees are highly likely to have husbands with college degrees owing to homogamous marriage trends (Blossfeld and Timm 2003) who are more likely to be able to provide for a family on one income. But not only do college degrees mean that women stay in (instead of having no effect or encouraging exit), but marriage also ceases to predict exits for the later cohort. Both of these pieces of evidence together confirm the rise in the dual-earner couple phenomenon in the 1980s in the United States and the phenomenon of 'work-rich' and 'work-poor' families, as described in the chapters by Golsch and Bukodi and Róbert (this volume). Women's labor market participation at the professional, knowledge-based level was in greater demand through this decade, possibly due to globalization forces.

As with marriage, children have no effect on women's exits from employment for the later cohort. For this cohort, full commodification and lifelong employment are stronger norms than for the previous cohorts.

Upward job-to-job transitions

Initial tests for cohort differences show that for upward mobility, all three cohorts are significantly different from each other (see Table 12.4).

Upward mobility chances depend partly on the duration in the current job: spending two or more years in the current job has a significantly depressive effect on the chance of later upward mobility. But interruptions in the job career have a different effect. A short gap (six months or fewer) can lead to a better job afterwards. But having a gap over seven months long hurts women's chances of upward mobility to the next job.

Labor force context and experience strengthen in relevance across cohorts. Women in the latest birth cohort show lower chances of upward mobility

Table 12.3   Job to nonemployment transitions for women in the United States[a]

Variable	Cohort 1942–45		Cohort 1946–49		Cohort 1950–53	
	Coeff	Sig.	Coeff	Sig.	Coeff	Sig.
Period-specific information						
Months in job < 12	−3.45***		−3.47***		−3.19***	
Months in job 13–24	−3.67***		−3.72***		−3.77***	
Months in job 25–36	−4.03***		−4.16***		−4.19***	
Months in job ≥ 37	−5.16***		−5.20***		−5.23***	
Labor force context						
Number of months in LF	−0.01***		−0.01***		−0.00***	
Number of jobs	0.09*		0.02		−0.01	
ISEI prestige score	−0.02***		−0.01***		−0.01***	
ISEI prestige score missing	−0.13		0.91***		0.88***	
Full-time 35 or more (ref)						
Part-time (1–34 hours)	0.16		0.34***		0.29***	
Hours missing	−0.35*		−0.34***		−0.21*	
Highest education obtained						
Less than HS degree	0.26**		0.11		−0.11	
HS degree (ref)						
Some college	0.06		0.00		0.02	
College degree	0.32***		0.12		−0.20**	
Family measures						
Married	0.24**		0.15***		0.04	
No children under 18 (ref)						
Youngest child is 0–5	0.33***		0.20*		−0.09	
Youngest child is 6–17	−0.14		−0.24**		−0.04	
Number of children	−0.09*		−0.13***		0.00	
Contextual measures						
Reside in South	−0.21**		−0.05		0.04	
African-American	−0.09		−0.07		−0.13*	
Episodes	816		1 935		1 970	
Total episodes	15 924		34 488		36 539	
Censored episodes	15 108		32 553		34 569	
−2*diff log likelihood	580		1 320		1 582	
Log likelihood (starting values)	−4 609		−10 773		−11 110	
Log likelihood (final estimates)	−4 319		−10 113		−10 319	

Notes: [a] Transition rate models; cohort differences are significant between middle and latest cohort
         * $p < 0.05$,   ** $p < 0.01$,   *** $p < 0.001$

Source: National Longitudinal Survey of Young Women; N = 4413

Table 12.4 Predictors of upward job transitions for women in the United States[a]

Variable	Cohort 1942–45		Cohort 1946–49		Cohort 1950–53	
	Coeff	Sig.	Coeff	Sig.	Coeff	Sig.
Constant	−2.65***		−2.60***		−2.58***	
Period-specific information						
Months in job < 12 (ref)						
Months in job 13–24	−0.20		−0.06		−0.01	
Months in job 25–36	−1.01***		−0.90***		−0.82***	
Months in job ≥ 37	−1.78***		−1.79***		−1.78***	
Months in interruption < 6	−0.03		0.28**		0.05	
Months in interruption 6–12	−0.43		−0.39**		−0.25*	
Months in interruption ≥ 13	−0.84***		−0.57***		−0.66***	
Labor force context						
ISEI prestige score	−0.05***		−0.05***		−0.05***	
ISEI prestige score missing	−0.67		−0.08		0.15	
Number of months in LF	−0.00		−0.00		−0.00**	
Number of jobs	0.02		0.01		−0.05*	
Full-time 35 or more (ref)						
Part-time (1–34 hours)	0.02		0.15**		0.23***	
Hours missing	0.10		−0.26		−0.12	
Holding a second job	0.16		0.07		0.45***	
Highest education obtained						
Less than HS degree	−0.59***		−0.39***		−0.13*	
HS degree (ref)						
Some college	0.15		0.43***		0.21***	
College degree	0.42***		0.78***		0.60***	
Family measures						
Married	−0.12		−0.15*		−0.12*	
No children under 18 (ref)						
Youngest child is 0–5	−0.12		−0.20*		−0.35***	
Youngest child is 6–13	−0.02		0.14		0.11	
Youngest child is 14–17	0.02		0.23		−0.22	
Number of children	0.07		0.02		0.02	
Contextual measures						
Reside in South	0.18*		0.12**		0.04	
African-American	−0.24*		−0.30**		−0.37***	
Episodes	585		1 435		1 790	
Total episodes	22 622		48 947		51 801	
Censored episodes	22 037		47 512		50 011	
−2*diff log likelihood	484		1 256		1 594	
Log likelihood (starting values)	−3 731		−8 978		−10 963	
Log likelihood (final estimates)	−3 489		−8 350		−10 166	

Notes: [a] Exponential models; cohort differences for upward mobility are significant
* $p < 0.05$, ** $p < 0.01$, *** $p < 0.001$

Source: National Longitudinal Survey of Young Women, N = 4413

after a longer time in the labor market generally (a stagnation effect) and with a rising number of previous jobs, factors that are not significant for the earlier-born cohorts. Job turmoil, indicated by the number of previous jobs, may also be an indicator of difficult-to-employ women who struggle from job to job. Work hours also play a role for the later birth cohort: compared with full-time employees, part-time employees find more opportunity for upward mobility. This may be because of the increased probability of moving up that comes from a lower starting point or because of the expansion of part-time work available for the later-born cohorts.

Some women hold more than one job. For the later cohort, holding a second job increases the chances of upward mobility. The chances are that a woman who takes a second job may be expecting the first one to end or able to choose between the better of the two eventually, making the second job an access point to the next position. As will be seen in the next table, the second job is also a predictor of downward mobility.

Educational characteristics influence chances of upward mobility across cohorts, and the flow is in the same direction for the lower and upper levels of education: lacking a high school degree has lost significance for predicting a lack of upward moves, while having at least some college is increasing the probability of upward moves. This reflects the change in the meaning of a high school degree, illustrating that, increasingly, it is not enough to secure stable and upwardly mobile employment. High school degrees for the later cohort are beginning to behave the way no degree once did for the earlier cohort, and some college is carrying the impacts for upward mobility in the later cohort that a high school degree had for the earlier cohort.

Family characteristics, finally, express telling indications of social change in the realm of paid work and family. Especially mothers of very young children in the later cohorts experience lower chances of upward mobility than their peers with no children at home, compared with earlier cohorts. The employed mothers in the earlier-born cohort are likely biased toward more ambition or need of employment than the group of women in the later cohort owing to stronger norms of full-time unpaid caregiving. These effects may be related to the rise in maternal employment overall for the later cohort, because the robustness of the effects is the only change.

Cohorts in the South once had higher upward mobility chances compared with their northern and western sisters, but these effects have dwindled for the later cohort. Being African-American has become a more robust indicator of declining chances of upward mobility, an unfortunate signal of the failure of affirmative action programs and the persistence of racial disadvantage.

Downward job-to-job transitions

For downward mobility, only the earliest and latest cohorts are statistically significantly different (see Table 12.5). Tenure in a job secures current

Table 12.5 Predictors of downward job transitions for women in the United States[a]

Variable	Cohort 1942–45		Cohort 1946–49		Cohort 1950–53	
	Coeff	*Sig.*	*Coeff*	*Sig.*	*Coeff*	*Sig.*
Constant	−7.44***		−7.13***		−7.14***	
Period-specific information						
Months in job < 12 (ref)						
Months in job 13–24	−0.09		−0.27**		−0.13	
Months in job 25–36	−0.69***		−0.83***		−0.85***	
Months in job ≥ 37	−1.86***		−1.86***		−1.59***	
Months in interruption < 6	0.38		0.53***		0.45***	
Months in interruption 6–12	0.25		0.17		−0.07	
Months in interruption ≥ 13	−0.58***		−0.38***		−0.19*	
Labor force context						
ISEI prestige score	0.05***		0.05***		0.04***	
ISEI prestige score missing	−0.76		−0.05		−0.23	
Number of months in LF	0.00		0.00		0.00***	
Number of jobs	−0.03		0.04		0.14***	
Full-time 35 or more (ref)						
Part-time (1–34 hours)	0.13		0.28***		0.23***	
Hours missing	−0.36		0.09		0.14	
Holding a second job	0.27		0.30		0.38**	
Highest education obtained						
Less than HS degree	0.50***		0.53***		0.25***	
HS degree (ref)						
Some college	−0.18		−0.24**		−0.22**	
College degree	−0.66***		−0.89***		−0.67***	
Family measures						
Married	−0.18		−0.28***		−0.18**	
No children under 18 (ref)						
Youngest child is 0–5	0.03***		−0.33***		−0.20	
Youngest child is 6–13	−0.06		−0.28*		0.07	
Youngest child is 14–17	0.16		−0.04		0.05	
Number of children	0.08		0.10*		0.05	
Contextual measures						
Reside in South	−0.11		0.03		0.11	
African-American	0.34**		0.15		0.08	
Episodes	392		966		1073	
Total episodes	21 616		47 006		49 837	
Censored episodes	21 224		46 040		48 764	
−2*diff log likelihood	301		759		690	
Log likelihood (starting values)	−2 639		−6 387		−7 081	
Log likelihood (final estimates)	−2 489		−6 007		−6 736	

Notes: [a] Exponential models; cohort differences are significant for earliest and latest cohorts
  * $p < 0.05$, ** $p < 0.01$, *** $p < 0.001$

Source: National Longitudinal Survey of Young Women; N = 4413

employment and decreases chances of downward moves. Essentially one could say that job tenure tends to stabilize careers, causing them to move neither up nor down. Change across cohorts comes into play when women take interruptions from the labor market. Here, a gap of fewer than six months significantly increases the odds that a woman in the later cohort will return to a job that is less prestigious than the one she left. Longer gaps, of over one year, decrease the odds of downward mobility for the earlier cohort, but this effect is declining for the later cohort.

Labor force experience is changing in its effect on downward mobility across cohorts. As with upward mobility, more experience (months in the labor force cumulatively) means a lower likelihood of change for the later cohort. But for this later cohort, having more jobs means a greater chance of downward mobility.

Part-time work increases downward mobility for the later cohort as well, compared with full-time work. Considering part-time work's effect on upward mobility as well, the findings together suggest that part-time employment is a sort of stepping-stone to both better and worse jobs for the later cohort. So is holding a second job.

Education influences downward mobility across cohorts identically to the way it influences upward mobility – there is a shift that no high school degree predicts downward moves for all cohorts but the effect is slightly less strong at predicting downward moves for the later cohort compared to a high school degree, and at least some college and college degrees are gaining in predictive power across cohorts for avoiding downward mobility.

Family and structural location matter only in a few instances: marriage reduces the likelihood of downward mobility, being African-American increases the likelihood for the earlier cohort. Mothers of young children in the earlier cohort experience a downward mobility penalty, but this effect disappears by the later cohort. These findings suggest that anti-discrimination legislation has had some impact to protect some groups at least from downward mobility, even if their upward mobility is not yet guaranteed.

DISCUSSION AND CONCLUSIONS

Evidence from the comparison of cohorts born almost a decade apart in the middle of the twentieth century reveals three trends: evidence of a rise in uncertainty for women's careers, evidence of the erosion of the female homemaker lifestyle for women and evidence of the consequences of educational expansion.

Evidence in the United States of rising uncertainty includes the fact that both having labor market involvement (more jobs and a longer tenure in the current job) is riskier over time for upward mobility and for staying in the labor market. Staying in one position, as measured by job tenure and overall experience, is a stabilizing force that depresses subsequent mobility opportunities. Interruptions to jobs hurt women's careers across cohorts. Variation in the employment career, measured by the presence of part-time work and a second simultaneous job, indicate turmoil in the form of more movement up *and* down the occupational prestige scale. Part-time work, furthermore, becomes a stepping-stone out of the labor market for later cohorts.

Female homemaking is in decline in the United States, as evidenced by the fact that marriage ceases to be a reason to exit and instead turns into a marker of labor market stability. Marriage reduces upward and downward moves over time, reduces chances of exits and increases chances of returns. Perhaps it makes sense that, after the Women's Movement, marriage would no longer be a reason to exit. But the presence of children is also counterintuitively related to job stability. Over time, children cease to cause downward moves for women but reduce upward moves. Caregiving thus can be seen as costly to advancement but contexualized and managed for the later cohorts.

One striking piece of evidence may point to value change within the United States. For the earlier-born cohort, the number of children used to *increase* odds of entry and *decrease* odds of exit, evidence that women in that cohort who were employed while parenting were doing so out of economic need or ambition. The later cohort is unaffected by the number of children on their job entries and exits, perhaps indicating that the decision for employment while parenting in the later-born cohort is based not exclusively on need or ambition but that other factors such as the desire to be employed and prior investment in career paths are playing a role. It could also be that exits are becoming less voluntary, less linked to family circumstances and more tied to market uncertainty. Women's employment in the United States has become a life stage that more and more women participate in, for a longer and longer period of their adult life courses, regardless of family or marital status.

Educational expansion seems to be affecting women's careers, with the value of specific degree levels shifting in importance: a high school degree protects the later cohort as much as no degree did for the earlier cohort; some college protects as well as high school degrees once did. As more women (and men) offer themselves on the labor market with higher degrees, employers can be more selective about the degree level of their employees. The lowest-educated stand to lose much in this process.

Finally, the results presented here indicated that racial and class stratification has more severe consequences over time. Do we see evidence of a bifurcation of the class structure? In that women without a high school degree have worse chances, and African-American women experience worse labor market chances over time in nearly every category, the picture does not indicate movement toward a classless society. The system seems to be failing some women in the United States in systematic ways. Repercussions are likely to be felt into future generations if the declining occupational realities of mothers continue to be modelled for, and repeated by, their children.

NOTES

1 I would like to extend deepest thanks to Daniela Grunow, Sandra Buchholz and Karin Kurz for extensive support with the data analysis techniques and to John Bendix and Daniela Grunow for invaluable comments to improve the text.
2 The last point can be debated, because high mobility is generally accepted in the United States and can make a woman more secure and upwardly mobile. At the height of the technology boom in the 1990s, for example, firms favored workers with more previous jobs because it meant they were more desirable on the labor market. Staying in a job meant stagnating. This would not hold for every industry and might not be true for the earlier cohorts or employment spells, thus this should be a two-tailed test.
3 The National Longitudinal Survey of Young Women is sponsored by the US Bureau of Labor Statistics and conducted by the Center for Human Resources, Ohio State University.
4 Sample weights are not used here because of the difficulty in using weights for a moving sample with rates of attrition over time. Because I am not making claims to averages in the population but rather speaking about trends in individual women's lives, leaving the data unweighted should not pose a great risk to the results on the connections between women's own circumstances and outcomes.
5 One exception, exits from employment, has statistically significant cohort differences only between the middle and later-born cohorts. In this case, the middle and later cohort differences are discussed.

BIBLIOGRAPHY

Avellar, S. and Smock, P.J. (2003) 'Has the price of motherhood declined over time? A cross-cohort comparison of the motherhood wage penalty', *Journal of Marriage and Family*, 65(3): 597–607.
Blossfeld, H.-P. and Huinink, J. (1991) 'Human-capital investments or norms of role transition? How women's schooling and career affect the process of family formation', *American Journal of Sociology*, 97(1): 143–68.
Blossfeld, H.-P. and Timm, A. (eds) (2003) Who marries whom? Educational systems as marriage markets in modern societies, Dordrecht: Kluwer Academic.
Blossfeld, H.-P., Buchholz, S. and Hofäcker, D. (2006) *Globalization, uncertainty, and late careers in society*, London: Routledge.
Blossfeld, H.-P., Klijzing, E., Mills, M. and Kurz, K. (eds) (2005) *Globalization, uncertainty, and youth in society*, London: Routledge.
Charles, M. and Bradley, K. (2002) 'Equal but separate? A cross-national study of sex segregation in higher education', *American Sociological Review*, 67(4): 573–99.
Cherlin, A. (1989) 'The trends: marriage, divorce, remarriage', in A.S. Skolnick and J.H. Skolnick (eds) *Family in transition* (6th edition), Glenview, IL: Scott, Foresman and Company.
Cohen, P.N. and Bianchi, S.M. (1999) 'Marriage, children, and women's employment: What do we know?', *Monthly Labor Review*, 122(21): 22–31.
Coontz, S. (1992) The way we never were: American families and the nostalgia trap, New York: Basic Books.

Dortch, S. (1997) 'Hey guys: hit the books – college enrollments', *American Demographics*, 12(9): 1–4.

Ehrenreich, B. (2001) *Nickel and dimed: on (not) getting by in America*, New York: Henry Holt and Company, LCC.

Erikson, R. and Goldthorpe, J.H. (1993) 'Introduction: industrial society and social mobility', *The constant flux: a study of class mobility in industrial societies*, Oxford: Clarendon Press.

Esping-Andersen, G. (1999) *Social foundations of postindustrial economies*, Oxford: Oxford University Press.

Fuchs, V. (1988) *Women's quest for economic equality*, Cambridge, MA: Harvard University Press.

Ganzeboom, H.B.G. and Treiman, D.J. (1996) 'International stratification and mobility file: conversion tools', Utrecht, Department of Sociology, www.fss.uu.nl/soc. Accessed 10 January 2004.

Grunow, D. Hofmeister, H. and Buchholz, S. (2006) 'Late 20th–Century persistence and decline of the female homemaker in Germany and the United States', *International Sociology*, 21(1): 101–31.

Guthrie, D. and Roth, L.M. (1999) 'The state, courts, and maternity policies in US organizations: specifying institutional mechanisms', *American Sociological Review*, 64(1): 41–63.

Herring, C. and Wilson-Sadberry, K.R. (1993), 'Preference or necessity? Changing work roles of black and white women, 1973–1990', *Journal of Marriage and the Family*, 55(2): 314–25.

Hirschl, T.A., Altobelli, J. and Rank, M.R. (2003) 'Does marriage increase the odds of affluence? Exploring the life course probabilities', *Journal of Marriage and Family*, 65(4): 927–38.

Jacobsen, J.P. and Levin, L.M. (1995) 'Effects of intermittent labor force attachment on women's earnings', *Monthly Labor Review*, 118(9): 14–19.

Kim, K. and Creighton, S. (1999) 'Participation in adult education in the United States: 1998–1999', Washington, DC, National Center for Education Statistics 2000-027.

Leibowitz, A. and Klerman, J.A. (1995) 'Explaining changes in married mothers employment over time', *Demography*, 32(3): 365–78.

Lelyveld, J. (ed.) (2001) *How Race is Lived in America*, New York: Henry Holt and Company.

Lipset, S.M. (1995) American exceptionalism: a double-edged sword, New York: W.W. Norton.

Marler, J.H. and Moen, P. (2002) 'Alternative employment arrangements: a gender perspective', Presentation in Session 859 at the *Annual Academy of Management Meetings*, Denver. 13 August 2002.

Marler, J.H., Tolbert, P.S. and Milkovich, G.T. (2003) 'Alternative employment arrangements', in P. Moen (ed.) *It's about time: couples and careers*, Ithaca, NY: Cornell University Press.

Mills, M., Blossfeld, H.-P. and Bernardi, F. (2006) 'Globalization, uncertainty and men's employment careers: a theoretical framework', in H.-P. Blossfeld, M. Mills, and F. Bernardi (eds) *Globalization, uncertainty and men's careers: an international comparison*, Cheltenham, UK and Northampton, MA, USA: Edward Elgar.

Stacey, J. (1991) Brave new families: stories of domestic upheaval in late twentieth century America, New York: Basic Books.

Stier, H. and Lewin-Epstein, N. (2001) 'Welfare regimes, family-supportive policies, and women's employment along the life-course', *American Journal of Sociology*, 106(6): 1731–60.

US Department of Commerce (2000) 'High school completion rates and number and distribution of 18-through 24-year-old completers not currently enrolled in high school or below, by background characteristics: October 2000', Washington, DC, US Census Bureau, Current Population Survey.

US Department of Education (2000) 'Percentage of undergraduates with nontraditional characteristics: 1992–93 and 1999–2000', Washington, DC, National Center for Education Statistics, National Postsecondary Student Aid Study (NPSAS: 2000).

US Department of Education (2001) 'Enrollment in degree-granting institutions, with alternative projections: Fall 1987 to Fall 2012' (Education Statistics Quarterly Edition), Washington, DC, National Center for Education Statistics, 'Fall Enrollment in Colleges and Universities' surveys, Integrated Postsecondary Education Data System surveys, and Enrollment in Degree-Granting Instititutions Model.

US Department of Labor (2002) 'College enrollment and work activity of 2001 high school graduates, table 383: college enrollment and labor force status of 2000 and 2001 high school completers, by sex and race/ethnicity: October 2000 and October 2001', Washington, DC, Bureau of Labor Statistics.

US Department of Labor (2004) 'History of federal minimum wage rates under the Fair Labor Standards Act, 1938–1996', US Department of Labor, Employment Standards Administration Wage and Hour Division.

Warner, D. and Hofmeister, H. (2006) 'Late career transitions among men and women in the United States', pp. 141–82 in H.-P. Blossfeld, S. Buchholz and D. Hofäcker (eds) *Globalization, uncertainty and late careers in society*, London: Routledge.

Woods, D.R. (2004) 'Das "adult worker model" in den USA und Großbritannien', in M. Schratzenstaller (ed.) *Wohlfahrtsstaat und Geschlechterverhältnis im Umbruch: Was kommt nach dem Ernährermodell?*, Wiesbaden: VS Verlag für Sozialwissenschaften.

Yoon, Y.H. and Waite, L.J. (1994) 'Converging employment patterns of black, white, and hispanic women – return to work after 1st birth', *Journal of Marriage and the Family*, 56(1): 209–17.

PART VI

Country-specific contributions on
family-oriented welfare regimes

13. Labor force dynamics and occupational attainment across three cohorts of women in urban Mexico

Emilio A. Parrado

INTRODUCTION

Globalization is likely to impact female labor force participation in a variety of ways depending on a country's institutional structure and degree of connection with the global economy. In this respect, Mexico stands out from the more developed societies of Europe and North America treated in this volume. While trade and capital investments are increasingly incorporating Mexico into the global economy, wide disparities in economic and institutional development remain between Mexico and more developed countries. As a result, relative to other countries, the intensity of the economic, social and political changes accompanying globalization has been particularly strong in Mexico. The country's close proximity to the United States, participation in the North American Free Trade Agreement (NAFTA), substantial foreign investments and long history of female employment in domestic and informal work set Mexico apart and potentially heighten the impact of globalization on women's work.

The direction of these effects, however, is unclear. Previous studies have shown that female employment in Mexico is highly responsive to socioeconomic change. Women's labor market entry has been greatly facilitated by educational expansion and declining fertility over time. Beyond personal characteristics, however, contextual forces have also shaped patterns of women's work in Mexico. Foreign capital investments, particularly in the maquiladora industry, affected occupational opportunities and increased women's labor market incorporation into blue-collar occupations. At the same time, the recurrent financial crises accompanying economic restructuring have triggered married women's labor market entry, particularly into domestic employment (Garcia and de Oliveira 1994; Parrado 2005; Tiano 1994).

Thus while globalization has encouraged Mexican women's labor market incorporation, improving their economic standing vis-à-vis men, it may have also constrained their occupational opportunities, increasing their representation in blue-collar and domestic employment relative to professional or clerical jobs. Unfortunately, surprisingly little is known about women's labor market trajectories and career opportunities and how they have changed under globalization (Escobar Latapi 1997; Filguera 2000; Klein and Tokman 2000). Studies on the social mobility of men have shown that economic restructuring policies aimed at incorporating Mexico into the global economy have been associated with stagnant career opportunities and even downward mobility, especially into informal sector employment (Parrado 2002).

Less is known about the effect of these policies and other contextual forces on women's work lives. The lack of longitudinal data that follows individuals as they age has prevented systematic analysis of women's life-time labor market opportunities. In addition, comparable data spanning different historical periods is necessary in order to assess the impact of globalization on women's career trajectories. Given the extent of economic reforms and the intensity of globalization in Mexico, we can expect women's work to have been significantly affected by economic restructuring well beyond changes in patterns of labor market entry.

Accordingly, this chapter analyzes the life-course dynamics of female employment in urban Mexico. Two main questions guide the empirical analysis. First, to what extent has globalization affected the degree of women's labor market attachment, that is, movements in and out of the labor force? Second, to what extent have globalization and economic restructuring policies affected women's occupational opportunities over the life course? The analytic strategy of the chapter is to compare patterns of labor market entries and exits and occupational class attainment after first employment across three cohorts of urban Mexican women representative of different economic and policy periods. The main argument presented here is that it is at the intersection of period conditions and life-course opportunities that we can best assess the extent to which globalization and economic restructuring policies affect women's work lives and employment opportunities in Mexico.

THE CONTEXT OF GLOBALIZATION IN MEXICO

During the past two decades, Mexico has become one the world's most aggressive 'new globalizers' (World Bank 2002). After the debt crises of the early 1980s, Mexico implemented a series of economic restructuring policies that included fiscal reforms, extensive privatization of state firms, labor market deregulation and common market formation such as NAFTA (Lustig 1992). These policies aimed at incorporating the country into the global economy and reorienting the model of development from inward- to outward-looking (Barkin and Rosen 1997; Dussel Peters 1997; ECLA 2002).

Three specific changes resulting from economic restructuring have affected the institutional context (Pyle 1999). First, with the goal of promoting fiscal austerity, productivity and competitiveness, the government implemented a series of structural adjustment programs that directly reduced the employment capacity of the public sector and removed a central channel for professional, clerical and service sector employment. Measures were taken to reduce the number of government employees, including hiring freezes. Teachers' wages were particularly affected by these policies. The educational system has historically been a central avenue for women's incorporation into skilled and professional occupations. However, between 1982 and 1998, teachers' salaries lost 67 percent of their real value, falling to the level of salaries in manual occupations (CIDAC 1992). This deterioration of teachers' salaries in recent decades has acted as a powerful disincentive to female employment in the educational system and has compromised efforts to improve the quality of education in Mexico.

In addition to the deterioration in public sector wages, wide-ranging privatization programs and the liquidation of public companies resulted in large-scale worker displacement. The employment effect of privatization in Mexico cannot be overstated. By 1993, only 210 of the 1155 state-owned companies that existed in 1982 had not been privatized, merged or liquidated (Teichman 1996). In order to maximize profit and increase efficiency, privatized firms reduced the number of white and blue-collar workers by more than half (La Porta and López-de-Silanes 1997). This also eliminated one of the central avenues of female employment in formal and clerical occupations, reducing the possibilities of higher occupational class attainment over the life course.

Second, the promotion of labor flexibility increased employment instability and promoted informal rather than formal sector employment (Rakowski 1994; Roberts 1989). In order to attract capital investment, measures were taken to lower employers' labor costs. The Mexican government implemented several 'solidarity' pacts, the first in December 1987, with select unions and the private sector in order to guarantee an abundant supply of cheap labor in the context of 'flexible specialization' in industrial relations (Dussel Peters 1998). As a result, between 1980 and 1995 the real minimum wage declined by nearly 65 percent in Mexico (Dávila Capalleja 1997). Male wages were hardest hit by these changes, prompting many women to enter the labor market to compensate for their husbands' declining income.

Third, the emphasis on integration into the global economy altered Mexico's path towards industrialization (Dussel Peters 1997). Through pressure from international financial institutions such as the International Monetary Fund and the World Bank, Mexico was encouraged to pursue its comparative advantage and promote trade integration. Contrary to earlier periods of export orientation, however, this shift not only involved concentrating on primary product production, but also expanding industrial exports, generally produced by multinational subsidiaries and other foreign-owned assembly plants in export processing zones.

Export orientation has been particularly successful in Mexico due to its close connection to the US and the signing of NAFTA in 1992. Between 1960 and 1998 exports of goods and services as percentage of GDP grew from 8 to 31 percent (see Figure 13.1), making Mexico the largest, most dynamic and diversified exporter in Latin America, with 90 percent of exports directed towards the US (ECLA 2002). However, the expansion of exports has been paralleled by a concomitant expansion of imports that grew from 11 to 33 percent in the same time period, with 88 percent originating in the US. Thus, the overall employment benefits of export orientation have been severely limited by the lack of linkages between exports and local industrial development in Mexico.

The main engine behind the new export orientation has been the maquiladora program (Cooney 2001). Initiated in 1965, the program was designed to promote foreign capital investment in Mexico and support

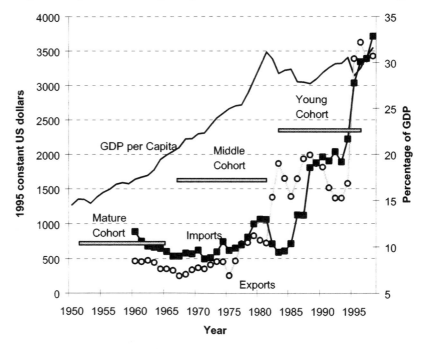

Source: 1998 National Retrospective Demographic Survey (EDER [Encuesta Demográfica Retrospectiva] 2000)

Figure 13.1   Trends in per capita GDP and trade in Mexico

American companies in their competition with Asia by granting duty-free imports of machinery, raw materials, parts and components to (mainly US-owned) assembly plants in Mexico. The final products were exported back to the United States, and taxes were paid only on the value added by Mexican workers.

The maquiladora industry has been a central stimulus to female employment in Mexico. The industry currently employs over 1 million workers, representing 27.3 percent of employment in manufacturing, and produces 53 percent of all Mexican exports (Dussel Peters 1997). In order to guarantee a cheap and flexible, even exploitable, labor force, maquiladora companies deliberately recruited young, single women. This was particularly the case during the initial stages of the program. In the 1960s, over 70 percent of the maquiladora work force was female (Gomez Luna 2001). This percentage has fallen to 45 percent in 2000 as the stagnant Mexican economy made maquiladora employment attractive for men as well. The end result has been a considerable expansion of employment opportunities for women in blue-collar and manual occupations.

Together, the reduced employment capacity of the state, increased flexibility of the labor force, deterioration of male wages and expansion of the maquiladora industry altered the institutional context guiding women's labor market attachment and career opportunities in Mexico. While these factors tended to encourage female labor force participation, the same conditions that limited occupational advancement for men are also likely to have constrained women's occupational attainment over time.

THEORIES OF FEMALE LABOR MARKET DYNAMICS AND THE MEXICAN CASE

In order to understand the changes in women's labor market dynamics associated with globalization, I use human capital, new international division of labor and household strategy perspectives as a framework for the analysis (Brinton, Lee and Parish 1995; Bustos and Palacios 1994). While these perspectives differ widely in emphasis, they are not necessarily incompatible. I expect elements of all three paradigms to structure the impact of globalization on women's work in Mexico.

Human capital explanations of female employment link the dynamics of market work predominantly to women's personal characteristics (Becker 1991; Mincer 1962). According to this perspective, women's work propensities are a direct function of their educational endowments and family responsibilities. More educated women have increased incentives to maintain a higher level of labor market attachment, since the opportunity costs of remaining at home increase with higher levels of education. At the same time, the dynamics of women's work are closely connected to family responsibilities. The greater family obligations of recently married women and those with young children reduce their labor market attachment.

There is very little room in this explanation for the role of contextual forces in shaping women's work. For the most part, this perspective expects countries to follow the logic of industrialism and move in a somewhat unidirectional manner towards increased modernization, urbanization and industrialization. This process will in turn expand occupational opportunities for women, increasing their labor market attachment and facilitating their incorporation into skilled professional and clerical occupations. As applied to Mexico, the human capital perspective would predict considerable variation in labor market dynamics associated with educational and family characteristics. At the same time, it would predict that over time modernization and the logic of industrialism would expand occupational opportunities, thereby increasing women's representation in professional and clerical occupations.

New international division of labor explanations of female labor force participation explicitly recognize that labor demand conditions directly affect women's work propensities. This perspective links changes in female employment to the expansion of multinational corporations and transnational assembly plants in developing countries (Nash and Fernández Kelly 1982). The shift of menial, low-paying jobs from the core to the periphery of the capitalist system has lead to expanded employment opportunities in areas reserved for young single women who can be easily dismissed once they marry or have children (Benería and Feldman 1992, Benería and Roldan 1987; Tinker 1990). The maquiladora industry in Mexico is a typical example of this type of change (Buitelaar and Perez 2000; Fernández Kelly 1982; Tiano 1994). Accordingly, a central expectation from this perspective is that through multinational corporations, globalization will affect labor demand conditions in Mexico in favor of blue-collar occupations. In addition, the high turnover rate characteristic of the maquiladora industry (in many cases exceeding 100 percent annually) is likely to produce a higher dynamism of labor market entries and exits, particularly among women employed in blue-collar occupations (Miller, Hom and Gomez-Mejia 2001).

Finally, household strategy explanations explicitly link the dynamics of female employment to the broader conditions prevalent in developing countries, including the industrial mix, stage in the industrialization process, and model of industrialization (Roberts and de Oliveira 1994; Standing 1989). According to this perspective, the internal market orientation of import-substitution industrialization promoted the expansion of formal and stable types of employment that tended to be reserved for men (Gonzalez de la Rocha 1994; Selby, Murphy and Lorenzen 1990). This model of development was more consistent with a relatively rigid gender division of labor within the household in which men were the sole providers for the family and women's economic activities were confined to the home.

Recurrent recessions and the application of structural adjustment programs during the 1980s and 1990s significantly altered the established gender division of labor. Since traditional male occupations suffered the most during recessions, the rigid specialization of gender roles became extremely risky. To protect against employment instability, families increasingly diversified their sources of income by incorporating other members of the household into the labor force, including women (Gonzalez de la Rocha 1994; de Oliveira and Ariza 1998). At the same time, globalization and economic restructuring contributed to reducing the conflict between family life and market work by expanding domestic and low-skilled service sector activities that are not always incompatible with family responsibilities.

Accordingly, the main expectations from this perspective are that the increased diversification of family survival strategies have resulted in a more dynamic female labor force in which women enter and leave the labor market at a higher rate, depending on economic opportunities and the need to substitute for male income (ECLA 1993; Rubery 1988). At the same time, the erosion of more formal types of female employment accompanying globalization and economic restructuring have constrained occupational attainment. In particular, globalization increased women's movements into domestic and informal sector employment throughout the life course (Chant 1991).

DATA AND METHODS

To assess the impact of globalization on women's work dynamics, I use data from the 1998 National Retrospective Demographic Survey (EDER – [Encuesta Demográfica Retrospectiva] 2000). The EDER is the first nationally representative survey of life histories in Mexico, and was designed to capture changes in life-course transitions across three generations of Mexican men and women. The analysis here is restricted to the female component of the survey residing in urban areas with population of 15 000 or more, the areas most likely to be affected by the forces of globalization

Figure 13.1 illustrates the periods represented by the three cohorts in relation to per capita GDP and trade in Mexico. The mature cohort, born between 1936 and 1938, entered the labor market around 1951 and is representative of the earlier period of Mexican economic development. The intermediate cohort, born between 1951 and 1953, entered the labor market around 1967 and is representative of a period of rapid economic growth when import substitution industrialization was at its peak. The young cohort, born between 1966 and 1968, entered the labor market around 1983, after the demise of import substitution industrialization and when economic restructuring policies were implemented. Ironically, the stagnant and unstable economic conditions experienced by the younger cohort during the 1990s coincide with Mexico's entry into the global economy and rapidly expanding international trade, as illustrated by trends in imports and exports as percentage of GDP.

The three periods captured by the cohorts also represent very different educational and family contexts. Access to education among urban women expanded dramatically across cohorts, with average years of completed education at age 30 increasing from 4.5 to 10.2 among the mature and young cohorts, respectively. The expansion of education was also accompanied by a delay in the timing of labor market entry. The average age at first job increased from 17.2 to 18.7 across cohorts. These changes in women's human capital characteristics also affected family life. The proportion ever married by age 30 declined from 93 to 82 percent, and the average age at marriage increased from 17 to 19 across the generations. In addition, Mexican women experienced a dramatic decline in fertility, with the average number of children at age 30 declining from 3.8 to 2.0 across the cohorts.

The EDER includes retrospective information on four employment-related dimensions: occupation, industry, position (employer, self-employed, piece-work employee, salaried employee or unpaid employee) and firm size. Using these dimensions, I was able to follow labor force attachment (cycles of employment and non-employment, including unemployment) and occupa-tional class location of women as they aged. In order to make the three generations comparable, the analysis is restricted to events occurring between the time of first employment and age 30. Thus, the analysis concentrates on changes in the labor market and occupational attainment during young adulthood, when the bulk of job mobility occurs (Balán, Browning and Jelin 1973; Bernhardt et al. 2001; Murphy and Welch 1990).

OCCUPATIONAL CLASSES AND MODEL SPECIFICATION

The analysis is separated into two parts. The first part concentrates on the dynamics of labor market exits and entries. The second part considers occupational class attainment over the life course. Any analysis of intragenerational occupational class attainment requires specific criteria for sorting jobs into particular class locations. This is especially challenging in the Latin American context where capitalist and non-capitalist forms of class relations coexist, complicating the application of standard classifications developed for more industrialized countries (Portes and Hoffman 2003). My occupational class classification follows Goldthorpe's (1980) definition of social classes that combines occupations whose incumbents share similar market and work conditions, including sources and levels of income, degree of economic security and chances of economic advancement, and location within the systems of authority and control governing the process of production.

As applied to women's work in Mexico, however, this typology requires slight modifications. Relative to more developed societies, Mexico suffers from an imperfect development of modern capitalist relations, with a large proportion of workers not formally incorporated into the legally regulated and currency-exchange economy (Jusidman 1992; Roberts and de Oliveira 1994). The structural segmentation of the Mexican labor market implies that any class definition should take into account the particular situation of informal workers. Thus, I modify Goldthorpe's typology by adding an occupational class category for informal workers, following the productive rationality approach definition of the informal sector proposed by International Labour Organization/Programa Regional del Empleo de America Latina y el Caribe (ILO/PREALC) (Jusidman 1992). This definition includes owners and workers (both paid and unpaid) in firms of fewer than six employees, and the self-employed, excluding domestic workers and professionals.

If globalization is associated with declining occupational opportunities, domestic employment could be a central avenue absorbing the rising supply of female workers. Domestic workers are also treated as a separate occupational class in my analysis. Domestic employment is the most common form of female employment in Mexico and is strongly embedded within the system of pervasive social inequality prevalent in Mexican society. The large proportion of women employed in domestic work and the low prestige and unfavorable working conditions associated with it justify a separate classification (Chaney and Castro 1989). Thus, the occupational classes are defined here as follows:

1   professionals: high and lower-grade professionals, administrators, officials, managers in large or small establishments and supervisors of non-manual employees;
2   clerical workers: routine non-manual, clerical employees, sales personnel and other rank-and-file service employees;
3   manual workers: lower grade technicians, supervisors of manual workers and manual wage workers in semi- and unskilled grades;
4   domestic workers: manual workers in domestic occupations;
5   informal workers: owners and workers in firms with less than six employees, casual vendors and unpaid family workers, excluding domestic workers and professionals.

The analyses apply discrete-time event history methods that follow individuals over time and estimate the likelihood of exiting or entering the labor market or changing occupational class status (Blossfeld, Hamerle and Mayer 1989; Yamaguchi 1991). The models follow a repeated event specification, with the estimation technique varying according to the dependent variable. In analyses where the outcome is the occurrence of an event, such as labor market exits and entries, the models are estimated using logistic regression. In cases where the specific destination of the move is of interest, such as occupational class destination, the models follow a competing risk specification and are estimated using multinomial logistic techniques (Blossfeld, Hamerle and Mayer 1989).

Four sets of variables are expected to affect the dynamics of female employment: structural constraints resulting from different socioeconomic contexts and periods of economic development, human capital endowments, family characteristics and past and current labor market experiences. The first set of variables captures the structural constraints present during different periods. Because the three cohorts of women are tracked across the same age range and for the same length of time, cohort effects enable us to illuminate the impact of period conditions on labor force dynamics.

The second set of variables measures the influence of human capital characteristics on female employment. Educational attainment and work experience are two central human capital dimensions expected to enhance both labor market attachment and upward mobility. In addition, migrant status is a reflection of the pursuit of new jobs and opportunities and is also expected to enhance market attachment and occupational attainment.

The third set of variables measures the constraints imposed by family life on market work. The effect of marriage is captured by dummy variables indicating marital duration. This set of variables distinguishes between single women, those in their first two years of marriage, and those in marriages of longer duration. The initial marriage period is expected to be a particularly strong deterrent to female labor market attachment and mobility due to strong norms against married women's employment and the high probability of young children in the first years of marriage. Other family responsibilities, particularly the number of children, are expected to limit job experimentation and constrain career moves.

The final set of variables measures employment experiences. The models control for the dependence of labor market dynamics on an individual's age by including a variable measuring age at labor market entry or exit. In addition, years in or out of the labor market is included to capture the baseline risk of experiencing a labor market change. Models of labor market entry and exit also control for occupational class to measure the different mobility propensities of particular occupational groups. I expect mobility to be lower among more skilled occupational classes, particularly professionals, and increase among less skilled classes. I also estimated interactions between cohort membership and socioeconomic characteristics and report results when significant.

RESULTS

Dynamics of labor force participation

While Mexican men are expected to participate in the labor force throughout most of their adult lives, women's careers remain far more intermittent and significantly dependent on personal characteristics and contextual forces. Over time, there has been a considerable expansion of female labor force participation in urban Mexico. The proportion of women ever working before age 30 increased from 58 percent among the mature cohort to 69 and 79 percent among the middle and young cohorts, respectively. At the same time, 55, 48 and 52 percent of ever working women in each cohort left the labor market at some point after first employment before age 30.

The dynamics of women's work remains highly dependent on family responsibilities, especially marriage (Garcia and de Oliveira 1994). Figure 13.2 plots the labor force participation rates of ever-married women in relation to the timing of marriage across cohorts. The y-axis is the percent of women working at a particular point in time and the x-axis depicts years before and after marriage, with 0 representing the year of marriage. Female labor force participation increases considerably in the years prior to marriage. Differences across cohorts seem to suggest that single women in the middle cohort achieved higher participation rates than young cohort women. However, this result is a function of the lower proportion of young cohort women marrying by age 30 relative to the middle cohort. It is actually the postponement of marriage that allowed greater labor market participation among young women in Mexico in recent decades.

Figure 13.2 clearly shows that marriage is a central constraint to labor force participation and that this result holds for all three cohorts. For instance, while 52 percent of ever married women in the middle cohort worked in the year prior to marriage, only 38 percent do so in the year of marriage and a scant 27 percent remained employed two years after marriage. A slightly less dramatic change is evidenced among the younger cohort, where 46 percent of women work in the years prior to marriage and 37 percent are still working two years after marriage.

However, while it is clear from Figure 13.2 that marriage constrains market work, the dynamics of female employment cannot be captured in the graph. A labor force participation rate of 37 percent after marriage can reflect a very heterogeneous labor force where 37 percent of women work continuously throughout their lives and the other 63 percent never work or a more homogeneous one in which around one-third of the female population enter and exit the labor market every year. While both scenarios produce the same participation rate, the latter implies a far more dynamic pattern of labor force attachment. In order to assess whether the labor market has become more or less dynamic as a result of globalization, I estimated different models

Source: 1998 National Retrospective Demographic Survey (EDER [Encuesta
                  Demográfica Retrospectiva] 2000)

Figure 13.2   Female labor force participation and marriage by cohort in Mexico

predicting the likelihood of labor market exits and re-entries among working
and non-working women.

Results reported in Table 13.1 show that cohort has a pronounced effect on
women's employment dynamics, strongly suggesting the impact of economic
restructuring policies on women's work. Consistent with expectations from
household survival strategies, globalization in Mexico has been associated
with a more fluid pattern of female employment. Columns 1 and 3 of Table
13.1 show a significant increase in the rate of labor market exits and entries
among women in the younger cohort relative to their middle cohort peers.
Specifically, younger cohort women are 57 percent (exp(0.455) = 1.57) more
likely to exit and 90 percent (exp(0.643) = 1.90) more likely to re-enter the
labor force than women in middle cohort.

The effects of socioeconomic and family characteristics on employment
dynamics follow expectations from human capital theories. Higher levels of
education are a central factor reducing the likelihood of labor market exit and

increasing the chances of returning to the labor force after not working. Likewise, women with greater work experience are more likely to return to the labor force than comparable women with fewer years of work experience. Being an internal migrant also increases the chances of women returning to the labor market. The search for better employment opportunities is a central

Table 13.1   *Discrete-time logit models predicting dynamics of labor market entries and exits for Mexican women*

	Labor market exits		Labor market entries	
	(1)	*(2)*	*(3)*	*(4)*
Constant	−3.75**	−3.67**	−6.31**	−6.12**
	(0.49)	(0.49)	(1.42)	(1.43)
Cohort				
Mature	−0.03	−0.06	−0.20	−0.09
	(0.19)	(0.19)	(0.54)	(0.55)
Middle (ref)				
Young	0.44**	0.18	0.64*	0.53
	(0.16)	(0.18)	(0.38)	(0.38)
Human capital characteristics				
Years of education	−0.06**	−0.06**	0.18**	0.18**
	(0.02)	(0.02)	(0.06)	(0.06)
Years of work exp.	−0.03	−0.03	0.21**	0.21**
	(0.02)	(0.02)	(0.06)	(0.06)
Internal migrant	−0.05	−0.06	0.54*	0.55*
	(0.14)	(0.15)	(0.33)	(0.33)
Family characteristics				
Single (ref)				
First two years married	1.17**	1.16**	−1.45**	−1.50**
	(0.17)	(0.17)	(0.61)	(0.61)
Three or more years married	0.34	−0.20	−0.79*	−0.82*
	(0.22)	(0.29)	(0.46)	(0.46)
Number of children	−0.31**	−0.29**	0.06	0.08
	(0.08)	(0.08)	(0.15)	(0.15)
Employment characteristics				
Age at market entry	0.07**	0.07**	−0.03	−0.04
	(0.02)	(0.02)	(0.05)	(0.05)
Years in labor market	0.00**	0.00**	−0.10*	−0.10*
	(0.00)	(0.00)	(0.06)	(0.06)
	(0.27)	(0.27)	(0.82)	(0.83)

Table 13.1   continued

	Labor market exits		Labor market entries	
	(1)	*(2)*	*(3)*	*(4)*
Occupational class				
Professional (ref)				
Clerical	0.54**	0.57**	0.85	0.87
	(0.25)	(0.25)	(0.79)	(0.79)
Manual	0.85**	0.90**	1.69**	1.69**
	(0.28)	(0.28)	(0.84)	(0.85)
Agriculture	−0.36	−0.33	1.95	1.83
	(0.78)	(0.78)	(1.37)	(1.38)
Domestic	0.66**	0.68**	0.95	−0.17
	(0.32)	(0.32)	(0.95)	(1.33)
Informal	0.61**	0.64**	1.75**	1.73**
	(0.27)	(0.27)	(0.82)	(0.83)
Socioeconomic and cohort interactions				
Young* 3 or more years in marriage		0.92**		
		(0.30)		
Young* domestic occupation				1.68*
				(0.95)
Chi-squared	117.1**	126.7**	68.1**	70.6**
Person-years	3 761		2 285	

Note: * p < 0.1, **p < 0.05

Source: 1998 National Retrospective Demographic Survey (EDER [Encuesta Demográfica Retrospectiva] 2000)

motivation for internal migration and is thus associated with shorter durations outside the labor force.

Consistent with the description presented in Figure 13.2, family characteristics are an important constraint on labor market attachment. The likelihood of exiting and not re-entering the labor force is particularly high during the first two years of marriage. After two years, however, marriage no longer encourages women to leave employment though it still inhibits re-entry among those who had left the labor market. It is important to note that the

account trends in education and family formation. The dependent variable in the analysis is changes in occupational class status that includes movements out of the labor force as a competing event. The model is estimated using a discrete-time multinomial logit specification that follows women as they age, with the reference category remaining in the same occupational status.

Results reported in Table 13.3 indicate that cohort effects, and by implication globalization and economic restructuring, are particularly important for understanding women's relative career opportunities. Specifically, results show a significant increase in the likelihood of women moving into manual employment among young relative to middle cohort women. Over time, the expansion of the maquiladora industry not only has increased women's likelihood of entering the labor market through blue-collar employment (Parrado 2005) but also has accelerated women's transition into manual occupations throughout their work lives.

At the same time, the diversification of family survival strategies and the deterioration of economic conditions resulting from structural adjustment programs reduced employment opportunities among the younger cohort and increased women's chances of moving into domestic work. Thus, while professional and clerical employment opportunities grew in the aggregate over time, they failed to keep pace with the rising human capital of Mexican women. Rather then fueling upward mobility, as human capital and modernization theories predict, globalization and economic restructuring actually undermined women's occupational attainment in Mexico. Once rising stocks of human capital are taken into account, women in the young cohort were more likely to be channeled into low-skilled manual and domestic occupations, as both new international division of labor and household survival strategy theories predict. This represents a significant reversal in trends towards greater occupational attainment among women and has ominous implications for subsequent career development and lifetime earnings among generations most affected by economic restructuring.

Following human capital expectations, a central factor predicting occupational destinations is educational attainment. More educated women are significantly less likely to leave the labor force, move into manual work, enter domestic occupations or move into the informal sector. At the same time, less experienced workers are especially prone to moving into less rewarding occupations, as years of work experience reduce the chances of women leaving the labor force, taking up manual occupations or moving into the informal sector.

In general, family responsibilities, both marriage and number of children, reduce women's propensities to experience an occupational class move. This general trend, however, is contradicted in two situations. First, consistent with the pattern of labor market exits soon after marriage, being in the first

Table 13.3   *Discrete-time multinomial logit model predicting occupational class attainment over the life course of urban Mexican women*

	Professional	Clerical	Manual	Domestic	Informal	Out of LF
Constant	−15.43**	−10.77**	−10.03**	−8.57**	−8.81**	−8.48**
	(1.73)	(1.09)	(0.95)	(1.35)	(0.80)	(0.49)
Cohort						
Mature	−0.20	−0.47	−0.51	0.67	−0.26	−0.26
	(0.85)	(0.54)	(0.49)	(0.59)	(0.37)	(0.21)
Middle (ref)						
Young	0.22	0.08	0.91**	1.37**	0.31	0.21
	(0.49)	(0.35)	(0.38)	(0.64)	(0.31)	(0.18)
Human capital characteristics						
Years of education	0.07	−0.02	−0.22**	−0.34**	−0.15**	−0.15**
	(0.05)	(0.04)	(0.04)	(0.08)	(0.03)	(0.02)
Years of work exp.	−0.05	−0.05	−0.07*	−0.04	−0.11**	−0.25**
	(0.07)	(0.05)	(0.04)	(0.06)	(0.04)	(0.30)
Internal migrant	0.39	−0.18	−0.17	0.35	−0.25	−0.15
	(0.50)	(0.33)	(0.35)	(0.66)	(0.28)	(0.17)
Family characteristics						
Single (ref)						
First two years married	−0.49	0.10	−0.12	−2.06**	−0.70	1.87**
	(0.78)	(0.45)	(0.45)	(1.06)	(0.45)	(0.19)
Three or more years married	−0.63	−0.82**	−1.57**	−3.49**	−1.51**	−0.41*
	(0.58)	(0.46)	(0.47)	(0.80)	(0.39)	(0.25)
Number of children	−0.85**	−0.64**	−0.32**	0.23*	−0.28**	−0.74**
	(0.36)	(0.24)	(0.16)	(0.12)	(0.14)	(0.10)
Employment characteristics						
Age at occupational class entry	0.44**	0.35**	0.37**	0.28**	0.34**	0.36**
	(0.07)	(0.05)	(0.04)	(0.06)	(0.04)	(0.02)
Years in occupational class	0.18**	0.05	0.17**	−0.02	0.15**	0.26**
	(0.08)	(0.07)	(0.05)	(0.09)	(0.05)	(0.03)
Chi-squared	846.0					
Person-years	5138					

Note: *p < 0.1, **p < 0.05

Source: 1998 National Retrospective Demographic Survey (EDER [Encuesta Demográfica Retrospectiva] 2000)

two years of marriage increases women's movement out of the labor force. However, after the first two years, this effect is reversed and women in their third or later year of marriage are less likely to change occupations than their single counterparts.

Second, while marriage reduces moves into domestic occupations, the number of children has the opposite effect. The negative effect of marriage on domestic class moves is especially strong, suggesting that domestic work is a state tolerated predominantly while single. As the number of children increases, women appear to be more likely to move into domestic jobs. This is consistent with a view of female employment as a dynamic survival strategy that is highly responsive to financial need and family status.

DISCUSSION

Globalization and the associated economic restructuring policies have significantly affected the dynamics of female work in Mexico. Starting in the mid-1980s and accelerating during the 1990s, the reduced employment capacity of the state, the deterioration of male incomes and the expansion of employment opportunities in the maquiladora industry altered the institutional context guiding women's work careers in Mexico. As individuals and families adapted to the changing economic environment, women's work became increasingly responsive to period conditions above and beyond their personal characteristics. The end result of this process has been that women's labor force participation has become increasingly intermittent and unstable and that occupational opportunities have declined relative to earlier generations.

This chapter focused on two dimensions of women's work, labor market attachment and occupational attainment. The analytic strategy of the study was to compare work dynamics across three cohorts of urban Mexican women representative of different period conditions. Human capital, international division of labor and household survival theories provided the framework for understanding changes to women's work opportunities over time in Mexico.

Results show that human capital, international division of labor and household survival theories capture different dimensions of women's labor market experience. Consistent with human capital expectations, increases in women's labor market attachment and occupational attainment in Mexico have resulted from the expansion of education and reduction of family responsibilities over time. However, labor demand conditions and institutional arrangements have also affected women's labor market dynamics. Consistent with international division of labor and household survival theories, the expansion of the maquiladora industry and structural adjustment programs have altered the dynamics of labor market entries and exits and affected the occupational opportunities available to women.

Over time, female employment has become more dynamic in Mexico. Economic fluctuations, deteriorating family incomes and labor flexibility have reduced women's labor market attachment and increased their propensity to enter and exit the labor force across cohorts. In marked contrast with earlier periods of economic development in Mexico, globalization has resulted in more volatile work trajectories. Instead of maintaining a stable work career, recent cohorts of Mexican women move in and out of the labor market at a higher rate. The implications of these changes are two-fold. On the one hand, the increased dynamism of the female labor force facilitated female employment by reducing the conflict between family life and market work. In recent decades Mexican women appear to be able to more easily adapt their labor force participation to family responsibilities and economic needs. On the other hand, instability undermines career development and the accumulation of work experience, limiting women's lifetime chances of achieving higher occupational status and upward mobility.

Occupational opportunities have indeed been significantly affected by globalization. Results show that relative to earlier periods of economic development in Mexico, globalization and economic restructuring policies have reduced women's chances of achieving 'good' jobs or at least jobs commensurate with women's socioeconomic characteristics. During periods of economic restructuring, occupational opportunities have failed to keep pace with improvements in women's human capital endowments. Instead, in recent decades Mexican women are increasingly being channeled into domestic employment, still the most typical form of female employment in Mexico. The increase in women's relative chances of domestic work over time represents an unfortunate deterioration of employment opportunities. Domestic work is a highly undesirable form of employment that offers few chances of upward mobility and is anchored at the bottom of the highly unequal occupational hierarchy in Mexico.

Overall, the analysis highlights the importance of mobility studies for assessing the changes in work experiences associated with globalization. A focus on income or static comparisons of occupational growth fail adequately to describe the full impact of economic restructuring on the life chances of Mexican women. The results presented above sound a strong warning to advocates of neoliberal policy reforms that have removed central avenues for women's occupational attainment but failed to generate the economic development necessary to provide employment opportunities in the private sector.

BIBLIOGRAPHY

Balán, J., Browning, H.L. and Jelin, E. (1973) *Men in a developing society. Geographic and social mobility in Monterrey, Mexico,* Austin, TX and London: University of Texas Press.

Barkin, D. and Rosen, F. (1997) 'Why the recovery is not a recovery?', *NACLA report on the Americas*, 30: 24–5.

Becker, G. (1991) *A treatise on the family*, Cambridge, MA: Harvard University Press.

Benería, L. and Feldman, S. (eds) (1992) *Unequal burden: economic crises, persistent poverty, and women's work*, Boulder, CO: Westview.

Benería, L. and Roldán, M. (1987) *The crossroads of class and gender. Industrial homework, subcontracting and household dynamics in Mexico City*, Chicago, IL: University of Chicago Press.

Bernhardt, A., Morris, M., Handcock, M.S. and Scott, M.S. (2001) *Divergent paths. Economic mobility in the new American labor market*, New York: Russell Sage Foundation.

Blossfeld, H.-P., Hamerle, A. and Mayer, K.U. (1989) *Event history analysis: statistical theory and application in the social sciences*, Hillsdale, NJ: Lawrence Erlbaum Associates.

Brinton, M., Lee, Y.-J. and Parish, W.L. (1995) 'Married women's employment in rapidly industrializing societies: examples from East-Asia', *American Journal of Sociology*, 100(5): 1099–130.

Buitelaar, R.M. and Perez, R.P. (2000) 'Maquila, economic reform and corporate strategies', *World Development*, 28(9): 1627–42.

Bustos, B. and Palacios, G. (eds) (1994) *El Trabajo Femenino en America Latina. Los Debates en la Decada de los Noventa*, Mexico: Universidad de Guadalajara.

Centro de Investigacion para el Desarrollo – CIDAC (1992) *Educacion para una economic competitiva. Hacia una estrategia de reforma*, Mexico.

Chaney, E.M. and Garcia Castro, M. (eds) (1989) *Muchachas no more: household workers in Latin America and the Caribbean*, Philadelphia, PA: Temple University Press.

Chant, S. (1991) *Women and survival in Mexican cities: perspectives on gender, labour markets and low-income households*, Manchester: Manchester University Press.

Cooney, P. (2001) 'The Mexican crises and the maquiladora boom. A paradox of development or the logic of neoliberalism?', *Latin American Perspectives*, 28: 55–83.

Dávila Capalleja, E.R. (1997) 'Mexico: the evolution and reform of the labor market', in S. Edwards and N. Lustig (eds) *Labor markets in Latin America: combining social protection with market flexibility*, Washington, DC: Brookings.

de Oliveira, O. and Ariza, M. (1998) 'Trabajo, familia y condicion femenina: una revision de las principales perspectivas de analisis', Programa de Estudios de la Mujer, Colegio de Mexico.

Dussel Peters, E. (1997) *La Economía de la Polarización: Teoría y Evolución del Cambio Estructural de las Manufacturas Mexicanas (1988–1996)*, Mexico City: UNAM.

Dussel Peters, E. (1998) 'Mexico's liberalization strategy, 10 years on: Results and alternatives', *Journal of Economic Issues*, 32(2): 351–63.

Economic Commission for Latin America and the Caribbean – ECLA (1993) *Cambios en el Perfil de la Familia: La Experiencia Regional*, Santiago: CEPAL.

Economic Commission for Latin America and the Caribbean – ECLA (2002) *Panorama Social de América Latina y el Caribe*, Santiago: CEPAL.

Encuesta Demográfica Retrospectiva (EDER) (2000) *Diseño muestral: Encuesta demográfica retrospectiva nacional*, Mexico City: INEGI.

Escobar Latapi, A. (1997) 'Men's and women's patterns of intra-generational mobility during Mexico's boom and crisis', in H.A. Selby and H. Browning (eds) *The socioeconomic effects of the crisis in Mexico*, Austin, TX: University of Texas Press.

Fernández Kelly, P. (1982) 'Las maquiladoras y las mujeres de Ciudad Juárez, México: paradojas de la industrialización bajo el capitalismo integral', in M. León (ed.) *Sociedad, subordinación y feminismo*, Bogotá: Asociación Colombiana para el Estudio de la Población.

Filguera (2000) *La Actualidad de Viejas Temáticas: Sobre Los Estudios de Clase, Estratificación y Movilidad Social en América Latina*, Santiago: CEPAL and United Nations.

Garcia, B. and de Oliveira, O. (1994) *Trabajo Femenino y Vida Familiar en Mexico*, Mexico City: El Colegio de Mexico.

Goldthorpe, J. (1980) *Social mobility and class structure in modern Britain*, Oxford: Clarendon Press.

Gomez Luna, M. E. (2001) *La industria maquiladora de exportacion y el empleo femenino*, Santiago: CEPAL.

Gonzalez de la Rocha, M. (1994) *The resources of poverty. Women and survival in a Mexican city*, Oxford: Blackwell.

Jusidman, C. (1992) *The informal sector in Mexico*, Mexico City: Secretaria del Trabajo y Prevision Social.

Klein, V. and Tokman, V. (2000) 'Social stratification under tension in a globalized era', *CEPAL Review*, 72: 7–29.

La Porta, R. and López-de-Silanes, F. (1997) 'The benefits of privatization – evidence from Mexico', World Bank Group, *Public Policy Journal* No. 117.

Lustig, N. (1992) *Mexico, the remaking of an economy*, Washington, DC: Brookings.

Miller, J.S., Hom, P.W. and Gomez-Mejia, L.R. (2001) 'The high costs of low wages: does maquiladora compensation reduce turnover?', *Journal of International Business Studies*, 32(3): 585–95.

Mincer, J. (1962) 'LFP of married women: a study of labor supply', in National Bureau of Economic Research (ed.) *Aspects of labor economics*, Princeton, NJ: Princeton University Press.

Murphy, K. and Welch, F. (1990) 'Empirical age-earnings profiles', *Journal of Labor Economics*, 8(2): 202–29.

Nash, J. and Fernández Kelly, M.P. (eds) (1982) *Women, men and the international division of labor*, Albany, NY: State University of New York Press.

Parrado, E.A. (2005) 'Globalization and transition to adulthood in Mexico', in H.P. Blossfeld, E. Klijzing, M. Mills and K. Kurz (eds) *Globalization, uncertainty, and youth in society*, London: Routledge.

Parrado, E.A. (2005) 'Economic restructuring and intra-generational class mobility in Mexico', *Social Forces*, 84(2).

Portes, A. and Hoffman, K. (2003) 'Latin American class structures: their composition and change during the neoliberal era', Working Paper Series, Center for Migration and Development, Princeton University.

Pyle, J. (1999) 'Third world women and global restructuring', in J. Chafetz (ed.) *Handbook of the sociology of gender*, New York: Kluwer.

Rakowski, C.A. (ed.) (1994) *Contrapunto: the informal sector debate in Latin America*, Albany, NY: SUNY Press.

Roberts, B.R. (1989) 'Employment structure, life cycle, and life chances: formal and informal sector in Guadalajara', in A. Portes, M. Castells and L.A. Benton (eds) *The informal economy studies in advanced and less developed countries*, Baltimore, MD: Johns Hopkins University Press.

Roberts, B.R. and de Oliveira, O. (1994) 'Urban growth and urban social structure in Latin America 1930–1990', in L. Bethel (ed.) *The Cambridge history of Latin America*, Vol. 6, Cambridge: Cambridge University Press.

Rubery, J. (ed.) (1988) *Women and recession*, London and New York: Routledge and Kegan Paul.

Selby, H.A., Murphy, A.D. and Lorenzen, S.A. (1990) *The Mexican urban household. Organizing for self defense*, Austin, TX: University of Texas Press.

Standing, G. (1989) 'Global feminization through flexible labor,' *World Development*, 17(7): 1077–95.

Teichman, J. (1996) *Privatization and political change in Mexico*, Pittsburgh, PA: Pittsburgh University Press.

Tiano, S. (1994) *Patriarchy on the line: labor, gender and ideology in the Mexican maquila industry*, Philadelphia, PA: Temple University Press.

Tinker, I. (ed.) (1990) *Persistent inequalities: women and world development*, New York: Oxford University Press.

World Bank (2002) *Globalization, growth, and poverty. Building an inclusive world economy*, Washington, DC: World Bank and Oxford University Press.

Yamaguchi, K. (1991) *Event history analysis*, Newbury Park, CA: Sage.

14. Mid-career women in contemporary Italy: economic and institutional changes

Maurizio Pisati and Antonio Schizzerotto

INTRODUCTION

Italy, in comparison to other advanced societies, has played a minor role in the process of globalization. Put another way, it could be said that Italy has suffered the consequences of the internationalization of economies and markets more than it has actively contributed to that process. A crucial reason is that the Italian production system is made up of a few large companies (less than 1 percent of all firms in Italy) and numerous medium and small firms (more than three-quarters of all firms in Italy have only two to five employees). Moreover, large companies and small firms both mainly operate in technologically mature sectors, and in most cases they are owned by individual families. The limited number of public companies gives rise to a rather narrow financial market and to restricted stock exchange activities, all the more so because foreign investors are kept out of the Italian economy by legal and bureaucratic constraints that make it difficult to establish a firm in Italy.

Obviously, Italy has undergone some of the structural shifts that some authors (for example, Mills and Blossfeld 2005) have associated with globalization. The intention is simply to stress that these changes have been less pronounced in Italy than in other nations. As a consequence, it sometimes proves rather difficult to separate the economic and social transformations attributable to generic processes of modernization from those specifically due to globalization.

Bearing this caveat in mind, it can be maintained that at least four significant changes, in principle attributable to the globalization process, are observable in today's Italy. First, the few large Italian companies began to relocate their branch offices and production plants abroad in the early 1960s; more recently, several medium-sized and small firms located in northeastern Italy have delocalized their factories to Eastern Europe and the Far East, where labor costs are much lower than in Italy. Second, since the early 1980s,

Italian governments have attempted to give greater flexibility to the workings of the labor market, with a marked intensification of such efforts since the late 1990s. Third, during the 1990s, the Italian government decided to privatize some state companies (or some of their departments), namely, those operating in electricity and natural gas distribution, as well as in the oil, foodstuffs, metallurgical and mechanical sectors. Fourth, information and communication technologies (ICTs) have spread rapidly not only among firms and public administration bodies, but also among families. Indeed, the proportion of Italian families owning a personal computer rose from about 10 percent in 1995 to 50 percent in 2003 and the proportion with Internet access more than doubled in three years (from 14 percent in 2000 to 37 percent in 2003). Finally, since 2000 the Italian economy has suffered the effects of the world financial crisis linked to ending the speculative bubble of the 'new economy' and the downturn in the world economy following the terrorist attack on the USA on 11 September 2001.

Over the past 20 years, a rather stagnant economy, the delocalization of medium-sized and small firms and the increasing diffusion of precarious employment relations have increased the economic and social insecurity of most Italians. Yet this greater uncertainty affects social groups and individuals to a different extent, and depends on their specific place in the class structure as well as on the institutional arrangements of contemporary Italy, which have in turn changed little over time.[1] Therefore, in order to determine how they have affected the life courses and employment prospects of mid-career women, one must examine the changes that have occurred in the most important components of these institutions.

Labor market regulation is a crucial institutional mechanism shaping the impact of social and economic insecurity. Since the post-World War II period the Italian labor market has been characterized by an opposition between insider and outsider workers. Insider employees today are mostly adult married men born between the late 1930s and the late 1950s living in central and northern regions of the country. By contrast, young people, women and those residing in the southern regions are overrepresented among the unemployed, precarious employees and informal workers.

This situation is the result of a long process that can be roughly divided into two main phases (Bernardi et al. 2000; Gualmini 1998; Reyneri 1996; Samek Lodovici 1997; Schizzerotto 2002). In the first, lasting from the late 1940s to the early 1980s, the main intent of Italian governments and trade unions was to regulate the demand side of the labor market in order to protect the incomes and jobs of full-time permanent employees in large and medium-sized firms. During this period various laws were enacted that established or revised unemployment subsidies, ordinary wage supplement funds and a special wage supplement fund. The latter was intended to ensure that redundant workers of large and medium-sized industrial firms not only received almost their entire wages for a very long period, but also maintained their employment contracts until firms had overcome their production crises. The goal of protecting employees against the risks of dismissal was pursued by further measures that prevented firms – initially those with more than 35 employees and subsequently also those with from 16 to 34 employees – from firing their workers on an individual basis.[2] Both firing and hiring procedures were controlled by law. More precisely, norms were introduced to regulate apprenticeship contracts, to impede firms from selecting new workers on an individual basis and to give the state monopoly over job placement services.

The above policies were both quite effective and had a number of unintended negative effects, in particular the increase of firms and jobs in the informal economy and increased unemployment among young people and women. These negative effects became particularly evident after the two oil shocks of the 1970s and the subsequent economic crises.

The second phase in regulation of the Italian labor market has consequently been characterized by relatively feeble attempts to remedy these consequences. The starting point of the second phase of Italian labor policies can be fixed in 1984, when a law was enacted that introduced work-training[3] and part-time contracts. Since 1984, governments have partly shifted their attention[4] to the supply side of the labor market, and efforts have been made to relax the formerly stringent employment protection rules. The most important set of measures to this end – known as the 'Treu Law' – were enacted in 1997. Specifically, the Treu Law: (a) introduced contract labor through employment agencies and fixed-term contracts; (b) raised the age limit on people who could be hired on the basis of apprenticeship and work-training contracts; (c) facilitated the hiring of part-time employees; and (d) allowed private employment agencies to operate. Unfortunately, several specifications in the law constrained the functioning of private employment agencies. Moreover, the application of atypical contracts was largely restricted to young people.[5]

In contemporary Italy, as in every advanced society, the school system plays an important mediating role between labor force supply and demand. As a consequence, education and its changes may affect the life courses and occupational prospects of individuals. From the early 1930s to the early 1960s the Italian school system was standardized, partly vocationally oriented and highly stratified (Barbagli 1974; Cobalti and Schizzerotto 1993; Schizzerotto and Cobalti 1998). The school-leaving age was set at 11, only elementary school (which lasted five years) was compulsory, and a quite sharp distinction was made between the academic and vocational tracks of both lower and upper secondary school. Moreover, only students from the academic tracks of the lower and higher secondary schools could enroll, respectively, in higher secondary schools and universities. In 1962, a law reforming compulsory lower secondary schooling came into force. The distinction between academic and vocational track at the lower secondary level was abolished, the reformed (three-year) lower secondary school became part of compulsory education and the school-leaving age was set at 14 (where it remained until 2003). In the late 1960s, the higher secondary school system underwent a reform that strengthened the theoretical components of its technical and vocational segments. In 1969, students from all higher secondary school tracks were allowed to enroll at university. As a consequence of the reforms, the Italian school system became unstratified and strongly increased the academic components of its curricula, but it still remained highly standardized.[6]

Such changes corresponded with a substantial increase in attendance rates at upper secondary school and university levels. More relevant to the topic here, however, is that among those born since 1958, the traditional gender differentials in educational chances have changed their sign, and young women are now on average better educated than young men (Pisati 2002). Occupational returns to education also have not declined over time, despite the growing supply of highly educated people and the lack of any practical training even in the vocational and technical tracks of the Italian post-compulsory schools (Cobalti and Schizzerotto 1994; Schizzerotto and Cobalti 1998).

Individual life courses and living standards depend, aside from labor market regulation and school qualification, on the welfare state regime, and that of Italy is notoriously family oriented. Consequently, protection against economic and social risks, as well as care for the dependent (children, the disabled, the old) is conceived as being mainly a task for families and kinship networks, while the state and local authorities do no more than act as a meager and rather particularistic last resort. Two areas of public policy are of particular relevance to the working lives of mid-career women: (a) unemployment and income measures, and (b) family supports.

The Italian welfare regime is rather ungenerous in the first area. It does not provide first-time job seekers and the self-employed with any form of unemployment benefits. Moreover, only a small minority of workers – those dependent from medium-sized and large firms – are eligible for the rather plentiful ordinary and special wage supplementation funds and enrolment in the mobility list. Wage supplementation funds are for temporarily redundant workers of large firms. These workers are not fired and continue to work for their firm, but their salaries are integrated or entirely paid by the state. The distinction between ordinary and special wage supplementation funds is based on the severity of the production crisis passed through by a firm and its expected duration. More precisely, the ordinary wage supplementation fund is intended to support workers experiencing a reduction of their usual working times for a limited period (usually one to three months), while special supplementation funds can extend up to three years and are for employees who are not working at all. In both cases the replacement rate is fixed at 80 percent of the amount of the lost salary. In its turn, the mobility list is addressed to workers collectively and definitely laid off by large firms.

These workers receive, from the state, 80 percent of their former pay and have to be hired first in cases of newly available workplaces.[7] All other categories of the unemployed receive only standard benefits, which are markedly low (about 30 percent of the last wage) and last for a maximum of six months (Bernardi et al. 2000; Negri and Saraceno 1998; Samek Lodovici 1997). The same applies to income support. The Italian welfare state lacks a universalistic measure that guarantees a minimum income level.[8] Only some minor financial transfers, intended to support people on low incomes, are provided by the state (Negri and Saraceno 1996; Saraceno and Naldini 2001).

Turning to public policies to support families and working parents, these can be roughly divided into three categories: (a) economic benefits; (b) measures directed at working mothers and fathers; and (c) services to families. Economic benefits consist of tax deductions and family allowances. Tax deductions have long been provided for any economically dependent family member; unfortunately, they are extremely low. Family allowances were introduced in the early 1930s for some categories of employees in the industrial sector, and they were subsequently extended to most dependent workers and pensioners. Since 1994, they have been paid to families whose pre-tax annual incomes are below a certain (quite low) threshold, which varies according to family size. Moreover, the specific amount of family benefit is in inverse proportion to the family income.

As regards measures intended to help women reconcile work and family responsibilities, Italy has had laws in place to protect working women against dismissal since the beginning of the twentieth century. In the 1960s, this protection was extended to cover the entire pregnancy period and the first year of the child's life. Moreover, employed mothers are now entitled to mandatory maternity leave, which starts two months before delivery and lasts for three months after it. During this period, they receive 80 percent of their pay. On demand, working mothers are also entitled to additional paid maternity leave of six months during the child's first year. In this case, the state pays a benefit equal to 30 percent of the wage. Moreover, during the first two years of a child's life, working mothers are entitled to take further unpaid leave, a right that has been extended to working fathers since the 1990s as well[9] (Pinnelli and De Rose 1995; Saraceno 1998; Saraceno and Naldini 2001).

Services to families are limited to public nurseries and preschools. While the latter are very widespread and have been attended by a substantial proportion of Italian children between the ages of three and five since the late 1960s, the former – established in nearly all Italian municipalities in 1971 – are far less available. An estimated 10 percent (at best) of infants aged from birth to two have been able to attend public nurseries in the last 15 years (Pinnelli and De Rose 1995; Saraceno 1998; Schizzerotto 1989).

The rather ungenerous Italian welfare regime results in families playing an important role in shaping the life chances of individuals. More precisely, families are expected to take care of children, unmarried young people and the elderly parents of spouses. The nuclear family pattern had predominated but it has been somewhat weakened since the 1960s by a moderate increase in separations and divorces, and a slow increase in non-marital cohabitations, reconstructed couples and lone parents. However, post-nuclear families are decidedly uncommon, and the traditional division of domestic labor between men and women, though it has attenuated compared with the past, is still widespread. As a consequence, women provide the primary, if not the only, family support for children, young people and elderly parents. This fact, and the limited availability of part-time jobs and flexible work schedules, may account for the generally low level of labor force participation among Italian women. However, the activity rates of women born since the late 1950s are increasing because of their better education and owing to the reduced stability of marriage. These factors may explain both the rising age at first marriage and the decline in fertility rates recently recorded in Italy.

HYPOTHESES

Since 1945, Italy has experienced several, though limited, economic changes that can be linked with the process of globalization. These changes have been accompanied by less pronounced alterations in cultural patterns, institutional arrangements and social structure – except for the size of occupational classes, the rates of educational attendance and the level of female participation in the labor market.

As a consequence, we maintain that certain of the hypotheses developed by the globalization thesis with reference to mid-career women are not immediately applicable to the Italian case. To clarify how those hypotheses could be specified so that they fit better with the possible effects of socioeconomic change on the working lives of Italian mid-career women, they are now listed and briefly discussed.

First, the globalization thesis posits an increase over time in the fragmentation of labor market participation of mid-career women, that is, a multiplication of labor market status changes during their work lives. Second, it maintains that job mobility rates should rise across birth cohorts. Third, it foresees a growth of the degree of insecurity deriving from increasing risks of both entering non-standard employment relations and experiencing un-employment. Fourth, it suggests that the effects exerted by family status on women's labor market participation have decreased over time.

By and large, we agree that the work–life pattern of mid-career Italian women should be more fragmented as one moves from the oldest birth cohort to the youngest. Yet we think that this trend should display some rise and fall, at least in the case of mid-career women born between the 1900s and 1950s. Most women born between 1900 and the early 1930s, besides carrying out domestic chores, were permanently employed as family workers in the agricultural sector, and thus should display few changes in their labor market status. During the 1950s and the late 1960s, Italy recorded a quite strong reduction in the activity rate of women accompanied by a pronounced shift of those employed from agriculture to industry and, though at a lesser extent, services and public sectors. Women reduced their level of participation in the labor market for two strictly linked reasons: first, because in that period the Italian economy was booming and salaries earned by men employed in industry and service sectors allowed men easily to maintain their families even though most women remained at home as housekeepers; and, second, because industry became the core sector of the Italian economy and produced a quite fast growth of both service sector and GDP. The latter, in turn, allowed a remarkable increase in the public expenditure. As a consequence, a huge proportion of adult men previously employed in agriculture, as well as all young people entering the labor market for the first time, found an occupation in industrial firms or, though less frequently, in the service and public sectors. This structural change of the Italian economy can explain why women's employment sectors also moved from agriculture to industry, services and public administration. The labor demand was declining in agriculture and rising in industry, the private tertiary sector and the public sector. Moreover, earnings of people employed in agriculture were strongly reducing, in relative terms, compared with those of individuals working in the industrial and tertiary sectors. Therefore, the few Italian (young and not married) women who wanted to find a job found definitely greater employment opportunities and better pay in the industrial and tertiary sectors. However, in that period job protection was not very stringent and unemployment risks, at least in the case of women employed by private firms, were definitely higher than they used to be in agriculture, where most, not to say all, women were employed as family workers and, as such, were not fireable.

As a consequence, the changes of labor market status undergone by mid-career women born between the mid-1930s and the late 1940s should be higher than those experienced by older cohorts. In the early 1970s, despite a worsening of the economic situation, job protection rules became very effective, as stressed above. Employed women born in the early 1950s benefited from the new norms and enjoyed rather stable employment relationships. We believe they changed the labor market status less frequently than did the previous cohort. Between the mid-1970s and the mid-1980s, the Italian business cycle became even more negative, and the welfare regime did not increase its income support and unemployment benefits, though this was also the time during which women grew better educated and marriages became less stable. As a consequence, a sizable proportion of women born after the late 1950s were induced to enter the labor market, even though their increased presence in the labor force contributed to a further rise in unemployment rates. Moreover, the quite rigid regulation of hiring and firing procedures in the official labor market generated a greater diffusion of informal jobs. Therefore, we hypothesize that women belonging to these younger birth cohorts underwent much more frequent changes in their labor market status than did their older counterparts. In the case of women born after the mid-1960s, a further reason for fragmentation of labor market experiences arose: the introduction in Italian legislation of temporary and fixed-term contracts.

Turning to the job mobility hypothesis, we also believe that the job mobility rates of mid-career Italian women should have grown across cohorts as an effect of both changes in the occupational structure and the spread of unstable employment relationships. Yet we expect the expansion of job mobility experiences should not be very pronounced, in part owing to the stability of occupational returns to education, and in part because of the rather rigid regulation of career steps in Italy that strongly restricts intragenerational mobility flows (Cobalti and Schizzerotto 1994; Pisati and Schizzerotto 1999).

So we maintain that increased insecurity across birth cohorts should not be very pronounced, because the introduction of non-standard contracts should have generated a reduction in the number of informal jobs and because the experience of unemployment should be rather uncommon among mid-career women born between 1900 and 1960.[10] The only remarkable exception to this rather stable trend should be represented by mid-career women belonging to the youngest cohort. Specifically, we expect to observe a sudden and remarkable growth of unemployment risks among such women because of the diffusion of non-standard contracts.

As for the reduction over time in the effects of family status on patterns of labor market participation among mid-career women, we agree with this hypothesis only in the case of marriage influences on the risks of unemployment and inactivity. In the past, most Italian women working for pay in dependent positions definitively left the labor market and become pregnant immediately after marriage. Moreover, employers, in order not to pay wages to their employees on maternity leave, usually forced newly hired unmarried women to sign a resignation letter – that was used to dismiss them when they got married. As a consequence, it was rather common in the past to observe recently married women, not yet pregnant, looking for a new job. Of late, many Italian married women in the labor force postpone the birth of the first child, and – thanks to the introduction of temporary employment relationships – fewer employers now ask newly hired unmarried women to sign the above-mentioned resignation letter. This is why we expect to observe a reduction, across cohorts, of marriage effects on the risks of being both unemployed and inactive among Italian mid-career women.

We do not think that anything similar has happened in the case of pregnancy and motherhood, however. We believe that their influence should be rather stable across birth cohorts. The work experiences of most married women born between the 1900s and the mid-1950s came to an end even before pregnancy and motherhood, and even among the few who remained in the labor market after getting married, pregnancy and the first child usually marked the beginning of a permanent condition of inactivity. Rather similar events should be observed among the mid-career women born since the late 1950s. The limited supply of family services for children younger than three makes it very difficult to reconcile family obligations and work duties. In the case of working mothers who either work on a part-time basis or are able to rely on a kinship network, this situation improves somewhat when children become eligible for preschool and primary school attendance.

Unfortunately, part-time jobs are quite uncommon, and women living in medium-sized and big towns often lack any kinship support simply because their parents or parents-in-law live elsewhere. As a consequence, inactivity continues to be the most common consequence of motherhood for many mid-career Italian women. The proportion of working mothers who definitely abandon the labor market is now much lower than in the past, though this is because of the increased number of highly educated women who achieve white-collar or service class positions and receive a high enough salary for them to be able to pay a nanny. Put another way, the negative net effect of motherhood (and pregnancy) on the chance of being in the labor market has remained quite stable during the twentieth century, and so have the countervailing positive net influences of a good education and a suitable occupation. The same mechanism should work in the case of unemployment. In the past, few mothers sought employment; today, those who participate in the labor market are highly educated women who are not unemployed and do not run serious risks of being so.

We expect to find similar situations in the case of the risks of experiencing informal jobs, temporary contracts and job mobility episodes. Regarding both informal jobs and temporary contracts, we would say that these relate more to the level of education and birth cohort than to family status. We are also inclined to suggest that today, as in the past, Italian working women display very flat career trajectories and possess very reduced chances of being intragenerationally mobile in any direction (Cobalti and Schizzerotto 1994; Pisati and Schizzerotto 1999).

DATA AND VARIABLES

The data used in this chapter come from the first wave of the Indagine Longitudinale sulle Famiglie Italiane (Italian Household Longitudinal Survey), carried out in 1997 by a consortium of three Italian universities (Trento, Milano-Bicocca and Bologna) and other non-academic institutions (Istituto Trentino di Cultura and Istat). The survey was based on a large sample (N = 9770) of non-institutionalized men and women aged 18 or older residing in Italy at the time of the interview (Schizzerotto 2002). The main aim of the survey was to collect complete event history data – from birth to the time of interview – as well as on several aspects of individuals' lives, including education, work and family. The data analyzed here pertain to mid-career women's participation in the labor market, with a focus on women who participated in the labor market for at least eight years before the age of 50. To exclude both the 'establishment' and the 'retirement' phases of women's careers from the analyses, only events that occurred after t_0 are considered, defined as the fifth year after entry into the first job, and before t_n defined as the time of the interview or the fiftieth birthday, whichever comes first.

In order to test the hypotheses presented in the previous section and to show the possible effects of globalization on mid-career women's labor market participation, we analyze how the latter has changed over time. We consider the labor market experiences of women belonging to eight birth cohorts: 1900 to 1924, 1925 to 1934, 1935 to 1944, 1945 to 1949, 1950 to 1954, 1955 to 1959, 1960 to 1964 and 1965 to 1969. The youngest cohort (1965 to 1969) has been excluded from some analyses, however, because sufficient observations are lacking. Moreover, for the sake of efficiency, in some analyses we aggregate the eight birth cohorts into a smaller number of categories. When comparing labor market experiences, it is generally important to adopt the same observation window for every subject included in the analysis so as to rule out the possibility that the differences observed are owing to dissimilarities in the length and/or temporal collocation of the individual observation windows. To avoid this possible source of bias in our analyses, we will consistently standardize the observation windows, restricting our attention to those events that occurred within five or ten years since t_0.

We adopt the following classification of labor market status: (a) self-employment; (b) permanent job (employee with a standard contract); (c) temporary job (employee with a fixed-term contract); (d) informal job (employee without a regular contract);[11] (e) unemployment;[12] and (f) inactivity.[13] Moreover, when studying job mobility, we will distinguish between upward, downward and lateral mobility. Upward mobility is defined here as any move between two jobs involving a 10 percent or larger increase in the de Lillo-Schizzerotto occupational desirability score (de Lillo and Schizzerotto 1985); downward mobility is defined as any move between two jobs involving a 10 percent or larger decrease in the de Lillo-Schizzerotto occupational desirability score; and lateral mobility is defined as any move between two jobs involving an increase or a decrease in the de Lillo-Schizzerotto occupational desirability score smaller than 10 percent.

RESULTS

In this section, we will illustrate the results of two kinds of analyses. First, we will try to test hypotheses regarding how mid-career women's patterns of labor market participation have changed over time. To this end, we will focus on three dimensions of labor market participation deemed particularly relevant to testing the globalization hypothesis: (a) fragmentation, defined as the propensity (or risk) of changing labor market status one or more times during a given period; (b) job mobility, defined as the propensity (or risk) of moving between different jobs during a given period; and (c) insecurity, defined as the propensity (or risk) of experiencing unemployment, informal employment or temporary employment during a given period.

We then turn our attention to the hypotheses regarding the effects of family status on mid-career women's patterns of labor market participation. Specifically, we will try to ascertain whether there have been changes over time in the influence of family status on the probability of being in the three insecure labor market statuses (unemployment, informal employment, temporary employment); the probability of being out of the labor force; and the probability of experiencing upward, downward and lateral job mobility.

Patterns of labor force participation

One of the main hypotheses of the globalization thesis is that the globalization process produces a strong and monotonic increase in the fragmentation of labor market participation at the individual level. As far as mid-career Italian women are concerned, the data illustrated in Figure 14.1 offer some support for this hypothesis.

First, the percentage of women who have changed their labor market status at least once during the periods under consideration has generally increased (upper panel). This shows up more clearly when we consider the five-year observation window, where one can observe that labor market status changes have more than doubled when one moves from the oldest to the youngest cohort, rising from 24.1 to 50.7 percent. Does this growth exhibit the monotonic positive trend posited by the globalization theorists? Not if we examine only the point estimates. Rather, the data support our hypothesis of a fluctuating trend that indicates greater fragmentation only among the youngest birth cohorts. If, on the other hand, we take proper account of the uncertainty that surrounds our point estimates – as represented by the 95 percent confidence intervals – we could conclude that the trend is compatible with the monotonicity assumption. In any case, there is no doubt that women belonging to the youngest cohorts have changed their labor market status more frequently than have their mothers and grandmothers.

The same conclusion can be reached by analyzing how the mean number of labor market status changes varied over time (lower panel): this quantity

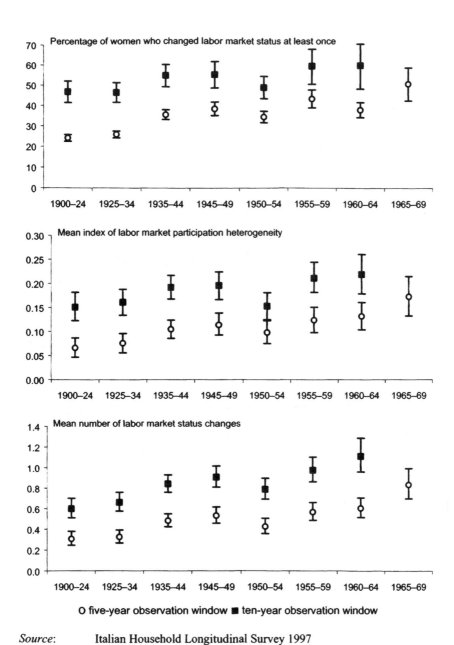

Source: Italian Household Longitudinal Survey 1997

Figure 14.1   *Percentage of Italian women who changed labor market status, mean index of labor market participation heterogeneity and mean number of changes by birth cohort and observation window: point estimates and 95 percent confidence intervals*

increased from 0.30 to 0.83 when we consider the five-year observation window, and from 0.60 to 1.11 when we consider the ten-year observation window. Once again, the available evidence suggests that the positive trends observed are compatible with the monotonicity assumption and therefore lends some support to the globalization thesis. However, it should be noted that the values under consideration are very low in all the cohorts observed, as we expected. This indicates that although mid-career women's labor market participation is significantly more fragmented than in the past, its mean level of fragmentation is still very low and is probably too low to be taken as a substantially significant effect of globalization.

The center panel of Figure 14.1 bears out this conclusion: when measured by the relative heterogeneity index,[14] the pattern exhibits a similarly positive trend, but again at very low levels.

One of the main sources of fragmentation is job mobility, which is the chance of changing jobs during one's working life. The globalization thesis expects to see a strong and monotonic increase in job mobility in every direction – upward, downward and lateral. The data depicted in Figure 14.2 seem to confirm this expectation for mid-career Italian women. First, the percentage of women who have experienced job mobility at least once during the periods under consideration has generally increased (upper panel). If we examine the five-year observation window, for instance, we can see that the proportion of women who have changed their job at least once during the five years in question has risen from 14.6 to 39.5 percent. The observed positive trends are compatible with the monotonicity assumption in both observation windows and therefore support the globalization thesis. However – as in the case of the mean number of labor market status changes just discussed – it should be noted that, though it has increased over time, the overall rate of job mobility appears quite low in all the cohorts under examination. Even in the youngest cohort, about 60 percent of all women working for pay have never changed their job during the observation period. This evidence weakens the globalization thesis and confirms that in Italy, job mobility is still a minority experience, as we suggested.

If we break down total job mobility into its components – downward, upward and lateral – our data exhibit mixed trends. Downward mobility (Figure 14.2, middle panel) has generally increased over time, but not monotonically: it has first grown, than slightly decreased and finally increased once again. On the other hand, the upward mobility rate (lower panel) shows a clear, monotonic positive trend (from 6.2 to 21.1 percent), especially when the five-year observation window is considered. Finally, the lateral mobility rate (see Pisati and Schizzerotto 2003) exhibits wide fluctuations around a generally positive trend.

Closely related to the concept of fragmentation is that of insecurity. The globalization thesis hypothesizes that labor market participation is becoming more insecure than in the past. In practice, this means that unemployment and

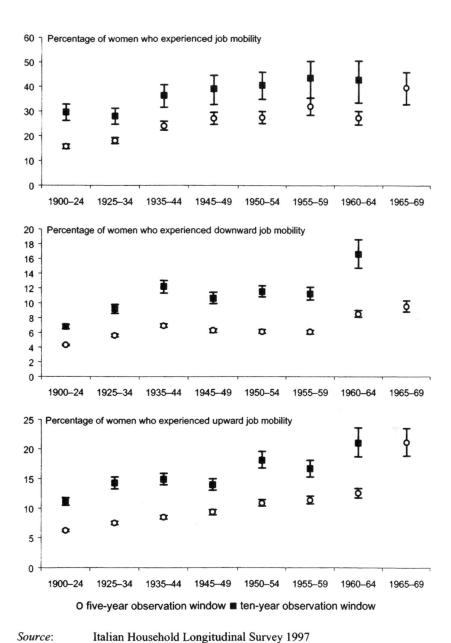

O five-year observation window ■ ten-year observation window

Source: Italian Household Longitudinal Survey 1997

*Figure 14.2   Percentage of Italian women who experienced job mobility,
downward job mobility and upward job mobility, by birth cohort and
observation window: point estimates and 95 percent confidence
intervals*

non-standard employment relationships (that is, informal and temporary employment) should be experienced by a growing number of people. As far as mid-career Italian women are concerned, the available evidence – summarized by the data reported in Figure 14.3 – gives mixed support for this hypothesis. The probability of experiencing unemployment (upper panel) did increase over time, but not following a monotonic trend. Therefore it is not entirely clear whether the globalization process should be taken to be mainly responsible for this trend.

Turning to informal employment, Figure 14.3 (center panel) shows that – contrary to expectations of globalization thesis – the percentage of women who have experienced this form of insecure employment has almost constantly declined from the 1900 to 1924 to the 1945 to 1949 cohort. However, from the 1945 to 1949 to the 1960 to 1964 cohort the proportion of women in informal employment remained rather stable. Moreover, in the youngest cohort (1965 to 1969) an upward shift has taken place whose origin may well be ascribed to the globalization process.

On the other hand, the probability of experiencing some kind of temporary employment (Figure 14.3, lower panel) has monotonically increased from the 1900 to 1924 to the 1960 to 1964 cohort onwards, thus confirming both the globalization thesis and our hypothesis. We would maintain this statement, despite the drop of almost five percentage points of the probability (from 19.6 to 14.3 percent) of experiencing temporary jobs recorded by women belonging to the 1965 to 1969 cohort. In our opinion this result does not represent a real reversing of the positive trend observed among older cohorts. Rather it should be interpreted as a temporary, and possibly casual, break in what is otherwise a quite consistently rising likelihood of falling into unstable, tough legal employment relations. Recent changes in the regulation of the Italian labor market, described in the first section, provide a rather sound basis for this expectation.

What conclusions can be drawn from this temporal analysis of the indicators of insecurity? Overall, the available evidence does offer some support for the globalization thesis. However, once again we must emphasize that although experiences of unemployment and temporary employment are generally more frequent, they still involve a relatively low number of women, so they are far from being a widespread feature of the female labor force. The same picture emerges when we analyze trends in the mean proportions of labor market time spent by mid-career women in the various labor market statuses. The largest amount of time (over 70 percent) is spent in self-employment or in standard (permanent) dependent jobs even in the youngest cohorts (Pisati and Schizzerotto 2003). This suggests that if globalization is at work in Italy, its effects on mid-career women's labor market participation are still not fully visible.

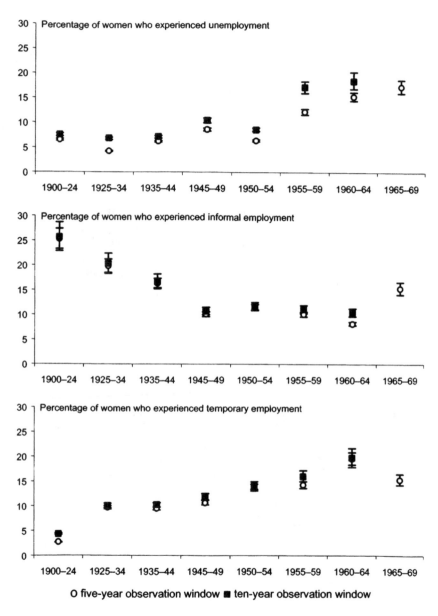

O five-year observation window ■ ten-year observation window

Source: Italian Household Longitudinal Survey 1997

Figure 14.3 *Percentage of Italian women who experienced unemployment, informal employment and temporary employment, by birth cohort and observation window: point estimates and 95 percentage confidence intervals*

The effects of family status

The globalization thesis further suggests that the effects exerted by family status on women's labor market participation have changed over time. Specifically, women's patterns of labor market participation should have grown ever less dependent on marriage, pregnancy and children. We contrasted this hypothesis with an alternative one, to the effect that the independence from family status holds only in the case of marriage influences on risks of unemployment and inactivity.

To test both hypotheses with regard to Italian mid-career women, we carried out two sets of analyses. First, we estimated changes over time in the effects exerted by four family-related variables (being married, being pregnant, having one or more children under age six and having one or more children ages six to 14) on the probability of being unemployed, having an informal job, having a temporary job and being inactive (out of the labor market) during the five-year observation window. Second, we estimated changes over time in the effects exerted by the same four family-related variables on the probability of experiencing downward, upward and lateral job mobility during the five-year observation window.[15]

To carry out the first set of analyses, we proceeded as follows. First, we created a person-month data set, that is, a data set in which each woman subject to analysis is represented by 60 records, one for each month in the five-year observation window. Next, we divided women into four birth cohorts: 1900 to 1934, 1935 to 1949, 1950 to 1959 and 1960 to 1969. Finally, for each birth cohort taken separately and for each of the four dependent variables of interest, we estimated a binomial logistic regression model with cluster-corrected standard errors. In each estimated model, the probability of interest was expressed as a function of the four family-related variables and a set of seven control variables: mother worked for pay, social class of origin, area of residence, level of education, age, age squared and period. For the purposes of our analysis, the quantities of interest are the point estimates – and the corresponding 95 percent confidence intervals – of the regression coefficients associated with the four family-related variables.

We proceeded in a similar fashion to carry out the second set of analyses. First, we divided women into four birth cohorts. Second, for each birth cohort taken separately and for each of the three kinds of job mobility of interest (upward, lateral and downward mobility), we estimated a discrete-time exponential regression model with cluster-corrected standard errors. In each estimated model, the probability of interest was expressed as a function of the four family-related variables and the set of seven control variables. Once again, for the purposes of our analysis, the quantities of interest are the point estimates and the corresponding 95 percent confidence intervals of the regression coefficients associated with the four family-related variables.

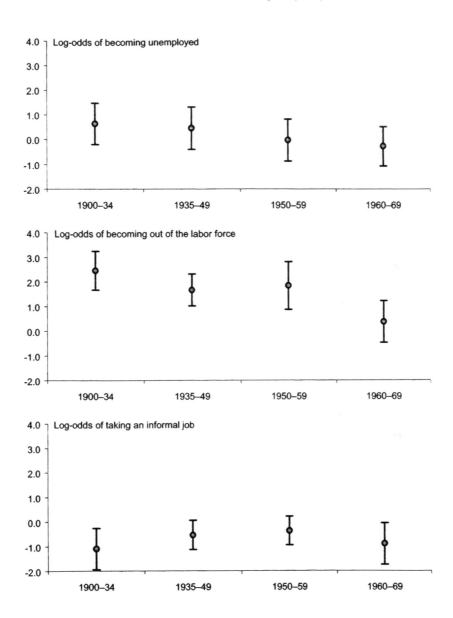

Source: Italian Household Longitudinal Survey 1997

Figure 14.4 *Marriage effects on the log-odds of transitions to unemployment, exiting the labor force, and taking an informal job during the five-year observation window in Italy, by birth cohort: point estimates and 95 percent confidence intervals*

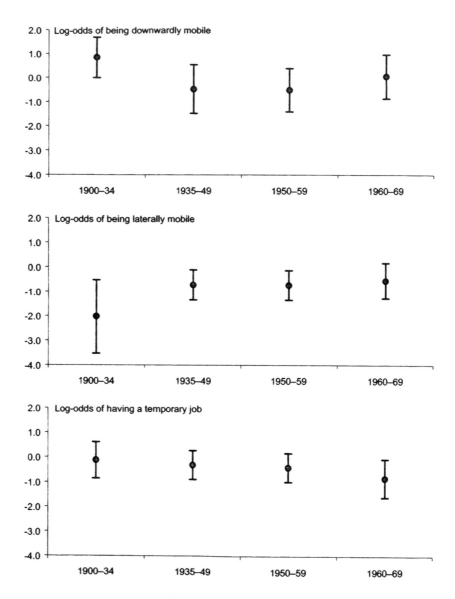

Source: Italian Household Longitudinal Survey 1997

Figure 14.5   *Marriage effects on the log-odds of Italian women moving downward or laterally or having a temporary job during the five-year observation window in Italy, by birth cohort: point estimates and 95 percent confidence intervals*

The available data do not allow us to draw firm conclusions about cohort differences in the effects of pregnancy and young children on women's labor market transitions. In fact, changes over time in the effects exerted by family status on mid-career women's labor market participation do not appear to follow any clear-cut trend, also owing to the fact that in most cases the uncertainty that surrounds the point estimates of regression coefficients – as represented by the 95 percent confidence intervals – is very large.[16] For some of the dependent variables analyzed (especially the three kinds of job mobility), the effect of having children does show some signs of decline, but the available evidence is too scattered to draw any reliable conclusions (Pisati and Schizzerotto 2003).

However, some patterns can be discerned regarding the effect of marriage, as shown in Figures 14.4 and 14.5. First, as posited by the globalization thesis and our hypotheses, the effect of being married shows a clear tendency to fade away across successive cohorts to predict being out of the labor force and unemployment (Figure 14.4). Specifically, the effect of this variable on the log-odds of being out of the labor force has decreased from 2.46 (earliest birth cohort) to 0.38 (latest birth cohort), a neat 85 percent drop in relative terms; likewise, its influence on the log-odds of being unemployed has weakened from 0.87 (oldest cohort) to around zero (youngest cohort). Yet, contrary to our hypotheses, but in accordance with the globalization thesis, the effects of being married on the log-odds of being downwardly and laterally mobile have also declined, respectively from 0.83 to 0.05 and from −2.03 to −0.56 (Figure 14.5). The only piece of counter-evidence in this picture, which turns out to be generally consistent with the globalization thesis, is the (negative) effect of being married on the log-odds of having a temporary job, which has increased over time from 0.12 to −0.87 (Figure 14.5).

DISCUSSION AND CONCLUSIONS

As we have repeatedly stressed, our analyses of Italian mid-career women neither falsify nor confirm the globalization thesis. To be more precise, we should say that our results fully support some of its hypotheses, provide extremely weak corroboration – if any – to others, and openly contradict still others.

The following specific predictions are clearly confirmed by the Italian data: (a) the monotonic increase of upward job mobility rates; (b) the monotonic increase in the proportions of women who have experienced temporary employment relations; (c) the monotonic reduction in the effect of being married on the chances of being unemployed, inactive, downwardly and laterally mobile. The following hypotheses have received far less convincing confirmation: (i) the fluctuating trend towards greater fragmentation in labor market participation; (ii) the rather low number of labor market status changes, even among the youngest birth cohorts; (iii) the nonmonotonic trend towards larger percentages of mid-career women who experience unemployment; and (iv) the rises and falls recorded by both downward and lateral job mobility rates. The results that apparently contradict the globalization thesis can be summarized as follows: (1) the quite monotonic decrease of the proportion of mid-career women entering informal jobs; (2) the increasing effects across birth cohorts of marriage on the risks of having a temporary job; and (3) the fluctuating over time effects of pregnancy and motherhood on patterns of labor market participation and job mobility chances.

In our initial assertions, we tried to anticipate possible explanations for the failure of certain predictions of the globalization thesis. Explanations include cultural patterns regarding the domestic division of labor between genders, the social role of the family, as well as the workings of the welfare regime and the regulation of labor market, all of which changed little and rather slowly during the twentieth century. As a consequence, they were quite effective in smoothing, or even impeding, possible effects deriving from economic changes.

However, there is one aspect of the transformations undergone by the pattern of labor market participation of Italian mid-career women that indeed matches the expectations of the globalization thesis: the fact that members of the youngest birth cohorts are currently suffering the highest overall degree of job instability ever recorded by working women in the twentieth century. Put another way, Italian mid-career women born since the late 1950s are the first generation of twentieth-century Italian women unable to improve their occupational perspectives, as compared with those enjoyed by their mothers.

It is debatable whether this very general result can be taken as convincing proof that Italian mid-career women are indeed experiencing the effects – though attenuated – of a genuine process of globalization or, more simply, the consequences of interactions between long-lasting modernization processes, negative economic circumstances and rather unbalanced (from an intergenerational perspective) attempts to reform labor market regulations.

NOTES

1   Obviously, the class structure has changed over time, particularly with respect to the size of individual classes, though their net effect on people's life chances have remained substantially the same (Schizzerotto 2002).

2   Individual dismissals are allowed only in cases of specific violations of laws and contracts and ascertained by a judge.

3   To be more precise, work-training contracts were introduced for the first time in 1977. Unfortunately, their regulation was so strict that almost no firm hired labor on that basis.

4   Despite the change mentioned in the text, interventions in favor of insider workers have not ceased. For instance, in 1991 a law regulating collective dismissals introduced a measure – called the 'mobility list' – which provides workers laid off by large and medium-sized firms with high unemployment benefits and re-employment facilities.

5   In an attempt to reduce the constraints impeding the operation of the 'Treu Law,' the Italian government issued a new set of rules known as the 'Biagi Law' in 2003. However, because the data we will analyze were collected in 1997, we do not describe it here.

6   In 1984, the Italian university system created PhD courses and introduced an intermediate university degree. In 2001, the organization of the university system moved closer to that of the UK and USA, and in 2003 a law was enacted that was intended to completely reform the Italian school system.

7   See note 5.

8   During the 1980s, some Italian regional administrations issued local regulations intended to offer universalistic income support for poor regional residents, which means that the minimum income level varies from region to region.

9   The rules on additional paid maternity leave were reformed and extended to fathers in 2000.

10 We expect to find relatively limited risks of unemployment among mid-career women born between the 1900s and 1960s, because of: (a) the large proportion of agricultural family workers in the oldest cohorts; (b) the good employment opportunities enjoyed by those in the labor market during the economic boom; and (c) the subsequent strong protection of the jobs of employed women.

11 Given the small number of respondents with part-time jobs, no attempt has been made to split dependent jobs into full-time and part-time jobs.

12 Unemployment is defined as the condition of being (a) without a job and (b) actively looking for one.

13 Inactivity is defined as the condition of being out of the labor force, that is, neither employed nor unemployed.

14 As used here, the *relative heterogeneity index* – also known as the *qualitative variation index* (Bohrnstedt and Knoke 1994) – expresses the propensity of women to spend the same time in all the six possible labor market statuses. The index takes values between 0 – corresponding to the case when a woman spends all the observed time in a single labor market status – and 1 – corresponding to the case when a woman spends exactly one-sixth of the observed time in each of the six possible labor market statuses.

15 For the sake of brevity, we have chosen to restrict our attention to the five-year observation window because this enabled us to include women belonging to the youngest cohorts in the analyses.

16 This high level of uncertainty mainly stems from the fact that the status/events that make up the dependent variables (unemployment, informal employment, temporary employment, inactivity and the various types of job mobility) are relatively infrequent and therefore do not offer enough 'examples' to estimate the effects of interest with sufficient precision. For example, out of 139 620 person-months analyzed, only 11 666 (8.4 percent) concern temporary job episodes, and even fewer – 5625 (4 percent) – are unemployment episodes.

BIBLIOGRAPHY

Barbagli, M. (1974) *Disoccupazione intellettuale e sistema scolastico in Italia*, Bologna: Il Mulino.

Bernardi, F., Layte, R., Schizzerotto, A. and Jacobs, S. (2000) 'Who exits unemployment? Institutional features, individual characteristics and chances of getting a job', in D. Gallie and S. Paugam (eds) *Welfare regimes and the experience of unemployment in Europe*, Oxford: Oxford University Press, pp. 218–39.

Bohrnstedt, G.W. and Knoke, D. (1994) *Statistics for social data analysis*, Itasca: F.E. Peacock.

Cobalti, A. and Schizzerotto, A. (1993) 'Inequality of educational opportunities in Italy', in Y. Shavit and H.-P. Blossfeld (eds) *Persistent inequality: changing educational stratification in thirteen countries*, Boulder, CO: Westview Press, pp. 155–76.

Cobalti, A. and Schizzerotto, A. (1994) *La mobilità sociale in Italia*, Bologna: Il Mulino.

de Lillo, A. and Schizzerotto, A. (1985) *La valutazione sociale delle occupazioni. Una scala di stratificazione occupazionale per l'Italia contemporanea*, Bologna: Il Mulino.

Gualmini, E. (1998) *La politica del lavoro*, Bologna: Il Mulino.

Mills, M. and Blossfeld, H.P. (2005) 'Globalization, uncertainty, and the early life course: a theoretical framework', in H.-P. Blossfeld, E. Klijzing, M. Mills and K. Kurz (eds) *Globalization, uncertainty, and youth in society*, London: Routledge.

Negri, N. and Saraceno, C. (1996) *Le politiche contro la povertà in Italia*, Bologna: Il Mulino.

Pinnelli, A. and De Rose, A. (1995) 'Italy', in H.-P. Blossfeld (ed.) *The new role of women. Family formation in western societies*, Boulder, CO: Westview Press, pp. 174–90.

Pisati, M. (2002) 'La partecipazione al sistema scolastico', in A. Schizzerotto (ed.) *Vite ineguali. Disuguaglianze e corsi di vita nell'Italia contemporanea*, Bologna: Il Mulino, pp. 141–86.

Pisati, M. and Schizzerotto, A. (1999) 'Pochi promossi, nessun bocciato. La mobilità di carriera in Italia in prospettiva comparata e longitudinale', *Stato e Mercato*, 56: 249–79.

Pisati, M. and Schizzerotto, A. (2003) 'Mid-career women in contemporary Italy', Globalife Working Paper No. 57, Chair of Sociology I, University of Bamberg, Germany.

Reyneri, E. (1996) *Sociologia del mercato del lavoro*, Bologna: Il Mulino.

Samek Lodovici, M. (1997) *Labour market regulation and unemployment in Italy*, Milano: Istituto per la Ricerca Sociale.

Saraceno, C. (1998) *Mutamenti della famiglia e politiche sociali in Italia*, Bologna: Il Mulino.

Saraceno, C. and Naldini, M. (2001) *Sociologia della famiglia*, Bologna: Il Mulino.

Schizzerotto, A. (1989) 'Dinamiche temporali e territoriali della scuola materna italiana', *Polis*, 3: 533–56.

Schizzerotto, A. (ed.) (2002) *Vite ineguali. Disuguaglianze e corsi di vita nell'Italia contemporanea*, Bologna: Il Mulino.
Schizzerotto, A. and Cobalti, A., (1998) 'Occupational returns to occupation in contemporary Italy', in Y. Shavit and W. Müller (eds) *From school to work. A comparative study of educational qualifications and occupational destinations*, Oxford: Clarendon Press, pp. 253–86.

15.   Hard choices: can Spanish women reconcile job and family?

Carles Simó Noguera

INTRODUCTION

Those countries previously closed off from global influences, including Spain, have become involved in a process of interdependence and integration into the global economy that affects not only their domestic institutions but also how those institutions are regulated. This chapter investigates the specific transformations of mid-career women's life courses in Spain brought about by globalization processes. Compared with men, Spanish women are strongly overrepresented in domestic tasks and play a unique role within the family as the main, if not the only, providers of care. As a consequence, since women's job opportunities and expectations are particularly affected by family formation processes, as well as by educational skills and previous job experience, I will assess the relationship between family formation and employment career pathways.

Spain's economic autarky began to erode before the end of the Franco dictatorship in 1975, and its economy became more exposed to international competition by the time the country joined the European Community a decade later. Today, governments actively work to make the Spanish economy more internationally competitive, in particular by removing state controls over the economy and by privatizing public companies. In this liberalization process, certain previously protected sectors are exposed to competition. The process of democratization and setting up a modern welfare system was accompanied by intense external transactions and contact that profoundly affected and transformed politics, society and culture, leading to difficult internal adjustments in government, production, labor and education. Government intervention in the labor market dealing with the diminution of labor costs, the protection of jobs, unemployment insurance and other changes led to sharp increases in unemployment. The highly segmented, male-oriented Spanish labor market thus experienced labor shifts and high rates of temporary work, deeply eroding the former sources of stability and security in jobs and careers. As Mills and Blossfeld (2005) state, the intensification of competition at the international level transforms work and leads to particular consequences for employment stability and job security (see also Heery and Salmon 2000; Ladipo and Wilkinson 2002).

Comparatively speaking, the Spanish labor market has very high levels of temporary employment and worker marginalization, a consequence of introducing so-called flexibility at the margin (Toharia and Malo 2000). Various regulations resulted in new sources of labor market segmentation, and those that particularly affect women will be reviewed here, mostly those that make it more difficult for them to find permanent, stable jobs. The centrality of women in the provision of care coupled with the weakness of the welfare system complicates women's employment.

Catholic doctrine and social mores had assigned Spanish women to household roles, so they had long been excluded from the paid labor market (Hakim 2003; Morcillo 1999; Simó, Castro Martín and Soro-Bonmatí 2005). But with the economic transformations, women have been increasing their labor market participation. Thus in Spain, increasing global competition, growing female labor force participation and educational expansion structurally transform and profoundly challenge both labor market and industrial relations as well as the traditional role of the family as provider of support and care. The male-breadwinner model is still important, but recent societal transformations have challenged Spanish women in their traditional roles in the dominant family model more. Other structural transformations have affected various industrial sectors, and that has molded the way in which women have been integrated into the Spanish labor market.

THE MAIN TRANSFORMATIONS OF THE LABOR FORCE

The new role of women

The restructuring of the Spanish economy during the 1970s and 1980s coincided with a substantial growth in the economically active population owing to the entry of larger birth cohorts and the increase in women's labor force participation, because of the remarkable expansion of women's education, mainly in tertiary education, as well as their rising aspirations to have a working career (Garrido and Requena 1996).

Education has been a major mechanism for modernization, secularization and social change in Spain since 1975, and the opportunities provided to all, and to women in particular, were designed to produce a more open, meritocratic society with increased social mobility (Hakim 2003). Compared with earlier generations, the 1950 to 1965 birth cohorts have much higher school-leaving ages, thereby reducing the earlier gender gap in education, and women have experienced a particularly rapid rise in enrollment and educational attainment figures (Baizán 2000). In fact, women's increasing participation in higher education coincides with men's stagnation in tertiary educational levels. Rising enrollment at Spanish universities during the 1970s and 1980s was mainly a result of feminization (Carabaña 2003).

Yet the strongly male-oriented Spanish labor market, in which women occupy a tangential, weak position, does not reflect these high female educational skill levels. Women must defy rigidly gendered structures in order to establish themselves in the labor market at all, and that is an important source of tension. The problem of over-education particularly affects the allocation in the labor force of women with tertiary education (Simó and Soro-Bonmatí 2002), and it does not seem to diminish much with age (García Serrano and Malo Ocaña 1997).

Moreover, such tensions are not only the cause of important shifts in female biographies but also the determinants of important transformations at the family level, such as postponing starting a family as a consequence of the difficulties faced by women in integrating into the labor market (Simó, Castro Martín and Soro-Bonmatí 2005). In Spain, highly educated women from young cohorts are significantly less likely to form a partnership or become mothers (Simó, Golsch and Steinhage 2002).

THE STRUCTURAL DIMENSIONS OF ECONOMIC TRANSFORMATION

These changes and tensions can be better understood with reference to the transformation of the Spanish economy along three main structural dimensions: (1) the composition of labor force and its feminization, (2) the industrial sectors and (3) market productivity and industrial relations. With respect to the first dimension, the eruption of unemployment in the later 1970s appears to have been the main factor molding the composition of the active population and it added a new dynamic to the labor market. Massive job losses (and a lack of job creation other than in the expanding service sector) meant the unemployment rates, very low in the early 1970s, went up to 8 percent in 1979 following the oil crisis, to 20 percent in 1984 after the economic restructuring of the early 1980s, and to 24 percent in 1994 following the recession in the 1990s.

However, the most important determinant of the transformation in the labor force is the increasing number of women participating (Simó and Soro-Bonmatí 2002). Although the feminization of the Spanish labor force is still far below European levels (Cousins 1994; Hakim 2003),[1] the speed of change has been remarkable, with the number of women working nearly tripling over the last 30 years.

A second structural dimension in the transformation of the Spanish economy lies in the distribution of employment across economic sectors. Severe crises in the textile and the metallurgical sectors from 1975 to 1985 brought about a deep restructuring in the manufacturing sector[2] that coincided with the dramatic decline of the agrarian sector and a steep rise in the service sector, a rise mainly owing to the creation of a modern administrative service and the explosion of tourism (Delgado and Castro Martín 1999; Tamames 1995). The proportion of service sector employment to total employment has increased by around 50 percent since 1977,[3] largely owing to women's entry: the service sector is the main source of women's employment, accounting for more than half of all employed women by 1976, and more than 80 percent by 2003. Figure 15.1 displays the increasing importance of women in the public sector and that gender parity is in sight. In the private sector, despite the rapid increase of female employment since 1986, there are currently only three women employed per five men. While the feminization of the public sector after 1986 has been very strong in absolute terms, it does not reach the levels recorded in a country such as Finland, where 90 percent of the employees in the public sector in 1990 were women (Szebehely 1998).

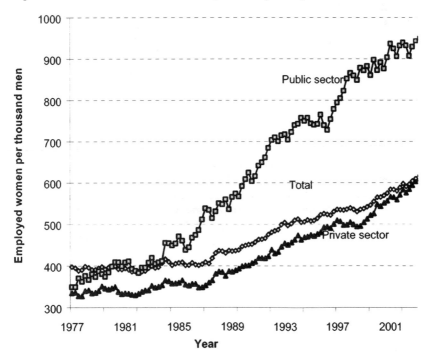

Source: Own elaboration using data from Spanish Institute for Statistics (INE), Spanish Labor Force Survey (EPA)

Figure 15.1   *The rise in the number of employed women per thousand men in the public and private sectors and in total in Spain*

Restructuring has also affected the third structural dimension, namely, how the Spanish economy is coordinated in terms of labor regulations and industrial relations. The transformations have challenged the relationship between the productive market and the labor force by increasing productivity and numerical flexibility[4] and decreasing labor costs; tensions lie with the simultaneous need to protect workers against rising instability. However, the greatest impact may have been in the reforms meant to improve the functioning of the labor market system. These fundamental, and new, regulations have deeply – and also negatively – affected first-time job seekers and labor market re-entrants. The next section focuses on how these regulations have evolved as well as the way they affect mid-life female occupational mobility.

LABOR MARKET REGULATIONS AND WOMEN'S EMPLOYMENT

In the patriarchal welfare system developed under the Franco dictatorship, the family was seen as the only institution responsible for providing individual care, support, and protection. Inspired by Catholicism, the state only put a few social services in place, since it did not see itself responsible for the provision of social welfare. In fact, the whole system of social welfare was sustained on the basis of women's unpaid family work, while the provision of 'bread' was assigned to men. This general norm accorded roles by gender and thus systematically excluded women from the labor force (Golsch 2003; Simó, Castro Martín and Soro-Bonmatí 2005).

Job security norms were inspired by this ideology as well under the Franco dictatorship. With the aim of protecting families, the government developed legal measures to shield (male) employment and restrict firing (Muñoz de Bustillo Llorente 2002), and the Spanish labor market was regulated by a system of corporatist representation and coordination (Martínez Alier and Roca Jusmet 1988). This was governed by familistic industrial relations in which working relationships were seen as long-term commitments. In sum, the labor market operated as a closed and regulated system almost exclusively for men.

The modern industrial relations enacted to substitute for the Francoist ones were mainly intended to introduce a more democratic regulation of labor and extended rights through the 1982 Workers' Statute. This is the main law defining industrial relations and labor protection, and it regulates the hiring and firing process, gives a central role to trade unions in collective bargaining and establishes an unemployment insurance system. Soon after its enactment, however, employers objected to the hiring and firing costs this statute imposed, as it hindered adopting measures to introduce functional and internal flexibility, and thus job creation.

This statute also did not foresee the integration of women into the closed and male-oriented labor market inherited from the previous regime. On the contrary: it gives priority to the male breadwinner and his stable employment. In fact, until the late 1990s when labor laws specifically designed to achieve higher rates of gender equality were passed, collective bargaining was the only means to protect the interests of female employees.

Once elected, the Socialist Party decided to launch new regulations to facilitate job creation, an important part of which was to introduce fixed-term contracts, which until then were only allowed for very specific reasons. However, this new 'flexibility at the margin' (Toharia and Malo 2000) was a new source of exclusion for women, because with these fixed-term contracts, job tenure was no longer a source of job security for new employees, though it remained intact for existing employees with permanent contracts (Golsch 2003; Simó, Golsch and Soro-Bonmatí 2002). In fact, since industrial relations were based on the premise of permanent employment, new employees were also excluded from the collective bargaining system (Segura 2001). Spanish trade unions also did not effectively protect the interests of new labor market entrants, among them women; instead their focus continued to be on the protection of permanent employees (De León 1999).

Employers quickly embraced fixed-term contracts, as they made it easier and cheaper to recruit new entrants and re-entrants (unemployed workers). Temporary employment rapidly expanded among the salaried labor force from 15 percent of men and 23 percent of women in 1987 to highs in 1997 of about 45 percent of men and 65 percent of women (see Figure 15.2), far exceeding the average in the European Union (EU) (Simó and Soro-Bonmatí 2002).

In sum, the recent segmentation of the Spanish labor market can be better understood considering both processes: building a system of democratic industrial relations and combating labor market rigidities. In the very closed[5] Spanish employment system and male-oriented labor market, such processes have exaggerated the differences between insiders and outsiders, and have hampered the entry of women and youth into the labor market (Blossfeld et al. 2005; Golsch 2003; Simó, Golsch and Steinhage 2002; Simó, Castro Martín and Soro-Bonmatí 2005). As a result, gender inequalities in the Spanish labor force remain very large compared with other European countries: female unemployment is more than double the level of male unemployment, and female employment is consistently more temporary than male employment (Hakim 2003; Laparra Navarro et al. 2002). While the share of all temporary contracts doubled from 1987 to 1991, the percentage of women holding such contracts has consistently been 5 to 10 percent higher than for men. However, gender inequalities are present not only in the labor market and industrial relations, but also in the underdevelopment of the Spanish welfare state. Patriarchal ideology constitutes a serious obstacle for women's integration in the labor market.

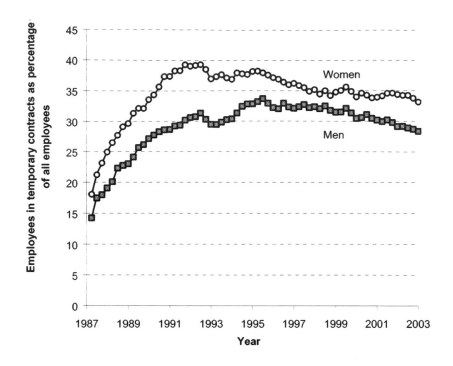

Source: Own elaboration using data from Spanish Institute for Statistics (INE),
Active Population Survey (EPA)

Figure 15.2   *Percentage of employees in temporary contracts by gender in Spain*

Weak support from the Spanish welfare state

A well-developed system of public welfare is decisive for a better initial
integration of women into the labor force and for easier re-integration after
spells of caregiving, as well as for reconciling family and work demands.
Indeed, welfare support may carry great weight for unemployed and
employed women moving in and out of the labor market by providing
security, yet the scope and generosity of welfare support varies enormously
among countries (Gauthier 1996; Sainsbury 1999).

The Spanish welfare state developed much later than in most Western
European nation-states and has not yet reached their level of development. In
2000, the amount spent on social programs as a percent of gross domestic
product was 20.1 percent for Spain compared with 27.3 percent as the EU
average: Sweden (at 32.3 percent) was the highest, while Ireland (14.1
percent) was the lowest (Muñoz de Bustillo Llorente 2002; Navarro 2003).[6]
Often termed 'family oriented' (Jurado Guerrero 1995), the Spanish welfare

state has been timidly expanding while dramatic changes in the labor market have been taking place, and considerable efforts were made to reduce the social costs of the resulting labor force adjustment (Simó, Golsch and Steinhage 2002). But still it is mainly the family and kinship networks that provide support, with a conspicuous absence of help from the welfare state compared with other countries (Esping-Andersen 1999; on Spanish family policies see Flaquer 2000). One of the main problems is the wholly inadequate provision of public nursery schools: only 8 percent of children under age three attend, in contrast to 44 percent of comparable children in Denmark, 40 percent in Sweden and 23 percent in France (Navarro and Quiroga 2003). Another problem is the minimal network of public social services supporting the elderly: daughters or daughters-in-law are their main care providers, both qualitatively and quantitatively. Only 2 percent of the elderly receive public support or publicly supported home care, as compared with 24 percent of elderly Danes and 17 percent of elderly Swedes (Navarro and Quiroga 2003; Rodríguez Cabrero 2003). As elsewhere in Europe, the Spanish population is aging, and in the absence of adequate public support, caring for elderly family members falls on the shoulders of women.

These omissions in public policy have critical consequences for women's careers, since women are still the main and almost exclusive providers of care for all members of the family; those women who want a career are confronted with the double burden of family duties and (mostly) full-time job requirements and enormous difficulties once they try to re-enter the labor market (Blossfeld 1997; Blossfeld and Drobnič 2001; Blossfeld and Hakim 1997; Cousins 1994).

Spanish women of all ages and young men are confronted with more instability in the labor market and more flexible work relations than are mid-career male workers (Simó, Golsch and Soro-Bonmatí 2002). But labor flexibility and its effects in the workplace itself (changes in timetables, positions and responsibilities) heighten the importance of the individual's job or career commitment while reducing the time available for the private sphere. Furthermore, because the individual is forced continuously to seek employment in the labor market, the uncertainty resulting from it becomes greater and greater. As a result of higher unemployment, more temporary contracts and thus greater uncertainty, young couples may see no alternative other than both of them having to work for pay. Consequently, although the male-breadwinner model is still important in Spain, with women's increasing participation in the labor market, the likelihood of dual-earner arrangements among young couples is increasing. In this sense, wives' employment can be viewed as a highly adaptive family strategy (Oppenheimer 1994).

The Spanish welfare state has not been successful in fulfilling the growing need for social policies that would make it easier for women to combine work and family, and labor market regulations have been neither designed to facilitate females' labor market integration, nor have changes in working relations proven sensitive to the new needs of the female population (Simó and Soro-Bonmatí 2002). This situation is worsened by the lack of part-time jobs, still rare in the formal labor market, including the public sector (Cousins 1994; Hakim 2003; Morán 1991).

In sum, the welfare system is maintained on the basis of the traditional male-breadwinner model, even though this no longer seems suited to the newer generations. Welfare provisions are still organized around gainful employment of male breadwinners (Esping-Andersen 1999), and while the permanent contracts are becoming more scarce, by and large permanent employees are less exposed to risks. The dominant ideology continues to see women as the main source of caregiving, despite the fact that they are increasingly integrating in the labor market; as a result, they are progressively confronted with the double burden of having to combine a labor market career and family obligations (Blossfeld and Hakim 1997). Accordingly, the lack of welfare support mainly affects women's jobs and careers. The modern Spanish welfare state, put in place with the democratization of the country, has not been successful in providing real alternatives. Women are not only confronted with an adverse atmosphere in the labor market, but are also faced with a series of needs and aspirations, which are difficult to reconcile.

HYPOTHESES

For women, the mid-life 'career' options are: (1) giving care (to husband or children) full-time; (2) being a caregiver while simultaneously working for pay; or (3) only working for pay. The choice is conditioned by education, skills, the opportunities provided by the labor market of obtaining a satisfying job, the possibilities of combining paid work with motherhood (dependent on family support, the extent of childcare facilities, the availability of part-time work), as well as by prevailing values, beliefs and social norms (Simó, Golsch and Steinhage 2002). One can formulate these considerations in terms of four hypotheses.

Women as outsiders

Until very recently, women have been seen as marginal workers or as outsiders who viewed industrial employment as a temporary adjunct to their primary roles as homemakers. In Spain, I expect to find that unmarried women have begun to approach male labor activity rates, and married women have enormously increased their labor force participation across cohorts as well (Cebrián López, Moreno Raymundo and Toharía Cortés 1997). However, despite the fact that women are increasing their investment in paid work, I expect that the Spanish labor market will continue to make their integration very difficult, both in terms of work prospects (very high levels of temporary work, high job turnover) and in hampering entry (Blossfeld et al. 2005; Simó, Golsch and Steinhage 2002; Simó and Soro-Bonmatí 2002). Such instability should be magnified when they re-enter the labor market after a caregiving period, as these women are outsiders and may well experience discrimination for having outdated skills and fewer networks (see Hofmeister, Blossfeld and Mills, this volume). Recent labor market segmentation also accentuates women's outsider position, meaning that I expect Spanish women to confront increasing job instability.

Forced choices

Women must work very hard to find a place in the Spanish labor market. On the one hand, they must compete with men within employment structures oriented to full-time male workers. On the other hand, as outsiders, they confront serious obstacles in the strongly segmented labor market. Such adverse contexts reduce the alternatives, so for mid-life women, family and paid work are hardly compatible in Spain. I expect homemakers who are completely out of the labor market to have the highest rate of births, while women still in education and female workers will have lower rates (Simó, Golsch and Steinhage 2002). Furthermore, I expect that women opting for both family and job suffer from more difficult adjustments to the labor market and higher levels of instability, while those with a strong job commitment may obtain a stable position at the expense of reducing family expectations. In sum, more and more Spanish women are being forced to choose between either having a career or being a homemaker/mother. The conditions needed for combining both have not yet crystallized (Simó, Golsch and Steinhage 2002). I expect that women opting for such both spheres will display worse career prospects than women who opt only for employment.

High exit costs

Once the investment in job or career is made, I expect that women will pay very high costs in terms of work instability and downward moves if they decide to stop for family reasons. The duration of job or career serves as a proxy for high job commitment or, conversely, as a disincentive to stopping for caregiving reasons. Thus, over time, the strong and long investments in a career exaggerate the conflict between job and family. Since women's job instability has increased mainly because of the increasing incidence of temporary work, the duration dependence of both job experience and unemployment (or caregiving) experience will be key factors for understanding security and commitment to a working career, and later career prospects. In contrast, female investment in caregiving and domestic tasks may erode job prospects. During the periods women stay out of the labor market their job opportunities diminish, so once they decide to re-enter the labor force, their job skills (and therefore opportunities) have decreased, their risk of downward moves has increased and their job opportunities are limited to low-wage and unskilled occupations. Thus, I expect a very important negative effect of both the duration of the job in the transition to caregiving and the duration of caregiving in the process of re-entering the labor market.

Human capital

Hakim (2003) asserts that human capital theory is clearly wrong to treat educational qualifications exclusively as an investment in an employment career and uses Bourdieu's arguments supporting the idea that cultural capital (specifically qualifications) can be invested in the marriage market as well as in the labor market. However, in Spain, education and occupational skills are crucial though not exclusive determinants for paid work. In order to compensate for their disadvantaged position in the labor market, I expect that women are likely to invest more than men in human capital. This higher investment is also necessary to compensate for the observed lower returns to human capital of Spanish women (San Segundo 1995). Indeed, the higher value that education has for women compared with men has already been demonstrated, at least with respect to the likelihood of finding a first job (Simó and Soro-Bonmatí 2002). Once they are in the labor market, women display an important mismatch (worse among women with tertiary education) between their educational qualifications and the occupational status of the job (Simó and Soro-Bonmatí 2002). Indeed, over-education affects women much more than men, and the mismatch does not diminish with age as fast among women as it does among men (García Serrano and Malo Ocaña 1997). In sum, in Spain, education plays a key role in female mid-life career chances, and not only in the process of entering the labor market. I expect that it is also a crucial buffer against the risk of having repeated short job spells, and it helps promote upward mobility.

DATA AND METHODS

I use the 1995 Spanish Fertility and Family Survey (FFS), a nationally representative household survey containing interviews with 4021 women (Delgado and Castro Martín 1999; Festy and Prioux 2002). While it includes complete education, job, partnership and maternity histories of individuals aged 18 to 49 at the date of the survey, it does not provide information that would allow one to infer the degree of labor security and flexibility, such as the type of working contract, industrial sector, firm size and whether employment was in the private or public sector. However, it permits one to discern different situations affecting mid-life women and to match time-dependent biographical characteristics.

These data have a serious limitation, however, as they do not distinguish between voluntary and involuntary unemployment. This problem enormously hampers the study of women's labor careers, since voluntary and involuntary unemployment may have opposite effects on the likelihood of searching for a new job.[7] However, these shortcomings are not an obstacle to investigate the hypotheses expressed above.

The survey retrospectively reconstructs the occupational career. In it, each job is defined as a period of three consecutive months or longer of paid employment, own-account work and unpaid work in family businesses or producer cooperatives. The existence of a gap between one job and the next is noted, and the main activity performed in the interval is also recorded. This allows the episodes between jobs in which women were unemployed or were students or homemakers to be identified. Finally, the current main activity also makes it possible to identify women who stopped working for pay and define their main activity as being homemakers. I include women aged 18 to 49, who have already had at least one job or are in a job, to study exit and re-entry processes. These analyses are limited to the members of the original sample who completed an interview and who have no disabilities. I use the entire women's job history and apply continuous time event history methods (Blossfeld, Blossfeld and Rohwer 2001; Hamerle and Mayer 1989). The modeling is based on the calculation of exponential rate models for five single transitions (from job to job, from job to unemployment, from job to caregiving, from unemployment to job and from caregiving to job) and for three competing risks directional moves (from job to job, job re-entry from unemployment and job re-entry from caregiving). All transitions are shown in Simó (2004); selected ones are presented in this chapter.

The Ganzeboom and Treiman prestige scale (1996) defines directional moves. Since the information on occupation is expressed in two-digit International Standard Classification of Occupations (ISCO) codes, I establish three competing destinations for all dependent processes for which it is possible to observe directional moves between occupations. A downward move is any job shift representing a step back in the prestige scale by 10 percent; a lateral move is any job shift that does not imply a change in the prestige scale or a change up to 10 percent; and upward moves are all those job shifts that represent a gain in the prestige scale bigger than 10 percent.

As explanatory covariates for social class, I use four groups of EGP (Erikson-Goldthorpe-Portocarero) occupational classes (Erikson and Gold-thorpe 1992):

1   'Services and self-employed with employees' include the EGP classes I (higher-grade professionals, administrators, and officials; managers in large industrial establishments; large proprietors), II (lower-grade

professionals, administrators, and officials; higher-grade technicians; managers in small industrial establishments; supervisors of non-manual employees) and IVa (small proprietors, artisans, with employees; or petty bourgeoisie with employees).

2   'Intermediate occupational groups' include the EGP classes IIIa (high grade routine non-manual employees), V (lower-grade technicians; supervisors of manual workers) and VI (skilled manual workers).

3   'Own account without employees' include the EGP classes IVb (small proprietors, artisans, without employees), IVc (farmers and smallholders; other self-employed workers in primary production).

4   'Precarious class' corresponds to the EGP classes IIIb (low-grade routine non-manual employees), VIIa (semi-skilled and unskilled manual workers) and VIIb (agricultural and other workers in primary production).

The models are based on a set of common covariates in order to ensure their comparability. In all dependent processes, the time control is expressed by means of covariates referring to the duration at risk. To observe the historical transformations, two main types of information are included: the labor market entry cohorts and the current calendar time. The accumulated experiences are thought of as a way of evaluating how the labor market career is affected by the duration of different biographical contexts. Individual human resources are expressed in levels of education and professional skills, while the degree of family constraints is indirectly observed by means of identifying the age of the youngest child.

DISCUSSION OF RESULTS

In the first part, I discuss the intensity of female job changes, in particular the increase of work termination. Two models outline these transitions across generations and across time; one for all labor market entry cohorts is not shown but indicates the significance of the cohort differences. The first model shown presents the cohorts that reached the labor market for the first time from 1955 to 1974, and the second model shows cohorts starting their first jobs from 1975 to 1994. Three transitions are examined: (1) job changes: the transition from job to job without a spell of unemployment in between, (2) job losses that place women in an unemployment period and (3) job terminations made mostly to provide care, referred to as job to caregiving transitions. The latter two are shown in the tables.

In the second part, the analysis evaluates directional class mobility that women experience when changing from one job to another. The goal is twofold: first, to observe the characteristics of women who have better chances on the labor market and the factors ensuring more successful job moves and, second, to point out the characteristics of women who work very short durations or who start working again after having been out of the labor market. The main interest here is to provide evidence of the difficulties Spanish women experience while trying to combine paid work and family obligations.

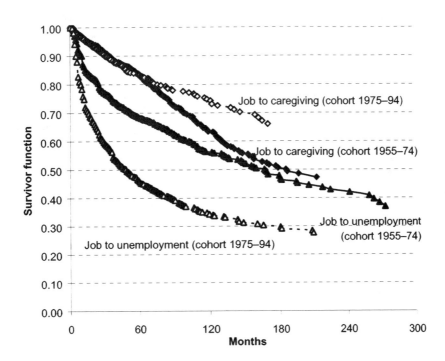

Source: 1995 Spanish Fertility and Family Survey, own elaboration

Figure 15.3   Months to transitions from job to caregiving and to unemployment by labor market cohorts, product-limit estimation

The increase of job instability

Figure 15.3 shows the survivor functions calculated for the transitions from job to job, from job to caregiving and from job to unemployment. The curves display differences between the two cohorts indicating that job-to-job changes become more frequent over time among the younger cohort, implying that women experience increasing job instability and this reinforces their outsider position. In the transition to caregiving, the velocity is the same for both cohorts in the first five years, but it decreases enormously for women belonging to the latest birth cohort. This confirms the expectations expressed in the hypothesis that women are separated into two disjunctive roles: workers or homemakers.

From job to job

As expected, the intensification of job-to-job changes corresponds to the existence of very short job durations (see Simó 2004). Although the survey does not provide information about the type of contract, there is no doubt that it is owing to the explosion of temporary contracts (refer to Figure 15.2): the negative effect of duration on further job moves becomes clearly stronger after three years of job tenure. Such effects inform us about an involuntary process characterized by instability and continuous reallocation. High rates of job changes do not seem to be the outcome of voluntary job searches made in order to improve professional conditions. These results support the forced choices hypothesis.

The high exit costs hypothesis is also supported: cumulative unemployment experience and previous job changes also predict additional job changes (table not shown). Women affected by previous unemployment, and without the protection of long job tenure contracts, are more likely to remain in outsider positions.

Educational-level effects are different between cohorts: women of the earliest birth cohorts with only a secondary education display a strong positive probability of job-to-job transitions, but education does not show any effect in the models of the latest birth cohorts. Moreover, education effects play no role once I control for professional classes. However, previous models have shown that prestige and education have important effects in reducing the rate of job change when professional classes are not controlled, meaning that though education does not provide insurance in favor of job stability, a higher-prestige job helps younger women avoid job turnover, as compared with women in the older cohort. This confirms the human capital hypothesis.

From job to unemployment

The results of the models for the transition from job to unemployment show evidence of increasing involuntary job shifts and job instability (see Table 15.1). A strongly negative period effect indicates a loss of protection for the latest birth cohort, protection that women of the earliest birth cohort (with more stable contracts) had experienced in previous times. The duration of job experience reduces the likelihood of falling into unemployment, but the accumulated duration of previous unemployment has a much stronger effect. The models for each cohort display a remarkable age effect: the likelihood of

Table 15.1 Exponential rate models of Spanish women's job to unemployment, job to caregiving transitions

Labor market entry cohorts	Job to unemployment		Job to caregiving	
	1955–74	1975–94	1955–74	1975–94
Years in the job				
Less than one year (ref.)				
From one year up to two years	−1.44***	−1.30***	−0.69***	−0.98***
From three years up to four years	−2.34***	−1.98***	−1.25***	−1.71***
Five and more years	−3.20***	−2.80***	−1.42***	−2.53***
Ages				
16 to 19 years old (ref.)				
20 to 29 years old	0.07	−0.08	0.27*	−0.03
30 to 39 years old	0.22**	−0.03	0.08	−0.12
40 to 49 years old	0.69**	−0.44	1.17**	−0.25
Job experience				
Duration of job experience	−0.00**	−0.01***	0.00	0.01
Duration of job experience (squared)	−0.00	−0.00	−0.00***	−0.00
Duration of caregiving experience				
Duration of caregiving experience	−0.01	0.00	0.02***	0.05***
Duration of caregiving experience (squared)	0.00	−0.00	−0.00***	−0.00***
Duration of unemployment experience				
Duration of unemployment experience	0.02***	0.03***	−0.03***	−0.08***
Duration of unemployment experience (squared)	−0.01***	−0.02***	0.01	0.05***
Classes (EGP-class scheme)				
Services and self-employed with employees (I & II & IVa)	−0.23	0.11	−0.48	−0.71***
Intermediate (IIIa & V& VI)	0.03	0.12*	−0.22*	−0.51***
Own-account (IVb & IVc)	−0.23	−0.05	0.09	−0.27
Precarious (IIIb, VIIa & VIIb) (ref.)				
Age of the youngest child				
Youngest child is three years old or older, or no child (ref.)				
Youngest child is younger than three	−0.06	−0.00	0.03	0.24
Constant	−2.64***	−2.60***	−4.06***	−4.33***
Number of events	576	1279	345	285
Number of episodes	1821	3237	1843	3292
Log likelihood (starting values)	−3648.38	−7122.72	−2363.85	−2017.60
Log likelihood (final estimates)	−2945.29	−5666.03	−2151.61	−1769.76

Note: Significance levels * p ≥ 0.9, ** p ≥ 0.95, *** p ≥ 0.99

Source: Spanish Fertility and Family Survey (FFS), women ages 18 to 49 who have already had at least one job or are in a job to study exit and re-entry processes

becoming unemployed increased strongly with age in the earliest birth cohort, yet age does not play any role in the latest birth cohort. This is evidence that unemployment is much more widespread in the latest birth cohort, and again confirms the outsider hypothesis. The high exit cost hypothesis is also demonstrated by the increasing impact of accumulated unemployment experience in the transition to unemployment, which becomes stronger for the latest birth cohort, while the effect of previous job experience seems to help this cohort more intensively.

From job to caregiving

In the transition from job to caregiving one can also see the negative effect of job duration (Table 15.1), which plays a much stronger role in the latest birth cohort (strong support for the exit cost hypothesis). In fact, the decrease of the rate after the first two years on the job is much more pronounced for women belonging to the later birth cohort. This is evidence that not only the investment in job career but also the difficulties women experience in combining job and domestic tasks makes the transition to caregiving less and less likely (forced choices hypothesis). This goes hand in hand with studies of parenthood in Spain indicating an increasing postponement of childbearing and a lowered overall birthrate (Simó, Golsch and Steinhage 2002).

The increasing coefficients found for the age covariates seem to illustrate that women in mid-career prefer to stop working for caregiving reasons once they have settled in the labor market. However, this only applies to the older cohort, though the coefficient is exaggerated as a consequence of our pooling selection process. Moreover, the accumulated duration of caregiving experiences displays a strong positive effect (high exit costs hypothesis), underscoring the difficulties for Spanish women of trying to combine job and family (forced choices hypothesis).

This selection process becomes more pronounced over time, as can be seen with the stronger positive coefficient for the later birth cohort than for the earlier birth cohort, and the effect of social class goes in the same direction. The higher the EGP-class, the less likely it is that women stop working in order to provide caregiving. In fact, women in precarious job positions are the most likely to become caregivers. Finally, the effect of period covariates is also relevant: as temporary work expanded after 1984, the likelihood of becoming a caregiver decreased. By contrast, women who entered the labor market before 1975 have a higher likelihood of stopping work in order to become caregivers than their younger compatriots (model not shown).

From unemployment to job, from caregiving to job

The chances of moving into employment from unemployment decline the longer the time in unemployment (not shown). Age also has a stronger effect when we control for the years in unemployment; the difficulties in finding a job are much greater for women after their forties, supporting the high exit costs hypothesis. Movement from caregiving to job is also conditioned on the duration in caregiving, making it less likely to move back into employment when one has spent a longer duration in caregiving. But even considering duration in caregiving, Spanish women have a lower likelihood of job re-entry from caregiving when they are over 40.

Directional job shifts: the worsening of women's labor prospects

We now turn to the observation of the professional prospects and the possibilities women have of establishing a good job career during their middle years. This is possible with statistical models that test the likelihood of transitions from job to job among three competing destinations: upward, lateral or downward moves. These job shifts can be related to voluntary steps to find a better job position, or may be necessary after the termination of very short job experiences that do not entitle women to employment benefits. Very short job experiences keep women permanently in search of the next job (Table 15.2).

Direct transitions from job to job

The duration at risk (time in the job position) constitutes an important determinant in explaining not only the rate of change – as we have seen before – but also the directional quality of the move. All moves are more likely after a shorter job duration compared with longer tenure, but the likelihood of downward moves in particular is highest early in a job and diminishes enormously from the third year in the job onwards.[8]

Concerning the effect of education, the general model displays only a significant coefficient for the secondary level, which seems to be a promoter of downward moves. This coincides with the evidence of the devaluation of the secondary educational skills and the 'ceiling effect', which says that women with higher educational degrees have less distance to go up.

The duration of accumulated caregiving experience and unemployment experience show positive but not statistically significant effects on downward mobility. Additionally, as we have seen before, the existence of previous job changes increases enormously the rate of job-to-job shifts, compared with female workers who never had a previous job change. However, this increasing effect is much stronger for downward moves, supporting the idea of the high costs that job shifts have for the career prospects of women. This is the result of the worsening of women's labor market prospects: the existence of previous job changes multiplies the chances of making job shifts, and this is much more a promoter of downward moves than lateral or upward ones.

Table 15.2 Competing risk exponential rate models of transitions for upward, lateral and downward job mobility of Spanish women

	All cohorts		
	Upward	*Lateral*	*Downward*
Duration at risk			
Less than one year (ref.)			
From one up to two years	−0.39	−0.63***	−1.20***
From three up to four years	−1.05***	−1.48***	−2.00***
Five and more years	−1.63***	−2.79***	−3.43***
Age	−0.00	−0.01**	−0.01
Age squared	−0.00	0.00*	0.00
Labor market entry cohort			
1955–74	0.22	0.41*	0.45
1975–94 (ref.)			
Educational level			
Compulsary education or no educational diploma (ref.)			
Secondary school, vocational training and not classified education	0.03	0.17	0.33*
Tertiary education	0.59	−0.10	0.48
Duration of job experience			
Duration of job experience	−0.00	−0.01*	−0.01
Duration of job experience (squared)	−0.00	−0.00	−0.00
Number of jobs	−0.03	−0.01	−0.03
Duration of caregiving experience			
Duration of caregiving experience	−0.00	0.00	0.02
Duration of caregiving experience (squared)	0.00	−0.00	−0.00
Duration of unemployment experience			
Duration of unemployment experience	0.04	0.01	0.02
Duration of unemployment experience (squared)	−0.07	−0.02	−0.01
Previous job changes			
There exist previous changes	1.69***	2.23***	2.92***
No previous changes (ref.)			
Prestige			
Prestige in job	−0.00	0.04***	0.01
Classes (EGP)			
Services and self-employed with employees (I & II & IVa)	−0.58	−0.79***	0.37
Intermediate groups (IIIa, V & VI)	−0.47**	−0.06	−0.11
Own-account (IVb & IVc)	−1.53	−0.84*	0.96***
Precarious (IIIb, VIIa & VIIb) (ref.)			

Table 15.2 continued

Age of the youngest child			
Youngest child is three years or older, or no child (ref.)			
Youngest child is less than three years old	−0.31	0.03	−0.19
Historical period when starting being at risk			
Before 1975 (ref.)			
1975–79	0.23	−0.03	−0.02
1980–84	0.72	0.02	0.13
1985–89	0.56	−0.03	−0.19
1990–94	0.30	−0.34	−0.06
Constant	−5.38***	−4.12***	−4.64***
Number of events	143	360	178
Number of episodes	5135	5135	5135
Log likelihood (starting values)		−5379.02	
Log likelihood (final estimates)		−4352.31	

Note: Significance levels   * ≥ 0.9,   ** ≥ 0.95,   *** ≥ 0.99

Source: Spanish Fertility and Family Survey (FFS), women ages 18 to 49 who have already had at least one job or are in a job to study exit and re-entry processes

Job re-entry from unemployment

I calculated two exponential rate models for job re-entry from unemployment transitions focusing on directional moves (models not shown, see Simó 2004). Upward moves are not related to very short episodes of unemployment, but downward moves are. Education displays no effect in women's upward or lateral moves at job re-entry from unemployment but it has a strong effect on downward moves. Women with secondary and tertiary level education are better able to avoid downward moves (human capital hypothesis). The likelihood of job re-entry from unemployment is lower for women with more previous unemployment experience. The likelihood of upward moves diminishes quickly for women in unemployment, proving that well-qualified women or those with skills in demand have an easier time finding new employment, after which there is a cumulation of disadvantage for the unemployed (costly job stops or past dependence hypothesis). In addition, women in high services and self-employed with employees have higher rates of upward moves after unemployment compared with the other EGP-class covariates, and a much lower rate of downward moves. Intermediate classes also prove to be important in avoiding downward moves. This confirms the expectations expressed in the human capital hypothesis.

Job re-entry from caregiving

Table 15.3 presents a model of three competing directional moves from job to job after a caregiving episode. The most important finding here is that the duration in caregiving has an inverse effect on the likelihood of returning to employment at all, and that women returning within one year have the best chances for lateral or upward moves. The likelihood of upward moves after caregiving is higher for women belonging to the latest labor market entry cohort compared with the earliest one, providing some evidence of an improvement in job prospects after caregiving over time.

Higher education protects women who re-enter the labor market after an episode of caregiving from downward moves to a degree. And the effects of previous professional class are explained by the 'ceiling effect' (the higher the class the stronger the likelihood of experiencing downward moves because movement up is no longer possible).

CONCLUSIONS

Recent labor market segmentation has accentuated Spanish women's outsider position, wherein women and youth are increasingly exposed to job instability. In Spain, women opting for a job career must invest much time and human capital compared with men and have extreme difficulty to combine job career and family. Women are being forced to choose between these two domains, which appear continually irreconcilable owing to scarce support from the welfare state and the male-oriented working relations. All this highlights the malfunctioning of the labor market, trade unions, working relations system, and welfare state, which, until very recently, have not seen the necessity of preparing the field for women's integration into the labor force. Higher education protects women from some labor market disadvantage, but disadvantage in terms of long periods of unemployment or unpaid caregiving as well as educational and occupational class show negative cumulative effects.

Table 15.3 Exponential rate models for job re-entry from caregiving for Spanish women

	Upward	Lateral	Downward
Years giving care at home			
Less than one year (ref.)			
From one year up to two years	−0.65**	−1.50***	−0.53
From three years up to four years	−0.96**	−2.14***	−1.34***
Five and more years	−1.59***	−2.79***	−2.10***
Duration of caregiving experience	−0.01***	−0.01***	−0.01***
Ages			
16 to 19 years old (ref.)			
20 to 29 years old	−0.24	0.23	−0.16
30 to 39 years old	0.07	−0.28	−0.07
40 to 49 years old	0.30	−0.53	−11.29
Labor market entry cohort			
1955–74	−0.56*	0.39*	−0.50
1975–94 (ref.)			
Educational level			
Compulsary education or no diploma (ref.)			
Secondary school, vocational training and not classified education	−0.04	−0.00	−0.04
Tertiary education	0.22	0.01	−0.97*
Previous professional class (EGP-class scheme)			
Services & self-employed with employees (I, II, IVa)	−0.68	−0.36	1.57***
Intermediate (IIIa & V& VI)	−0.11	−0.50**	0.90***
Own-account (IVb & IVc)	0.37	−0.29	0.84
Precarious (IIIb, VIIa & VIIb) (ref.)			
Age of the youngest child			
Youngest child is three years or older, or no child (ref.)			
Youngest child younger than three years old	−0.09	−0.25	0.03
Period			
Getting the job before 1975 (ref.)			
In 1975–79	−0.13	0.02	−0.03
In 1980–84	−0.46	0.17	−0.62
In 1985–89	−0.67	0.29	−0.60
In 1990–94	−2.07***	0.19	−0.97
Constant	−2.92***	−2.61***	−3.59***
Number of events	92	217	83
Number of episodes		636	
Log likelihood (starting values)		−2856.78	
Log likelihood (final estimates)		−2180.34	

Note: Significance levels $* \geq 0.9$, $** \geq 0.95$, $*** \geq 0.99$

Source: See Table 15.2

NOTES

1 Greece (29.8 percent) and Spain (31.5 percent) have the lowest proportion of women in the labor force (Ramos-Díaz 2003).
2 For these industrial sectors, the very low levels of productivity and high production costs reduced the ability to compete (Tamames 1995). About two million jobs were lost from 1976 to 1985, most in agriculture (850 000) and manufacturing (820 000), but many in construction (440 000). During this period, the service sector created about 160 000 positions (Garrido and Requena 1996: 28).
3 The numbers are from Toharia et al. (1997) who have collected several series of harmonized data on Spanish employment since the 1970s.
4 In Spain, fundamental regulatory aspects have been oriented to increase numerical flexibility, while other types of flexibility (organizational, functional) that could improve a firm's efficiency in production processes have still to be adopted. This is an important aspect, which contrasts with Wood's (1989) suggestion that 'it ought to be possible to admit of the importance of flexibility without assuming that this involves a fundamental change in the mode of regulation' (pp. 1–2).
5 The Spanish labor market has become a clear example of a dual labor market (Lindbeck and Snower 1987), segmented into 'insiders' with permanent contracts (predominantly adult males) who are difficult to fire and are thus insured against the risk of being laid off, and 'outsiders' with fixed-term contracts (predominantly younger workers and women) who endure poor working conditions, employment instability and few opportunities for advancement.
6 From 1993 onwards, the health system, the family support services, the nursery schools, the services at home for dependent persons, and the institutions for the elderly show relative weakness with respect to the EU average (Navarro 2003).
7 This has also been a problem in a previous investigation concerning the partnership transition (Simó, Golsch and Steinhage 2002).
8 The stronger likelihood of downward mobility is significant for the earliest labor market entry cohort, but this is a consequence of the selecting pool after having controlled for historical period, since the observations are reduced to the female job changes made from 1975 onwards.

BIBLIOGRAPHY

Baizán, P. (2000) 'Transition to adulthood in Spain', in M. Corijn and E. Klijzing (eds) *Transitions to adulthood in Europe: from a matter of standard to a matter of choice*, Deventer: Kluwer Academic.
Blossfeld, H.-P. (1997) 'Women's part-time employment and the family cycle: a cross-national comparison', in H.-P. Blossfeld and C. Hakim (eds) *Between equalization and marginalization. Part-time working women in Europe and the United States*, Oxford: Oxford University Press, pp. 315–24.
Blossfeld, H.-P. and Drobnič, S. (eds) (2001) *Careers of couples in contemporary societies. A cross-national comparison of the transition from male breadwinner to dual-earner families*, Oxford: University Press.
Blossfeld, H.-P. and Hakim, C. (1997) 'Introduction: a comparative perspective on part-time work', in H.-P. Blossfeld and C. Hakim (eds) *Between equalization and*

marginalization. Part-time working women in Europe and the United States, Oxford: Oxford University Press, pp. 315–24.

Blossfeld, H.-P. and Rohwer, G. (2001) *Techniques of event history modelling,* Hillsdale, NJ: Lawrence Erlbaum Associates.

Blossfeld, H.-P., Hamerle, A. and Mayer, K.U. (1989) *Event history analysis. Statistical theory and application in the social sciences,* Hillsdale, NJ: Lawrence Erlbaum Associates.

Blossfeld, H.-P., Klijzing, E., Mills, M. and Kurz, K. (2005) *Globalization, uncertainty, and youth in society,* London: Routledge.

Carabaña, J. (2003) 'Educación y movilidad social', in V. Navarro (ed.) *El estado de bienestar en España,* electronic book based on the seminar 'El Estado de Bienestar en España', Universidad Internacional Menéndez, 18 and 19 December 2003.

Cebrián López, I., Moreno Raymundo, G. and Toharía Cortés, L. (1997) '¿Es diferente el desajuste educativo de las mujeres?', *ICE-Mujer y Economía,* 760: 129–43.

Cousins, C. (1994) 'A comparison of the labour market position of women in Spain and the UK with reference to the flexible labour debate', *Work, Employment and Society,* 8(1): 45–67.

De León, M. (1999) 'La dimensión política del sistema de protección español y su repercusión en estructuras de género', in J.A. Garde (ed.) *Políticas sociales y Estado de bienestar en España. Informe 1999,* Valladolid: Editorial Trotta, pp. 767–93.

Delgado, M. and T. Castro Martín (1999) *Fertility and family surveys in countries of the ECE region, standard country report Spain, economic studies No. 10i,* Geneva: United Nations Economic Commission for Europe.

Erikson, R. and Goldthorpe, J.H. (1992) *The constant flux. A study of class mobility in industrial societies,* Oxford: Clarendon Press.

Esping-Andersen, G. (1999) *Social foundations of postindustrial economies,* Oxford: Oxford University Press.

Festy, P. and Prioux, F. (2002) *An evaluation of the fertility and family surveys project,* New York and Geneva: United Nations.

Flaquer, L.L. (2000) *Les polítiques familiars en una perspectiva comparada,* Barcelona: Fundació La Caixa.

Ganzeboom, H.B. and Treiman, D.J. (1996) 'Internationally comparable measures of occupational status for the 1988 international standard classification of occupations', *Social Science Research,* 25: 201–39.

García Serrano, C. and Malo Ocaña, M.A. (1997) '¿Es diferente el desajuste educativo de las mujeres?', *ICE. Mujer y Economía,* 760: 117–43.

Garrido, L. and Requena, M. (1996) *La emancipación de los jóvenes en España,* Madrid: Instituto de la Juventud. Ministerio de Trabajo y Asuntos Sociales.

Gauthier, A.H. (1996) *The state and the family: a comparative analysis of family policies in industrialized countries,* Oxford: Clarendon Press.

Golsch, K. (2003) 'Employment flexibility in Spain and its impact on transitions to adulthood', *Work, Employment and Society,* 17(4): 691–718.

Hakim, C. (2003) *Models of the family in modern societies: ideals and realities,* Aldershot: Ashgate.

Heery, E. and Salmon, J. (eds) (2000) *The insecure workforce,* London and New York: Routledge.

Jurado Guerrero, T. (1995) 'Legitimation durch Sozialpolitik? Die spanische Beschäftigungskrise und die Theorie des Wohlfahrtsstaates', *KZfSS*, 47: 727–52.

Ladipo, D. and Wilkinson F. (2002) 'More pressure, less protection', in B. Burchell, D. Ladipo and Wilkinson F. (eds) *Job insecurity and work intensification*, London and New York: Routledge.

Laparra Navarro, M., González, R., Macías, A., Pérez, B. and Silva, J. (2002) 'Social quality and the policy domain of employment', in *European foundation of social quality: social quality and the policy domain of employment*, Amsterdam.

Lindbeck, A. and Snower, D. (1987) 'Efficiency wages versus insiders and outsiders', *European Economic Review*, 31: 407–16.

Martínez Alier, J. and Roca Jusmet, J. (1988) 'Economía política del corporativismo en el Estado español: Del franquismo al posfranquismo', *Revista Española de Investigaciones Sociológicas*, 41: 25–62.

Mills, M. and Blossfeld, H.-P. (2005) 'Globalization, uncertainty and the early life course: a theoretical framework', in H.-P. Blossfeld, E. Klizjing, M. Mills and K. Kurz (eds) *Globalization, uncertainty, and youth in society*, London: Routledge.

Morán, M.P. (1991) 'Las Mujeres y el Empleo en España 1987–90', *Revista de Economía y Sociología del Trabajo*, 13–14: 88–103.

Morcillo, A.G. (1999) *True catholic womanhood: gender ideology in Franco's Spain*, DeKalb, IL: Northern Illinois University Press.

Muñoz de Bustillo Llorente, R. (2002) 'Spain and the neoliberal paradigm', CEPA Working Paper 2002-02, Center for Economic Policy Analysis, New School University.

Navarro, V. (ed.) (2003) *El estado de bienestar en España*, electronic book based on the seminar 'El Estado de Bienestar en España', Universidad Internacional Menéndez, 18 and 19 December 2003.

Navarro, V. and Quiroga, A. (2003) 'La protección social en España' in V. Navarro (ed.) *El estado de bienestar en España*, electronic book based on the seminar 'El Estado de Bienestar en España', Universidad Internacional Menéndez, 18 and 19 December 2003.

Oppenheimer, V.K. (1994) 'Women's rising employment and the future of the family in industrial societies', *Population and Development Review*, 20: 293–342.

Ramos-Díaz, J. (2003) 'Empleo precario en España: una asignatura pendiente', in V. Navarro (ed.) *El estado de bienestar en España*, electronic book based on the seminar 'El Estado de Bienestar en España', Universidad Internacional Menéndez, 18 and 19 December 2003.

Rodríguez Cabrero, G. (2003) 'La protección social a las personas en situación de dependencia en España', in V. Navarro (ed.) *El estado de bienestar en España*, electronic book based on the seminar 'El Estado de Bienestar en España', Universidad Internacional Menéndez, 18 and 19 December 2003.

Sainsbury, D. (1999) *Gender and welfare state regimes*, Oxford: Oxford University Press.

San Segundo, M.J. (1995) 'Los rendimientes económicos del capital humano', *Economistas*, 69: 376–83.

Segura, J. (2001) 'La reforma del mercado de trabajo español: Un panorama', *Revista de Economía Aplicada*, 25(9): 157–90.

Simó, C. (2004) 'Spanish women trapped by a hard election. Are they able to reconcile job and family?', GLOBALIFE Working Paper No. 58, Chair of Sociology I, University of Bamberg.

Simó, C. and Soro-Bonmatí, A. (2002) 'Early careers of young people in Spain: new evidence from the FFS and EPA', GLOBALIFE Working Paper No. 30, Chair of Sociology I, University of Bamberg.

Simó, C., Castro Martín, T. and Soro-Bonmatí, A. (2005) 'The effects of the globalization process on the transition into adulthood. The Spanish case', in H.-P. Blossfeld, E. Klijzing, M. Mills and K. Kurz (eds) *Globalization, uncertainty, and youth in society*, London: Routledge.

Simó, C., Golsch, K., Soro-Bonmatí, A. (2002) 'Globalization and occupational mobility in adult male job careers in Spain', GLOBALIFE Working Paper No. 35, Chair of Sociology I, University of Bamberg.

Simó, C., Golsch, K. and Steinhage, N. (2002) 'Increasing uncertainty in the Spanish labor market and entry into parenthood', *GENUS*, 58 (1): 77–119.

Szebehely, M. (1998) 'Changing divisions of care-work: caring for children and frail elderly people in Sweden', in J. Lewis (ed.) *Gender, social care and welfare state restructuring in Europe*, Aldershot: Ashgate, pp. 257–83.

Tamames R. (1995) *La Economía Española, 1975–1995*, Madrid: Ediciones Temas de Hoy, S.A.

Toharia, L., Albert, I., Cebrián, C., García Serrano, C., García Mainar, I., Malo, M.A., Moreno, G. and Villagómez, E. (1997) *El Mercado de Trabajo en España*, Madrid: McGraw-Hill.

Toharia, L. and Malo, M.A. (2000) 'The Spanish experiment: pros and cons of flexibility at the margin', in G. Esping-Andersen and M. Regini (eds) *Why deregulate labour markets?*, Oxford: Oxford University Press, pp. 307–35.

Wood, S. (1989) 'The transformation of work?', in S. Wood (ed.) *The transformation of work? Skill, flexibility and the labour process*, London: Unwin Hyman, pp. 1–43.

PART VII

Conclusions

16. The impact of gender role attitudes on women's life courses

Detlev Lück

INTRODUCTION

In the first chapter of this volume, Hofmeister, Blossfeld and Mills introduced a general theoretical framework for analyzing globalization effects on women's life courses. The present chapter suggests additional explanations that would have been difficult to include in the previous chapters in a systematic way since quantitative research needs to simplify the highly complex social reality.

In this chapter, I explain the impact of subjectivity and of culture on women's mid-career labor market involvement. The emphasis is on attitudes and values,[1] social values and norms, and how these affect women's career choices between working in the labor market (for pay) and working in the household (as unpaid caregivers). I demonstrate that cross-national differences and social change do not only reflect institutional but also cultural differences and change. It might be satisfying to give explanations that refer only to institutions (or to culture). However, including both views can resolve some contradictions that do not follow a strictly 'rational choice' model in women's career trajectories.

After a short theoretical discussion of the advantages and disadvantages of adding cultural explanations to the theoretical framework, I present empirical results.

THE IMPACT OF SUBJECTIVITY: EXTENDING THE MODEL

Subjectivity forms social reality in different ways. The following description distinguishes micro-level from macro-level effects, as well as effects of structured and of unstructured aspects of subjectivity.

What is 'subjectivity'?

The realist theory of cognition, that 'people around us perceive the world the same way as we do, and that this perception mirrors an objectively given reality,' is the basis for many sociological theories of action, such as homo economicus (Spranger 1950). It assumes people were fully informed about their (objective) situations and would evaluate these according to objective economic incentives. The majority of social scientists would probably no longer defend this assumption explicitly. In practice, however, hypotheses and interpretations show that homo economicus is still alive and the assumption of the realist theory of cognition is often still implicitly made. The aim of introducing subjectivity in this chapter is to overcome this assumption in all its consequences.

At the individual level, subjectivity can mean individual perception of reality: these are beliefs about what is real, independent of whether these beliefs are true. It can also mean individual evaluation of reality: this includes beliefs about the desirability and importance of the things one perceives as real. It can also mean individual attitudes and values: beliefs about what should and should not be. At the aggregate level, subjectivity as it is can appear as an aspect of culture: as belief systems, public opinion, social values, social norms, and so on.

Micro-level effects of actors' subjective perception

On the individual level, these perceptions, evaluations, attitudes and values can be measured to a certain extent, which enables us to explain action. Rational action explanations have included subjectivity: the SEU model employs subjective expected utility (SEU), with assumed costs and benefits (Langenheder 1975; Opp, Burow-Auffahrt and Hartmann 1984). These partly refer also to values and preferences as aspects of the subjective perceived utility (Easterlin 1973; Nauck 1989). Further developed rational choice models (Esser 1990; 1996) even assume that action under certain circumstances might not be rational at all.

These approaches are still unsatisfactory, inasmuch as these subjective preferences only play a role within a process of rational decision-making. Therefore, a more appropriate way of including individual beliefs should model rational calculation and individual beliefs as equal (interacting) factors in an extended theory of action.

Macro-level effects of subjective perception of actors

What does subjectivity mean for effects on the macro-level? As long as individual beliefs are not measured, they appear as 'blurriness' (Schulze 1993), as a weakening of correlations that might measure the impact of objective utilities on women's decisions. Hypotheses will need to be formulated probabilistically rather than deterministically, without changing the predicted direction of correlations or the explanation for them.

Once individual beliefs are measured, they can help to increase explained variance. In the following, the argumentation and the analyses will concentrate on attitudes and values. There is a lot of evidence for their impact on action in general (Fuchs and Rohrschneider 2001; Inglehart 1977; 1989; 1997; Klages 1984; 1988; 1993), as well as on women's careers specifically (Inglehart 1989, pp. 177ff; 1997, pp. 267ff; Klein 1990), although this impact is not yet fully understood (Höllinger, 1991).

I assume that values and attitudes regarding the *importance* of having a partner, having children, being in the labor market, having a high social status and so forth might influence women in their negotiations with their partners and their career paths or choices of how to balance job and family. Their influence is to weigh the subjectively perceived benefits or costs within women's decisions. However, they only interact with objectively given benefits or costs.

I also assume that values and attitudes regarding the '*right*' gender roles should have an even stronger effect: the beliefs (or stereotypes) of men as more rational and women as more emotional, or that it is not feminine to give instructions or not masculine to change diapers – these beliefs might affect women's choices of how to balance job and family, independently whether they are linked or interacting with any given objective reality. They could be considered as additional 'benefits' or 'costs.' And since they are only subjectively perceived and not rational, I might rather speak of 'satisfaction' or 'dissatisfaction' with a certain choice. People acting according to these beliefs make decisions that might seem irrational from an economic point of view. Nevertheless the subjective reality of the actor turns out to be at least as relevant as the given objective reality.

Data from the International Social Survey Program (ISSP) mainly offer indicators for this second group of values and attitudes, and here significant deviations from expectations based on economic models might be most clearly evident.

Culture, mediated by social values and norms

Further interesting ways to extend models appear once one realizes that subjective perceptions and beliefs do not only create blurriness or 'white noise,' but are structured as well. These structures appear as aspects of culture (or subculture).

Values are based either on experiences or on socialization. Both are usually shared with many others in society, especially in the closer social environment or generation. Therefore values – then called social values – tend to be specific for societies and social groups, despite all variance within the group. They tend to come in belief-systems: in sets of perceptions, evaluations and social values that affect all aspects of life. These belief-systems have proven to be strongly linked to religion. On the macro-level, social values or belief-systems can be used to explain cross-cultural differences in or social change of women's life courses. However, these belief-systems also imply norms, which empirically can hardly be distinguished from social values.

From a micro perspective, the difference between values and norms is fundamental: whereas acting according to values means following an individually shared strong belief that the action or its purpose is desirable per se, acting according to norms means following expectations of the social environment, seeking positive and avoiding negative sanctions. Acting according to values implies a strong motivation and identification with one's action and may even defy rules of the society. Acting according to norms means following these rules and can imply backing down from external pressure and violating personal principles. From a macro perspective, however, the difference is marginal: if one focuses on societies or social groups, a *social* value is a belief that is dominant within this collective. Such predominant values are translated into norms, which means the majority that sets public opinion raises the expectation that everyone (including minorities with deviant beliefs) acts according to these predominant values. Norms have been included in SEU models, where they are called constraints (Elster 1987).

The consequences of introducing norms (or social values) into the model are similar to when individual values are introduced. Only in this case, women act according to the predominant beliefs in their society or social environment and not necessarily according to their *own* beliefs.

The relationship of culture and welfare regimes

If I talk about culture as a competing or complementary explanation to the institutional structure of welfare regimes, then I need to ask about the interaction between the two.

Here, culture is understood as structure of social values and norms, shaping non-rational behavior through socialization and through social expectations. Welfare regimes are structures of institutional economic incentives and burdens that define the frame actors face. It can be argued that culture is shaped by welfare regimes, since the impact of institutions on rational behavior will, in the long run, lead to routines and finally to beliefs legitimizing those routines. I can also argue that welfare regimes are shaped by culture since the only plausible reason why a certain government is elected in order to organize the welfare state in a certain way is the society's cultural background.

Ethnic minorities might help us in estimating the empirically true relationship between the two structures. Ethnic minorities share a welfare system with the majority group but do not share the cultural background. Such minorities often show significant differences in gender (and other) behavior from the majority (BMfSFJ 2000; Breuer 1998; Herwartz-Emden 2000; Herwartz-Emden and Westphal 1999; Nauck 2002; Riedo 1991), even into the second generation (Worbs and Heckmann 2003), but they also deviate from the gender behavior in their home countries. That might indicate that both structures have some influence.

Pfau-Effinger (1996; 1997) offers a compromise by arguing for 'gender arrangements' that result from an interaction between a 'gender order' and a 'gender culture,' which mostly stabilize one another but sometimes are in conflict. 'Gender order' means the institutional frame of action, referred to as welfare regimes by Esping-Andersen. 'Gender culture' means dominant beliefs in society about the appropriate gender relations. This chapter suggests that gender culture is the model for the additional explanations.

HYPOTHESES

The discussion of cultural aspects raises a number of questions that will be tested in the empirical part of this chapter, formulated as hypotheses:

1 A woman will make career decisions between working in the labor market (for pay) and working in the household (as an unpaid caregiver) partly based on what she considers to be gender-appropriate; that is, on her gender-related values and attitudes.
2 A woman will make career decisions between working in the labor market and working in the household partly based on belief-systems, on dominant gender-related social values and norms in a given society. This influence, just like that of individual values, should be measurable in addition to the influence of welfare regimes.
3 Individual values and attitudes as well as social values and norms cannot be (fully) explained by welfare regimes. They reflect a broader cultural background such as traditional religious belief-systems.

DATA AND METHODS

Data

The empirical analyses are based on ISSP data, which are collected using a standardized (and translated) questionnaire administered by national research teams in almost 30 countries. In 1988, 1994 and 2002, the focus was on

'Family and Changing Gender Roles.' The ISSP is one of the few data sets that provides both cross-national and longitudinal information on gender and family attitudes (GESIS/ZA 2001).

Unfortunately, the ISSP is not a panel study, so changes over time can only be studied on an aggregate level. Controlling for cohorts will nevertheless give an idea whether changes are because of age, generation or period effects, and whether they *only* happen at the macro-level or also individually. Causal analyses only make sense with individual data and therefore will need to be cross-sectional. These cross-sectional analyses are computed for 1994, because the 2002 wave is not yet completely available and documented.

Cross-national data sets are inherently problematic and the ISSP is no exception: question wording will not be identical because of translation or the need to adapt formulations. Response categories vary, as do sampling techniques, and questions are answered in differing cultural contexts. I thus only interpret results robust enough to be found in different, comparable countries; outlier results for a single country that could be due to methodological problems are ignored.

Sub-samples from the ISSP data are drawn according to four criteria:

1   Only North American and European countries, Australia and New Zealand are followed. For the causal analyses, the Netherlands and Spain are dropped because several explanatory variables are missing for them.
2   Measuring values, the focus is on women since their (value-based) decisions are to be explained. Beliefs of women and men are relevant only for modeling the influence of norms in women's social environment.
3   For the causal analyses, only women with a steady partner are of interest, as for them variation in commitment to job versus family can be assumed.
4   Whenever age or cohort effects are not controlled for, analyses focus on women aged 20 to 50, since they are more likely to be confronted with the choice between parenting and job career.

Methods and measures

The goal of this chapter is to test whether there is evidence for the influence of institutions or culture on women's life courses with respect to their choices about employment and about household work. This is tested in two steps. First, regression models take the *woman's employment* (full-time, half-time or not employed) in various stages of her family career[2] as dependent variables. In the second step, indicators for the *division of labor within the household* are taken as dependent variables.

Several available indicators might equally well represent economic incentives *or* cultural background.[3] They are controlled for insofar as they are comparable among the countries[4] but not interpreted. These variables are: birth cohort, presence of a steady life-partner, presence of own children, experience of own mother's employment during the respondent's childhood, school education (represented by seven dummy variables) and individual income[5] (represented by ten dummy variables for income deciles in society). This basic model provides a reference point to compare how much *additional* variance may be explained by specific additional variables that can be interpreted more unambiguously in favor or disfavor of the hypotheses.

For testing the impact of attitudes and values, the following variables are included in the analysis: four items representing specific attitudes towards female employment in various stages of a family career; individual scores on two dimensions representing more general abstract beliefs with regard to gender roles (these are introduced in the following sections); and religiosity (church attendance) and individual religious denomination. Religious domination is measured by five dummy variables for being Catholic, Anglican, Lutheran, other Protestant, of another religious domination or atheist. For testing the impact of norms, the presence of values regarding gender roles, of religious denominations and religiosity in societies are included in the analysis.

The impact of welfare regimes can only be tested indirectly. The nation or society the respondent lives in (represented by 19 dummy variables) is included in the analysis. Interpreted is the surplus of variance explained by countries over the variance explained by country-specific norms giving a rather overestimated magnitude. With the division of labor within the household being the dependent variable, the woman's current employment status is added as an explanation to the models. Its impact is interpreted according to rational choice.

Measuring norms and values

What is typically measured (in the ISSP as well) is the degree of agreement with statements about more or less specific situations that are often framed in the terms of current public debate (such as 'Women should contribute to household income'). As a result, respondents might answer according to a value or a norm, or both, but they also might answer with reference to a specific situation (for example, a second household income is financially needed) or context (for example, the government is planning to reduce tax breaks for non-employed partners raising children). It can be assumed that many such items measure values and norms and specific attitudes at the same time, though each only to a certain degree.

I cope with this problem of validity by operationalizing values as dimensions: as tendencies of reaction that are situation-unspecific. Statistic-ally, dimensions are measured by factors combining highly inter-correlated items that ask about closely related, situation-specific attitudes. If there is variance measured simultaneously by different items, then this variance does not depend on the specific situation or context of one single question. The individual score on a dimension is interpreted as an individual value. Looking at the society as a whole, the dominant value will be interpreted as a social value, translated into a norm within this society.

The structure of norms and values towards family and employment

Which dimensions can be found and which items belong to these dimensions? In the ISSP 1994, 18 items[6] can be considered to be measuring attitudes toward gender roles (or what women should or should not do) regarding household, family or jobs. These items were included in a series of factor analyses.[7] Despite differences in the details across nations, cohorts, or social groups, a robust core structure of factors could be found. It includes two dimensions, each represented by three items.

Dimension 1 is labeled 'support for traditional gender roles' and represents an approval of the 'male breadwinner/female homemaker model' in which the female role is to be responsible for taking care of children and the household. It combines the items:

(a)   'Do you agree or disagree? A husband's job is to earn money; a wife's job is to look after the home and family.'
(b)   'Do you agree or disagree? It is not good if the man stays at home and cares for the children and the woman goes out to work.'
(c)   'Do you agree or disagree? People who have never had children lead empty lives.'

Dimension 2 is labeled 'support for female employment,' statistically largely independent from dimension 1 and thus cannot be read as a counter-position to it. Instead, it refers to the question of whether women should *just* stay home and raise children, irrespective of whether the main responsibilities are shared in a male-breadwinner way. This second dimension combines the items:

(a)   'Do you agree or disagree? Both the husband and wife should contribute to the household income.'
(b)   'Do you agree or disagree? Having a job is the best way for a woman to be an independent person.'
(c)   'Do you agree or disagree? Most women have to work these days to support their families.'

RESULTS OF CAUSAL ANALYSES

This section will look for evidence of a causal impact of cultural background in general, and values and norms in particular. Before I look at micro-level analyses, I shall have a brief look at macro-level data.

Macro-level analyses: welfare regimes, cultural background or gender arrangements?

In cross-national comparison, aggregate data seem to provide clear support for the theoretical assumptions of rational choice approaches. High employment rates among women in Anglo-Saxon and Scandinavian societies, for example, seem to lend support to the welfare regime arguments, with women in liberal countries being pushed into the labor market by economic necessity and women in social-democratic countries being pulled by policies. Without disproving these assumptions, I show that alternative interpretations are possible.

The remarkable statistical correlations between welfare regimes and patterns of gender behavior do not prove direct causal relationships. After all, welfare regimes basically match with cultural areas, visible for example in specific linguistic or religious traditions. The social-democratic welfare regimes are represented by heavily Lutheran Scandinavian countries whose languages are strongly related, while the liberal welfare regimes are typically Protestant-dominated, English-speaking countries. The cluster Esping-Andersen (1990) described as a 'conservative' welfare regime has a more diverse cultural background and set of institutions, which has led other authors (Ferrara 1996; Lessenich 1994) to divide it into two categories: the 'conservative' and the 'Southern European' regimes. The Southern European (or 'family-oriented') regime contains countries with a Latin-based language and a strong Roman Catholic influence, while the 'conservative' regime (as used in this volume) are mainly Germanic countries of continental Europe with strong influences of both Roman Catholic *and* Lutheran churches. Of course, there are countries that do not fit properly: Ireland (Southern and Northern) for example combines strong Catholicism with Anglo-Saxon influence and the English language, an ambiguity that is reflected in attempts to define its welfare regime(s) (Obinger and Wagschal 1998).

Durkheim has shown (1999, pp. 162f) that differing religious dominations come with different self-perceptions and basic approaches to life. With Max Weber (1988 [1920]), I might even be tempted to interpret these differences as a measure of the degree of societal modernity, with Protestantism and especially Calvinism or similar Protestant variations, as an environment that supports rationalization.

The picture becomes clearer with a look at the 'values map' (Inglehart 1997; Inglehart and Carballo 1997). Like this chapter, Inglehart and Carballo look at belief-structures using similar items and methods. But they compare societies based on the World Values Survey, which makes their results useful to confirm the findings based on ISSP data. Also they focus on culture as a whole employing a much larger set of variables, which gives interesting hints about the broader context of cultural change.

Inglehart and Carballo find belief-structures organized around two core dimensions, 'modernization' and 'post-modernization.' The first is a Weberian conceptualization of the transition from traditional or patrimonial to secular-rational authority. The second is a values shift away from largely survival concerns (food, shelter) in western societies after World War II toward well-being connected to personal autonomy and the environment. Inglehart (1977) called this earlier the 'Silent Revolution' with values change from 'materialism' to 'post-materialism.'

Inglehart and Carballo find the distribution of societies on these two dimensions highly linked to religious dominations referring to 'historically Protestant' and 'historically Catholic.' They argue that values connected to predominant churches in past centuries 'persist as a part of the cultural heritage of given nations' (Inglehart and Carballo 1997, p. 43). This helps to understand the differences between societies that are similar in other respects such as Germany and Austria. Historically, Protestant societies are at the forefront on both dimensions of cultural change but, as I will show, it is the dimension of post-modernization that helps us better understand national differences in gender role attitudes.

I cannot reproduce the 'values map' with ISSP data. But I can plot a quite similar map. Figure 16.1 shows the dimensions 'support for traditional gender roles' and 'support for female employment' plotted onto a two-dimensional map. Different shapes used for various countries distinguish among the customarily assigned welfare regimes. The scales measure the share of those in a society above the median, taken over all societies in the analyses; thus, the average of all societies is 50 percent along both axes, so countries are grouped around the midpoint (50 percent, 50 percent) of the figure.

Support for traditional gender roles turns out to spread societies across the conceptual map similar to Inglehart and Carballo's post-modernization dimension 'survival concerns – well-being' (only laterally reversed). This is not too surprising since Inglehart and Carballo's dimension includes items like 'woman needs children,' 'child needs both parents,' or support for the women's movement (Inglehart and Carballo 1997, pp. 36, 39) that could easily be interpreted as support for traditional gender roles as well. This social value then reflects something like a low degree of (post-)modernity and is slowly shrinking over time. Support for female employment, however, does not seem to have an impact on female employment. It is rather affected by other factors. Looking at the positions of societies and welfare regimes in the 'values map' or the 'gender values map' (Figure 16.1) I find strong similarities, especially regarding the dimension 'support for traditional gender roles'/(lack of) post-modernization.

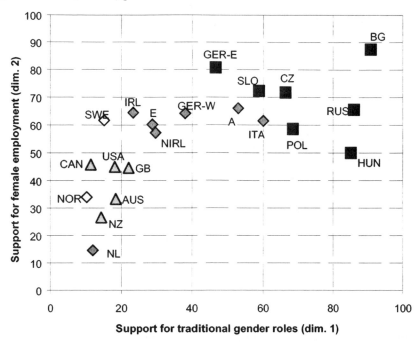

Note: Support for Traditional Gender Roles (first axis): Factor combining the items 'Do you agree or disagree? ... A husband's job is to earn money; a wife's job is to look after the home and family', ... 'It is not good if the man stays at home and cares for the children and the woman goes out to work,' and '... People who have never had children lead empty lives.' Support for Female Employment (second axis): Factor combining the items 'Do you agree or disagree? ... Having a job is the best way for a woman to be an independent person, '... Most women have to work these days to support their families', and '... Both the husband and wife should contribute to the household income.'

Source: ISSP 1994, own computation, women between 20 and 50, weighted data

Figure 16.1   *Support for traditional gender roles and for female employment by nation, 1994*

The broader context Inglehart and Carballo find helps us to answer which causal model to assume behind the statistical correlations. In terms of religious domination and the degree of kinship of languages, cultural roots are obviously older than the institutions that determine welfare regimes. Therefore, there is (at least *also*) a cultural background of societies that shapes their institutions, and thus also the according welfare regime.

I further ask whether gender-specific behavior is based directly and only on institutions (which again are influenced by cultural traditions) or whether a direct impact of culture on gender-specific behavior also exists. The earlier-mentioned research about ethnic minorities might indicate that both institutions and cultural heritage influence behavior. I also ask whether values shape individual behavior. The fact that some aspects of a cultural heritage like religion or ethnicity influence gender reality does not imply that every aspect of culture does. With aggregate analyses, this question cannot be answered to my satisfaction. I only can state that the described phenomena are interrelated. There may even be a symmetrical interrelation between gender culture and a gender order, as Birgit Pfau-Effinger (1996; 1997) has suggested in an effort to correct Esping-Andersen's model.

Micro-level analyses: What influences values?

Now, I turn to systematically testing the previously formulated hypotheses with micro-level data. I start with hypothesis 3: Individual values and attitudes as well as social values and norms cannot be (fully) explained by welfare regimes. At a minimum they also reflect a broader cultural background such as traditional religious belief-systems.

In the previous section, I demonstrated that social values and norms reflect traditional religious belief-systems. This section concentrates on what influences individual values. Dependent variables in regression models test the dimensions 'support for traditional gender roles' and 'support for female employment.'

Each table shows a series of regression models. The left column (Model 1) always shows the basic model using only ambiguous explaining variables that are controlled for but not interpreted. The basic model's corrected R^2 serves as a reference point to compare how much additional variance can be explained by specific additional variables: by individual religious domination and religiosity (Model 2), by predominant religious belief-systems in society (Model 4), by society as a dummy variable (Model 6) and so forth. A big R^2 size over the basic model (ΔR^2) is interpreted as a strong impact.

There is a clear and strong impact of religion and religiosity on individual gender-related values (see Table 16.1). Surprisingly, this impact is found only for the religious characteristics of the society (Model 3, $\Delta R^2 = 0.225$). Individually shared religious domination or religiosity might have some influence as well (Model 2, $\Delta R^2 = 0.092$), but it is almost negligible

Table 16.1   Regression analysis: support for traditional gender roles, 1994

Dependent variable: 'support for traditional gender roles' (v12/v13/v31)	Model	(1)	(2)	(3)	(4)	(5)	(6)	(7)
	cor. R^2 =	.228	.320	.453	.458	.513	.516	.521
Independent variables	ΔR^2 =		.092	.225	.230	.285	.288	.293
Birth cohort								
1920/earlier		.093***	.084***	.069***	.059***	.077***	.086***	.075***
1921–30		.117***	.095***	.074***	.065***	.076***	.084***	.076***
1931–40		.080***	.058***	.047***	.039***	.038***	.046***	.040***
1941–50 (ref)								
1951–60		-.033**	-.041***	-.036**	-.035**	-.041***	-.038**	-.037***
1961–70		-.060***	-.063***	-.061***	-.057***	-.055***	-.058***	-.053***
1971/later		-.046***	-.039**	-.047***	-.042***	-.042***	-.053***	-.049***
Is there a steady life-partner?		-.024*	.004	.008	.008	.014	.015	.013
Are/were there children?		.161***	.127***	.106***	.104***	.092***	.085***	.084***
Own mother was working before respondent was 14		.093***	.055***	-.028**	-.019*	-.045***	-.055***	-.048***
Education								
None		.059***	.035***	.011	.011	.004	.001	.001
Primary, uncompleted		.169***	.143***	.081***	.081***	.051***	.048***	.049***
Primary, completed		.167***	.189***	.137***	.142***	.119***	.119***	.123***
Secondary, uncompleted		.037**	.047***	.034***	.036***	.019*	.024*	.027**
Secondary, completed (ref)								
University, uncompleted		-.074***	-.094***	-.064***	-.068***	-.038***	-.039***	-.041***
University, completed		-.120***	-.110***	-.102***	-.098***	-.085***	-.089***	-.086***
Personal income								
Lowest decile		.051***	.034*	.058***	.053***	.062***	.069***	.065***
2nd decile		.002	-.020	-.005	-.005	.044***	.041***	.043***
3rd decile		.018	.015	.018	.015	.015	.019	.018
4th decile		-.009	-.022	-.012	-.012	.035**	.030**	.032**
5th decile (ref)								
6th decile		-.010	-.026*	-.025*	-.025*	.002	-.003	-.003
7th decile		-.015	-.023	-.020*	-.017	-.011	-.017	-.012
8th decile		-.010	-.016	-.027**	-.026*	-.009	-.012	-.010
9th decile		.014	.004	-.021*	-.018	-.001	-.006	-.004
Highest decile		.014	.002	-.021*	-.021*	-.010	-.013	-.012
Religion								
Catholic				.129***		.043**	.027*	.021
Anglican				-.062***		.027**	.016	.014
Lutheran				-.112***		.009	-.001	-.001
Other Protestant				.009		.054***	.043***	.038***
Other				.232***		.045**	.019	.018
Atheist (ref)								
Church attendance (0 = never, 5 = weekly or more)				.006		.069***	.065***	.076***

Table 16.1　continued

Dependent variable: 'support for traditional gender roles' (v12/v13/v31)	Model	(1)	(2)	(3)	(4)	(5)	(6)	(7)
	cor. R^2 =	.228	.320	.453	.458	.513	.516	.521
Independent variables	ΔR^2 =		.092	.225	.230	.285	.288	.293
USA							-.079***	-.102***
Canada							-.127***	-.138***
Australia							-.109***	-.113***
New Zealand							-.085***	-.094***
Great Britain							-.073***	-.076***
Northern Ireland							-.037***	-.052***
Ireland							-.052***	-.073***
Italy							.068***	.054***
Sweden							-.119***	-.114***
Norway							-.144***	-.131***
Austria							.042***	.035***
West Germany (ref)								
East Germany							-.001	.010
Hungary							.275***	.269***
Slovenia							.079***	.073***
Czech Republic							.112***	.119***
Poland							.099***	.083***
Bulgaria							.247***	.248***
Russia							.262***	.238***
Share of... in society								
Catholics				.284***	.261***	.020		
Anglicans				-.195***	-.198***	-.085***		
Lutherans				-.255***	-.254***	-.037		
Other Protestants				-.030**	-.049***	-.008		
Other religious dominations				.238***	.201***	.085***		
Weekly church attenders				-.299***	-.324***	-.087***		
Supporters of traditional gender roles						.494***		
Supporters of female employment						-.064***		

Source:　ISSP 1994, own computation, only women, weighted data, all countries except the Netherlands, Spain, Japan, Republic of Philippines, and Israel. Dependent variable: factor
combining the items 'Do you agree or disagree? A husband's job is to earn money; a wife's
job is to look after the home and family,' 'Do you agree or disagree? It is not good if the
man stays at home and cares for the children and the woman goes out to work,' and 'Do
you agree or disagree? People who have never had children lead empty lives.'

compared to the societal religious belief system, influencing gender behavior through norms. Having individual and societal religious belief-systems in the model (Model 4) explains hardly any more variance than having just the latter ($\Delta R^2 = 0.230$).

Taking more specific gender-related norms into the model (Model 5) – the support for traditional gender roles and the support for female employment in society[8] – I get even stronger results ($\Delta R^2 = 0.285$). But since it is the percentage of people sharing the explained value that is interpreted as a societal norm here, this model is in danger of being a partly circular explanation. However, it becomes clear that women's individual values certainly do reflect religious belief-systems in society, working through norms rather than through personally shared beliefs.

A further confirmation can be found in the beta-coefficients of the single items. Almost all of these show significant and strong effects in directions consistent with previous results.

Welfare regimes seem to have some influence on values as well. However, compared with the cultural background, it is relatively low. Adding 18 dummy variables for the 19 societies (with West Germany being the reference) into the model (Model 6) increases the corrected R^2 by 0.288. If I compare this surplus to the $\Delta R^2 = 0.230$ surplus items for religion and religiosity are offering (Model 4) then I find society dummies adding $\Delta(\Delta R^2) = 0.058$ more. This 'surplus of the surplus' could be interpreted as an impact of nation-specific institutions.

Even though this is rather a *maximum* for an impact, I can assume that welfare regimes do have a – subtle – impact on values as well. This can be concluded from a look at the beta coefficients. The effects match very well with the clustering of welfare regimes. Living in Norway or Sweden, social-democratic regimes makes it much less likely that one will support traditional gender roles. The same is true for Canada, Australia and the USA, followed by other 'liberal' countries, including (Catholic!) Ireland. Very strong positive effects are found in East European countries, especially Bulgaria, Russia and Hungary.

Micro-level analyses: Explaining individual behavior

In order to test hypothesis 2, the dependent variable changes, and gender-related behavior is to be explained: a woman will make career decisions between working in the labor market and working in the household partly based on belief-systems, on dominant gender-related social values and on norms in a given society.

As dependent variables, several indicators are available and are used in two steps: the first operationalizes women's employment and the second operationalizes the division of labor in the household. In the first step, a set of four items is of interest: asking whether the woman was full-time, part-time or not employed for each of the four phases in the family cycle: after marriage and before the first child was born, before the last child went to school, once all children had reached school age and after the last child moved out of the woman's household.[9] These four items are taken as dependent variables initially, with results for the employment of women with preschool children being presented (Table 16.2).

In the second step, to measure the division of labor in the household, I use a set of five items, including who does certain tasks more often: doing the laundry, undertaking small repairs in the home, caring for sick family members, grocery shopping and deciding what to have for dinner. In these models the woman's (current) employment status is added as an explaining variable (for reasons of space the results are not presented here but see Lück 2004). The models of women's employment only adequately explain two of the household labor items: doing laundry and caring for sick family members.

Do the predominant religious belief-systems in society have a direct impact on a woman's employment? The evidence (Model 3, $\Delta R^2 = 0.100$) at first sight does not seem overwhelming. However, it has to be noted that the explained variance in Table 16.2 is generally lower than in Table 16.1, which means that gender-related behavior is socially less determined (by the available indicators) than gender-related values are. Relative to this lower degree of determination, the predominant belief-systems in society do show a strong impact.

The most theoretically interesting item regarding employment is the phase when women have preschool children, because in this phase employment conflicts with a typically female role. However, similar results can be found when the dependent variable is 'employment of mothers with school-age children,' 'after children moved out of the house,' or 'after marriage and before she has children.'

The woman's own religious orientation, again, turns out to be a bad predictor (Model 2, $\Delta R^2 = 0.037$). Controlling for the religious character of the society (Model 4, $\Delta R^2 = 0.100$), individual religious beliefs do not add any further explained variance at all.

Bad predictors are also the gender-specific social values or norms. The support for traditional gender roles or for female employment in society also add hardly any further explained variance (Model 5, $\Delta R^2 = 0.103$). It is possible that the variance explained by social values and norms is already largely taken away by the items on religion in the model. It is possible that the ways of causal influence are more complicated than the models are able to capture.

Turning to the woman's share of housekeeping as the dependent variable, I find similar, but less convincing results. Relatively speaking, the dominant religious belief-systems in society again explain a large share of the variance ($\Delta R^2 = 0.049$), with individual beliefs and gender-specific norms being less important. The beta coefficients show significant effects, mostly in expected

Table 16.2   Regression analysis: employment of mother with preschool child, 1994

Dep. variable: employment of mother with pre-school child (v59/v63)	Model	(1)	(2)	(3)	(4)	(5)	(6)	(7)	(8)
	cor. R^2 =	.116	.153	.216	.216	.219	.290	.238	.238
Indep. variables	ΔR^2 =		.037	.100	.100	.103	.174	.122	.122
Birth cohort									
1920/earlier		-.044***	-.033**	-.041***	-.040***	-.038**	-.037**	-.040***	-.038**
1921–30		-.055***	-.052***	-.063***	-.061***	-.058***	-.059***	-.062***	-.059***
1931–40		-.011	-.011	-.027*	-.024	-.025*	-.028*	-.031*	-.029*
1941–50 (ref)									
1951–60		.044**	.029*	.043**	.037**	.035**	.020	.039*	.032*
1961–70		.002	-.006	-.006	-.004	-.007	-.022	-.013	-.013
1971/later		-.058***	-.067***	-.063***	-.067***	-.068***	-.059***	-.067***	-.071***
Own mother was working before respondent was 14		.264***	.215***	.147***	.146***	.139***	.103***	.138***	.136***
Education									
None		.004	-.011	-.012	-.015	-.018	-.014	-.014	-.017
Primary, uncompleted		.010	-.008	-.021	-.022	-.028*	-.032**	-.028*	-.028*
Primary, completed		-.076***	-.082***	-.094***	-.096***	-.111***	-.087***	-.094***	-.096***
Secondary, uncompleted		-.102***	-.094***	-.103***	-.102***	-.111***	-.099***	-.076***	-.074***
Secondary, completed									
University, uncompleted		.017	.010	.008	.013	.022	.006	.021	.026*
University, completed		.071***	.065***	.065***	.066***	.068***	.030*	.071***	.072***
Religion									
Catholic			-.009		.019	.015	-.001		.016
Anglican			-.118***		-.011	-.012	-.009		-.014
Lutheran			-.096***		-.030	-.032	-.026		-.028
Other Protestant			-.101***		-.035*	-.035*	-.018		-.037*
Other			.079***		.007	.007	.009		.008
Atheist (ref)									
Church attendance (0 = never, 5 = weekly, more)			-.079***		-.031*	-.031*	.005		-.035*
USA							.033*		.045**
Canada							.040**		.038*
Australia							-.049**		-.049**
New Zealand							-.060***		-.055***
Great Britain (UK without Northern Ireland)							-.013		-.013
Northern Ireland							-.011		-.004
Ireland							-.049***		-.053***
Italy							.059***		.052***
Sweden							.042**		.045**
Norway							.015		.022
Austria							.048***		.041**

Table 16.2   continued

Dep. variable: Model employment of mother with pre-school child (v59/v63)	(1)	(2)	(3)	(4)	(5)	(6)	(7)	(8)
cor. R^2 =	.116	.153	.216	.216	.219	.290	.238	.238
Indep. variables ΔR^2 =		.037	.100	.100	.103	.174	.122	.122
West Germany (ref)								
East Germany							.196***	.193***
Hungary							.129***	.127***
Slovenia							.181***	.174***
Czech Republic							.097***	.090***
Poland							.098***	.095***
Bulgaria							.165***	.156***
Russia							.231***	.207***
Societal (national) share of:								
Catholics			-.138***	-.154***	-.154***	-.155***		
Anglicans			-.301***	-.300***	-.229***	-.221***		
Lutherans			-.318***	-.305***	-.207***	-.197***		
Other Protestants			-.102***	-.086***	-.038	-.043*		
Other dominations			-.076***	-.082***	-.095***	-.082**		
Weekly church attenders			-.164***	-.155***	-.115***	-.116***		
Societal (national) share of supporters for:								
Traditional gender roles						.096***	.179***	
Female employment						.055**	-.032	
Respondent supports traditional gender roles						-.042**		
Respondent supports female employment							.090***	
Respondent supports employment of mothers with a preschool child								.244***

Source: ISSP 1994, own computation, only women with a steady partner, weighted data, all countries except the Netherlands, Spain, Japan, Republic of Philippines, and Israel. Dependent variable: 'Did you work outside the home full-time, part-time, or not at all ... When a child was under school age?' or for male respondents: 'What about your spouse/partner at that time: Did she ...?'

directions: Catholic societies, for example, provide a higher likelihood of women being responsible for housework. This confirms that the measured influence exists. However, the predictability of housework is generally very low. It is likely that women's responsibilities in housework are less socially structured than women's employment careers, since the first is a less formal and more flexible commitment than the latter.

Hypothesis 1 is tested by using the same models: a woman will make career decisions between working in the labor market (for pay) and working in the household (as an unpaid caregiver) partly based on what she considers to be 'gender appropriate' according to her gender-related values and attitudes.

Individual gender-related values affect women's choices in a similarly strong way, as religious belief-systems in society do. In explaining employment of women with a preschool child (Table 16.2), individual values by themselves show almost the identical strong impact ($\Delta R^2 = 0.102$, not in the table). Controlling for all other indicators for cultural influence, items regarding religious beliefs (of the individual and in the society) and for gender-related norms, individual values still show a very remarkable additional influence (Model 6, as compared with Model 5, $\Delta(\Delta R^2) = 0.071$). The fact that this influence is slightly lower than the impact of individual values alone is not surprising since individual values themselves are influenced by societal belief-systems (see above).

The beta coefficients confirm the effect of individual values on behavior. General support for female employment has a strong positive effect on a woman herself being employed. The effect of support for female employment in a particular family phase is even stronger. Similar results can be seen with the woman's employment status in other stages of her family career being the dependent variable.

Also when explaining the woman's responsibilities in housekeeping, individual values add to the picture. Again, they have a strong impact by themselves ($\Delta R^2 = 0.050$), and some additional impact when controlling for religious belief-systems in society and for individual religiosity ($\Delta(\Delta R^2) = 0.018$).

Unlike for individual religious domination and religiosity, the more abstract and general individual orientations, the individual gender-specific beliefs are an important predictor for explaining behavior. Whereas religious belief-systems have an impact mainly inasmuch as they are predominant in society and work through norms, with gender-specific beliefs the level of individual values becomes central.

Hypotheses 1 and 2 come with an additional remark: this influence (of belief-systems in a given society), like the influence of individual values, should be measurable in addition to the influence of welfare regimes. This implies that there is also an institutional influence. Do welfare regimes have an impact on gender-specific behavior as well?

They do, though it is relatively weak. Looking at the influence on women's employment with preschool children (Table 16.2), the dummy variables for societies (Model 7) add $\Delta R^2 = 0.122$ to the basic model. This surplus is higher by $\Delta(\Delta R^2) = 0.022$ than the impact of the cultural background

(Model 3). This 'surplus of the surplus' again leaves some evidence for a welfare regime effect. But it is less important than the impact of cultural predictors.

It is also interesting to look at the impact on housekeeping responsibilities. Here I can include the woman's current employment status as an explaining variable, which brings in a micro-level indicator for rational choice. I would imagine that employed women take over less responsibility in the household than women out of the labor market. This effect is not too strong either, but visible ($\Delta R^2 = 0.012$). Dummy variables for societies add $\Delta R^2 = 0.066$ to the basic model, which leaves $\Delta(\Delta R^2) = 0.017$ as an estimated welfare regime effect.

All in all, evidence points to both an institutional and a cultural impact on women's decisions between employment career and housekeeping responsibilities. But welfare regimes, like other economic incentives or obstacles, turn out to be less important, compared with the norms set by religious belief-systems in society and with the individual values regarding the 'right' gender relationship.

CHANGE OF VALUES AND NORMS OVER TIME

Assuming that values and norms do have an impact on women's life courses in balancing an employment career versus housekeeping, *cultural differences* and *cultural change* become important in understanding cross-national differences and change of women's life courses.

The indicators of interest are the dimension 'support for traditional gender roles,' and the three items used to calculate it. Unfortunately, not all three ISSP waves include all three items of interest, so the analyses therefore concentrate on the item 'Do you agree or disagree? ... A husband's job is to earn money; a wife's job is to look after the home and family' being the strongest available indicator (Figure 16.2).

Basic Trends

As a generalization, it seems that support for traditional gender roles has been declining across Europe over the most recent 14 years of the study. But the downward trend is not uniform, and there are striking differences in the levels.

In some Anglo-Saxon countries – for example, Australia, New Zealand and in the United Kingdom – only a slight change, if any at all, can be found. These countries had little support for the male-breadwinner concept in 1988. Some Central European societies – for example, West Germany, Austria – started with a high support in 1988, but since then have moved strongly toward more gender-egalitarian social values. I therefore could surmise that

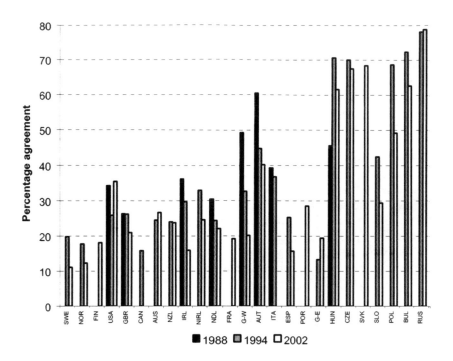

Note: Variable: 'Do you agree or disagree? ... A husband's job is to earn
             money; a wife's job is to look after the home and family.' Columns
             represent answer categories 1 'strongly agree,' 2 'agree,' and 3
             'neither agree nor disagree' (out of five possible) combined

Source: ISSP 1988, 1994, 2002, own computation, women between 20 and 50,
             weighted data

Figure 16.2   *Acceptance of male-breadwinner model, cross-national comparison,
             1988, 1994, 2002*

the overall trend is not toward complete disapproval of traditional gender
roles, but rather that societies are moving toward a *lower level* of support –
where the decline stops and gender-related values re-stabilize.

However, if this is true, the level of long-term re-stabilization, is not the
same for all societies. There are societies that have already reached a rather
gender-egalitarian norm and are still moving, such as Sweden and Norway.
And there are others, such as Italy or Hungary, that are not showing a clear
cultural change over the last 14 years of the study and seem to maintain a
higher support for the male-breadwinner concept.

Eastern Europe leaves a slightly different impression by comparison. According to Figure 16.2, there was a strong increase between 1988 and 1994 in Hungary (being the only country to participate in ISSP before 1991), followed by a decrease in the late 1990s (also visible in other Eastern European societies). The peak comes at a time of exceptionally strong social change. In this time of high economic vulnerability, uncertainty and anomie, it is easy to assume that value structures are reacting with a temporary re-traditionalization, a 'transition shock' (Lück and Hofäcker 2003, p. 38) that might have occured in several post-socialist societies.

East Germany provides a special case, for unlike other former communist societies, it shows an extremely low level of support for traditional gender roles. Like other Eastern European societies, it managed to establish female employment as self-evident. But it additionally managed to free women from the double burden of employment and childcare by introducing a generous infrastructure of professional childcare. It also managed to create a highly secular society with only a small minority of Lutheran Christians. These unique circumstances probably made it possible to establish East Germany as one of the most gender-egalitarian cultures that one can find.

Generation effects or period effects?

It is possible to interpret developments in aggregate data in two ways. One is to argue that as in society as a whole, individuals in the society change their beliefs over time. The other is to assert that new birth cohorts, born and raised in the society, establish different values than the older cohorts whom they replace. In this way, society can go through a value shift without a single individual changing his or her beliefs. The first interpretation is known as the *period effect*, the second as the *generation effect*. Which of the two is taking place when there are value changes and to what degree? This has been the subject of intense debate (Bürklin, Klein and Ruß 1994; Inglehart 1977, pp. 21ff; Klages 1984, pp. 41ff; 1988, pp. 53ff).

To answer the question which effect(s) lie(s) behind the cultural change visible in Figure 16.2, cohort analyses were calculated for every single society, inasmuch as data existed extending more than one year. In Figure 16.3, the more striking examples are presented. Again I find an unexpected result. Not only are both period and generation effects evident, but the existence of the two effects is country-specific!

In the USA, for example, *only* the generation effect is (clearly) visible. The support for traditional gender roles is rather stable within the cohorts in all three ISSP waves. At least, it does not shift in a clear direction. That the USA as a society has moved toward more gender equality – in the late 1980s and early 1990s – is owing to the natural exchange of generations, with younger generations having different views on this issue than the older generations. At the same time, the overall shift is slowing down as intergenerational

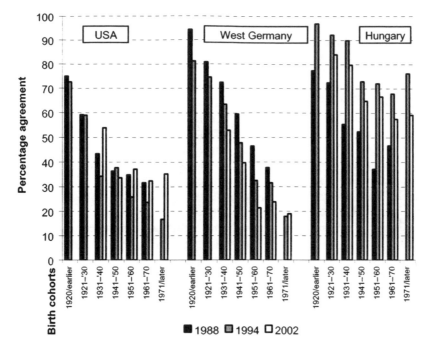

Note: Variable: 'Do you agree or disagree? ... A husband's job is to earn
                 money; a wife's job is to look after the home and family.' Columns
                 represent answer categories 1 'strongly agree,' 2 'agree,' and 3
                 'neither agree nor disagree' (out of five possible) combined

Source: ISSP 1988, 1994, 2002, own computation, weighted data

*Figure 16.3   Acceptance of male-breadwinner model at three interview waves
                 across cohorts for the USA, West Germany and Hungary*

differences become much smaller than they were among older cohorts. The
Netherlands, Great Britain and New Zealand are other examples where I find
only a generational effect.

In the USA, I also find some evidence for a re-traditionalization in the late
1990s (Figure 16.2), which in the cohort-analysis seems to occur as an
additional period effect. This trend, however, should be confirmed by further
data when possible.

The picture is quite different in West Germany. Here I see an even stronger
generation effect that is causing ongoing cultural change across *all* cohorts in
the analysis. But I additionally witness a shift *within* cohorts, with every
single birth cohort decreasing its support for the male-breadwinner concept,
in some cases very remarkably. The amount of decrease and its consistency

over *all* birth cohorts cannot be interpreted as random deviations but rather as a combination of both generation and period effects, which are speeding up the overall cultural change in society. A similar picture, with both effects overlapping and supporting each other can be found in Ireland, Spain and Sweden.

Hungary provides still another model. Looking at the period effect, I find the 'transition shock,' mirrored in the fact that every single cohort makes an upwards leap in 1994 showing extraordinary strong support for traditional gender roles at least temporarily, and then every single cohort leaps back down in 2002. As was true at the aggregate level in 2002, every single cohort is still at a more traditional level than in 1988. Either Hungarian society is still recovering from the 'transition shock,' or the shock of introducing capitalism is leaving individuals permanently with more traditional values than they had in the 1980s.

Also, cultural change across cohorts occurs. Among elder cohorts it is shifting toward more gender equality, among the youngest cohorts it seems to support the re-traditionalization of society, leaving those born in the 1950s as the most gender egalitarian cohort. This peak might have to do with political change as well. However, the back shift in the youngest cohort was already visible in 1988 data – in a pre-transition year – so the interpretation is less clear.

SUMMARY

This chapter has argued that it is not only national institutions and welfare regimes that are shaping women's life courses, but that 'gender culture' as Pfau-Effinger describes it (1996; 1997) plays an important role as well. It has looked at women's decisions to follow an employment career versus the decision to become a mother and homemaker.

Empirical analyses have shown that these decisions have a lot to do with a woman's individual values and attitudes regarding the 'gender-appropriate' career track. And they have a lot to do with social values and norms, connected to the predominant religious belief-systems in the woman's societies. I also have shown that a woman's individual gender-related values are affected by the religious belief-systems in her society. What is less important is the woman's individual religious beliefs.

Cross-national differences and changes in women's life courses therefore cannot be understood solely as a function of the institutional filters welfare regimes provide. Welfare regimes do affect women's career tracks as well, but it might be more appropriate to frame this influence with Pfau-Effinger's concept of 'gender arrangements' (1996; 1997) linking 'gender order' and 'gender culture.'

Linking results to Inglehart and Carballo, I have found that cross-cultural differences and change of gender culture are embedded in a broader context of social changes that could be referred to as 'modernization' (in a Weberian sense of rationalization) on the one hand, and as a values shift away from survival concerns after World War II toward well-being concerns. Cross-national differences and change of women's life courses are also embedded in these processees of cultural change.

NOTES

1   Attitudes, defined as specific beliefs, are assumed to have a stronger impact on behavior than values (though on fewer aspects). Values are defined as more general and abstract beliefs. However, terms such as 'specific values' or 'general attitudes' blur this distinction. ISSP data also does not allow me to measure values in a way that clearly distinguishes them from attitudes. Therefore, both attitudes and values are treated as one category.

2   The stages are: before children are born, with preschool children, with school-age children and after all children have moved out of the household.

3   Education, for example, might have an effect because of the human capital women achieve with it or because of the different social class, strata or lifestyle they get socialized into. A similar ambiguity exists for personal or household income. A cohort impact might reflect an institutional change over time or cultural change (value change) over generations.

4   This means a lot of compromises: income variables are not only measured in different currencies, but also partly as monthly, as yearly, as net and partly as gross income. Therefore, only income deciles within a given country could be used. Self-classification of social class was dropped as was an urban–rural indicator because these variables were included only in some countries.

5   Household income is also available, but it cannot be used along with individual income in the same model, because they are too highly inter-correlated. So two versions were tested, which produced quite comparable results. Here only the version with individual income is presented.

6   These are: v4 to v18 and v29 to v31.

7   The analyses included correlations, principal components factor analyses (varimax rotation) and reliability analyses, repeated for all countries, for single countries and for specific sub-samples (for example, women aged 25 to 50).

8   Represented by the share of people in society who are strong supporters, according to a dichotomous indicator.

9   The categories 'full-time,' 'part-time' or 'not employed' are assumed to be metrical in Table 16.2, and the dependent variable includes all three answers. However the results remain similar (at a lower level of explained variance) if I use a dummy variable instead.

430   *Conclusions*

BIBLIOGRAPHY

Breuer, R. (1998) *Familienleben im Islam. Traditionen, Konflikte, Vorurteile,* Freiburg im Breisgau: Herder.

Bundesministerium für Familie, Senioren, Frauen und Jugend (BMfSFJ) (2000) *Sechster Familienbericht. Familien ausländischer Herkunft,* Drucksache 14/4357.

Bürklin, W., Klein, M. and Ruß, A. (1994) 'Dimensionen des Wertewandels. Eine empirische Längsschnittanalyse zur Dimensionalität und der Wandlungsdynamik gesellschaftlicher Wertorientierungen', *Politische Vierteljahresschrift,* 35(4): 580–606.

Durkheim, É. (1999) *Der Selbstmord,* Frankfurt a.M.: Suhrkamp.

Easterlin, R.A. (1973) 'Relative economic status and the American fertility swing', in E.B. Sheldon (ed.) *Family economic behaviour. Problems and prospects,* Philadelphia, PA and Toronto: Lippincott.

Elster, J. (1987) *Subversion der Rationalität,* Frankfurt a.M.: Campus.

Esping-Andersen, G. (1990) *The three worlds of welfare capitalism,* Cambridge: Polity Press.

Esser, H. (1990) 'Habits, frames und rational choice. Die Reichweite von Theorien der rationalen Wahl (am Beispiel der Erklärung des Befragtenverhaltens)', *Zeitschrift für Soziologie,* 19: 231–47.

Esser, H. (1996) 'Die Definition der Situation', *Kölner Zeitschrift für Soziologie und Sozialpsychologie,* 48(1): 1–34.

Ferrara, M. (1996) 'The 'Southern Model' of welfare in social Europe', *Journal of European Social Policy,* 6(1): 17–37.

Fuchs, D. and Rohrschneider, R. (2001) 'Der Einfluß politischer Wertorientierungen auf Regimeunterstützung und Wahlverhalten', in H.-D. Klingemann and M. Kaase (eds) *Wahlen und Wähler: Analysen aus Anlass der Bundestagswahl 1998,* Wiesbaden: Westdeutscher Verlag.

GESIS/ZA (2001). The International Social Survey Programme. ISSP 1985–1996, 1998. Data and Documentation, www.gesis.org. Accessed 5 December 2005.

Herwartz-Emden, L. (2000) 'Einwandererfamilien. Geschlechterverhältnisse, Erziehung und Akkulturation', *Schriften des Instituts für Migrationsforschung und Interkulturelle Studien der Universität Osnabrück, Nr. 9,* Osnabrück: Rasch.

Herwartz-Emden, L. and Westphal, M. (1999) 'Frauen und Männer, Mütter und Väter. Empirische Ergebnisse zu Veränderungen der Geschlechterverhältnisse in Einwandererfamilien', *Zeitschrift für Pädagogik,* 45(6): 885–902.

Höllinger, F. (1991) 'Frauenerwerbstätigkeit und Wandel der Geschlechtsrollen im internationalen Vergleich', *Kölner Zeitschrift für Soziologie und Sozialpsychologie,* 43(4): 753–71.

Inglehart, R. (1977) *The silent revolution,* Princeton, NJ: Princeton University Press.

Inglehart, R. (1989) *Culture shift in advanced industrial society,* Princeton, NJ: Princeton University Press.

Inglehart, R. (1997) *Modernization and postmodernization. Cultural, economic, and political change in 43 societies,* Princeton, NJ: Princeton University Press.

Inglehart, R. and Carballo, M. (1997) 'Does Latin America exist? And is there a confucian culture? A global analysis of cross-cultural differences', *PS: Political Science & Politics,* 30: 34–46.

Klages, H. (1984) *Wertorientierungen im Wandel. Rückblick, Gegenwartsanalysen, Prognosen.* Frankfurt a.M. and New York: Campus.

Klages, H. (1988) *Wertedynamik. Über die Wandelbarkeit des Selbstverständlichen,* Osnabrück: Verlag A. Fromm.

Klages, H. (1993) *Traditionsbruch als Herausforderung. Perspektiven der Wertewandelsgesellschaft,* Frankfurt a.M. and New York: Campus.

Klein, T. (1990) 'Postmaterialismus und generatives Verhalten', *Zeitschrift für Soziologie,* 19(1): 57–64.

Langenheder, W. (1975) *Theorie menschlicher Entscheidungshandlungen,* Stuttgart: Enke.

Lessenich, S. (1994) 'Three worlds of welfare capitalism' – oder vier? Strukturwandel arbeits- und sozialpolitischer Regulierungsmuster in Spanien', *Politische Vierteljahresschrift,* 35(2): 224–44.

Lück, D. (2004) 'Cross-national comparison of gender role attitudes and their impact on women's life courses', GLOBALIFE Working Paper No. 67, Chair of Sociology I, University of Bamberg, Germany.

Lück, D. and Hofäcker, D. (2003) 'Rejection and acceptance of the male breadwinner model', GLOBALIFE Working Paper No. 60, Chair of Sociology I, University of Bamberg, Germany.

Nauck, B. (1989) 'Individualistische Erklärungsansätze in der Familienforschung: Die rational-choice-Basis von Familienökonomie, Ressourcen- und Austauschtheorie', in R. Nave-Herz and M. Markefka (eds) *Handbuch der Familien- und Jugendforschung. Band 1: Familienforschung,* Neuwied: Luchterhand.

Nauck, B. (2002) 'Dreißig Jahre Migrantenfamilien in der Bundesrepublik. Familiärer Wandel zwischen Situationsanpassung, Akkulturation, Segregation und Re-migration', in R. Nave-Herz (ed.) *Kontinuität und Wandel der Familie in Deutschland: Eine zeitgeschichtliche Analyse,* Stuttgart: Lucius und Lucius.

Obinger, H. and Wagschal, U. (1998) 'Drei Welten des Wohlfahrtsstaates? Das Strafizierungskonzept in der clusteranalytischen Überprüfung', in S. Lessenich and I. Ostner (eds) *Welten des Wohlfahrtskapitalismus. Der Sozialstaat in vergleichender Perspektive,* Frankfurt a.M. and New York: Campus, pp. 109–35.

Opp, K.-D., Burow-Auffahrt K. and Hartmann, P. (1984) *Soziale Probleme und Protestverhalten,* Opladen: Westdeutscher Verlag.

Pfau-Effinger, B. (1996) 'Analyse internationaler Differenzen in der Erwerbsbeteiligung von Frauen – theoretischer Rahmen und empirische Ergebnisse', *KZfSS,* 48(4): 462–92.

Pfau-Effinger, B. (1997) 'Zum theoretischen Rahmen für die Analyse internationaler Differenzen in der gesellschaftlichen Integration von Frauen', in S. Hradil (ed.) *Differenz und Integration: die Zukunft moderner Gesellschaften. Verhandlungen des 28. Kongresses der Deutschen Gesellschaft für Soziologie in Dresden 1996,* Frankfurt a.M.: Campus.

Riedo, R. (1991) 'Ausländerfamilien', in T. Fleiner-Gerster, P. Gilliand and K. Lüscher (eds) *Familien in der Schweiz,* Fribourg: Universitätsverlag Freiburg.

Schulze, G. (1993) *Die Erlebnisgesellschaft. Kultursoziologie der Gegenwart,* Frankfurt a.M.: Campus.

Spranger, E. (1950) *Lebensformen. Geisteswissenschaftliche Psychologie und Ethik der Persönlichkeit,* Tübingen: Niemeyer.

Weber, M. (1988 [1920]) 'Askese und kapitalistischer Geist', in M. Weber (ed.) *Gesammelte Aufsätze zur Religionssoziologie, Band I*, Tübingen: J.C.B. Mohr (Paul Siebeck) (UTB).

Worbs, S. and Heckmann, F. (2003) *Islam in Deutschland: Aufarbeitung des gegenwärtigen Forschungsstandes und Auswertung eines Datensatzes zur zweiten Migrantengeneration*, Studie im Auftrag des Bundesministeriums des Inneren, efms.

17. Women's careers in an era of uncertainty: conclusions from a 13-country international comparison

Heather Hofmeister and
Hans-Peter Blossfeld[1]

INTRODUCTION

Women's increasing ties to the labor market in modern societies have helped to enhance their equality and reduce their oppression. The goal of this book has been to test for evidence that these changes might be reversing owing to globalization for women in 13 countries: Germany, the Netherlands, Sweden, Denmark, Hungary, Estonia, the Czech Republic, Poland, Britain, the United States, Mexico, Italy and Spain. We examine whether the processes of globalization in the second half of the twentieth century accelerate patterns of labor market attachment by expanding the amount and variety of work available, or if these processes reverse trends toward equality by concentrating women in positions of low security and disempowerment in the labor market at various points along the life course, even if their attachment has increased. Women without access to quality employment must rely on alternative sources of support such as earner/breadwinners – fathers, sons, husbands – or the state. In fact, many systems are, or until recently were, designed around the idea that women will obtain their security from partners. The dire and even life threatening consequences for unpartnered, widowed, abused, abandoned or divorced women are ignored or accepted. But even the security of male breadwinners and the state are increasingly challenged under globalization in almost all of the countries under study (Blossfeld et al. 2005; Blossfeld, Buchholz and Hofäcker 2006; Blossfeld, Mills and Bernardi 2006).

Since the early 1960s, rates of mid-life women's paid work have been steadily increasing in all modern societies. But this is a picture in the aggregate. Our volume has examined the role of employment in individual women's lives with a cohort-level comparison wherever possible. We intended particularly to test whether successive cohorts of women in mid-life are experiencing rising labor market attachment – shorter spells of absence from the labor market – and whether women are experiencing rising employment insecurity, measured as more movement to unemployment, more difficult returns to the labor market from a state of unemployment or caregiving, or more downward mobility over time. We also sought to understand the ways in which institutions and individual characteristics affect the probability of a woman experiencing any of these effects. In this concluding chapter, we summarize the answers to these questions based on the nation-specific case studies in this volume. We find evidence pointing to increased labor market attachment and the reduction in employment quality for women in most of our countries, as companion volumes have also found for youth (Blossfeld et al. 2005) and for mid-career men in unprotected employment regimes (Blossfeld, Mills and Bernardi 2006). Family systems, as with national systems, do not operate in isolation. It stands to reason that the difficulties of youth becoming established in the labor market, the lengthening of youth's residence in the parental home and the rising challenge for some men in providing financial security and stability for their families would have an impact on mid-life women's employment. In a hostile labor market, women's earnings become all the more essential for their families. The irony and tragedy occurs with the failure of employment systems to adapt to the urgency and importance of female employment. Systems, societies and policy makers who assume a woman's earnings are legitimately marginalized – as 'pin money' or just for extras like vacations and dining out – create dangerous consequences for women and children and fail at their task to ensure full and equal human rights for their citizens.

Interpreting reasons for and consequences of changes in the work careers of women at the national level over time is a delicate task; the most accurate interpretations rely on our national experts who understand the context and the dynamics within a country. Our results are drawn from the separate country-specific chapters in this volume, which described the unique context of women's employment within a specific country over the past decades. These include the conservative welfare regimes of Germany (Buchholz and Grunow, this volume) and the Netherlands (Kalmijn and Luijkx, this volume), the social-democratic regimes of Sweden (Korpi and Stern, this volume) and Denmark (Grunow and Leth-Sørensen, this volume), the post-socialist regimes of Hungary (Bukodi and Róbert, this volume), Estonia (Helemäe and Saar, this volume) the Czech Republic (Hamplová, this volume) and Poland (Plomien, this volume), the liberal regimes of the United Kingdom (Golsch, this volume) and the United States (Hofmeister, this volume) and the family-oriented regimes of Mexico (Parrado, this volume), Italy (Pisati and Schizzerotto, this volume) and Spain (Simó Noguera, this volume). These country-specific experts engaged in an empirical examination of the intragenerational employment transitions of women, which included the study of upward and downward job mobility, transition into unemployment, transition into caregiving and re-entry into the labor market following unemployment or caregiving. We furthermore draw conclusions from the comparative examination of welfare regimes (Hofäcker, this volume) and of the role of gender attitudes and cultural frameworks (Lück, this volume).

GLOBALIZATION AND WOMEN'S CAREERS

Globalization has ambivalent but mostly negative implications for women's employment, largely depending on the welfare state and the country-specific employment regime. As globalization has expanded the informal sector and created demand for workforces to be summoned in times of need and dismissed in times of reduced demand, women, as historic outsiders in the labor market, have seen their careers become more turbulent in most countries of this study (see Table 17.1). In this section we answer the four main questions posed in the introduction: whether globalization has contributed to a rise in mid-life women's labor market attachment, what has happened to the quality of that employment, how individual characteristics matter, and how national contexts matter.

A rise in mid-life labor market attachment?

Our first research question asked whether globalization fosters a rise in women's mid-life labor force attachment. To summarize in broad strokes, women in countries with a historically weak attachment to the labor market saw their attachment strengthen; women in countries with a strong attachment saw that attachment weaken. But there are exceptions. In the introductory chapter we presented a figure showing an s-curve of women's labor market attachment, with predictions about the consequences of movement over time along a continuum from weak attachment to strong attachment. Here we present a modified version of that figure showing the actual movement of women's labor market attachment in the countries of this study (see Figure 17.1).

In countries at the upper right end of the curve who had achieved higher levels of women's full-time secure employment, the results of this volume indicate movement in all three directions – up, down and straight ahead – for women in countries represented at this point. Sweden has managed to protect its workforce for the most part, and women's strong integration in the labor market means they are not disproportionately disadvantaged by globalization, a straight-ahead path (Korpi and Stern, this volume). In Estonia and the Czech Republic, attachment remains high (Helemae and Saar, this volume; Hamplová, this volume). Denmark's government created a release valve of well-compensated caregiving exit possibilities that were used by women who

Table 17.1 Results of the 13-country comparison of women's labor market attachment and employment and career uncertainty over time

Welfare regime	Labor market attachment		Employment and career uncertainty	
	Rising (stable)	Decreasing	Rising (stable)	Decreasing
Conservative	Germany The Netherlands		Germany (The Netherlands)	
Social democratic	Sweden	Denmark	(Sweden) (Denmark)	
Post-socialist	(Estonia) (Czech Republic)	Hungary Poland	Hungary Estonia Czech Republic Poland	
Liberal	Great Britain United States		Great Britain United States	
Family-oriented	Italy Spain	Mexico	Mexico Italy Spain	

otherwise might have been unemployed, making a downturning path slightly away from previous levels of labor market attachment (Grunow and Leth-Sørensen, this volume). Some Hungarian and Polish women have taken the opportunity to leave the labor market now that the Iron Curtain has fallen and full-time employment is no longer mandatory, which marks their pathway away from full attachment (Bukodi and Róbert, this volume; Plomien, this volume). How this process will settle out in the forthcoming decades is an important topic for future research.

For countries along the other points of the continuum, with the exception of Mexico, women experienced a rise in labor market attachment across cohorts in the phase of globalization. We discuss reasons below.

Declining levels of women's labor market attachment: Denmark, Hungary, Poland and Mexico

Our research indicates a variety of reasons why some countries experience declines in women's labor market attachment. Denmark put in place a popular high-impact personal leave alternative to unemployment (for education, sabbatical, or caregiving) which dropped the level of female labor market attachment over the course of the 1990s (Grunow and Leth-Sørensen, this volume). In Hungary and Poland, women are less attached to the labor market because rates of women's labor market involvement were already so high that there was only one direction to go, which was down, now that the political regime no longer mandates full-time work for all adults (Bukodi and Róbert, this volume; Plomien, this volume). When the markets opened up, employment became optional at least for some women with secure-income alternatives. The ability to leave the labor market for caregiving is often a mark of affluence.

In Mexico, we describe women's labor market attachment as declining because the new industries moving in under NAFTA have made flexible employment and temporary work more possible (Parrado, this volume). The expanding employment forms are domestic help and the maquiladora industries that employ young women at drastically depressed wages. Since women in this country still bear the overwhelming majority of responsibility for the household and caregiving responsibilities, such employment has enabled them to take time off as needed when caregiving demands are more intense, provided they have other sources of income such as a stable breadwinner, a condition that should not be taken for granted.

Rising levels of women's labor market attachment: Spain, Italy, Germany, The Netherlands, Sweden, Britain, the United States

The effects of globalization on other members of a woman's family system have been established in volumes by Blossfeld et al. (2005) and Blossfeld, Mills and Bernardi (2006). In short, globalization makes the transition to first employment for youth less secure, which has the effect of young people residing longer with their parents and postponing family and partnership formation. Younger men, North American men and men from Eastern European countries are experiencing more difficulties attaching to and staying in the labor market. The logical consequence of these changes is that that many women's life courses will also change, because women's lives are linked to and integrated with the lives of other members of the family. Rising labor market attachment may be fostered in women's life courses directly through market change that opens opportunities for women and/or indirectly through the career turbulence of close family members, such as husbands and adult children, which increases the urgency of women's earnings.

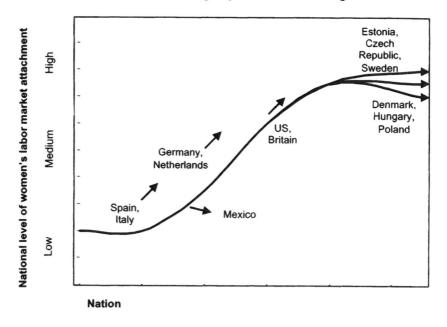

Key:
   Direction globalization forces push women's labor market
                  attachment

*Figure 17.1   Empirical illustrative summary of macro-level
                changes in women's labor market attachment over
                time under processes of globalization*

Another interpretation for the rise in women's labor market attachment stems from the rise in tolerance for, and practice of, married women's employment (see Lück, this volume). In many countries, married women's employment is strongly on the rise because marriage is no longer a reason for exiting, meaning that women who were employed at the time of marriage stay employed. Our models confirm that, across cohorts and countries, marriage is losing its depressive effect on women's labor market attachment.

A third explanation for the rise in women's labor market attachment is the rise in information and communication technologies. A more specific analysis of the relationship between high-technology jobs and women's career opportunities is therefore a fruitful area for future research.

We now turn to country-specific reasons for the rise in women's labor market attachment. We had hypothesized that women in conservative and family-oriented welfare regimes with historically low levels of overall female employment would increase their attachment to the labor market over time owing to the expansion of flexible jobs. Indeed, women in other family-oriented countries have experienced a rising attachment to the labor market, but more strongly coinciding with declining family formation, not necessarily with a rise in flexible jobs. It is increasingly common for women in Spain and Italy to remain childless or have fewer children than their mothers or older sisters had (Pisati and Schizzerotto, this volume). Blame may lie with the problems in reconciling employment and family owing to the lack of market or government support for alternatives to mother-care (Simó Noguera, this volume). A traditional male-oriented workplace culture denies women promotion opportunities or makes advancement take longer, while the rise in education for women makes women better qualified, adding to the frustration of the situation.

Women in Germany, though in a conservative welfare regime, show tendencies similar to those of the family-oriented countries in the sense that they tend to choose between employment and family careers, rather than maintaining both simultaneously. Women remain in the labor market longer in Germany in the later-born cohorts, but they still exit at high rates when children are born (Buchholz and Grunow, this volume). The lack of an inclusive childcare policy and the strong cultural expectations for mothers' constant care and attention for German children discourage women from trying to mix employment and family, especially when the children are very young. Once children have grown, the strong insider labor market has effectively closed behind them, and re-entry to careers once children are more independent is difficult for German women. This seemingly modern welfare state and robust and sophisticated economy is grafted onto a strongly traditional society where the expectations for men's and women's roles, deeply rooted in tradition and church teachings, play an invisible but strong hand in constructing women's (and men's) life courses.

Women in the Netherlands have experienced a consistent rise in labor market attachment in the last decades of the twentieth century (Kalmijn and Luijkx, this volume). The probability of Dutch women leaving the labor market has continuously declined while the chances of re-entering the labor market have continuously increased. In these senses, the careers of Dutch women have become more stable. At the same time, Kalmijn and Luijkx find that job mobility has increased over time, suggesting that careers have also become more versatile. As was also the case for Germany, marriage no longer plays a strong role in women's employment exits, but children remain a reason to exit.

Swedish women have acquired increasingly secure positions on the labor market: employment rates, working hours and job stability have all increased (Korpi and Stern, this volume). Domestic policies in the forms of expansion of the public sector and reforms in regulations regarding parental leave, daycare, part-time work and taxation have drastically transformed the conditions for female employment in Sweden. Though unemployment increased in Sweden in the 1990s, Korpi and Stern suggest that these increases are not a sign of globalization because the effects were not disproportionately concentrated in manufacturing or among the various educational groups.

The United States and Britain provide contrasting cases within the liberal welfare regime of reasons for women's rising attachment. Women in the United States have achieved a high level of labor market integration, as in Sweden (Hofmeister, this volume). Also like Sweden, women and men in the United States experience changes in the labor market in similar ways. But unlike Sweden, this similar experience in the United States stems from a lack of protection of workers rather than extensive protection of workers. In the United States, expanding education for women, the rising insecurity of men's employment, the rise in the standard of living expectations and the rise in divorce rates contribute to the growing attachment of women to the labor market in a context that, rather than marginalizing women's employment, has liberalized women's careers to the point where women can be found, in some cases in the majority, in many industries and fields that were formerly dominated by men. The price American women pay is in maintaining an unencumbered, unhindered 'male-type' work career trajectory in a context where they are in fact simultaneously raising children and keeping the household running with their after-hours labor.

In Britain, labor market segregation of women translates to low-pay, low-advancement careers for women (Golsch, this volume). These careers make the integration of work and family easier and thus foster the attachment of more women to the labor market for a greater proportion of their lives, but at a price. British women in marginal jobs experience a higher probability of unemployment.

We find it important to distinguish among three different types of consequences of globalization on women's employment. The first is the level of temporal flexibility. The second is the quality of jobs, whether they are secure lifelong-type jobs or precarious short-term. The third is whether the labor market attachment is in actual employment or in unemployment. Any expansion in employment possibilities in nearly all countries seem to be counteracted by rollbacks in the quality of formerly secure jobs, the insecurity of the newly created jobs and rising unemployment. These findings are consistent with our hypothesis that the pressures of globalization encourage the market to shift risk to individuals, especially the most vulnerable, who include youth and women wishing to return to paid work from an extended period of caregiving. We now turn to a discussion of the quality of women's new employment trajectories.

The quality of women's employment

We asked what consequences globalization brings not only to the attachment of women to the labor market, but also to the quality of women's employment, whether the uncertainty in women's careers has increased (see Table 17.1). The employment restructuring fueled by globalization has partly jeopardized women's job security by creating more insecure jobs than in the past. We specifically examined whether increased employment flexibilization hinders the further integration of women into the skilled and mostly full-time positions of the internal labor market, exposing them to greater career uncertainty, or whether skilled women are particularly integrated through more flexible work forms created by the knowledge-intensive economy. Our second hypothesis summarized our expectation that increased competition would compel firms to reduce (or at least not improve) benefits for marginal, flexibilized workers. What we find is that, indeed, flexible work remains marginalizing. As this form of work expands and is filled primarily by women, the employment and career uncertainty of women in nearly all countries rises (Germany, Hungary, Estonia, Czech Republic, Poland, Britain, United States, Mexico, Italy and Spain) or in the best case remains stable (the Netherlands, Sweden and Denmark).

We also studied whether the escalating restructuring of employment conditions affects the movement of mid-life women into unskilled jobs (downward mobility), skilled jobs (upward mobility), unemployment and unpaid caregiving. We find globalization accelerating mid-life women's re-entrance to the labor market even as it makes those transitions harder to accomplish with the rise in unemployment. We find that unemployment is on the rise in all countries, including Sweden, but the human capital of individual women tempers the probability of staying unemployed.

No later-born cohort of women in these national studies experienced an overall rise in career certainty compared with previous cohorts. Evidence from countries where labor market participation of women has been high for many decades suggests that there is more to this explanation than only the selection of highly motivated, achievement-oriented women into the labor market in earlier cohorts. Those women who experienced stable rates of career certainty (rather than declining rates) are in the Netherlands, Sweden and Denmark, three countries that have a high degree of women's labor

market participation and, formally or informally, alternative employment
tracks for women, with high degrees of occupational segregation and part-
time work. These countries have been open to international markets and trade
over a longer period of time, enabling them perhaps to react more flexibly to
the newest demands of an international market while maintaining social
support for their citizens. Another feature of these countries conforms to our
third hypothesis. We found that overall the public sector did offer protection
for women from the uncertainties introduced by globalization. Thus countries
with high levels of female employment in the public sector such as the
Netherlands, Sweden and Denmark offered many women some extra shelter
from the uncertainties introduced by globalization.

The differential allocation of jobs

Third, we asked whether there are certain groups of women who are more
likely to be unemployed or in lower-quality jobs. Indeed, structural position
contributes a great deal to the likelihood of women's job quality, as we
expected. Individual levels of education and job experience, as expected, play
a role. Women with strong skills in new 'knowledge-based' areas, high
education and youth on their side tend to leave unemployment relatively
quickly and to advance to better jobs, leaving behind a ghetto of unemployed
or career-stagnated women who tend to be older, have less labor market
experience, less education and more previous spells of unemployment.
Education was, in country after country, a strong predictor of which women
have and maintain career ties across their life courses with opportunities for
advancement. There is a cumulation of advantage, and the processes of
globalization, which restructure the labor market and increase flexible and
short-term employment, do not aid women who find themselves repeatedly
losing jobs. There is less work for unskilled labor, as we expected. In fact,
evidence suggests that the processes of assortative class allocation in the
labor market are deepened and solidified by globalization.

But the presence of another earner also contributes to the selectivity
women can adopt when choosing to accept a job, as we hypothesized.
Women with breadwinners can afford to accept only better positions and turn
down worse ones, whereas single mothers, divorced women and widows tend
to have fewer options as the need for an income supersedes issues of job
quality. Women with more young children at home tend to suffer
disadvantages on the labor markets compared with other women. This
finding may be a consequence of the way women are forced to prioritize
between either family work or paid work; those who choose family work
ahead of paid work chronologically experience penalties in the labor market
owing to employer assumptions that they cannot be (as) serious about their
jobs. Other explanations include labor market absences and childcare
difficulties.

The difficulties later cohorts of women experience in the labor market may be partly explained by selection bias across cohorts, because earlier birth cohorts of women who had employment careers were overcoming stronger stigmas against female employment in order to have their careers and thus represent a more selective and ambitious group of women workers. By comparison, later-born cohorts of women represent a broader cross-section of education and aspiration because of their numbers. But the same outcome arriving from a variety of methods, samples and cohort definitions in this volume suggests that there is something else to the story.

The role of national context

A final question asked how national contexts and welfare regimes influence the availability of the compromises between work and family demands for mid-career women, the quality of women's employment and inequality among women. Countries differ significantly with respect to the configuration of relationships among employers, workers, families and the state (Esping-Andersen 1999; Orloff 2002). The inclusion of countries that are structurally different allowed us to gain an empirically grounded theoretical understanding of how globalization has impacted on women's mid-career life courses across a variety of contexts.

There are distinct variations among modern countries in terms of the importance of not only labor market agreements but also the availability of state-sponsored family supports or market-driven alternatives to women's unpaid care, all of which impact on the mid-life options and pathways of women tremendously. We find that in some countries spells of unemployment tend to be short (Sweden, Denmark) and expansion of the public and service sectors greatly enhances women's employment opportunities despite fluctuations in the national economy. These nations share a social-democratic welfare regime philosophy that does impact on women's life courses. In other countries (Italy, Spain, Germany), the lack of provisions for women's caregiving means women make choices between paid work and family: they reduce the number of children or avoid them altogether if they are committed to careers. This trend also follows welfare regime logics.

Countries with few protections and a laissez-faire social policy regarding female and child poverty tend to leave poor women in the position of seeking informal solutions to childcare and accepting jobs almost regardless of the levels of constraints or the low quality of the position (United States, Estonia). British women are more vulnerable to unemployment when they have flexible, short-term, fixed-term and marginal work. But a means-tested benefit system and flat-rate entitlements in Britain may contribute to a lack of incentive for either partner in poor households to seek employment. Women living in countries undergoing large-scale economic reforms such as the former socialist countries are the most vulnerable with the most potential to gain and lose.

Herein may be the most important story of this volume. Thanks to the expertise of Bukodi, Róbert, Helemäe, Saar, Hamplová and Plomien, this volume illustrates – in a way none have before – the drastic consequences on employment and family life that have occurred owing to the fall of the Iron Curtain. Each has reported on the shift from required full-time employment of women to the stark choices available among unemployment or full-time employment. Maternity leave may be increasingly insecure as these countries face economic pressures and expenses in the process of modernizing their economies and infrastructures. Part-time employment is rarely available, though much coveted, but the financial demands of households often require two full-time incomes. In a cultural context where a woman's place was in the home at the same time that the law required her full-time paid labor, resulting in a phenomenally taxing double burden in the former socialist countries, it is little surprise that gender attitudes have moved back toward a male-breadwinner–female-homemaker preference in these countries since the collapse of socialism; such an attitude is a luxury to idealize, even if the constraints of the market do not permit its expression in reality.

The contribution of Lück in Chapter 16 highlights the story behind the national and welfare regime differences. He finds that culture influences both welfare regime arrangements and women's attitudes toward employment and family. This culture is marked by linguistic and religious distinctions that made a significant difference in the attitudes women had toward combining employment and family across national contexts. Gender attitudes of women have been liberalizing between 1998 and 2002 for women in all cohorts, with the exception of the post-socialist countries. Here one can observe what he calls a 'transition shock' in 1994, which adjusted back to the trend by 2002.

We asked in the introduction whether dominant cultural norms will shift toward women's labor market participation and generate attitudinal and institutional support growing within other relevant institutions across societies, or whether, instead, we would see attitudinal extremes forming based on access to power and privilege. Evidence from Chapter 16 suggests that the tolerance for women's paid work is increasing across cohorts, across countries, over time, regardless of national, religious or class divisions. The starting points vary, but the direction seems consistent in all globalized societies under study across a 14-year spread.

PATHWAYS IN AND OUT OF UNCERTAINTY

In the introduction, we laid out pathways in and out of uncertainty in Figure 1.3. One of the hypothesized generators of uncertainty was a weakening of state support. We find some evidence that in countries where state support has been weakened (the United States, Britain, Estonia), women are increasing their attachment to the labor market, and in countries where state support is strengthened (Denmark), women have decreased their attachment. But this may be just one of several factors contributing to differences in women's attachment.

We also imagined that a rise in unemployment for women would mean increasing dependence on male earners or on state support. Anecdotal evidence and overviews suggest that this is happening, though further research would be needed to confirm the causality.

We also imagined that a weakening in the reliability of the earnings of the male breadwinner would cause women to increase their labor market attachment. Indeed, this seems to be the case. A more extensive use of couple-level data would be a fruitful area for future research. The knowledge of couple-level dynamics are of crucial importance for understanding the role of uncertainty in an individual's life course. We also advocate for research on the strategies available to women after marital dissolution in longitudinal and international comparative perspective.

CONSEQUENCES FOR WOMEN AND FAMILIES

The fact that mid-life women still hold primary responsibility for the household has enormous implications for women's careers and families. This heavy responsibility and the likelihood of women interrupting – or being expected to interrupt – work careers for caregiving responsibilities at various points along the life course makes it difficult for mid-life women to compete with unencumbered workers (men) in internal labor markets and for full-time secure positions. Women who do wish to compete with men in internal labor markets in many countries attempt to remedy this problem by avoiding family formation (Italy, Spain, Germany).

Alternative employment tracks

In other countries (the Netherlands, Sweden), alternative employment tracks for mothers have been created and often even institutionalized. These alternatives place women 'between equalization and marginalization' in the labor market – rarely able to compete with men for power, prestige or earnings, but also not fully excluded. Through the combination of state and employer support, many of these women are able to maintain professional identities and contribute to society while being able to care for family and private life more effectively than women who are forced to execute both roles as if the other did not exist. The consequences are varied: statistical discrimination against women in certain professional occupations, the feminization of certain occupations at the expense of their pay and prestige, a continuing dependence on male earnings in households, but full acceptance of the legitimacy of women's contributions in portions of the public sphere and respect for their earnings contributions at home. In Sweden, there are social policies designed to increase men's involvement in the private sphere, an initiative that may eventually open opportunities further for women in the public sphere.

More temporally flexible jobs theoretically should bring some mid-life women into the labor market who previously had difficulties reconciling paid work with unpaid care duties. But we find a pattern in countries as diverse as Italy, Hungary, the Czech Republic and Estonia that the continued lack of part-time work opportunities of any kind, to say nothing of high-quality upwardly mobile part-time jobs, severely limits the ability of women to combine employment and caregiving.

Structural constraints on families under the logic of capitalism

The difficulties faced by women in the labor market may come down to a fundamental logic of capitalism: workers who lack political power are vulnerable, as are groups who become convinced that when their work has intrinsic value, emotional value, it automatically loses its financial value. The historic 'separate spheres' capitalist dichotomy of the loving home versus the cold heartless marketplace frames women's employment decisions in stark either/or choices in ways that men's employment decisions never face.

If in fact caregiving and other unpaid work in society were as attractive as high-quality paid employment, we should see many more highly qualified men rushing into caregiving and domestic work. The fact is that these tasks and roles are avoided by most men. Men's earnings have been historically successfully framed as family caregiving, but women's earnings have not. But framing of earnings-as-care would not prevent men who wish to physically caregive from doing so. Rather the high level of career penalty associated with caregiving seems to be a strong disincentive to caregiving for men. The existence of these constraints and penalties that would apply to any active caregiver, male or female, suggests that carework is devalued and marginalized by society and is a testimony to the power of the market that employer interests predominate over the interests of the family. The low wages paid to women engaged in professional childcare further illustrate the devaluation of care. The costs to care on careers exist not only for men but also for women, though; why is it that men appear to avoid these constraints for themselves while passing these costs on to their wives? That the earnings penalties and job insecurity of parenthood are passed on to women rather than being shared across parents reflects men's greater structural position within the family and within society. It also illustrates the individualism inherent in the economic system even as states use couples and households as the unit of analysis for tax policies and as justification for statistical wage and hiring discrimination against women.

Other structural constraints exist to varying degrees that limit the options available to women (or to men) that would help balance their competing demands in most countries. The timing of the workday, workweek and work year are typically out of synchronization with school and childcare schedules. It is difficult to secure childcare in many countries, or childcare is abundant but the quality is poor, or quality care is too expensive relative to the wages of women. Some education systems limit the possibilities for women to return to train for new careers. Vast geographic distances and/or poor transportation linkages among workplaces, homes and potential caregivers hinder mobility. The list can go on and would be specific to each country context. Men would experience the same practical constraints or penalties for taking time out of the labor market for caregiving coupled with the social stigma of 'feminized work.'

POLICY IMPLICATIONS

Investing in women's careers and in women's ability to engage in simultaneous caregiving and earning is an investment in women's equality and in the well-being of the next generation. Women make reliable, conscientious workers; mothers have strong incentives to provide the best possible care and financial security for their children, which means they tend to meet supportive employers and government policies more than halfway toward accomplishing the goals of all parties. As the globalization of work loosens the traditional configurations of the workplace and opens the possibility of flexibility, the time is ripe for invoking win-win changes that help parents, not only mothers, rear the next generation and support this one. Toward this end, we recommend several policy directions.

The first and most important policy recommendation is more a value recommendation, and that is to value care. One of the main sources of difficulty with work and family conflict and with female employment is the lack of value placed on caregiving labor. For example, mothers' care is uncounted in calculations of the gross national product even though it is vital for the production work of every society. Unpaid caregiving within households is a taken-for-granted sacrifice from individual women for the good of society. This kind of sacrifice is asked of no other group. As women increasingly have other options, more choose away from the unpaid, undervalued caregiving at home and the effect on the birthrate is felt in many countries. Those who are paid to care are paid extremely low wages. The low pay scale stems partly from the low value on care and also from the fact that much purchased care is paid for privately in many countries. Since few households can afford to pay out of pocket for expensive care, employed women, who are already paid on average less than men in comparable positions, are forced to exploit other women by paying even lower wages for caregiving. When underpaid caregivers have no time to care for their own children and must leave them in self-care, poor-quality care or with relatives, sometimes in distant home countries (Ehrenreich and Hochschild 2002), the cycle becomes sadly ironic. If a system of valuing care could be designed around the attitude that all of us were once children and must cooperate for the care of the next generation rather than focusing every family for itself, systems of inequality based on class and gender could be radically transformed.

A second policy recommendation is that in situations where mothers do take time off from paid employment, mothers should be welcomed back to the labor market rather than denied opportunities upon return. Mothers' incomes raise the possibilities for their children's health and education, and provide additional sources of tax revenue for societies that are coping with increased demands on the welfare state. Women's incomes also help secure old age for couples by providing an extra revenue stream for savings toward retirement. Mothers' employment gives children an additional model of responsible productive adulthood. Since women's and mothers' employment, like men's and fathers' employment, is here to stay, we might as well support it by eliminating the obstacles to continued employment and adequate compensation in the interest of women's and families' well-being. It would be sensible to open employment opportunities to mothers entering the labor market for the first time after raising families and provide educational opportunities for non-traditional-aged students so that women (and men) could return to the labor market with new skills and for second or third careers. Destigmatizing older or non-standard-aged workers would also be essential in this process.

In a new world of women's employment opportunities, men must play a stronger role at home. As a third policy recommendation, if other countries follow the lead of Sweden in providing incentives for couples to share caregiving and domestic responsibilities, the level of understanding for the diversity of adult responsibilities and the respect for caregiving would undoubtedly rise. People tend to develop compassion and empathy from having personal experience in a role. Men with firsthand responsibility for childcare and household maintenence may be better able and willing to re-design workplaces and governments to take into account the needs of all kinds of adult workers. Instead, our current workplaces primarily cater to and reward workers who can act disembodied and disengaged from the variety of adult tasks that a thriving society naturally asks of its adult citizens. When there are more points of similarity across men's and women's life courses, the opportunity for compassion and cooperation should increase and the systematic devaluing of women should decline, with consequences such as the reduction in domestic violence, the maximization of individuals' talents and abilities regardless of gender and the upbringing of the first generation of children raised with a healthy respect for their mothers as well as their fathers and, by extension, also for themselves and each other.

Concrete policy recommendations include investing in education all along the life course, reducing bureaucratic barriers to re-training and re-entry, enabling a better fit between diverse job markets and housing with opportunities for work to come to the workers and workers to go to the work, even workers in families, and invest in the training, pay and support of caregiving for children and for elders. If we make the costs of Fordism visible in terms of the private toll on households for the care of workers and their offspring (the future workers), the movement toward a post-Fordist system may be made easier and may be designed better for the way families actually live and work.

Call for further research

We recognize the limitations of this study to the OECD-type countries of North America and Europe. For future research, we recommend extending quantitative, longitudinal analyses to countries like China, India, Thailand, Vietnam and the Philippines, where the economies are expanding rapidly owing to globalization and to South America, Africa and the Near East, where geo-political conflicts have created enormous turbulence in individual life courses. How are women adapting to the tremendous changes and protecting and providing for their families in these situations? Researchers such as Jody Heymann (2003), Barbara Ehrenreich and Arlie Russell Hochschild (2002) and their collaborators have begun to address important questions about women's work worldwide; we advocate for longitudinal studies that highlight these processes.

CONCLUDING REMARKS

The changes in women's mid-life work entries, exits and re-entries to paid work and family caregiving, and their job mobility within paid work over the last few decades are in nearly every country in our comparison. It is not the case that 'the rising tide lifts all boats' when it comes to globalization's effects on women's job opportunities; rather, the boats that float and get ahead on the rough waters of globalization tend to be those manned by women with university degrees.

It has been said that as the family goes, so goes the society. Given the centrality of the roles of wife and mother in the lives of women historically, we might add that as the woman goes, so goes the family. As long as rising uncertainty is affecting men's and women's career trajectories, these impacts will be felt by families and in turn by societies for many generations. The impact of globalization on women's careers has profound implications indeed, as do the roles of institutions shaped by culture in mediating these effects.

NOTE

[1] The authors would like to thank Daniela Grunow, Detlev Lück and John Bendix for helpful comments on an earlier version of this chapter.

BIBLIOGRAPHY

Blossfeld, H.-P., Buchholz, S. and Hofäcker, D. (2006) *Globalization, uncertainty, and late careers in society*, London: Routledge.

Blossfeld, H.-P., Klijzing, E., Mills, M. and Kurz, K. (eds) (2005) *Globalization, uncertainty, and youth in society*, London: Routledge.

Blossfeld, H.-P., Mills, M. and Bernardi, F. (2006) *Globalization, uncertainty, and men's careers: an international comparison*, Cheltenham, UK and Northampton, MA, USA: Edward Elgar.

Ehrenreich, B. and Hochschild, A. (2002) *Global woman: nannies, maids, and sex workers in the new economy*, New York: Metropolitan/Owl Books.

Esping-Andersen, G. (1999) *Social foundations of postindustrial economies*, Oxford: Oxford University Press.

Heymann S.J. (ed.) (2003) *Global inequalities at work: work's impact on the health of individuals, families, and societies*, New York: Oxford University Press.

Orloff, A.S. (2002) 'Women's employment and welfare regimes: globalization, export orientation and social policy in Europe and North America,' *Social Policy and Development Programme Paper*, 12(June), Florence: United Nations Research Institute for Social Development.

Index

adult worker model 32, 308
Australia 415, 418, 419, 421, 424, 425
Austria 414, 415, 418, 421, 424, 425

Belgium 415
belief-systems *see* cultural values
birth rate *see* fertility rates
Blossfeld, Hans-Peter 3–31, 433–50
Britain
  British Household Panel Survey 26,
    275–6, 283
  career maturity hypothesis 282
  career uncertainty 441
  caregiving, unpaid 281, 284, 285,
    288–94
  childcare, private 49, 280
  childcare, public 279
  children, effect on employment 38,
    279, 280–82, 285, 289–93, 421
  cohabitation 289, 292
  collective bargaining 276, 280
  competition 281
  deregulation 275, 276, 277, 278, 282
  divorce 289, 292
  dual-earner household 281, 285
  education 275, 278–9, 283, 285, 287,
    289–96
  education expansion 281–2
  education, tertiary 279, 287, 289, 292,
    293, 295
  employment interruptions 281, 284,
    285, 288–94
  employment protection 11, 52, 276–7,
    280, 281, 283
  employment regulation 279, 280
  family responsibilities 280, 281, 284,
    285, 288–94, 440
  fixed-term contracts 284, 286–7, 289,
    294–5, 443
  full-time employment 277, 279, 281,

    286–7, 289, 294, 295
  gender role attitudes 279–80, 282,
    415, 418, 424, 427
  generational effect 427
  and globalization 275, 280–83, 438
  homemaker model 280
  individualistic mobility regime 281,
    282–3
  job competition 282, 283
  job mobility 277, 278, 281, 282–3,
    284, 286–8, 294–6
  job security 232, 275, 277, 279, 281,
    282, 290, 440
  labor force participation 35, 38, 46,
    47, 275–301, 436, 438, 440, 445
  labor market exit 281, 286–8
  labor market flexibility 275–8,
    280–82, 286–8, 290–91, 294, 443
  labor market re-entry 277, 279, 280,
    284, 286–8, 291, 292
  liberalization 275
  male employment 232, 275, 279, 281,
    290, 291, 293, 294
  male-breadwinner model 248, 425
  marginal employment 286–7, 289,
    295, 440, 443
  marriage 281, 289, 292
  maternity leave 280
  national minimum wage 277
  New Deal 277, 279, 280
  outsourcing 277
  parental leave 279
  part-time employment 40, 41, 44,
    276–8, 280–81, 284, 286–7, 289,
    294, 295
  paternity leave 279
  private sector 277, 281, 285, 287, 289,
    295
  public sector 46, 277, 281, 286, 287,
    289, 295

recessions 278
service sector 47
short-term contracts 276, 278–9, 440,
    443
single parents 280, 289, 292
social integration 275, 279, 440
subcontracting 277
taxation 277, 280, 281
Third Way 277
trade unions 277, 280
unemployment 50, 51, 276–9, 281,
    283–95, 440, 443
unemployment benefits 277
unskilled workers 282–3
vocational training 278, 283, 287
wage levels 276, 277, 281, 440
welfare state 18, 276–8, 279–80, 281,
    294, 304, 307, 443, 445
working hours 284, 294
see also liberal regime
Buchholz, Sandra 37, 39, 61–83, 144,
    207, 304, 305
Bukodi, Erzsébet 171–98, 205, 224
Bulgaria 415, 418, 419, 422, 425

Canada 35, 38–40, 44, 46–7, 50–52,
    418–19, 421, 425
capital mobility 116–19
capitalism 446–7
career
    advancement 5–6, 23, 24–5, 32, 33,
        61–2, 84, 151
    buffering effect 68
    multiple 21
    see also labor force participation
caregiving, unpaid 6, 7, 67, 76, 412, 423,
    441, 443, 447
    family-oriented regime 376–7, 380,
        383–5, 388–9, 391–4, 396,
        446
    liberal regime 281, 284, 285, 288–94,
        311, 316
    post-socialist regime 183, 185,
        188–91, 201, 215, 446, 448
    see also employment interruptions;
        family responsibilities
childcare options 9, 13, 16, 45, 71
    employer-provided 45, 49
    lack of 13–16, 18, 19, 22, 442
    see also family responsibilities

childcare, private
    conservative regime 49, 50
    family-oriented regime 49
    liberal regime 49, 50, 280, 306
    post-socialist regime 259
    social-democratic regime 49–50, 147
childcare, public 18, 19, 45, 49–50, 147
    conservative regime 48, 66, 69, 86,
        426, 439, 443
    family-oriented regime 19, 39, 48, 49,
        356, 360, 383, 443
    liberal regime 18, 48, 53, 279, 305,
        307, 443
    post-socialist regime 48, 177, 183,
        200, 225, 230–31, 234, 259–61,
        443
    social-democratic regime *see under*
        Denmark; Sweden
children, effect on employment 71,
    420–24, 442
    conservative regime 39, 88, 97–8,
        105, 107–9, 422, 439
    family-oriented regime *see under*
        Italy; Mexico; Spain
    liberal regime *see under* Britain;
        United States
    post-socialist regime *see under* Czech
        Republic; Estonia; Hungary;
        Poland
    social-democratic regime 38, 145–7,
        153–8, 160, 162
class differences, occupational
    conservative regime 67, 91, 94,
        99–102, 442
    family-oriented regime 336–8, 343–7,
        357, 387–8
    liberal regime 40
    post-socialist regime 176–7, 181–2,
        186–8, 191–2, 232–3, 235–41,
        257, 259
    social-democratic regime 442
closed employment system 10, 20, 86,
    201, 210, 225, 280–81, 376, 380–81
cohabitation
    conservative regime 88, 92, 95, 97,
        99, 101, 105, 107–8
    family-oriented regime 357
    liberal regime 285, 289, 292
    post-socialist regime 178, 193, 203
    social-democratic regime 162

see also marriage; partnership
dependence
collective bargaining 4, 20, 87, 202, 276,
 280, 380, 381
see also trade unions
communism *see under* Czech Republic;
 Estonia; Hungary; Poland
competition
 conservative regime 62, 67, 68, 69,
  70, 80, 89
 and deregulation *see* deregulation
 family-oriented regime 19
 and ICT *see* ICT
 liberal regime 281, 282, 283, 304,
  305, 306
 post-socialist regime 259, 266
 social-democratic regime 15, 143
 see also international trade;
  liberalization
conservative regime 14–16, 44, 413,
 436, 439
 childcare, private 49, 50
 childcare, public 48, 49, 53, 66, 69,
  86, 426, 439, 443
 children, effect on employment 39, 88,
  97–8, 105, 107–9, 422, 439
 class differences, occupational 67, 91,
  94, 99–102, 442
 cohabitation 88, 92, 95, 97, 99, 101,
  105, 107–8
 competition 62, 67, 68, 69, 70, 80, 89
 deregulation 68
 divorce 66, 88
 dual-earner model 150
 education 63–4, 74–8, 88, 99, 101–4,
  106, 173
 education expansion 63, 67, 68, 69,
  73, 88
 education, tertiary 88, 227, 229, 235,
  242
 employment interruptions 62, 64,
  72–9, 89, 92–3, 96, 98–109
 employment protection 52, 90–91
 family formation 69–70, 76, 88, 439,
  443, 445
 fertility rates 88, 92, 98
 fixed-term contracts 43, 62, 64, 68,
  86, 87
 full-time employment 99, 101–2
 gender role attitudes *see under*

Germany; Netherlands
globalization 68–70, 89–92, 98, 438,
 442
homemaker model 76
industrial sector 64, 67–8
international trade 86, 442
job mobility 62, 64, 70–76, 79, 89–93,
 96–100, 102–10, 440
job security 62, 65, 68, 281
job stability 64, 68–9, 70
labor force participation *see under*
 Germany; Netherlands
labor market exits 71, 76, 89–93, 96,
 98–100, 102–3, 108–10, 439
labor market flexibility 51, 64, 68, 69,
 72, 73, 86–7, 89, 92, 103, 439
labor market re-entry *see under*
 Germany; Netherlands
male employment 64–9, 86–8, 90
male-breadwinner model 14–15, 66,
 68, 69–70, 73–9, 425, 427
marginal employment 64, 445
marriage 76, 88, 97–9, 101, 105,
 107–9, 440
maternity leave 14, 146
one-and-a-half breadwinner model
 14–15
parental leave 66
part-time employment 19, 40–42, 44,
 62, 64–6, 86–7, 99, 101–2, 442
private sector 73, 74–5, 88
public sector *see under* Germany;
 Netherlands
religion 413
service sector 47, 53, 64, 67, 88
social integration 44, 65, 80
taxation 14, 66
temporary contracts 86, 87
trade unions 86
unemployment 51, 62, 64–5, 67–73,
 86–8
unemployment benefits 65
unskilled employment 64, 67
vocational training 63–4, 145
wage levels 86, 200, 202, 225, 226,
 228–31
welfare state 65–7, 69, 76, 79, 443
working hours 44, 86, 87, 94, 99, 102,
 104
see also Germany; Netherlands

contracts 4, 34, 35, 40, 53, 54, 231
  see also fixed-term contracts;
     short–term contracts; temporary
     contracts
cultural values 5, 6, 9, 15, 17, 21–2,
  33–4
  changes over time 424–8
  generation effect 426–8
  and welfare regime 407–11, 413–16,
    419, 423, 444
  see also class differences,
    occupational; gender role
    attitudes; religion
Czech Republic
  agriculture 229, 238, 240, 241, 242
  career uncertainty 441
  caregiving, unpaid 446
  central planning 224, 225, 226
  childcare, public 48, 225, 230–31, 234
  children, effects on employment
    225–6, 228, 234, 237, 239–40,
    422
  class differences, occupational 232–3,
    235, 236, 237–40, 241
  and communism 10, 224–5, 229, 231,
    235
  deregulation 225, 232, 237, 243
  dual-earner model 225
  economic reforms 225–9
  education 226, 227, 229, 235, 237–40,
    241
  education, tertiary 227, 229, 235, 242
  employment interruptions 234, 236,
    237, 240–43
  'employment miracle' 228
  employment protection 52, 225, 226
  family formation 230, 236
  family responsibilities 228, 230–32,
    233–4, 236
  FDI 236, 241
  fertility rates 230, 231
  full-time employment 44, 225, 226,
    228, 234
  GDP 226, 227, 228, 229
  gender roles, support for traditional
    415, 418
  and globalization 10, 225, 231–4, 237,
    435, 438
  human capital theory 233
  ICT in 232, 233

  industrial sector 229, 236
  international trade 226, 227, 231
  job mobility 225–6, 229, 232–7,
    240–43
  job security 232–3, 441
  labor force participation 37, 44, 46–7,
    224–46, 252, 255, 435–6, 438
  labor market exits 225, 229, 237
  labor market flexibility 225
  labor market re-entry 225, 234, 237
  liberalization 225, 226, 229, 231, 232
  male employment 226, 227, 228, 233
  male-breadwinner model 425
  marriage 230, 233
  maternity leave 230, 234, 237, 241,
    243
  MNCs 233
  parental leave 230, 234
  part-time employment 41, 42, 225,
    226, 228, 446
  private sector 226, 231, 239–42
  public sector 46, 239, 240, 242
  retirement, early 227
  self-employment 233, 235, 236, 238,
    240, 241, 242
  service sector employment 47, 229,
    233, 236, 239
  Social Transformation survey 234
  Stratification Survey 26
  taxation 229
  unemployment 51, 226–8, 232–4,
    236–7, 254
  unemployment benefits 227
  unskilled workforce 238, 240, 241,
    242
  vocational training 237, 241, 242
  wage levels 225, 226, 228, 229, 230,
    231
  welfare state 225, 227, 228, 230
  WTO and OECD membership 226,
    231
  see also post-socialist regime

Denmark
  adult education 145
  career uncertainty 441–2
  caregiving, unpaid 160, 164
  childcare, private 49, 147
  childcare, public 48, 145, 147–8,
    150–51, 154–6, 383

children, effect on employment 143,
 145–7, 153–8, 160, 162
class differences, occupational 442
cohabitation 162
competition 143
deregulation 144
dual-earner model 150
economic boom 144
education 143, 144–5, 148, 150–58,
 161
education expansion 144, 151
education, tertiary 145, 153, 154–5,
 157–8, 161, 162
elderly care 145, 383
employment interruptions 143, 150,
 151, 152
Employment Miracle 147–9, 152, 156
employment protection 52, 142, 147
family formation 144, 152
family responsibilities 143, 145–6,
 148, 150–54, 156–9, 161–2
fertility rates 155, 158, 161
full-time employment 153, 159
GDP 149, 153
gender role attitudes 143, 148
and globalization 435–6, 438
human capital theory 151, 156
income redistribution 144, 145
industrial revolution, second 144
institutional framework 143, 144–9,
 150–52
international trade 442
job mobility 143, 146, 147, 150,
 151–3, 155, 156, 157–8
job security 163
labor force participation 35, 46–7,
 142–67, 435–8, 441–2
labor force re-entry 146, 160–62
labor market exits 143, 150, 151,
 154–6, 157–60, 435
labor market flexibility 51, 142, 143,
 147–8, 152
Labor Market Research 26, 142, 152
male employment 143, 146, 148, 153
male-breadwinner model 143, 148,
 151, 157
marriage 162
maternity leave 146–7, 150
parental leave 146–7, 149, 150, 151,
 154, 157, 162, 163

part-time employment 41, 159, 442
PLAs (paid leave arrangements)
 148–53, 156, 159, 160
private sector 143, 149, 159, 160, 443
public sector 46, 143, 145–6, 159–60,
 442–3
service sector 47, 144
taxation 144, 145, 150
unemployment 50–51, 142–3, 147–50,
 152–62, 443
unemployment benefits 147–8, 156
unskilled workforce 144, 151–2, 162
vocational training 145
wage levels 143, 146–7, 153, 155,
 156, 158
welfare state 142–4, 147, 156, 435–7,
 445
working hours 153, 159
see also social-democratic regime
deregulation 4, 20, 144, 171
and competition 8, 9, 11
conservative regime 68
family-oriented regime 330
liberal regime 275–8, 282, 304
post-socialist regime 16–17, 220, 225,
 232, 237, 243
social-democratic regime 144
developing countries 117, 119, 334
diffusion of information *see* ICT
divorce 62, 69, 433, 442
conservative regime 66, 77–8, 88, 95
family-oriented regime 357
liberal regime 289, 292, 302, 305,
 308, 440
post-socialist regime 179, 187, 189,
 190, 192, 207, 208, 259, 265
see also marriage; single parents
downsizing 11, 64, 306
dual-earner model 16, 17, 32, 178, 442
conservative regime 150
family-oriented regime 383
liberal regime 281, 285, 304, 317
post-socialist regime 178, 225, 257
social-democratic regime 17, 145–6,
 150, 444

economic interdependence, and
 globalization 9, 275, 376
education 5–6, 8–10, 19–20, 23, 33–4,
 64, 116, 144

adult 145, 181, 202, 304, 448, 449
conservative regime 63–4, 74–8, 88,
    99, 101–4, 106, 173
family-oriented regime *see under*
    Italy; Mexico; Spain
and gender roles 64, 88, 417
liberal regime *see under* Britain;
    United States
over-education 181, 378, 386
post-socialist regime *see under* Czech
    Republic; Estonia; Hungary;
    Poland
social-democratic regime 127–30,
    132–5, 143–5, 148, 150–58, 161,
    440
see also knowledge-based economy;
    vocational training
education expansion
conservative regime 63, 67, 68, 69,
    73, 88
family-oriented regime 329, 336,
    340–41, 355, 358, 360, 377–8
liberal regime 281–2, 304, 306, 440
post-socialist regime 173
social-democratic regime 132, 144,
    151
education, tertiary
conservative regime 88, 227, 229,
    235, 242
family-oriented regime 354, 355,
    377–8, 386, 394, 395
liberal regime *see under* Britain;
    United States
post-socialist regime *see under* Czech
    Republic; Estonia; Hungary;
    Poland
social-democratic regime 125, 130,
    132–5, 145, 153–5, 157–8, 161,
    162
elderly care 19, 145, 183, 383
employment interruptions
conservative regime 62, 64, 72–9, 89,
    92–3, 96, 98–102, 103–9
family-oriented regime 339, 368,
    385–6
liberal regime 281, 284, 285, 288–94
post-socialist regime 182, 205–6,
    211
social-democratic regime 46, 125–9,
    132–7, 143, 150–52, 445

see also family responsibilities; labor
    market exit; labor market re-entry
employment protection 11, 17, 20,
    50–52, 90
conservative regime 52, 90–91
family-oriented regime 52, 353–4,
    358, 376, 380, 393
liberal regime *see under* Britain;
    United States
post-socialist regime 17, 52, 201, 204,
    209, 225, 226
social-democratic regime 52, 142,
    147
employment restructuring 3–4, 6, 7, 20,
    32–58
Esping-Andersen, G. 43–4, 65, 248, 279,
    413, 416
Estonia
adult education 202
agriculture 203, 213, 214, 215, 216,
    219
career uncertainty 441
caregiving, unpaid 201, 205, 210, 215,
    217–19, 446
childcare, public 200, 443
children, effect on employment 205–6,
    210, 214–18
closed employment system 201
cohabitation 203
collective bargaining system 202
and communism 10, 199–203, 212–19
deregulation 220
divorce 207, 208
economic reform 200–202, 204, 209
education 202, 205, 207–10, 213–19
education, tertiary 207
Employment Contract Law 202
employment interruptions 205–6, 211
employment protection 201, 202, 204,
    209
family formation 203, 206, 208
family responsibilities 209, 210, 213
Fertility and Family Survey 205, 211
full-time employment 44, 206
GDP 200, 201, 204
gender equity 199, 200, 203, 205–7,
    208, 215
Germany, trade with 202
and globalization 10, 200, 208–9, 435,
    438

as individualist mobility regime 204, 209, 210
industry, heavy 203
inflation 201
international competition 200, 201, 202
job mobility 209–10, 211, 212–14
job stability 199, 201, 204, 210, 214, 217, 219
labor force participation 36–9, 44, 46–7, 199–223, 435–6, 438, 445
Labor Force Survey 26, 211
labor market exit 205, 211, 215–16
labor market flexibility 201
labor market location 209–10, 215
labor market re-entry 201, 207, 210, 212, 217
as liberal regime 205
male employment 200, 203, 204, 208, 210
marriage 208, 213, 214, 217–18, 219
maternity leave 200, 205–6, 207, 218
migration 201
National Labor Market Board 202
parental leave 203
part-time employment 201, 206, 446
pension age 207
poverty 443
private sector 202, 205, 207, 209–10, 213–14, 216, 219
public sector employment 46, 202, 207, 209, 213–16, 219
recessions 201, 204
retirement, early 39, 201
self-employment 201
service sector 47
short-term contracts 201, 202
single-parent households 207, 208
subcontracting 200
taxation 205
trade unions 204
unemployment 199, 201, 204, 207, 209, 210–12, 215–17
unemployment benefits 201, 202, 204–5, 217
unskilled employment 211
vocational training 207–8
wage levels 200, 202
welfare state 201, 202–3, 204, 205–7, 208, 445

working hours 206
see also post-socialist regime
ethnic minorities 309–10, 312, 316, 318–22, 409, 416
see also migrant status
European Union 86–8, 120, 382
employment 86, 178, 203, 254–5, 381
see also individual countries

family formation 8, 22–3, 33–4, 61, 84, 144, 309–10
conservative regime 69–70, 76, 88, 439, 443, 445
family-oriented regime 345, 368–71, 376, 445
liberal regime 280, 303, 308, 315–16, 318–22
post-socialist regime 178–9, 187–90, 192, 203, 206, 208, 230, 236
social-democratic regime 144, 152
family responsibilities 5, 6, 9, 11–12, 16, 21–4, 34, 39–40, 45, 248, 407, 439, 442, 445, 448–9
career penalties 446
conservative regime 62, 64–7, 69–71, 76–80, 89, 92, 97–8, 101, 108, 110
family-oriented regime 39, 334–6, 338–9, 343, 345–6, 355–7, 360, 376, 382–5, 437
liberal regime 280–81, 284–5, 288–94, 306–7, 309, 311, 440
and men 446–7
post-socialist regime *see under* Czech Republic; Estonia; Hungary Poland
social-democratic regime 143, 145–6, 148, 150–54, 156–62, 164
see also childcare; employment interruptions; gender role attitudes; welfare state
family-oriented regime 14, 15, 19, 44, 413, 436, 439
agricultural industry 39, 47
caregiving, unpaid 376–7, 380, 383–5, 388–9, 391–4, 396, 446
childcare, private 49
childcare, public 19, 39, 48, 49, 356, 360, 383, 443

children, effect on employment *see
    under* Italy;Mexico; Spain
class differences, occupational 336–8,
    343–7, 357, 387–8
cohabitation 357
competition 19
cultural background 413
deregulation 330
divorce 357
dual-earner model 383
education *see under* Italy; Mexico;
    Spain
education expansion 329, 336,
    340–41, 355, 358, 360, 377–8
education, tertiary 354, 355, 377–8,
    386, 394, 395
elderly care, lack of 19
employment interruptions 339, 368,
    385–6
employment protection 52, 353–4,
    358, 376, 380, 393
family formation 345, 368–71, 376,
    445
family responsibilities 39, 334–6,
    338–9, 343, 345–6, 355–7, 360,
    376, 382–5, 437
fertility rates 19, 329, 336, 357, 359,
    368, 371, 385, 392, 439, 443
fixed-term contracts 43, 44, 53, 354,
    381
full-time employment 44, 385
gender role attitudes 335, 343, 357,
    379, 381, 415, 418, 425, 428
globalization *see under* Italy; Mexico;
    Spain
homemaker model 384, 385, 387, 390
human capital theory 333–4, 336, 338,
    340–41, 343–5, 386, 396
industrial employment 47
international trade 336
job mobility 336, 338, 377, 385, 387,
    390, 393–5
job security 281, 357, 359, 362,
    364–6, 377, 381, 386
job stability 331, 377, 380–81, 383,
    385, 388–90, 392
labor force participation 36–9, 44,
    46–53, 329–401, 436–9
labor market exits 334–5, 337–8,
    340–43, 359, 369, 385–8, 390–92

labor market flexibility 19, 50–51,
    331, 333, 353, 377, 380–81, 386,
    437, 439
labor market re-entry 359, 380, 381,
    383, 385–7, 392–3, 395–6
male employment 330–31, 333, 339,
    376, 378, 380–81, 383–5
male-breadwinner model 334, 377,
    380–81, 383–5, 425
marginal employment 377, 384–5,
    390
marriage 334, 336, 338–43, 345–60,
    368–70, 371, 384, 386
maternity leave 19, 356
part-time employment 19, 41, 42, 354,
    357, 359–60, 384, 446
poverty 343, 356, 358
private sector 330–31, 352–4, 358,
    376, 379, 386
public sector 46, 352–3, 358, 379,
    384, 386
religion 19, 377, 380, 413
self-employment 39, 40, 44, 53, 337,
    355, 366, 387–8, 391
service sector 47, 331, 358, 378–9,
    387–8, 391
single parents 357
social integration 53, 381–4
taxation 333, 356
temporary contracts 359, 362, 366–8,
    370, 376–7, 381–2, 385, 387–8
trade unions 331, 353, 380, 381
unemployment *see under* Italy;
    Mexico; Spain
unemployment benefits 19, 353–4,
    355–6, 357, 358, 376, 380
unskilled employment 337, 386,
    388
vocational training 354, 355, 394
wage levels 10, 331, 333, 352–6, 358,
    437
welfare state 353, 355–8, 376–7,
    380–84, 443
working hours 44
see also Italy; Mexico; Spain
FDI 4, 86, 118, 120, 122, 236, 241, 329,
    331–3, 352
see also international trade
fertility rates
    conservative regime 88, 92, 98

family-oriented regime *see under*
Italy; Mexico; Spain
liberal regime 184, 230, 231
post-socialist regime 184, 230, 231
social-democratic regime 155, 158,
161
Finland 379, 425
fixed-term contracts 15, 40, 43, 62, 85
conservative regime 43, 62, 64, 68,
86, 87
family-oriented regime 43, 44, 53,
354, 359, 381
liberal regime 43, 44, 284, 286–7,
289, 294–5, 443
post-socialist regime 43, 178, 184
flexibility *see* labor market flexibility
France 40, 47–9, 51, 52, 53, 248, 383,
425
full-time employment 3, 5, 14–18,
20–22, 34, 44, 200, 419, 441
conservative regime 99, 101–2
family-oriented regime 385
liberal regime *see under* Britain;
United States
post-socialist regime 44, 206, 225–6,
228, 234, 437
social-democratic regime 123, 153,
159

gender role attitudes 22, 32, 37, 44, 57,
64, 66, 248–9, 334–5, 405–32, 410,
443, 448–9
conservative regime *see under*
Germany; Netherlands
in education 88, 417
family-oriented regime 335, 343, 357,
379, 381, 415, 418, 425, 428
liberal regime 18, 279–80, 282, 415,
418–19, 424, 426–7, 427
macro-level analysis 413–16
micro-level analysis 416–24
post-socialist regime *see under* Czech
Republic; Estonia; Hungary;
Poland
social-democratic regime 16, 124,
129, 143, 148, 415, 418–19, 425,
428, 445
subjectivity, impact 405–9, 413–16
support for 412–19, 424–5
'winner-takes-all' model 203

see also culture; family
responsibilities; individualization;
male-breadwinner model
generation effect 426–8
Germany
agricultural sector 64
'baby boom' generation 67
career uncertainty 441
caregiving, unpaid 64, 65, 67, 71,
76–80
childcare, private 49
childcare, public 48, 66, 69, 426, 439,
443
children, effect on employment 422,
439
decentralization 64
demographic fluctuations 67
deregulation 68
divorce 66, 77–8
downsizing 64
dual-earner model 63
education 63–4, 74–5, 76, 77–8, 173
education expansion 63, 67, 68, 69, 73
education, tertiary 63–4, 74–5, 77–8,
315
employment interruption 62, 64, 66,
72, 73, 74–5, 76–9
employment protection 52
employment relations 64–7
Estonia, trade with 202
family formation 69–70, 76, 439, 443
family responsibilities 62, 64, 65,
66–7, 69–71, 76–9
firm size reduction 64
fixed-term contracts 62, 64, 68
gender roles attitudes 65–7, 415, 418,
424, 426, 427–8
generation effect 427–8
globalization 68–70, 438
'golden age' 64, 67
homemaker model 76
industrial sector 64, 67–8
institutional filters 63–8
job mobility 62, 64, 70–71, 72–3,
74–5, 76, 79
job security 62, 65, 68, 281
job stability 64, 68–9, 70
labor force participation 36, 46, 47,
61–83, 436, 438, 439
labor market exit 439

labor market exits 71, 76
labor market flexibility 64, 65, 67, 68,
    69, 72, 73
labor market re-entry 62, 65, 67, 68,
    71–2, 73, 76, 79, 439
Life History Study 26, 70
male employment 64, 65, 66–7, 68, 69
male-breadwinner model 66, 68,
    69–70, 73–9, 425, 427
marginal employment 64
market trends 63–8
marriage 76, 440
maternity leave 146
oil price shock 64
outsourcing 64
parental leave 66
part-time employment 40, 41, 42, 62,
    64, 65, 66
pensions 65, 66
private sector 64, 73, 74–5
public sector 46, 47, 64, 67, 73, 74–5
religious beliefs 414, 426, 439
service sector 47, 64, 67
taxation 14, 66
unemployment 51, 62, 64, 65, 67, 68,
    69, 70, 71–2, 73
unemployment benefits 65
unskilled employment 64, 67
vocational training 63–4, 145
wage levels 64, 65, 229
welfare state 65–7, 69, 76, 79, 443
working hours 44
see also conservative regime
globalization 4, 6, 8–12, 14, 16, 21,
    32–58, 224, 232
    conservative regime 68–70, 89–92,
        98, 438, 442
    and economic interdependence 9, 275,
        376
    and employment restructuring 3–4, 6,
        7, 20, 32–58, 442
    family-oriented regime *see under*
        Italy; Mexico; Spain
    and institutional structures 12–22
    liberal regime 275, 280–83, 302–8,
        316–17, 438
    market volatility 9, 10, 12, 62, 117
    networks 8, 9, 275, 303
    policy implications 447–9
    political 27, 50, 149, 150, 247, 251

post-socialist regime *see under* Czech
        Republic; Estonia; Hungary;
        Poland
    social-democratic regime 124, 130,
        132, 435, 435–6, 438, 440
    timescale 90
    and uncertainty 4, 8, 9, 11, 14, 24–6,
        67
    and women's careers 435–44
    and youth employment 12, 437–8
    see also international trade; job
        mobility; job security; labor
        market flexibility; modernization
Golsch, Katrin 275–301, 381
Grunow, Daniela 61–83, 142–67

Hamplová, Dana 224–46
Heckscher–Ohlin model 116, 117
Helemäe, Jelena 199–223
Hofäcker, Dirk 32–58, 304, 426, 433–50
Hofmeister, Heather 3–31, 144, 207,
    302–26, 433–50
homemaker model 21, 22, 32, 334, 412,
    444
    conservative regime 76
    family-oriented regime 384, 385, 387,
        390
    liberal regime 27, 280, 322
    post-socialist regime 183, 188, 194
    social-democratic regime 126, 127–8
homogamy 182, 194–5, 309, 317
household labor *see* gender role attitudes
human capital theory 23
    family-oriented regime 333–4, 336,
        338, 340–41, 343–5, 386, 396
    post-socialist regime 171–5, 181–2,
        196, 233, 261
    social-democratic regime 151, 156
Hungary
    adult education 181
    agriculture 176, 181, 187, 188, 192
    career uncertainty 441
    caregiving, unpaid 183, 185, 188–91,
        446
    childcare, public 177, 183
    children, effect on employment 177,
        179, 182, 184, 188, 191, 193, 422
    cohabitation 178, 193
    communism 10, 171–5, 181–3, 185–9,
        191–2, 195, 254

divorce 179, 187, 189, 190, 192
dual-earner model 178
education 171–5, 177–8, 180–82,
    186–92
education expansion 173
education, tertiary 173, 175, 177, 181,
    186–7, 189–93
elderly care 183
employment interruptions 182
employment protection 52
family formation 178–9, 187, 188–90,
    192
family responsibilities 171–2, 177–8,
    182, 437
fertility rates 184
fixed-term contracts 178
full employment, mandatory 437
gender role attitudes 172, 175–6, 415,
    418–19, 425–6, 428
generation effect 428
and globalization 10, 181, 182, 196,
    438
homemaker model 183, 188, 194
Household Panel Survey 26, 171, 184
human capital investment 171–5,
    181–2, 196
international competition 172
job flexibility 177–8, 183
job mobility 171–98
job security 177–8, 186
labor force participation 36, 37, 46,
    47, 171–98, 252, 255, 436–8
labor market exit 174, 179, 181, 182,
    183, 188, 437
labor market re-entry 172, 174–6, 180,
    183, 186, 189–91, 193
lifelong learning 174
male employment 171–2, 174–9, 182,
    188–9, 194
male-breadwinner model 179, 425–6,
    427
marriage 178–9, 182, 184, 187–90,
    192–3
maternity leave 174, 180, 182–3,
    188–91, 193
occupational structure 176–7, 181,
    182, 186–8, 191–2
over-education 181
part-time employment 41, 42, 177–8,
    180, 446

poverty 176, 180, 182
private sector 178, 182, 187, 192
public sector 46, 176, 178, 181, 192
self-employment 178, 183
service sector 47, 176, 182, 187,
    188
short-term contracts 175
social integration 191
trade unions 180
transition shock 428
unemployment 51, 172, 175–8, 181–3,
    185–9, 191–2, 195, 254
unskilled employment 177, 178
vocational training 173, 174, 189
wage levels 175, 176–7, 178
welfare state 178, 179–80, 182
working hours 178
see also post-socialist regime

ICT 4, 8, 11–12, 21, 23, 84, 88, 90,
    232–3, 303–4, 353, 439
individualization 20, 23–4, 53, 204,
    209–10, 232, 446–7
'blurriness' 406, 407
see also life course; subjectivity
industrialization 10, 117, 119, 122
    deindustrialization 118, 209
inequality *see* gender role attitudes
informal workers 330, 335, 337, 342,
    344, 353–4, 359, 362, 366–9
innovation 9, 10, 21, 69
insider-outsider divide 91
institutional filters 9, 33, 34, 44–52
institutional structures, and globalization
    12–22
international trade 4, 8–12, 33, 84,
    115–19, 144, 352
    conservative regime 86, 442
    family-oriented regime 336
    post-socialist regime 172, 200–202,
        226–7, 231, 247, 376, 377
    social-democratic regime 116–20,
        122, 442
    see also FDI; globalization
investment, foreign *see* FDI
Ireland 248, 382, 413, 415, 418–19, 421,
    425, 428
ISSP (International Social Survey
    Program) 407, 410, 411, 412, 414,
    424

Italy
  agricultural industry 39, 358
  career uncertainty 441
  caregiving, unpaid 446
  childcare, private 49
  childcare, public 48, 356, 360, 443
  children, effect on employment
      359–60, 368, 371, 421
  cohabitation 357
  divorce 357
  economic crises 353, 354
  education 354, 357
  education expansion 355, 358, 360
  education, tertiary 354, 355
  employment interruptions 368
  employment protection 52, 353, 354,
      358
  employment relations 353
  family formation 368–71, 445
  family responsibilities 39, 355, 356–7,
      360
  FDI, lack of 352
  fertility rates 19, 357, 359, 368, 371,
      439, 443
  fixed-term contracts 354, 359
  GDP 358
  gender role attitudes 357, 415, 418,
      425
  and globalization 352, 357, 361, 362,
      364, 366, 371, 438
  Household Longitudinal Survey 26,
      360
  ICT 353
  industry sector 358
  informal workers 353–4, 359, 362,
      366–9
  job mobility 355–6, 357, 359, 361,
      362–3, 364–5, 370
  job security 353, 357, 359, 362,
      364–6
  labor force participation 36, 37, 47,
      352–75, 436, 438
  labor market exit 359, 369
  labor market flexibility 19, 353
  labor market re-entry 359
  male-breadwinner model 425
  marriage 357, 358, 359–60, 368–70,
      371
  maternity leave 356
  occupational classes 357

  part-time employment 19, 42, 354,
      357, 359, 360, 446
  paternity leave 356
  poverty 356, 358
  private sector 352, 353, 354, 358
  public sector 352, 353, 358
  religion 19
  self-employment 39, 355, 366
  service sector 47, 358
  single parents 357
  SMEs 352, 353, 354
  taxation 356
  temporary contracts 353, 359, 362,
      366–8, 370
  trade unions 353
  Treu Law 354
  unemployment 51, 353, 354, 356,
      358–9, 360, 362, 364–7, 368–70,
      371
  unemployment benefits 353–4, 355–6,
      357, 358
  vocational training 354, 355
  wage levels 352, 353–4, 355, 356, 358
  welfare state 353, 355–7, 358, 443
  see also family-oriented regime

Japan 120
job mobility 6–9, 12, 19, 91, 441
  conservative regime 62, 64, 70–76,
      79, 89–93, 96–100, 102–10, 440
  family-oriented regime 336, 338, 377,
      385, 387, 390, 393–5
  liberal regime 277, 278, 281–4,
      286–8, 294–6, 303, 312, 314,
      317–22
  post-socialist regime 209–14, 225–6,
      229, 232–7, 240–43
  social-democratic regime 16, 123–5,
      130–37, 143, 146–7, 150–53,
      155–8
  see also life course
job security 4, 11, 13–14, 20, 64, 91,
      441, 446
  conservative regime 62, 65, 68, 281
  family-oriented regime 281, 357, 359,
      362, 364–6, 377, 381, 386
  liberal regime 18, 232, 275, 277, 279,
      281, 282, 290, 304–5, 309, 440
  post-socialist regime 177–8, 186, 199,
      201, 204, 232–3

Luijkx, Ruud 84–112, 174

male employment 3, 5, 7–8, 85
  conservative regime 64–9, 86–8, 90
  family-oriented regime 330–31, 333,
    339, 376, 378, 380–81, 383–5
  liberal regime 232, 275, 279, 281,
    290–91, 293–4, 304, 440
  post-socialist regime *see under* Czech
    Republic; Estonia; Hungary;
    Poland
  social-democratic regime 126, 143,
    146, 148, 153, 440
male-breadwinner model 5, 9, 21–2, 24,
    32, 34, 407, 442, 445–6
  conservative regime 66, 68, 69–70,
    73–9, 425, 427
  erosion of 62, 73–9, 424
  family-oriented regime 334, 377,
    380–81, 383–5, 425
  liberal regime 248, 302, 304–5, 307,
    309, 311, 316, 425, 427
  post-socialist regime 173, 179, 425–6,
    427, 444
  social-democratic regime 143, 148,
    151, 157, 248–9, 425
  support for 412, 444
  see also gender role attitudes
marginal employment 4, 11, 13, 15, 20,
    40, 434
  conservative regime 64, 445
  family-oriented regime 377, 384–5,
    390
  liberal regime 18, 286–7, 289, 295,
    440, 443
  post-socialist regime 258
  social-democratic regime 445
marriage 24–6, 84, 87–9, 92, 173, 248,
    420, 438–9
  conservative regime 76, 88, 97–9,
    101, 105, 107–9, 440
  family-oriented regime 334, 336,
    338–43, 345–60, 368–70, 371,
    384, 386
  instability of 34, 69
  liberal regime 281, 289, 292, 302,
    309, 313, 316–22
  post-socialist regime 178–9, 182, 184,
    187–90, 192–3, 208, 213–14,
    217–19, 230, 233

social-democratic regime 162
  see also cohabitation; divorce;
    partnership dependence
maternity leave 13, 17, 18, 248
  conservative regime 14, 146
  family-oriented regime 19, 356
  liberal regime 18, 280
  post-socialist regime *see under* Czech
    Republic; Estonia; Hungary;
    Poland
  social-democratic regime 123, 146–7,
    150
Mexico
  agricultural industry 39, 342
  career uncertainty 441
  children, effect on employment 334,
    338, 343, 345–7
  competitiveness 331
  deregulation 330
  economic restructuring 329–31, 334,
    335, 337, 345
  education 331, 336, 338, 345–6
  educational expansion 329, 336,
    340–41
  employment interruptions 339
  employment protection 52
  export orientation 332, 336
  family formation 345
  family responsibilities 39, 334–6,
    338–9, 343, 345–6, 437
  FDI 329, 331–3
  fertility rates 329, 336
  financial crises 329, 330
  GDP 332, 336
  gender role attitudes 335, 337, 343
  and globalization 329–33, 335–6,
    339–40, 343–5, 438
  human capital theory 333–4, 336, 338,
    340–41, 343–4, 345
  industrialization 329–31, 334, 335,
    345
  informal sector employment 330, 335,
    337, 342, 344
  international trade 336
  job mobility 336, 338
  job stability 331
  labor force participation 36, 37, 46,
    47, 329–51, 436–8
  labor market exits 334, 335, 337–8,
    340–43, 345–6

labor market flexibility 50, 331, 333, 437
labor market re-entry 334, 335, 337–8, 340–43
male employment 330, 331, 333, 339
manual workers 337, 343, 344, 345
maquiladora industry 329, 332–3, 334, 345, 437
marriage 334, 336, 338, 339, 340, 341, 342–3, 345–7
migrant workforce 341–2, 346
MNCs 331, 334
NAFTA 329, 330, 332, 437
National Retrospective Demographic Survey (EDER) 26, 335, 336
occupational class differences 336–8, 343, 344–7
part-time employment 41, 42
poverty 343
private sector 330, 331
professional sector 337, 342, 343, 344
public sector 46, 331, 337, 342, 344
recessions 335
religion 19
self-employment 39, 337
service sector 47, 329–31, 337, 342–4, 347, 437
solidarity pacts 331
structural adjustment programs 335
taxation 333
temporary employment 437
trade unions 331
unemployment 51
unskilled employment 337
wage levels 331, 333, 437
see also family-oriented regime
migrant status 201, 211, 338, 341–2, 346
see also ethnic minorities
Mills, Melinda 3–31
MNCs 118, 120, 122, 233, 331, 334
mobility *see* job mobility
modernization 17, 84–5, 87, 90, 92, 94, 98, 109, 144, 334, 344–5, 352, 372, 414–15
see also globalization

Netherlands
career investments measure 94–5
career uncertainty 89, 91, 441–2
childcare, private 49, 50
childcare, public 48, 86
children, effect on employment 39, 88, 97–8, 105, 107–9
closed employment system 86
cohabitation 88, 97, 99, 101, 105, 107–8
collective bargaining 87
competition 89
demographic transition 88, 90
divorce rate 88, 95
education 88, 99, 101, 102–3, 104, 106
education expansion 88
education, tertiary 88
employment interruption 89, 92, 93, 96, 98–109
employment protection 52, 90–91
employment regulations 86
family formation 88
Family and Households Surveys 26, 92–3
family responsibilities 89, 92, 97–8, 101, 108, 110
FDI 86
fertility rates 88, 92, 98
fixed-term contracts 43, 86, 87
full-time employment 99, 101–2
gender role attitudes 87–9, 415, 427, 445
generational effect 427
and globalization 89–92, 98, 438, 442
ICT sector 88, 90
international trade 86, 442
job mobility 89–92, 93, 96–7, 98–100, 102–10, 440
job stability 440
labor agreements 86–7
labor force participation 36, 47, 84–112, 436, 438–4
labor market exit 439
labor market exits 89–93, 96, 98–100, 102–3, 108–10
labor market flexibility 86–7, 89, 92, 103
labor market re-entry 89, 91–3, 96, 98–101, 103, 109, 439
male employment 86, 87–8, 90
male-breadwinner model 425
marginal employment 445

marriage 88, 97–9, 101, 105, 107–9, 440

occupational class differences 91, 94, 99–102, 442

one-and-a-half breadwinner model 14

part-time employment 40–42, 44, 86–7, 99, 101–2, 442

'polder' model 86

private sector 88

public sector 88, 90, 98–101, 104, 106, 109–10, 442

secondary employment 86

service sector 47, 53, 88

temporary employment 86, 87

tourism, international 86

trade unions 86–7

unemployment 86, 87–8

wage levels 86

women in male jobs 99, 100, 101, 104, 106, 110

working hours 86, 87, 94, 99, 102, 104

see also conservative regime

networks

global 8, 9, 275, 303

kinship 191, 208, 280, 305, 306, 355, 360, 383, 385

New Zealand 415, 418, 421, 424, 425, 427

Norway 415, 418, 419, 421, 425

one-and-a-half breadwinner model 14–15, 42

outsourcing 62, 64, 120, 277, 306

parental leave 11, 22, 37

conservative regime 66

liberal regime 279, 307

post-socialist regime 37, 203, 230, 234, 258–61, 264

social-democratic regime 16, 123–4, 146–7, 149–51, 154, 157, 162–3, 440

Parrado, Emilio A. 329–51

part-time employment 4, 11, 14–17, 19, 32, 34, 40–43, 85, 419

conservative regime 19, 40–42, 44, 62, 64–6, 86–7, 99, 101–2, 442

family-oriented regime 19, 41, 42, 354, 357, 359–60, 384, 446

liberal regime *see under* Britain; United States

post-socialist regime *see under* Czech Republic; Estonia; Hungary; Poland

social-democratic regime 41, 159, 442

see also labor market flexibility; temporary contracts; working hours

partnership dependence 24, 25, 66, 179, 184, 203, 275, 378, 438

see also cohabitation; marriage

paternity leave 279, 356

Pisati, Maurizio 352–75

Plomien, Ania 247–71

Poland

abortion law 264

agriculture 257

career uncertainty 441

childcare, private 259

childcare, public 259–61

children and employment, effects of 261, 422

class differences, occupational 257, 259

command economy 253, 256, 257

and communism 10, 247–50, 252–3, 256–7

competition 259, 266

divorce 259, 265

dual earner model 257

education 251, 256, 257, 259, 260, 261

Employment Act 262

EQUAL initiative 264

EU membership 247–8, 251, 262, 263–5

family responsibilities 250, 251, 259–61, 264, 437

full employment, mandatory 437

gender role attitudes 249–52, 256–8, 260–63, 415, 418

and globalization 10, 247, 438

human capital theory 261

ICT 247

international trade 247

Labor Code 262, 264

labor force participation 247–71, 436–8

Labor Force Surveys 26

labor market exits 254, 437
labor market policy 262
male employment 253–8, 261
male-breadwinner model 425
marginal employment 258
maternity leave 251, 259, 260
National Action Plan for Women 251,
263
NGOs 263
parental leave 258, 259, 260, 261, 264
part-time employment 251, 257–8,
259, 264
pensions 258–9
poverty 251, 255, 257, 259, 263
private sector 257
public sector 257
religion 17, 27
retirement 258–9, 263
service sector 257
single mothers 251
state policies 249–52
trade unions 263
unemployment 247, 251, 252–6,
258–9, 261, 262
unemployment benefits 262
violence against women 251
wage levels 251, 256–7, 258, 259,
261, 262
welfare state 249, 250, 253, 257,
258–9, 260, 262, 263
Women's Movement 266–7
see also post-socialist regime
Portugal 425
post-socialist regime 14, 15, 17–18, 44,
426, 436, 444
agriculture 229, 238, 240–42
caregiving, unpaid 183, 185, 188–91,
201, 215, 446
childcare, private 259
childcare, public 18, 48–9, 177, 183,
200, 225, 230–31, 234, 259–61,
443
children, effect on employment *see
under* Czech Republic; Estonia;
Hungary; Poland
class differences, occupational 176–7,
181–2, 186–8, 191–2, 232–3,
235–41, 257, 259
cohabitation 178, 193, 203
communism, collapse of 10, 17,

171–5, 181–9, 191–2, 195, 225,
229, 231, 247–54, 256–7
competition 259, 266
deregulation 17, 220, 225, 232, 237
divorce 179, 187, 189, 190, 192, 207,
208, 259
dual-earner model 17, 178, 225, 257,
444
education *see under* Czech Republic;
Estonia; Hungary; Poland
education expansion 173
education, tertiary *see under* Czech
Republic; Estonia; Hungary;
Poland
employer discrimination 37
employment interruptions 182, 205–6,
211
employment protection 17, 52, 201,
202, 204, 209, 225, 226
family formation 178–9, 187–90, 192,
203, 206, 208, 230, 236
family responsibilities *see under*
Czech Republic; Estonia;
Hungary; Poland
fertility rates 184, 230, 231
fixed-term contracts 43, 184
full-time employment 17, 43, 44, 206,
225–6, 228, 234, 437, 444
gender role attitudes *see under* Czech
Republic; Estonia; Hungary;
Poland
globalization 10, 181–2, 196, 200,
208–9, 225, 231–4, 237, 247,
435, 438
homemaker model 183, 188, 194
human capital theory 171–5, 181–2,
196, 233, 261
industry sector 37, 229, 236
international trade 172, 200–202,
226–7, 231, 247, 376, 377
job mobility 209–14, 225–6, 229,
232–7, 240–43
job security 177–8, 186, 199, 201,
204, 232–3
job stability 210, 214, 217, 219, 233
labor force participation 36–9, 44,
46–54, 171–271, 435, 436–8, 445
labor market exits 174, 179, 181–3,
188, 205, 211, 215–16, 225, 229,
237, 254, 437

labor market flexibility 51, 177–8, 183, 201, 225
labor market re-entry *see under* Czech Republic; Estonia; Hungary; Poland
male employment *see under* Czech Republic; Estonia; Hungary; Poland
male-breadwinner model 173, 179, 425–6, 427, 444
marginal employment 258
market economy transition 53
marriage 178–9, 182, 184, 187–90, 192, 193, 208, 213–14, 217–19, 230, 233
maternity leave *see under* Czech Republic; Estonia; Hungary; Poland
parental leave 37, 203, 230, 234, 258–61, 264
part-time employment *see under* Czech Republic; Estonia; Hungary; Poland
poverty 176, 180, 182, 251, 255, 257, 259, 263, 443
private sector *see under* Czech Republic; Estonia; Hungary; Poland
public sector *see under* Czech Republic; Estonia; Hungary; Poland
religion 17, 27
retirement, early 37, 39
self-employment 39, 130–32, 178, 201, 233, 235–6, 238, 240–42
service sector 47, 144, 176, 182, 187, 188, 257
short-term contracts 17, 201, 202
single parents 207, 208, 251
social integration 191
taxation 205, 229
trade unions 180, 204, 263
transition shock 37, 53, 426, 444
unemployment *see under* Czech Republic; Estonia; Hungary; Poland
unemployment benefits 201, 202, 204, 205, 217, 227, 262
unskilled employment 176–7, 186–8, 192–3, 211, 238, 240–42

vocational training 173, 174, 189, 207–8, 237, 241, 242
wage levels 17, 175–8, 200, 202, 225–6, 228–31, 251, 256–9, 261–2
welfare state 178–80, 182, 201–8, 225, 227–8, 230, 445
working hours 41, 43, 178, 206
see also Czech Republic; Estonia; Hungary; Poland
poverty 24
family-oriented regime 343, 356, 358
liberal regime 306–8, 443
post-socialist regime 176, 180, 182, 251, 255, 257, 259, 263, 443
private sector 4, 8, 9, 11, 34, 37, 115, 144
conservative regime 73, 74–5, 88
family-oriented regime 330–31, 352–4, 358, 376, 379, 386
liberal regime 18, 277, 281, 285, 287, 289, 295, 304
post-socialist regime *see under* Czech Republic; Estonia; Hungary; Poland
social-democratic regime 126–9, 132–3, 136–7, 143, 149, 159–60, 440, 442–3, 446
productivity 11, 21, 116–17, 118
public sector 11, 34, 37, 45–8, 115
conservative regime *see under* Germany; Netherlands
family-oriented regime 46, 352–3, 358, 379, 384, 386
liberal regime 18, 46–7, 277, 281, 286–7, 289, 295, 302
post-socialist regime *see under* Czech Republic; Estonia; Hungary; Poland
social-democratic regime 16, 46, 143, 145, 146, 159–60, 442, 443

race *see* ethnic minorities
rational choice models 9, 208, 405, 406–8, 411, 413, 424
relationships *see* cohabitation; divorce; life course; marriage; partnership dependence
religion 17, 19, 27, 377, 380, 408, 411, 413–14, 416–23, 426, 439, 444

see also cultural values
retirement, early 37, 39, 201, 227
    see also welfare state
Ricardian trade theory 116, 117, 118
Róbert, Péter 171–98, 224
Russia 415, 418, 419, 422, 425

Saar, Ellu 199–223
Schizzerotto, Antonio 352–75
self-employment 34, 39–40, 43, 53
    with employees 40
    family-oriented regime 39, 40, 44, 53,
        337, 355, 366, 387–8, 391,
        394–5, 397
    liberal regime 44
    post-socialist regime 39, 130–32, 178,
        183, 201, 233, 235–6, 238,
        240–42
    see also labor market flexibility
service sector 6, 16, 33, 34, 45–8, 84,
        118
    conservative regime 47, 53, 64, 67, 88
    family-oriented regime 47, 331, 358,
        378–9, 387–8, 391
    liberal regime 47, 53, 303
    post-socialist regime 47, 144, 176,
        182, 187, 188, 257
    social-democratic regime 16, 47, 119,
        120–21, 144
short-term contracts 4, 231, 442
    liberal regime 276, 278–9, 305, 306,
        440, 443
    post-socialist regime 17, 175, 201,
        202
    social-democratic regime 127
Simó Noguera, Carles 376–401
single parents 14, 18, 124, 442
    family-oriented regime 357
    liberal regime 18, 280, 289, 292, 307,
        308
    post-socialist regime 207, 208, 251
skills *see* vocational skills
Slovakia 425
Slovenia 415, 418, 422, 425
social integration 6, 15, 27, 32–4, 38, 43,
        441
    conservative regime 44, 65, 80
    family-oriented regime 53, 381–4
    liberal regime 27, 44, 53, 275, 279,
        440

post-socialist regime 191
social-democratic regime 44, 46, 52,
        134, 137, 435
social-democratic regime 14–16, 43–4,
        413, 436
    caregiving, unpaid 160, 164
    childcare, private 49–50, 147
    childcare, public *see under* Denmark;
        Sweden
    children, effect on employment 38,
        145–7, 153–8, 160, 162, 448
    class differences, occupational 442
    cohabitation 162
    competition 15, 143
    cultural background 413
    dual-earner model 17, 145–6, 150,
        444
    education 127–30, 132–5, 143–5, 148,
        150–58, 161, 440
    education expansion 132, 144, 151
    education, tertiary 125, 130, 132–5,
        145, 153–5, 157–8, 161, 162
    employment interruptions 46, 125–9,
        132–7, 143, 150–52, 445
    employment promotion programs 46
    employment protection 52, 142, 147
    family formation 144, 152
    family responsibilities 143, 145–6,
        148, 150–54, 156, 157–9,
        161–2
    fertility rates 155, 158, 161
    fixed-term contracts 43
    full-time employment 123, 153, 159
    gender role attitudes 16, 124, 129,
        143, 148, 415, 418–19, 425, 428,
        445
    globalization 124, 130, 132, 435,
        435–6, 438, 440
    homemaker model 126, 127–8
    human capital theory 151, 156
    international trade 116–20, 122, 442
    job mobility 16, 123–5, 130–37, 143,
        146–7, 150–53, 155–8
    job security 163
    job stability 128–9, 440
    labor force participation 35–6, 38,
        43–4, 46–53, 115–67, 435–8,
        440–42
    labor market exits 137, 143, 150–51,
        154–60, 435

labor market flexibility 16, 51, 142–3, 147–8, 152
labor market re-entry 146, 160–62
male employment 126, 143, 146, 148, 153, 440
male-breadwinner model 143, 148, 151, 157, 248–9, 425
marginal employment 445
marriage 162
maternity leave 123, 146–7, 150
parental leave 16, 123–4, 146–7, 149–51, 157, 162, 440
part-time employment 16, 40, 41, 42, 159, 442
PLAs (paid leave arrangements) 148–53, 156, 159, 160
private sector 126–9, 132–3, 136–7, 143, 149, 159–60, 440, 442–3, 446
public sector 16, 46, 143, 145–6, 159–60, 442, 443
reduced-full-time work 16
religion 413
service sector 16, 47, 119, 120–21, 144
short-term contracts 127
social integration 44, 46, 52, 134, 137, 435
taxation 124, 144, 145, 150, 249, 440
unemployment 16, 50–51, 124–6, 129–31, 142–3, 147–50, 152–62, 440, 443
unemployment benefits 147–8, 156
unskilled employment 144, 151–2, 162
vocational training 16, 145
wage levels 137, 143, 146–7, 153, 155, 156, 158
welfare state 123–4, 142–4, 147, 156, 413, 435–7, 440, 445, 448
working hours 126, 129, 153, 159, 440
see also Denmark; Sweden
social security *see* welfare state
Spain
agricultural industry 39, 379
care provision, unpaid 376–7, 380, 383–5, 388–9, 391–4, 396
career uncertainty 383, 441
childcare, private 49

childcare, public 48, 383, 443
children, effect on employment 39, 378, 391, 395
closed employment system 201
collective bargaining 380, 381
cultural pressures 377, 380
democratization process 10, 376, 377, 381
dual-earner role 383
economic crises 378–9
education 376, 385, 386, 390, 393, 394, 395
education expansion 377–8
education, over-education 378, 386
education, tertiary 377–8, 386, 394, 395
elderly care 383
employment interruptions 385–6
employment protection 52, 376, 380, 393
EU membership 376
family formation 376, 445
family responsibilities 39, 376, 382, 383–4, 385
Fertility and Family and Labor Force Surveys 26, 386
fertility rates 385, 392, 439, 443
fixed-term contracts 43, 44, 53, 381
full-time employment 385
GDP 382
gender role attitudes 379, 381, 415, 428
generation effect 428
and globalization 10, 376, 377, 438
homemaker model 384, 385, 387, 390
human capital theory 386, 396
international trade 376, 377
job mobility 377, 385, 387, 390, 393–5
job security 281, 377, 381, 386, 390
job stability 377, 380, 383, 385, 388–90, 392
labor force participation 36, 37, 38, 39, 46, 376–401, 436, 438
labor market exit 385–6, 387, 388, 390–92
labor market flexibility 19, 377, 380, 381, 386
labor market re-entry 380, 381, 383, 385, 386, 387, 392–3, 395–6

labor market regulations 380–84
labor market segmentation 377, 381,
    385
liberalization 376
male employment 376, 378, 380, 381,
    383, 384, 385
male-breadwinner role 377, 380, 381,
    384, 425
manufacturing industry 378–9
marginal employment 377, 384–5,
    390
marriage 384, 386
occupational groups 387–8
outsiders, women as 384–5, 390
part-time employment 19, 42, 384
private sector 376, 379, 386
public sector 46, 379, 384, 386
recession 378
religion 19, 377, 380
secularization 377
self-employment 39, 44, 53, 387–8,
    391, 394, 395, 397
service sector 47, 378, 379, 387–8,
    391
social integration 381–4
temporary employment 376, 377,
    381–2, 383, 385
tourism 379
trade unions 380, 381
unemployment 51, 376, 378, 381–3,
    385, 387–96
unemployment benefits 376, 380
unskilled employment 386
vocational training 394
welfare state 376, 377, 380, 381,
    382–4, 443
Workers' Statute 380
see also family-oriented regime
Stern, Charlotta 115–41
stratification 63, 157, 248, 249, 266,
    323, 354–5
subcontracting 40, 200
subjectivity 405–9, 413–16
see also individualization
Sweden
    agriculture 120, 121
    career uncertainty 441–2
    childcare, private 49
    childcare, public 48, 123–4, 145, 249,
        383, 440

children, effect on employment 38,
    126, 129, 421, 448
deindustrialization 120–21
dual-earner model 145–6
education 127–8, 129–30, 132–5, 440
education expansion 132
education, tertiary 125, 130, 132–5
elderly care 383
employment interruptions 125–9,
    132–7, 445
employment protection 52
Estonia, trade with 202
'father-month' 123
FDI 120, 122
full-time employment 123
GDP 119
gender role attitudes 124, 129, 415,
    418–19, 425, 428, 445
generation effect 428
and globalization 124, 130, 132, 435,
    438, 440
homemaker model 126, 127–8
housewife tax deduction 124
institutional structures 123–4
and international trade 116–19,
    119–20, 122, 442
job mobility 123, 124, 125, 130–37
job stability 128–9, 440
labor force participation 35–6, 38, 46,
    47, 115–41, 435–6, 438, 440,
    441–2
labor market exits 137
labor market flexibility 51
Level of Living and Labor Force
    Surveys 26, 125, 130
male breadwinner model 248–9, 425
male employment 126, 440
manufacturing sector 119, 120–22,
    124, 126–30, 132, 134–7, 440
marginal employment 445
maternity leave 123
MNCs 120, 122
occupational segregation 442
OECD Jobs Study 119–20
outsourcing 120
parental leave 123, 124, 440
part-time employment 41, 123, 124,
    126, 129, 440, 442
pensions 123
private sector 126–9, 132–7, 443, 446

public sector 12, 46, 121, 127–9,
132–3, 136–7, 440, 442–3, 446
recession 120, 122, 127, 129
self-employment 39, 130–31, 132
service sector 47, 119, 120–21
short-term contracts 127
social integration 46, 134, 137, 435
structural change causes 121–2
taxation 124, 249, 440
unemployment 124, 125, 126, 129–30,
131, 440, 443
wage levels 137
welfare state 123–4, 382, 448
working hours 126, 129, 440
see also social-democratic regime

taxation 4, 11, 14, 448
conservative regime 14, 66
and employment discrimination 13,
447
family-oriented regime 333, 356
liberal regime 277, 280, 281, 307
post-socialist regime 205, 229
social-democratic regime 124, 144,
145, 150, 249, 440
telecommuting 12, 40
temporary contracts 34, 85, 231–2
conservative regime 86, 87
family-oriented regime 359, 362,
366–8, 370, 376–7, 381–2, 385,
387–8
see also labor market flexibility
trade unions 4, 18, 20
conservative regime 86
family-oriented regime 331, 353, 380,
381
liberal regime 18, 277, 280, 305
post-socialist regime 180, 204, 263
see also collective bargaining
training *see* vocational training
Treiman prestige scale 70–71, 74–5, 131,
235, 312, 387

uncertainty
differential distribution of 309
economic 84, 85, 89, 91, 258, 265,
303, 308–9, 383, 441–2
and globalization 4, 8, 9, 11, 14, 24–6,
67
in men's careers 61

pathways 444–5
see also job security; job stability
unemployment 6–7, 12, 16, 17–18, 20,
24–5, 62, 115, 117, 150, 437,
440–42, 445
added worker effect 291
conservative regime 51, 62, 64–5,
67–73, 86–8
discouragement from working 13, 19,
123, 254, 290, 316
family-oriented regime *see under*
Italy; Mexico; Spain
liberal regime 50–51, 276–9, 281,
283–95, 304–5, 310–11, 316,
440, 443
post-socialist regime *see under* Czech
Republic; Estonia; Hungary;
Poland
short-term 50, 85
social-democratic regime 50–51,
124–6, 129–31, 142–3, 147–50,
152–62, 440, 443
unemployment benefits 19
conservative regime 65
family-oriented regime 19, 353–4,
355–8, 376, 380
liberal regime 277, 304, 311
post-socialist regime 201, 202, 204,
205, 217, 227, 262
social-democratic regime 147–8,
156
unions *see* trade unions
United Kingdom *see* Britain
United States
adult education 304
adult worker model 308
career uncertainty 303, 308–9
caregiving, unpaid 311, 316
childcare, private 49, 50, 306
childcare, public 305, 307, 443
children, effect on employment 38,
302–3, 305, 309, 313, 315, 316,
421
competitiveness 304, 305, 306
demographic controls 309–10, 312,
316, 318–22
deregulation 304
divorce 302, 305, 308, 440
downsizing 306
dual earner model 304, 317

education 302, 303, 306–7, 309,
    314–15, 317, 318–22
education expansion 304, 306, 440
education, tertiary 207, 306–7, 309,
    314–15, 317, 318–22
employment interruptions 305, 306,
    309, 313, 317
employment protection 11, 52, 302,
    303, 305, 307, 440
Equal Pay Act 307
family formation 303, 308, 315, 316,
    318–22
Family and Medical Leave Act 307
family responsibilities 306, 307, 309,
    311, 440
Family Support Act 307
fertility rates 302, 308
full-time employment 18, 305, 307,
    309, 311, 313, 318–22
gender role attitudes 415, 418, 419,
    426–7
generation effect 426–7
and globalization 302, 303–8, 316,
    317, 438
health insurance 18, 304, 307
homemaker model 322
homogamy 309, 317
ICT 303–4
individualism 304, 307
job mobility 303, 312, 314, 317–22
job security 232, 304, 305, 309,
    440
knowledge-based sector 303, 317
labor force participation 35–6, 46, 47,
    302–26, 436, 438, 440, 445
labor market exits 303, 305, 309, 311,
    317
labor market flexibility 303–4, 305,
    306
labor market re-entry 303–6, 309, 311,
    314–16
male employment 232, 304, 440
male-breadwinner model 302, 304–5,
    307, 309, 311, 316, 425, 427
marriage 302, 309, 313, 316, 317,
    318–22
minimum wage 307
'mommy penalty' 305
NAFTA (North American Free Trade
    Agreement) 305

National Longitudinal Survey of
    Young Women 26, 310
outsourcing 306
parental leave 307
part-time employment 40–41, 44, 305,
    307, 309, 313, 318–22
pensions 18, 304
poverty 306, 307–8, 443
private sector 304
public sector 46, 302
racial background 309–10, 312, 316,
    318–22
religion 314
retirement 304, 305, 307
service sector 47, 303
short-term contracts 305, 306
single mothers 307, 308
social integration 440
taxation 307
trade unions 305
unemployment 50, 51, 304, 305,
    310–11, 316
unemployment benefit 304, 311
vocational training 307
wage levels 10, 302, 304–7, 309
welfare state 304, 305, 307–8, 445
working hours 306, 309, 311, 313,
    318–21
see also liberal regime
unskilled employment 6, 12, 115,
    117–18, 122, 124, 128–9, 138,
    151–2, 441, 442
conservative regime 64, 67
family-oriented regime 337, 386,
    388
liberal regime 282–3
post-socialist regime 176–7, 186–8,
    192–3, 211, 238, 240, 241, 242
social-democratic regime 144, 151–2,
    162

vocational training 9, 10, 12, 13, 16,
    19–21
conservative regime 63–4, 145
family-oriented regime 354, 355, 394
liberal regime 278, 283, 287
post-socialist regime 173, 174, 189,
    207–8, 237, 241, 242
social-democratic regime 16, 145
see also education

wage levels 4, 5, 10, 11, 17–20, 23, 64, 115, 248, 446–8
  conservative regime 86, 200, 202, 225, 226, 228–31
  family-oriented regime 10, 331, 333, 352–6, 358, 437
  liberal regime 10, 18, 302, 304–7, 309
  post-socialist regime 17, 175–8, 200, 202, 225–6, 228–31, 251, 256–9, 261–2
  social-democratic regime 137, 143, 146–7, 153, 155, 156, 158
welfare regimes *see* conservative regime; family-oriented regime; liberal regime; post-socialist regime; social-democratic regime
welfare state 3, 6, 8–9, 11–14, 16, 18, 23–6, 33–4, 45, 171, 248–9, 443–4
  childcare *see* childcare
  conservative regime 65–7, 69, 76, 79, 443
  and cultural values 407–9, 411, 413–16, 419, 423, 444
  family-oriented regime 353, 355–8, 376–7, 380–84, 443
  liberal regime 18, 276–81, 294,
    304–5, 307–8, 423, 443, 445
  retirement, early 37, 39, 201, 227
  post-socialist regime 178–80, 182, 201–8, 225, 227–8, 230, 445
  social-democratic regime 123–4, 142–4, 147, 156, 413, 435–7, 440, 445, 448
  see also family responsibilities
Women's Movement 266–7, 310, 323, 414
work characteristics, dependent 40–43
work councils 20
work experience, importance of 103
working hours 4, 11, 12, 35, 64
  conservative regime 44, 86, 87, 94, 99, 102, 104
  liberal regime 284, 294, 306, 309, 311, 313, 318–21
  post-socialist regime 41, 43, 178, 206
  social-democratic regime 126, 129, 153, 159, 440
  see also part-time employment
World Values Survey 414

youth employment 12, 278, 381, 396, 434, 437–8, 438, 441